SILVER SPONSORS

Charles Aronberg, MD

Drew A. Brodsky, MD

Jeffrey Cao, MD

John Differding, MD

Fiquet H. Duckworth, MD

Sally Fisher, MD

Donald D. Forrester, MD

George Guthrie, MD

Keith Hanson, MD

Vivian Houng, MD

M. Walter Johnson, MD

Albert Lui, MD

John McDougall, MD

Ernest C. Miller, MD

Mary O'Connell, MD

Susan E. Ritter, MD

Robert Rowen, MD

Rhoda Ruttenberg, MD

Fredric Schroeder, MD

Gary Silverman, DO

Samara Solan, MD

Michelle Spring, MD

Terri Su, MD

Diane Tanenbaum, MD

Glenn L. Wiltse, MD

Michal Young, MD

Nutrition Guide for Clinicians

Second Edition

NEAL D. BARNARD, MD, EDITOR IN CHIEF
RICK WEISSINGER, MS, RD
BRENT J. JASTER, MD
SCOTT KAHAN, MD, MPH
CHARLES SMYTH, EDITOR

PCRM

PHYSICIANS COMMITTEE FOR RESPONSIBLE MEDICINE
WASHINGTON, DC

Physicians Committee for Responsible Medicine
5100 Wisconsin Ave., NW, Suite 400
Washington, DC 20016
202-686-2210
www.pcrm.org

ISBN-13: 978-0-9664081-7-1

$19.95 (U.S.)

ACKNOWLEDGEMENTS

The authors wish to acknowledge the generous assistance of many people who made this book possible. First, we thank the many reviewers, listed below, who lent their expertise to this project, and Adrian Petre, MD, DMD, and Aparna Sundaram, DO, MPH, for their assistance in drafting the original manuscript. Doug Hall supervised the production of this book and helped establish its editorial and conceptual framework. Proofreading was conducted by Isabel Clark, Lynne Crane, and Marla Reece-Hall. Leonard Rosenbaum compiled the book's index.

Neal D Barnard, MD
Rick Weissinger, MS, RD
Brent Jaster, MD
Scott Kahan, MD
Charles Smyth

REVIEWERS

ALLERGY

Anne M Lent, MD
National Jewish Health
Denver, CO

CARDIOLOGY

David T Nash, MD
Upstate Medical University
Syracuse, NY

John J Pippin, MD, FACC
Physicians Committee for
Responsible Medicine
Washington, DC

Rajnish Prasad, MD, FACC
Cardiovascular Medicine, PC
Marietta, GA

DERMATOLOGY

Avanta P Collier, MD
University of Colorado Denver
Department of Dermatology
Aurora, Colorado

Robert P Dellavalle, MD, PhD, MSPH
Veterans Affairs Medical Center
Denver, CO

Richard L Gallo, MD, PhD
University of California, San Diego
San Diego, CA

EAR, NOSE, AND THROAT

Carol A Foster, MD
University of Colorado Denver
School of Medicine
Aurora, CO

Todd T Kingdom, MD, FACS
University of Colorado Denver
Denver, CO

ENDOCRINOLOGY

Steven Edelman, MD
University of California, San Diego
Veterans Affairs Medical Center
San Diego, CA

Alireza Falahati-Nini, MD, FACE
St Mark's Hospital
Salt Lake City, UT

Michael Salzman, MD, MS
Albany, NY

Mark Sklar, MD, FACP, FACE
Georgetown University Medical
Center
Washington, DC

Jack H Turco, MD
Dartmouth Medical School
Hanover, NH

EPIDEMIOLOGY

James R Cerhan, MD, PhD
Mayo Clinic College of Medicine
Rochester, MN

FAMILY MEDICINE

Douglas T Baska, DO
Florida Medical Clinic
Zephyrhills, Florida

Robert Alan Bonakdar, MD, FAAFP
Scripps Center for Integrative
Medicine
La Jolla, CA

Adam E Perrin, MD, FAAFP
University of Connecticut School of
Medicine
Middletown, CT

William M Simpson, Jr, MD
Medical University of South
Carolina
Charleston, SC

Deborah Sogge-Kermani, MD
Crow Agency, MT

Alan M Weaver, DO
Sturgeon, MO

Pamela L Wible, MD
Eugene, OR

GASTROENTEROLOGY

David H Alpers, MD
Washington University School of
Medicine
St Louis, MO

Lawrence J Cheskin, MD, FACP
Johns Hopkins Bloomberg School
of Public Health
Baltimore, MD

Michael F Leitzmann, MD, DrPH
Institute of Epidemiology and
Preventive Medicine
University of Regensburg
Regensburg, Germany

HEMATOLOGY/ONCOLOGY

Keith I Block, MD
University of Illinois College of
Medicine
Block Center for Integrative Cancer
Care
Institute for Integrative Cancer
Research & Education
Evanston, IL

Donald Doll, MD
University of Missouri
Columbia, MO

Kathryn Hassell, MD
University of Colorado Denver
Denver, CO

Carl F Myers, MD
US Oncology
Yuma, AZ

Gordon Alan Saxe, MD, PhD
University of California, San Diego
Moores UCSD Cancer Center
La Jolla, CA

INFECTIOUS DISEASE

John Koeppe, MD
University of Colorado Denver
Denver, CO

Marilyn E Levi, MD
University of Colorado Denver
Denver, CO

INTERNAL MEDICINE

Jack D McCue, MD
University of California, San
Francisco
San Francisco, CA

Anne Nedrow, MD
Oregon Health & Science University
Portland, OR

Gretchen Serota, MD
Cincinnati, OH

Diane Snustad, MD, FACP
University of Virginia
Charlottesville, VA

NEPHROLOGY

Moshe Levi, MD
University of Colorado Denver
Denver, CO

David M Spiegel, MD, FACP
University of Colorado Denver
Denver, CO

NEUROLOGY

Aysha Akhtar, MD, MPH
North Potomac, MD

Jan J Golnick, MD
Neurological and Headache Center
Omaha, NE

Alexander R Lim, MD
The Neurological Clinic
Corpus Christi, TX

David Perlmutter, MD, FACN
Perlmutter Health Center
Naples, FL

Rand S Swenson, DC, MD, PhD
Dartmouth Medical School
Hanover, NH

NUTRITION

Rayane AbuSabha, PhD, RD
The Sage Colleges
Troy, NY

Indira K Devadas, MS, RD, LD
Veterans Affairs Maryland Health
Care System
Baltimore Rehabilitation Extended
Care Center
Baltimore, MD

Teresa Fung, ScD
Simmons College
Boston, MA

Lawrence H Kushi, ScD
Kaiser Permanente
Oakland, CA

Amy Joy Lanou, PhD
University of North Carolina,
Asheville
Asheville, NC

Susan Levin, MS, RD
Physicians Committee for
Responsible Medicine
Washington, DC

Reed Mangels, PhD, RD, LD
Nutrition Advisor, The Vegetarian
Resource Group
Baltimore, MD

Lorraine Sirota, EdD, RD, FADA
Brooklyn College
Brooklyn, NY

Dr Wilhelm Stahl
Heinrich-Heine University
Düsseldorf, Germany

Caroline Trapp, MSN, APRN, BC-
ADM, CDE
Premier Internists and Northwest
Internal Medicine
Division of Millennium Medical
Group, PC
Southfield, MI

Dulcie Ward, RD, LD
Portland, OR

OBESITY

James O Hill, PhD
University of Colorado Denver
Denver, CO

OBSTETRICS AND GYNECOLOGY

Anthony R Scialli, MD
Tetra Tech Sciences
Arlington, VA

OPHTHALMOLOGY

Greg Diamond, MD
Hudson Valley Eye Surgeons
Fishkill, New York

Lee R Duffner, MD
Hollywood, FL

Marnix Heersink, MD
Eye Center South
Dothan, AL

Stephen R Kaufman, MD
Case Western Reserve University
School of Medicine
Cleveland, OH

Bruce A Winters, MD, FACS
University of California, Davis
School of Medicine
Sacramento, CA

Karlette J Winters, MD, FACS
Roseville, CA

PEDIATRIC GASTROENTEROLOGY, HEPATOLOGY, AND NUTRITION

Jonathan E Teitelbaum, MD,
FAAP, AGAF
The Children's Hospital at
Monmouth Medical Center
Drexel University School of
Medicine
Long Branch, NJ

PEDIATRIC OTOLARYNGOLOGY

Peggy E Kelley, MD
University of Colorado Denver
The Children's Hospital
Aurora, CO

PEDIATRIC PULMONOLOGY

Gwendolyn S Kerby, MD
University of Colorado Denver
The Children's Hospital
Aurora, CO

Monica Federico, MD
University of Colorado Denver
The Children's Hospital
Aurora, CO

PEDIATRICS

Kathi Kemper, MD, MPH
Second Opinion Clinic, Brenner
Children's Hospital
Wake Forest University Health
Sciences
Winston-Salem, NC

Allan E Kornberg, MD, MBA, FAAP
National Initiative for Children's
Healthcare Quality
Cambridge, MA

PHYSICAL MEDICINE AND REHABILITATION

William Joel Paule, MD
Ventura, CA

Keith WL Rafal, MD, MPH
Brown University
Rehabilitation Hospital of Rhode
Island
Healing Choices, PC
Providence, RI

PLASTIC SURGERY

Gordon K Lindberg, MD, PhD
University of Colorado Denver
Aurora, CO

PSYCHIATRY

Debbie R Carter, MD
University of Colorado Denver
Aurora, CO

Mary N Cook, MD
University of Colorado Denver
The Children's Hospital
Aurora, CO

Donald L Feinsilver, MD
Medical College of Wisconsin
Milwaukee, WI

Robert E Feinstein, MD
University of Colorado Denver
School of Medicine
Aurora, CO

Josephine Howard, MD
University of California, San
Francisco
San Francisco, CA

PULMONOLOGY

Ronald Balkissoon, MD, MS, MSc,
DIH, FRCP (C)
National Jewish Health
University of Colorado Denver
School of Medicine
Denver, CO

Brooke G Judd, MD
Dartmouth Medical School
Hanover, NH

Jerry A Nick, MD
National Jewish Health
University of Colorado Denver
Denver, CO

Milene Saavedra, MD
National Jewish Health
Denver, CO

Robert A Winn, MD
University of Colorado Denver
School of Medicine
Aurora, CO

RHEUMATOLOGY

James D Katz, MD, FACP, FACR
The George Washington University
Washington, DC

Gary Jay Silverman, DO, FACR
Midwestern University
Glendale, AZ

TOXICOLOGY

Michael Wilson, PhD
  Denver, CO

UROLOGY

Michael J Andrews Jr, MD
  Danville Urologic Clinic
  Danville, VA

Fernando J Kim, MD, FACS
  Denver Health Medical Center
  University of Colorado Denver
  Denver, CO

Arnold M Kwart, MD, FACS
  Washington Hospital Center
  Washington, DC

Shandra Wilson, MD
  University of Colorado Denver
  Denver, CO

CONTENTS

Important Notice to Reader

SECTION I: NUTRITION IN DISEASE PREVENTION AND MEDICAL TREATMENT

1. Nutrition in Clinical Medicine

In 1957, a surgeon named Denis Burkitt first encountered a puzzling form of childhood cancer. The condition, which came to be called Burkitt's lymphoma, caused a massive swelling of the jaw and was often fatal. But Burkitt noticed something peculiar: The disease followed a geographic pattern, never appearing far from the equator and the east coast of Africa. He painstakingly identified the cause—a virus (now known as Epstein-Barr) transmitted by an insect vector—and then found an effective treatment.[1] His lifesaving work was acclaimed throughout the world of medicine.

Soon thereafter, Dr. Burkitt set his sights on larger medical epidemics, whose solutions were hidden in a much bigger geographical puzzle. He noticed that the great bulk of diseases occurring in the Western world—heart disease, diabetes, obesity, and many others—were surprisingly rare in rural Africa. During 20 years of surgical practice in Africa, he removed only 2 gallbladders, something he might have done on a single morning in any London hospital. Many other conditions, from appendicitis to colon cancer, were rare in Africa, but common in Europe. He ruled out genetics as the main explanation, because people moving from one country to another eventually assumed the same risks as the populations in their adopted homes.

Burkitt proposed that the culprit was diet. In Europe and the Americas, diets bore no resemblance to a fiber-rich African diet. On the contrary, they were fiber-depleted and laden with fat, cholesterol, and sugar. His work, and that of other medical pioneers, launched a major rethinking of the fundamental causes of illness. Previously, nutrition had been thought to play a fairly minor role in health. Yes, there were rare deficiency states, such as pellagra or scurvy, but these were little more than details on medical school examinations. The major killer diseases were thought to have more to do with genes and bad luck than diet. But this new breed of researchers held that nutrition was decisive. It was a fundamental contributor to the major diseases that filled doctors' waiting rooms throughout the Western world.

Burkitt proposed that health authorities should spend less time dealing with the results of bad diets and more time encouraging people to change the way they eat. To continue to treat illnesses while ignoring prevention, he said, was like a plumber mopping up a kitchen floor rather than turning off the tap in an overflowing sink. A new focus on nutrition and prevention could turn the tide in the epidemics of our time.

Evolving Knowledge in Nutrition

Just as new medications often have advantages over previous ones, diet approaches evolve as well, with new dietary methods building on previous ones and research studies putting diets to the test. Heart-healthy diets are a case in point. For decades, cardiologists have encouraged heart patients to switch from red meat to white meat, trim away chicken skin, and stay physically active. These steps were modestly helpful. Following such guidance, an average patient experienced roughly a 5% drop in low density lipoprotein (LDL or "bad") cholesterol.[2]

However, in 1990, a Harvard-trained physician named Dean Ornish published the results of a study using a much more vigorous regimen.[3] His research participants had significant heart disease. His experimental treatment included a low-fat, vegetarian diet, smoking cessation, modest exercise, and stress management. The diet was logical: Foods from plants have no cholesterol and no animal fat. For comparison, his study included a control group that received the usual care that doctors provide for heart patients.

The results made medical history. Not only did the program reduce cholesterol far more effectively than previous diets, it visibly changed the disease process itself. Angiograms done before and after the one-year intervention showed that participants in the control group gradually worsened. But the patients in the experimental group had a very different experience. Their coronary arteries were beginning to open up again, so much so that signs of reversal were clearly evident in 82% of participants within the first year.

In 1999, Dr. Caldwell Esselstyn, a Cleveland Clinic surgeon, published the results of a remarkable 12-year study integrating nutrition with medications.[4] In a group of patients with severe heart disease, he used a diet similar to that used by Dr. Ornish. For any patient whose total cholesterol remained above 150 mg/dl despite the diet, he added cholesterol-lowering medications. In the ensuing 12 years, the research participants had no cardiac events. The combination of the diet and judiciously used medications made the patients practically heart-attack-proof.

Then, in 2005, David Jenkins, from the University of Toronto, took things a step further. He emphasized foods with known cholesterol-lowering properties—oats, soy, and certain nuts, for example. In four weeks' time, LDL cholesterol fell nearly 30%.[5] As research has moved forward, our idea of an effective diet has advanced as well.

The same sort of trend has occurred in the approach to cancer. For many years, lifestyle advice from cancer authorities was limited to avoiding tobacco and getting regular checkups. But it has become clear that diet plays a major role in cancer risk. We now encourage all patients to include more fruits and vegetables in their routines, to focus on foods that are rich in antioxidants, and to limit fat and boost fiber.

More recently, nutritional steps have been tested not only for cancer prevention, but for cancer survival. Studies of individuals diagnosed with breast or prostate cancer have shown that diet may make a major difference in the ensuing years.

Safe and Effective

Dietary approaches are often remarkably effective. The cholesterol-lowering power of the diets used by Drs. Ornish, Esselstyn, and Jenkins rivals that of typical cholesterol-lowering medications. Their effect on blood glucose control rivals that of oral diabetes drugs.[6] For migraines or arthritis, not everyone improves with dietary adjustments that eliminate common dietary triggers, but many do; in controlled clinical trials, sometimes simple diet changes bring dramatic improvements.

Unlike the undesirable side-effects we associate with medications, healthful diet changes bring desirable side-effects. People who adjust the menu in hopes of reducing their cholesterol get the bonus of losing unwanted weight. Their blood pressure drifts downward as well. If they have diabetes, it comes under better control, and they may be able to reduce their need for medication.

While many still think of medications as "conventional medicine" and dietary changes as "alternative therapies," a growing number of clinicians would turn the definitions around. For many conditions, attention to diet and lifestyle is the foundation of good clinical care. Medications, surgery, or other treatments should be used when diet and lifestyle changes do not apply or are not, by themselves, sufficient for the task at hand.

New clinicians come to find that problems they had once regarded as strictly medical, or perhaps even genetic—diabetes and coronary disease, for example—have major nutritional antecedents. As time goes on, they start to see nutritional problems everywhere. The role of nutrition is indeed greater than most clinicians and patients realize. At the same time, not all problems have nutritional connections, and, even for nutrition-related conditions, medical diagnosis and treatment have as important a role now as ever.

This book summarizes the most effective dietary interventions for common conditions and provides information to help patients and their families make healthful changes. A major trend in research, which is reflected here, is a renewed emphasis on plant-based diets. The diets now being offered to heart patients and the vegetable-and-fruit-rich diets advocated for cancer prevention are very different from the diets that are familiar to most patients and doctors. However, many doctors find these diets useful, and many patients will find them lifesaving. Readers will also find details on dietary factors that have adverse health consequences. There is no shortage of unhealthful foods in everyday life, and they exact a large and growing health toll. It is important to educate patients about these dietary risks.

How to Use This Book

We suggest that readers consult the introductory chapters devoted to basic nutrition topics and then look at chapters relevant to the conditions they see in practice. We also encourage a look at the supporting references.

Clinicians should not feel that they must be nutrition experts able to provide detailed diet counseling. But just as clinicians need to know when to order an x-ray whether or not they know how the radiographic equipment works, they also need to know when a nutritional intervention is needed and how to refer patients appropriately.

This guide is updated regularly. It therefore goes without saying that no edition of the guide can be held to be the definitive work on nutrition. Science moves on, and we look forward to the day when the information in this book, which may seem remarkable to many readers today, is eclipsed by new findings and new nutritional tools.

Each chapter was written by one or more physicians and a nutrition expert, and was reviewed by appropriate medical specialists. While the authors are pleased to present this clinical tool, we appreciate readers' pointing out typographical errors and opportunities for improving future editions. Nutrition is as controversial as any other science—perhaps more so—and we welcome readers' suggestions and criticisms. We also look forward to hearing from readers who would like to serve as reviewers for subsequent editions.

Finally, we should note that this work was originally intended to remedy the absence of clinically oriented nutrition information in the curricula of many medical schools. We hope readers will find ways to tackle the same problem. A new emphasis on prevention and nutrition in medical practice will be empowering for clinicians and potentially lifesaving for patients.

References

1. Burkitt DP. The discovery of Burkitt's lymphoma. *Cancer.* 1983;51:1777-1786.

2. Hunninghake DB, Stein EA, Dujovne CA, et al. The efficacy of intensive dietary therapy alone or combined with lovastatin in outpatients with hypercholesterolemia. *N Engl J Med.* 1993;328:1213-1219.

3. Ornish D, Brown SE, Scherwitz LW, Billings JH, Armstrong WT, Ports TA. Can lifestyle changes reverse coronary heart disease? *Lancet.* 1990;336:129-133.

4. Esselstyn CB Jr. Updating a 12-year experience with arrest and reversal therapy for coronary heart disease (an overdue requiem for palliative cardiology). *Am J Cardiol.* 1999;84:339-341.

5. Jenkins DJ, Kendall CW, Marchie A, et al. Direct comparison of a dietary portfolio of cholesterol-lowering foods with a statin in hypercholesterolemic participants. *Am J Clin Nutr.* 2005;81:380-387.

6. Barnard ND, Cohen J, Jenkins DJ, et al. A low-fat, vegan diet improves glycemic control and cardiovascular risk factors in a randomized clinical trial in individuals with type 2 diabetes. *Diab Care.* 2006;29:1777-1783.

2. Macronutrients in Health and Disease

Carbohydrate, protein, and fat are essential for health maintenance, growth, reproduction, immunity, and healing. Deficits or excesses of any of these nutrients may compromise these processes, resulting in poor health outcomes, which vary depending on the macronutrient in question and the life stage of the affected person.

In decades past, research on nutrition and disease frequently focused on the problems caused by diets that provided inadequate intakes of protein, calories, or micronutrients. Concerns that such deficient diets could lead to poor growth and development or might result in weight loss in the hospitalized elderly were appropriate. Currently, however, an excess of macronutrients is a far greater threat to health and well-being in developed countries and in many developing nations as well. Obesity has become a driving force behind common chronic diseases.

This chapter focuses on the basics of macronutrients—their roles, sources, and requirements.

Carbohydrate

Carbohydrate, in the form of starches and sugars, is the main energy source in the human diet, providing 50% or more of total calories. Carbohydrate-containing foods can be classified in several clinically relevant ways:

Simple vs. Complex Carbohydrate

The term *simple carbohydrate* refers to monosaccharides and disaccharides. Common monosaccharides include glucose and fructose, while common disaccharides include sucrose. Figure 1, Figure 2, and Figure 3 represent the chemical structures of glucose, fructose, and sucrose.

Figure 1: Glucose (monosaccharide)

$C_6H_{12}O_6$

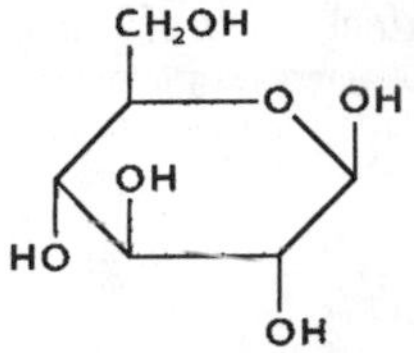

Figure 2: Fructose (monosaccharide)

$C_6H_{12}O_6$

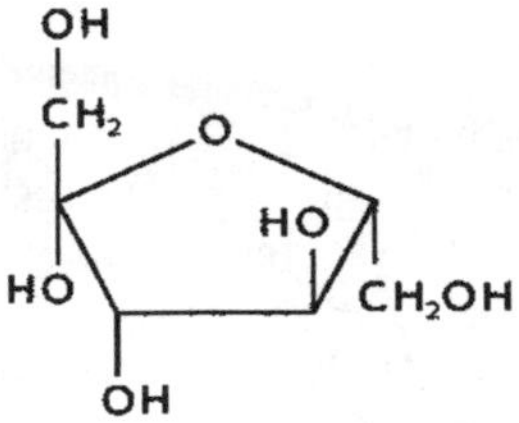

Figure 3: Sucrose (disaccharide)

$C_{12}H_{22}O_{11}$

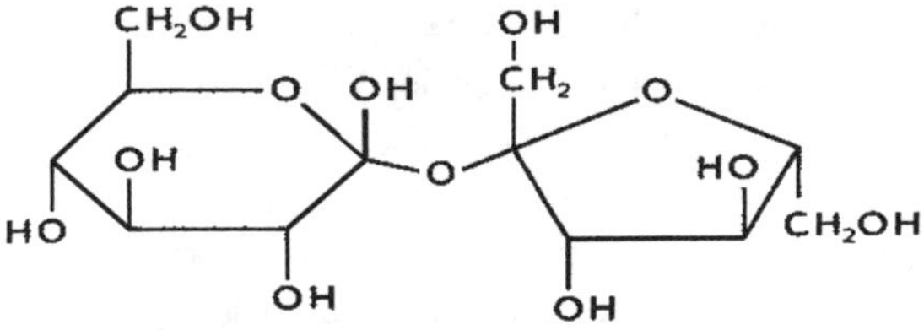

Complex carbohydrate refers to polysaccharides; the term is synony-mous with "starch." The health benefits of carbohydrate-containing foods are largely limited to those rich in complex (rather than simple)

carbohydrate. Foods high in simple carbohydrate include table sugar, fruit, and milk. Foods high in complex carbohydrate include grains, legumes, starchy vegetables, pasta, and breads. Starches are branched carbohydrates that include glycogen ("animal starch"), amylopectin, amylose, and cellulose (Figures 4 and 5), an important source of dietary fiber (see below).

Figure 4: Cellulose

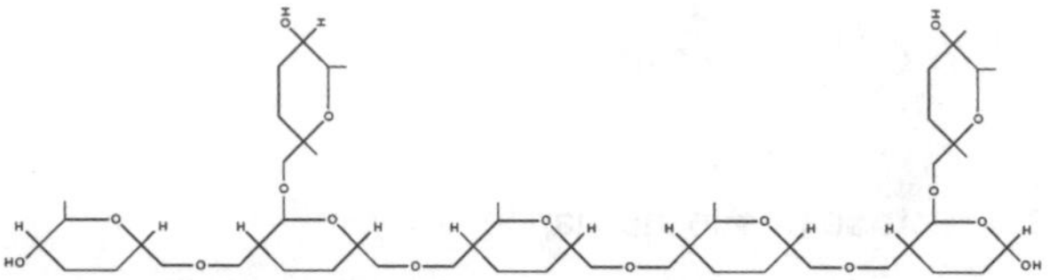

Figure 5: Partial Structure of Amylose

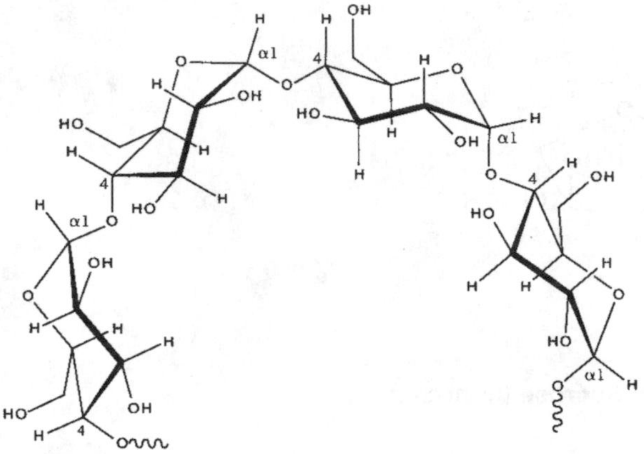

Refined vs. Unrefined Carbohydrates

Refining is a process by which the fibrous outer bran coating of grains is removed. By this process, brown rice is converted to white rice, for example, or whole wheat is converted to white flour, greatly reducing fiber content. Note that a food can be rich in complex carbohydrate but also be refined. White rice and white bread, for example, are refined grain products, but they retain their complex carbohydrate.

Glycemic index. The glycemic index was first presented in 1981 as a means of quantifying the effects of carbohydrate-rich foods on blood glucose concentrations.[1] The glycemic index of a food is determined by feeding a portion containing 50 g of carbohydrate to 10 healthy people after an overnight fast. Blood glucose is tested at 15- to 30-minute intervals over the next 2 hours, and the results are compared with those obtained by feeding the same amount of glucose. A glycemic index below 100 means the food has less effect on blood sugar, compared with glucose. A higher number means the test food has a greater effect.[1]

Distinctions between various kinds of carbohydrate are clinically important. Diets high in sugars and refined carbohydrate may cause elevations of plasma triglyceride concentrations. However, diets high in low–glycemic index foods and fiber tend to have the opposite effect, leading to significant reductions in triglycerides.[2]

In studies of individuals with diabetes, a meta-analysis of 14 prior studies with a total of 356 participants showed that diets emphasizing low-glycemic-index foods reduce hemoglobin A1c (the principal clinical measure of long-term blood glucose control) by about 0.3 to 0.4 percentage points. In some studies, the difference was as much as 0.6 points.[3] Studies showed a similar benefit for both type 1 and type 2 diabetes.

Diets that are high in carbohydrate and fiber and low in fat and cholesterol have clinical utility in prevention and management of several diseases, including obesity and weight-related conditions such as diabetes and hypertension. Dietary fiber promotes satiety, and its intake is inversely associated with body weight and body fat.[4]

Although carbohydrate intake is the main determinant of plasma glucose, available evidence indicates that people who consume approximately 3 servings per day of whole-grain foods have a 20% to 30% lower risk of developing type 2 diabetes than individuals consuming <3 servings per week.[5] Low-fat, high-carbohydrate, high-fiber diets also significantly reduce the need for insulin and oral hypoglycemic agents in patients with type 2 diabetes.[6] Such diets are also associated with significant improvements in blood lipid concentrations, blood pressure, and indices of atherosclerosis (see Dyslipidemias chapter) and appear to be useful for preventing and treating some intestinal disorders (see Constipation, Inflammatory Bowel Disease, Peptic Ulcer Disease, and Gastroesophageal Reflux Disease chapters).

Clinicians should be aware that patients sometimes mistakenly blame carbohydrate for weight or health problems, based on the tenets of popular low-carbohydrate weight-loss diets. Patients may need to be reminded that carbohydrate is essential to human health. Complex carbohydrates, in unprocessed or minimally processed forms, are staple foods in the diets of countries where chronic diseases are rarely seen. In areas of changing dietary patterns, where carbohydrate-rich foods become displaced by fat- and protein-rich foods, several chronic diseases become much more common. In Japan, for example, the Westernization of the diet occurring in the latter half of the 20th century meant a sharp decrease in rice consumption and an increase in meat and total fat intake, with corresponding increases in obesity, diabetes, cardiovascular disease, and other health problems.[7] In studies of Japanese adults over the age of 40, diabetes prevalence was between 1% and 5% prior to 1980. By 1990, prevalence of the disease had increased to 11% to 12%.[7]

Carbohydrate Intolerance

Lactose intolerance. Intolerance of certain kinds of carbohydrate is common and may mimic medical disorders. Lactase, the enzyme in the jejunum that cleaves the milk sugar lactose, normally disappears sometime after the age of weaning. Its disappearance is gradual and extremely variable in age of onset. For some, the enzyme disappears in early childhood; in others, it wanes in late adulthood. The nonpersistence of lactase was once regarded as an abnormal condition, referred to as *lactose intolerance*. It is now known to be the biological norm, occurring in the vast majority of individuals. For most whites, however, lactase persists throughout life, a condition referred to as *lactase persistence*.

After lactase disappearance, the consumption of milk or other lactose-containing products can cause bloating, cramping, diarrhea, and flatulence, which may be mistaken for a number of gastrointestinal diseases.[8] Some authorities advise individuals with these symptoms to limit their consumption of lactose-containing products to small amounts consumed throughout the day, or to use lactase-treated dairy products, soymilk, rice milk, or other substitutes. However, after the age of weaning, there is no nutritional requirement for either milk or milk substitutes, and their inclusion in the diet is based on preference rather than nutritional needs.

Sucrase deficiency. This condition is rare in the general public. It has been reported in adults with renal calculi,[9] and one study found sucrase deficiency in 31% of a population of individuals with HIV.[10]

Fructose malabsorption. Fructose malabsorption can also cause significant gastrointestinal symptoms (eg, bloating, cramps, osmotic diarrhea) that may not respond to medications or surgical interventions.[11]

However, fructose malabsorption is only likely to be problematic for individuals consuming concentrated amounts of this sugar (eg, beverages with high-fructose corn syrup), as opposed to those eating reasonable quantities of fruit.[12] Malabsorption appears to be a problem mainly with fructose intakes exceeding 25 grams per meal, although in patients with functional bowel disease, malabsorption may occur with amounts <15 g.[13]

Congenital carbohydrate intolerances. Congenital carbohydrate intolerances are rare but life-threatening. These conditions include sucrase-maltase deficiency, glucose-galactose malabsorption, and alactasia (a total absence of lactase).[14]

Protein

Protein supports the maintenance and growth of body tissues. The amino acids that make up proteins are used for the synthesis of nucleic acids, cell membranes, hormones, neurotransmitters, and plasma proteins that serve transport functions and exert the colloid osmotic pressure needed to maintain fluid in vascular space. Protein is also the second-largest energy store, second to adipose tissue because of the large amount of muscle tissue that is a labile source of amino acids for gluconeogenesis, although carbohydrate (in the form of glycogen) is used between meals as a primary source.

The Food and Nutrition Board of the Institute of Medicine has determined that 9 amino acids are indispensable for all age groups.[15] They must be obtained from the diet to provide amounts required to maintain health, although the body synthesizes both essential and nonessential amino acids to varying degrees. The essential amino acids are:

- Isoleucine
- Leucine
- Lysine
- Methionine
- Phenylalanine
- Threonine
- Tryptophan
- Valine
- Histidine

During growth and in various disease states, several other amino acids (arginine, cysteine, glutamine, glycine, proline, tyrosine) are regarded as conditionally indispensable.[16] The term *conditionally indispensable* applies when endogenous synthesis cannot meet metabolic need (eg, under special pathophysiologic circumstances, including prematurity in infants and severe catabolic stress in adults).[15]

The effects of certain conditionally indispensable amino acids may be of interest to clinicians involved in the care of critically ill patients. One of these is glutamine, a precursor of both adenosine triphosphase (ATP) and nucleic acids.[17] Depletion of glutamine through hypercatabolic/hypermetabolic illness may result in enterocyte and immunocyte starvation,[18] and glutamine enrichment of enteral or parenteral feedings limits nitrogen loss and improves outcome (significantly reducing bacteremia, sepsis, and hospital stay) in critically ill patients who are post-surgery or in the intensive care unit (ICU).[19,20] In addition, glutamine significantly increases plasma concentrations of taurine,[21] an amino acid with antihypertensive, antiarrhythmic, and positive inotropic effects.[18] This may be important for patients with chronic kidney disease, in whom low intracellular taurine concentrations are common and who are at high risk for cardiac events.

Cysteine is a conditionally indispensable amino acid in infants, one that may promote nitrogen retention in immature infants especially.[22] As a precursor of glutathione, cysteine also plays important roles in antioxidant defense and regulation of cellular events (including gene expression, DNA and protein synthesis, cell proliferation and apoptosis, signal transduction, cytokine production, and the immune response).[23] Patients with liver disease cannot meet their requirements for cysteine due to diminished activity of transsulfuration pathways.[18] The importance of cysteine is also underscored by its role in synthesizing N-acetylcysteine (NAC), a glutathione precursor with important clinical and preventive effects. These include reducing the risk of exacerbations and improving symptoms in patients with chronic bronchitis;[24] significantly reducing the risk of radiocontrast-induced nephropathy;[25] and reducing the expression of a number of cancer risk markers in humans.[26] Patients with cirrhosis may benefit from supplementation with specific (eg, branched-chain) amino acids (see Cirrhosis chapter).

Although a deficiency of dietary protein is clearly detrimental, many chronic conditions may be caused or exacerbated by an excess of protein, particularly animal protein. These include osteoporosis, kidney stones, chronic kidney disease, and possibly certain cancers. Food from plant sources can supply protein in the amount and quality adequate for all ages.[27,28]

The major difference between diets providing animal protein and those providing plant proteins appears to be that, while plant foods contain all essential amino acids, some are limited in lysine or sulfur-containing amino acids. The amino acids provided by various plant foods, however, tend to complement each other, and it is not necessary to intentionally combine foods.[31] The natural combinations of foods in typical vegetarian diets provide more than adequate amounts of complete protein. Soy products provide protein with a biological value as high as that of animal protein. Because plant sources of protein are free of cholesterol and low in saturated fat and provide dietary fiber and various phytochemicals, they present advantages over animal protein sources.

Protein requirements are increased in certain conditions. These include severe acute illness, burn injury, and end-stage renal disease. (See Burns and End-Stage Renal Disease chapters for further information.) In some studies of nursing home residents, protein deficiency has emerged as a concern.[29]

Protein needs are influenced by life stage. Protein requirements are highest in the growing years, with infants up to 12 months and children 1 to 3 years of age requiring 1.5 g/kg and 1.1 g/kg, respectively. Requirements for protein remain high relative to adult needs during the period from growth to puberty (ages 4 to 13 years), at 0.95 g/kg, and are reduced to near-adult levels (0.85 g/kg) from 14 to 18 years of age. Pregnancy and lactation also increase protein needs, to 1.1 g/kg of maternal prepregnancy weight for the former and 1.3 g/kg for the latter.[30]

For healthy adults, the Estimated Average Requirement (EAR) set by the Institute of Medicine (IOM) is considerably lower (0.66 g/kg/d), 47 and 38 grams per day for men and women, respectively.[31] In addition, the intake of adequate protein-sparing calories (see below) allows for maintenance of lean body mass at roughly this level of intake.[28]

Most adults in Western countries consume more protein than the recommended EAR and RDA of 0.66 g/kg/d and 0.8 g/kg, respectively. In fact, the Continuing Survey of Food Intakes indicated protein intakes at 1.5g/kg, roughly double the requirement,[31] while other studies have found that less than 30% to 50% of US adults consume dietary protein in amounts that could be considered moderate (ie, at or near recommended levels of intake).[32] Excessive intakes may contribute to risk for certain chronic diseases (see below).

Energy adequacy spares protein. When considering protein requirements, it is important to consider the number of calories available for nitrogen sparing (ie, calories from both carbohydrate and protein). A ratio of 150 nonprotein calories per gram of nitrogen (provided by 6.25 g of protein) is considered sufficient for protein sparing. Thus, a healthy 60-kg woman consuming 0.8 g protein per kg body weight would consume approximately 7.7 grams of nitrogen and would require approximately 1,152 calories to remain in nitrogen equilibrium. Without these energy sources, proteins will be deaminated and used to meet energy needs. In illness, protein sparing does not occur to any appreciable extent (see below).[33]

Illness causes protein catabolism and affects interpretation of serum protein values. In well-nourished individuals experiencing mild-to-moderate illness, negative nitrogen balance can occur over the short term, mainly in skeletal muscle. Protein storage will be restored once appetite, intake, and activity resume pre-illness levels. In this context, additional dietary protein is not required.

In critically ill patients and those with chronic illnesses involving infection and inflammation, protein requirements exceed the norm, and significant losses of protein occur.[34,35] Serum proteins commonly used to assess protein status are often influenced by the presence of illness. These include albumin, prealbumin, transthyretin, and retinol-binding protein. In otherwise healthy individuals, reduced protein and calorie intake does not cause hypoalbuminemia. However, in the presence of infection, liver and kidney diseases, surgery, and other conditions involving elevated metabolic rate, immune activation, and inflammation, cytokines direct protein synthesis toward that of acute-phase proteins, with subsequent reduction in serum proteins.[36] Alternatively, cytokines will direct amino acids toward energy production rather than protein synthesis.[33] In terms of measuring the effectiveness of nutrition intervention, transthyretin and retinol-binding protein have the greatest clinical utility, because these are the earliest to rise when acute-phase protein levels decrease.[36]

In metabolically stressed patients, both inadequate and excessive protein can cause problems. Even brief periods of protein-calorie deprivation can tip the balance from anabolism to catabolism in critically ill patients. Protein requirements in the range of 1.25 to 2.0 g/kg have been recommended for the critically ill by the American Society for Enteral and Parenteral Nutrition,[37] and intakes in the range of 1.2 to 1.5 g/kg have been found helpful for promoting the healing of pressure ulcers.

However, others have noted no additional reduction in body protein losses at levels above 1.2 g/kg protein.[34] Clinical judgment regarding protein needs may therefore be essential for treating patients on an individualized basis.

Overfeeding of protein can also cause problems, including acidosis and azotemia. In patients not given adequate water, hypertonic dehydration (tube feeding syndrome) may result from obligate water losses that occur due to higher urea production.[33] Acute toxic effects of excess protein intake are rare, but they are seen in cases of inborn errors of amino acid metabolism and in patients with hemorrhagic esophageal varices, which precipitates encephalopathy in patients with liver disease.[19] In certain conditions (eg, chronic kidney disease), diets that provide lower amounts of protein than the Dietary Reference Intakes (DRI) have been useful for improving clinical status (see Chronic Kidney Disease chapter).

Additional dangers of excess protein intake include idiopathic hypercalciuria;[38] greater risk for type 2 diabetes;[39] and, when protein constitutes >35% of total energy intake, hyperaminoacidemia, hyperammonemia, hyperinsulinemia, nausea, and diarrhea.[40] Other dangers associated with excess protein intake are related mainly to animal protein. These include gout, osteoporosis, and certain cancers (see individual chapters in this book for further information).

Fats

Dietary fats are the least-required macronutrient, with only a few grams per day needed for the absorption of fat-soluble vitamins A, D, E, and K, among other functions. Foods contain combinations of saturated and unsaturated fats. Substantial quantities of saturated fat are found in dairy products, eggs, meats, and tropical oils, while unsaturated fats predominate in liquid fats (eg, vegetable oils). The latter are subdivided into monounsaturated fats (predominant in olive and canola oils) and polyunsaturated fats (found in nuts, seeds, seed oils, and, to a lesser extent, in meats).

Only the polyunsaturated fatty acids (PUFA) are essential to human nutrition, since the body does not synthesize these. PUFA have roles as structural components of cell membranes and as signaling molecules (eg, eicosanoids).[41] The essential fatty acids (EFA) include linoleic acid (an omega-6 fatty acid) and alpha-linolenic acid (an omega-3 fatty acid).

The Institute of Medicine recommends a ratio of dietary linoleic (omega-6) to alpha-linolenic (omega-3) acid intake of 10:1; however, this figure is controversial (some suggest a higher intake of omega-3). The suggested ratio of intake for different age groups is listed in Table 1, EFA Requirements (g/d).[30]

Table 1:
Recommended Ratio of Linoleic Acid to Alpha-Linolenic Fatty Acid, by Age Group, EFA Requirements (g/d)

Age	Omega-6	Omega-3
Infants (0-6 months)	4.4	0.5
Infants (7-12 months)	4.6	0.5
Children (1-3 years)	7.0	7.0
Children (4-8 years)	10.0	0.9
Males (9-13)	12.0	1.2
Females (9-13)	10.0	1.0
Males (14-18)	16.0	1.6
Females (14-18)	11.0	1.1
Males (19-50)	17.0	1.6
Females (19-50)	12.0	1.1
Males (51->70)	14.0	1.6
Females (51->70)	11.0	1.1
Pregnancy	13.0	1.4
Lactation	13.0	1.3

The IOM Food and Nutrition Board currently recommends a range of fat intake of 20% to 35% of total energy intake.[30] This too is controversial, given that good health outcomes have been achieved with considerably lower levels of fat intake. Most individuals can meet their EFA needs by consuming very small amounts of fat per day (~14 g, or 0.5 oz), although many people are eating far more than this (~85 g or 3 oz/day, on average).[42]

This level of excess consumption of fats is problematic because EFA derivatives are raw materials for eicosanoids (ie, prostaglandins, leukotrienes, and thromboxanes), hormone-like chemicals with short-lived but powerful effects. Eicosanoids play significant roles in immune function, inflammation, thrombosis, proliferation, reproduction, gastroprotection, and hemostasis, in addition to other functions.[43] The omega-6 polyunsaturated fatty acid linoleic acid and the omega-3 polyunsaturated fatty acid alpha-linolenic acid are metabolized to long-chain fatty acids (arachidonic and eicosapentanoic acids, respectively), which are the precursors for the eicosanoids. These long-chain derivatives are also found in some food products, with arachidonic acid being present in meat, eggs, and dairy products, and eicosapentanoic acid found in fish. These food sources are not required, however, as eicosanoids are produced in the body.

The type and amount of PUFA consumed (omega-6 vs. omega-3) are important considerations. Certain kinds of eicosanoids will predominate when omega-6 fats are in plentiful supply, as is the case with Western diets.[44] These include prothrombotic thromboxanes (eg, thromboxane A2); immunosuppressive prostaglandins (eg, prostaglandin E2); and proinflammatory leukotrienes (eg, leukotriene B4). Reducing the intake of omega-6 fatty acids (particularly arachidonic acid from animal products) while proportionately increasing the intake of omega-3 fatty acids results in the production of eicosanoids with reduced potential to do harm (eg, thromboxane A3, prostaglandin E3, and leukotriene B5).[44]

The need to limit fat. Of all the macronutrients, fat has the greatest potential to cause disease when consumed in excess. Saturated fats in particular tend to raise cholesterol and triglyceride concentrations (see Obesity and Dyslipidemias chapters for further information). Reducing saturated fat is important for controlling blood lipids. Beyond that, reducing total fat (not just replacing saturated with unsaturated fatty acids) is helpful for reducing the excess weight that contributes significantly to cardiovascular disease and other chronic health problems. Fat provides 9 calories per gram, more than twice that of protein or carbohydrate. Individuals who are successfully maintaining significant weight loss typically consume less than 25% of their total daily calories from fat.[45]

Intake of polyunsaturated and monounsaturated fatty acids should also be limited. PUFA are particularly sensitive to lipid peroxidation, resulting in generation of reactive oxygen species (superoxide and hydroxyl radicals, hydrogen peroxide, singlet oxygen, hypochlorous acid). Diets that are both low in antioxidants (eg, Western diets) and high in PUFA may result in a condition termed *oxidative stress*,[46] which damages DNA, proteins, and carbohydrates, thereby contributing to a spectrum of common chronic diseases.[47] Peroxidation of PUFA in low-density lipoprotein (LDL) increases the amount of oxidized LDL, a key stimulus for atherosclerosis progression.

In general, fatty foods provide very few nutrients. Other than essential fatty acids, vegetable oils provide only vitamins E and K, which can be obtained from other sources. Ideally, fats should not be added to meals. Rather, they should be consumed in modest amounts from foods that are a vehicle for other essential nutrients. For example, nuts provide essential fatty acids, magnesium, copper, folic acid, potassium, fiber, and vitamin E.[48]

References

1. Jenkins DJ, Wolever TM, Taylor RH, et al. Glycemic index of foods: a physiological basis for carbohydrate exchange. *Am J Clin Nutr.* 1981;34:362-366.

2. Jenkins DJ, Wolever TM, Kalmusky J, et al. Low-glycemic index diet in hyperlipidemia: use of traditional starchy foods. *Am J Clin Nutr.* 1987;46:66-71.

3. Brand-Miller J, Hayne S, Petocz P, Colagiuri S. Low-glycemic index diets in the management of diabetes. *Diab Care.* 2003;26:2261-2267.

4. Slavin JL. Dietary fiber and body weight. *Nutrition.* 2005;21:411-418.

5. Venn BJ, Mann JI. Cereal grains, legumes and diabetes. *Eur J Clin Nutr.* 2004;58:1443-1461.

6. Barnard RJ, Massey MR, Cherny S, O'Brien LT, Pritikin N. Long-term use of a high-complex-carbohydrate, high-fiber, low-fat diet and exercise in the treatment of NIDDM patients. *Diabetes Care.* 1983;6:268-273.

7. Kuzuya T. Prevalence of diabetes mellitus in Japan compiled from literature. *Diab Res Clin Practice.* 1994;24(suppl):S15-S21.

8. Rusynyk RA, Still CD. Lactose intolerance. *J Am Osteopath Assoc.* 2001;101(suppl 4, pt 1):S10-S12.

9. Belmont JW, Reid B, Taylor W, et al. Congenital sucrose-isomaltase deficiency presenting with failure to thrive, hypercalcemia, and nephrocalcinosis. *BMC Pediatr.* 2002;2:4.

10. Gudmand-Hoyer E, Skovbjerg H. Disaccharide digestion and maldigestion. *Scand J Gastroenterol.* 1996;216(suppl):111-121.

11. Johlin FC Jr, Panther M, Kraft N. Dietary fructose intolerance: diet modification can impact self-rated health and symptom control. *Nutr Clin Care.* 2004;7:92-97.

12. Choi YK, Johlin FC Jr, Summers RW, Jackson M, Rao SS. Fructose intolerance: an under-recognized problem. *Am J Gastroenterol.* 2003;98:1348-1353.

13. Riby JE, Fujisawa T, Kretchmer N. Fructose absorption. *Am J Clin Nutr.* 1993;58(suppl):748S-753S.

14. Levin RJ. Carbohydrates. In: Shils ME, Olson JA, Shike M, Ross AC, eds. *Modern Nutrition in Health and Disease.* 9th ed. Baltimore, MD: Williams & Wilkins; 1999:49-65.

15. Institute of Medicine. *Dietary Reference Intakes for Energy, Carbohydrate, Fiber, Fat, Fatty Acids, Cholesterol, Protein, and Amino Acids (Macronutrients).* Washington, DC: National Academies Press; 2005:593-594.

16. Pencharz PB, Ball RO. Different approaches to define individual amino acid requirements. *Annu Rev Nutr.* 2003;23:101-116.

17. Reeds PJ. Dispensable and indispensable amino acids for humans. *J Nutr.* 2000;130:1835S-1840S.

18. Furst P, Stehle P. What are the essential elements needed for the determination of amino acid requirements in humans? *J Nutr.* 2004;134(suppl 6):1558S-1565S.

19. Soeters PB, van de Poll MC, van Gemert WG, Dejong CH. Amino acid adequacy in pathophysiological states. *J Nutr.* 2004;134(suppl 6):1575S-1582S.

20. Boelens PG, Nijveldt RJ, Houdijk AP, Meijer S, van Leeuwen PA. Glutamine alimentation in catabolic state. *J Nutr.* 2001;131(suppl 9):2569S-2577S.

21. Boelens PG, Houdijk AP, de Thouars HN, et al. Plasma taurine concentrations increase after enteral glutamine supplementation in trauma patients and stressed rats. *Am J Clin Nutr.* 2003;77:250-256.

22. Heird WC. Amino acids in pediatric and neonatal nutrition. *Curr Opin Clin Nutr Metab Care.* 1998;1:73-78.

23. Wu G, Fang YZ, Yang S, Lupton JR, Turner ND. Glutathione metabolism and its implications for health. *J Nutr.* 2004;134:489-492.

24. Stey C, Steurer J, Bachmann S, Medici TC, Tramer MR. The effect of oral N-acetylcysteine in chronic bronchitis: a quantitative systematic review. *Eur Respir J.* 2000;16:253-262.

25. Duong MH, MacKenzie TA, Malenka DJ. N-acetylcysteine prophylaxis significantly reduces the risk of radiocontrast-induced nephropathy: comprehensive meta-analysis. *Catheter Cardiovasc Interv.* 2005;64:471-479.

26. De Flora S, Izzotti A, D'Agostini F, Balansky RM. Mechanisms of N-acetylcysteine in the prevention of DNA damage and cancer, with special reference to smoking-related end-points. *Carcinogenesis.* 2001;22:999-1013.

27. American Dietetic Association. Position of the American Dietetic Association and Dietitians of Canada: Vegetarian diets. *J Am Diet Assoc.* 2003;103:748-765.

28. Millward DJ. Optimal intakes of protein in the human diet. *Proc Nutr Soc.* 1999;58:403-413.

29. Crogan NL, Corbett CF, Short RA. The minimum data set: predicting malnutrition in newly admitted nursing home residents. *Clin Nurs Res.* 2002;11:341-353.

30. Institute of Medicine. *Dietary Reference Intakes for Energy, Carbohydrate, Fiber, Fat, Fatty Acids, Cholesterol, Protein, and Amino Acids (Macronutrients).* Washington, DC: National Academies Press; 2005.

31. Institute of Medicine. *Dietary Reference Intakes for Energy, Carbohydrate, Fiber, Fat, Fatty Acids, Cholesterol, Protein, and Amino Acids.* Washington, DC: National Academies Press; 2002.

32. Kerstetter JE, O'Brien KO, Insogna KL. Dietary protein, calcium metabolism, and skeletal homeostasis revisited. *Am J Clin Nutr.* 2003;78(suppl 3):584S-592S.

33. Mechanick JI, Brett EM. Nutrition support of the chronically critically ill patient. *Crit Care Clin.* 2002;18:597-618.

34. Reid CL. Nutritional requirements of surgical and critically-ill patients: do we really know what they need? *Proc Nutr Soc.* 2004;3:467-472.

35. Matthews DE. Proteins and amino acids. In: Shils ME, Olson JA, Shike M, Ross AC, eds. *Modern Nutrition in Health and Disease.* 9th ed. Baltimore, MD: Williams & Wilkins; 1999:11-48.

36. Raguso CA, Dupertuis YM, Pichard C. The role of visceral proteins in the nutritional assessment of intensive care unit patients. *Curr Opin Clin Nutr Metab Care.* 2003;6:211-216.

37. American Society of Parenteral and Enteral Nutrition. *Standards of Practice and Clinical Guidelines for Nutritional Support.* Dubuque, Iowa: Kendall Hunt Publishing Company; 2002.

38. Liebman SE, Taylor JG, Bushinsky DA. Idiopathic hypercalciuria. *Curr Rheumatol Rep.* 2006;8:70-75.

39. Krebs M. Amino acid-dependent modulation of glucose metabolism in humans. *Eur J Clin Invest.* 2005;35:351-354.

40. Bilsborough S, Mann N. A review of issues of dietary protein intake in humans. *Int J Sport Nutr Exerc Metab.* 2006;16:129-152.

41. Sweeney B, Puri P, Reen DJ. Modulation of immune cell function by polyunsaturated fatty acids. *Pediatr Surg Int.* 2005;21:335-340.

42. Centers for Disease Control. Intake of Calories and Selected Nutrients for the United States Population, 1999-2000. Available at: http://www.cdc.gov/nchs/data/nhanes/databriefs/calories.pdf. Accessed November 26, 2005.

43. Tapiero H, Ba GN, Couvreur P, Tew KD. Polyunsaturated fatty acids (PUFA) and eicosanoids in human health and pathologies. *Biomed Pharmacother.* 2002;56:215-222.

44. Simopoulos AP. Evolutionary aspects of diet and essential fatty acids. *World Rev Nutr Diet.* 2001;88:18-27.

45. Wing RR, Hill JO. Successful weight loss maintenance. *Annu Rev Nutr.* 2001;21:323-341.

46. Jones PJH, Kubow S. Lipids, sterols, and their metabolites. In: Shils ME, Olson JA, Shike M, Ross AC, eds. *Modern Nutrition in Health and Disease.* 9th ed. Baltimore, MD: Williams & Wilkins; 1999:67-94.

47. Cross CE, Halliwell B, Borish ET, et al. Oxygen radicals and human disease. *Ann Intern Med.* 1987;107:526-545.

48. Hu FB. Plant-based foods and prevention of cardiovascular disease: an overview. *A J Clin Nutr.* 2003;78(suppl 3):544S-551S.

---

3. Micronutrients in Health and Disease

Twenty-eight essential vitamins and minerals play key roles in the metabolism of protein, carbohydrate, and fat, as well as in the structure of the human body (eg, vitamin K in bone matrix, calcium in bone tissue). Many micronutrients are also important antioxidants (eg, vitamins C and E) or act as cofactors for antioxidant enzymes (eg, selenium in glutathione peroxidase). Several trace minerals, though not considered essential, are being studied for their roles in human nutrition. Examples include silicon for bone health[1] and vanadium for stimulation of glucose transport.[2]

Although vitamin deficiency diseases (eg, pellagra) are no longer widespread, suboptimal micronutrient intake is common. Recent studies show that 10% to 75% of Americans take in less than the recommended dietary allowance (RDA) for many micronutrients (eg, zinc, folate, iron, vitamins B_6 and B_{12}), and between 5% and 50% of Americans consume less than half the RDA for many micronutrients.[3] While what constitutes sufficient intake is controversial for some nutrients, it is clear that a surprisingly large number of people are undernourished for certain micronutrients, even as they are overly nourished with respect to macronutrients.

Insufficient micronutrient intake has short-term and long-term implications for disease risk. As an example, immune function is adversely affected by poor intakes of nearly every essential vitamin and mineral.[4] Thus, diets lacking essential micronutrients may, theoretically at least, affect health over the short term by impairing resistance to viral or bacterial infection. Among longer-term problems, a lack of nutrients required for DNA methylation and gene stability may increase the risk for certain cancers.[3]

The following sections address issues of greatest concern to clinicians: deficiency states, diet-drug interactions, and at-risk populations. Three reference tables are included at the end of this chapter: Table 1, Conditions That May Be Improved by Nutritional Supplements; Table 2, Vitamin Functions, Deficiency Diseases, Toxicity Symptoms, and Dietary Reference Intakes; and Table 3, Mineral Functions, Deficiency Diseases, Toxicity Symptoms, and Dietary Reference Intakes.

Vitamin Deficiency States

Vitamin B_{12}. Vitamin B_{12} deficiency affects 10% to 15% of individuals over age 60, mainly due to poor absorption.[5] (See Megaloblastic Anemia chapter.)

Vitamin C. Deficiency of vitamin C, which manifests as scurvy in its most severe form, is a condition most clinicians would presume to be long gone. Nevertheless, vitamin C deficiency or depletion was found in 5% to 17% of participants in the Third National Health and Nutrition Examination Survey,[6] in 30% of a sample of hospice patients,[7] in 68% of a population of hospitalized elderly patients,[8] and in individuals who eat meat-based diets and avoid fruits and vegetables.[9] In smokers, the risk for vitamin C deficiency is roughly 4 times greater than in nonsmokers.[6]

Vitamin D. Soft and deformed bones characterize rickets, a vitamin D deficiency disease that affects infants and children. Although rickets is presumed to be an infrequent problem in the United States due to vitamin D fortification of milk, these efforts have not been entirely successful, and resurgence of this disease has occurred for a number of reasons. The natural source of vitamin D is sun exposure. However, life in urban areas or at extremes of latitude makes sunlight a less predictable source. Vitamin D is naturally present in few foods (eg, oily fish, egg yolk), many of which people do not eat for reasons of preference or health. This has prompted the American Academy of Pediatrics to recommend 200 international units (IU) of supplemental vitamin D for infants, children, and adolescents ingesting less than 500 mL per day of vitamin D-fortified formula or milk.[10]

Intakes that are considered either deficient or insufficient have also been found in young women and elderly persons who lack sun exposure.[11] These low intakes are a risk factor for autoimmune disease and some cancers.[12] Certain drugs (eg, phenytoin, phenobarbital) can also decrease blood levels of vitamin D, resulting in both osteopenia and osteomalacia.[13]

Some evidence suggests that a "functional" vitamin D deficiency state may be caused by a high calcium intake due to dairy intake and calcium supplements and may influence the risk for prostate cancer. In one study, although higher calcium intake was not appreciably associated with total or nonadvanced prostate cancer, men with intakes of 1,500 to 1,999 mg per day of calcium had nearly double the risk for advanced and fatal prostate cancer. Men consuming 2,000 mg per day or more had a risk almost 2.5 times greater, compared with men whose long-term calcium intakes were 500 to 749 mg per day. These risks have been attributed to elevated blood calcium concentrations that decrease production of the active form of vitamin D (calcitriol). Under normal circumstances, vitamin D's presumed anti-cancer differentiation, and regulation of the invasiveness, angiogenesis, and metastatic potential of prostate cancer cells.[14] Vitamin D adequacy reduces the risk of osteoporosis (see Osteoporosis chapter) and may also reduce risk of cardiovascular disease through inhibition of vascular smooth effects include inhibition of cellular proliferation, promotion of muscle proliferation, suppression of vascular calcification, changes in cytokine profile from pro- to anti-inflammatory types, and down-regulation of the renin-angiotensin system.[15]

Considerable evidence suggests that certain subgroups (eg, elderly persons) do not meet vitamin D requirements due to lack of sun exposure.[16] Multiple vitamin formulas typically contain 400 IU of vitamin D, an amount that meets or exceeds the recommended intakes for all age groups except those over 70 years. Some evidence suggests, however, that current recommended intakes may be insufficient for elderly persons, as well as for individuals in other age groups, and these recommendations are being re-evaluated.[17]

Mineral Deficiencies

Iron. Deficiency of this mineral occurs with a frequency ranging from 2% of pubescent and adult males to 16% of menstruating females,[18] and iron deficiency-related anemia is the most common cause of anemia in pregnancy.[19] (See Iron Deficiency Anemia chapter.)

Calcium. Intakes of calcium at levels significantly below dietary reference intakes (DRI) are common in a large segment of the US population. After 10 years of age, both males and females get, on average, roughly half the recommended intake.[20] A significant body of evidence, however, indicates that a more moderate calcium intake may be adequate. While calcium intakes below 400 mg per day may reduce bone development, intakes above this level do not appear to correlate with bone mineral density or to reduce fracture risk. Other factors, particularly targeted physical activity, do appear to more precisely reflect bone density in this population.[21] Data from the Nurses' Health Study do not support the hypothesis that a higher total calcium or dairy calcium intake in adults is protective against hip or forearm fracture.[22]

Concerns about high calcium intakes have arisen from studies indicating a higher risk of prostate cancer among men consuming more dairy products or calcium (see Prostate Cancer chapter) and a higher risk of kidney stones under certain circumstances (see Kidney Stones chapter).

Magnesium. Clinical deficiency of blood magnesium is rare in the general population, but it should be suspected in individuals with chronic diarrhea, patients with hypocalcemia or refractory hypokalemia, and those given certain medications (see below).[23,24] Individuals developing or having hypomagnesemia may show neuromuscular hyperexcitability,[23] and hypocalcemia is a sign of severe hypomagnesemia (<1.0 mEq/L, 0.5 mmol/L).[24] Hypomagnesemia occurs in up to 12% of hospitalized patients and in as many as 60% to 65% of Intensive Care Unit (ICU) patients.[24] In the Third National Health and Nutrition Examination Survey (NHANES III), 68% of adults consumed less than the recommended daily allowance (RDA) for magnesium, and 19% consumed less than 50% of the RDA.[25] Hypomagnesemia was found in 27% of healthy lean children and 55% of obese children in one study,[26] and the condition occurs in 25% to 38% of individuals with diabetes.[27] (See Diabetes chapter.) Magnesium deficiency may result from poor intake of foods rich in this mineral, such as green vegetables, nuts, seeds, dried beans, and whole grains.

Antioxidants and Phytochemicals

Antioxidant vitamins (vitamins C and E), carotenoids, and minerals that are constituents of antioxidant enzymes (eg, zinc, magnesium, and manganese in superoxide dismutase; selenium in glutathione peroxidase) are essential for minimizing free-radical reactions and the resulting destruction of cellular structures. However, clinical trials indicate that simply adding supplemental antioxidant nutrients to a typical American diet does not reduce the risk for common diseases such as cardiovascular disease and cancer.[28] Evidence suggests that a healthful overall diet is required—namely, a diet that is both low in factors that promote disease and high in antioxidant nutrients.

In addition, an increasing body of evidence indicates that the presence of nonvitamin, nonmineral antioxidants (eg, phytochemicals) in foods is responsible for the majority of antioxidant effects.[29] In general, populations eating greater amounts of phytochemical-containing foods (eg, fruits, vegetables, whole grains) have a significantly lower mortality risk[30] and a lower risk for cardiovascular disease, cancer, diabetes mellitus, hypertension, and arthritis.[31,32] Population studies do not, however, typically isolate the effect of micronutrients, and they also involve significant macronutrient differences, compared with unmodified diets. Nevertheless, these studies suggest that any additional nutrients should be supplemental to, and not substituted for, a plant-based diet.

At-Risk Populations

Certain groups are likely to be deficient in micronutrients and to need dietary adjustments or supplementation. The following nutritional choices may result in poor or deficient intakes of essential nutrients:

Alcohol abuse. Lower blood concentrations of vitamins C and E, carotenoids, and selenium have been found in alcohol-dependent patients, compared with low-alcohol consumers.[33,34] Alcohol abusers may miss B vitamins through poor food intake and may lose B vitamins due to the diuretic effect of alcohol; these (particularly thiamine) must be replaced to prevent neurologic sequelae, including Wernicke-Korsakoff syndrome.[35] Folate intake may be especially important for alcohol consumers. For example, individuals who consume as little as one-half of a serving of alcohol per day appear to be at twice the risk for breast cancer when folate intakes are below recommendations (ie, at <335 µg/d), compared with those with higher intakes.[36]

Western dietary pattern. Individuals who eat a Western diet generally have reduced intakes of several micronutrients, compared with individuals following plant-based diets, although these reduced intakes may not represent frank deficiencies. Vitamin C deficiency has been found in individuals who eat meat-based diets and shun fruits and vegetables.[9,37] In the European Investigation into Cancer and Nutrition study of 65,429 men and women, individuals avoiding meat and other animal products had much higher intakes of fiber, folate, and vitamins C and E, compared with omnivores.[38] Other surveys of vegetarians also determined higher intake of vitamins C and E, in addition to potassium[39] and dietary fiber,[40] compared with omnivores. Pregnant vegetarian women had significantly lower risk for folate deficiency than omnivores had.[41]

According to the Institute of Medicine (IOM), current and international dietary guidelines call for obtaining at least 90% of vitamin A in the form of provitamin A carotenoids, and US residents obtain less than 40%, with the balance coming from animal products.[23] This results in lower blood levels of carotenoids, and these reduced levels are consistent with a greater risk for many chronic diseases, compared with the risk for individuals eating recommended amounts (ie, 5 servings/day) of fruits and vegetables.[23]

Iron overload, although less common than iron deficiency, occurs in roughly 0.5% of whites and results from hereditary hemochromatosis (HHC), an autosomal recessive disorder caused in most cases by the C282Y and H63D mutation in the HFE gene on chromosome 6p21.3.[42] However, in spite of the frequency of this disorder, it is not solely responsible for HHC-related diseases, such as diabetes and liver disease.[43] Even in the absence of the gene for hemochromatosis, evidence shows that individuals in Western, meat-eating populations may have iron stores far in excess of those needed for health.[44] These individuals may be at greater risk for heart disease, cancer, and diabetes, risks that appear to be greatest among elderly persons.[45] Among elderly participants in the Framingham Heart Study, 13% had high iron stores, while approximately 3% were found to have iron deficiency.[45]

Smokers. Smokers often have poorer diets in general than nonsmoking individuals, and they generally consume fewer fruits and vegetables and more saturated fat.[46] Moreover, even after adjustment for differences in diet, smokers have significantly lower blood levels of several carotenoids and vitamin C.[47]

Inappropriately restricted diets. Nutritional deficiency can result from overly stringent dietary restrictions, particularly those that suggest elimination of the most nutrient-rich foods (eg, vegetables, fruits, and whole grains). Such diets may be practiced by individuals who are dealing with what they suspect are problematic reactions to foods[48,49] and who do not seek alternative sources of essential nutrients. Individuals who consume low-carbohydrate, high-meat diets may have vitamin C intakes that are nearly 50% lower than those of persons eating more plant-based diets.[50]

Elderly persons, particularly those in hospitals or long-term care facilities, and individuals following unsupplemented vegan diets are at risk for deficiency of vitamins B_{12} and D. With appropriate supplementation, a vegan diet has nutritional advantages, compared with unmodified diets.[51] Alcohol-dependent individuals are at risk for folate, B_6, B_{12}, and thiamin deficiencies. Poor intakes and subclinical deficiencies in these and other groups, along with the increased risk for chronic diseases that may follow, have led to the suggestion that all adults take a multiple vitamin daily.[52]

Vitamin dependency disorders resulting from inborn errors of metabolism are rare, but they require lifelong treatment with certain vitamins. Examples of these include multiple carboxylase deficiencies that are biotin-responsive[53] and pyridoxine-dependent seizures.[54]

Drug-Diet Interactions

Drug-diet interactions can cause increased needs for certain micronutrients. Electrolyte imbalances are probably the most common micronutrient deficiency states and are often caused by medications.[13]

Folic acid deficiency may occur due to treatment with many anticonvulsants (eg, phenytoin, carbamazepine, phenobarbital, valproic acid) and may subsequently increase the risk for birth defects.[55] Through an antagonizing effect on folate, these same drugs also significantly increase certain indicators of cardiovascular risk, such as homocysteine and possibly lipoprotein(a).[56] Available data indicate that folic acid treatment can significantly reduce homocysteine in children on anticonvulsant medications.[57] Additional studies are needed to test the initial observation that B-vitamin supplements (folate, pyridoxine, and riboflavin) reduce certain other cardiovascular risk factors, including von Willebrand factor and lipoprotein, that are elevated in adults on anticonvulsant treatment.[58]

Many side effects of methotrexate treatment (gastrointestinal intolerance, stomatitis, alopecia, and cytopenia) are due to folate antagonism. However, it is thought that these effects may be avoided by combining a folate-rich diet with minimal folate supplementation (ie, multiple vitamins) and by reducing the dose of methotrexate if necessary.[59] American College of Rheumatology guidelines indicate that supplementation with additional folic acid or folinic acid (Leucovorin) may prevent treatment side effects without compromising therapeutic efficacy.[60] Although doses of 2.5 mg to 5.0 mg reduce the side effects of methotrexate without significantly altering effectiveness, higher amounts (eg, 15 mg) have resulted in worsening of rheumatoid arthritis (RA) symptoms.[53]

Vitamin B_{12} absorption decreases as a result of long-term acid suppression therapy (eg, proton pump inhibitors) and can exacerbate the already-declining absorption of this vitamin caused by atrophic gastritis.[61] Long-term treatment with metformin also decreases B_{12} absorption,[62] apparently as a result of inhibiting a calcium-dependent process that normally promotes ileal uptake of the B_{12}-intrinsic factor complex. Preliminary data indicate that this effect is ameliorated by calcium supplementation.[63]

Hypokalemia frequently results from commonly used diuretics, amphotericin B, corticosteroids, antipseudomonal penicillins, and insulin, while hyperkalemia may result from heparin,[13] as well as from potassium-sparing diuretics and poor kidney function.[64]

Hypomagnesemia and **thiamine** deficiencies frequently result from treatment with diuretics, and the former can also occur due to administration of amphotericin B, aminoglycoside antibiotics, and cyclosporine.[13,24] Cisplatin therapy may cause hypomagnesemia.[65]

Hypocalcemia may result from foscarnet by forming a complex with ionized calcium.[13] It may also occur in patients given bisphosphonates who have unrecognized hypoparathyroidism, impaired renal function, or vitamin D deficiency.[66]

Sodium imbalances may occur due to the ubiquitous presence of sodium and phosphorus in foods; deficiencies of these electrolytes are less common. Hyponatremia, however, can occur from carbamazepine and thiazide diuretics, while hypernatremia can result from drugs that cause diarrhea (eg, lactulose).

Micronutrients in Clinical Practice

Certain diseases or conditions increase nutrient needs. For example, diseases that cause malabsorption (chronic cholestasis, abetalipoproteinemia, celiac disease, and cystic fibrosis) result in vitamin E deficiency and the need for supplementation.[67] Clinicians should encourage patients to obtain these nutrients primarily from foods, rather than supplements, due to the presence of other nutrients in whole foods and their potentially synergistic effects.[68] For example, vitamin E supplements only contain α-tocopherol, but food sources of vitamin E include γ-tocopherol (a scavenger of reactive oxygen and nitrogen radicals and inhibitor of cyclooxygenase)[69] and tocotrienols, which have both antioxidant and nonantioxidant benefits that alpha-tocopherol does not possess.[70]

Similarly, patients may be tempted to purchase dietary supplements containing carotenoids (eg, lutein/zeaxanthin) to prevent or treat certain eye diseases (see Cataract chapter and Macular Degeneration chapter). Although some studies indicate a benefit for supplements, many have found a protective association with carotenoids in foods. The latter may be a preferable source, because macular pigment density increases to a greater degree (43%) when lutein is combined with other antioxidants, compared with lutein alone (36% increase).[71] Emerging evidence also suggests that higher lutein intake is associated with progression of macular degeneration in the context of diets higher in easily peroxidized polyunsaturated fat (ie, linoleic acid).[72] Until further data are available, lutein and other micronutrients should be obtained from food primarily, and in supplement form only if recommended by a physician.

Certain individuals may require nutrients in amounts that exceed RDAs for healthy adults. Such individuals may also benefit from supplementation with nonessential or conditionally essential micronutrients (eg, carnitine, coenzyme Q10).

The three tables on the following pages show the relationship between micronutrients and health.

Table 1:

Conditions that May Be Improved by Nutrient Supplementation

Disease	Nutrient(s)	Rationale
Anemia, microcytic	Iron	Increased need in high-risk groups (eg, pregnant adolescents).
Anemia, pernicious	Vitamin B_{12}	Risk for deficiency in elderly individuals, post-gastrectomy patients.
Burn injury	Vitamins A, D & E; carotenoids; selenium, zinc, copper	Burns reduce blood levels; increases are needed to support immune function.
Celiac sprue	Vitamins D, E & K; B-vitamins; iron, calcium, zinc, magnesium	Restricted diet increases risk of deficiency.
Congestive heart failure	Thiamine, magnesium	Loss due to diuretics may further compromise cardiac function.
Cystic fibrosis	Vitamins A, D, E, K & C; selenium, zinc	Malabsorption of fat-soluble vitamins is common. CF patients have lower blood levels of antioxidants and greater oxidative stress.
Eating disorders	Multivitamin/ mineral, calcium, vitamin D	Poor intake; evidence of deficiency; reversal of osteoporosis in patients with anorexia nervosa
End-stage kidney disease	B-vitamins, vitamin C	Losses due to dialysis treatment.
Inflammatory bowel disease	Beta-carotene, vitamins C, D & E; selenium, zinc	Malabsorption.
Macular degeneration	Vitamins C & E, beta-carotene; zinc, copper, lutein	Antioxidants reduce oxidative stress in the macula.
Osteoporosis	Calcium, vitamin D	At risk populations include elderly individuals and persons on long-term corticosteroid treatment.

Table 2:
Vitamin Functions, Deficiency Diseases, Toxicity Symptoms, and Dietary Reference Intakes**

Vitamin	Functions/Roles in metabolism	Deficiency Symptoms	Toxicity Symptoms	Recommended Dietary Allowance
Vitamin A	Bone growth, reproduction, cell division, immunity, cell differentiation	Clinical: Night blindness; total blindness (rare in the U.S.) Subclinical: May increase risk for respiratory and diarrheal infections; decrease growth rate; slow bone develop-ment; and decrease likelihood of survival from serious illness	Birth defects, liver abnormalities, reduced bone mineral density; central nervous system disorders (eg, pseudotumor cerebri)	**Adults (Age 19+):** Males: 900 µg Females: 700 µg **Infants/children:** 0-6 months:* 400 µg 7-12 months:* 500 µg 1-3 years: 300 µg 4-8 years: 400 µg 9-13 years: 600 µg 14-18 years (males): 900 µg 14-18 years (females): 700 µg **Pregnancy:** Age ≤18: 750 µg Age 19+: 770 µg **Lactation:** Age ≤18: 1,200 µg Age 19+: 1,300 µg

Vitamin D	Maintenance of normal blood levels of calcium and phosphorus; promotes bone mineralization; regulates cell growth, differentiation, immune function	In children: rickets In adults: osteomalacia	Nausea, vomiting, poor appetite, constipation, weakness, and weight loss; mental status changes; hypercalcemia; calcinosis	**Adults:*** Ages 19-50: 5 μg/200 IU Ages 51-70: 10 μg/400 IU Ages 70+: 15 μg/600 IU **Infants/children:*** 1-18 years: 5 μg/200 IU **Pregnancy/ lactation:*** 5 μg/200 IU
Vitamin E	Antioxidant (protects cells against free radicals); plays role in immune function and in DNA repair; inhibits cell proliferation, platelet aggregation, and monocyte adhesion[1]	Nerve degeneration in hands and feet	Can influence coagulation in some persons with drug-induced vitamin K deficiency; anti-platelet effect	**Adults (19+ years):** 15 mg **Infants/children:** 0-6 months:* 4 mg 7-12 months:* 5 mg 1-3 years: 6 mg 4-8 years: 7 mg 9-13 years: 11 mg 14-18 years: 15 mg **Pregnancy:** 15 mg **Lactation:** 19 mg

TABLE 2 CONTINUED ON NEXT PAGE

TABLE 2 CONTINUED

Vitamin	Functions/Roles in Metabolism	Deficiency Symptoms	Toxicity Symptoms	Recommended Dietary Allowance
Vitamin K	Coenzyme for synthesis of proteins involved in blood coagulation and bone metabolism	Increase in prothrombin time; in severe cases, hemorrhagic events	None currently known	**Adults (19+ years):***
				Males: 120 μg
				Females: 90 μg
				Infants/children/adolescents:*
				0-6 months: 2 μg
				7-12 months: 2.5 μg
				1-3 years: 30 μg
				4-8 years: 55 μg
				9-13 years: 60 μg
				14-18 years (males): 120 μg
				14-18 years (females): 75 μg
				Pregnancy/lactation:*
				Girls ≤18 years: 75 μg
				Adults 19 + years: 90 μg

**Sources: National Institutes of Health, Office of Dietary Supplements Web site (http://dietary-supplements.info.nih.gov/)

¹see Azzi A Zingg. Nonantioxidant activities of vitamin E. *Curr Med Chem.* 2004;11:1113-1133.

Institute of Medicine. *Dietary Reference Intakes for Vitamin A, Vitamin K, Arsenic, Boron, Chromium, Copper, Iodine, Iron, Manganese, Molybdenum, Nickel, Silicon, Vanadium, and Zinc.* Washington, D.C.: National Academies Press, 2000.

Institute of Medicine. *Dietary Reference Intakes for Vitamin C, Vitamin E, Selenium, and Carotenoids.* Washington, D.C.: National Academies Press, 2000.

* IOM did not set an RDA for vitamins in this age group. Instead, an Adequate Intake (AI) is used. According to the Institute of Medicine, "The AI is a recommended average daily nutrient intake level, based on experimentally derived intake levels or approximations of observed mean nutrient intake by a group (or groups) of apparently healthy people that are assumed to be adequate. An AI is established when there is insufficient scientific evidence to determine an Estimated Average Requirement (EAR)."

Vitamin	Functions/Roles in Metabolism	Deficiency Symptoms	Toxicity Symptoms	Recommended Dietary Allowance
Vitamin C	Antioxidant; biosynthesis of connective tissue components (collagen, elastin, fibronectin, proteoglycans, bone matrix, and elastin-associated fibrillin); carnitine, and neurotransmitters	Scurvy (involves deterioration of elastic tissue); follicular hyperkeratosis, petechiae, ecchymoses, coiled hairs, inflamed and bleeding gums, perifollicular hemorrhages, joint effusions, arthralgia, and impaired wound healing; dyspnea, edema, Sjögren syndrome, weakness, fatigue, depression	Nausea, abdominal cramps, and diarrhea (from supplements)	**Adults (≥19 years):** Males: 90 mg Females: 75 mg **Infants/children:** 0-6 months:* 40 mg 7-12 months:* 50 mg 1-3 years: 15 mg 4-8 years: 25 mg 9-13 years: 45 mg 14-18 years (males): 75 mg 14-18 years (females): 65mg **Pregnancy:** Age ≤18: 80 mg Age 19-50: 85 mg **Lactation:** Age ≤18: 115 mg Age 19+: 120 mg

TABLE 2 CONTINUED ON NEXT PAGE

TABLE 2 CONTINUED

Vitamin	Functions/Roles in Metabolism	Deficiency Symptoms	Toxicity Symptoms	Recommended Dietary Allowance
Thiamine (B₁)	Coenzyme in the metabolism of carbohydrates and branched-chain amino acids	Anorexia; weight loss; mental changes such as apathy, decrease in short-term memory, confusion, and irritability; muscle weakness; cardiomegaly; beriberi (polyneuritis)	Oral forms: None currently known Parenteral: Pruritus (rare: 1% of patients); extremely rare anaphylactic reaction IOM conclusion: Even high-dose IV use is relatively safe	**Adults (≥ 19 years):** Males: 1.2 mg Females: 1.1 mg **Infants/children:** 0-6 months:* 0.2 mg 7-12 months:* 0.3 mg 1-3 years: 0.5 mg 4-8 years: 0.6 mg 9-13 years: 0.9 mg 14-18 years (males): 1.2 mg 14-18 years (females): 1.1 mg **Pregnancy/lactation:** 1.4 mg
Riboflavin (B₂)	Coenzyme in numerous redox reactions	Ariboflavinosis; sore throat; hyperemia and edema of pharyngeal and oral mucous membranes; cheilosis; angular stomatitis;	None currently known	**Adults (Age 19+):** Males: 1.3 mg Females: 1.1 mg **Infants/children:** 0-6 months:* 0.3 mg 7-12 months:* 0.4 mg

Micronutrient	Function	Deficiency	Toxicity	RDA
		glossitis (magenta tongue); seborrheic dermatitis; normochromic, normocytic anemia		1-3 years: 0.5 mg 4-8 years: 0.6 mg 9-13 years (males): 0.9 mg 14-18 years (males): 1.3 mg 9-13 years (females): 0.9 mg 14-18 years (females): 1.0 mg **Pregnancy:** 1.4 mg **Lactation:** 1.6 mg
Niacin (B₃)	Coenzyme in numerous redox reactions	Pellagra (pigmented rash, vomiting, constipation or diarrhea, bright red tongue; neurological symptoms including depression, apathy, headache, fatigue, and loss of memory)	From nicotinamide: nausea, vomiting, and signs and symptoms of liver toxicity (at intakes of 3 g/day); from nicotinic acid: same signs at 1.5 g/day (most toxicity related to pharmacologic use); hepatotoxicity (at doses of 3-9 g/day); blurred vision, toxic amblyopia, macular edema (doses of 1.5-5g/day)	**Adult males and males ≥age 14:** 16.0 mg **Adult females and females ≥age 14:** 14.0 mg **Infants/children:** 0-6 months:* 2.0 mg 7-12 months:* 4.0 mg 1-3 years: 6.0 mg 4-8 years: 8.0 mg 9-13 years: 12.0 mg **Pregnancy:** 18.0 mg **Lactation:** 17.0 mg

TABLE 2 CONTINUED ON NEXT PAGE

TABLE 2 CONTINUED

Vitamin	Functions/Roles in Metabolism	Deficiency Symptoms	Toxicity Symptoms	Recommended Dietary Allowance
Pantothenic acid (B_5)	Component of coenzyme A; cofactor and acyl group carrier for many enzymatic processes, and acyl carrier protein, a component of the fatty acid synthase complex	Extremely rare; irritability and restlessness; fatigue; apathy; malaise; sleep disturbances; gastro-intestinal complaints such as nausea, vomiting, and abdominal cramps; neurobiological symptoms such as numbness, paresthesias, muscle cramps, staggering gait	None currently known	**Adults (Ages 19+):*** 5.0 mg **Infants/children/adolescents:*** 0-6 months: 1.7 mg 7-12 months: 1.8 mg 1-3 years: 2.0 mg 4-8 years: 3.0 mg 9-13 years: 4.0 mg 14-18 years: 5.0 mg **Pregnancy:*** 6.0 mg **Lactation:*** 7.0 mg
Pyridoxine (B_6)	Coenzyme in the metabolism of amino acids, glycogen, and sphingoid bases	Seborrheic dermatitis, microcytic anemia, epileptiform convulsions	Sensory neuropathy with high (≥100 mg) supplementary intake	**Adults:** Ages 19-50: 1.3 mg Age 51+ (males): 1.7 mg Age 51+ (females): 1.5 mg **Infants/children:** 0-6 months:* 0.1 mg 7-12 months:* 0.3 mg

	Coenzymes are involved in DNA synthesis; amino acid interconversions; single-carbon metabolism; methylation reactions	Early sign: hypersegmented neutrophils Late sign: macrocytic anemia (weakness, fatigue, difficulty concentrating, irritability, headache, palpitations, shortness of breath)	None in healthy individuals; may decrease phenytoin levels and trigger seizures in patients with seizure disorder may precipitate or exacer-bate neuropathy in vitamin B_{12} deficient individuals		
				1-3 years:	0.5 mg
				4-8 years:	0.6 mg
				9-13 years:	1.0 mg
				14-18 years (males):	1.3 mg
				14-18 years (females):	1.2 mg
				Pregnancy:	1.9 mg
				Lactation:	2.0 mg
Folic acid				**Adults (Ages 19+):**	400 μg
				Infants/children:	
				0-6 months:*	65 μg
				7-12months:	80 μg
				1-3 years:	150 μg
				4-8 years:	200 μg
				9-13 years:	300 μg
				14-18 years:	400 μg
				Pregnancy:	600 μg
				Lactation:	500 μg

* IOM did not set an RDA for vitamins in this age group. Instead, an Adequate Intake (AI) is used. According to the Institute of Medicine, "The AI is a recommended average daily nutrient intake level, based on experimentally derived intake levels or approximations of observed mean nutrient intake by a group (or groups) of apparently healthy people that are assumed to be adequate. An AI is established when there is insufficient scientific evidence to determine an Estimated Average Requirement (EAR)."

TABLE 2 CONTINUED ON NEXT PAGE

TABLE 2 CONTINUED

Vitamin	Functions/Roles in Metabolism	Deficiency Symptoms	Toxicity Symptoms	Recommended Dietary Allowance
Vitamin B$_{12}$	Cofactor for methionine synthase and L-methyl-malonyl-CoA mutase; essential for normal blood formation and neurologic function	Pernicious anemia; neurologic manifestations (sensory disturbances in the extremities; motor disturbances, including abnormalities of gait); cognitive changes (loss of concentration; memory loss, disorientation and frank dementia); visual disturbances; insomnia; impotency; and impaired bowel and bladder control	None currently known	**Adults (Age 19+):** 2.4 μg **Infants/children:** 0-6 months:* 0.4 μg 7-12 months:* 0.5 μg 1-3 years: 0.9 μg 4-8 years: 1.2 μg 9-13 years: 1.8 μg 4-18 years: 2.4 μg **Pregnancy:** 2.6 μg **Lactation:** 2.8 μg
Biotin	Coenzyme in bicarbonate-dependent carboxylation reactions (eg, acetyl-CoA carboxylase, pyruvate carboxylase)	Dermatitis, conjunctivitis, alopecia, and central nervous system abnormalities (depression, lethargy, hallucinations, and paresthesia of the extremities)	None currently known	**Adults (Age 19+):*** 30 μg **Infants/children:*** 0-6 months: 5 μg 7-12 months: 6 μg 1-3 years: 8 μg 4-8 years: 12 μg 9-13 years: 20 μg 14-18 years: 25 μg **Pregnancy:*** 30 μg **Lactation:*** 35 μg

Choline	Synthesis and release of acetylcholine; precursor for the synthesis of cell membrane components (phospholipids and sphingomyelin), platelet activating factor, and betaine (important in metabolism of homocysteine)	Steatosis, liver damage	Fishy body odor, sweating, salivation, hypotension, mild hepatotoxicity	**Adults:***	
				Males (age 19+):	550 mg
				Females (age 19+):	425 mg
				Infants/children:*	
				0-6 months:	125 mg
				7-12 months:	150 mg
				1-3 years:	200 mg
				4-8 years:	250 mg
				9-13 years:	375 mg
				14-18 years (males):	550 mg
				14-18 years (females):	400 mg
				Pregnancy:*	450 mg
				Lactation:*	550 mg

Source: Institute of Medicine. *Dietary Reference Intakes for Thiamin, Riboflavin, Niacin, Vitamin B6, Folate, Vitamin B12, Pantothenic Acid, Biotin, and Choline* (1998) and Institute of Medicine (IOM). *Dietary Reference Intakes for Vitamin C, Vitamin E, Selenium, and Carotenoids.* Washington, D.C.: National Academies Press, 2000.

* IOM did not set an RDA for vitamins in this age group. Instead, an Adequate Intake (AI) is used. According to the Institute of Medicine, "The AI is a recommended average daily nutrient intake level, based on experimentally derived intake levels or approximations of observed mean nutrient intake by a group (or groups) of apparently healthy people that are assumed to be adequate. An AI is established when there is insufficient scientific evidence to determine an Estimated Average Requirement (EAR)."

Table 3:
Mineral Functions, Deficiency Diseases, Toxicity Symptoms, and Dietary Reference Intakes*

Mineral	Biochemical Role/ Function	Deficiency Symptoms	Toxicity Symptoms	Recommended Dietary Allowance or AI*
Calcium	Component of teeth and bones; mediates vascular contraction and vaso-dilation, muscle contraction, nerve transmission, and glandular secretion	Reduced bone mass and osteoporosis	Hypercalcemia; increased risk for kidney stones (with supplements); milk-alkali syndrome; possible increase in risk for prostate cancer (see Prostate Cancer chapter)	**Adults:*** Ages 19-50: 1,000 mg; Age 51+: 1,200 mg; **Infants/children/adolescents:*** 0-6 months: 210 mg; 7-12 months: 270 mg; 1-3 years: 500 mg; 4-8 years: 800 mg; 9-18 years: 1,300 mg; **Pregnancy/lactation:*** Age ≤18: 1,300 mg; Age 19+: 1,000 mg

Phosphorus	Component of most biological membranes and nucleotides and nucleic acids; buffering of acid or alkali excesses; temporary storage and transfer of the energy derived from metabolic fuels; activation of many catalytic proteins through phosphorylation	Anorexia, anemia, muscle weakness, bone pain, rickets and osteomalacia, general debility; may be seen in persons recovering from alcoholic bouts; in diabetic keto-acidosis; in refeeding with calorie-rich sources without paying attention to phosphorus needs; & with AL-containing antacids	Metastatic calcification, skeletal porosity, interference with calcium absorption	**Adults (Age 19+):** 700 mg
				Infants/children:
				0-6 months:* 100 mg
				7-12 months:* 275 mg
				1-3 years: 460 mg
				4-8 years: 500 mg
				9-18 years: 1,250 mg
				Pregnancy/lactation:
				Age ≤18: 1,250 mg
				Age 19+: 700 mg

TABLE 3 CONTINUED ON NEXT PAGE

TABLE 3 CONTINUED

Mineral	Biochemical Role/Function	Deficiency Symptoms	Toxicity Symptoms	Recommended Dietary Allowance or AI*
Magnesium	Required cofactor for over 300 enzymes, including ones involved in anaerobic and aerobic energy generation, glycolysis, and oxidative phosphorylation; DNA and RNA synthesis; activation of adenylate cyclase; sodium, potassium-ATPase activity; has a calcium channel-blocking effect	Hypocalcemia; neuro-muscular hyperexcitability & latent tetany; insulin resistance and impaired insulin secretion	GI disturbance (diarrhea, nausea, abdominal cramping, paralytic ileus); more likely to occur with impaired renal function	**Adults:** Ages 19-30 Males: 400 mg Females: 310 mg Ages 31+ Males: 420 mg Females: 320 mg **Infants/children:** 0-6 months:* 30 mg 7-12months:* 75 mg 1-3 years: 80 mg 4-8 years: 130 mg 9-13 years: 240 mg 14-18 years (males): 410 mg 14-18 years (females): 360 mg **Pregnancy:** Ages ≤18: 400 mg Ages 19-30: 350 mg Ages 31-50: 360 mg **Lactation:** Ages ≤18: 360 mg

| | | | | | Ages 19-30: | 310 mg |
| | | | | | Ages 31-50: | 320 mg |

Source: Institute of Medicine. *Dietary Reference Intakes for Calcium, Phosphorus, Magnesium, Vitamin D, and Fluoride.* Washington, D.C.: National Academies Press, 1997.

* IOM did not set an RDA for vitamins in this age group. Instead, an Adequate Intake (AI) is used. According to the Institute of Medicine, "The AI is a recommended average daily nutrient intake level, based on experimentally derived intake levels or approximations of observed mean nutrient intake by a group (or groups) of apparently healthy people that are assumed to be adequate. An AI is established when there is insufficient scientific evidence to determine an Estimated Average Requirement (EAR)."

Potassium	Neural transmission, muscle contraction, vascular tone	Cardiac arrhythmias; muscle weakness; leg discomfort; extreme thirst; frequent urination; confusion; glucose intolerance; increased blood pressure; increased salt sensitivity; increased risk for kidney stones; increased bone turnover	Fatigue, weakness, tingling, numbness, or other unusual sensations; paralysis, palpitations, difficulty breathing; cardiac arrhythmias; GI distress		**Adults & children:**	
					≥14 years of age:*	4,700 mg
					Infants/children:*	
					0-6 months:	400 mg
					7-12 months:	700 mg
					1-3 years:	3,000 mg
					4-8 years:	3,800 mg
					9-13 years:	4,500 mg
					Pregnancy:*	4,700 mg
					Lactation:*	5,100 mg

TABLE 3 CONTINUED ON NEXT PAGE

TABLE 3 CONTINUED

Mineral	Biochemical Role/Function	Deficiency Symptoms	Toxicity Symptoms	Recommended Dietary Allowance or AI*
Sodium	Maintenance of extra-cellular volume and plasma osmolality; is an important determinant of the membrane potential of cells and the active transport of molecules across cell membranes	Brain swelling, resulting in loss of appetite, nausea, vomiting, headache, mental status changes (confusion, irritability, fatigue, hallucinations); muscle weakness; convulsions	Elevated blood pressure; increased risk for cardiovascular disease and stroke; neurologic symptoms (confusion, coma, paralysis of the lung muscles)	**Adults:*** 19-50 years: 1,500 mg 51-70 years: 1,300 mg 70+ years: 1,200 mg **Infants/children:*** 0-6 months: 120 mg 7-12 months: 370 mg 1-3 years: 1,000 mg 4-8 years: 1,200 mg 9-18 years: 1,500 mg **Pregnancy:*** 1,500 mg **Lactation:*** 2,300 mg
Chloride	Important component of gastric juice as hydrochloric acid	Hypochloremic metabolic alkalosis. In infants, hypochloremia results in growth failure, lethargy, irritability, anorexia, gastrointestinal symptoms, and weakness; may also	Dehydration, fluid loss, hyper-natremia	**Adults:*** 19-50 years: 2,300 mg 51-70 years: 2,000 mg >70 years: 1,800 mg **Infants/children:*** 0-6 months: 180 mg 7-12 months: 570 mg 1-3 years: 1,500 mg

	result in hypokalemia, metabolic alkalosis, hematuria, hyper-aldosteronism, and increased plasma renin	4-8 years:	1,900 mg
		9-18 years:	2,300 mg
		Pregnancy:*	2,300 mg
		Lactation:*	2,300 mg

Source: Institute of Medicine. *Dietary Reference Intakes for Water, Potassium, Sodium, Chloride, and Sulfate.* Washington, D.C.: National Academies Press, 2004.

* IOM did not set an RDA for vitamins in this age group. Instead, an Adequate Intake (AI) is used. According to the Institute of Medicine, "The AI is a recommended average daily nutrient intake level, based on experimentally derived intake levels or approximations of observed mean nutrient intake by a group (or groups) of apparently healthy people that are assumed to be adequate. An AI is established when there is insufficient scientific evidence to determine an Estimated Average Requirement (EAR)."

TABLE 3 CONTINUED ON NEXT PAGE

TABLE 3 CONTINUED

Mineral	Biochemical Role/ Function	Deficiency Symptoms	Toxicity Symptoms	Recommended Dietary Allowance or AI*
Iron	Component of enzymes necessary for oxidative metabolism; heme proteins (hemoglobin, myoglobin, cytochromes); participates in electron transfer	Impaired physical work performance, develop-mental delay, cognitive impairment, anemia	Fatigue, anorexia, dizziness, nausea, vomiting, headache, weight loss, shortness of breath	**Adults:** Males 19+ & females 51+: 8 mg Females (age 19-50): 18 mg **Infants/children:*** 0-6 months:* 0.27 mg 7-12 months: 11 mg 1-3 years: 7 mg 4-8 years: 10 mg 9-13 years: 8 mg 14-18 years (males): 11 mg 14-18 years (females): 15 mg **Pregnancy:** 27 mg **Lactation:** 14-18 years: 10 mg 19-50 years: 9 mg
Zinc	Component of enzymes (RNA polymerase, alkaline phosphatase); structural role for some enzymes and in protein	Growth retardation, hair loss, diarrhea, delayed sexual maturation and	GI symptoms (epi-gastric pain, nausea, vomiting, abdominal cramps, diarrhea); impaired immune response; reduced copper status	**Adults (Age 19+):** Males: 11 mg Females: 8 mg **Infants/children:*** 0-6 months:* 2 mg

	Function	Deficiency	Toxicity	
	folding; anti-oxidant function as part of zinc-copper superoxide dismutase	impotence, eye and skin lesions, loss of appetite, delayed wound healing		7 months to 3 years: 3 mg 4-8 years: 5 mg 9-13 years: 8 mg 14-18 years (males): 11 mg 14-18 years (females): 9 mg **Pregnancy:** 14-18 years: 12 mg 19+ years: 11 mg **Lactation:** ≤ 18 years: 13 mg 19+ years: 12 mg
Copper	Component of metallo-enzymes (oxidases; eg, monoamine oxidase; lysyl oxidase used for collagen and elastin production; cytochrome c oxidase; dopamine β mono-oxygenase); part of zinc-copper SOD	Defects in connective tissue; anemia; immune and cardiac dysfunction	GI symptoms (abdominal pain, nausea, vomiting, cramps, diarrhea)	**Adults (Age 19+):** 900 µg **Infants/children:*** 0-6 months:* 200 µg 7-12 months:* 220 µg 1-3 years: 340 µg 4-8 years: 440 µg 9-13 years: 700 µg 14-18 years: 890 µg **Pregnancy:** 1000 µg **Lactation:** 1300 µg

TABLE 3 CONTINUED ON NEXT PAGE

TABLE 3 CONTINUED

Mineral	Biochemical Role/Function	Deficiency Symptoms	Toxicity Symptoms	Recommended Dietary Allowance or AI*
Chromium	Potentiation of insulin action; mobilizes the glucose transporter, GLUT4, to the plasma membrane; enhances tyrosine phosphorylation of the insulin receptor	Rare; found in patients on TPN prior to inclusion of Cr+3; symptoms included weight loss, neuropathy, and impaired glucose tolerance	None for Cr+3; Cr+6 is a known carcinogen when inhaled, and oral ingestion (20 mg/l) causes GI symptoms (abdominal pain, nausea, vomiting, diarrhea)	**Adults:*** Males (age 19-50): 35 µg Females (age 19-50): 25 µg Males (age 50+): 30 µg Females (age 50+): 20 µg **Infants/children/adolescents:*** 0-6 months: 0.2 µg 7-12 months: 5.5 µg 1-3 years: 11 µg 4-8 years: 15 µg 9-13 years (males): 25 µg 9-13 years (females): 21 µg 14-18 years (males): 35 µg 14-18 years (females): 24 µg **Pregnancy:*** 30 µg **Lactation:*** 45 µg

Sources: Institute of Medicine. *Dietary Reference Intakes for Vitamin A, Vitamin K, Arsenic, Boron, Chromium, Copper, Iodine, Iron, Manganese, Molybdenum, Nickel, Silicon, Vanadium, and Zinc.* Washington, D.C.: National Academies Press, 2000; National Institutes of Health, Office of Dietary Supplements Web site (http://dietary-supplements.info.nih.gov/)

* IOM did not set an RDA for vitamins in this age group. Instead, an Adequate Intake (AI) is used. According to the Institute of Medicine, "The AI is a recommended average daily nutrient intake level, based on experimentally derived intake levels or approximations of observed mean nutrient intake by a group (or groups) of apparently healthy people that are assumed to be adequate. An AI is established when there is insufficient scientific evidence to determine an Estimated Average Requirement (EAR)."

Selenium	Defense against oxidative stress, regulation of thyroid hormone action, and regulation of the redox status of vitamin C and other molecules, through selenoproteins; eg, oxidant defense enzymes such as glutathione peroxidase; iodothyronine deiodinases	Keshan disease (cardiomyopathy in pediatric population); skeletal muscle disorders manifested by muscle pain, fatigue, proximal weakness, and serum creatine kinase (CK) elevation	Selenosis (gastrointestinal upset, hair loss, white blotchy nails, garlic breath odor, fatigue, irritability, and mild nerve damage); hair and nail brittleness and loss	**Adults (Age 19+):** 55 µg
				Infants/children: *
				0-6 months: 15 µg
				7-12 months: 20 µg
				1-3 years: 20 µg
				4-8 years: 30 µg
				9-13 years: 40 µg
				14-18 years: 55 µg
				Pregnancy: 60 µg
				Lactation: 70 µg

TABLE 3 CONTINUED ON NEXT PAGE

TABLE 3 CONTINUED

Mineral	Biochemical Role/Function	Deficiency Symptoms	Toxicity Symptoms	Recommended Dietary Allowance or AI*	
Iodine	Component of the thyroid hormones thyroxine (T4) and triiodothyronine (T3)	Mental retardation, hypothyroidism, goiter, cretinism, and varying degrees of other growth and developmental abnormalities	Burning of the mouth, throat, and stomach; abdominal pain; fever; nausea, vomiting; diarrhea; weak pulse; cardiac irritability; coma; cyanosis; thyroid enlargement (goiter) from increased TSH stimulation; increased risk of thyroid papillary cancer; iodermia; hyperthyroidism	**Adults (Age 19+):** 150 μg	
				Infants/children:*	
				0-6 months:*	110 μg
				7-12 months:*	130 μg
				1-3 years:	90 μg
				4-8 years:	90 μg
				9-13 years:	120 μg
				14-18 years:	150 μg
				Pregnancy:	220 μg
				Lactation:	290 μg
Manganese	Component of metallo-enzymes (arginase, manganese superoxide dismutase, pyruvate carboxylase)	Dermatitis, hypo-holesterolemia	Neurotoxicity	**Adults (Age 19+):***	
				Males:	2.3 mg
				Females:	1.8 mg
				Infants/children:*	
				0-6 months:	3.0 μg
				7-12 months:	0.6 mg
				1-3 years:	1.2 mg
				4-8 years:	1.5 mg

				9-13 years (males): 1.9 mg
				9-18 years (females): 1.6 mg
				14-18 years (males): 2.2 mg
				Pregnancy:* 2.0 mg
				Lactation:* 2.6 mg
Molybdenum	Component of sulfite oxidase, xanthine oxidase, aldehyde oxidase, enzymes involved in catabolism of sulfur-containing amino acids, purines, and pyridines	Rare; initially seen in patients on TPN, before addition of MO to standard TPN regimes; resulted in tachycardia, headache, night blindness, low serum uric acid	Reproductive effects as observed in animal studies; with occupational exposure, hyper-uricemia, and gout symptoms	**Adults (Age 19+):** 45 µg
				Infants/children:*
				0-6 months:* 2 µg
				7-12 months:* 3 µg
				1-3 years: 17 µg
				4-8 years: 22 µg
				9-13 years: 34 µg
				14-18 years: 43 µg
				Pregnancy/lactation: 50 µg

Sources: Institute of Medicine. *Dietary Reference Intakes for Vitamin A, Vitamin K, Arsenic, Boron, Chromium, Copper, Iodine, Iron, Manganese, Molybdenum, Nickel, Silicon, Vanadium, and Zinc.* Washington, D.C.: National Academies Press, 2000; National Institutes of Health, Office of Dietary Supplements Web site (http://dietary-supplements.info.nih.gov/)
* IOM did not set an RDA for vitamins in this age group. Instead, an Adequate Intake (AI) is used. According to the Institute of Medicine, "The AI is a recommended average daily nutrient intake level, based on experimentally derived intake levels or approximations of observed mean nutrient intake by a group (or groups) of apparently healthy people that are assumed to be adequate. An AI is established when there is insufficient scientific evidence to determine an Estimated Average Requirement (EAR)."

References

1. Bisse E, Epting T, Beil A, Lindinger G, Lang H, Wieland H. Reference values for serum silicon in adults. *Anal Biochem.* 2005;337:130-135.

2. Srivastava AK, Mehdi MZ. Insulinomimetic and anti-diabetic effects of vanadium compounds. *Diabet Med.* 2005;22:2-13.

3. Ames BN, Wakimoto P. Are vitamin and mineral deficiencies a major cancer risk? *Nat Rev Cancer.* 2002;2:694-704.

4. Corman LC. Effects of specific nutrients on the immune response. Selected clinical applications. *Med Clin North Am.* 1985;69:759-791.

5. Baik HW, Russell RM. Vitamin B_{12} deficiency in the elderly. *Annu Rev Nutr.* 1999;19:357-377.

6. Hampl JS, Taylor CA, Johnston CS. Vitamin C deficiency and depletion in the United States: the Third National Health and Nutrition Examination Survey, 1988 to 1994. *Am J Public Health.* 2004;94:870-875.

7. Mayland CR, Bennett MI, Vitamin C deficiency in cancer patients. *Palliat Med.* 2005;19:17-20.

8. Paillaud E, Merlier I, Dupeyron C, Scherman E, Poupon J, Bories PN. Oral candidiasis and nutritional deficiencies in elderly hospitalised patients. *Br J Nutr.* 2004;92:861-867.

9. Levin NA, Greer KE. Scurvy in an unrepentant carnivore. *Cutis.* 2000;66:39-44.

10. Gartner LM, Greer FR. Section on Breastfeeding and Committee on Nutrition. American Academy of Pediatrics. Prevention of rickets and vitamin D deficiency: new guidelines for vitamin D intake. *Pediatrics.* 2003;111(pt 1):908-910.

11. Calvo MS, Whiting SJ, Barton CN. Vitamin D fortification in the United States and Canada: current status and data needs. *Am J Clin Nutr.* 2004;80(suppl 6):1710S-1716S.

12. Holick MF. Vitamin D: importance in the prevention of cancers, type 1 diabetes, heart disease, and osteoporosis. *Am J Clin Nutr.* 2004;79:362-371.

13. Brown RO, Dickerson RN. Drug-nutrient interactions. *Am J Manag Care.* 1999;5:345-352.

14. Giovannucci E, Liu Y, Stampfer MJ, Willett WC. A prospective study of calcium intake and incident and fatal prostate cancer. *Cancer Epidemiol Biomarkers Prev.* 2006;15:203-210.

15. Zittermann A, Schleithoff SS, Koerfer R. Putting cardiovascular disease and vitamin D insufficiency into perspective. *Br J Nutr.* 2005;94:483-492.

16. Heaney RP. Barriers to optimizing vitamin D3 intake for the elderly. *J Nutr.* 2006;136:1123-1125.

17. Cranney A, Horsley T, O'Donnell S, et al. Effectiveness and safety of vitamin D in relation to bone health. *Evid Rep Technol Assess* (Full Rep). 2007;158:1-235.

18. Centers for Disease Control and Prevention. Iron deficiency—United States, 1999-2000. *MMWR.* 2002;51:897-899.

19. Cuervo LG, Mahomed K. Treatments for iron deficiency anaemia in pregnancy. *Cochrane Database Syst Rev.* 2001;(2):CD003094.

20. Newmark HL, Heaney RP, Lachance PA. Should calcium and vitamin D be added to the current enrichment program for cereal-grain products? *Am J Clin Nutr.* 2004;80:264-270.

21. Lanou AJ, Berkow SE, Barnard ND. Calcium, dairy products, and bone health in

children and young adults: a reevaluation of the evidence. *Pediatrics.* 2005;115:736-743.

22. Feskanich D, Willett WC, Stampfer MJ, Colditz GA. Milk, dietary calcium, and bone fractures in women: a 12-year prospective study. *Am J Public Health.* 1997;87:992-997.

23. Institute of Medicine. *Dietary Reference Intakes for Calcium, Magnesium, Vitamin D, and Fluoride.* Washington, DC: National Academy Press; 2000:190-249.

24. Agus ZS. Hypomagnesemia. *J Am Soc Nephrol.* 1999;10:1616-1622.

25. King DE, Mainous AG III, Geesey ME, Woolson RF. Dietary magnesium and C-reactive protein levels. *J Am Coll Nutr.* 2005;24:166-171.

26. Huerta MG, Roemmich JN, Kingston ML, et al. Magnesium deficiency is associated with insulin resistance in obese children. *Diabetes Care.* 2005;28:1175-1181.

27. de Lordes Lima M, Cruz T, Pousada JC, Rodrigues LE, Barbosa K, Cangucu V. The effect of magnesium supplementation in increasing doses on the control of type 2 diabetes. *Diabetes Care.* 1998;21:682-686.

28. U.S. Preventive Services Task Force. Routine vitamin supplementation to prevent cancer and cardiovascular disease: recommendations and rationale. *Ann Intern Med.* 2003;139:51-55.

29. Cao G, Russell RM, Lischner N, Prior RL. Serum antioxidant capacity is increased by consumption of strawberries, spinach, red wine or vitamin C in elderly women. *J Nutr.* 1998;128:2383-2390.

30. Michels KB, Wolk A. A prospective study of variety of healthy foods and mortality in women. *Int J Epidemiol.* 2002;31:847-854.

31. Kris-Etherton PM, Hecker KD, Bonanome A, et al. Bioactive compounds in foods: their role in the prevention of cardiovascular disease and cancer. *Am J Med.* 2002;113(suppl 9B):71S-88S.

32. Fraser GE. Associations between diet and cancer, ischemic heart disease, and all-cause mortality in non-Hispanic white California Seventh-day Adventists. *Am J Clin Nutr.* 1999;70(suppl 3):532S-538S.

33. Bergheim I, Parlesak A, Dierks C, Bode JC, Bode C. Nutritional deficiencies in German middle-class male alcohol consumers: relation to dietary intake and severity of liver disease. *Eur J Clin Nutr.* 2003;57:431-438.

34. Gueguen S, Pirollet P, Leroy P, et al. Changes in serum retinol, alpha-tocopherol, vitamin C, carotenoids, zinc and selenium after micronutrient supplementation during alcohol rehabilitation. *J Am Coll Nutr.* 2003;22:303-310.

35. Thomson AD, Cook CCH, Touquet R, Henry JA. The Royal College of Physicians report on alcohol: guidelines for managing Wernicke's encephalopathy in the Accident and Emergency Department. *Alcohol and Alcoholism.* 2002;37:513-521.

36. Stolzenberg-Solomon RZ, Change SC, Leitzmann MF, et al. Folate intake, alcohol use, and postmenopausal breast cancer risk in the Prostate, Lung, Colorectal, and Ovarian Cancer Screening Trial. *Am J Clin Nutr.* 2006;83:895-904.

37. Akikusa JD, Garrick D, Nash MC. Scurvy: forgotten but not gone. *J Paediatr Child Health.* 2003;39:75-77.

38. Davey GK, Spencer EA, Appleby PN, Allen NE, Knox KH, Key TJ. EPIC-Oxford: lifestyle characteristics and nutrient intakes in a cohort of 33,883 meat-eaters and 31,546 non meat-eaters in the UK. *Public Health Nutr.* 2003;6:259-269.

39. Thane CW, Bates CJ. Dietary intakes and nutrient status of vegetarian preschool children from a British national survey. *J Hum Nutr Diet.* 2000;13:149-162.

40. Alexander H, Lockwood LP, Harris MA, Melby CL. Risk factors for cardiovascular disease and diabetes in two groups of Hispanic Americans with differing dietary habits. *J Am Coll Nutr.* 1999;18:127-136.

41. Koebnick C, Heins UA, Hoffman I, Dagnelie PC, Leitzmann C. Folate status during pregnancy in women is improved by long-term high vegetable intake compared with the average western diet. *J Nutr.* 2001;131:733-739.

42. Fuchs J, Podda M, Packer L, Kaufmann R. Morbidity risk in HFE associated hereditary hemochromatosis C282Y heterozygotes. *Toxicology.* 2002;180:169-181.

43. Beutler E. The HFE Cys282Tyr mutation as a necessary but not sufficient cause of clinical hereditary hemochromatosis. *Blood.* 2003;101:3347-3350.

44. Lauffer RB, ed. *Iron and Human Diseases.* Boca Raton, FL: CRC Press; 1992.

45. Fleming DJ, Tucker KI, Jacques PF, Dallal GE, Wilson PW, Wood RJ. Dietary factors associated with the risk of high iron stores in the elderly Framingham Heart Study cohort. *Am J Clin Nutr.* 2002;76:1375-1384.

46. Ma J, Hampl JS, Betts NM. Antioxidant intakes and smoking status: data from the continuing survey of food intakes by individuals 1994-1996. *Am J Clin Nutr.* 2000;71:774-780.

47. Dietrich M, Block G, Norkus EP, et al. Smoking and exposure to environmental tobacco smoke decrease some plasma antioxidants and increase gamma-tocopherol in vivo after adjustment for dietary antioxidant intakes. *Am J Clin Nutr.* 2003;77:160-166.

48. Fairfield KM, Fletcher RH. Vitamins for chronic disease prevention in adults: scientific review. *JAMA.* 2002;287:3116-3126.

49. Liu T, Howard RM, Mancini AJ, et al. Kwashiorkor in the United States: fad diets, perceived and true milk allergy, and nutritional ignorance. *Arch Dermatol.* 2001;137:630-636.

50. Greene-Finestone LS, Campbell MK, Evers SE, Gutmanis IA. Adolescents' low-carbohydrate-density diets are related to poorer dietary intakes. *J Am Diet Assoc.* 2005;105:1783-1788.

51. Turner-McGrievy GM, Barnard ND, Scialli AR, Lanou AJ. Effects of a low-fat, vegan diet and a Step II diet on macro- and micronutrient intakes in overweight, postmenopausal women. *Nutrition.* 2004;20:738-746.

52. Fletcher RH, Fairfield KM. Vitamins for chronic disease prevention in adults: clinical applications. *JAMA.* 2002;287:3127-3129.

53. Seymons K, De Moor A, De Raeve H, Lambert J. Dermatologic signs of biotin deficiency leading to the diagnosis of multiple carboxylase deficiency. *Pediatr Dermatol.* 2004;21:231-235.

54. Grillo E, da Silva RJ, Barbato JH Jr. Pyridoxine-dependent seizures responding to extremely low-dose pyridoxine. *Dev Med Child Neurol.* 2001;43:413-415.

55. Lewis DP, Van Dyke DC, Stumbo PJ, Berg MJ. Drug and environmental factors associated with adverse pregnancy outcomes. Part I: Antiepileptic drugs, contraceptives, smoking, and folate. *Ann Pharmacother.* 1998;32:802-817.

56. Tumer L, Serdaroglu A, Hasanoglu A, Biberoglu G, Aksoy E. Plasma homocysteine and lipoprotein (a) levels as risk factors for atherosclerotic vascular disease in epileptic children taking anticonvulsants. *Acta Paediatr.* 2002;91:923-926.

57. Huemer M, Ausserer B, Graninger G, et al. Hyperhomocysteinemia in children treated with antiepileptic drugs is normalized by folic acid supplementation. *Epilepsia.* 2005;46:1677-1683.

58. Apeland T, Mansoor MA, Pentieva K, McNulty H, Seljeflot I, Strandjord RE. The effect

of B-vitamins on hyperhomocysteinemia in patients on antiepileptic drugs. *Epilepsy Res.* 2002;51:237-247.

59. Endresen GK, Husby G. Folate supplementation during methotrexate treatment of patients with rheumatoid arthritis. An update and proposals for guidelines. *Scand J Rheumatol.* 2001;30:129-134.

60. American College of Rheumatology Subcommittee on Rheumatoid Arthritis Guidelines. Guidelines for the management of rheumatoid arthritis: 2002 update. *Arthritis Rheum.* 2002;46:328-346.

61. Wolters M, Strohle A, Hahn A. Cobalamin: a critical vitamin in the elderly. *Prev Med.* 2004;39:1256-1266.

62. Bailey CJ, Turner RC. Metformin. *N Engl J Med.* 1996;334:574-579.

63. Bauman WA, Shaw S, Jayatilleke E, Spungen AM, Herbert V. Increased intake of calcium reverses vitamin B_{12} malabsorption induced by metformin. *Diabetes Care.* 2000;23:1227-1231.

64. Sica D. Antihypertensive therapy and its effects on potassium homeostasis. *J Clin Hypertens* (Greenwich). 2006;8:67-73.

65. Lajer H, Daugaard G. Cisplatin and hypomagnesemia. *Cancer Treat Rev.* 1999;25:47-58.

66. Maalouf NM, Heller HJ, Odvina CV, Kim PJ, Sakhae K. Bisphosphonate-induced hypocalcemia: report of 3 cases and review of literature. *Endocr Pract.* 2006;12:48-53.

67. Aslam A, Misbah SA, Talbot K, Chapel H. Vitamin E deficiency induced neurological disease in common variable immunodeficiency: two cases and a review of the literature of vitamin E deficiency. *Clin Immunol.* 2004;112:24-29.

68. Jacobs DR Jr, Steffen LM. Nutrients, foods, and dietary patterns as exposures in research: a framework for food synergy. *Am J Clin Nutr.* 2003;78(suppl 3):508S-513S.

69. Halliwell B, Rafter J, Jenner A. Health promotion by flavonoids, tocopherols, tocotrienols, and other phenols: direct or indirect effects? Antioxidant or not? *Am J Clin Nutr.* 2005;81(suppl 1):268S-276S.

70. Schaffer S, Muller WE, Eckert GP. Tocotrienols: constitutional effects in aging and disease. *J Nutr.* 2005;135:151-154.

71. Anon. Lutein and zeaxanthin. Monograph. *Alt Med Rev.* 2005;10:128-135.

72. Vu HT, Robman L, McCarty CA, Taylor HR, Hodge A. Does dietary lutein and zeaxanthin increase the risk of age related macular degeneration? The Melbourne Visual Impairment Project. *Br J Ophthalmol.* 2006;90:389-390.

4. Nutritional Requirements Throughout the Life Cycle

We need essential amino acids, carbohydrate, essential fatty acids, and 28 vitamins and minerals to sustain life and health. However, nutritional needs vary from one life stage to another. During intrauterine development, infancy, and childhood, for example, recommended intakes of macronutrients and most micronutrients are higher relative to body size, compared with those during adulthood. In elderly persons, some nutrient needs (eg, vitamin D) increase, while others (eg, energy and iron) are reduced.

The National Academy of Sciences has published recommendations for Dietary Reference Intakes (DRI)[1] that are specific for the various stages of life. It should be noted, however, that the DRIs are not designed for individuals who are either chronically ill or who are at high risk for illness due to age, genetic, or lifestyle factors (eg, smoking, alcohol intake, strenuous exercise). Clinicians must make their own judgments regarding nutrient requirements in such cases based on available information (see table).

In this chapter, we will examine nutrient needs throughout the life cycle. Two major themes emerge:

First, the predominant nutritional problem in developed countries is overnutrition. It has led to unprecedented epidemics of obesity and chronic diseases. Clinicians can assist patients in making the dietary shifts necessary to prevent overnutrition and its sequelae.

Second, a renewed emphasis on vegetables, fruits, whole grains, and legumes can help prevent weight problems and chronic illnesses, including cardiovascular disease,[2] diabetes,[3] and cancer,[4] among others.[5] Plant-based diets meet or exceed recommended intakes of most nutrients and have the advantage of being lower in total fat, saturated fat, and cholesterol than typical Western diets,[6] with measurable health benefits.[7]

Excess Calorie Intakes: A Risk Factor Common to All Age Groups

The major nutritional problems encountered in developed countries are excess macronutrient intake (especially saturated fat, protein, and sugar) and insufficient intake of the fiber and micronutrients provided by vegetables, fruits, grains, and legumes.

Overnutrition begins early. Pregnant and lactating women are encouraged to eat more because they are "eating for two." While it is true that an expectant mother must provide nutrition for both herself and her developing baby, the increased energy requirement of pregnancy amounts to no more than about 300 calories per day.[1] Excessive nutrient intake may result in excessive weight gain, conferring a greater risk for cesarean section and other complications of pregnancy and delivery.[8]

Overfed infants and children may develop dietary habits and perhaps even metabolic characteristics that have lifelong consequences.[9-11] Higher-than-recommended energy intakes at 4 months of age have been shown to predict greater weight gain before 2 years and risk for obesity in childhood and adulthood.[12,13] Therefore, caretakers should select foods conducive to healthy body weights and restrain their desire to promote child growth through overfeeding.

Adolescents face a similar problem. Many teens consume higher-than-recommended amounts of fat, saturated fat, sodium, and sugars, thereby increasing the risk for adolescent and adult obesity, among other health problems.[14] The increased prevalence of excess body weight in adolescents is correlated with escalating risk for type 2 diabetes.[15] This does not mean that adolescents are well nourished, however. In spite of their higher energy intake, adolescents frequently fail to achieve required intakes of essential micronutrients (eg, vitamins A and C).[16] This problem is compounded by the fact that roughly 60% of female and more than 25% of male adolescents are dieting to lose weight at any given time, and between 1% and 9% report using maladaptive habits, such as purging, to do so.[17]

Adults in developed countries are at particular risk from excess energy intake. While a significant percentage of North Americans (5% to 50%) consume less than half the recommended intake of micronutrients,[18] energy balance is typically far in excess of needs. In Western countries, dietary staples (eg, meat, dairy products, vegetable oils, and sugar) are more energy-dense than in traditional Asian or African cultures, where grains, legumes, and starchy vegetables are larger parts of the diet. This problem is aggravated by increases in food portion sizes and in the availability and consumption of calorie-dense, nutrient-poor fast foods.[19] As a result, this age group is experiencing an epidemic of obesity-related diseases, including coronary heart disease, hypertension, diabetes, and cancer. The metabolic syndrome, often triggered by obesity, is a common problem in elderly persons and is associated with greater risk for premature mortality.[20] These circumstances indicate a need for diets that are micronutrient-dense while modest in fat and energy.

Fertility

The role of nutrition in fertility has been the subject of a limited body of research focusing particularly on the role of antioxidants, other micro-nutrients, and alcohol. However, while nutritional and lifestyle factors may affect fertility directly, they also influence risk for several diseases that impair fertility, including polycystic ovarian syndrome, endometrio-sis, and uterine fibroids (see relevant chapters).

In females, some studies suggest a potential role for high-dose (750 mg/d) vitamin C and combinations of antioxidants, iron, and arginine supplements in achieving pregnancy.[21] Celiac disease, an immune-me-diated condition triggered by gluten, can also impair fertility in women by causing amenorrhea, inducing malabsorption of nutrients needed for organogenesis, and resulting in spontaneous abortion. In affected individuals, fertility may be improved by a gluten-free diet.[22] Obesity is also associated with decreased fertility in women.

In males, infertility may occur by disruption of the normal equilibrium between the production of reactive oxygen species by semen and ox-ygen-radical scavengers. This may occur through smoking, infection of the reproductive tract, varicocele,[23] and perhaps through poor diet as well. The result is oxidative damage to sperm. Controlled studies of high-dose combinations of supplementary antioxidants (vitamins C, >200 mg/d; vitamin E, 200 to 600 IU/d; selenium, 100 to 200 μg/d) found improved sperm motility and morphology and increased preg-nancy rates, particularly in former smokers.[23]

Carnitine is concentrated within the epididymis and contributes directly to the energy supply required by sperm for maturation and motility.[24] Treat-ment with carnitine or acetylcarnitine (1.0 to 2.0 g/d) increases the number and motility of sperm and the number of spontaneous pregnancies.[23,24]

Alcohol consumption is associated with decreased fertility in both women[25] and men.[26] In males, alcohol consumption contributes to im-potence and to a reduction of blood testosterone concentrations and impairment of Sertoli cell function and sperm maturation.[26]

Pregnancy and Lactation

Pregnant and lactating women have increased requirements for both macronutrients and micronutrients. The failure to achieve required in-takes may increase risk for certain chronic diseases in their children, sometimes manifesting many years later.[10,11] For instance, studies of the Dutch famine during World War II (in which rations were progres-sively cut from 1400 cal/d in August 1944 to 1000 cal/d in December, and ultimately to 500 cal/d) found that undernutrition during mid- to late pregnancy increased the risk for glucose intolerance and resulted in greater progression of age-related hypertension.[27] Malnutrition of women during early pregnancy correlated with higher body weights of their offspring as adults, along with increased risk for coronary heart disease and certain central nervous system anomalies.[10,27,28]

Protein requirements in pregnancy rise to 1.1 g/kg/d (71 g) to allow for fetal growth and milk production. The source of protein may be as important as the quantity, however. Some evidence suggests that protein requirements can be more safely met by vegetable than by animal protein. Meat is a major source of saturated fat and cholesterol; it is also a common source of ingestible pathogens[29] and a rich source of arachidonic acid, a precursor of the immunosuppressive eicosanoid PGE2.

Pregnant women also should not meet their increased need for protein by the intake of certain types of fish, such as shark, swordfish, mackerel, and tilefish, which often contain high levels of methylmercury, a potent human neurotoxin that readily crosses the placenta.[30] Other mercury-contaminated fish, including tuna and fish taken from polluted waters (pike, walleye, and bass), should be especially avoided.[31] There is no nutritional requirement for fish or fish oils. Vegetable protein sources, aside from meeting protein needs, can help meet the increased needs for folate, potassium, and magnesium and provide fiber, which can help reduce the constipation that is a common complaint during pregnancy.

Pregnant and/or lactating women also require increased amounts of vitamins A, C, E, and certain B vitamins (thiamine, riboflavin, niacin, pyridoxine, choline, cobalamin, and folate). Folate intake is especially important for the prevention of neural tube defects and should be consumed in adequate amounts prior to conception; evidence shows that average intakes are only ~60% of current recommendations.[32] Folate intakes were noted to be poorest in women eating a typical Western diet and highest in women eating vegetarian diets.[33] Pregnant women also require increased amounts of calcium, phosphorus, magnesium, iron, zinc, potassium, selenium, copper, chromium, manganese, and molybdenum.[1] Prenatal vitamin-mineral formulas are suggested to increase the likelihood that these nutrient needs will be met.

Infancy and Early Childhood

Requirements for macronutrients and micronutrients are higher on a per-kilogram basis during infancy and childhood than at any other developmental stage. These needs are influenced by the rapid cell division occurring during growth, which requires protein, energy, and nutrients involved in DNA synthesis and metabolism of protein, calories, and fat. Increased needs for these nutrients are reflected in DRIs for these age groups,[1] some of which are briefly discussed below.

Energy. While most adults require 25 to 30 calories per kg, a 4 kg infant requires more than 100 cals/kg (430 calories/day). Infants 4 to 6 months who weigh 6 kg require roughly 82 cals/kg (490 calories/day). Energy needs remain high through the early formative years. Children 1 to 3 years of age require approximately 83 cals/kg (990 cals/d). Energy requirements decline thereafter and are based on weight, height, and physical activity.

As an energy source, breast milk offers significant advantages over manufactured formula. Breast-feeding is associated with reduced risk for obesity,[34] allergies, hypertension, and type 1 diabetes; improved cognitive development; and decreased incidence and severity of infections. It is also less costly than formula feeding.[35]

Water. Total water requirements (from beverages and foods) are also higher in infants and children than for adults. Children have larger body surface area per unit of body weight and a reduced capacity for sweating when compared with adults, and therefore are at greater risk of morbidity and mortality from dehydration.[36] Parents may underestimate these fluid needs, especially if infants and children are experiencing fever, diarrhea, or exposure to extreme temperatures (eg, in vehicles during summer).

Essential fatty acids. Requirements for fatty acids on a per-kilogram basis are higher in infants than adults (see below). Through desaturation and elongation, linolenic and alpha-linolenic acids are converted to long-chain fatty acids (arachidonic and docosahexanoic acids) that play key roles in the central nervous system. Since both saturated fats and trans fatty acids inhibit these pathways,[37] infants and children should not ingest foods that contain a predominance of these fats.

Adolescence and Adulthood

The Institute of Medicine recommends higher intakes of protein and energy in the adolescent population for growth. For most micronutrients, recommendations are the same as for adults. Exceptions are made for certain minerals needed for bone growth (eg, calcium and phosphorus).[38] However, these recommendations are controversial, given the lack of evidence that higher intakes are an absolute requirement for bone growth. Evidence is clearer that bone calcium accretion increases as a result of exercise rather than from increases in calcium intake.[39]

Micronutrient needs in adults 19 to 50 years of age differ slightly according to gender. Males require more of vitamins C, K, B_1, B_2, and B_3; choline; magnesium; zinc; chromium; and manganese. Menstruating females require more iron, compared with males of similar age.

Later Years

Due to reductions in lean body mass, metabolic rate, and physical activity, elderly persons require less energy than younger individuals need. Some DRIs for elderly persons differ from those of younger adults. For example, in order to reduce the risk for age-related bone loss and fracture, the DRI for vitamin D is increased from 200 IU/d to 400 IU/d in individuals 51 to 70 years of age and from 200 IU/d to 600 IU/d for those >70 years of age. Suggested iron intakes drop from 18 mg per day in women ages 19 to 50 to 8 mg/d after age 50, due to iron conservation and decreased losses in postmenopausal women, compared with younger women.[1]

Some elderly persons have difficulty getting adequate nutrition because of age- or disease-related impairments in chewing, swallowing, digesting, and absorbing nutrients.[40] Nutrient status may also be affected by decreased production of digestive enzymes, senescent changes in the cells of the bowel surface, and drug-nutrient interactions[40] (see Micronutrients chapter). The results can be far-reaching. For example, a study in elderly long-term-care residents demonstrated frequent deficiency in selenium, a mineral important for immune function.[40] In turn, impaired immune function affects susceptibility to infections and malignancies. The role of vitamin B_6 in immunity also presents a rationale for higher recommended intakes for elderly persons.[41]

Nutritional interventions should first emphasize healthful foods, with supplements playing a judicious secondary role. Although modest supplementary doses of micronutrients can both prevent deficiency and support immune function (see Upper Respiratory Infection chapter), overzealous supplementation (eg, high-dose zinc) may have the opposite effect and result in immunosuppression.[42] Multiple vitamin-mineral supplements have not been consistently shown to reduce the incidence of infection in elderly individuals.[43] The effects of multiple vitamin-mineral supplementation on cancer risk may be mixed, with some studies showing benefit[44] and others showing increased cancer risk related to supplement use (eg, increased risk for prostate cancer[45] and non-Hodgkin lymphoma in women).[46] Risks may be specific to certain nutrients. For example, high calcium intake has been associated with prostate cancer risk (see Prostate Cancer chapter), while other micronutrients have protective effects.

Alcohol intake can be a serious problem in elderly persons. The hazards of excess alcohol intake include sleep disorders, problematic interactions with medications, loss of nutrients, and a greater risk for dehydration, particularly in those who take diuretics. Roughly one-third of elderly persons who overuse or abuse alcohol first develop drinking problems after the age of 60 years.[47]

Conclusion

Requirements for energy and micronutrients change throughout the life cycle. Although inadequate intake of certain micronutrients is a concern, far greater problems come from the dietary excesses of energy, saturated fat, cholesterol, and refined carbohydrate, which are fueling the current epidemics of obesity and chronic disease. Clinicians can assist patients in choosing foods that keep energy intake within reasonable bounds, while maximizing intakes of nutrient-rich foods, particularly vegetables, fruits, legumes, and whole grains.

Changing Nutrient Needs through the Life Cycle	
Life Stage	**Change in Nutrient Needs**
Pregnancy*	Increased requirements: energy, protein, essential fatty acids, vitamin A, vitamin C, B-vitamins (B_1, B_2, B_3, B_5, B_6, B_{12}, folate, choline) & calcium, phosphorus,** magnesium, potassium, iron, zinc, copper, chromium, selenium, iodine, manganese, molybdenum
Life Stage	**Change in Nutrient Needs**
Lactation*	Increased requirements: vitamins A, C, E, all B-vitamins, sodium, magnesium** Decreased requirements: iron
Infancy, childhood*	Increased requirements: energy, protein, essential fatty acids

Adolescence*	Increased requirements: energy, protein, calcium, phosphorus, magnesium, zinc (females only)
Early adulthood (ages 19-50)	Increased requirements for males, compared with females: vitamins C, K; B$_1$, B$_2$, B$_3$, and choline; magnesium, zinc, chromium, manganese Increased requirements for females, compared with males: iron
Middle age (ages 51-70)*	Increased requirements: vitamin B$_6$, vitamin D
Elderly (age 70+)*	Increased requirements: vitamin D Decreased requirements: energy; iron (females only)

* Relative to adult requirements for those 19-50 years of age (and on a per-kg basis for macronutrients).

** Applies only to individuals under age 18.

For detailed nutrient recommendations, see chapters on Macronutrients and Micronutrients.

References

1. Institute of Medicine. *Dietary Reference Intakes for Energy, Carbohydrate, Fiber, Fat, Fatty Acids, Cholesterol, Protein, and Amino Acids (Macronutrients).* Washington, DC: National Academies Press, 2005.

2. Hu FB. Plant-based foods and prevention of cardiovascular disease: an overview. *Am J Clin Nutr.* 2003;78(suppl 3):544S-551S.

3. Jenkins DJ, Kendall CW, Marchie A, et al. Type 2 diabetes and the vegetarian diet. *Am J Clin Nutr.* 2003;78(suppl 3):610S-616S.

4. Nishino H, Murakoshi M, Mou XY, et al. Cancer prevention by phytochemicals. *Oncology.* 2005;69(suppl 1):38-40.

5. Fraser GE. Associations between diet and cancer, ischemic heart disease, and all-cause mortality in non-Hispanic white California Seventh-day Adventists. *Am J Clin Nutr.* 1999;70(suppl 3):532S-538S.

6. Messina V, Mangels AR. Considerations in planning vegan diets: children. *J Am Diet Assoc.* 2001;101:661-669.

7. Fraser GE. Vegetarianism and obesity, hypertension, diabetes, and arthritis. In: *Diet, Life Expectancy, and Chronic Disease: Studies of Seventh-day Adventists and Other Vegetarians.* New York: Oxford University Press; 2003:129-148.

8. Kabiru W, Raynor BD. Obstetric outcomes associated with increase in BMI category during pregnancy. *Am J Obstet Gynecol.* 2004;191:928-932.

9. Nicklas T, Johnson R. American Dietetic Association. Position of the American Dietetic Association: dietary guidance for healthy children age 2 to 11 years. *J Am Diet Assoc.* 2004;104:660-677.

10. Roseboom TJ, van der Meulen JH, Ravelli AC, Osmond C, Barker DJ, Bleker OP. Effects of prenatal exposure to the Dutch famine on adult disease in later life: an overview. *Mol Cell Endocrinol.* 2001;185:93-98.

11. Jackson AA. Nutrients, growth, and the development of programmed metabolic function. *Adv Exp Med Biol.* 2000;478:41-55.

12. Ong KK, Emmett PM, Noble S, Ness A, Dunger DB, and the ALSPAC Study Team. Dietary energy intake at the age of 4 months predicts postnatal weight gain and childhood body mass index. *Pediatrics.* 2006;117:e503-e508.

13. Baird J, Fisher D, Lucas P, Kleijnen J, Roberts H, Law C. Being big or growing fast: systematic review of size and growth in infancy and later obesity. *BMJ.* 2005;331:929-935.

14. Whitlock EP, Williams SB, Gold R, Smith PR, Shipman SA. Screening and interventions for childhood overweight: a summary of evidence for the US Preventive Services Task Force. *Pediatrics.* 2005;116:e125-e144.

15. Vivian EM. Type 2 diabetes in children and adolescents--the next epidemic? *Curr Med Res Opin.* 2006;22:297-306.

16. Paeratakul S, Ferdinand DP, Champagne CM, Ryan DH, Bray GA. Fast-food consumption among US adults and children: dietary and nutrient intake profile. *J Am Diet Assoc.* 2003;103:1332-1338.

17. Daee A, Robinson P, Lawson M, Turpin JA, Gregory B, Tobias JD. Psychologic and physiologic effects of dieting in adolescents. *South Med J.* 2002;95:1032-1041.

18. Ames BN, Wakimoto P. Are vitamin and mineral deficiencies a major cancer risk? *Nat Rev Cancer.* 2002;2:694-704.

19. Isganaitis E, Lustig RH. Fast food, central nervous system insulin resistance, and obesity. *Arterioscler Thromb Vasc Biol.* 2005;25:2451-2462.

20. Firdaus M. Prevention and treatment of the metabolic syndrome in the elderly. *J Okla State Med Assoc.* 2005;98:63-66.

21. Agarwal A, Gupta S, Sharma RK. Role of oxidative stress in female reproduction. *Reprod Biol Endocrinol.* 2005;3:28-42.

22. Stazi AV, Mantovani A. A risk factor for female fertility and pregnancy: celiac disease. *Gynecol Endocrinol.* 2000;14:454-463.

23. Agarwal A, Nallella KP, Allamaneni SS, Said TM. Role of antioxidants in treatment of male infertility: an overview of the literature. *Reprod Biomed Online.* 2004;8:616-627.

24. Sinclair S. Male infertility: nutritional and environmental considerations. *Altern Med Rev.* 2000;5:28-38.

25. Eggert J, Theobald H, Engfeldt P. Effects of alcohol consumption on female fertility during an 18-year period. *Fertil Steril.* 2004;81:379-383.

26. Emanuele MA, Emanuele NV. Alcohol's effects on male reproduction. *Alcohol Health Res World.* 1998;22:195-201.

27. Kyle UG, Pichard C. The Dutch Famine of 1944-1945: a pathophysiological model of long-term consequences of wasting disease. *Curr Opin Clin Nutr Metab Care.* 2006;9:388-394.

28. St Clair D, Xu M, Wang P, et al. Rates of adult schizophrenia following prenatal exposure to the Chinese famine of 1959-1961. *JAMA*. 2005;294:557-562.

29. Fessler DM. Luteal phase immunosuppression and meat eating. *Riv Biol*. 2001;94:403-446.

30. Evans EC. The FDA recommendations on fish intake during pregnancy. *J Obstet Gynecol Neonatal Nurs*. 2002;31:715-720.

31. Jarup L. Hazards of heavy metal contamination. *Br Med Bull*. 2003;68:167-182.

32. Siega-Riz AM, Bodnar LM, Savitz DA. What are pregnant women eating? Nutrient and food group differences by race. *Am J Obstet Gynecol*. 2002;186:480-486.

33. Koebnick C, Heins UA, Hoffmann I, Dagnelie PC, Leitzmann C. Folate status during pregnancy in women is improved by long-term high vegetable intake compared with the average Western diet. *J Nutr*. 2001;131:733-739.

34. Owen CG, Martin RM, Whincup PH, Smith GD, Cook DG. Effect of infant feeding on the risk of obesity across the life course: a quantitative review of published evidence. *Pediatrics*. 2005;115:1367-1377.

35. Leung AK, Sauve RS. Breast is best for babies. *J Natl Med Assoc*. 2005;97:1010-1019.

36. Krous HF, Nadeau JM, Fukumoto RI, Blackbourne BD, Byard RW. Environmental hyperthermic infant and early childhood death: circumstances, pathologic changes, and manner of death. *Am J Forensic Med Pathol*. 2001;22:374-382.

37. Ascherio A, Willett WC. Health effects of trans fatty acids. *Am J Clin Nutr*. 1997;66(suppl 4):1006S-1010S.

38. Institute of Medicine. *Dietary Reference Intakes for Calcium, Phosphorus, Magnesium, Vitamin D, and Fluoride*. Washington, DC: National Academies Press; 1997.

39. Lanou AJ, Berkow SE, Barnard ND. Calcium, dairy products, and bone health in children and young adults: a reevaluation of the evidence. *Pediatrics*. 2005;115:736-743.

40. Chernoff R. Micronutrient requirements in older women. *Am J Clin Nutr*. 2005;81:1240S-1245S.

41. Institute of Medicine. *Dietary Reference Intakes for Thiamin, Riboflavin, Niacin, Vitamin B6, Folate, Vitamin B12, Pantothenic Acid, Biotin, and Choline*. Washington, D.C.: National Academies Press, 1998.

42. Bogden JD. Influence of zinc on immunity in the elderly. *J Nutr Health Aging*. 2004;8:48-54.

43. El-Kadiki A, Sutton AJ. Role of multivitamins and mineral supplements in preventing infections in elderly people: systematic review and meta-analysis of randomised controlled trials. *BMJ*. 2005;330:871-876.

44. Watkins ML, Erickson JD, Thun MJ, Mulinare J, Heath CW Jr. Multivitamin use and mortality in a large prospective study. *Am J Epidemiol*. 2000;152:149-162.

45. Stevens VL, McCullough ML, Diver WR, et al. Use of multivitamins and prostate cancer mortality in a large cohort of US men. *Cancer Causes Control*. 2005;16:643-650.

46. Zhang SM, Giovannucci EL, Hunter DJ, et al. Vitamin supplement use and the risk of non-Hodgkin's lymphoma among women and men. *Am J Epidemiol*. 2001;153:1056-1063.

47. Barrick C, Connors GJ. Relapse prevention and maintaining abstinence in older adults with alcohol-use disorders. *Drugs Aging*. 2002;19:583-594.

5. Basic Diet Orders: Teaching Patients Good Health Practices

The hospital is more than a place for treatment. It can be a place for learning. Picture this scenario:

A man arrives at the emergency room after an accident at a construction site. He has a compound fracture and a leg laceration with significant blood loss. After his initial treatment, he is admitted. His improvement is quick, and by day 2, he is medically stable and reasonably comfortable. His doctor arrives for a visit. After checking the wound sites and vital signs, the doctor sits down for a serious talk.

"You are going to come through this accident just fine," the doctor says. "You'll be out of the hospital before you know it. I don't expect any residual problems at all. You're going to be okay." Then the doctor's expression turns more serious. "While you're here, let's tackle another problem. As I understand it, you've been smoking two packs a day for quite some time now. While you're here, let me help you stop. These injuries won't kill you, but tobacco very likely will, and this is as good a time as any to deal with it."

The patient bites his lip. But he realizes the doctor is right. He had wanted to quit, of course, and now—stuck in a nonsmoking hospital—that is exactly what is going to happen, whether he likes it or not.

Later on, the same doctor sits down with another patient, this one hospitalized for a hip replacement. The patient also has a long-standing weight problem, poorly controlled hypertension, and a high cholesterol level. He has had two prior heart attacks, but has not followed through on suggestions that he change his diet. The doctor's speech sounds nearly identical:

"You are going to come through the surgery just fine," the doctor says. "You'll be out of the hospital in no time. But while you're here, let's tackle a more serious problem. I am going to ask the hospital staff to help you learn some healthy eating habits."

In the chart, the doctor orders a dietetic consultation and a healthful diet, explaining to the patient that this is a chance to try some healthful foods. Whether the patient keeps it up after discharge is his business. But the doctor is going to use the hospitalization to its full advantage.

None of this had anything to do with the man's hip, of course. But it had everything to do with what threatened his life over the long run.

Both patients told their families about what the doctor had said. And both families were mightily impressed.

These patients came to truly respect their doctor. Yes, they were a bit unsure about quitting smoking and rearranging long-standing eating habits. But, like many patients, they were well aware that they were not succeeding at tackling their problems on their own. They appreciated a caregiver who looked beyond the presenting complaint to what really threatened their long-term health. The doctor saw the problems they had been unable to solve and helped these patients to address them.

Helping Patients Adopt Healthy Diets

Although the value of healthy diets and lifestyles in preventing and treating disease is well established, too few health care providers raise these issues with their patients. The Behavioral Risk Factor Surveillance System surveyed approximately 13,000 obese individuals in 50 states, and found that only 42% had been advised by a health care provider to lose weight.[1]

Surveys show that physicians and medical students feel ill-prepared to address nutritional questions.[2] Aside from a lack of information, physicians are often concerned about patients' ability to stick to lifestyle changes. They may also face a lack of reimbursement and significant time pressures, among other problems.[1-3] Despite these reservations, the fact that patients seek out, respect, and are motivated by advice from physicians[4] indicates that clinic visits and hospital stays present important opportunities to effect major nutritional changes that improve health.

Partly in response to a growing consensus that practicing physicians and medical students should learn about nutrition, the National Institutes of Health developed the *Nutrition Guide for Training Physicians*.[5] This publication is designed to help physician-educators integrate essential medical nutrition knowledge and behavioral skills into undergraduate and graduate medical curricula.

Hospitalization as a Teaching Opportunity

Every hospitalization is a chance to help patients overcome problems that may be much more serious than the presenting complaint. Doctors do this every day:

An emergency physician treats a burn in a pediatric patient. But before closing the chart, he calls social services, because he suspects child abuse. That single action may have spared the child untold years of mistreatment.

An orthopedic surgeon treats a man's broken wrist. But before discharge, he has a frank talk about the alcoholism that led to the accident and arranges outpatient treatment.

A geriatric specialist can't find anything wrong with his patient's back. But with a few carefully chosen questions, he goes beyond the complaint of back pain. He discovers that the patient has no appetite, is sleeping poorly, and has lost interest in his usual activities. With the patient's permission, he arranges a psychiatric consultation for depression.

Child abuse, alcoholism, and depression are serious problems that are often hidden, and a physician who spots them makes a big difference.

If you are treating a typical North American population, you will confront equally deadly problems on a daily basis. Half of the patients in your practice will eventually die of cardiovascular disease. Many of the remainder will one day succumb to cancer. Along the way, diabetes, renal disease, chronic weight problems, and other serious health conditions will take their toll.

Depending on your specialty, these may not be your problems, of course. And, with ever-increasing time pressures, it is tempting to ignore the diet patterns that contribute to the presenting problems that you see. But hospitalization can be a time for a new beginning. You have the patient's attention, and with very little effort you can make a huge difference. The actions described below are the basic tools for getting the patient the help he or she needs.

Request a dietetic consultation. A registered dietitian can provide the nutritional counseling that you may not have the time or expertise for. If possible, extend the consultation into the post-hospitalization period. The process of diet change takes time, and patients always need continuing support.

Work as a team. In a weight management program at 80 general practice sites, a combination of physicians, nurses, and dietitians specializing in obesity was able to achieve weight loss of ≥5% of body weight in one-third of the patients. In addition, roughly 50% of patients attended all clinic appointments, and 40% of this sub-group also maintained weight loss ≥5% at 12 months.[6] These results suggest that, while a team approach will not conquer all nutrition-related problems at the first attempt, a significant number of patients respond well to it. A team approach should be combined with the use of an effective diet prescription, as described below.

A team approach also provides more expertise on the topics of interest to patients and saves time for physicians. Although questions regarding weight loss are especially common, a wide range of other topics come up routinely. Diet-drug interactions are a key topic. Unfortunately, physicians receive minimal training on informing patients about such interactions, in spite of this being a requirement of the Joint Commission on Accreditation of Healthcare Organizations.[2] A registered dietitian can be a helpful consultant to both physician and patient.

Call the dietary department. At some point, call the dietary department manager to let him or her know that you will be ordering healthful meals frequently. Surprising as it may sound, hospital dietary services are not necessarily thinking about the fat and cholesterol of the foods they serve. A single call or visit will help the dietary staff understand your goals and let them know that you appreciate their help. Let them know that you plan to request healthful diets (see below) on a regular basis.

Talk to the patient. Explain to the patient that you are interested in providing good care, not only for the presenting complaint, but for all aspects of health during the hospital stay. A common complaint among patients is that doctors (1) seem to know little about nutrition; (2) favor pharmaceutical prescriptions over dietary interventions; and (3) underestimate patients' interest in nutrition and ability to change. Patients appreciate a doctor who helps them in this area, even if that help consists only of a special diet order and a referral to a knowledgeable dietitian. Patients are barraged by dietary messages of all kinds, from fad diet books to advertising claims. You can help them find their way through the thicket of information and misinformation.

Studies suggest that clinicians have the most success in helping patients modify diet, exercise, or smoking habits when they elicit and acknowledge patients' concerns, support their efforts to change, offer choices about treatment options, and provide relevant information—all while minimizing pressure and control.[7] An authoritarian finger-wagging approach is likely to lead to rebellion, avoidance, or behavior changes that are only short-lived.[8]

For patients on medication, it is important to point out that medications work more effectively when combined with the diet prescribed. Poor food choices can negate the effect of medications. For example, foods high in sodium oppose the effects of diuretic medications, while foods high in saturated fat (eg, meat, eggs, and dairy products) oppose the benefits of cholesterol-lowering drugs. Many frequently prescribed medications designed for common ailments have additional benefits for patients. These include the anti-inflammatory benefits of statins,[9] the benefits of antidiabetic medications on endothelial dysfunction,[10] and the ability of ACE inhibitors and angiotensin receptor blocking drugs to significantly reduce the risk for type 2 diabetes.[11] However, diets high in saturated fat and low in protective fiber and antioxidants can do the opposite by increasing inflammation,[12] causing endothelial dysfunction[13] and increasing the risk for type 2 diabetes (see Diabetes chapter).

At outpatient visits, it is useful to ask the patient about his or her diet, just as you would about smoking. A dietitian can be extremely helpful with follow-up.

Encourage an optimal diet. Diet studies show that patients sometimes follow their doctors' orders and sometimes do not, but the more significant the changes are that their doctors recommend, the more changes patients actually accomplish.[14] If a doctor recommends as close to an optimal diet as possible, the likelihood of patients making at least some healthful changes is higher than if the doctor recommends only minor changes.

A contrary view is that, for many patients, recommended diet changes may be more effective if they are gradual, stepwise,[15] and communicated with the understanding that perfection is not expected. This view is common among clinicians, but is at odds with clinical experience with other types of lifestyle changes, such as smoking cessation or substance abuse treatment, in which case flexibility often leads to failure.

A reasonable solution is to prescribe an optimal diet, while avoiding any semblance of moralizing when patients have lapses. It should be recognized that guilt and secrecy often characterize dietary behavior. A physician can coach patients through the routine difficulties of diet change, while helping patients set aside guilt and blame.

Give the patient a clear path to follow. It is easy to give vague advice about "eating right" or "trying to cut back on calories," but it is much more helpful to provide the patient with clear expectations and a specific diet plan. The receipt of a physician's advice to change diet and exercise habits strongly predicts attempts by patients to actually initiate and follow through with these changes.[16] On the other hand, failure to communicate the purpose of treatment has been linked to noncompliance with therapeutic regimens. Compliance improves when physicians have better communication skills and when patients feel that they have more information and are actively participating in treatment planning.[17] Most patients need to hear a health message several times before putting the new information into practice.[4]

Many patients are new to preparing healthful meals. They appreciate referrals to books, Web sites, health-oriented grocery stores, cooking classes, and supportive organizations. Dietitians also also provide detailed and practical information. Hospital dietary or patient education departments may have nutrition or cooking classes, or can be encouraged to do so.

Welcome resistance. Mental health professionals know that when patients express resistance to change, it does not mean they are unwilling to change; it means they are expressing their concerns along the way. Many physicians misinterpret resistance as opposition, when, in reality, it is simply a way to discuss the challenges raised by the diet change. So when a patient says, "I don't like to cook," it is an opportunity for a dietitian to think through healthy simple meals or restaurant choices. A patient who says he could never give up certain favorite foods is showing a need for healthful alternatives. Resistance is a predictable stage in the process of change.

Clinicians often misjudge their patients' motivation.[18] Many patients are far more motivated than their caregivers give them credit for. Although behavior change is an inexact science, change can occur through successive approximations of desired behaviors. Physicians can help by taking an interest in nutrition, by recognizing that patients' resistance is to be expected but is rarely deep-seated, and by providing a supportive relationship.

Provide healthful basic diet orders. If a special diet is not ordered, patients will be provided a standard hospital diet. However, a special diet can provide an opportunity to introduce healthful habits, albeit briefly.

To tackle patients' diet-related health problems, the most broadly applicable diet orders, and the orders recommended unless other considerations apply, are as follows:

- Vegetarian diet, low-fat, nondairy
- Dietetic consultation

Although the dietary regimen may sound more demanding than the patient may need, it has been shown to be as acceptable to patients as other therapeutic diets.[19,20] It is also the only dietary approach that removes all cholesterol and animal fat from the patient's diet. As outlined in the first chapter of this book, evidence has shown this type of diet to be more effective for metabolic control, compared with other diets (see Coronary Heart Disease, Dyslipidemias, Diabetes, Hypertension, and Obesity chapters). Low-fat, vegetarian diets allow for weight reduction without a specific calorie restriction. This diet order will allow the patient to try out new foods and new tastes, without having to do any of the preparation.

Generally speaking, there are no contraindications to such orders. All hospitals are equipped to carry them out. However, some patients need additional orders, such as a sodium restriction for hypertension or a gluten-free diet for celiac disease.

Involve the family. After discharge, the family can either support or derail the patient's newfound eating habits. Ideally, they will serve as allies in the healing process. They are also likely to be at risk for the same diet-related problems the patient is displaying. With a single set of diet orders and dietetic follow-up, you can help them all.

References

1. Galuska DA, Will JC, Serdula MK, Ford ES. Are health care professionals advising obese patients to lose weight? *JAMA.* 1999;282:1576-1578.

2. Mihalynuk TV, Knopp RH, Scott CS, Coombs JB. Physician informational needs in providing nutritional guidance to patients. *Fam Med.* 2004;36:722-726.

3. Truswell AS, Hiddink GJ, van Binsbergen JJ, Kok F, van Weel C. Empowering family doctors and patients in nutrition communication. *Eur J Clin Nutr.* 2005;59(suppl 1):S1-3.

4. Blackburn GL. Teaching, learning, doing: best practices in education. *Am J Clin Nutr.* 2005;82(suppl 1):218S-221S.

5. National Heart, Lung, and Blood Institute. Nutrition curriculum guide for training physicians. Washington, D.C.: National Institutes of Health, 2002.

6. McQuigg M, Brown J, Broom J, et al. Empowering primary care to tackle the obesity epidemic: the Counterweight Programme. *Eur J Clin Nutr.* 2005;59(suppl 1):S93-100.

7. Williams GC, McGregor HA, Sharp D, et al. Testing a self-determination theory intervention for motivating tobacco cessation: supporting autonomy and competence in a clinical trial. Health Psychol. 2006;25:91-101.

8. Williams GC, Quill TE, Deci EL, Ryan RM. "The facts concerning the recent carnival of smoking in Connecticut" and elsewhere. *Ann Intern Med.* 1991;115:59-63.

9. Arnaud C, Burger F, Steffens S, et al. Statins reduce interleukin-6-induced C-reactive protein in human hepatocytes: new evidence for direct antiinflammatory effects of statins. *Arterioscler Thromb Vasc Biol.* 2005;25:1231-1236.

10. Sarafidis PA, Lasaridis AN. Actions of peroxisome proliferator-activated receptors-gamma agonists explaining a possible blood pressure-lowering effect. *Am J Hypertens.* 2006;19:646-653.

11. Abuissa H, Bel DS, O'keefe JH Jr. Strategies to prevent type 2 diabetes. *Curr Med Res Opin.* 2005;21:1107-1114.

12. Basu A, Deveraj S, Jialal I. Dietary factors that promote or retard inflammation. *Arterioscler Thromb Vasc Biol.* 2006;26:995-1001.

13. Abeywardena MY. Dietary fats, carbohydrates and vascular disease: Sri Lankan perspectives. *Atherosclerosis.* 2003;171:157-161.

14. Barnard ND, Akhtar A, Nicholson A. Factors that facilitate compliance to lower fat intake. *Arch Fam Med.* 1995;4:153-158.

15. Barlow SE, Dietz WH. Obesity evaluation and treatment: Expert Committee recommendations. The Maternal and Child Health Bureau, Health Resources and Services Administration and the Department of Health and Human Services. *Pediatrics.* 1998;102:E29.

16. Koster FR, Verheijden MW, Baartmans JA. The power of communication. Modifying behaviour: effectively influencing nutrition patterns of patients. *Eur J Clin Nutr.* 2005;59 (suppl 1):S17-S21.

17. Bellamy R. An introduction to patient education: theory and practice. *Med Teach.* 2004; 26:359-365.

18. Verheijden MW, Bakx JC, Van Weel C, Van Staveren WA. Potentials and pitfalls for nutrition counseling in general practice. *Eur J Clin Nutr.* 2005;59 (suppl 1):S122-128.

19. Barnard ND, Scherwitz LW, Ornish D. Adherence and acceptability of a low-fat, vegetarian diet among patients with cardiac disease. *J Cardiopulm Rehab.* 1992;12:423-431.

20. Barnard ND, Scialli AR, Turner-McGrievy GM, Lanou AJ. Acceptability of a very-low-fat, vegan diet compares favorably to a more moderate low-fat diet in a randomized, controlled trial. *J Cardiopulm Rehab.* 2004;24:229-235.

6. Resources for Patients

Web Resources

For patients with Internet access, *www.NutritionMD.org* is a noncommercial Web site designed to accompany this book. It provides health and dietary information for clinicians and the lay public and walks patients through the steps of a diet make-over. It also allows them to develop individualized menus, drawing from a database of hundreds of recipes, complete with automated nutrient analyses, and shopping lists. For patients without Internet access, you may wish to print out fact sheets from *www.NutritionMD.org* for use as patient handouts.

The Cancer Project, *www.CancerProject.org*, is a subsidiary of the Physicians Committee for Responsible Medicine focusing on dietary information for cancer prevention and survival. This site includes a full downloadable version of The Survivor's Handbook and a nutrition guide for cancer survivors, as well as a directory of free nutrition and cooking classes that are suitable for anyone seeking a healthier diet.

Dr. McDougall's Health and Medical Center, *www.drmcdougall.com*, offers up-to-date medical, health, and nutrition information, and low-fat vegetarian recipes.

The Vegetarian Resource Group Web site, *www.vrg.org,* offers free recipes, information regarding vitamins and minerals and the health benefits of vegan diets, and access to vegetarian publications.

The National Cancer Institute's 5 A Day for Better Health Web site, *http://5aDay.gov,* allows users to create their own cookbooks of free downloadable fruit and vegetable recipes.

Books

Barnard, Neal. *Food for Life.* New York: Harmony Books; 1993.

Barnard, Neal. *Foods That Fight Pain.* New York: Harmony Books; 1998.

Barnard, Neal. *Breaking the Food Seduction.* New York: St. Martin's Press; 2003.

Barnard, Neal. *Dr. Neal Barnard's Program for Reversing Diabetes.* New York: Rodale; 2007.

Campbell, T. Colin and Thomas M. Campbell. *The China Study: Startling Implications for Diet, Weight Loss and Long-Term Health.* Dallas, TX: BenBella Books; 2004.

Diehl, Hans. *Dynamic Health: A Simple Plan to Take Charge of Your Life.* Lake Mary, FL: Strang Communications; 2003.

Esselstyn, Caldwell. *Prevent and Reverse Heart Disease: The Revolutionary, Scientifically Proven, Nutrition-Based Cure.* New York: Avery; 2007.

Freston, Kathy. *Quantum Wellness: A Practical and Spiritual Guide to Health and Happiness.* New York: Weinstein Books; 2008.

Lavine, Jay. *The Eye Care Sourcebook.* Chicago: Contemporary Books; 2001.

McDougall, John A. *The McDougall Program: 12 Days to Dynamic Health.* New York: Plume Books; 1990.

McDougall, John A. *The McDougall Program for Maximum Weight Loss.* New York: Plume Books; 1994.

Ornish, Dean. *Dr. Dean Ornish's Program for Reversing Heart Disease.* New York: Ballantine Books; 1990.

Ornish, Dean. *Eat More, Weigh Less.* New York: Harper Collins; 1993.

Cookbooks

Alexander, Nanci. *The Sublime Restaurant Cookbook.* Summertown, TN: Book Publishing Company; 2009.

Davis, Brenda. *Becoming Vegan: The Complete Guide to Adopting a Healthy Plant-Based Diet.* Summertown, TN: Book Publishing Company; 2000.

Grogan, Bryanna Clark. *The (Almost) No Fat Cookbook: Everyday Vegetarian Recipes.* Summertown, TN: Book Publishing Company; 1994.

Grogan, Bryanna Clark. *20 Minutes to Dinner.* Summertown, TN: Book Publishing Company; 1997.

McDougall, Mary, and John McDougall. *The New McDougall Cookbook.* New York: Plume Books; 1993.

McDougall, Mary, and John McDougal. *The McDougall Quick & Easy Cookbook.* New York: Plume Books; 1999.

Pirello, Christina. *Christina Cooks: Everything You Always Wanted to Know About Whole Foods But Were Afraid to Ask.* New York: HP Books; 2004.

Oser, Marie. *The Enlightened Kitchen: Eat Your Way to Better Health.* Hoboken, NJ: John Wiley & Sons; 2002.

Wasserman, Debra, and Reed Mangels, PhD, RD. *Simply Vegan.* Baltimore, MD: The Vegetarian Resource Group; 2006.

DVDs

A New Approach to Nutrition and Diabetes. Neal Barnard, MD. Washington, DC: Physicians Committee for Responsible Medicine; 2008.

Eating Right for Cancer Survival. Neal D. Barnard, MD, Sualua Tupolo, and Stephanie Beine, RD. Washington, DC: The Cancer Project; 2009.

Food for Life: Unlocking the Power of Plant-Based Nutrition. Neal Barnard, MD. Washington, DC: Physicians Committee for Responsible Medicine; 2009.

Heart Health: Unlocking the Power of Plant-Based Nutrition for a Healthy Heart. Neal Barnard, MD. Washington, DC: Physicians Committee for Responsible Medicine; 2009.

McDougall Made Easy. John McDougall, MD. Santa Rosa, CA, 2009.

McDougall Made Irresistible. John McDougall, MD. Santa Rosa, CA 2009.

Weight Control: Unlocking the Power of Plant-Based Nutrition for Weight Control. Neal Barnard, MD. Washington, DC: Physicians Committee for Responsible Medicine; 2009.

SECTION II: NUTRITIONAL DISORDERS

7. Protein-Calorie Malnutrition

Protein-calorie malnutrition results in two similar but distinct diseases, marasmus and kwashiorkor.

Marasmus is defined simply as chronic deprivation of energy needed to maintain body weight. Its extreme form is characterized by severe weight loss and cachexia.[1] Marasmus is further characterized by subnormal body temperature, decreased pulse and metabolic rate, loss of skin turgor, constipation, and starvation diarrhea, consisting of frequent, small, mucus-containing stools.[2]

Kwashiorkor is a somewhat more complex disease. It is characterized by edema, low capillary-filtration rate, hypoalbuminemia, and dermatitis.

Derived from an African term meaning "the disease that occurs when the next baby is born," kwashiorkor was initially thought to result from a diet high in calories (mainly carbohydrates, such as maize) yet deficient in protein. However, infection, aflatoxin poisoning, and oxidative stress may also play causative roles.[1,3] Edema, a defining characteristic of kwashiorkor, resolves with treatment, despite continuing hypoalbuminemia, suggesting that the edema is due to leaky cell membranes, low capillary filtration rates, high concentrations of free iron, and free radicals that increase capillary permeability.[4] Kwashiorkor is further distinguished from marasmus by the following findings:

- Massive edema of the hands and feet
- Profound irritability
- Anorexia
- Dermatologic symptoms (desquamative rash, hypopigmentation)
- Alopecia or hair discoloration
- Fatty liver
- Loss of muscle tone
- Anemia and low blood concentrations of albumin, glucose, potassium, and magnesium[5,6]

Kwashiorkor may also involve severe, life-threatening hypophosphatemia (<1.0 mg/dL), which has been found to triple the mortality rate compared with that of children who have normal phosphorus levels.[7]

Overall, in impoverished regions of Africa, marasmus is more prevalent than kwashiorkor.[8] These conditions are most commonly seen in areas that are both impoverished and affected by human immunodeficiency virus (HIV) infection. Evidence indicates that HIV-infected children in Africa have more than twice the incidence of marasmus, compared with uninfected children (16% vs 7%).

Protein-calorie malnutrition is also found in developed countries under unusual circumstances, including anorexia nervosa and cancer. The condition has also been found in infants placed on severely restricted diets[9,10] and in 5% of a population of patients who requested Roux-en-Y gastric bypass surgery to control obesity.[11]

Both marasmus and kwashiorkor can lead to impaired immune responses; cell-mediated immunity is particularly affected.[2] The result is greater susceptibility to and mortality from infectious disease. Immune function can be normalized by refeeding.[5] The same cannot always be said for the extensive physical and mental retardation that may occur.[2]

Treatment

Individuals treated for protein-energy malnutrition are at risk for refeeding syndrome, in which hypophosphatemia, hypokalemia, and hypomagnesemia may lead to disturbances in the cardiac, neurologic, gastrointestinal, respiratory, hematologic, skeletal, and endocrine systems. Guidelines have been developed to help prevent these complications and to establish a transition to normalcy. Treatment consists of 2 phases: stabilization and rehabilitation.

The initial (stabilization) phase proceeds from days 1 through 7. It consists of treatment and prevention of hypoglycemia, hypothermia, dehydration, and infection; correction of electrolyte imbalance and micronutrient deficiencies; and a cautious feeding regimen.

A rehabilitation phase proceeds from weeks 2 through 6. It consists of achievement of catch-up growth; provision of sensory stimulation and emotional support; and preparation for follow-up after recovery.

These initial 2 steps are followed by protocols for the treatment of shock and anemia; management of associated conditions; and guidelines for individuals who fail to respond.[12]

References

1. Fuhrman MP, Charney P, Mueller CM. Hepatic proteins and nutrition assessment. *J Am Diet Assoc.* 2004;104:1258-1264.

2. Castiglia PT. Protein-energy malnutrition (kwashiorkor and marasmus). *J Pediatr Health Care.* 1996;10:28-30.

3. Hendrickse RG. Of sick turkeys, kwashiorkor, malaria, perinatal mortality, heroin addicts and food poisoning: research on the influence of aflatoxins on child health in the tropics. *Ann Trop Med Parasitol.* 1997;91:787-793.

4. Sive AA, Dempster WS, Malan H, et al. Plasma-free iron: a possible cause of edema in kwashiorkor. *Arch Dis Child.* 1997;76:54-56.

5. Cunningham-Rundles S, McNeeley DF, Moon A. Mechanisms of nutrient modulation of the immune response. *J Allergy Clin Immunol.* 2005;115:1119-1128.

6. Manary MJ, Broadhead RL, Yarasheski KE. Whole-body protein kinetics in marasmus and kwashiorkor during acute infection. *Am J Clin Nutr.* 1998;67:1205-1209.

7. Manary MJ, Hart CA, Whyte MP. Severe hypophosphatemia in children with kwashiorkor is associated with increased mortality. *J Pediatr.* 1998;133:789-791.

8. Bakaki P, Kayita J, Moura Machado JE, et al. Epidemiologic and clinical features of HIV-infected and HIV-uninfected Ugandan children younger than 18 months. *J Acquir Immune Defic Syndr.* 2001;28:35-42.

9. Kuhl J, Davis MD, Kalaaji AN, et al. Skin signs as the presenting manifestation of severe nutritional deficiency: report of 2 cases. *Arch Dermatol.* 2004;140:521-524.

10. Carvalho NF, Kenney RD, Carrington PH, et al. Severe nutritional deficiencies in toddlers resulting from health food milk alternatives. *Pediatrics.* 2001;107:E46.

11. Faintuch J, Matsuda M, Cruz ME, et al. Severe protein-calorie malnutrition after bariatric procedures. *Obes Surg.* 2004;14:175-181.

12. Ashworth A, Khanum S, Jackson A, et al. Guidelines for the inpatient treatment of severely malnourished children. World Health Organization; 2003. Available at: http://www. who.int/nutrition/publications/guide_inpatient_text.pdf. Accessed December 3, 2007.

8. Obesity

Obesity has become a worldwide epidemic. In the United States, more than 60% of the population is overweight or obese. Weight conditions are typically classified based on body mass index (BMI), which is calculated by the following formula:

$$BMI = \frac{weight\ (kilograms)}{height^2\ (meters)}$$

Overweight is defined as a BMI between 25 and 29.9 kg/m^2, and obesity is defined as a BMI of 30 kg/m^2 or greater.

Although genetic factors influence body weight, diet and lifestyle have a major effect as well. The number of overweight and obese people in the United States increased by one-third between 1990 and 2000, due in part to larger portion sizes, increased availability of high-calorie foods such as cheese and soft drinks, and decreased physical activity.

Obesity is a strong risk factor for several chronic diseases, including dyslipidemia, cardiovascular and cerebrovascular disease, venous thromboembolism, hypertension, type 2 diabetes, cholelithiasis, gout, several types of cancer (particularly those arising in the breast, prostate, and colon), dementia, sleep apnea, pseudotumor cerebri, osteoarthritis (hip/knee), and infertility. Abdominal fat, compared with other fat distributions, is generally a stronger indicator of health-problem risk.

Risk Factors

In addition to the contributions of increased energy intake and decreased physical activity to the risk of obesity, genetic factors play an important role. Dozens of genes coding for hormones, neurotransmitters, and receptors have been associated with weight control. Several mechanisms are being investigated as a basis for possible pharmacologic therapies. These include leptin, ghrelin, and melanocortin. Depression, anxiety, and eating disorders may also contribute to habits that promote unhealthy weight gain.

Diagnosis

An evaluation of obesity requires a complete history and physical examination, with special attention to medications, herbal remedies, nutritional and exercise history, risk factors for coronary artery disease, and family history of thyroid and cardiac diseases.

BMI calculation is commonly used to estimate the severity of overweight.

Anthropometric measures include waist circumference, waist-to-hip circumference ratio, and body-fat determination, which is usually based on skin-fold thickness or bioimpedance.

Laboratory testing includes fasting glucose and insulin concentration, thyroid-stimulating hormone and free T4 hormone levels, renal function, lipid panel, complete blood count (CBC), and aspartate aminotransferase (AST) to screen for hepatic steatosis.

Treatment

The therapeutic essentials for treating obesity are diet, exercise, and lifestyle modification that reduce energy intake and increase energy expenditure. Nutritional interventions are discussed below. Physical activity helps to retain lean body mass and may better prepare patients to keep weight off after the initial loss,[1] in comparison with food restriction alone.

Pharmacotherapy

Several medical therapies are available, and more are under study. However, results of pharmacotherapy are generally modest, and weight is often regained once the medication is discontinued.[2] Evidence of long-term benefits is scarce. Recent evidence suggests that a combination of pharmacotherapy and behavior therapy achieves better results than either modality used alone.[3]

Medications that are commonly used (but not necessarily recommended) include:

Appetite suppressants. Examples are sibutramine, phentermine, benzphetamine, phendimetrazine, and diethylpropion.

Orlistat. This gastric lipase inhibitor decreases the absorption of dietary fat. However, when using this medicine, it is necessary to supplement diet with fat-soluble vitamins and phytonutrients.

Other medications may be useful in certain patients with diabetes, depression, or seizure disorders.

Surgery

Bariatric surgery has been used successfully in morbidly obese patients (BMI >40). Gastric bypass and banding are the most frequently used surgeries. Complications such as nutrient malabsorption and infection are common and lead to the 1% to 2% mortality risk associated with these procedures.

Lifestyle Modification

Certain personality and behavioral factors are characteristic of those who succeed at maintaining weight loss. These factors include developing coping skills that prevent using food for comfort; increasing self-efficacy with respect to weight control;[4] engaging in high levels of physical activity (approximately 1 hour per day); choosing a low-calorie, low-fat diet; eating breakfast regularly; self-monitoring weight;

and maintaining a consistent eating pattern through the 7-day week.[5] The characteristic behaviors of those who keep weight off are documented and updated through the National Weight Control Registry, available at: http://www.nwcr.ws/.[5]

Dietary Supplements

Patients should be advised to avoid dietary supplements promoting weight loss. Reviews of their effectiveness indicate a lack of efficacy for chitosan, chromium picolinate, Garcinia cambogia, glucomannan, guar gum, hydroxy-methylbutyrate, Plantago psyllium, pyruvate, yerba mate, and yohimbe.[6] Ephedra-containing formulas have been found effective for weight control, particularly when combined with aspirin. However, the risk-to-benefit ratio of this combination is prohibitively high due to potential adverse cardiovascular effects of ephedra, as well as potential gastrointestinal damage caused by aspirin.

Nutritional Considerations

Although genetic factors contribute to obesity, the increased prevalence of this condition during the last century (particularly in the last three decades) confirms that environmental factors play a major role.[7] The Western diet, which provides highly palatable, energy-dense foods rich in fat and sugar, is conducive to weight gain. These foods activate reward systems in the brain, up-regulate the expression of hunger signals, and blunt the response to satiety signals, promoting overconsumption.[8]

Common short-term restrictive diets that focus on limiting portion sizes tend not to produce long-term weight loss. A better approach is a permanent change in the *type* of foods individuals select and in the physical activity they include in their routines. Individuals who consume foods lower in energy density and higher in water and fiber (eg, salads, soups, vegetables, and fruits), instead of foods high in energy density, experience early satiety and spontaneously decrease food intake. This strategy has produced weight loss in several clinical studies.[9] By allowing for the intake of larger portions that provide satiety,[10,11] it fosters continued adherence.

The following steps reduce the energy density of the diet and promote weight control:

Reducing dietary fat. Dietary fat holds more than twice as many calories per gram as protein and carbohydrate (9 calories per gram of fat, compared with 4 for protein or carbohydrate), and it promotes passive overconsumption of energy. These factors may explain why the prevalence of overweight worldwide is directly related to the percentage of fat in the diet, and why low-fat diets have been consistently shown to promote moderate weight loss.[12] Common sources of fat are meats, dairy products, fried foods, and added oils.

Choosing foods high in complex carbohydrates and fiber. Populations in Asia, Africa, and elsewhere with diets high in complex carbohydrates tend to have a low incidence of obesity. The whole grains and legumes in these diets also provide fiber. Fiber is filling but contributes little to overall calorie intake. Studies show that fiber intake is inversely associated with body weight and body fat.[13]

Following low-fat, vegetarian diets. Several studies have found that vegetarians tend to be slimmer than omnivores, which is not surprising given that grains, legumes, vegetables, and fruits are low in fat and high in complex carbohydrates and fiber.[14] Randomized trials show that low-fat vegan diets promote greater weight loss than typical low-fat diets and that they also improve plasma lipids, insulin sensitivity, and other measures.[10] A study of a vegetarian diet in heart patients, used in combination with exercise and stress management, showed sustained weight loss over a 5-year period.[15]

Minimizing sugars. Sucrose, high-fructose corn syrup, and other sugars add calories without producing satiety. A systematic review of epidemiological and clinical studies found positive associations between intake of sugar-sweetened beverages and both weight gain and obesity in children and adults.[16]

Low-carbohydrate diets have been popular, but they have not been found superior to either low-fat, high-carbohydrate, or calorie-controlled diets over a 12-month period.[17] Low-carbohydrate diets may increase plasma low-density lipoprotein concentrations, sometimes severely, in approximately one-third of users. They also cause a sustained increase in urinary calcium losses.[18] In the Women's Health Initiative Dietary Modification Trial, weight loss was greatest in women who both decreased fat intake and consumed more fruit, vegetables, and fibrous carbohydrate.[19]

Orders

See Basic Diet Orders chapter.

Vegetarian diet, nondairy, low-fat.

What to Tell the Family

Obesity contributes to many chronic illnesses, but it may be prevented and successfully treated in most individuals through a diet low in fat and sugar and high in fiber, along with regular physical activity. Well-planned, low-fat vegan and vegetarian diets are particularly healthful and effective.

The family plays an essential role in supporting the diet and lifestyle changes that can prevent and treat weight problems. Family members are likely to benefit from these same changes.

References

1. Hill JO, Wyatt HR. Role of physical activity in preventing and treating obesity. *J Appl Physiol.* 2005;99:765-770.

2. Padwal R, Li SK, Lau DC. Long-term pharmacotherapy for obesity and overweight. *Cochrane Database Syst Rev.* 2004;(3):CD004094.

3. Wadden TA, Berkowitz RI, Womble LG, et al. Randomized trial of lifestyle modification and pharmacotherapy for obesity. *N Engl J Med.* 2005;353:2111-2120.

4. Byrne SM. Psychological aspects of weight maintenance and relapse in obesity. *J Psychosom Res.* 2002;53:1029-1036.

5. Wing RR, Phelan S. Long-term weight loss maintenance. *Am J Clin Nutr.* 2005;82(suppl 1):222S-225S.

6. Pittler MH, Ernst E. Dietary supplements for body-weight reduction: a systematic review. *Am J Clin Nutr.* 2004;79:529-536.

7. Tremblay A, Perusse L, Bouchard C. Energy balance and body-weight stability: impact of gene-environment interactions. *Br J Nutr.* 2004;92(suppl 1):S63-S66.

8. Erlanson-Albertsson C. How palatable food disrupts appetite regulation. *Basic Clin Pharmacol Toxicol.* 2005;97:61-73.

9. Rolls BJ, Ello-Martin JA, Tohill BC. What can intervention studies tell us about the relationship between fruit and vegetable consumption and weight management? *Nutr Rev.* 2004;62:1-17.

10. Barnard ND, Scialli AR, Turner-McGrievy G, Lanou AJ, Glass J. The effects of a low-fat, plant-based dietary intervention on body weight, metabolism, and insulin sensitivity. *Am J Med.* 2005;118:991-997.

11. Ello-Martin JA, Ledikwe JH, Rolls BJ. The influence of food portion size and energy density on energy intake: implications for weight management. *Am J Clin Nutr.* 2005;82(suppl 1):236S-241S.

12. Jequier E, Bray GA. Low-fat diets are preferred. *Am J Med.* 2002;113(suppl 9B):41S-46S.

13. Berkow S, Barnard ND. Vegetarian diets and weight status. *Nutr Rev.* 2006;64:175-188.

14. Slavin JL. Dietary fiber and body weight. *Nutrition.* 2005;21:411-418.

15. Ornish D, Scherwitz LW, Billings JH, et al. Intensive lifestyle changes for reversal of coronary heart disease. *JAMA.* 1998;280:2001-2007.

16. Malik VS, Schulze MB, Hu FB. Intake of sugar-sweetened beverages and weight gain: a systematic review. *Am J Clin Nutr.* 2006;84:274-288.

17. Astrup A, Meinert Larsen T, Harper A. Atkins and other low-carbohydrate diets: hoax or an effective tool for weight loss? *Lancet.* 2004;364:897-899.

18. Yancy WS, Olsen MK, Guyton JR, Bakst RP, Westman EC. A low-carbohydrate, ketogenic diet versus a low-fat diet to treat obesity and hyperlipidemia. *Ann Int Med.* 2004;140:769-777.

19. Howard BV, Manson JE, Stefanick ML, et al. Low-fat dietary pattern and weight change over 7 years: the Women's Health Initiative Dietary Modification Trial. *JAMA.* 2006;295:39-49.

SECTION III: EYE, EAR, NOSE, AND THROAT

9. Age-Related Macular Degeneration

Age-related macular degeneration (ARMD) is a degenerative disease of the macula, the central part of the retina. There are two forms of ARMD: a "dry" form marked by degenerative changes in the macula without bleeding or leakage of fluid; and a "wet" form, which often occurs in association with dry ARMD and exhibits leakage and/or bleeding from new blood vessel growth beneath the retina. Central vision, which is necessary for fine visual tasks and many daily activities, is threatened by ARMD. Consequently, ARMD is the most common cause of legal blindness (20/200 or worse in both eyes) among elderly Americans. ARMD pathogenesis is not well understood.

Changes usually seen in early stages of dry ARMD include subretinal yellowish deposits (drusen) and chorioretinal atrophy. Visual loss in dry macular degeneration tends to have a slow progression and uncommonly results in severe loss of central vision. In addition, dry ARMD can transform to wet ARMD. The wet form of ARMD involves abnormal vessel growth (neovascularization) into the subretinal space, causing leakage of fluid and/or bleeding. Resultant vision loss can occur suddenly or over the course of a few weeks.

Dry ARMD is almost always bilateral; wet ARMD is often unilateral.[1] Acute (days to weeks) or unilateral changes require immediate ophthalmologic evaluation. Dry ARMD may cause slow recovery of vision after leaving sunlight and going indoors. Symptoms of wet ARMD include distortion of straight lines (although this may also occur in dry ARMD) and (rarely) changes in color perception. As the disease progresses, a central blind spot may occur. For example, when an affected individual looks directly at another person's face, the nose (or larger area) may appear absent or distorted.

Risk Factors

Persons of white, non-Hispanic race/ethnicity generally have a higher prevalence of ARMD.[2,3] Blacks have the lowest risk.[3]

Established risk factors include:

Age. ARMD rarely occurs in persons under age 55. The prevalence is 0.8% in those aged 70 and older, increasing to 16% in those over 90.[4]

Smoking. Individuals who smoke have a relative risk of 2.0 and greater, compared with those who have never smoked. Risk may remain elevated for 15 or more years after smoking cessation.[5]

Family history. Genetic factors are linked to ARMD and, combined with smoking, substantially increase risk.

Additional possible risk factors include nutritional deficiencies (see Nutritional Considerations below) and overweight.

Studies of the relationship of hypertension and sunlight exposure on macular degeneration show conflicting results. Cataract surgery as a possible risk factor needs further research.

Diagnosis

ARMD is diagnosed by the characteristic appearance of the macula, on dilated examination or by slit-lamp microscopy.

Slit-lamp photography of the macula is sometimes performed to document progression.

Fluorescein angiography detects the presence and location of any subretinal neovascularization.

Treatment

Vitamins C, E, beta-carotene and zinc are potentially valuable therapies (see Nutritional Considerations).

Gingko biloba is under investigation for a possible role in treatment. It improved visual acuity in a small study[6] and a larger, more recent study.[7] Further investigation is warranted.

Dry ARMD

No specific medical or surgical treatment for the dry form of ARMD exists. Laser therapy needs further study.

Wet ARMD

If fluorescein angiography reveals classic neovascularization, **thermal laser photocoagulation** or **photodynamic (laser) therapy** may be used. However, recurrences are common.

Photodynamic therapy (PDT), which is performed after intravenous injection of verteporfin that differentially enters neovascular tissue, offers limited benefit to patients with several forms of wet ARMD.[8]

For neovascular ARMD, **VEGF inhibitors** ranibizumab, bevacizumab (off-label use), and pegaptanib are options for treatment. Further studies are ongoing.

Intravitreal steroid injections are under study.

Submacular surgery is generally not recommended, except possibly when large hemorrhages are present.

Macular translocation surgery has many complications, but could be a viable alternative for those who are not candidates for laser therapy. However, it remains unclear which patients, if any, are best served by this invasive approach.

Nutritional Considerations

Dietary factors appear to play an important role in ARMD. In epidemiologic studies, the following factors are associated with reduced risk of onset or progression of the disease:

Maintenance of ideal weight. Studies have found a higher risk for ARMD in association with measures of adiposity, including body mass index (BMI) and waist/hip ratio.[9-11] Regular exercise is associated with lower risk for ARMD.[9,12]

Low fat intake. Studies have found associations between high intakes of saturated fat and cholesterol and ARMD.[13,14] Other studies have implicated vegetable fat and total fat intake in ARMD.[15-17] People who regularly consumed processed baked goods had double the risk of ARMD, compared with those who did not regularly consume these foods; the effect may relate to adverse effects on blood lipids or inflammation.[15] Some studies have suggested that fish intake is associated with reduced prevalence of ARMD, at least among certain populations, presumably due to its omega-3 content.[13, 15-17] However, two recent systematic reviews have concluded that the evidence for a protective effect of omega-3 fatty acids on ARMD is insufficient.[18,19]

High consumption of fruits and vegetables. Lutein and zeaxanthin are the principal carotenoids in the macular region of the retina. They are abundant in dark-green, leafy vegetables and appear to play an important role in prevention of macular degeneration.[20] Several studies have found that people with high intake of fruits and vegetables had a significantly lower risk for ARMD compared with those who have low intakes.[21,22] The Eye Disease Case Control Study found that individuals in the highest quintile of carotenoid intake had a 43% lower risk for ARMD compared with those in the lowest quintile. Intakes of collard greens and spinach, both rich in lutein, were found to be the most protective. The Health Professionals Follow-Up Study and Nurses' Health Study found inverse associations between higher fruit intakes (3 or more servings per day) and lower risk for neovascular age-related maculopathy.[23]

Antioxidant supplements. In the Age-Related Eye Disease Study, individuals with moderate or advanced ARMD who received 500 mg of vitamin C, 400 IU of vitamin E, 15 mg of beta carotene, and 80 mg of zinc oxide (and 2 mg cupric oxide to prevent copper deficiency) had significantly reduced progression of their disease, compared with subjects receiving a placebo.[24] Caution is advised, however, for several reasons: This evidence derives from a single study. Also, beta-carotene supplementation may increase lung cancer risk among smokers. Finally, daily doses of vitamin E exceeding 400 IU may increase cardiovascular and all-cause mortality.[25]

In the lutein antioxidant supplementation trial (LAST), a 10-mg supplement of lutein taken daily, alone or with an antioxidant vitamin combination, increased macular pigment density and improved visual function when compared with a placebo.[26] Lutein supplementation also improved visual performance (visual acuity and glare sensitivity) in other controlled trials.[27] Due to a saturation of transport mechanisms for these carotenoids, some individuals do not achieve increases in macular pigment density, in spite of increases in blood levels of lutein and zeaxanthin following supplementation.[28] Other individuals may not benefit if they are overweight, because lutein and zeaxanthin will be taken up by adipose tissue, rather than by the macula.[29] An ophthalmologist should make patient-specific recommendations, because the age of the patient, disease severity, duration of treatment, and potential inhibitory effect of lutein supplementation on other carotenoids should be taken into account.

Orders

See Basic Diet Orders chapter.

Emphasize fresh fruits and vegetables, particularly leafy greens, such as collard or turnip greens, kale, spinach.

Consider the following supplements in consultation with an ophthalmologist: Vitamin C 500 mg, vitamin E 400 IU, beta-carotene 15 mg, zinc oxide 80 mg, and cupric oxide 2 mg daily.

Lutein, dosed per ophthalmologist recommendations.

Smoking cessation.

What to Tell the Family

Appropriate medical care and self-care can slow the loss of vision due to ARMD. It is helpful to encourage smoking cessation and a diet that is low in fat and cholesterol and high in fruits and vegetables. That means including at least 1 serving daily of a dark leafy green vegetable, such as spinach, kale, collards, or turnip greens, along with 3 servings of fresh fruit. This diet is also beneficial to family members, who may have a higher risk of ARMD. Supplemental lutein and certain vitamins and minerals (C, E, beta-carotene, and zinc/copper oxide) may be beneficial, but their use should be supervised by an ophthalmologist. Low-vision aids (such as special lighting and magnifiers) are available through eye clinics.

References

1. Quillen DA. Common causes of vision loss in elderly patients. *Am Fam Physician.* 1999;60:99-108.

2. Klein R, Clegg L, Cooper LS, et al. Prevalence of age-related maculopathy in the Atherosclerosis Risk in Communities Study. *Arch Ophthalmol.* 1999;117:1203-1210.

3. Klein R, Klein BE, Knudtson MD, et al. Prevalence of age-related macular degeneration in 4 racial/ethnic groups in the multi-ethnic study of atherosclerosis. *Ophthalmology.* 2006;113:373-380.

4. Weih LM, VanNewkirk MR, McCarty CA, Taylor HR. Age-specific causes of bilateral visual impairment. *Arch Ophthalmol.* 2000;118:264-269.

5. Seddon JM, Willett WC, Speizer FE, Hankinson SE. A prospective study of cigarette smoking and age-related macular degeneration in women. *JAMA.* 1996;276:1141-1146.

6. Lebuisson DA, Leroy L, Rigal G. Treatment of senile macular degeneration with Ginkgo biloba extract. A preliminary double-blind drug vs. placebo study [in French]. *Presse Med.* 1986;15:1556-1558.

7. Fies P, Dienel A. Ginkgo extract in impaired vision--treatment with special extract EGb 761 of impaired vision due to dry senile macular degeneration [in German]. *Wien Med Wochenschr.* 2002;152:423-426.

8. Photodynamic therapy of subfoveal choroidal neovascularization in age-related macular degeneration with verteporfin: one-year results of 2 randomized clinical trials--TAP report. Treatment of age-related macular degeneration with photodynamic therapy (TAP) Study Group. *Arch Ophthalmol.* 1999;117:1329-1345.

9. Seddon JM, Cote J, Davis N, Rosner B. Progression of age-related macular degeneration: association with body mass index, waist circumference, and waist-hip ratio. *Arch Ophthalmol.* 2003;121:785-792.

10. Schaumberg DA, Christen WG, Hankinson SE, Glynn RJ. Body mass index and the incidence of visually significant age-related maculopathy in men. *Arch Ophthalmol.* 2001;119:1259-1265.

11. Smith W, Mitchell P, Leeder SR, Wang JJ. Plasma fibrinogen levels, other cardiovascular risk factors, and age-related maculopathy: the Blue Mountains Eye Study. *Arch Ophthalmol.* 1998;116:583-587.

12. Klein R, Klein BE, Tomany SC, Cruickshanks KJ. The association of cardiovascular disease with the long-term incidence of age-related maculopathy: the Beaver Dam Eye Study. *Ophthalmology.* 2003;110:1273-1280.

13. Smith W, Mitchell P, Leeder SR. Dietary fat and fish intake and age-related maculopathy. *Arch Ophthalmol.* 2000;118:401-404.

14. Mares-Perlman JA, Brady WE, Klein R, VandenLangenberg CM, Klein BE, Palta M. Dietary fat and age-related maculopathy. *Arch Ophthalmol.* 1995;113:743-748.

15. Seddon JM, Cote J, Rosner B. Progression of age-related macular degeneration: association with dietary fat, transunsaturated fat, nuts, and fish intake. *Arch Ophthalmol.* 2003;121:1728-1737.

16. Cho E, Hung S, Willett WC, et al. Prospective study of dietary fat and the risk of age-related macular degeneration. *Am J Clin Nutr.* 2001;73:209-218.

17. Seddon JM, Rosner B, Sperduto RD, et al. Dietary fat and risk for advanced age-related macular degeneration. *Arch Ophthalmol.* 2001;119:1191-1199.

18. Hodge WG, Barnes D, Schachter HM, et al. Evidence for the effect of omega-3 fatty acids on progression of age-related macular degeneration: a systematic review. *Retina.* 2007;27:216-221.

19. Hodge WG, Schachter HM, Barnes D, et al. Efficacy of omega-3 fatty acids in preventing age-related macular degeneration: a systematic review. *Ophthalmology.* 2006;113:1165-1172.

20. Ribaya-Mercado JD, Blumberg JB. Lutein and zeaxanthin and their potential roles in disease prevention. *J Am Coll Nutr.* 2004;23(suppl 6):567S-587S.

21. Goldberg J, Flowerdew G, Smith E, Brody JA, Tso MOM. Factors associated with age-related macular degeneration: an analysis of data from the First National Health and Nutrition Examination Survey. *Am J Epidemiol.* 1998;128:700-710.

22. Seddon JM, Ajani UA, Sperduto RD, et al. Dietary carotenoids, vitamins A, C, and E, and advanced age-related macular degeneration. Eye Disease Case-Control Study Group. *JAMA.* 1994;272:1413-1420.

23. Cho E, Seddon JM, Rosner B, Willett WC, Hankinson SE. Prospective study of intake of fruits, vegetables, vitamins, and carotenoids and risk of age-related maculopathy. *Arch Ophthalmol.* 2004;122:883-892.

24. Age-Related Eye Disease Study Research Group. A randomized, placebo-controlled, clinical trial of high-dose supplementation with vitamins C and E, beta-carotene, and zinc for age-related macular degeneration and vision loss: AREDS report no. 8. *Arch Ophthalmol.* 2001;119:1417-1436.

25. Miller ER 3rd, Pastor-Barriuso R, Dalal D, Riemersma RA, Appel LJ, Guallar E. Meta-analysis: high-dosage vitamin E supplementation may increase all-cause mortality. *Ann Intern Med.* 2005;142:37-46.

26. Richer S, Stiles W, Statkute L, Pulido J, Frankowski J, Rudy D. Double-masked, placebo-controlled, randomized trial of lutein and antioxidant supplementation in the intervention of atrophic age-related macular degeneration: the Veterans LAST study (Lutein Antioxidant Supplementation Trial). *Optometry*. 2004;75:216-230.

27. Olmedilla B, Granado F, Blanco I, Vaquero M. Lutein, but not alpha-tocopherol, supplementation improves visual function in patients with age-related cataracts: a 2-y double-blind, placebo-controlled pilot study. *Nutrition* 2003;19:21-24.

28. Trieschmann M, Beatty S, Nolan JM, et al. Changes in macular pigment optical density and serum concentrations of its constituent carotenoids following supplemental lutein and zeaxanthin: the LUNA study. *Exp Eye Res*. 2007;84:718-728.

29. Hammond BR Jr, Ciulla TA, Snodderly DM. Macular pigment density is reduced in obese subjects. *Invest Ophthalmol Vis Sci*. 2002;43:47-50.

10. Cataract

Cataract is an opacification of the crystalline lens of the eye. The condition is responsible for approximately half of all cases of severe vision loss in the world, affecting an estimated 15 million people. Opacities can be either diffuse or localized, and cataracts are usually classified according to the region of the lens affected: cortical, nuclear, posterior subcapsular, or mixed. Loss of transparency occurs when lens proteins become oxidized.

Symptoms are progressive, not painful, and usually bilateral. Specific symptoms may include:

Blurred or "double" vision

Excessive glare during night driving and in bright sunlight

Halo effect around lights

Deterioration of distance vision more than of near vision

Risk Factors

Compared with whites, African Americans have an elevated level of legal blindness due to cataracts. There is also a slightly higher prevalence of cataracts in women and in persons with limited education.

Age.

Family history of cataract.

Diabetes mellitus.

Corticosteroids. Systemic, topical, or inhaled steroids increase risk of posterior subcapsular cataracts.

Smoking is a dose-related risk factor. Overall, it roughly doubles risk. Quitting may partially reverse the disease in the nuclear and posterior subcapsular forms.

Alcohol use. See Nutritional Considerations below.

Extensive sunlight exposure; ie, photo-oxidation secondary to UV-B. Risk is dose-related.[1]

Lead exposure.

Abnormal serum lipids (chylomicrons, triglycerides, VLDL, low HDL).

Excess body weight.[2,3] Compared with participants with BMI less than 23 kg/m2, those with BMI greater than or equal to 30 kg/m^2 had a 36% higher risk of any type of cataract.[3]

High dairy consumption in certain individuals[4,5] or **deficient galac-tokinase activity.**[5-8]

Risk of cataract is also increased by the use of **phenothiazines, ocular radiation exposure, trauma, uveitis,** and **malnutrition.**

Diagnosis

Ophthalmologists typically diagnose cataracts by directly viewing the opacified layers of the lens with the slit lamp biomicroscope. Cataracts can also be detected with the direct ophthalmoscope. In a room with dim illumination and the focusing dial of the ophthalmoscope set at "0," the doctor observes the patient at arm's length. Opacified areas of the lens may appear as silhouettes within the red reflex, or the red reflex may be darker than normal.

Treatment

Treatment is surgical, although use of a long-acting mydriatic drop, such as atropine or homatropine, in patients with early posterior subcapsular cataract can sometimes delay the need for surgery. Cataract extraction involves removal of the lens and possible replacement with an artificial intraocular lens. This surgery is generally elective and should be considered only in people whose vision with the best possible eyeglasses is insufficient to meet their needs.

Nutritional Considerations

Epidemiologic studies have shown associations between several nutritional factors and cataract risk. These factors have not been tested in controlled intervention trials, however. The principal factors under study are described below.

Maintaining serum lipids within established norms. Researchers have identified relationships between elevated levels of triglycerides, chylomicrons, and VLDL and increased cataract risk.[9,10] There appears to be an inverse association between HDL concentrations and cataract risk.[9,11]

Modifying fat intake. Cataract risk may be influenced by the type and amount of dietary fat. Compared with those eating the least fat (25% of calories), those eating the highest amount (37%) had a 10% greater risk for cataract.[12,13] Women consuming the highest percentage of energy from essential fatty acids (6% of calories from linoleic acid and ~0.7% calories from alpha-linolenic acid) had over twice the risk for cataract, compared with those consuming the least (4% and ~0.5%, respectively).[13]

In the Nurses Health Study involving more than 71,000 women, eating fish >3 times per week was associated with a 12% lower risk for cataract extraction compared with women eating the least fish.[12] The Blue Mountains Eye Study found a roughly 40% lower cataract risk in individuals who consumed the highest amount of total omega-3 fatty acids, but found no protective effect from fish consumption alone.[14]

Avoiding dairy products. Persons with heterozygous galactokinase deficiency[15] and elderly persons who have diminished activity of this enzyme are at greater risk for cataract.[16] Dairy products, which contribute most of the galactose to the diet, should be avoided in these patients.

Eating more fruits and vegetables. Since antioxidant-rich diets have been associated with a lower risk of cataract, incorporation of more vegetables and fruits may prevent or slow the condition's progression.[17]

Consuming more carotenoid-containing vegetables. The consumption of higher intakes of lutein and zeaxanthin, two carotenoids present in dark green, leafy vegetables and corn, has been associated with a reduced risk of cataract in several large epidemiological studies.[18] Within the crystalline lens, these carotenoids may protect against cataract by preventing the oxidation of lens proteins.[18]

Emphasizing antioxidant-rich foods. Some evidence suggests that high doses of antioxidants help prevent cataract formation[19] and that the antioxidant vitamins C and E may retard the progression of cataract. Good sources of vitamin C include citrus fruits, peppers, tropical fruits, cantaloupe, strawberries, kiwifruits, cruciferous vegetables, tomatoes, potatoes, and sweet potatoes. Good sources of vitamin E include wheat germ, cooked spinach, soymilk, many varieties of nuts, sunflower seeds, mangoes, and olive, peanut, and vegetable oils.

Avoidance of alcohol. Compared with nondrinkers, individuals who consumed more than 2 glasses per week of any type of alcohol (beer, wine, or distilled spirits) had a 13% higher risk for nuclear opacity.[20] In the Swedish Mammography Cohort study of nearly 35,000 women, having 1 drink per day was associated with a 7% greater risk for cataract extraction compared with avoiding alcohol. [21]

Protein intake. Several studies have shown that higher protein intakes are associated with a reduced cataract risk.[14] In the Blue Mountains Eye Study II involving a 5-year follow-up of more than 2,300 individuals over 49 years of age, an estimated protein intake of 107 grams per day was associated with a roughly 70% lower risk for posterior subcapsular cataract, when compared with a protein intake of 71 grams per day. Possible explanations for these findings include an association of high protein intakes with certain nutrients considered to be protective against cataract (eg, beta-carotene, zinc) and prevention of osmotic stress to the lens through albumin, which is maintained by a high protein intake.[14] However, the potential benefit for cataract prevention must be weighed against the risk of diseases associated with excess intake of protein (eg, kidney stones; see Nephrolithiasis chapter) and of the fat and cholesterol that often accompany protein.

Orders

See Basic Diet Orders chapter.

In cases of galactokinase deficiency, avoid dairy products.

Control of plasma lipid concentrations (see Dyslipidemias chapter).

Limit sun exposure.

Smoking cessation.

Alcohol restriction.

What to Tell the Family

It is important for the patient and family to understand that cataract is not a cancer and that harm rarely occurs to the remainder of the eye structure. The decision as to when to have surgery depends upon the patient's perceived degree of disability. When surgery is necessary, the chance for restoration of vision is excellent.

Supplements of lutein or other antioxidants should not take the place of a diet rich in dark, leafy green vegetables. The possible benefit associated with vegetables may be partially due to the presence of other phytochemicals that have not yet been fully identified. Since family members of cataract patients are also at risk for cataract, their adoption of a similar healthful diet is advantageous. The family can also help the patient avoid tobacco, excessive sunlight, and alcohol exposure. These diet and lifestyle changes offer many other health benefits as well.

References

1. West SK, Duncan DD, Munoz B, et al. Sunlight exposure and risk of lens opacities in a population-based study. The Salisbury Eye Evaluation Project. *JAMA.* 1998;280:714-718.

2. Schaumberg DA, Glynn RJ, Christen WG, Hankinson SE, Hennekens CH. Relations of body fat distribution and height with cataract in men. *Am J Clin Nutr.* 2000;72:1495-1502.

3. Weintraub JM, Willett WC, Rosner B, Colditz GA, Seddon JM, Hankinson SE. A prospective study of the relationship between body mass index and cataract extraction among US women and men. *Int J Obes Relat Metab Disord.* 2002;26:1588-1595.

4. Simoons FJ. A geographic approach to senile cataracts: possible links with milk consumption, lactase activity, and galactose metabolism. *Dig Dis Sci.* 1982;27:257-264.

5. Couet C. Lactose and cataract in humans: a review. *J Am Coll Nutr.* 1991;10:79-86.

6. Skalka HW, Prchal JT. Presenile cataract formation and decreased activity of galactosemic enzymes. *Arch Ophthalmol.* 1980;98:269-273.

7. Skalka H, Prchal J. Presenile cataracts. *Arch Ophthalmol.* 1984;102:507.

8. Elman MJ, Miller MT, Matalon R. Galactokinase activity in patients with idiopathic cataracts. *Ophthalmology.* 1986;93:210-215.

9. Hiller R, Sperduto RD, Reed GF, D'Agostino RB, Wilson PW. Serum lipids and age-related lens opacities: a longitudinal investigation: the Framingham Studies. *Ophthalmology.* 2003;110:578-583.

10. Goodrich ME, Cumming RG, Mitchell P, Koutts J, Burnett L. Plasma fibrinogen and other cardiovascular disease risk factors and cataract. *Ophthalmic Epidemiol.* 1999;6:279-290.

11. Klein BE, Klein R, Lee KE. Cardiovascular disease, selected cardiovascular disease risk factors, and age-related cataracts: the Beaver Dam Eye Study. *Am J Ophthalmol.* 1997;123:338-346.

12. Lu M, Cho E, Taylor A, Hankinson SE, Willett WC, Jacques PF. Prospective study of dietary fat and risk of cataract extraction among US women. *Am J Epidemiol.* 2005;161:948-959.

13. Lu M, Taylor A, Chylack LT Jr, et al. Dietary fat intake and early age-related lens opacities. *Am J Clin Nutr.* 2005; 81:773-779.

14. Townend BS, Townend ME, Flood V, et al. Dietary macronutrient intake and five-year incident cataract: the Blue Mountains eye study. *Am J Ophthalmol.* 2007;143:932-939.

15. Stambolian D, Scarpino-Myers V, Eagle RC Jr, Hodes B, Harris H. Cataracts in patients heterozygous for galactokinase deficiency. *Invest Ophthalmol Vis Sci.* 1986;27:429-433.

16. Birlouez-Aragon I, Ravelontseheno L, Villate-Cathelineau B, Cathelineau G, Abitbol G. Disturbed galactose metabolism in elderly and diabetic humans is associated with cataract formation. *J Nutr.* 1993;123:1370-1376.

17. Christen WG, Liu S, Schaumberg DA, Buring JE. Fruit and vegetable intake and the risk of cataract in women. *Am J Clin Nutr.* 2005;81:1417-1422.

18. Vu HT, Robman L, Hodge A, McCarty CA, Taylor HR. Lutein and zeaxanthin and the risk of cataract: the Melbourne visual impairment project. *Invest Ophthalmol Vis Sci.* 2006;47:3783-3786.

19. Cumming RG, Mitchell P, Smith W. Diet and cataract: The Blue Mountains Eye Study. *Ophthalmology.* 2000;107:450-456.

20. Morris MS, Jacques PF, Hankinson SE, Chylack LT Jr, Willett WC, Taylor A. Moderate alcoholic beverage intake and early nuclear and cortical lens opacities. *Ophthalmic Epidemiol.* 2004;11:53-65.

21. Lindblad BE, Hakansson N, Philipson B, Wolk A. Alcohol consumption and risk of cataract extraction: a prospective cohort study of women. *Ophthalmology.* 2007;114:680-685.

11. Glaucoma

Glaucoma is a group of eye diseases characterized by optic nerve damage that is usually associated with elevated intraocular pressure. It can cause permanent visual field loss and possible blindness.[1] Glaucoma is the second-leading cause of blindness worldwide after cataract, but, unlike with cataract, blindness caused by glaucoma is irreversible.

The four principal types of glaucoma are primary open-angle, angle closure, secondary, and congenital.

The most common form of this disease, primary open-angle glaucoma (POAG), is the focus of this chapter. This condition is an asymptomatic, progressive process that can irreversibly affect peripheral visual fields and, ultimately, central vision. A basic ophthalmologic exam can diagnose glaucoma if elevated intraocular pressure or optic disc "cupping" is present, but identification of unaffected or at-risk eyes is not as simple.

Angle-closure glaucoma generally occurs in an anatomically predisposed eye. As intraocular pressure mounts, the eye often becomes red and painful, but sometimes nausea is the principal symptom. Relief of the elevated pressure must occur emergently in most cases to avoid severe visual loss or blindness. There are many causes of secondary glaucoma, such as cataract, inflammation, derangement of the eye anatomy due to blunt trauma, neovascularization in diabetic retinopathy, pigment dispersion syndrome, pseudoexfoliation, and central retinal vein occlusion.

Risk Factors

There are 4 major risk factors for POAG.[2]

Age. There is <1% prevalence in persons under age 65, approximately 1% at 70 years, and 3% at 75 years.[2]

Elevated intraocular pressure. However, high intraocular pressure is not necessary or sufficient for glaucoma pathogenesis.

Race. Prevalence is 4 to 5 times greater among African Americans, compared with whites, and reaches 11% in African Americans aged 80 and over. The age-adjusted rate of blindness due to glaucoma is 6 times higher in African Americans, with blindness onset averaging 10 years earlier, compared with whites.[3,4]

Family history. There is a relative risk of 3.7 in siblings of the affected person and 2.2 in those with affected parents.[5]

Additional risk factors include corticosteroid use, high blood pressure (a risk factor for elevated intraocular pressure),[6,7] cardiovascular disease, diabetes,[6,8] homocysteine elevation,[9,10] low diastolic perfusion pressure, hypothyroidism, and myopia.[11]

Diagnosis

POAG is generally asymptomatic, and major visual field loss can occur prior to any visual symptoms.

Fundus examination is required for diagnosis, along with visual field testing (confrontational visual field testing is not sufficiently accurate to diagnose glaucoma) and measurement of intraocular pressure. Most persons with POAG will have an untreated intraocular pressure above 21 mmHg at some point in the disease,[12] compared with a normal intraocular pressure of about 15.3 for women and 15.5 for men.[13]

The American Academy of Ophthalmology describes POAG as chronic, generally bilateral, often asymmetrical, and with all of the following in one or both eyes:[14]

- Optic nerve or retinal nerve fiber layer damage (including thinning or notching in the optic disc rim, defects in the nerve fiber, or progressive change), or characteristic visual field abnormalities without other explanation.

- Adult onset.

- Normal anterior angles.

- No factors known to cause secondary open-angle glaucoma.

Treatment

Lowering intraocular pressure is effective for reducing visual field loss in many patients.[15,16] More evidence is needed to confirm that these results translate to other patient populations, such as individuals with severe POAG.

The target for intraocular pressure is individualized. Pressure must be lowered until no further damage occurs. Because the disease is generally asymptomatic until severe damage has occurred, many patients do not use their medicines or follow up as recommended. Compliance should be monitored closely.

Methods of lowering intraocular pressure include eye drops, systemic medications, laser treatment, and surgery.

Topical Medication

Beta-blockers, carbonic anhydrase inhibitors, and alpha-adrenergic agonists decrease aqueous production. Beta-blockers are first-line drugs, unless contraindicated for pulmonary or cardiovascular reasons. Topical carbonic anhydrase inhibitors are preferred over systemic preparations because of multiple adverse side effects with systemic use. Adrenergic agonists (ie, brimonidine) have potential (although uncommon) adverse ocular and systemic side effects.

Prostaglandins, alpha-adrenergic agonists, and cholinergic agonists increase aqueous outflow. Prostaglandin analogues are also first-line agents, which may be used in conjunction with beta-blockers. Cholinergic agonists have several adverse ocular side effects.

Systemic Therapy

Gingko biloba has improved visual field test results in patients with normal-tension glaucoma[17] but requires cautious use because of its anticoagulant effect.

Other systemic medications, such as carbonic anhydrase inhibitors, are associated with many adverse side effects and are second-line agents.

Laser Therapy

Trabeculoplasty (laser application to tissues for aqueous absorption in the angle between the cornea and iris) is often effective in the short term, but repeat therapy is often needed, and the laser may cause new damage.

Laser therapy or cryotherapy can also be used to destroy the ciliary body, which produces the aqueous humor.

Surgery

Surgery creates an alternative pathway for aqueous flow, but there is no clear advantage to early surgery over medical therapy.[18,19] Surgery is generally reserved for patients with severe disease and can be associated with blinding complications, particularly infection.

Nutritional Considerations

High blood pressure, obesity, and diabetes are risk factors for elevated intraocular pressure. A diet that helps maintain normal blood pressure and blood glucose concentrations may help reduce the risk for this disease, although no controlled trials have demonstrated the ability of diet to prevent or treat glaucoma (see Hypertension and Diabetes chapters).

Studies have noted associations between obesity and both intraocular pressure and ocular hypertension.[20] The links between obesity and intraocular pressure have been theorized to be the result of excessive intraorbital adipose tissue development, increases in blood viscosity and episcleral venous pressure, and impairment of aqueous outflow.[20] Evidence does not yet indicate that losing excess weight reduces the risk for glaucoma, although significant decreases in intraocular pressure were reported in humans during weight loss (0.4 to 1.5kg) associated with religious fasting.[21]

Orders

See Basic Diet Orders chapter.

Ophthalmology consultation.

What to Tell the Family

It is essential for the patient to have regular ophthalmologic examinations, since affected individuals cannot assess treatment efficacy on their own. Significant optic nerve damage can occur prior to any symptoms. Failure to use glaucoma medications as prescribed can result in severe visual damage. Family members should also be screened for glaucoma by an ophthalmologist or optometrist.

References

1. Weinreb RN, Khaw PT. Primary open-angle glaucoma. *Lancet*. 2004;363:1711-1720.

2. Leske MC. The epidemiology of open-angle glaucoma: a review. *Am J Epidemiol*. 1983;118:166-191.

3. Sommer A, Tielsch JM, Katz J, et al. Racial differences in the cause-specific prevalence of blindness in East Baltimore. *N Engl J Med*. 1991;325:1412-1417.

4. Tielsch JM, Sommer A, Katz J, et al. Racial variations in the prevalence of primary open-angle glaucoma. The Baltimore Eye Survey. *JAMA*. 1991;266:369-374.

5. Tielsch JM, Katz J, Sommer A, et al. Family history and risk of primary open- angle glaucoma. The Baltimore Eye Survey. *Arch Ophthalmol*. 1994;112:69-73.

6. Hennis A, Wu SY, Nemesure B, Leske MC; Barbados Eye Studies Group. Hypertension, diabetes, and longitudinal changes in intraocular pressure. *Ophthalmology*. 2003;110:908-914.

7. Nemesure B, Wu SY, Hennis A, Leske MC; Barbados Eye Studies Group. Factors related to the 4-year risk of high intraocular pressure: the Barbados Eye Studies. *Arch Ophthalmol*. 2003;121:856-862.

8. Distelhorst JS, Hughes GM. Open-angle glaucoma. *Am Fam Physician*. 2003;67:1937-1944.

9. Puustjarvi T, Blomster H, Kontkanen M, Punnonen K, Terasvirta M. Plasma and aqueous humour levels of homocysteine in exfoliation syndrome. *Graefes Arch Clin Exp Ophthalmol*. 2004;242:749-754.

10. Leibovitch I, Kurtz S, Shemesh G, et al. Hyperhomocystinemia in pseudoexfoliation glaucoma. *J Glaucoma*. 2003;12:36-39.

11. Girkin CA, McGwin G Jr, McNeal SF, et al. Hypothyroidism and the development of open-angle glaucoma in a male population. *Ophthalmology*. 2004;111:1649-1652.

12. American Academy of Ophthalmology. Preferred practice pattern, primary open-angle glaucoma. American Academy of Ophthalmology, 1996.

13. Klein BE, Klein R, Linton KL. Intraocular pressure in an American community. The Beaver Dam Eye Study. *Invest Ophthalmol Vis Sci*. 1992;33:2224-2228.

14. American Academy of Ophthalmology. Preferred practice pattern guideline, primary open-angle glaucoma. American Academy of Ophthalmology, 2005.

15. Heijl A, Leske MC, Bengtsson B, et al. Reduction of intraocular pressure and glaucoma progression: results from the Early Manifest Glaucoma Trial. *Arch Ophthalmol*. 2002;120:1268-1279.

16. Higginbotham EJ, Gordon MO, Beiser JA, et al. The Ocular Hypertension Treatment Study: topical medication delays or prevents primary open-angle glaucoma in African American individuals. *Arch Ophthalmol*. 2004;122:813-820.

17. Quaranta L, Bettelli S, Uva MG, et al. Effect of ginkgo biloba extract on preexisting visual field damage in normal tension glaucoma. *Ophthalmology.* 2003;110:359-362.

18. Lichter PR, Musch DC, Gillespie BW, et al. Interim clinical outcomes in the Collaborative Initial Glaucoma Treatment Study comparing initial treatment randomized to medications or surgery. *Ophthalmology.* 2001;108:1943-1953.

19. Janz NK, Wren PA, Lichter PR, et al. The Collaborative Initial Glaucoma Treatment Study: interim quality of life findings after initial medical or surgical treatment of glaucoma. *Ophthalmology.* 2001;108:1954-1965.

20. Cheung N, Wong TY. Obesity and eye diseases. *Surv Ophthalmol.* 2007;52:180-195.

21. Dadeya S, Kamlesh, Shibal F, Khurana C, Khanna A. Effect of religious fasting on intra-ocular pressure. *Eye.* 2002;16:463-465.

12. Allergic Rhinitis and Sinusitis

Allergic rhinitis is a common disease affecting at least 60 million people in the United States. In sensitized individuals, allergens cause release of chemical mediators from mast cells in the nasal mucosa. These mediators may cause rhinorrhea; sinus congestion; sneezing; and eye, palate, and nasal pruritis. In addition, rhinitis may result in postnasal drip, which, in turn, may lead to a cough, sleep disturbance, and fatigue. In allergic individuals, rhinitis is often seasonal and may worsen significantly during the pollen seasons (spring and fall). Rhinitis may also result from year-round exposures—to mold or animal dander, for example.

Sinusitis, also known as rhinosinusitis, is an inflammatory process of the paranasal sinuses. The most common causes are viral upper airway infections and allergies. Acute bacterial rhinosinusitis is a secondary event occurring in approximately 2% of cases of viral infection; it may also occur in allergic individuals. One common cause of acute sinusitis is a secondary bacterial infection, which occurs in ~2% of viral infections. Common causes of subacute and chronic sinusitis include allergen and irritant exposure.

Risk Factors

Though controversial, possible risk factors for allergic rhinitis and sinusitis include:

Allergic Rhinitis

- History of atopy in patient or family.
- First-born child.
- Birth during a pollen season.
- Early introduction of infant formula and food. Breast-feeding for 3 to 6 months may reduce risk.
- Maternal and other smoking exposure in first year of life.
- The role of early exposure to indoor allergens (dust mites, animal dander, mold) is unclear. Some evidence suggests that exposure early in life may increase the risk of developing allergic sensitization, while other evidence suggests a protective effect from such exposure. The "hygiene hypothesis" holds that individuals become "desensitized" with early and repeated exposure and, thus, do not mount an allergic reaction when exposed to various allergens. In addition, air pollution and gas stove fume exposure may also play a role in allergy development, although this theory requires additional study.

Sinusitis

- Allergic rhinitis.
- Nasogastric intubation.
- Dental infection.
- Barotrauma.
- Cystic fibrosis or other ciliary abnormalities.
- Chemical irritation.
- Obstruction: nasal septum deviation, tumor, granuloma, or foreign body.

Diagnosis

Allergic Rhinitis

The diagnosis of allergic rhinitis is based on consistent findings in the history and physical examination, including a seasonal pattern of rhinorrhea, congestion, and pruritis, as well as positive skin tests for sensitivity to aeroallergens.

Pale or bluish nasal mucosa, edematous turbinates with or without drainage, and "cobblestoning" of the oropharynx may be visible on examination. A transverse nasal crease, subcutaneous venodilation under the eyes, and mouth breathing may be signs of allergic rhinitis. Young children may make a clicking sound while rubbing their soft palates with their tongues. Rhinoscopy can allow visualization of polyps, septal deviation, foreign bodies, and tumors.

The diagnosis may be confirmed by prick skin testing, which consists of placing a series of liquid extracts containing various allergens on a patient's back and gently pricking the skin. A positive response consists of erythema (redness) and swelling in the designated area after 20 minutes of observation. Negative skin tests usually exclude an "allergic" or IgE-mediated origin, yet they may not reflect a "nonallergic"/irritant or "vasomotor" reaction.

Other tests, such as blood eosinophils, serum IgE, and the radioallergosorbent test (RAST) to aeroallergens, are not necessary in most clinical situations.

Sinusitis

Sinusitis may include purulent nasal discharge, persistent cough, headache, sinus pressure (especially when leaning forward), fever, and teeth or facial pain at sinus sites. Chronic allergic rhinitis may predispose an individual to both acute and chronic sinusitis. Although acute and chronic sinusitis may be asymptomatic, they often cause a decreased sense of smell (anosmia) and halitosis and may exacerbate asthma due to mucosal inflammation of the nasal and paranasal sinus cavities.

In cases of complicated acute, refractory (chronic), or recurrent sinusitis, a sinus CT scan may help to determine the presence of infection, anatomical abnormalities, tumors, and degree of mucosal disease.

Treatment

Allergic Rhinitis

Avoidance of inciting factors is the most effective treatment. The following measures are also helpful:

- **Nasal irrigation** with hypertonic saline solution may improve symptoms.

- **Antihistamines**, oral or intranasal, improve allergic rhinitis symptoms and are most effective when taken prior to allergen exposure. Antihistamines are ideal for individuals with mild and intermittent symptoms. Common side effects include sedation and dry mouth and eyes, although second-generation antihistamines generally have a better sedation profile.

- **Intranasal steroids** are extremely effective therapy and improve nasal congestion more effectively than antihistamines. Unlike oral antihistamines, nasal steroids must be taken consistently to be effective. They may also improve asthma symptoms.

- **Immunotherapy** injections have been shown to significantly improve nasal symptoms and asthma control. Injections need to be given on a regular basis and may take as long as 6 months to relieve symptoms.

- **Leukotriene antagonists (zileuton)** and **leukotriene receptor antagonists (montelukast, zafirlukast)** help decrease nasal and ocular inflammation.

- **Nasal cromolyn** inhibits mast cell mediator release. It is most effective when taken before allergen exposure and is less effective in preventing nasal symptoms than nasal steroids. The safety profile may be better than steroids for children.

- For allergic conjunctivitis, **ophthalmic drops** may be used (eg, olaptadine and other combination drugs, cromolyn, antihistamines, NSAIDs).

- **Nasal decongestant sprays** should only be used temporarily (a few days). Prolonged use may result in a "rebound" effect (ie, tachyphylaxis), in which nasal congestion worsens upon withdrawal of medication. These medications are effective prior to elevation gain (eg, on mountains, in airplanes) or before initiating nasal steroid use.

- **Oral decongestants,** such as pseudoephedrine, do not cause tachyphylaxis and are effective in relieving acute nasal congestion. However, caution must be taken in hypertensive patients.

- **Nasal ipratroprium bromide** may be most helpful in children needing an alternative to steroids, and it is highly effective in treating rhinorrhea without nasal congestion.

- **NSAIDs** (short-term use) improve systemic sequelae, such as cough.

Sinusitis

- **Nasal irrigation** with hypertonic saline solution may improve symptoms.

- **Symptomatic treatment** with antihistamines and decongestants, and nonsteroidal anti-inflammatory drugs (NSAIDs) for systemic sequelae, such as cough, congestion, and fatigue, may be helpful over the short term.

- In presumed cases of acute bacterial sinusitis, **antibiotics** may be effective but are not always necessary for initial therapy.

- **Amoxicillin, trimethoprim-sulfamethoxazole,** and **doxycycline** are initial options for acute bacterial sinusitis. **Amoxicillin-clavulanate** and select **cephalosporins/fluoroquinolones** are needed to cover resistant bacteria.

- Recurrent/chronic disease requires aggressive treatment with **intranasal steroids** and **nasal saline flushes**. A CT scan of the sinuses may be indicated.

Nutritional Considerations

Nutritional factors may help prevent allergies. Limited evidence suggests that longer duration of breast-feeding and avoidance of early introduction of potentially allergenic foods may reduce the likelihood of allergic sensitization. In an Italian study, new mothers were advised to breast-feed their infants and to avoid introducing commonly allergic foods (whole cow's milk, eggs, fish, nuts, and cocoa) during the first year of life. Mothers who did breast-feed were also asked to limit dairy products and avoid eggs in their own diets, as well as to avoid exposure to other sources of allergens (smoking, day care attendance prior to age 2) as much as possible. These interventions greatly reduced allergic symptoms, including allergic rhinitis.[1]

Studies suggest that, among individuals with allergic rhinitis, dietary fatty acids and antioxidants may influence the production of allergic mediators, including histamine and leukotrienes, and may thereby play a role in the treatment (and possibly the prophylaxis) of allergic rhinitis and sinusitis.

Some evidence suggests that children who eat less saturated fat and cholesterol and more omega-3 fats have less risk of developing rhinitis. Consumption of butter by children[2] and of liver by adolescents[3] has been associated with greater frequency of allergic rhinitis. In contrast, use of an omega-3 fatty acid supplement, paired with a multiple vitamin-mineral formula containing selenium, was shown to decrease the number of episodes of sinus symptoms and acute sinusitis in children.[4]

Limited evidence also suggests that blood levels of vitamins C and E are lower in children with chronic sinusitis than in controls.[5] The intake of citrus fruit or kiwi fruit, both high in vitamin C, has been associated with lower frequency of rhinitis in children.[6] Vitamin E has immunologic effects that might improve rhinitis symptoms, including suppression of neutrophil migration and inhibition of immunoglobulin E (IgE) production.[2] Vitamin E intake from foods was protective against hay fever in an adult population.[7] Patients with hay fever taking vitamin E supplements during pollen season experienced lower nasal symptom scores than those of placebo takers.[8] Additional studies are needed to determine if food or supplemental sources of ascorbic acid and vitamin E benefit sufferers of allergic rhinitis.

A botanical treatment called butterbur (*Petasites hybridus*) significantly reduces both histamine and leukotriene production in sufferers of allergic rhinitis.[9] Benefits have been shown to be similar to those of a prescription antihistamine (Cetirizine), without causing Cetirizine's sedating side effects.[10,11]

Orders

See Basic Diet Orders chapter.

Smoking cessation.

What to Tell the Family

Allergic rhinitis and sinusitis are common yet treatable illnesses. Dietary adjustments may play a role in prevention and, to some extent, in treatment—and they have no problematic side effects. Women who plan to have children should be encouraged to breast-feed (and withhold any dairy products for at least the first 6 months of life) and not smoke to decrease the risk of allergic rhinitis and therefore sinusitis in their children. Families should adopt the same changes as the patient to improve their own health and encourage patient compliance.

References

1. Marini A, Agosti M, Motta G, Mosca F. Effects of a dietary and environmental prevention program on the incidence of allergic symptoms in high atopic risk infants: three years' follow-up. *Acta Paediatr Suppl.* 1996;414:1-21.

2. Farchi S, Forastiere F, Agabiti N, et al. Dietary factors associated with wheezing and allergic rhinitis in children. *Eur Respir J.* 2003;22:772-780.

3. Huang SL, Lin KC, Pan WH. Dietary factors associated with physician-diagnosed asthma and allergic rhinitis in teenagers: analyses of the first Nutrition and Health Survey in Taiwan. *Clin Exp Allergy.* 2001;31:259-264.

4. Linday LA, Dolitsky JN, Shindledecker RD. Nutritional supplements as adjunctive therapy for children with chronic/recurrent sinusitis: pilot research. *Int J Pediatr Otorhinolaryngol.* 2004;68:785-793.

5. Unal M, Tamer L, Pata YS, et al. Serum levels of antioxidant vitamins, copper, zinc, and magnesium in children with chronic rhinosinusitis. *J Trace Elem Med Biol.* 2004;18:189-192.

6. Forastiere F, Pistelli R, Sestini P, et al. Consumption of fresh fruit rich in vitamin C and wheezing symptoms in children. SIDRIA Collaborative Group, Italy (Italian Studies on Respiratory Disorders in Children and the Environment). *Thorax.* 2000;55:283-288.

7. Nagel G, Nieters A, Becker N, Linseisen J. The influence of the dietary intake of fatty acids and antioxidants on hay fever in adults. *Allergy.* 2003;58:1277-1284.

8. Shahar E, Hassoun G, Pollack S. Effect of vitamin E supplementation on the regular treatment of seasonal allergic rhinitis. *Ann Allergy Asthma Immunol.* 2004;92:654-658.

9. Thomet OA, Simon HU. Petasins in the treatment of allergic diseases: results of pre-clinical and clinical studies. *Int Arch Allergy Immunol.* 2002;129:108-112.

10. Schapowal A, and the Petasites Study Group. Randomized controlled trial of butter-bur and cetirizine for treating seasonal allergic rhinitis. *BMJ.* 2002;324:144-146.

11. Schapowal A, and the Petasites Study Group. Treating intermittent allergic rhinitis: a prospective, randomized, placebo and antihistamine-controlled study of Butterbur extract Z 339. *Phytotherapy Research.* 2005;19:530-537.

---

13. Acute Otitis Media

Acute otitis media (AOM) is an inflammatory process of the middle ear. The condition may occur at any age but mainly affects children, peaking between 6 months and 2 years of age. An estimated 30% of all antibiotics prescribed for children in the United States are prescribed for AOM.[1] Common specific symptoms include pain, otorrhea, and temporary hearing loss; vertigo occasionally occurs. Nonspecific findings are more common in young children and include fever, irritability, reduced activity or expressivity, vomiting, diarrhea, and decreased appetite. An upper respiratory infection often precedes AOM, and resultant congestion can obstruct the eustachian tube, creating an accumulation of middle-ear secretions and a potential breeding ground for infections. Spread of infection from the inner ear may result in mastoiditis, or, uncommonly, meningitis, carotid artery thrombosis, and disease of other contiguous structures. Allergies can also contribute to eustachian tube dysfunction and predispose to chronic otitis media.

Risk Factors

Indigenous North American populations have a greater incidence of aggressive AOM. Risk factors include:

Age <10 years. Peak is between 6 months and 24 months.

Male gender.

Pacifier use.[2] Bottle feeding may also increase risk, as noted below.

Day care attendance.

Tobacco smoke exposure.

Air pollution.[3]

Hereditary factors.

Low socioeconomic status.

Fall and winter months.

Allergies.

Diagnosis

Diagnosis requires an acute history, otalgia or erythema of the tympanic membrane, and a middle-ear effusion. Effusion can be demonstrated by a bulging and immobile tympanic membrane (or one with decreased mobility as demonstrated with pneumatic otoscopy), an air-fluid level, or otorrhea.[4]

An erythematous tympanic membrane should not be presumed to be due to AOM. Only 15% of such cases are caused by AOM.[5]

To ensure a correct diagnosis, immobility of the tympanic membrane should be demonstrated. Tympanometry or acoustic reflectometry may substitute for pneumatic otoscopy when the presence of middle-ear effusion is uncertain.

Bacterial culture of a middle ear aspirate is only indicated in the case of immunosuppression, severe illness (with AOM as the likely source), or refractory AOM.

Treatment

Suggestions in the Nutritional Considerations section below should be considered early in the treatment of AOM; they may reduce the need for other treatments, which can often be difficult and taxing.

Decongestants and antihistamines have no proven benefit in AOM.

Several treatment options are available for otalgia.

NSAIDs and **acetaminophen** may improve symptoms, although objective findings may not be apparent.[6]

Benzocaine/antipyrine (Auralgan) otic solution and **Otikon Otic** (an herbal preparation including garlic) may also reduce pain.[7,8]

The American Academy of Pediatrics and the American Academy of Family Physicians make the following recommendations regarding use of antibiotics for AOM:[4]

- All patients under 6 months of age should receive antibiotics, even if the diagnosis of AOM is uncertain.

- Patients aged 6 months to 2 years should receive antibiotics if the diagnosis is clear. If the diagnosis is uncertain, antibiotics should be given if otalgia is moderate to severe, or if the patient's temperature is ≥39°C. Otherwise, observation may be considered.

- Patients older than 2 years with a definite diagnosis of AOM should start an antibiotic if otalgia is moderate to severe, or if fever reaches 39°C. Otherwise, observation may be considered.

- Observation alone is permissible only if rapid initiation of antibiotics and follow-up can be guaranteed. Antibiotics should be started if no improvement occurs in 2 to 3 days.

- **Amoxicillin**, 80 to 90 mg/kg divided into 2 doses for 10 days, is the first-line therapy. In mild to moderate cases in children 6 years and older, treatment for 5 to 7 days may be adequate.[4]

- For penicillin-allergic patients, **cephalosporins** may be used, provided patients did not develop hives or anaphylaxis with penicillin. **Macrolides** or **trimethoprim-sulfamethoxazole** may also be used, but bacteria are often resistant to these medications.

- **Amoxicillin/clavulanate** is used in severe illnesses or when broader coverage is desired.

Recurrent ear infections may warrant additional treatments, such as prophylactic antibiotics, tympanostomy, and adenoidectomy.

- **Tympanostomy** is indicated for severe or recurrent otitis media, or persistent, serous effusion.

- **Adenoidectomy** (with or without tonsillectomy) may benefit those who have recurrent AOM despite tympanostomy. Adenoidectomy may also reduce future AOM episodes when it occurs concomitantly with tympanostomy.[9]

Nutritional Considerations

Bottle feeding may increase risk. Breast-feeding for at least 3 months appears to be protective against AOM.[2]

Although most AOM follows viral infection, food and other environmental allergies can result in chronic otitis media in 35% to 40% of cases.[10] Diets that eliminate foods suspected of causing allergy have resulted in improvement in 86% of affected children, and most relapse when the offending foods are reintroduced.[11] These occurrences may be related to immunoglobulin G (IgG)-food antigen complexes, particularly those of cow's milk protein.[12] Children with otitis media have some evidence of poor antioxidant status[13,14] and poorer zinc and iron status than healthy controls,[15] indicating a need for improved diets.

Orders

See Basic Diet Orders chapter.

Consider an elimination diet. For guidelines, see Anaphylaxis and Food Allergy chapter.

What to Tell the Family

Acute otitis media may be prevented in some cases by breast-feeding, avoiding crowded environments (such as day care), preventing exposure to tobacco smoke and (food) allergens, refraining from use of a pacifier, and providing a diet with adequate micronutrients to support immune function. Antibiotic therapy is not always necessary and is contingent on signs and symptoms of bacterial infection. Repeated episodes of infection may require surgery.

References

1. Nyquist AC, Gonzales R, Steiner JF, Sande MA. Antibiotic prescribing for children with colds, upper respiratory tract infections, and bronchitis. *JAMA*. 1998;279:875-877.

2. Uhari M, Mantysaari K, Niemela M. A meta-analytic review of the risk factors for acute otitis media. *Clin Infect Dis*. 1996;22:1079-1083.

3. Brauer M, Gehring U, Brunekreef B, et al. Traffic-related air pollution and otitis media. *Environ Health Perspect*. 2006;114:1414-1418.

4. American Academy of Family Physicians and American Academy of Pediatrics. Clinical Practice Guideline. Diagnosis and Management of Acute Otitis Media. 2004. Available at: www.aafp.org/PreBuilt/final_aom.pdf. Accessed December 21, 2006.

5. Pelton SI. Otoscopy for the diagnosis of otitis media. *Pediatr Infect Dis J*. 1998;17:540-543.

6. Bertin L, Pons G, d'Athis P, et al. A randomized, double-blind, multicenter controlled trial of ibuprofen versus acetaminophen and placebo for symptoms of acute otitis media in children. *Fundam Clin Pharmacol*. 1996;10:387-392.

7. Hoberman A, Paradise JL, Reynolds EA, Urkin J. Efficacy of Auralgan for treating ear pain in children with acute otitis media. *Arch Pediatr Adolesc Med*. 1997;151:675-678.

8. Sarrell EM, Mandelberg A, Cohen HA. Efficacy of naturopathic extracts in the management of ear pain associated with acute otitis media. *Arch Pediatr Adolesc Med*. 2001;155:796-799.

9. Coyte PC, Croxford R, McIsaac W, et al. The role of adjuvant adenoidectomy and tonsillectomy in the outcome of the insertion of tympanostomy tubes. *N Engl J Med*. 2001;344:1188-1195.

10. Bernstein JM. The role of IgE-mediated hypersensitivity in the development of otitis media with effusion: a review. *Otolaryngol Head Neck Surg*. 1993;109(pt 2):611-620.

11. Nsouli TM, Nsouli SM, Linde RE, O'Mara F, Scanlon RT, Bellanti JA. Role of food allergy in serous otitis media. *Ann Allergy*. 1994;73:215-219.

12. James JM. Respiratory manifestations of food allergy. *Pediatrics*. 2003;111(pt 3):1625-1630.

13. Cemek M, Dede S, Bayiroglu F, Caksen H, Cemek F, Yuca K. Oxidant and antioxidant levels in children with acute otitis media and tonsillitis: A comparative study. *Int J Pediatr Otorhinolaryngol*. 2005;69:823-827.

14. Yariktas M, Doner F, Dogru H, Yasan H, Delibas N. The role of free oxygen radicals on the development of otitis media with effusion. *Int J Pediatr Otorhinolaryngol*. 2004;68:889-894.

15. Bondestam M, Foucard T, Gebre-Medhin M. Subclinical trace element deficiency in children with undue susceptibility to infections. *Acta Paediatr Scand*. 1985;74:515-520.

SECTION IV: HEMATOLOGY

14. Iron Deficiency Anemia

Anemia is a condition in which too few red blood cells are in circulation. Iron deficiency is the most frequent cause of anemia; it results from inadequate levels of iron in the body, causing decreased production of red blood cells. Symptoms are nonspecific and include weakness and fatigue, irritability and mood swings, headache, exercise intolerance, decreased appetite (especially in children), pica (which may include chewing ice), pallor (in dark-pigmented persons, pallor may be evident in sclera and palmar surfaces), shortness of breath, and restless leg syndrome.

The most common cause of iron deficiency is blood loss, usually through menorrhagia or gastrointestinal bleeding. The condition may also be caused by inadequate iron intake, increased iron utilization due to rapid growth (as in infancy, adolescence, and pregnancy), malabsorption (eg, celiac disease or previous gastric surgery, including gastric bypass), phlebotomy, hemolysis, or other rare instances such as intense athletic training. Anemia develops after iron stores (found mainly in the liver, spleen, bone marrow, and the blood itself) are depleted.

According to the Centers for Disease Control and Prevention (CDC),[1] an estimated 7% of toddlers, 4% to 5% of children, 9% to 16% of menstruating females, and 2% of pubescent and adult males have iron deficiency, with smaller percentages having anemia. Mild iron deficiency with depleted iron body stores may produce symptoms without resulting in anemia.

Risk Factors

Age. Children have a greater risk of iron deficiency anemia due to rapid growth, particularly in the first 2 years of life.

Gender. Women generally consume less iron than men do (because of lower energy requirements), but a female patient may have a greater need for iron, depending on her stage of life. On average, a menstruating woman loses 30 to 45 mg of iron per month. Pregnancy and delivery together use about 1 gram of maternal iron. On average, breast-feeding a child uses a total of about 1 gram of maternal iron in the first year.

Peptic ulcer disease and gastritis. These disorders lead to blood loss, which can deplete iron stores. Aspirin and nonsteroidal anti-inflammatory drugs (NSAIDs) are often contributing factors.

Malignancy. Esophageal, gastric, and other gastrointestinal cancers often cause occult bleeding.

Excessive exercise. Blood losses may occur due to intense exercise—eg, "foot strike" hemolysis in distance runners. Increased sweating also results in iron losses. Such losses may predispose adolescent female athletes in particular to frank anemia.[2]

Dietary and absorptive factors (see Nutritional Considerations below).

Diagnosis

Laboratory testing is necessary to diagnose iron deficiency anemia. A complete blood count (CBC) reveals a low hematocrit and hemoglobin concentration and usually a decreased mean corpuscular volume. The red blood cell distribution width (RDW) is elevated. Iron deficiency is one of the most common causes of an elevated platelet count.

The current preferred means of diagnosis is a serum ferritin test, which reflects total body iron stores. Note, however, that ferritin is an acute-phase reactant that may be elevated in cases of inflammation, infection, malignancy, and liver disease, producing a false-negative result.

A blood smear may reveal hypochromic, microcytic red blood cells. However, such cells are also found in the context of other disorders, such as anemia of chronic disease and thalassemia.

Additional useful tests include transferrin (often measured indirectly as the total iron-binding capacity, which is elevated in iron deficiency) and serum iron, which is usually decreased. These tests are less reliable during acute illnesses or in patients with severe chronic diseases. Transferrin is also elevated in women who are pregnant or using oral contraception.

Bone marrow biopsy to determine marrow iron stores was a standard means of diagnosis in the past but now is rarely necessary to diagnose iron deficiency anemia.

An interesting finding is that the ingestion of beets in a person with iron deficiency may cause red-tinged urine. In persons with normal iron levels, the beet pigment loses its color through a redox reaction with ferric ions.[3]

Treatment

Treatment involves resolving the patient's iron deficiency, as well as addressing the underlying etiology (eg, ulcer, malignancy, menorrhagia, dietary deficiency, iron malabsorption). A careful dietary and menstrual history, hemoccult evaluation, endoscopy, or appropriate imaging may reveal the cause. Caution is essential, however, as some patients may have two sources of anemia, such as peptic ulcer and colon cancer.

Nonenteric-coated oral iron supplements are the first line of therapy. Ferrous sulfate is most commonly used and has the greatest bioavailability, but it may also lead to more stomach upset than the gluconate or fumarate forms. Enteric-coated tablets are often poorly absorbed, as they can pass intact through the duodenum (the site of highest iron absorption). Typical adult dosage is 325 mg of ferrous sulfate taken up to 3 times daily.

Dairy products should be avoided because they interfere with the absorption of oral iron (see Nutritional Considerations below). Supplements should be taken on an empty stomach, if tolerated, and at least 2 hours before, or 4 hours after, antacids.

Simultaneous intake of **ascorbic acid** increases absorption of iron. For example, a glass of orange juice contains sufficient vitamin C to significantly increase iron absorption from foods.

If the patient does not tolerate oral supplements or in cases of poor absorption, intramuscular and intravenous iron treatments are available.

Dosage is usually tailored to the magnitude of deficiency balanced with gastrointestinal upset and constipation.

After 2 weeks of maximal ferrous sulfate treatment, laboratory values generally show improvement; values typically normalize after 2 months. Supplementation continued for 6 additional months should replenish iron stores. However, if anemia is due to internal bleeding, stopping iron supplementation when values normalize will allow an assessment as to whether blood loss persists.

Nutritional Considerations

Dietary iron is available in two forms. Heme iron is found in animal muscle and blood, whereas nonheme iron is found both in animal products and in a variety of plant-based foods.

Heme iron in the diet is absorbed at a relatively constant rate of about 23%, independent of other dietary factors. Nonheme iron absorption varies, depending on other dietary factors, as described below. As body stores of iron decrease, the percentage of nonheme iron absorbed increases significantly.

Iron deficiency is common in developing countries (30% to 70%).[4] In industrialized countries, the prevalence of iron deficiency is much lower—roughly 20%—due partly to iron fortification of grain products.[4] However, only one-third to one-half of iron-deficient individuals actually have iron deficiency anemia.[5]

Individuals infected with *Helicobacter pylori* may be especially at risk for iron deficiency. *H pylori* competes with the host for iron and reduces the amount of vitamin C in gastric secretions.[6] Iron therapy becomes unnecessary after eradication of *H pylori* and may be ineffective for treating iron deficiency anemia unless patients receive antimicrobial treatment.[7]

Healthful sources of iron include greens and legumes. Although the myth persists that meat is a preferred iron source, a balanced vegetarian diet that includes legumes, fortified grains, and green vegetables easily provides adequate iron. Studies have shown that the incidence of iron deficiency anemia is no greater among individuals consuming a healthy vegetarian diet than among omnivores.[8]

Dairy products and eggs decrease iron absorption. Caseins from milk and certain forms of calcium inhibit iron absorption.[9] In addition, infants who are allergic to cow's milk may be particularly susceptible to intestinal blood losses due to the irritating effect of dairy products.[5] Iron status measured as serum ferritin is inversely associated with greater consumption of dairy products in toddlers, particularly when they displace foods that contain iron or that facilitate iron absorption.[10] Eggs (especially yolks) also appear to inhibit iron absorption.[11,12]

Fruits and vegetables aid the absorption of nonheme iron. Fruits and vegetables contain vitamin C and organic acids (eg, citric acid) that keep iron in a reduced form, allowing for better absorption of nonheme iron. Vitamin A and carotenoids also appear to enhance iron absorption by overcoming the inhibiting effect of polyphenols and phytates (found in whole grains) on iron absorption. Adding vitamin A to an iron supplement regimen has also been shown to result in greater anemia reduction than iron alone produces.[7]

Tea, coffee, and cocoa should not be consumed with meals if poor iron status is suspected. Polyphenols in these beverages inhibit the absorption of nonheme iron. Black tea appears to be the most potent in this regard.[9]

Adequate iron intake before pregnancy can help prevent anemia in both mothers and infants. Iron deficiency is more common in women of childbearing age, especially during pregnancy.[5] The physiologic need for iron increases almost 10-fold during pregnancy and lactation, and iron deficiency in the first trimester results in significantly poorer indicators of fetal growth, neural development, and behavior in offspring, compared with what happens when mothers have adequate iron status.[13] In mothers with iron deficiency, exclusive breast-feeding often results in iron deficiency in infants.[14] Without adequate iron stores prior to conception, iron supplementation may be necessary during pregnancy (see below).

Breast milk contains significant iron. Human milk and cow's milk contain similar concentrations of iron (0.5 mg/100 ml), although breast-feeding is preferable for many reasons (see Healthy Diets at All Stages of Life chapter). Unfortified infant formula contains about 20% of the iron found in breast milk, whereas fortified formula has over twice the iron concentration. Despite this higher level, iron in breast milk is more absorbable than that in soy-based or dairy-based formulas.

Iron supplementation should be individualized. The CDC recommends that iron supplementation be individualized based on hemoglobin screening of at-risk individuals.[15] Iron supplementation should be avoided in cases lacking documented need because excess iron stores are associated with greater risks for colon cancer, coronary heart disease, and insulin resistance.[16,17]

Alcohol intake enhances iron absorption but should not be used as a means of regulating iron status. Consumption of any amount of alcohol is associated with a 40% reduction in the risk of iron deficiency anemia. However, the prevalence of markers of iron overload, which may be more harmful than mild reductions in iron status, was found to be significantly elevated among individuals who consumed >2 alcoholic drinks per day.[18] Increasing alcohol consumption is obviously not a recommended treatment for improving a person's iron status.

Orders

See Basic Diet Orders chapter.

Avoid tea, coffee, and cocoa with meals.

What to Tell the Family

Iron deficiency anemia is usually preventable and highly treatable. A diet of fortified grains, legumes, nuts and seeds, and fruits and vegetables can provide for healthy iron balance. During times of increased iron requirements or when an iron deficiency has been diagnosed, iron supplementation may be needed. Simple blood tests can accurately assess a person's iron status.

References

1. Centers for Disease Control and Prevention. Iron Deficiency—United States, 1999-2000. *MMWR.* 2002;51:897-899.

2. Shaskey DJ, Green GA. Sports haematology. *Sports Med.* 2000;29:27-38.

3. Tunnessen WW, Smith C, Oski FA. Beeturia: A sign of iron deficiency. *Am J Dis Child.* 1969;117:424-426.

4. Ramakrishnan U, Yip R. Experiences and challenges in industrialized countries: control of iron deficiency in industrialized countries. *J Nutr.* 2002;132:820S-824S.

5. Burke W, Imperatore G, Reyes M. Iron deficiency and iron overload: effects of diet and genes. *Proc Nutr Soc.* 2001;60:73-80.

6. Salgueiro J, Zubillaga M, Goldman C, et al. Review article: is there a link between micronutrient malnutrition and Helicobacter pylori infection? *Aliment Pharmacol Ther.* 2004;20:1029-1034.

7. Kostaki M, Smaragdi F, Themistocles K. Refractory iron-deficiency anaemia due to silent Helicobacter pylorigastritis in children. *Eur J Pediatr.* 2003;162:177-179.

8. Craig WJ. Iron status of vegetarians. *Am J Clin Nutr.* 1994;59:1233S-1237S.

9. Camara-Martos F, Amaro-Lopez MA. Influence of dietary factors on calcium bioavailability: a brief review. *Biol Trace Elem Res.* 2002;89:43-52.

10. Thane CW, Walmsley CM, Bates CJ, Prentice A, Cole TJ. Risk factors for poor iron status in British toddlers: further analysis of data from the National Diet and Nutrition Survey of children aged 1.5-4.5 years. *Public Health Nutr.* 2000;3:433-440.

11. Hallberg L, Hulthen L. Prediction of dietary iron absorption: an algorithm for calculating absorption and bioavailability of dietary iron. *Am J Clin Nutr.* 2000;71:1147-1160.

12. Stekel A, Amar M, Calvo E, et al. Nutritional significance of interactions between iron and food components. *Arch Latinoam Nutr.* 1983;33:33-41.

13. Beard JL. Effectiveness and strategies of iron supplementation during pregnancy. *Am J Clin Nutr.* 2000;71:1288S-1294S.

14. Yurdakok K, Temiz F, Yalcin SS, Gumruk F. Efficacy of daily and weekly iron supplementation on iron status in exclusively breast-fed infants. *J Pediatr Hematol Oncol.* 2004;26:284-288.

15. Centers for Disease Control and Prevention. Recommendations to prevent and control iron deficiency in the United States. *MMWR Recomm Rep.* 1998;47(RR-3):1-29.

16. Bioavailability of iron, zinc, and other trace minerals from vegetarian diets. *Am J Clin Nutr.* 2003;78:633S-639S.

17. Fernandez-Real JM, Lopez-Bermejo A, Ricart W. Cross-talk between iron metabolism and diabetes. *Diabetes.* 2002;51:2348-2354.

18. Ioannou GN, Dominitz JA, Weiss NS, Heagerty PJ, Kowdley KV. The effect of alcohol consumption on the prevalence of iron overload, iron deficiency, and iron deficiency anemia. *Gastroenterology.* 2004;126:1293-1301.

15. Megaloblastic Anemia

Megaloblastic anemia is characterized by enlarged and oval-shaped red blood cells and is frequently caused by vitamin B_{12} (cobalamin) or folate deficiency. Numerous hematologic and neurologic abnormalities can result from the impaired DNA processes due to inadequate B_{12} or folate concentrations.

Vitamin B_{12} deficiency causes subacute combined neurologic degeneration, which can be severe and sometimes irreversible. Neurologic defects may occur with or without anemia. The signs and symptoms include:

- Paresthesias of the hands and feet.

- Symmetrical and progressive spastic and ataxic weakness.

- Loss of deep tendon reflexes.

- Irritability and mental status changes (megaloblastic madness).

Other symptoms of vitamin B_{12} or folate deficiency may include fatigue, weakness, glossitis, gastrointestinal problems (eg, diarrhea), decreased appetite, changes in taste, and weight loss. These symptoms sometimes precede anemia. However, megaloblastic anemia is often asymptomatic until the condition is quite severe.

Risk Factors

Vitamin B_{12} deficiency may result from:

Intrinsic factor deficiency. Intrinsic factor is required for vitamin B_{12} absorption. A deficiency can occur congenitally or through chronic gastritis, gastrectomy, or autoimmune processes directed at intrinsic factor or the gastric parietal cells that produce it. When anemia results from an intrinsic factor deficiency, it is called pernicious anemia.

Malabsorption. Small bowel and pancreatic disease and alcohol abuse contribute to poor B_{12} absorption. Elderly persons may also have reduced B_{12} absorption.

Other gastric disease. Occasionally, individuals with *H pylori* gastritis, total or partial gastrectomy, or gastric bypass may develop a B_{12} deficiency.

Medications. Metformin (reversible with calcium supplements), proton pump inhibitors, H2-blockers, antacids, and antibiotic use (with subsequent bacterial overgrowth) may inhibit B_{12} absorption.

HIV infection. Weight loss and diarrhea in HIV/AIDS are associated with B_{12} deficiency.[1]

Fish tapeworm. Fish tapeworm competes for available B_{12}.

Dietary deficiency. See Nutritional Considerations below.

Folate deficiency may result from:

Alcohol abuse. Alcohol interferes with the enterohepatic cycle and absorption of folate.

Malabsorption. Malabsorptive diseases, such as inflammatory bowel disease and sprue, decrease folate absorption.

Pregnancy and breast-feeding. Because fetal and infant growth requires increased folate, pregnancy and breast-feeding may deplete a woman's folate stores. In turn, an exclusively breast-fed infant whose mother is folate-deficient will not receive adequate folate.

Medications. Intake of certain medications, such as methotrexate, phenytoin, and trimethoprim, may lead to folate deficiency.

Hemolysis and exfoliative dermatitis. Both conditions increase the demand for folate.

Vitamin B_{12} deficiency. Because vitamin B_{12} is responsible for the formation of the metabolically active form of folic acid, its deficiency can lead to folate deficiency.

Dietary deficiency. See Nutritional Considerations below.

Diagnosis

The complete hematologic picture includes:

- Large bone marrow precursor cells of neutrophils and erythrocytes (macro-ovalocytes) with an elevated mean corpuscular volume (MCV). Note: An elevated MCV may not be present if iron deficiency is concurrent.

* Hypersegmented neutrophil nuclei (6 lobes or greater or several 5-lobed cells).

* A complete blood count (CBC) showing anemia. Severe anemia is possible with occasional hemoglobin values <5.0 g/dL.

* Normal or depressed reticulocyte counts.

* Marked lactate dehydrogenase (LDH) elevation (in the thousands) due to ineffective red blood cell production.

* Thrombocytopenia and neutropenia.

Bone marrow biopsy is usually not necessary for diagnosis, but typically shows megaloblastosis and hypercellularity with erythroid and myeloid hyperplasia.

Additional tests must be conducted to distinguish between folate and vitamin B_{12} deficiencies because the hematologic indices revealed by blood smear review and bone marrow aspirate are similar for both deficiency types.

Serum B_{12} and folate and/or red blood cell folate concentration should be measured. Serum folate can be acutely elevated after a folate-rich meal, whereas red blood cell folate more accurately measures actual stores.

If the serum B_{12} and folate results are not diagnostic, additional testing can be performed. Note that serum folate and vitamin B_{12} assays may be rendered unreliable by pregnancy, alcohol intake, acute nutrition change, or medication use. In these instances, additional tests may aid diagnosis.

Serum methylmalonic acid is elevated in vitamin B_{12} deficiency and is usually normal in folate deficiency.

Deficiency of vitamin B_{12} or folate will elevate homocysteine.

Because hypothyroidism can be associated with pernicious anemia, screening with a thyroid-stimulating hormone (TSH) level should be considered in patients with B_{12} deficiency.

Treatment

Identification of the underlying cause of vitamin B_{12} or folate deficiency is necessary to ensure adequate long-term treatment.

Vitamin B_{12}

Vitamin B_{12} injections (1000 μg) are usually given daily for 1 week, then weekly for 4 weeks, and then monthly until hematologic indices have stabilized. Patients with continued risk of deficiency should remain on monthly injections. Oral B_{12} (1000-2000 μg/day) may be substituted in highly compliant patients. At high intakes, the vitamin enters the body through diffusion. Vitamin B_{12} sublingual preparations and a nasal gel are also available for maintenance therapy when compliance is ensured.

Folate

Oral folate (1 mg) taken daily for several months usually corrects the deficiency.

Doses up to 5 mg may be used if indicated.

Concomitant B_{12} deficiency must be ruled out, as folate supplementation can mask the hematologic signs of B_{12} deficiency, leading to irreversible neurologic injury if not treated. This masking is particularly likely to occur in patients routinely prescribed folate for other medical reasons (eg, sickle cell anemia).[2]

Nutritional Considerations

Vitamin B_{12}

In individuals following omnivorous diets, dietary vitamin B_{12} is usually adequate. However, some people, particularly elderly persons, have poorer B_{12} absorption due to atrophic gastritis or hypochlorhydria. The use of histamine H_2-receptor blockers or proton pump inhibitors may also interfere with the breakdown of vitamin B_{12} from food and interfere with B_{12} absorption. In these situations, low-dose crystalline B_{12} supplements may prevent B_{12} deficiency. In cases of intrinsic factor deficiency, intramuscular injections or high-dose supplements (1 mg/day) will prevent or treat pernicious anemia.[3]

Persons who have had gastric bypass surgery are at risk for B_{12} deficiency.[4,5] Individuals who have followed vegan diets for many years without taking B_{12} supplements and their exclusively breast-fed infants are also at risk. In these groups, the risk for vitamin B_{12} deficiency is easily eliminated with supplementation.[4] Individuals who abuse alcohol and those with celiac disease are also at higher risk for deficiency.[6,7] Individuals infected with *Helicobacter pylori* may also be at risk. A concurrent inhibition of vitamin B_{12} and folate absorption caused by this organism may result in pernicious anemia. [8]

Folate

Due to fortification of grain products with folic acid, anemia resulting from folate deficiency is becoming less frequent. However, alcoholism often leads to poor folate intake and, combined with alcohol's anti-folate effect, may lead to deficiency.[9]

An autosomal-recessive inborn error of metabolism causes thiamine-responsive megaloblastic anemia (also known as Rogers syndrome).[10] Pharmacologic doses of thiamine (25-200 mg/day) correct the hematologic abnormalities associated with this condition.[11]

Caution is necessary in prescribing folate supplements. As noted above, folic acid can mask signs of vitamin B_{12} deficiency.

Orders

See Basic Diet Orders chapter.

Restrict alcohol use. A psychiatric referral, along with substance abuse counseling and Alcoholics Anonymous meetings or other community-based support, may be necessary.

Vitamin B_{12} supplementation, intramuscular or oral as indicated.

Oral folate supplementation (rule out B_{12} deficiency prior to treatment).

What to Tell the Family

Megaloblastic anemia is typically caused by a vitamin B_{12} or folate deficiency and can be easily treated. Appropriate supplementation, increased consumption of folate-rich foods, and reduction of alcohol use can help prevent recurrence. In vegan diets, oral vitamin B_{12} supplementation is necessary. If the primary cause of deficiency is alcohol use, the patient will likely need multilevel support facilitated through the primary care provider.

References

1. Balt CA. An investigation of the relationship between vitamin B_{12} deficiency and HIV infection. *J Assoc Nurses AIDS Care.* 2000;11:24-28, 31-35.

2. Dhar M, Bellevue R, Carmel R. Pernicious anemia with neuropsychiatric dysfunction in a patient with sickle cell anemia treated with folate supplementation. *N Engl J Med.* 2003;348:2204-2207.

3. Baik HW, Russell RM. Vitamin B_{12} deficiency in the elderly. *Annu Rev Nutr.* 1999;19:357-377.

4. Grange DK, Finlay JL. Nutritional Vitamin B_{12} deficiency in a breastfed infant following maternal gastric bypass. *Pediatr Hematol Oncol.* 1994;11:311-318.

5. Drummond JF, White DK, Damm DD. Megaloblastic anemia with oral lesions: a consequence of gastric bypass surgery. *Oral Surg Oral Med Oral Pathol.* 1985;59:149-153.

6. Dahele A, Ghosh S. Vitamin B_{12} deficiency in untreated celiac disease. *Am J Gastroenterol.* 2001;96:745-750.

7. Quigley EM, Carmichael HA, Watkinson G. Adult celiac disease (celiac sprue), pernicious anemia and IgA deficiency: case report and review of the relationships between Vitamin B_{12} deficiency, small intestinal mucosal disease and immunoglobulin deficiency. *J Clin Gastroenterol.* 1986;8:277-281.

8. Salgueiro J, Zubillaga M, Goldman C, et al. Review article: is there a link between micronutrient malnutrition and Helicobacter pylori infection? *Aliment Pharmacol Ther.* 2004;20:1029-1034.

9. Lindenbaum J, Roman MJ. Nutritional anemia in alcoholism. *Am J Clin Nutr.* 1980;33:2727-2735.

10. Singleton CK, Martin PR. Molecular mechanisms of thiamine utilization. *Curr Mol Med.* 2001;1:197-207.

11. Bappal B, Nair R, Shaikh H, et al. Five years followup of diabetes mellitus in two siblings with thiamine responsive megaloblastic anemia. *Indian Pediatrics.* 2001;38:1295-1298.

16. Sickle Cell Disease

Sickle cell disease (SCD) is an autosomal recessive condition in which red blood cells become sickle-shaped and fragile. This results in hemolytic anemia and recurrent vaso-occlusion in the microvasculature due to increased red blood cell adhesion and retention. Acute vaso-occlusion causes severe pain in the musculoskeletal system, abdomen, and other areas. Other acute vaso-occlusive complications include splenic sequestration and/or infarct and the acute chest syndrome associated with pulmonary infarcts. Large vessel stroke occurs in the setting of stenotic blood vessels due to chronic vessel wall injury.

Hemoglobin S (HbS) is characterized by a single change in the amino acid sequence of the β-globin chain and is responsible for creating the abnormal red cell morphology. Individuals who are heterozygous for the HbS gene generally have no symptoms or sequelae of SCD, but they are said to have sickle cell trait; ie, they are carriers of the HbS gene. Their offspring could be affected if the other parent is heterozygous or homozygous for the gene or carries another abnormal hemoglobin gene.

Other SCD variants include hemoglobin SC, a heterozygous combination of HbS and hemoglobin C, and hemoglobin S and β-thalassemia (hemoglobin Sβ^+-thalassemia or Sβ°-thalassemia). These conditions cause SCD, although the symptoms and complications may be less severe than those in the homozygous condition. The remainder of this chapter will focus on SCD that results from homozygous HbS.

Acute signs and symptoms may include pain in the hands and feet, fever, immunocompromise due to splenic sequestration/infarction, priapism, chest pain, shortness of breath, fatigue, pallor, tachycardia, jaundice, and urinary symptoms. Chronic complications include delayed growth/puberty, retinopathy, chronic lung and kidney disease, cardiovascular disease, avascular necrosis of the hips and shoulders, bone infarcts, and leg ulcers.

Risk Factors

The disease occurs most often among people whose ancestry can be linked to sub-Saharan Africa, South America and Central America, the Caribbean, India, and the Middle East and Mediterranean regions. A Texas study showed the disease to be about 300 times more common in African Americans (approximately 3 per 1,000) than in whites, and 3 times more common in individuals of Hispanic ethnicity than in non-Hispanic whites.[1] Approximately 1 in 12 African Americans carry sickle cell trait.

Diagnosis

Prenatal screening is possible through chorionic villous sampling if the fetus is at risk for SCD. Other prenatal tests may be routinely available in the near future.

Universal newborn screening by electrophoresis (or other diagnostic testing) is performed in every U.S. state. Sickle cell anemia is indicated by the presence of fetal hemoglobin (hemoglobin F) and hemoglobin S and an absence of hemoglobin A.

Electrophoretic findings for sickle cell anemia are:

- Hemoglobin S at 85% to 98% (normally 0%).

- Hemoglobin A at 0% (normally 95%–98%).

- Hemoglobin F at 2% to 15% (normally 0.8%–2.0%).

Additional findings are likely to include a normochromic, normocytic anemia; reticulocytosis; and sickle cells (and other abnormal findings, including polychromasia) visible on peripheral blood smear. Other findings consistent with hemolysis may also be present.

Subsequent to diagnosis, patients should undergo periodic testing, which includes complete blood count (CBC), iron studies, liver function tests, and tests of renal function, such as urinalysis, blood urea nitrogen (BUN), and creatinine. These data can be compared with those assessed during exacerbations to guide medical management.

Treatment

In the acute pain setting, analgesics, warm compresses, and oral and intravenous fluids are appropriate interventions. Complementary therapies, such as hypnosis, relaxation techniques, and biofeedback, may also be helpful.

Preventive Strategies

Comprehensive and multidisciplinary care is essential. Education of both patient and family may help prevent complications of the disease.

Influenza and pneumococcus vaccines should routinely be used. **Pneumococcal prophylaxis** (oral penicillin V 125-250 mg twice daily) should be taken continuously by children with sickle cell anemia until age 5. Children with a history of splenectomy or severe pneumonia may need further prophylaxis.

Folic acid should be taken in doses of 1 mg daily.

Transcranial Doppler may identify children at risk for stroke. Those at higher risk should be offered a chronic blood transfusion program.[2]

Routine eye exams should monitor for proliferative retinopathy.

Assessment for chronic complications, including chronic lung and kidney disease, should be performed periodically, especially in older children and adults.

Analgesia

Narcotics are often required for pain relief. Initial boluses with patient-controlled anesthesia for subsequent pain control are appropriate strategies.

Morphine sulfate and **hydromorphone** are first-line agents. Hydromorphone is more concentrated and therefore beneficial in fluid-restricted patients. Morphine synthetics, such as fentanyl, can also be used. Meperidine is not recommended.

Nonnarcotic analgesia may also be helpful. **Ketorolac** is especially helpful for bone pain and is as effective as meperidine.[3] Note: Ulcer prophylaxis is needed and renal function should be monitored. **Tramadol** can be used for outpatient management and is less likely than narcotics to lead to dependence.

Lesser-potency analgesics, including nonsteroidal anti-inflammatory drugs (NSAIDs), are likely important adjuncts to the above narcotic agents, but they have not been well studied in this context.

Antibiotics

Infections cause nearly 50% of SCD–induced mortality. Patients who have febrile episodes, without other symptoms, need broad-spectrum antibiotic coverage (eg, ceftriaxone). Depending on the severity of the fever and prophylactic penicillin status (in children), antibiotics can be administered intravenously or intramuscularly and on an inpatient or outpatient basis.

Meningitis, bacteremia, osteomyelitis, urinary tract infections, and acute chest syndrome require specific antibiotic regimens.

Blood Transfusions

Transfusions may be of the simple or exchange type. It is important that patients are not transfused acutely above a hemoglobin of 10 g/dL, which can lead to increased blood viscosity. Strategies and formulas have been devised to help calculate appropriate volumes to be transfused in both children and adults.

Simple transfusions restore blood volume and oxygen-carrying capacity in individuals with SCD.

Partial-exchange transfusions may be required during a severe acute complication (eg, acute chest syndrome) to prevent increased blood viscosity. Exchange therapy lowers the risk of stroke[2] and may also prevent other end-organ damage and reduce iron loading, compared with simple transfusion.

Transfusion therapy is not indicated for uncomplicated SCD pain events.

Alloimmunization (antibody formation after blood transfusion) is approximately 6 times more common in persons with SCD compared with other anemias, and the cost to ensure more strictly matched blood can be high. A racially and ethnically diverse blood supply can help reduce the likelihood of alloimmunization.

Other Treatments

Hydroxyurea stimulates the production of hemoglobin F. In addition, hydroxyurea may reduce the number of acute pain episodes and acute chest syndrome attacks.

Erythropoietin's ability to stimulate production of hemoglobin F is less clear, but if hydroxyurea produces a less than adequate stimulus, substitution or addition of erythropoietin may be tried empirically.[4]

Hematopoietic cell transplantation and **gene therapy** are potentially curative treatment strategies but remain experimental.

Magnesium supplementation may reduce the number of acute pain episodes. More thorough study of its role is under way.

Niprasan, an herbal product, may prevent pain episodes. Further study is warranted.[5]

Inhaled nitric oxide, poloxamer 188, nasal cromolyn sodium, and anticoagulation may have roles in SCD treatment. Further study is needed.

Nutritional Considerations

Patients with sickle cell anemia have greater than average requirements for both calories and micronutrients. During sickle cell crises, energy intake can be especially poor. Children frequently hospitalized for sickle cell disease (SCD) commonly show poor linear growth, lean body mass, and reduced fat-free mass. For reasons that are poorly understood, many patients are deficient in essential micronutrients. A diet emphasizing fruits, vegetables, whole grains, and legumes will provide a greater proportion of essential nutrients than a typical Western diet, and appropriate supplementation (1-3 times the recommended intakes for most essential nutrients) can prevent deficiency and may decrease the likelihood of disease exacerbation.

High-calorie, nutrient-dense diet. The average energy intake of sickle cell patients is typically below the suggested allowance for calories during the quiescent phase of the disease, and it drops to roughly half the recommended levels during times of illness requiring hospitalization.[6] As a result, children with SCD have impaired growth and significantly lower fat and fat-free mass, compared with unaffected individuals.[7] Standard nutritional assessment methods used to calculate energy needs typically underestimate resting energy expenditure in persons with SCD.[8,9] A careful nutritional assessment and the addition of energy supplements are indicated.

Adequate fluid consumption to maintain hydration. Sickling of erythrocytes increases in SCD patients who exercise in the heat without consuming fluids, compared with those who maintain well-hydrated status.[10]

Micronutrient status may need correction. Blood levels of several vitamins and minerals, including vitamin A and carotenoids,[11,12] vitamin B$_6$,[13] vitamin C,[14] vitamin E,[15] magnesium,[16] and zinc,[17,18] are often low in individuals with SCD. These deficiencies cause a significant depreciation in blood-antioxidant status in these patients,[19] and the resulting oxidative stress may precipitate vaso-occlusion–related acute chest syndrome.[20] Studies indicate that vitamin-mineral supplements of certain nutrients (vitamins C and E, zinc, magnesium) or treatment with a combination of high-dose antioxidants can reduce the percentage of irreversibly sickled cells.[15,21-24]

Omega-3 fatty acid supplements. The serum phospholipids of children with SCD contain reduced proportions of both the parent (alpha-linolenic acid) and the long-chain omega-3 polyunsaturated fatty acids (eicosapentanoic acid [EPA] and docosahexanoic acid [DHA]), compared with healthy controls.[25,26] Long-chain omega-3 fatty acids (EPA, DHA) increase the fluidity of red blood cell membranes,[27] which may prevent sickle cell crisis.[28] A small preliminary study indicated that the antithrombotic effect of fish oil (0.1 g/kg/day) reduced the number of painful episodes requiring hospitalization, compared with olive oil treatment.[27] However, this finding has not yet been confirmed in controlled trials.

Orders

See Basic Diet Orders chapter.

High-potency multiple vitamin with minerals,1 tablet by mouth daily. For patients with iron overload due to frequent transfusions, supplements containing any amount of iron should be avoided.

Nutrition consultation for assessment, to advise patient regarding specific dietary recommendations, and to arrange follow-up as needed.

Protein-calorie supplements, per nutrition consultant.

What to Tell the Family

Good nutrition can help safeguard healthy growth in children with sickle cell disease and may reduce the risk of complications. A registered dietitian can advise the patient and family on how to meet macronutrient and micronutrient needs. Supplemental nutrients may be required and ordered by the physician.

References

1. Strahan JE, Canfield MA, Drummond-Borg LM, Neill SU. Ethnic and gender patterns for the five congenital disorders in Texas from 1992 through 1998. *Tex Med.* 2002;98:80-86.

2. Adams RJ, McKie VC, Hsu L, et al. Prevention of a first stroke by transfusions in children with sickle cell anemia and abnormal results on transcranial Doppler ultrasonography. *N Engl J Med.* 1998;339:5-11.

3. Grisham JE, Vichinsky EP. Ketorolac versus meperidine in vaso-occlusive crisis: A study of safety and efficacy. *Int J Pediatr Hematol Oncol.* 1996;3:239.

4. Rodgers GP, Dover GJ, Uyesaka N, Noguchi CT, Schechter AN, Nienhuis AW. Augmentation by erythropoietin of fetal hemoglobin response to hydroxyurea in sickle cell patients. *N Engl J Med.* 1993;328:73-80.

5. Wambebe C, Khamofu H, Momoh JA, et al. Double-blind, placebo-controlled, randomised cross-over clinical trial of NIPRISAN in patients with sickle cell disorder. *Phytomedicine.* 2001;8:252-261.

6. Malinauskas BM, Gropper SS, Kawchak DA, et al. Impact of acute illness on nutritional status of infants and young children with sickle cell disease. *J Am Diet Assoc.* 2000;100:330-334.

7. Barden EM, Kawchak DA, Ohene-Frempong K, et al. Body composition in children with sickle cell disease. *Am J Clin Nutr.* 2002;76:218-225.

8. Williams R, Olivi S, Mackert P, et al. Comparison of energy prediction equations with measured resting energy expenditure in children with sickle cell anemia. *J Am Diet Assoc.* 2002;102:956-961.

9. Barden EM, Zemel BS, Kawchak DA, et al. Total and resting energy expenditure in children with sickle cell disease. *J Pediatr.* 2000;136:73-79.

10. Bergeron MF, Cannon JG, Hall EL, et al. Erythrocyte sickling during exercise and thermal stress. *Clin J Sport Med.* 2004;14:354-356.

11. Gray NT, Bartlett JM, Kolasa KM, et al. Nutritional status and dietary intake of children with sickle cell anemia. *Am J Pediatr Hematol Oncol.* 1992;14:57-61.

12. Tangney CC, Phillips G, Bell RA, et al. Selected indices of micronutrient status in adult patients with sickle cell anemia (SCA). *Am J Hematol.* 1989;32:161-166.

13. Segal JB, Miller ER III, Brereton NH, et al. Concentrations of B vitamins and homocysteine in children with sickle cell anemia. *South Med J.* 2004;97:149-155.

14. Westerman MP, Zhang Y, McConnell JP, et al. Ascorbate levels in red blood cells and urine in patients with sickle cell anemia. *Am J Hematol.* 2000;65:174-175.

15. Marwah SS, Blann AD, Rea C, et al. Reduced vitamin E antioxidant capacity in sickle cell disease is related to transfusion status but not to sickle crisis. *Am J Hematol.* 2002;69:144-146.

16. Zehtabchi S, Sinert R, Rinnert S, et al. Serum ionized magnesium levels and ionized calcium-to-magnesium ratios in adult patients with sickle cell anemia. *Am J Hematol.* 2004;77:215-222.

17. Zemel BS, Kawchak DA, Fung EB, et al. Effect of zinc supplementation on growth and body composition in children with sickle cell disease. *Am J Clin Nutr.* 2002;75:300-307.

18. Riddington C, De Franceschi L. Drugs for preventing red blood cell dehydration in people with sickle cell disease. *Cochrane Database Syst Rev.* 2002;(4):CD003426.

19. Blann AD, Marwah S, Serjeant G, et al. Platelet activation and endothelial cell dysfunction in sickle cell disease is unrelated to reduced antioxidant capacity. *Blood Coagul Fibrinolysis.* 2003;14:255-259.

20. Klings ES, Farber HW. Role of free radicals in the pathogenesis of acute chest syndrome in sickle cell disease. *Respir Res.* 2001;2:280-285.

21. Jaja SI, Ikotun AR, Gbenebitse S, et al. Blood pressure, hematologic and erythrocyte fragility changes in children suffering from sickle cell anemia following ascorbic acid supplementation. *J Trop Pediatr.* 2002;48:366-370.

22. Ohnishi ST, Ohnishi T, Ogunmola GB. Sickle cell anemia: a potential nutritional approach for a molecular disease. *Nutrition.* 2000;16:330-338.

23. De Franceschi L, Bachir D, Galacteros F, et al. Oral magnesium supplements reduce erythrocyte dehydration in patients with sickle cell disease. *J Clin Invest.* 1997;100:1847-1852.

24. Muskiet FA, Muskiet FD, Meiborg G, et al. Supplementation of patients with homozygous sickle cell disease with zinc, alpha-tocopherol, vitamin C, soybean oil, and fish oil. *Am J Clin Nutr.* 1991;54:736-744.

25. Glew RH, Casados JK, Huang YS, et al. The fatty acid composition of the serum phospholipids of children with sickle cell disease in Nigeria. *Prostaglandins Leukot Essent Fatty Acids.* 2002;67:217-222.

26. VanderJagt DJ, Trujillo MR, Bode-Thomas F, Huang YS, Chuang LT, Glew RH. Phase angle and n-3 polyunsaturated fatty acids in sickle cell disease. *Arch Dis Child.* 2002;87:252-254.

27. Tomer A, Kasey S, Connor WE, et al. Reduction of pain episodes and prothrombotic activity in sickle cell disease by dietary n-3 fatty acids. *Thromb Haemost.* 2001;85:966-974.

28. Ballas SK, Smith ED. Red blood cell changes during the evolution of the sickle cell painful crisis. *Blood.* 1992;79:2154-2163.

SECTION V: ONCOLOGY

17. Diet During Cancer Treatment

There are no standard evidence-based recommendations for diet therapy during cancer treatment, due in part to the heterogeneous nature of this disease. Loss of appetite and severe weight loss (cachexia) are common in many cancer patients, and significant weight loss at the time of diagnosis—as well as malnutrition that may occur during the course of the disease—is a predictor of poor outcome.[1] Malnutrition also impairs the response to chemotherapy.[2] Due to these risks, the National Cancer Institute (NCI) suggests early nutrition screening and intervention, as well as close monitoring and evaluation of patients throughout all phases of cancer treatment and recovery.[1]

Nutritional Assessment Goals, Criteria, and Methodology

The goals of nutrition assessment and therapy include prevention or reversal of nutrient deficiencies; preservation of lean body mass; increased tolerance for anticancer treatments with a minimization of nutrition-related side effects and complications; decreased risk for infection through support of immune function; facilitation of recovery and healing; and maintenance of strength, energy, and quality of life.[3]

NCI recommends 2 methods of assessing nutritional status in cancer patients:

The **Prognostic Nutrition Index (PNI)** uses body weight, skin-fold thickness, serum albumin and transferrin concentrations, and delayed cutaneous hypersensitivity to classify patients into categories of nutritional status that predict clinical outcome.[4]

The **Patient-Generated Subjective Global Assessment (PG-SGA)** includes weight history, food intake, symptoms, and function, which are evaluated in the context of weight loss, disease, and metabolic stress. These findings, along with a nutrition-related physical examination, generate a score indicating the need for nutrition intervention.[3]

Additional criteria suggesting a need for oral, enteral, or parenteral nutrition support include:[3]

- presenting at less than 80% of ideal weight
- unintentional weight loss of more than 10% of usual weight
- nutrient malabsorption due to disease, short bowel syndrome, or anticancer therapy
- fistulas or draining abscesses
- inability to eat or drink for more than 5 days

Potential Risk of Aggressive Nutrition Therapy

Because weight loss and malnutrition are often significant in individuals fighting malignancy, clinical efforts frequently focus on increasing protein and energy intake by any means acceptable to patients, including use of the same type of cuisine that might have contributed to the initial development of the malignancy and that may be associated with poorer long-term survival. Although identification of nutrition problems and treatment of nutrition-related symptoms have been shown to stabilize or reverse weight loss in 50% to 88% of oncology patients,[3] there is little evidence that these patients survive longer than patients whose weight loss is less aggressively treated. Evidence suggests that *ad libitum* diets high in fat, sugar, and animal protein may, by increasing cancer growth factors and stimulating cellular events leading to immune suppression and inflammation, foster cell proliferation and metastasis, interfere with effective treatment, and potentially worsen survival. These issues await further research.

Weight loss that may lead to cachexia should be differentiated from healthful weight loss in overweight individuals. In certain cancers (eg, breast and colon), higher weight and/or greater percent body fat have been associated with increased mortality after diagnosis. One study of 526 individuals with colon cancer found that every 10% increase in body fat was associated with a 33% decrease in cancer survival.[5] Caution should therefore be exercised in trying to prevent weight loss in individuals for whom such loss would otherwise be therapeutic, particularly in light of findings that adipocytes secrete adipocytokines (eg, leptin) that have an agonistic effect on cancer growth.[6]

Recommendations for nutrition-related side effects. Current nonspecific nutrition recommendations for patients with cancer provided by the NCI are described below.[3]

Gastrointestinal disturbances. The National Cancer Institute, the National Comprehensive Cancer Network (a not-for-profit alliance of 20 cancer care centers throughout the United States), and the American Cancer Society suggest the following dietary strategies to control the nausea and vomiting associated with chemotherapy:[3,7-9]

- Eat prior to cancer treatments and have small, frequent meals.

- Eat bland, soft, easy-to-digest foods rather than heavy meals.

- Slowly sip fluids throughout the day.

- Avoid foods that are likely to cause nausea. For some patients, these include spicy foods, greasy foods, and foods that have strong odors.

- Eat dry foods such as crackers, breadsticks, or toast throughout the day.

- Sit up or lie with the upper body raised for one hour after eating.

- Avoid eating in a room that has cooking odors or that is overly warm. Keep the living space at a comfortable temperature and with plenty of fresh air.

- Rinse out the mouth before and after eating.

- Suck on hard candies such as peppermints or lemon drops if the mouth has a bad taste.

- If these suggestions do not prevent vomiting, a clear liquid diet is suggested, with progression to a full liquid diet and then a soft diet (ie, bland foods that are softened by cooking, mashing, puréeing, or blending) as tolerated.

In addition to these suggestions, the National Comprehensive Cancer Network and the American Cancer Society suggest behavioral strategies for the "anticipatory" type of nausea and vomiting that occur as a conditioned response to many cancer therapies. These include self-hypnosis, progressive muscle relaxation, biofeedback, guided imagery, and systematic desensitization.[9,10]

Control of diarrhea and constipation. For diarrhea, NCI recommendations include consuming foods high in sodium and potassium (eg, broth, sports drinks, and bananas, peach and apricot nectar, and boiled or mashed potatoes) and bland, low-fiber foods (eg, rice, noodles, farina or cream of wheat, smooth peanut butter, white bread, canned, peeled fruits, and well-cooked vegetables), as well as avoiding very hot, cold, or caffeinated foods or beverages. Recommendations for constipation include a high-fiber diet (with physician approval, due to potentially undesirable effects in certain cancers), along with maintenance of physical activity and consumption of a hot drink about half an hour before the usual time for a bowel movement, in the context of a high total fluid volume (at least 64 oz per day).[3]

Anorexia. Suggestions provided by the NCI for this condition are not geared toward its root causes but instead relate to strategies that may prevent its sequalae. These include planning menus in advance; eating frequent meals and snacks that are easy to prepare; adding liquid calorie sources (eg, juices, soups, milkshakes, and fruit smoothies); eating small, frequent (every 2 hours), high-calorie meals; snacking between meals; seeking foods that appeal to the sense of smell; and experimenting with different foods.[3]

Radiation enteritis. Symptoms of radiation enteritis include nausea, vomiting, abdominal cramping, tenesmus, and watery diarrhea. According to the National Cancer Institute, a diet that is lactose-free, low in fat, and low in residue can be effective in symptom management.[1] However, evidence supporting this approach is minimal[11] and requires confirmation in controlled trials.

Chemotherapy-related mucositis and stomatitis. Oral cooling with ice chips for 30 minutes before bolus administration of chemotherapy (eg, 5-FU) prevented mucositis[12] and reduced symptoms by roughly half compared with a control group in one study.[13] Practical dietary suggestions for dealing with this symptom include eating foods cold or at room temperature rather than warm or hot and eating soft foods that are easy to chew and swallow while avoiding foods that are coarse in texture, difficult to chew (eg, crackers, granola, toast, raw vegetables), or irritating (eg, salty or spicy foods and citrus products).[1] In patients treated with chemotherapy for a variety of cancers, oral glutamine (2 g/m^2 delivered in a swish-and-swallow form or up to 4 g/d orally) decreased the severity and duration of oropharyngeal mucositis in addition to significantly reducing pain and the need for IV narcotics and parenteral nutrition in two studies.[14,15] Glutamine supplementation was also found to decrease the incidence and severity of diarrhea, neuropathy, cardiotoxicity, and hepatic veno-occlusive disease that accompany the use of many chemotherapeutic agents.[16]

Hypogeusia. Blunted taste sensation often occurs in patients undergoing chemotherapy and radiation. It occurs in up to 70% of chemotherapy-treated patients and may contribute to lack of appetite and poor dietary intake, which, in turn, can worsen a patient's health status.[17]

Treatment with zinc sulfate (45 mg/d) reduces the occurrence of hypogeusia and speeds recovery of taste acuity in patients with head and neck cancer.[18]

Prevention of foodborne illness due to neutropenia. Avoidance of all possible sources of microbial contamination is suggested, including raw foods or those that cannot easily be decontaminated[3] (see chapter on Foodborne Illness).

In addition to the above considerations, some evidence supports the use of the following interventions:

Selenium supplements. In women receiving chemotherapy for ovarian cancer, selenium supplementation (200 μg/d) significantly increased white blood cell count and decreased hair loss, abdominal pain, weakness, malaise, and loss of appetite in one study.[19] Short-term treatment with high doses of selenium (4000 μg/d) reduces nephrotoxicity and bone marrow suppression in cisplatin-treated patients.[20] Further clinical trials are needed to establish the benefit and lack of toxicity of selenium doses in excess of Dietary Reference Intakes.

Specialized enteral formulas. In research studies, patients who received surgical treatment for gastric or head and neck cancers and were fed formulas containing arginine, glutamine, omega-3 fatty acids, RNA, or a combination of these had superior outcomes compared with patients receiving standard enteral formulas. The experimental group demonstrated higher levels of total and T lymphocytes, T helper and natural killer cells[21] and a significant reduction in postoperative infections and wound complications.[22] However, further study is needed to confirm the superiority of specialized over standard formulas with respect to immune parameters and infection rates.

Behavioral interventions. Published studies support the effectiveness of behavioral interventions for chemotherapy-related nausea and vomiting, including hypnosis, guided imagery, relaxation, and distraction.[9]

Studies suggest that diet changes may reduce the likelihood of recurrence or other poor outcomes for certain types of malignancy. (See Breast Cancer, Prostate Cancer, and Ovarian Cancer chapters for additional information.)

Orders

See Basic Diet Orders chapter.

Nutrition consultation. The dietitian should counsel the patient and family on meeting the patient's energy needs and make recommendations regarding protein-calorie supplements.

What to Tell the Family

Patients with cancer are often undernourished and malnourished. These problems may contribute to impaired treatment outcomes and increased morbidity. However, a more enlightened nutritional approach to diet than encouraging patients to eat *ad libitum* is needed both during and after cancer therapy. The family can help the patient make the necessary diet changes.

References

1. National Cancer Institute. Nutrition in Cancer Care (PDQ): Nutrition Implications of Cancer Therapies. Available at: http://www.cancer.gov/cancertopics/pdq/supportivecare/nutrition/HealthProfessional/page4. Accessed December 15, 2006.

2. Andreyev HJ, Norman AR, Oates J, Cunningham D. Why do patients with weight loss have a worse outcome when undergoing chemotherapy for gastrointestinal malignancies? *Eur J Cancer.* 1998;34:503-509.

3. National Cancer Institute. Nutrition in Cancer Care (PDQ): Nutrition Therapy. Available at: http://www.cancer.gov/cancertopics/pdq/supportivecare/nutrition/HealthProfessional/page5#Section_148. Accessed December 15, 2006.

4. Rivadeneira DE, Evoy D, Fahey TJ 3rd, Lieberman MD, Daly JM. Nutritional support of the cancer patient. *CA Cancer J Clin.* 1998;48:69-80.

5. Haydon AM, Macinnis RJ, English DR, Giles GG. Effect of physical activity and body size on survival after diagnosis with colorectal cancer. *Gut.* 2006;55:62-67.

6. Housa D, Housova J, Vernerova Z, Haluzik M. Adipocytokines and cancer. *Physiol Res.* 2006;553:233-244.

7. American Cancer Society. How Are Nausea and Vomiting Treated? Available at: http://www.nccn.org/patients/patient_gls/_english/_nausea_and_vomiting/4_treatment.asp. Accessed August 11, 2005.

8. National Cancer Institute. Chemotherapy and You: Support for People with Cancer. Available at: http://www.nci.nih.gov/cancertopics/chemotherapy-and-you/page4#C4. Accessed August 9, 2005.

9. Finley JP. Management of cancer cachexia. *AACN Clin Issues.* 2000;11:590-603.

10. National Comprehensive Cancer Network. How Is Nausea and Vomiting Treated? Available at: http://www.nccn.org/patients/patient_gls/_english/_nausea_and_vomiting/4_treatment.asp. Accessed December 15, 2006.

11. Stryker JA, Bartholomew M. Failure of lactose-restricted diets to prevent radiation-induced diarrhea in patients undergoing whole pelvis irradiation. *Int J Radiat Oncol Biol Phys.* 1986;12:789-792.

12. Scully C, Epstein J, Sonis S. Oral mucositis: a challenging complication of radiotherapy, chemotherapy, and radiochemotherapy: part 1, pathogenesis and prophylaxis of mucositis. *Head Neck.* 2003;25:1057-1070.

13. Cascinu S, Fedeli A, Fedeli SL, et al. Oral cooling (cryotherapy), an effective treatment for the prevention of 5-fluorouracil-induced stomatitis. *Eur J Cancer B Oral Oncol.* 1994;30B:234-236.

14. Aquino VM, Harvey AR, Garvin JH, et al. A double-blind randomized placebo-controlled study of oral glutamine in the prevention of mucositis in children undergoing hematopoietic stem cell transplantation: a pediatric blood and marrow transplant consortium study. *Bone Marrow Transplant.* 2005;36:611-616.

15. Anderson PM, Schroeder G, Skubitz KM. Oral glutamine reduces the duration and severity of stomatitis after cytotoxic cancer chemotherapy. *Cancer.* 1998;83:1433-1439.

16. Savarese DM, Savy G, Vahdat L, et al. Prevention of chemotherapy and radiation toxicity with glutamine. *Cancer Treat Rev.* 2003;29:501-513.

17. Yamagata T, Nakamura Y, Yamagata Y, et al. The pilot trial of the prevention of the increase in electrical taste thresholds by zinc containing fluid infusion during chemotherapy to treat primary lung cancer. *J Exp Clin Cancer Res.* 2003;22:557-563.

18. Ripamonti C, Zecca E, Brunelli C, et al. A randomized, controlled clinical trial to evaluate the effects of zinc sulfate on cancer patients with taste alterations caused by head and neck irradiation. *Cancer.* 1998;82:1938-1945.

19. Sieja K, Talerczyk M. Selenium as an element in the treatment of ovarian cancer in women receiving chemotherapy. *Gynecol Oncol.* 2004;93:320-327.

20. Hu YJ, Chen Y, Zhang YQ, et al. The protective role of selenium on the toxicity of cisplatin-contained chemotherapy regimen in cancer patients. *Biol Trace Elem Res.* 1997;56:331-341.

21. Wu GH, Zhang YW, Wu ZH. Modulation of postoperative immune and inflammatory response by immune-enhancing enteral diet in gastrointestinal cancer patients. *World J Gastroenterol.* 2001;7:357-362.

22. Riso S, Aluffi P, Brugnani M, et al. Postoperative enteral immunonutrition in head and neck cancer patients. *Clin Nutr.* 2000;19:407-412.

18. Thyroid Cancer

Thyroid cancers are uncommon, accounting for less than 1% of all cancers. However, incidence has risen significantly during the past half century, possibly the result of radiation therapy to the head and neck used to treat benign childhood conditions in the mid-1900s.

Patients usually present with a solitary thyroid nodule. Although most nodules are benign, all patients with a thyroid nodule should be evaluated for thyroid cancer. Associated symptoms that raise suspicion for thyroid cancer include hoarseness, dysphagia or odynophagia, and adenopathy.

The majority of thyroid cancers are papillary or follicular carcinomas. Medullary carcinoma and anaplastic carcinoma are far less common. Papillary and follicular carcinomas are well-differentiated tumors that respond well to treatment, with cure rates exceeding 90%. Medullary carcinoma, which accounts for just 5% of cases, is a cancer of the calcitonin-producing C cells of the thyroid and may be associated with multiple endocrine neoplasia type 2 (MEN 2) syndromes. Anaplastic carcinoma is a rare but aggressive cancer with a poor prognosis.

Risk Factors

Female gender. Nearly three-fourths of thyroid malignancies occur in women, making this cancer the eighth most common female malignancy.

Radiation exposure. Head and neck radiation, especially during infancy, is a strong risk factor for all thyroid cancers.

Genetics. Relatives of thyroid cancer patients have a 10-fold greater risk. In addition, medullary carcinoma may be inherited, either as part of MEN 2 syndromes or as an isolated familial disease. Rearrangements of the *RET* and *TRK* genes are found in some papillary carcinomas.

Overweight. Excess weight may increase the risk for thyroid cancer. A study of approximately 2 million individuals in Norway who were followed for 23 years indicated that obesity (BMI >30 kg/m^2) was associated with thyroid cancer incidence. Specifically, risk in women in BMI categories 30 to 34.9, 35 to 39.9, and >40.0 increased by 27%, 33%, and 38% respectively, compared with risk in women with a BMI of 18.5 to 24.9. A similar increase was found in risk for men with a BMI >30.[1]

Diagnosis

Evaluation should begin with thyroid function tests, including **thyroid-stimulating hormone** (TSH) and thyroxin, to check for hyperthyroidism or hypothyroidism.

Fine-needle aspiration biopsy is the best diagnostic test and will establish the diagnosis in most cases.

Ultrasound may detect nodules and distinguish solid from cystic lesions.

Radioactive iodine uptake scan (thyroid scintigraphy) evaluates whether a nodule takes up iodine to distinguish functioning thyroid nodules (those that produce thyroid hormone) from nonfunctioning nodules. Functioning nodules are rarely malignant. Nonfunctioning nodules may be malignant and require a fine-needle aspiration biopsy.

Serum calcitonin concentration may be elevated in medullary carcinomas.

Treatment

Thyroidectomy is the primary therapy for most thyroid cancers. Resection is often followed by postoperative radioactive iodine ablation of residual thyroid tissue and potential metastases.

Lifelong thyroid hormone replacement therapy is necessary for all surgical patients.

Treatment may include radiation and chemotherapy as an adjuvant to surgery or for palliation, primarily for patients with medullary or anaplastic thyroid cancer.[2]

Nutritional Considerations

In epidemiologic studies, certain dietary patterns are associated with reduced risk for thyroid cancer. As noted above, obesity increases risk. As is the case with many other types of cancer, eating more fruits and vegetables, avoiding animal fat, and replacing animal products with plant-based foods appear to have a protective effect.

Avoiding animal products. Persons who consume large amounts of butter and cheese have 2.1-fold and 1.4-fold higher risk for thyroid cancer, respectively, than those who consume small amounts of these foods.[3] High intakes of processed fish products and chicken were associated with roughly double the risk for thyroid cancer,[4] while frequent pork consumption raised the risk by about 1.6-fold.[5] Retinol, a form of vitamin A obtained from animal products, including eggs and milk, increased the risk for thyroid carcinoma 1.5-fold in persons with the highest intakes compared with the risk in those who had the lowest intakes.[6]

Increasing vegetables and fruits. A diet that includes large amounts of fruits and vegetables appears to reduce thyroid cancer risk by roughly 10% to 30%.[5,7] Individuals with higher intake of beta-carotene appear to have half the risk for thyroid cancer compared with persons with the lowest intake.[6]

In addition, it may be that certain components of a traditional Asian diet lower the risk for thyroid cancer. Studies have found that cancer and other thyroid diseases occur more often among Asian immigrants to the United States than among Asians in their native countries.[8] The explanation may relate not only to the relative scarcity of animal products in an Asian diet compared with a Western diet, but also to the inclusion of soy and tea. When comparing lowest with highest intakes of soy foods, women consuming the greatest amount had a 30% to 44% lower risk for thyroid cancer.[9] Tea consumption (>3 cups/day), another characteristic of traditional Asian diets, conferred a 70% lower risk for thyroid cancer in women.[10]

Orders

See Basic Diet Orders chapter.

What to Tell the Family

Thyroid cancer, like many other cancers, is a disease that may be influenced by diet and lifestyle, although evidence does not yet permit a firm conclusion. Limited evidence suggests that avoiding fatty foods and increasing fruits and vegetables reduces the risk that this disease will develop. These diet changes are easier when the whole family makes them together.

The role of diet and lifestyle after diagnosis has not been well studied. Surgery remains the treatment of choice, followed by appropriate chemotherapy or radiation.

References

1. Engeland A, Tretli S, Akslen LA, Bjorge T. Body size and thyroid cancer in two million Norwegian men and women. *Br J Cancer.* 2006;95:366-370.

2. Sherman SI. Thyroid carcinoma. *Lancet.* 2003;361:501-511.

3. Franceschi S, Levi F, Negri E, Fassina A, La Vecchia C. Diet and thyroid cancer: a pooled analysis of four European case-control studies. *Int J Cancer.* 1991;48:395-398.

4. Memon A, Varghese A, Suresh A. Benign thyroid disease and dietary factors in thyroid cancer: a case-control study in Kuwait. *Br J Cancer.* 2002;86:1745-1750.

5. Markaki I, Linos D, Linos A. The influence of dietary patterns on the development of thyroid cancer. *Eur J Cancer.* 2003;39:1912-1919.

6. D'Avanzo B, Ron E, La Vecchia C, Francaschi S, Negri E, Zleglar R. Selected micronutrient intake and thyroid carcinoma risk. *Cancer.* 1997;79:2186-2192.

7. Bosetti C, Negri E, Kolonel L, et al. A pooled analysis of case-control studies of thyroid cancer. VII. Cruciferous and other vegetables (International). *Cancer Causes Control.* 2002;13:765-775.

8. Haselkorn T, Stewart SL, Horn-Ross PL. Why are thyroid cancer rates so high in Southeast Asian women living in the United States? The Bay Area thyroid cancer study. *Cancer Epidemiol Biomarkers Prev.* 2003;12:144-150.

9. Horn-Ross PL, Hoggatt KJ, Lee MM. Phytoestrogens and thyroid cancer risk: the San Francisco Bay Area thyroid cancer study. *Cancer Epidemiol Biomarkers Prev.* 2002;11:43-49.

10. Mack WJ, Preston-Martin S, Bernstein L, Qian D. Lifestyle and other risk factors for thyroid cancer in Los Angeles County females. *Ann Epidemiol.* 2002;12:395-401.

19. Lung Cancer

Lung cancer is the most common cause of cancer death for men and women worldwide. It is the most frequently occurring cancer in men and the third most frequent in women. Lung cancer usually develops within the epithelium of the bronchial tree and subsequently invades the pulmonary parenchyma. In advanced stages, it invades surrounding organs and may metastasize throughout the body.

The most common histologic types are:

Epidermoid (squamous cell) carcinoma (about 40% of lung cancer cases). This is the most common form, located centrally in the lung. The carcinoma arises from a dysplastic epithelial focus in one of the bronchi, presenting the cytologic and nuclear features of atypia. Eventually, it invades the pulmonary parenchyma.

Adenocarcinoma (about 25% of cases). The lesions are peripheral or central, arising from the epithelium of small airways and showing evidence of glandular activity (sometimes producing mucin). Adenocarcinomas have a characteristic growth pattern along the alveolar septa, without destroying the underlying lung architecture.

Small cell (oat cell) carcinoma (about 20% of cases). This form involves the wall of a major bronchus, arising from specialized neuroendocrine cells (K cells) in the lungs, which show extensive mitotic activity and foci of necrosis. The tumor is commonly a central, perihilar mass. Virtually all small cell cancers are attributable to tobacco use.

Large cell (undifferentiated) carcinoma (about 15% of cases). This is a bronchogenic tumor with large pleomorphic cells containing prominent nucleoli. The cells are poorly differentiated and metastasize early.

Risk Factors

Smoking. Tobacco smoking accounts for approximately 90% of lung cancers. Initially, tobacco smoke irritates the bronchial epithelium and paralyzes the respiratory cilia, depriving the respiratory mucosa of its defense and clearance mechanisms. The carcinogens in tobacco smoke then act on the epithelium, giving rise to atypical cells, which form the first stage of cancer: carcinoma in situ. After metaplastic transformation, the cancer invades bronchial and pulmonary tissues and subsequently metastasizes hematogenously or via lymphatics. Additional risk factors include:

Passive smoking. Epidemiologic evidence suggests an increased risk of approximately 20% to 25% in nonsmokers regularly exposed to secondhand smoke.[1]

Occupation. Exposure to manipulated asbestos, chromium and nickel (heavy metals), benzopyrene, acroleine, nitrous monoxide, hydrogen cyanide, formaldehyde, nicotine, radioactive lead, carbon monoxide, insecticides or pesticides containing arsenic, glass fibers, and coal dust increases workers' risk of bronchopulmonary cancer.

Family history. Investigations show a 14-fold higher frequency of lung carcinomas in smokers with a family history of lung cancer.[2] Risk is also increased in individuals with Li-Fraumeni syndrome, resulting from an inherited mutation in the *p53* gene.[3]

Immunosuppression. The risk of oncogenesis increases with conditions that weaken the immune system (eg, immunosuppressive medications, diseases, or malnutrition).

Air pollution. The mortality rate from lung cancer is 2 to 5 times higher in industrialized areas than in less polluted rural areas.

Inflammation. Chronic and recurrent respiratory diseases act as chronic irritants and play an oncogenic role (eg, tuberculosis, chronic bronchitis, recurrent pneumonias).

Ionizing radiation. Radiation exposure (x-rays, radon gas) increases carcinogenic risk in a dose-dependent manner. Lung cancer is 10 times more frequent in uranium miners than in the general population.

Diet and nutrition. See Nutritional Considerations below.

Diagnosis

Primary Symptoms

Lung cancer has an insidious onset, and the disease is usually well developed by the time of diagnosis. Clinical signs and symptoms that suggest lung cancer are:

- Generalized weakness and fatigue.
- Cough. About 93% of lung cancer patients complain of an initial cough, which gradually worsens. Chronic irritation of the bronchial epithelium will cause a persistent cough that can be dry, productive, spastic, and refractory to symptomatic treatment. When the tumor erodes the lung capillaries, the cough is often accompanied by hemoptysis.

- Chest pain, which is often pleuritic. This commonly occurs when the tumor invades the pleural folds or the thoracic wall and ribs, causing pleural effusion.

- Loss of weight and appetite.

- Persistent fever.

- Clubbing of fingers and toes.

- Dyspnea. This is a late symptom, caused by airway obstruction or compression.

- Atelectasis.

- Lymphadenopathy in the axilla, latero-cervically, or supraclavicularly.

- Hoarseness. This symptom is caused by the compression of the laryngeal recurrent nerve in the mediastinum by the tumoral growth.

- Dysphagia. It occurs when the tumor invades or compresses the esophagus.

- Pericardial complications. These are frequent and due to direct invasion and metastatic spread.

- Recurring infections, such as bronchitis and pneumonia, with moderate fever.

Metastatic Symptoms

- Signs and symptoms vary according to the organ or site affected.

- Bone pain and limitations of use occur with bony metastases.

- Neurologic changes (such as weakness or numbness, dizziness, or recent seizure onset) occur when tumors invade or compress nerves.

- Jaundice results from metastatic invasion and/or compression of the liver and biliary canals.

- Masses may appear near the surface of the body due to cancer spreading to the skin or to regional lymph nodes.

Laboratory Tests and Clinical Procedures

Chest x-ray can detect lesions up to 2 years before symptoms appear. It defines tumor size and location and can track progression or remission.

Bronchoscopy facilitates diagnosis through tissue biopsy. Bronchoscopic lavage allows for cytologic and histologic analysis, which can detect cancer before radiologic changes.

Computed tomography (CT) accurately reveals tumor location and size.

CT-guided percutaneous fine-needle aspiration of pulmonary nodules allows for cytologic examination.

Erythrocyte sedimentation rate (ESR) is usually elevated in malignant disease. It is a nonspecific finding, however, as ESR is also commonly elevated in tuberculosis and other pulmonary infections.

Ultrasound examination allows differentiation of cystic versus solid tumors. It also allows guidance of thoracentesis needle.

Radioactive pulmonary scan, with radioisotopes injected into the bloodstream, is better than x-ray for precise and extended visualization of tumoral lesions.

Bronchography with contrast dyes allows visualization of distal bronchi, stenosis, and infarcts.

Phlebography allows visualization of axillary or subclavicular enlarged lymph nodes. Phlebography through the vena cava and azygos vein reveals mediastinal compression and infiltration.

Pleuracentesis gives the diagnosis in 80% of cases where pleural invasion occurs.

Lymph node biopsy is of great diagnostic value when enlarged lymph nodes are present and accessible.

Mediastinoscopy allows for a biopsy of hilar and mediastinal ganglia and is positive in nearly 40% of all lung cancer cases. It allows direct visualization of possible mediastinal invasions that could contraindicate surgery.

Treatment

Medical treatment of lung cancer involves combinations of surgery, radiation, and chemotherapy. Treatment is largely palliative, although early detection and treatment of the cancerous process may significantly improve prognosis and prolong survival.

Surgery. The main treatment for squamous cell carcinoma, adenocarcinoma, and large cell cancer is surgery, unless the tumor is unresectable or the patient is not a surgical candidate. Surgery can involve partial removal of diseased lung areas (segmentectomy, lobectomy, bronchopulmonary resection with bronchoanastomosis), or total lung removal (simple or radical pneumonectomy), with removal of metastatic lymph nodes.

Chemotherapy. Chemotherapy is the primary treatment for small cell cancer and some other types. However, it has serious side effects, such as myelosuppression, neutropenia with infection, thrombocytopenia, nausea, vomiting, and alopecia, without improving significantly the life expectancy and survival rate. Doxorubicin may cause cardiomyopathy, vincristine and cisplatin are potentially neurotoxic, and cyclophosphamide may cause hemorrhagic cystitis. In 2006, the FDA approved treatment with a monoclonal antibody drug (bevacizumab) in conjunction with carboplatin and paclitaxel. This regimen can have severe side effects, including hemorrhage and neutropenia.

Radiation therapy. Radiation may reduce tumor bulk to allow surgical resection. Radiation is usually recommended in early stages of cancer if surgery is contraindicated or as an adjunct to surgery. A serious side effect is the "irradiated lung," with symptoms of radiation pneumonitis (dyspnea, cough, chest pain, fever, and malaise) and later pulmonary fibrosis, with severe alteration of pulmonary parenchyma. Irradiation also depresses immune function.

Three-dimensional conformal radiation therapy. A new and innovative therapeutic technique, 3D CRT increases the radiation dose delivered to a tumor and improves local control, allowing less irradiation of adjacent tissues than the conventional two-dimensional technique.

Fast-neutron radiotherapy. This therapy leverages high linear energy transfer to increase the effectiveness of radiation.

Symptomatic treatments. An important part of the therapeutic plan is treatment of the symptoms that accompany lung cancer and its metastatic manifestations. Pain may be mild or severe and requires analgesic anti-inflammatory drugs or opioid derivates. Pain in the thoracic wall can be treated with infiltrations of affected nerves with anesthetic substances or alcohol. Hemoptysis can be treated with procoagulants, such as vitamin K. Sleep disorders due to pain, lack of appetite, dyspnea, cough, and asthenia may also respond to focused treatment. Superinfections are common and should be treated with appropriate antibiotics, antifungals, and expectorants.

Nutritional Considerations

Although environmental exposures (particularly tobacco smoke and, to a lesser extent, air pollution, asbestos, and radon) are the chief causes of lung cancer, diet also plays a surprisingly important role. Research on the relationships between diet, smoking, and lung cancer risk is complicated by the fact that smokers tend to have lower intakes and/ or lower blood levels of many protective nutrients, compared with non-smokers. Nonetheless, certain patterns have emerged.

Overall, evidence suggests that individuals (eg, Seventh-day Adventists) eating plant-based diets rich in vegetables and fruits may be at lower risk for lung cancer, independent of tobacco use. The aspects of the diet associated with reduced risk are avoiding meat and saturated fat, consuming antioxidant-rich fruits and vegetables, and limiting alcohol, as described below:

Avoiding meat and saturated fat. Some studies suggest that vegetarian diets are associated with lower risk for lung cancer.[4] Increased risk is also associated with regular consumption of red meat,[5] particularly ham, sausage, and liver,[6] saturated fat,[7] and dairy products.[8,9] The NIH-AARP study of more than 500,000 individuals found a 20% greater risk for lung cancer in persons eating the most red meat (approximately 60 g/d) compared with those eating the least (10 g/d).[10]

Consumption of fruits and vegetables. Several studies show that individuals with diets rich in vegetables and fruits have reduced risk for lung cancer, independent of smoking. The European Prospective Investigation into Cancer (EPIC) study of more than 478,000 individuals found inverse associations between fruit intake and lung cancer in nonsmokers, in addition to inverse associations between vegetable intake and lung cancer in smokers.[11]

Nutrients that appear responsible for these protective benefits include carotenoids (as opposed to vitamin A found in animal products); vitamin C;[12,13] sulfur compounds in cruciferous vegetables (broccoli, cauliflower, cabbage);[14] flavonoids;[15] and folic acid.[16,17] A comprehensive antioxidant index that summarized the collective intake of carotenoids, flavonoids, vitamins E and C, and selenium among male smokers found that those with the highest antioxidant consumption had a significantly lower risk for lung cancer than those with the lowest antioxidant intakes.[18] There appears to be no decrease in lung cancer incidence in persons taking antioxidant supplements, with the exception of individuals with poor selenium status who take selenium supplements.[19] Beta-carotene supplements may actually raise lung cancer risk, at least in certain subgroups.[20,21]

Limiting alcohol intake. Several studies suggest that regular intake of higher amounts of beer and spirits increases lung cancer risk up to 3 times that of nondrinkers.[22,23] In the European Prospective Investigation into Cancer and Nutrition (EPIC), high chronic alcohol intake (≥60 g/d, about 5 drinks) was associated with a roughly 30% greater lung cancer risk when compared with low intake (0.1 to 4.9 g/d; approximately 1 drink per week). However, moderate alcohol intakes (5 to 15 g/d; 1 drink or less each day) were associated with a roughly 20% to 25% lower risk for lung cancer, a finding also noted in prior studies.[23,24]

It remains unclear whether these associations represent cause and effect. The link between high alcohol intake and lung cancer may reflect an association with smoking or a carcinogenic effect of acetaldehyde, an alcohol metabolite, and the ability of alcohol to activate carcinogens through an increase in cytochrome P450.[25] The hypothetical basis for a protective effect of moderate alcohol use may be anti-inflammatory actions, antioxidant components of alcoholic beverages (eg, flavonoids in red wine and beer), and/or induction of DNA repair enzymes or carcinogen detoxification enzymes.[25]

Orders

Smoking cessation.

Lung cancer prevention: See Basic Diet Orders chapter.

Treatment of lung cancer: There are as yet no specific guidelines for dietary interventions associated with improved survival. However, see Diet During Cancer Treatment chapter for general guidelines.

What to Tell the Family

In the case of lung cancer, prevention is clearly the most effective strategy. Family members and the patient should be encouraged to quit smoking. Smoking is the primary risk factor for lung cancer, and those who quit smoking experience a gradual risk reduction over time. This lower risk may be enhanced in persons who avoid alcohol and eat a diet low in saturated fat and high in fruits and vegetables. Family members can encourage each other to follow a healthful diet. In the process, everyone benefits.

References

1. Bofetta P, Trichopoulos D. Cancer of the lung, larynx, and pleura. In: Adami H-O, Hunter D, Trichopoulos D, eds. *Textbook of Cancer Epidemiology*. Oxford, England: Oxford University Press; 2002:248-280.

2. Sellers TA, Bailey-Wilson JE. Familial predisposition to lung cancer. In: Roth JA, Cox JD, Hong WD, eds. *Lung Cancer*. Malden, Mass: Blackwell; 1998:57-71.

3. Malkin D, Li FP, Strong LC, et al. Germ line *p53* mutation in a familial syndrome of breast cancers, sarcomas, and other neoplasms. *Science.* 1990;250:1233-1238.

4. Frentzel-Beyme R, Claude J, Eilber U. Mortality among German vegetarians: first results after five years of follow-up. *Nutr Cancer.* 1988;11:117-126.

5. Alavanja MC, Field RW, Sinha R, et al. Lung cancer risk and red meat consumption among Iowa women. *Lung Cancer.* 2001;34:37-46.

6. Ozasa K, Watanabe Y, Ito Y, et al. Dietary habits and risk of lung cancer death in a large-scale cohort study (JACC Study) in Japan by sex and smoking habit. *Jpn J Cancer Res.* 2001;92:1259-1269.

7. Mulder I, Jansen MC, Smit HA, et al. Role of smoking and diet in the cross-cultural variation in lung-cancer mortality: the Seven Countries Study. Seven Countries Study Research Group. *Int J Cancer.* 2000;88:665-671.

8. Kesteloot H, Lesaffre E, Joossens JV. Dairy fat, saturated animal fat, and cancer risk. *Prev Med.* 1991;20:226-236.

9. Mettlin C. Milk drinking, other beverage habits, and lung cancer risk. *Int J Cancer.* 1989;43:608-612.

10. Cross AJ, Leitzmann MF, Gail MH, Hollenbeck AR, Schatzkin A, Sinha R. A prospective study of red and processed meat intake in relation to cancer risk. *PLoS Med.* 2007;4:e325.

11. Linseisen J, Rohrmann S, Miller AB, et al. Fruit and vegetable consumption and lung cancer risk: updated information from the European Prospective Investigation into Cancer and Nutrition (EPIC). *Int J Cancer.* 2007;121:1103-1114.

12. Miller AB, Altenburg HP, Bueno-de-Mesquita B, et al. Fruits and vegetables and lung cancer: Findings from the European Prospective Investigation into Cancer and Nutrition. *Int J Cancer.* 2004;108:269-276.

13. Yong LC, Brown CC, Schatzkin A, et al. Intake of vitamins E, C, and A and risk of lung cancer. The NHANES I epidemiologic follow-up study. First National Health and Nutrition Examination Survey. *Am J Epidemiol.* 1997;146:231-243.

14. Neuhouser ML, Patterson RE, Thornquist MD, Omenn GS, King IB, Goodman GE. Fruits and vegetables are associated with lower lung cancer risk only in the placebo arm of the beta-carotene and retinol efficacy trial (CARET). *Cancer Epidemiol Biomarkers Prev.* 2003;12:350-358.

15. Neuhouser ML. Dietary flavonoids and cancer risk: evidence from human population studies. *Nutr Cancer.* 2004;50:1-7.

16. Shen H, Wei Q, Pillow PC, Amos CI, Hong WK, Spitz MR. Dietary folate intake and lung cancer risk in former smokers: a case-control analysis. *Cancer Epidemiol Biomarkers Prev.* 2003;12:980-986.

17. Voorrips LE, Goldbohm RA, Brants HA, et al. A prospective cohort study on antioxidant and folate intake and male lung cancer risk. *Cancer Epidemiol Biomarkers Prev.* 2000;9:357-365.

18. Wright ME, Mayne ST, Stolzenberg-Solomon RZ, et al. Development of a comprehensive dietary antioxidant index and application to lung cancer risk in a cohort of male smokers. *Am J Epidemiol.* 2004;160:68-76.

19. Reid ME, Duffield-Lillico AJ, Garland L, Turnbull BW, Clark LC, Marshall JR. Selenium supplementation and lung cancer incidence: an update of the nutritional prevention of cancer trial. *Cancer Epidemiol Biomarkers Prev.* 2002;11:1285-1291.

20. Goodman GE, Thornquist MD, Balmes J, et al. The Beta-Carotene and Retinol Efficacy Trial: incidence of lung cancer and cardiovascular disease mortality during 6-year follow-up after stopping beta-carotene and retinol supplements. *J Natl Cancer Inst.* 2004;96:1743-1750.

21. Albanes D, Heinonen OP, Taylor PR, et al. Alpha-Tocopherol and beta-carotene supplements and lung cancer incidence in the alpha-tocopherol, beta-carotene cancer prevention study: effects of base-line characteristics and study compliance. *J Natl Cancer Inst.* 1996;88:1560-1570.

22. Bandera EV, Freudenheim JL, Vena JE. Alcohol consumption and lung cancer: a review of the epidemiologic evidence. *Cancer Epidemiol Biomarkers Prev.* 2001;10:813-821.

23. Prescott E, Gronbaek M, Becker U, Sorensen TI. Alcohol intake and the risk of lung cancer: influence of type of alcoholic beverage. *Am J Epidemiol.* 1999;149:463-470.

24. Kubik AK, Zatloukal P, Tomasek L, et al. Dietary habits and lung cancer risk among non-smoking women. *Eur J Cancer Prev.* 2004;13:471-480.

25. Rohrman S, Linseisen J, Boshuizen HC, et al. Ethanol intake and risk of lung cancer in the European Prospective Investigation into Cancer and Nutrition (EPIC). *Am J Epidemiol.* 2006;164:1103-1114.

20. Gastric Cancer

Gastric cancer is the second most common malignancy worldwide and the 11th most common in the United States. Prevalence has been decreasing over the last century, likely due to better methods of food preservation, improved sanitation, and lower infectious disease rates. In addition, improved screening techniques—especially in Japan and other high-risk areas—have led to a decrease in mortality. Nonetheless, gastric cancer remains one of the most lethal malignancies, with the 5-year survival rate in the United States less than 20%.

More than 90% of cases are adenocarcinomas, which are derived from glandular tissue. Tumors are classified as either intestinal or diffuse. In the intestinal type, which is far more common, tumors grow as discrete masses and eventually erode through the stomach wall into nearby organs. The diffuse type is less common overall, but is more prevalent in younger patients and carries a poorer prognosis. Diffuse tumors are poorly differentiated cancers with little cell cohesion. As a result, they grow outward along the submucosa of the stomach, widely enveloping the stomach without producing a discrete mass.

Tumors tend to be asymptomatic until the disease is advanced. The most common symptoms of advanced tumors are weight loss, early satiety, abdominal pain, nausea, and vomiting. Less common symptoms include dysphagia, melena, a palpable abdominal mass, and ascites.

Risk Factors

Incidence varies greatly by geographic area and race. Areas of highest incidence include Japan, Korea, Chile, and parts of Eastern Europe. African Americans, Asian Americans, and Latinos have a higher incidence than other demographic groups in the United States. Other risk factors are:

Helicobacter pylori **infection.** Chronic infection is a strong risk factor for gastric cancer of the distal stomach and may be responsible for up to 90% of distal gastric cancers.

Chronic gastritis, pernicious anemia, partial gastrectomy. A history of any of these conditions may increase risk.

Genetics. A positive family history and blood type A are associated with an increased risk. The roles of specific genes are still unclear.

Gender. Males have twice the risk of females.

Diet. Factors strongly associated with an increased risk include high intake of salted, smoked, and pickled foods, and low intake of fruits and vegetables. (See Nutritional Considerations below.)

Age. The disease is rare before age 40, and the incidence increases steadily thereafter.

Tobacco use.

Alcohol use. Although alcohol has long been considered a risk factor, conclusive evidence for its role in gastric cancer has yet to be demonstrated. However, the concomitant use of alcohol and tobacco appears to increase the risk of gastric cancer more than use of tobacco alone.

Diagnosis

In Japan, where there is a particularly high incidence of gastric cancer, mass screening programs of asymptomatic individuals using endoscopy or upper GI series identify early cases that may be curable with immediate treatment. As a result, survival rates have improved significantly. However, due to the relatively low incidence of gastric cancer in the United States, mass screening is not currently recommended.

Upper GI endoscopy with biopsy is diagnostic.

Barium swallow with upper GI series has historically been used to diagnose gastric cancer and may reveal ulceration, mass, or distortion of the stomach wall. However, false-negatives are frequent, and barium swallow has particularly poor sensitivity in identifying early stage disease. Endoscopy offers important advantages; notably, direct visual examination of suspicious lesions and biopsy, which is required for definitive diagnosis.

CBC may reveal iron deficiency anemia.

CT scan and endoscopic ultrasound are used for staging and to evaluate for metastatic disease.

Treatment

Complete surgical resection offers the only hope for cure. Unfortunately, most tumors are already advanced at diagnosis and not amenable to full resection. Total or subtotal gastrectomy is indicated for tumors confined to the stomach. Resection of adjacent organs may be required if the tumor has spread.

Early detection by appropriate screening may decrease the need for further treatment and improve survival. Experience in Japan shows that patients with early cancers may elect to be treated with endoscopic mucosal resection, a low-cost and relatively safe alternative to surgery.[1] Thus far, however, this experience has not been duplicated in Western countries.

Surgery, chemotherapy, or radiation may be used for palliation.

Nutritional Considerations

During the 20th century, the incidence of stomach cancer consistently declined in those countries where refrigeration supplanted other methods of food preservation. Gastric cancer is associated with the carcinogenic effect of nitrosamines, compounds derived from nitrates used to preserve meats. High sodium intakes appear to be responsible for the high rates of gastric cancer in cultures where processed (salted) fish and processed, high-sodium soy foods are consumed frequently. In epidemiologic studies, a protective effect has been noted for plant-rich diets, especially those high in fruits, vegetables, and whole grains.[2] Consumption of these foods is inversely related to gastric cancer mortality.[3] In observational studies, the following dietary factors are associated with reduced risk:

Avoidance of animal products, particularly those containing nitrates. Cholesterol and animal protein intakes are associated with several subtypes of gastric and esophageal cancer.[4] The European

Prospective Investigation Into Cancer and Nutrition (EPIC) study involving 521,457 men and women found that the highest intake of processed red meat (45 grams for women/85 grams for men, compared with 13 grams for women/19 grams for men, respectively) was associated with a 62% increase in risk for gastric (non-cardia) cancer. This study also found twice the risk for stomach cancer in association with higher total meat intake (118-187 g/d, compared with 60-91 g/d in women and men, respectively).[5] Findings from the Swedish Mammography Cohort involving more than 51,000 women indicated that nitrates may be an important contributor to this phenomenon, revealing a 2-fold greater risk in women with the highest intakes of these preservatives, compared with the risk in women who had the lowest intakes.[6] Preserved fish that contains nitrates and/or salt is also associated with increased risk.[7] In persons with a family history of gastric cancer and high red meat consumption, the risk for gastric cancer is roughly 25 times that of individuals with no history and low meat intake.[8] Red meat contains particularly high levels of heme iron; individuals taking in the highest amount of this nutrient had roughly 3 times the risk for upper digestive tract cancer (predominantly gastric cancer), compared with those consuming the lowest amount.[9]

Eating more fruits and vegetables. Fruit intake is inversely related to gastric cancer incidence, and high vegetable consumption is associated with as much as a 30% reduction in risk, compared with low intakes.[10] Three explanations have been suggested for the apparent anticancer effects of fruits and vegetables: the inhibiting effect of vitamin C and other antioxidants on nitrosamine formation; the effects of carotenoids,[11] flavonoids,[12] and sulfur compounds in *Allium* species of vegetables, including garlic and onion;[13] and the total antioxidant potential of the diet, particularly in *H pylori*-infected persons.[14]

Replacing refined grains with whole grains. Whole grain and dietary fiber intake is associated with greatly reduced risk for gastric cancer.[15,16] In contrast, several reports show that high consumption of carbohydrates from refined grain products increases risk,[17,18] possibly because fruit and vegetable consumption may be lower in these cases.[19]

Avoiding highly salted foods. Sodium is a gastric irritant, and table salt intake is associated with gastric cancer risk, especially in Asians, who frequently eat salted fish,[20] processed or salted foods,[21] and fermented soy foods with added sodium.[22]

Maintenance of a healthy body weight. Obesity is a risk factor for adenocarcinoma of the gastric cardia and esophagus. Persons with a higher body mass index (BMI) have 2 to 4 times the risk of those with lower BMI, and the most obese have nearly 9 times the risk.[23,24] (See Obesity chapter.)

Diet and survival in gastric cancer. Although the role of diet in gastric cancer prognosis needs further study, data indicate that patients whose diets were lower in animal fat, animal protein, and nitrosamines before diagnosis had approximately half the risk of death from this cancer, compared with other patients.[25]

Orders

See Basic Diet Orders chapter.

Limit intake of salted and pickled foods.

Avoid foods preserved with nitrates.

What to Tell the Family

Diet plays an important role in the prevention of gastric cancer, which remains one of the leading causes of cancer-related death worldwide. Animal products, especially those preserved with nitrates, are associated with increased risk of gastric cancer and other cancers. A diet that includes regular servings of fruits, vegetables, and whole grains may reduce that risk, in addition to its other health benefits. The whole family would do well to incorporate these dietary changes into their lifestyle.

References

1. Rembacken B, Fujii T, Kondo H. The recognition and endoscopic treatment of early gastric and colonic cancer. *Best Pract Res Clin Gastroenterol.* 2001;15:317-336.

2. McCullough ML, Robertson AS, Jacobs EJ, Chao A, Calle EE, Thun MJ. A prospective study of diet and stomach cancer mortality in United States men and women. *Cancer Epidemiol Biomarkers Prev.* 2001;10:1201-1205.

3. Ocke MC, Bueno-de-Mesquita HB, Feskens EJ, Kromhout D, Menotti A, Blackburn H. Adherence to the European Code Against Cancer in relation to long-term cancer mortality: intercohort comparisons from the Seven Countries Study. *Nutr Cancer.* 1998;30:14-20.

4. Mayne ST, Risch HA, Dubrow R, et al. Nutrient intake and risk of subtypes of esophageal and gastric cancer. *Cancer Epidemiol Biomarkers Prev.* 2001;10:1055-1062.

5. Gonzalez CA, Jakszyn P, Pera G, et al. Meat intake and risk of stomach and esophageal adenocarcinoma within the European Prospective Investigation Into Cancer and Nutrition (EPIC). *J Natl Cancer Inst.* 2006;98:345-354.

6. Larsson SC, Bergkvist L, Wolk A. Processed meat consumption, dietary nitrosamines and stomach cancer risk in a cohort of Swedish women. *Int J Cancer.* 2006;119:915-919.

7. Jakszyn P, Gonzalez CA. Nitrosamine and related food intake and gastric and oesophageal cancer risk: a systematic review of the epidemiological evidence. *World J Gastroenterol.* 2006;12:4296-4303.

8. Palli D, Russo A, Ottini L, et al. Red meat, family history, and increased risk of gastric cancer with microsatellite instability. *Cancer Res.* 2001;61:5415-5419.

9. Lee DH, Anderson KE, Folsom AR, Jacobs DR Jr. Heme iron, zinc and upper digestive tract cancer: the Iowa Women's Health Study. *Int J Cancer.* 2005;117:643-647.

10. Lunet N, Lacerda-Vieira A, Barros H. Fruit and vegetables consumption and gastric cancer: a systematic review and meta-analysis of cohort studies. *Nutr Cancer.* 2005;53:1-10.

11. De Stefani E, Boffetta P, Brennan P, et al. Dietary carotenoids and risk of gastric cancer: a case-control study in Uruguay. *Eur J Cancer Prev.* 2000;9:329-334.

12. Garcia-Closas R, Gonzalez CA, Agudo A, Riboli E. Intake of specific carotenoids and flavonoids and the risk of gastric cancer in Spain. *Cancer Causes Control.* 1999;10:71-75.

13. Fleischauer AT, Poole C, Arab L. Garlic consumption and cancer prevention: meta-analyses of colorectal and stomach cancers. *Am J Clin Nutr.* 2000;72:1047-1052.

14. Serafini M, Bellocco R, Wolk A, Ekstrom AM. Total antioxidant potential of fruit and vegetables and risk of gastric cancer. *Gastroenterology.* 2002;123:985-991.

15. Chen H, Tucker KL, Graubard BI, et al. Nutrient intakes and adenocarcinoma of the esophagus and distal stomach. *Nutr Cancer.* 2002;42:33-40.

16. Jacobs DR Jr, Slavin J, Marquart L. Whole grain intake and cancer: a review of the literature. *Nutr Cancer.* 1995;24:221-229.

17. Jedrychowski W, Popiela T, Steindorf K, et al. Nutrient intake patterns in gastric and colorectal cancers. *Int J Occup Med Environ Health.* 2001;14:391-395.

18. Chatenoud L, La Vecchia C, Franceschi S, et al. Refined-cereal intake and risk of selected cancers in Italy. *Am J Clin Nutr.* 1999;70:1107-1110.

19. Jansen MC, Bueno-de-Mesquita HB, Rasanen L, et al. Consumption of plant foods and stomach cancer mortality in the seven countries study. Is grain consumption a risk factor? Seven Countries Study Research Group. *Nutr Cancer.* 1999;34:49-55.

20. Tsugane S, Sasazuki S, Kobayashi M, Sasaki S. Salt and salted food intake and subsequent risk of gastric cancer among middle-aged Japanese men and women. *Br J Cancer.* 2004;90:128-134.

21. Ji BT, Chow WH, Yang G, et al. Dietary habits and stomach cancer in Shanghai, China. *Int J Cancer.* 1998;76:659-664.

22. Wu AH, Yang D, Pike MC. A meta-analysis of soyfoods and risk of stomach cancer: the problem of potential confounders. *Cancer Epidemiol Biomarkers Prev.* 2000;9:1051-1058.

23. Lagergren J, Bergstrom R, Nyren O. Association between body mass and adenocarcinoma of the esophagus and gastric cardia. *Ann Intern Med.* 1999;130:883-890.

24. Chow WH, Blot WJ, Vaughan TL, et al. Body mass index and risk of adenocarcinomas of the esophagus and gastric cardia. *J Natl Cancer Inst.* 1998;90:150-155.

25. Palli D, Russo A, Saieva C, Salvini S, Amorosi A, Decarli A. Dietary and familial determinants of 10-year survival among patients with gastric carcinoma. *Cancer.* 2000;89:1205-1213.

21. Pancreatic Cancer

Pancreatic cancer is the fourth most common cancer and the fifth most common cause of cancer-related mortality. Little is known about etiologic agents, but tobacco use is probably the most important modifiable risk factor.

More than 90% of pancreatic cancers are adenocarcinomas, which are discussed here. Less common pancreatic tumors include endocrine tumors, carcinoid tumors, and lymphoma.

The characteristic presentation includes an insidious onset of weight loss, fatigue, anorexia, and gnawing abdominal or back pain. The most common symptom is epigastric pain with radiation to the back, which often improves upon bending forward. In addition, painless jaundice, dark urine, acholic stools, pruritis, migratory thrombophlebitis, or Courvoisier sign (a palpable, nontender gallbladder) may be present.

Unfortunately, by the time symptoms appear, the cancer has generally become quite advanced. At the time of diagnosis, more than 80% of patients have advanced tumors marked by either local extension into adjacent organs (such as the liver) or distant metastases, resulting in a poor long-term survival rate. Most patients die within a year of diagnosis.

Risk Factors

Males and African Americans have a slightly higher risk. Additional risk factors include the following:

Smoking.

Age. The condition is rare before age 45. Incidence increases with age.

Family history. About 5% to 10% of patients with pancreatic cancer have a first-degree relative with the disease.

Genetics. Mutations in the *p16*, *K-ras*, *CDKN2A*, *p53*, and *BRCA* genes appear to increase the risk.

Obesity. Overweight and obesity clearly increase the risk of pancreatic cancer.

Periodontal disease. Preliminary studies suggest that men with this condition may have an increased risk of pancreatic cancer. This may be due to an inflammatory state induced by periodontal disease.[1]

Asbestos exposure.

Dietary factors (see Nutritional Considerations).

Diagnosis

Abdominal CT scan is the most common diagnostic test for pancreatic cancer. It will reveal the extent of the disease and may identify metastases.

Biopsy is necessary for a definitive diagnosis.

MRI (with or without angiography) or laparoscopy may determine resectability.

Ultrasound, endoscopic ultrasound, and endoscopic retrograde cholangiopancreatography (ERCP) are used for tumor staging.

Laboratory analysis should include a complete blood count, liver function tests, amylase, lipase, and tumor-associated antigens, such as carcinoembryonic antigens (CEA) and cancer antigen (CA) 19-9. Levels of alkaline phosphatase and bilirubin may be elevated if the bile duct is obstructed or if liver metastases are present.

Treatment

Despite advances in treatment, the prognosis for pancreatic cancer remains poor, and surgical resection is the only curative treatment. However, curative operations are possible in only 10% to 15% of patients. Common surgical procedures include pancreaticoduodenectomy (the Whipple procedure), which involves removal of the duodenum, head of the pancreas, and gallbladder, and total or distal pancreatectomy. Treatment with chemotherapy and/or radiation following surgery may improve survival rates.

If the tumor is unresectable, palliation may be attempted via radiation, chemotherapy, or surgical intervention to relieve bile duct and GI tract obstructions.

Allow for liberal use of narcotic analgesics for pain control.

Nutritional Considerations

The risk for pancreatic cancer appears to be significantly related to insulin resistance. Obesity, diabetes, lack of exercise, and macronutrients known to worsen insulin resistance (saturated fat, high glycemic index carbohydrates) are associated with increased risk.

The risk for pancreatic cancer appears to be lower in persons who eat more fiber, fruits, and vegetables, and in persons following vegetarian diets.[2-4] In epidemiologic studies, several dietary factors are associated with reduced risk:

Avoiding animal products. Several studies have shown that pancreatic cancer risk increases with higher intake of meat and of saturated fat from animal products. The Swedish Mammography Cohort study of more than 61,000 women found a 75% higher risk for pancreatic cancer in women eating 4 or more servings per week of red meat compared with those eating less than 1.5 servings.[5] Similarly, the Multiethnic Cohort study of 190,000 white, black, Latino, Japanese-American, and Native Hawaiians residing in Hawaii and Los Angeles found a 50% greater risk in association with the highest intakes of red meat compared with the lowest (26 g/d compared with 3 g/d) and the highest intakes of pork compared with the lowest (~10 g/d compared with <0.5 g/d).[6] These relationships may result from the carcinogenic effects of heterocyclic amines (HCAs) frequently found in cooked poultry, fish, and red meat[7] or of nitrates used in some prepared meat products.[8] In international studies, per capita consumption of meat, eggs, and milk correlated with mortality rates for pancreatic cancer.[9] Conversely, intake of beans, lentils, other vegetarian protein sources, peas, and dried fruits is associated with significantly reduced risk for pancreatic cancer.[3]

Reducing fat intake. In a group of 27,111 male smokers aged 50-69 years who were followed for a 12-year period, those who ate the most saturated fat had a significantly higher risk for pancreatic cancer, compared with nonsmokers who ate the least saturated fat.[10] Some have suggested that the ability of saturated fat to increase insulin-like growth factor 1,[11] a known risk factor for pancreatic cancer mortality,[12] may also have contributed to these findings. Although the relationships do not appear to be as strong for total fat as for animal fat, even fat from vegetable sources may increase pancreatic cancer risk. In a Swedish study, fried foods were associated with greater risk for pancreatic cancer,[13] and women who ate the most fat had three times the risk for this cancer as those eating the least fat.[14] The relationship may be due to the effect of high-fat diets on insulin resistance, a possible risk factor for pancreatic cancer.[15]

Increasing consumption of fruits, vegetables, and fiber. Numerous data link consumption of fruits, vegetables, and fiber with lower risk for pancreatic cancer. One report implicated both oxidative stress and oxidative stress-associated inflammation as causes of pancreatic cancer.[16] This association may explain the correlation between high intakes of fruits, vegetables, and certain antioxidants found in these foods with lower risk for this cancer. Another study found that women who ate the most fruit had a 63% lower risk of pancreatic cancer, and those who ate the most vegetables and fiber had a 70% lower risk, compared with women eating the smallest quantities of these foods.[14] Risk was also lower among individuals with higher serum levels of lycopene (a carotenoid particularly prevalent in tomato products and watermelon),[17] and men whose lycopene intake was highest had a 69% lower risk than men with the lowest lycopene intake.

Persons with the highest intakes of beta-carotene and total carotenoids had a 40% lower risk compared with those with the lowest intakes.[2] Persons eating the highest amount of vitamin C appear to have about half the risk for pancreatic cancer as those with the least vitamin C in their diets.[4,18] It is unclear, however, whether these associations relate specifically to these food constituents or to another aspect of vegetables and fruits; evidence indicates that dietary fiber, folate, or certain kinds of vegetables may be especially protective. Persons with the highest intake of fiber had a 55% lower risk for pancreatic cancer than those eating the least fiber,[4] a relationship that may be mediated by the beneficial effect of fiber on insulin sensitivity.[19] In a cohort of nearly 82,000 Swedish men and women, those consuming more than 3 servings per week of cruciferous vegetables had a 30% lower risk, compared with those eating less than 1 serving per week.[20] In the same cohort, the highest intake of folate from foods (>350 µg/d) was associated with a 75% lower risk for pancreatic cancer when compared with those whose intake was <200 µg/d.[21]

Weight control. Exercise and weight control also appear to reduce risk for pancreatic cancer. Individuals who performed the greatest amount of moderate to strenuous physical activity had roughly half the risk as those getting the least exercise.[15] Overweight individuals may derive the most protection from exercise; the risk for pancreatic cancer is inversely related to physical activity in persons with a body mass index >25.[22]

Vitamin D. Compared with individuals consuming less than 150 IU of vitamin D per day, individuals consuming at least 300-600 IU daily had a 40% lower risk for pancreatic cancer in a study of 120,000 health professionals.[23] Among smokers, the opposite result was found in the Alpha-Tocopherol, Beta-Carotene Cancer Prevention Study. Pancreatic cancer risk was 3 times greater among smokers with the highest blood levels of vitamin D compared with those with the lowest levels.[24]

Avoiding sugar-containing soft drinks. In a study of 138,000 men and women, the intake of 3 or more servings per week of soft drinks was associated with a significantly greater risk for pancreatic cancer. However, this risk was limited to women with a BMI >25 kg/m² and women getting the least physical activity. Both groups experienced roughly twice the risk for this cancer, compared with women with a BMI <25 kg/m² and those with high levels of activity.[25]

Diet and Prognosis for Pancreatic Cancer

Few studies have examined the effect of dietary changes on survival after diagnosis. One study found a 4-fold increase in median survival (13 months versus 3 months) in patients with pancreatic cancer who followed a macrobiotic diet (composed mainly of whole grains, land and sea vegetables, beans, legumes, and small amounts of fruit) compared with those eating omnivorous diets.[26] Further studies are needed to establish relationships between diet and pancreatic cancer survival.

Orders

See Basic Diet Orders chapter.

Smoking cessation.

Exercise prescription.

What to Tell the Family

Pancreatic cancer typically has a poor prognosis. While dietary factors appear to play a role in risk and possibly in survival, further studies are necessary to clarify these relationships.

References

1. Michaud D, Joshipura K, Giovannucci E, Fuchs C. A prospective study of periodontal disease and pancreatic cancer in US male health professionals. *J Natl Cancer Inst.* 2007;99:171-177.

2. Nkondjock A, Ghadirian P, Johnson KC, Krewski D, and the Canadian Cancer Registries Epidemiology Research Group. Dietary intake of lycopene is associated with reduced pancreatic cancer risk. *J Nutr.* 2005;135:592-597.

3. Mills PK, Beeson WL, Abbey DE, Fraser GE, Phillips RL. Dietary habits and past medical history as related to fatal pancreas cancer risk among Adventists. *Cancer.* 1988;61:2578-2585.

4. Howe GR, Ghadirian P, Bueno de Mesquita HB, et al. A collaborative case-control study of nutrient intake and pancreatic cancer within the search programme. *Int J Cancer.* 1992;51:365-372.

5. Larsson SC, Hakanson N, Permert J, Wolk A. Meat, fish, poultry and egg consumption in relation to risk of pancreatic cancer: a prospective study. *Int J Cancer.* 2006;118:2866-2870.

6. Nothlings U, Wilkens LR, Murphy SP, Hankin JH, Henderson BE, Kolonel LN. Meat and fat intake as risk factors for pancreatic cancer: the multiethnic cohort study. *J Natl Cancer Inst.* 2005;97:1458-1465.

7. Anderson KE, Sinha R, Kulldorff M, et al. Meat intake and cooking techniques: associations with pancreatic cancer. *Mutat Res.* 2002;506-507:225-231.

8. Coss A, Cantor KP, Reif JS, Lynch CF, Ward MH. Pancreatic cancer and drinking water and dietary sources of nitrate and nitrite. *Am J Epidemiol.* 2004;159:693-701.

9. Ghadirian P, Thouez JP, PetitClerc C. International comparisons of nutrition and mortality from pancreatic cancer. *Cancer Detect Prev.* 1991;15:357-362.

10. Stolzenberg-Solomon RZ, Pietinen P, Taylor PR, Virtamo J, Albanes D. Prospective study of diet and pancreatic cancer in male smokers. *Am J Epidemiol.* 2002;155:783-792.

11. Giovannucci E, Pollak M, Liu Y, et al. Nutritional predictors of insulin-like growth factor I and their relationships to cancer in men. *Cancer Epidemiol Biomarkers Prev.* 2003;12:84-89.

12. Lin Y, Tamakoshi A, Kikuchi S, et al. Serum insulin-like growth factor-I, insulin-like growth factor binding protein-3, and the risk of pancreatic cancer death. *Int J Cancer.* 2004;110:584-588.

13. Gerhardsson de Verdier M. Epidemiologic studies on fried foods and cancer in Sweden. *Princess Takamatsu Symp.* 1995;23:292-298.

14. Lyon JL, Slattery ML, Mahoney AW, Robison LM. Dietary intake as a risk factor for cancer of the exocrine pancreas. *Cancer Epidemiol Biomarkers Prev.* 1993;2:513-518.

15. Hanley AJ, Johnson KC, Villeneuve PJ, Mao Y, and the Canadian Cancer Registries Epidemiology Research Group. Physical activity, anthropometric factors, and risk of pancreatic cancer: results from the Canadian enhanced cancer surveillance system. *Int J Cancer.* 2001;94:140-147.

16. Hine RJ, Srivastava S, Milner JA, Ross SA. Nutritional links to plausible mechanisms underlying pancreatic cancer: a conference report. *Pancreas.* 2003;27:356-366.

17. Burney PG, Comstock GW, Morris JS. Serologic precursors of cancer: serum micronutrients and the subsequent risk of pancreatic cancer. *Am J Clin Nutr.* 1989;49:895-900.

18. Lin Y, Tamakoshi A, Hayakawa T, Naruse S, Kitagawa M, Ohno Y. Nutritional factors and risk of pancreatic cancer: a population-based case-control study based on direct interview in Japan. *J. Gastroenterol.* 2005;40:297-301.

19. McKeown NM. Whole grain intake and insulin sensitivity: evidence from observational studies. *Nutr Rev.* 2004;62:286-291.

20. Larsson SC, Hakansson N, Naslund I, Bergkvist L, Wolk A. Fruit and vegetable consumption in relation to pancreatic cancer risk: a prospective study. *Cancer Epidemiol Biomarkers Prev.* 2006;15:301-305.

21. Larsson SC, Hakansson N, Giovannucci E, Wolk A. Folate intake and pancreatic cancer incidence: a prospective study of Swedish women and men. *J Natl Cancer Inst.* 2006;98:407-413.

22. Michaud DS, Giovannucci E, Willett WC, Colditz GA, Stampfer MJ, Fuchs CS. Physical activity, obesity, height, and the risk of pancreatic cancer. *JAMA.* 2001;286:921-929.

23. Skinner HG, Michaud DS, Giovannucci E, Willett WC, Colditz GA, Fuchs CS. Vitamin D intake and the risk for pancreatic cancer in two cohort studies. *Cancer Epidemiol Biomarkers Prev.* 2006;15:1688-1695.

24. Stolzenberg-Solomon RZ, Vieth R, Azad A, et al. A prospective nested case-control study of vitamin D status and pancreatic cancer risk in male smokers. *Cancer Res.* 2006;66:10213-10219.

25. Schernhammer ES, Hu FB, Giovannucci E, et al. Sugar-sweetened soft drink consumption and risk of pancreatic cancer in two prospective cohorts. *Cancer Epidemiol Biomarkers Prev.* 2005;14:2098-2105.

26. Carter JP, Saxe GP, Newbold V, Peres CE, Campeau RJ, Bernal-Green L. Hypothesis: dietary management may improve survival from nutritionally linked cancers based on analysis of representative cases. *J Am Coll Nutr.* 1993;12:209-226.

22. Colorectal Cancer

Colon cancer is the third most common malignancy worldwide and the second leading cause of cancer-related mortality. It accounts for 10% of cancer deaths in the United States. Although the disease is common and often lethal, risk is significantly reduced with regular screenings and timely removal of precancerous lesions. Evidence also suggests that dietary habits may influence both cancer incidence and progression.

More than 95% of colon cancers are adenocarcinomas, which originate from glandular tissue. Presenting symptoms and complications depend on the location of the tumor. General symptoms include abdominal pain, a change in bowel habits, decreased caliber of stool, and constitutional symptoms, such as weight loss, weakness, and fatigue. Right-sided tumors may additionally present with melena or occult bleeding and/or a right-sided abdominal mass. Left-sided tumors may cause constipation, diarrhea, and, especially with distal left-sided and rectal tumors, hematochezia. Further, patients with left-sided tumors are at much higher risk of intestinal obstruction, which may present with nausea, vomiting, absence of bowel movements and flatus, and abdominal distention.

Local spread and distant metastases are common. Between 15% and 20% of patients initially present with metastases, most commonly to the regional lymph nodes, liver, lungs, and peritoneum.

Risk Factors

Age: Incidence increases with age; 90% of cases occur in patients over age 50.

Family history: 25% of patients have a positive family history. There is a several-fold increased risk if 1 or more first-degree relatives have colon cancer.

Environment: Incidence is highest in developed countries. Individuals migrating from areas of low incidence to areas of high incidence eventually assume a risk similar to that of their adopted country.

Diet: Numerous studies have detected associations between diet and the development of colon cancer, as described below in Nutritional Considerations.

Tobacco use.

Hereditary syndromes (eg, familial polyposis, Lynch syndrome).

Inflammatory bowel disease: Both ulcerative colitis and Crohn disease predispose to colon cancer. There appears to be a higher risk with ulcerative colitis (as much as a 5-fold to 15-fold increased risk) than with Crohn disease.

Overweight: A number of studies, including the NIH-AARP Diet and Health Study involving more than 500,000 women and men, have found a linear relationship between excess weight and death from colon cancer.[1] Individuals with a BMI ≥40 have a roughly 45% greater risk for colorectal cancer, compared with those who are at a healthy weight (BMI 18.5 to 24.9). Individuals who are mildly or moderately obese appear to have a 10% and approximately 35% greater risk, respectively.[2]

In contrast to the above factors, physical activity may be protective. In a study of more than 120,000 female teaching professionals, among women who had never used hormone therapy, exercising for 4 or more hours per week was associated with roughly half the risk for colon cancer, compared with the risk for women who exercised 30 minutes per week or less.[3] Possible mechanisms include reduction in weight or in blood concentrations of insulin or insulin-like growth factor.[4]

Hormone replacement therapy may influence risk. Data from the Women's Health Initiative suggest a reduced risk of colorectal cancer in postmenopausal women using hormone replacement therapy.[5,6]

Diagnosis

Guiac-positive stools should prompt evaluation with a colonoscopy. Complete blood count may reveal microcytic anemia from chronic blood loss. Patients with anemia and ferritin levels of 100 ng/mL or less should undergo colonoscopy for further evaluation.[7]

Colonoscopy with biopsy identifies colonic growths and may allow for removal of early lesions. Barium enema is not as sensitive as colonoscopy and does not allow for polyp removal. "Virtual colonoscopy" using CT or MRI is under investigation but is less sensitive than colonoscopy.

Tumor markers (CEA, CA 125, CA 19-9, CA 50, CA 195) are not sufficiently specific for general screening, but they can be used to determine prognosis and to monitor for disease recurrence.

Metastatic workup includes liver function tests and CT scans of the thorax, abdomen, and pelvis. CT scan is also used for clinical staging. The TNM (Tumor, Node, Metastasis) classification is the preferred system for tumor staging:

- **TNM stage I:** Tumor is localized to the mucosa and submucosa.
- **TNM stage II:** Tumor has extended into the muscle layer but without lymph node involvement.
- **TNM stage III:** Regional lymph node involvement.
- **TNM stage IV:** Distant metastases.

Treatment

Surgical resection is the definitive treatment and is often curative for early cancers. A combination of surgical resection and adjuvant chemotherapy (eg, 5-fluorouracil, leucovorin, oxaliplatin) is indicated for advanced cancers. Radiation and chemotherapy are mainstays of treatment for rectal cancers, in addition to surgical resection.

Liver metastases are treated by resection, chemoembolization, or direct arterial infusion chemotherapy into the hepatic artery. Avastin, an angiogenesis inhibitor, has been approved by the FDA as a first-line treatment for metastatic colon cancer when administered in conjunction with 5-fluorouracil and leucovorin.

Patients at risk for colorectal cancer should be counseled on the potential preventive benefits of weight control and regular exercise, as well as those of the dietary changes noted below.

Nutritional Considerations

Diet is a major contributor to colon cancer risk. Several lines of evidence implicate meats (particularly red meat and processed meat) in colon cancer risk. The main associations are presumed to be due to macronutrients (such as saturated fat) found in meat products, as well as to carcinogens found in or formed as a result of cooking and processing of meats. Conversely, plant-based and vegetarian diets are associated with lower incidence of colon cancer,[8] probably due to the absence of meat, as well as to the inclusion of protective plant constituents. The following factors are associated with reduced risk of colorectal cancer:

Avoidance of meat products. Consumption of meat, particularly red and processed meat, is associated with increased risk of colorectal cancer. Based on a review of 16 cohort and 71 case-control studies on red meat and 14 cohort and 44 case-control studies on processed meat, the World Cancer Research Fund and American Institute for Cancer Research concluded in 2007 that "convincing" evidence supports a causal relationship between consumption of these products and colorectal cancer risk.[9] Risk increases with increasing consumption. Risk of colorectal cancer increases, on average, by 21% for every 50 grams of processed meat consumed daily. A 50-gram serving is approximately the size of a typical hot dog.

In the European Prospective Investigation into Cancer and Nutrition (EPIC) study involving more than 480,000 individuals, those eating ≥160 g/d of red or processed meat had a 70% greater risk for colorectal cancer than persons eating >20 g/d.[10] Similarly, the Cancer Prevention Study II (CPS II) Nutrition Cohort, involving more than 148,000 persons, determined that individuals eating the highest amount of red meat and processed meat were at 50% and 70% greater risk for colon cancer and rectal cancer, respectively, compared with those eating the lowest amount.[11]

The role of white meat in colon cancer remains unclear. Some studies have found no increase in risk associated with frequent white meat consumption. However, in one study, Seventh-day Adventist men who ate white meat ≥1 time per week had a risk roughly 3.3 times that for those who abstained from eating white meat.[12]

The association between meat and colon cancer risk has variously been explained by the presence of nitrosamines,[13] polycyclic aromatic hydrocarbons (PAH), and heterocyclic amines (carcinogens formed as a result of high-temperature cooking)[14] and by the pro-oxidant effects of heme iron.[15] A high cholesterol intake,[16] higher serum cholesterol,[17] and higher levels of oxidized LDL[18] are also associated with greater colorectal cancer risk. High-cholesterol foods such as eggs may also increase risk of proximal colon cancer.[19]

High-fiber foods. Studies in Western countries have so far provided only modest support for the ability of high-fiber diets to reduce colorectal cancer risk. A pooled analysis of prospective cohort studies found that individuals with higher intakes of dietary fiber (23 to 41 g/d for men and 20 to 35 g/d for women) had a non-statistically significant (6%) lower risk for colorectal cancer compared with those with the lowest intakes.[20] Some have suggested that higher fiber intakes than are typically found in Westernized diets may be necessary for a more robust preventive effect.[21] The Multiethnic Cohort Study of nearly 200,000 women and men found a nearly 40% lower risk for colorectal cancer in men who ate more than 35 grams of fiber per day, compared with those who ate roughly 13 grams per day.[22]

There may be a more substantial role for fiber in preventing precursor lesions. Investigators have demonstrated a role for fiber in reducing the risk for adenomatous polyps[23-25] and decreasing the risk for polyp recurrence in women who follow a high-fiber, low-fat diet[26] or a fiber-supplemented diet plus vitamins.[27] In addition, a combination of a low-fat diet and high-fiber intake (as 25 g additional wheat bran) significantly reduced the incidence of colorectal adenomas, although either intervention alone did not.[28] However, the Polyp Prevention Trial, a randomized multicenter clinical trial of a low-fat, high-fiber, high-fruit and vegetable diet, found no effect of diet on recurrence of adenomas of the large bowel, even eight years after randomization.[29]

The best-established mechanism for the potential of fiber to reduce the risk of cancerous or precancerous lesions derives from the ability of insoluble fiber to reduce fecal bile acid concentrations.[27] Some have also suggested that the potential preventive effect of fiber-containing foods may be due to an association with micronutrients, including carotenoids;[30] sulfur compounds in garlic;[31,32] or glucosinolates found in Brassica vegetables,[33] which accelerate Phase II detoxification of potential carcinogens.

Many foods high in fiber are also high in magnesium, a nutrient that may reduce the risk for colorectal cancer through its role in promoting genomic stability and DNA repair.[34] High magnesium intakes were associated with lower risk for colorectal cancer in the Swedish Mammography Cohort, which included more than 61,000 women,[35] and lower risk for colon cancer in the Iowa Women's Health Study of more than 35,000 women.[36] However, in the Netherlands Cohort Study including 58,279 men and 62,573 women, magnesium intake was significantly and inversely associated with the risk for colorectal cancer only in individuals with a body mass index (BMI) of ≥ 25 kg/m^2.[34]

Individuals eating the most refined carbohydrates (eg, sucrose, refined starches) appear to have roughly twice the risk for developing colon cancer, compared with those who eat the least amount.[37,38]

Foods high in folic acid and vitamin B6. Leafy green vegetables, beans, and whole grains are good sources of folate, an important determinant of DNA methylation, which affects maintenance of DNA integrity and stability.[39] Although a relationship between folate and other dietary factors may account for benefits, evidence indicates that individuals eating the most folate have a 39% lower risk for colon cancer[40] and a 25% lower risk for colorectal cancer than do persons eating the lowest amount.[41] Similarly, vitamin B6 is involved in DNA methylation and suppresses tumorigenesis by reducing cell proliferation, oxidative stress, angiogenesis, and other mechanisms.[42] Individuals who consume the highest amounts of vitamin B6 or have the highest blood levels of pyridoxal phosphate have a 34% to 44% lower risk for colorectal cancer compared with those who have the lowest B6 intakes or pyridoxal phosphate blood levels.[43,44]

Limiting alcohol use. Several studies show that alcohol consumption (≥1 drink per day) is independently associated with the risk of colorectal adenoma or cancer.[45]

Vitamin D and calcium. Higher intakes of both calcium and vitamin D are associated with lower risk for colorectal cancer,[46] and supplemental forms of calcium and vitamin D may be inversely associated with recurrence of colorectal adenoma.[47] The purported ability of calcium and calcium-containing foods to reduce risk for colorectal cancer may be due to calcium's effect on proliferation, differentiation, apoptosis, and binding of bile acids that may act as mutagens in the colon.[48] A lower risk for colon cancer was found in persons whose calcium intake was 700 mg per day, compared with those who have lower intakes; the additional benefit of higher intakes was minimal.[49] The Cohort of Swedish men study involving >45,000 men showed that those who consumed ≥2 servings of dairy products each day had roughly 45% lower risk for this cancer when compared with those having <2 servings/day, a finding in agreement with a meta-analysis of case-control and cohort studies.[48] Calcium and dairy products may be double-edged swords, however, reducing risk of colon cancer but increasing risk of prostate cancer (see Prostate Cancer chapter). In some studies, the cancer risk-reducing effect was abolished when vitamin D was not present or when the effect of calcium was dependent on high intake of this vitamin.

A recent meta-analysis showed that high blood levels of 25(OH) vitamin D (corresponding to a daily dose of 1,000 to 2,000 IU of vitamin D3) were associated with a roughly 50% lower risk for colorectal cancer.[50]

Selenium-containing foods. Combined data from the Wheat Bran Fiber Trial, the Polyp Prevention Study and Polyp Prevention Trial,[51] and the Diet and Health Study indicated that individuals with the highest blood selenium levels had a 40% lower risk for colorectal adenoma and a 30% lower risk for adenoma recurrence[51] compared with individuals with the lowest levels.

Tea. Frequent black tea consumption is associated with a lower risk for colon and rectal cancer.[52-54] Several studies have found a lower risk for colorectal cancers in Chinese populations drinking green tea.[55] In a study of nearly 70,000 Chinese women, drinking green tea on a regular basis (at least 3 times per week) was associated with a roughly 40% lower risk for development of colorectal cancer, compared with less frequent consumption.[55] It has not yet been established that frequent green tea intake reduces the risk for this cancer in Western populations, however.

Nutrition and Colorectal Cancer Survival

In a study of more than 1,000 individuals with stage III colon cancer receiving chemotherapy, those who scored highest on a scale measuring a Western dietary pattern high in meat, refined grains, and desserts had a three times greater risk for cancer recurrence or mortality, compared with those who had the lowest score.[56] A "prudent" diet, emphasizing vegetables, fruits, poultry, and fish, was not significantly associated with disease recurrence or mortality.

Diet Orders

Vegetarian, low-fat, high-fiber.

What to Tell the Family

The risk for colon cancer may be reduced through a plant-based diet and healthy lifestyle. Even after cancer diagnosis and treatment, diet and lifestyle changes may be helpful, reducing the risk of recurrence. Family members can help by supporting the patient in adopting healthful diet and lifestyle habits and by adopting such habits themselves.

References

1. Adams KF, Leitzmann MF, Albanes D, et al. Body mass and colorectal cancer risk in the NIH-AARP cohort. *Am J Epidemiol.* 2007;166:36-45.

2. Calle EE, Rodriguez C, Walker-Thurmond K, Thun MJ. Overweight, obesity, and mortality from cancer in a prospectively studied cohort of U.S. adults. *N Engl J Med.* 2003;348:1625-1638.

3. Mai PL, Sullivan-Halley J, Ursin G, et al. Physical activity and colon cancer risk among women in the California Teachers Study. *Cancer Epidemiol Biomarkers Prev.* 2007;16:517-525.

4. Wei EK, Ma J, Pollak MN, et al. A prospective study of C-peptide, insulin-like growth factor-I, insulin-like growth factor binding protein-1, and the risk of colorectal cancer in women. *Cancer Epidemiol Biomarkers Prev.* 2005;14:850-855.

5. Chlebowski RT, Wactawski J, Ritenbaugh C, et al. Estrogen plus progestin and colorectal cancer in postmenopausal women. *N Engl J Med.* 2004;350:991-1004.

6. Nelson HD, Humphrey LL, Nygren P, et al. Postmenopausal hormone replacement therapy: scientific review. *JAMA.* 2002;288:872-881.

7. Sawhney MS, Lipato T, Nelson DB, Lederle FA, Rector TS, Bond JH. *Am J Gastroenterol.* 2007;102:82–88.

8. Fraser GE. Associations between diet and cancer, ischemic heart disease, and all-cause mortality in non-Hispanic white California Seventh-day Adventists. *Am J Clin Nutr.* 1999;70(suppl 3):532S-538S.

9. World Cancer Research Fund/American Institute for Cancer Research. Food, Nutrition, Physical Activity, and the Prevention of Cancer: A Global Perspective. Washington, DC: AICR; 2007:284.

10. Norat T, Bingham S, Ferrari P, et al. Meat, fish, and colorectal cancer risk: the European Prospective Investigation into cancer and nutrition. *J Natl Cancer Inst.* 2005;97:906-916.

11. Chao A, Thun MJ, Connell CJ, et al. Meat consumption and risk of colorectal cancer. *JAMA.* 2005;293:172-182.

12. Singh PN, Fraser GE. Dietary risk factors for colon cancer in a low-risk population. *Am J Epidemiol.* 1998;148:761–774.

13. Le Marchand L, Donlon T, Seifried A, Wilkens LR. Red meat intake, CYP2E1 genetic polymorphisms, and colorectal cancer risk. *Cancer Epidemiol Biomarkers Prev.* 2002;11:1019-1024.

14. Murtaugh MA, Ma KN, Sweeney C, Caan BJ, Slattery ML. Meat consumption patterns and preparation, genetic variants of metabolic enzymes, and their association with rectal cancer in men and women. *J Nutr.* 2004;134:776-784.

15. Lee DH, Anderson KE, Harnack LJ, Folsom AR, Jacobs DR Jr. Heme iron, zinc, alcohol consumption, and colon cancer: Iowa Women's Health Study. *J Natl Cancer Inst.* 2004;96:403-407.

16. Jarvinen R, Knekt P, Hakulinen T, Rissanen H, Heliovaara M. Dietary fat, cholesterol, and colorectal cancer in a prospective study. *Br J Cancer.* 2001;85:357-361.

17. Yamada K, Araki S, Tamura M, et al. Relation of serum total cholesterol, serum triglycerides, and fasting plasma glucose to colorectal carcinoma in situ. *Int J Epidemiol.* 1998;27:794-798.

18. Suzuki K, Ito Y, Wakai K, et al. Serum oxidized low-density lipoprotein levels and risk of colorectal cancer: a case-control study nested in the Japan Collaborative Cohort Study. *Cancer Epidemiol Biomarkers Prev.* 2004;13:1781-1787.

19. Steinmetz KA, Potter JD. Egg consumption and cancer of the colon and rectum. *Eur J Cancer Prev.* 1994;3:237-245.

20. Park Y, Hunter DJ, Spiegelman D, et al. Dietary Fiber Intake and Risk of Colorectal Cancer: A Pooled Analysis of Prospective Cohort Studies. *JAMA.* 2005;294:2849-2857.

21. Leach JD. Evolutionary perspective on dietary intake of fibre and colorectal cancer. *Eur J Clin Nutr.* 2007;61:140-142.

22. Nomura AM, Hankin JH, Henderson BE, et al. Dietary fiber and colorectal cancer risk: the multiethnic cohort study. *Cancer Causes Control.* 2007;18:753-764.

23. Martinez ME, McPherson RS, Levin B, Glober GA. A case-control study of dietary intake and other lifestyle risk factors for hyperplastic polyps. *Gastroenterology.* 1997;113:423-429.

24. Martinez ME, McPherson RS, Annegers JF, Levin B. Association of diet and colorectal adenomatous polyps: dietary fiber, calcium, and total fat. *Epidemiology.* 1996;7:264-268.

25. Peters U, Sinha R, Chatterjee N, et al. Dietary fiber and colorectal adenoma in a colorectal cancer early detection program. *Lancet.* 2003;361:1491-1495.

26. McKeown-Eyssen GE, Bright-See E, Bruce WR, et al, and the Toronto Polyp Prevention Group. A randomized trial of a low-fat, high-fiber diet in the recurrence of colorectal polyps. *J Clin Epidemiol.* 1994;47:525-536.

27. Macrae F. Wheat bran fiber and development of adenomatous polyps: evidence from randomized, controlled clinical trials. *Am J Med.* 1999;106:38S-42S.

28. MacLennan R, Macrae F, Bain C, et al. Randomized trial of intake of fat, fiber, and beta carotene to prevent colorectal adenomas. *J Natl Cancer Inst.* 1995;87:1760-1766.

29. Lanza E, Yu B, Murphy G, et al. The polyp prevention trial continued follow-up study. *Cancer Epidemiol Biomarkers Prev.* 2007;16:1745-1752.

30. Nkondjock A, Ghadirian P. Dietary carotenoids and risk of colon cancer: case-control study. *Int J Cancer.* 2004;110:110-116.

31. Levi F, Pasche C, La Vecchia C, Lucchini F, Franceschi S. Food groups and colorectal cancer risk. *Br J Cancer.* 1999;79:1283-1287.

32. Steinmetz KA, Kushi LH, Bostick RM, Folsom AR, Potter JD. Vegetables, fruit, and colon cancer in the Iowa Women's Health Study. *Am J Epidemiol.* 1994;139:1-15.

33. Voorrips LE, Goldbohm RA, van Poppel G, Sturmans F, Hermus RJ, van den Brandt PA. Vegetable and fruit consumption and risks of colon and rectal cancer in a prospective cohort study: The Netherlands Cohort Study on Diet and Cancer. *Am J Epidemiol.* 2000;152:1081-1092.

34. van den Brandt PA, Smits KM, Goldbohm RA, Weijenberg MP. Magnesium intake and colorectal cancer risk in the Netherlands Cohort Study. *Br J Cancer.* 2007;96:510-513.

35. Larsson SC, Bergkvist L, Wolk A. Magnesium intake in relation to risk of colorectal cancer in women. *JAMA.* 2005;293:86–89.

36. Folsom AR, Hong CP. Magnesium intake and reduced risk of colon cancer in a prospective study of women. *Am J Epidemiol.* 2006;163:232–235.

37. Satia-Abouta J, Galanko JA, Martin CF, Ammerman A, Sandler RS. Food groups and colon cancer risk in African Americans and Caucasians. *Int J Cancer.* 2004;109:728-736.

38. Bostick RM, Potter JD, Kushi LH, et al. Sugar, meat, and fat intake, and nondietary risk factors for colon cancer incidence in Iowa women (United States). *Cancer Causes Control.* 1994;5:38-52.

39. Kim YI. Folate and DNA methylation: a mechanistic link between folate deficiency and colorectal cancer? *Cancer Epidemiol Biomarkers Prev.* 2004;13:511-519.

40. Larsson SC, Giovannucci E, Wolk A. A prospective study of dietary folate intake and risk of colorectal cancer: modification by caffeine intake and cigarette smoking. *Cancer Epidemiol Biomarkers Prev.* 2005;14:740-743.

41. Sanjoaquin MA, Allen N, Couto E, Roddam AW, Key TJ. Folate intake and colorectal cancer risk: a meta-analytical approach. *Int J Cancer.* 2005;113:825-828.

42. Komatsu S, Yanaka N, Matsubara K, Kato N. Antitumor effect of vitamin B6 and its mechanisms. *Biochim Biophys Acta.* 2003;1647:127-130.

43. Larsson SC, Giovannucci E, Wolk A. Vitamin B6 intake, alcohol consumption, and colorectal cancer: a longitudinal population-based cohort of women. *Gastroenterology.* 2005;128:1830-1837.

44. Wei EK, Giovannucci E, Selhub J, Fuchs CS, Hankinson SE, Ma J. Plasma vitamin B6 and the risk of colorectal cancer and adenoma in women. *J Natl Cancer Inst.* 2005;97:684-692.

45. Bailey LB. Folate, methyl-related nutrients, alcohol, and the MTHFR 677C-->T polymorphism affect cancer risk: intake recommendations. *J Nutr.* 2003;133(suppl 1):3748S-3753S.

46. Garland C, Shekelle RB, Barrett-Connor E, Criqui MH, Rossof AH, Paul O. Dietary vitamin D and calcium and risk of colorectal cancer: a 19-year prospective study in men. *Lancet.* 1985;1:307-309.

47. Hartman TJ, Albert PS, Snyder K, et al. The association of calcium and vitamin D with risk of colorectal adenomas. *J Nutr.* 2005;135:252-259.

48. Larsson SC, Bergkvist L, Rutegård J, Giovannucci E, Wolk A. Calcium and dairy food intakes are inversely associated with colorectal cancer risk in the Cohort of Swedish Men. *Am J Clin Nutr.* 2006;83:667-673.

49. Wu K, Willett WC, Fuchs CS, Colditz GA, Giovannucci EL. Calcium intake and risk of colon cancer in women and men. *J Natl Cancer Inst.* 2002;94:437-446.

50. Gorham ED, Garland CF, Garland FC, et al. Optimal vitamin D status for colorectal cancer prevention: a quantitative meta analysis. *Am J Prev Med.* 2007;32:210-216.

51. Jacobs ET, Jiang R, Alberts DS, et al. Selenium and colorectal adenoma: results of a pooled analysis. *J Natl Cancer Inst.* 2004;96:1669-1675.

52. Michels KB, Willett WC, Fuchs CS, Giovannucci E. Coffee, tea, and caffeine consumption and incidence of colon and rectal cancer. *J Natl Cancer Inst.* 2005;97:282–292.

53. Su LJ, Arab L. Tea consumption and the reduced risk of colon cancer: results from a national prospective cohort study. *Public Health Nutr.* 2002;5:419–425.

54. Zheng W, Doyle TJ, Kushi LH, Sellers TA, Hong CP, Folsom AR. Tea consumption and cancer incidence in a prospective cohort study of postmenopausal women. *Am J Epidemiol.* 1996;144:175–182.

55. Yang G, Shu XO, Li H, et al. Prospective cohort study of green tea consumption and colorectal cancer risk in women. *Cancer Epidemiol Biomarkers Prev.* 2007;16:1219-1223.

56. Meyerhardt JA, Niedzwiecki D, Hollis D, et al. Association of dietary patterns with cancer recurrence and survival in patients with stage III colon cancer. *JAMA.* 2007;298:754-764.

23. Breast Cancer

One in 8 women in the United States will be diagnosed with invasive breast cancer during her lifetime.[1] Breast cancer is the most commonly diagnosed cancer in women, constituting more than 1 in 4 cancers in females in the United States. It is second only to lung cancer as a cause of cancer death in women, accounting for over 40,000 deaths annually. Until recently, the incidence of breast cancer had been increasing year by year. Beginning in 2002, age-adjusted incidence rates began to decline.

The incidence of breast cancer in men is about 1% of the rate in women. In both genders, the incidence increases with age. Most of the cancers are invasive at the time of diagnosis; only about 20% represent carcinoma in situ. More than 85% of the invasive tumors are infiltrating ductal carcinoma. Other histologic types are infiltrating lobular, medullary, mucinous, and tubular carcinomas.

Risk Factors

Individuals in higher socioeconomic status (SES) categories generally have greater risk of developing breast cancer—as high as double the incidence in comparison with the lowest SES. The mediating factor is believed to be differing reproductive patterns in various SES groupings.[2] Breast cancer aggressiveness and mortality are higher in African American women, compared with whites.[3-5]

The role of oral contraceptives in breast cancer risk remains unsettled. The effect, if any, is very small.[6-8] Breast cancer risk is not associated with induced abortion.[9-12] Most studies have not shown increased risk from silicone breast implants, electromagnetic fields, electric blankets, hair dyes, or organochlorines.[13]

The following are widely accepted breast cancer risk factors:

Age. Incidence increases sharply until age 45 to 50 years. Incidence continues to increase with age after menopause, but at a slower rate.[14] The rate of increase in incidence stabilizes in later years and declines near age 80.[15] Mean age at diagnosis is 65 years.

Family history. Risk increases with an increasing number of first- or second-degree relatives with breast cancer history.

Genetic factors. The presence of *BRCA1* or *BRCA2* gene mutations increases breast cancer risk.

Reproductive events. These include early menarche, late menopause, older age at first birth, nulliparity, and lower parity.

Radiation exposure. Radiation exposure is one of the few exogenous factors that have been clearly demonstrated to increase breast cancer risk.

The following factors are also associated with breast cancer risk and may play etiologic roles:

Shorter duration of breast-feeding. Several cohort and case-control studies show protective benefits of breast-feeding. A multinational case-control study of nearly 150,000 women showed a decreased risk of 4.3% for each year of breast-feeding and 7% for each pregnancy.[16]

Obesity. Elevated estrogen levels, presumably due to peripheral aromatization of androstenedione to 1-estrone in adipose tissue, may increase breast cancer risk in overweight postmenopausal women.[17] Higher birth weight and greater weight gain are also associated with an increased risk. In contrast, excess body fat may be associated with decreased risk of premenopausal breast cancer.

Physical inactivity. Physically active women are less likely to develop breast cancer, compared with sedentary women. Exercise may decrease risk by reducing circulating estrogen and androgen concentrations and increasing sex-hormone binding globulin concentrations.[18] In the Prostate, Lung, Colorectal, and Ovarian Cancer Screening Trial involving nearly 39,000 women, roughly 4 hours per week of exercise was associated with a >20% reduction in these women's risk for breast cancer, compared with the risk for women reporting no physical activity.[19] Some evidence indicates that exercise may impart this benefit regardless of hormone receptor subtype (ie, ER+/PR+ or ER-/PR-) or menopausal status.[20]

Higher endogenous serum estrogen concentrations. Women with higher concentrations of circulating estrogen have a higher risk of developing breast cancer.[21] In a clinical trial with 7,705 women, those whose serum estradiol concentrations were in the highest tertile had twice the risk for invasive postmenopausal breast cancer, compared with women with lower estradiol concentrations.[22]

Proliferative benign breast disease (with or without atypia).

Ovarian cancer.

Previous breast cancer. A first breast cancer may increase risk for subsequent unrelated breast cancer.[23]

Hormone replacement therapy (HRT). The Women's Health Initiative (WHI) trial showed a higher risk of breast cancer (RR=1.26) among women taking a combined estrogen-progestin preparation for approximately 5 years, compared with those who used a placebo.[24] This finding had been demonstrated previously, as well. Unopposed estrogens may have a lesser risk in comparison with combination HRT for eligible women, but this treatment carries other risks, such as thromboembolism. Studies link HRT to lobular cancers.[25,26] The incidence of such cancers doubled from 1987 to 1999, a period of steady increase in use of combination HRT, without significant change in ductal cancer incidence.[1] HRT also accelerates growth in estrogen and progesterone receptor-positive tumors.

As noted above, age-adjusted breast cancer incidence began to fall in the United States in mid-2002, a reduction that was only observed in women age 50 and older. This occurred almost immediately after prescriptions for HRT began to decline steeply following the 2002 report of findings from the Women's Health Initiative study of an increased risk of breast cancer among postmenopausal women using combination hormone replacement therapy (both estrogen and progestin). A cause-effect relationship between HRT and breast cancer risk is strongly supported by the temporal nature, specificity, and biological plausibility of this association.

Elevated blood glucose. The Nurses' Health Study found that postmenopausal women with diabetes had a slightly greater risk for breast cancer.[27] Other studies have found greater risk for breast cancer in nondiabetic women with higher levels of fasting glucose.[28,29]

Insufficient vitamin D. In a pooled analysis of two studies examining vitamin D and risk of breast cancer, women whose serum 25(OH) D levels were in the lowest quintile (<13 ng/dL) had twice the odds of developing breast cancer as those whose levels were in the highest quintile (>52 ng/dL.) An inverse dose-response relationship was detected, suggesting that the lower the circulating vitamin D level, the higher the risk of breast cancer.[30] The authors reported that a level of 50 ng/dL could be achieved by oral intake of 2,000 IU of vitamin D_3, coupled with moderate, regular sun exposure.

Increased birth weight. In a review of 26 studies that examined the association between weight at birth and subsequent risk of breast cancer, the majority of studies detected associations between birth weight and premenopausal, but not postmenopausal, disease.[31] This suggests that breast cancer risk may be influenced by the intrauterine environment (eg, by increased levels of biologically active growth factors).

Diagnosis

Breast self-examination and clinical examination by a health care provider are used for screening, although the efficacy remains controversial. Mammography screening clearly decreases mortality for women over 50 years of age. Women usually receive initial screenings at 40 to 50 years but may begin earlier depending on individual risk factors.

Presenting signs and symptoms of breast cancer may include palpable breast mass (most common), dimpling, or pain; nipple inversion or unilateral nipple discharge (especially when bloody or watery); and *peau d'orange* ("orange peel skin"), erythema, or other skin changes.

All breast lumps should be evaluated thoroughly with mammography, ultrasound, or fine-needle aspiration biopsy (FNAB). Mammography is not usually recommended in women under 35 years. FNAB and ultrasound determine whether the lump is a simple cyst or a complex/solid mass.

A suspicious mass on mammogram requires tissue sample, and a mass not certainly benign requires ultrasound (or magnified or spot compression mammography).

An FNAB with bloody aspirate must be cytologically evaluated.

Recurrent/residual lumps must be re-evaluated and may need core or excisional biopsy. Solid cysts may still be diagnosed with cells from the needle. Benign cells require a mammogram, and nondiagnostic cells require repeat FNAB, core, or excisional biopsy.

Complex cysts or solid masses on ultrasound need FNAB, core, or excisional biopsy for definitive evaluation.

It is important to follow up all masses that were determined to be benign, using appropriate guidelines.

Treatment

Treatment is based on the TNM staging system: primary tumor size, regional lymph node involvement, and presence of distant metastasis. Surgery, radiation, and chemotherapy (including hormone therapy) are involved in primary treatment of breast cancer. Many possible algorithms exist, and each patient's presentation should be evaluated to determine the best treatment.

Factors that will affect the prognosis and preferred treatment are the size of the tumor, degree of invasiveness, lymph node involvement, menopausal status, age, hormone receptor status, and other tumor markers such as presence of HER2/neu receptors. Tumor histology is less important than invasiveness. Invasive disease usually requires surgical and nodal resection and postoperative adjuvant therapy, whereas in situ disease usually only requires surgery. An exception to this rule is inflammatory breast cancer, which typically calls for chemotherapy prior to surgical excision.

The choice of primary therapy often presents difficulties for doctors and patients because of patients' nonmedical priorities. Breast-conserving procedures, such as lumpectomy or segmental mastectomy followed by radiation, may be considered in the case of smaller, unifocal tumors and/or larger breasts where a good cosmetic result is anticipated. Mastectomy virtually eliminates the risk of local recurrence but does not confer higher overall survival compared with more limited surgery. Occasionally, radiation may be required after a mastectomy, such as in the case of a chest wall recurrence.

Primary treatment of breast cancer also usually includes excision of all or a sample of axillary lymph nodes. When axillary nodes are positive, chemotherapy or hormonal therapy is generally recommended. However, axillary node dissection carries risks of lymphedema. Alternatively, sentinel node biopsy, a newer and increasingly common form of nodal examination, can be performed, reducing the risk of lymphedema. However, discovery of a cancerous node on sentinel node biopsy may still necessitate further axillary lymph node removal or irradiation.

Women with estrogen-receptor-positive or progesterone-receptor-positive cancers may benefit from adjuvant treatment with tamoxifen and/or aromatase inhibitors such as exemestane or anastrozole. Conversely, women who are receptor-negative may benefit from adjuvant chemotherapy, particularly if they are under 50 years or premenopausal. Hormonal therapy or chemotherapy is often used in the treatment of recurrent or systemic disease. Women who have aggressive, unresponsive tumors, but who are positive for HER-2/neu receptor, frequently respond to trastuzumab, a drug therapy created to target HER-2/neu protein.

Among high-risk women without breast cancer, tamoxifen taken for 5 years decreases the risk of developing breast cancer by 50% or more.[32]

Genetic tests may help identify those who are most likely to benefit from treatment, though further investigation of their utility is necessary.

Nutritional Considerations

Researchers have long noted the low incidence of breast cancer in countries where traditional diets based on plant foods prevail.[33-35] A striking increase in breast cancer incidence has been noted in immigrants who have abandoned traditional diets (eg, rice, vegetables, soy foods) and adopted Western diets high in meat, dairy products, and fat.[36] These observations have led scientists to hypothesize that diet-related factors, particularly obesity, play a key role in breast cancer risk. Part of this risk may be related to an increase in estrogen production from adipose tissue and to eating fatty, low-fiber foods that maintain elevated circulating estrogen concentrations.[37,38] Certain micronutrients, such as folate, that are commonly found in vegetables and fruits may also play a protective role. However, it may be that risk depends on dietary *patterns*, rather than on intake of individual foods or nutrients.

Prevention

The key issues that epidemiologic studies have identified as related to reduced risk include:

Maintenance of healthy body weight. Both the Women's Health Initiative (WHI) study, which included nearly 86,000 women,[39] and the Swedish Mammography Cohort study, involving nearly 52,000 women, as well as numerous other studies, indicate that breast cancer risk increases significantly with overweight and obesity.[40]

Reducing or eliminating alcohol. Alcohol intake is associated with a linear increase in incidence of breast cancer up to 5 drinks a day. Women who consumed 2 (approximately 30 g ethanol) or more drinks per day had a relative risk of 1.41 compared with nondrinkers.[41] Even 1 drink daily increases risk 9% to 10%.[41,42] The risk is additive with HRT.[43] Increased risk of breast cancer due to alcohol use may be mediated by the effect on sex hormone levels.

Avoidance of a Western dietary pattern. Diets in Western countries, high in meat and fat (particularly saturated and omega-6 fatty acids) and low in fruits, vegetables, legumes, whole grains, and fiber, are linked to higher breast cancer risk, although the specific aspects of this dietary pattern that account for this risk have not been clearly separated. Breast cancer is less prevalent in countries where diets are mainly plant-based, high in fruits, vegetables, grains, and legumes.[44,45] Incidence increases successively in first- and second-generation immigrants to North America.[13,16] Specific dietary factors under investigation for a potentially helpful role are described below, and it should be noted that research attention is focusing more on overall dietary patterns than on the effects of specific foods or single nutrients.[47]

a. Limiting or avoiding meat. In the Nurses' Health Study II involving over 90,000 women, higher intakes of red meat (more than 5-7 servings/week, compared with 3 or fewer servings/week) were associated with a 40% greater breast cancer risk in women with the more commonly diagnosed estrogen-receptor-positive / progesterone-receptor-positive breast cancer.[48] Similarly, in the UK Women's Cohort Study involving more than 35,000 women, those consuming the most red meat (an average of 2 oz/d compared with none) had a roughly 40% greater risk for breast cancer. In this same study, a high intake of all processed meats (>20 g/d) was associated with an approximately 65% greater risk for postmenopausal breast cancer, compared with not eating processed meat.[49] It is not yet clear whether these associations reflect the effect of meat-based diets on hormone concentrations, the presence of carcinogens (eg, heterocyclic amines, polycyclic aromatic hydrocarbons), or other factors.

b. Reducing fat. The relationship between fat intake and breast cancer is controversial. Data from international correlational studies support an association between fat intake and breast cancer risk.[50] Prospective studies within Western countries have been less convincing regarding a relationship between total fat intake and breast cancer risk, but some have indicted specific types of fat. In a 20-year follow-up study of more than 80,000 postmenopausal women in the Nurses' Health Study, neither the quantity nor specific type of fat intake in midlife was associated with greater breast cancer risk.[51] In the Nurses' Health Study II involving more than 90,000 women, those in the highest quintile of fat intake had a slightly increased risk for premenopausal breast cancer, attributed mainly to the intake of high-fat dairy products and red meat.[45] Similarly, the National Institutes of Health (NIH)-AARP Diet and Health Study involving nearly 189,000 women found that consumption of 40% of calories from fat was associated with a more than 30% greater risk for postmenopausal breast cancer, compared with eating half as much fat. Further analysis of subtype of fat consumed (ie, saturated, monounsaturated, polyunsaturated) indicated that only saturated fat was significantly associated with risk.[52]

High-fat diets (not just saturated fat) tend to promote weight gain, which may be associated with greater breast cancer risk (see above). Increased adiposity leads to higher serum estrogen levels, which, in turn, may also be associated with greater breast cancer risk. Dietary factors may also influence the age of menarche, which can also increase lifetime estrogen exposure.[53] Animal fat and animal protein intake are also associated with elevated levels of insulin-like growth factor-1 (IGF-1).[54] IGF-1 may, in turn, be associated with other established risk factors for breast cancer (eg, breast density).[55]

Aside from reducing saturated fat intake, there may be benefit in reducing consumption of omega-6 fats (arachidonic acid, linoleic acid). A 2005 study showed that postmenopausal women with the highest vegetable oil intake (a common source of omega-6 fats), in comparison with those consuming the least, had more than double the risk for breast cancer.[56] One presumptive mechanism, aside from a possible effect of fat on estrogen production, is an increase in formation of prostaglandin E_2 (an eicosanoid that triggers proliferation of tumor cells) through the cyclooxygenase (COX) enzyme. A role for this mechanism is supported by the fact that regular use of COX-inhibitory drugs (ASA and other NSAIDs) has been associated with a reduced breast cancer risk.[57,58]

The Women's Health Initiative (WHI) Dietary Modification Trial, which included 48,835 women, tested a diet that aimed to reduce fat intake to 20% of energy and to increase vegetable and fruit consumption. Selected participants were consuming more fat than the US average at study baseline. The actual fat intake achieved by study participants averaged 24% of energy at 1 year and drifted upward toward baseline values by the study's end. After 8.1 years of follow-up, breast cancer risk was 9% lower in the intervention group, compared with a control group, although this result did not reach statistical significance. One exception was for progesterone-receptor-negative tumors, for which the risk decreased by 24% (P=.001).[59] While the study results fueled pessimism about the ability of dietary changes to significantly alter breast cancer risk, it should be noted that the intervention diet included much more fat, meat, and dairy products than the Asian diets associated with lower cancer risk.

c. High-fiber diets. Dietary fiber interrupts the enterohepatic circulation of estrogen by binding unconjugated estrogens in the gastrointestinal tract.[60] High-fiber, low-fat diets reduce serum estradiol, which is known to be associated with breast cancer risk.[61] A large study of postmenopausal women found that those eating the most fiber had the lowest risk for breast cancer. In this group risk was even lower among women eating the least fat.[62] In addition to its influence on circulating estrogens, fiber has other physiologic effects that may reduce cancer risk. High-fiber diets help keep blood glucose levels within normal limits and lower the risk for adult-onset diabetes, both of which have been related to increased breast cancer risk.[28,29]

d. Fruits, vegetables, and legumes. Fruits and vegetables have a number of bioactive components that may confer protection against breast cancer. Folate may be especially important in women who consume alcohol.[63] Foods that contain folic acid (green leafy vegetables, legumes, oranges) are likely to be more effective than folate supplements, due to the presence of other protective factors (eg, fiber, beta-carotene, vitamin C, and phytochemicals). The European Investigation into Cancer and Nutrition (EPIC) study concluded that fruit and vegetable intake was not related to breast cancer risk.[64] However, a study that examined the risk for breast cancer in association with higher scoring on healthy dietary patterns (eg, the Alternate Healthy Eating Index, Recommended Food Score, or Alternate Mediterranean Diet) concluded that the vegetable component of these dietary patterns was protective against estrogen receptor-negative breast cancer. [65]

Consumption of legumes (including soy products) that are high in isoflavones and lignans is also associated with lower risk for breast cancer, an effect that is greater if intake of these foods begins before or during adolescence.[63] A greater intake of isoflavones was also found to protect against breast cancer in a study of more than 21,000 native Japanese women,[66] and a meta-analysis of epidemiologic studies indicated a 30% lower risk for premenopausal women and a nearly 25% lower risk for postmenopausal women who consumed the most soy.[67] Further evidence of the benefit of legumes and was noted in the Nurses' Health Study II, in which eating beans or lentils twice per week was associated with a 25% lower risk, compared with consuming those foods less than once per month.[68]

Survival after Diagnosis

The following considerations apply to recurrence and survival after diagnosis:

Lower body weight. Breast cancer patients with greater-than-average body weight experience a shortened survival time,[69] and Japanese women who have less body fat are more likely to survive breast cancer.[70] In the Nurses' Health Study, weight before diagnosis was positively associated with breast cancer recurrence and death.[71] Even differences in body weight within or near the normal range may influence mortality. A Shanghai study of women previously treated for breast cancer showed that, compared with women with a body mass index <23.0, mortality was higher in those with a body mass index of 23.0–24.99, and greater still among those with a body mass index of ≥25.[72]

Lower-fat diets. In Japan and certain other countries, age-adjusted death rates for breast cancer increased when high-fat foods (particularly butter and margarine, cheese, ham and sausage, and dairy products) became available.[73] Prospective studies suggest that women consuming less fat at the time of diagnosis, and perhaps those who later alter their diets to reduce fat intake, have a better prognosis.[74,75]

Results from a large randomized clinical trial, the Women's Intervention Nutrition Study (WINS), showed that postmenopausal women previously treated for breast cancer who ate a low-fat diet were less likely to develop a recurrence or a new primary cancer, compared with those who ate a more typical diet.[76] Risk of recurrence or new primary cancers was reduced by 24% for all breast cancers and by 42% for estrogen-receptor-negative cancers.

Fruits and vegetables. Diets high in fruits and vegetables may enhance survival from breast cancer. The Women's Healthy Eating and Living (WHEL) study combined a low-fat diet with an additional emphasis on vegetables and fruits for postmenopausal women previously treated for breast cancer. The intervention was predicated on earlier observational studies that had detected associations of either body weight or diet composition with disease-free or overall survival.[77,78] Women in the intervention group (an intensive arm fostering 5 daily vegetable servings plus 16 oz of vegetable juice; 3 fruit servings; 30 g of fiber; and 15% to 20% of energy intake from fat) of the WHEL study reduced serum concentrations of estradiol, bioavailable estradiol, estrone, and estrone sulfate.[79] Within the comparison group (a less intensive arm fostering 5 fruit and vegetable servings per day), variations in carotenoid concentrations in the blood (a marker for vegetable and fruit intake) were inversely associated with risk of recurrence or new primary cancers.[79] After follow-up for 5-11 years, those in the comparison group who consumed 5 or more daily servings of fruits and vegetables and engaged in an average of 30 minutes of walking 6 days per week had roughly half the mortality risk of those who either had less vegetable and fruit intake or who were less physically active.[80] However, no differences were observed between the intervention and comparison groups with respect to either disease-free survival or overall survival, suggesting that increasing vegetable and fruit intake beyond 5 servings per day was not associated with further benefits.[81]

More recent findings from the Long Island Breast Cancer Study Project involving more than 1200 women have also revealed a survival advantage with a change in diet. Women eating roughly 5-6 servings of fruits and vegetables per day had a roughly 25% lower all-cause mortality risk, compared with those consuming 0-2.5 daily servings. However, this was not significant after adjustment for age and energy intake, and exercise was not considered as a variable.[82]

Part of the apparent benefit may be attributable to the combinations of carotenoids, folate, and phytochemicals present in these foods.[63] In the National Breast Screening Study, a significantly lower risk of dying from breast cancer was observed with higher intakes of vitamin C and beta-carotene, 2 nutrients found in fruits and vegetables.[83]

Orders

During active treatment, dietary orders should be written in consultation between the treating physician and a consulting dietitian.

After treatment, a low-fat, vegetable-rich, plant-based diet.

Exercise prescription (30 minutes per day of walking or equivalent energy expenditure).

Alcohol cessation or minimization.

What to Tell the Family

The families of breast cancer patients play 2 key roles. The first is to assist the patient who is undergoing treatment, which can be arduous at times. Particularly important is helping the patient make diet and lifestyle changes that can support good health. Second, breast cancer sometimes runs in families. It is important for family members to not only have regular screening for the disease, but to also reduce their risk to the extent possible through the diet and lifestyle changes noted above.

References

1. National Cancer Institute. Surveillance Epidemiology and End Results: SEER. Available at: http://seer.cancer.gov/csr/1975_2000/results_merged/topic_lifetime_risk.pdf. Accessed December 12, 2005.

2. Kelsey JL, Fischer DB, Holford TR, et al. Exogenous estrogens and other factors in the epidemiology of breast cancer. *J Natl Cancer Inst*. 1981;67:327-333.

3. Trock BJ. Breast cancer in African American women: Epidemiology and tumor biology. *Breast Cancer Res Treat*. 1996;40:11-24.

4. Chevarley F, White E. Recent trends in breast cancer mortality among white and black U.S. women. *Am J Public Health.* 1997;87:775-781.

5. Weiss HA, Brinton LA, Brogan D, et al. Epidemiology of in situ and invasive breast cancer in women aged under 45. *Br J Cancer.* 1996;73:1298-1305.

6. Hankinson SE, Colditz GA, Manson JE, et al. A prospective study of oral contraceptive use and risk of breast cancer. *Cancer Causes Control.* 1997;8:65-72.

7. Marchbanks PA, McDonald JA, Wilson HG, et al. Oral contraceptives and the risk of breast cancer. *N Engl J Med.* 2002;346:2025-2032.

8. Collaborative Group on Hormonal Factors in Breast Cancer. Breast cancer and hormonal contraceptives: collaborative reanalysis of individual data on 53,297 women with breast cancer and 100,239 women without breast cancer from 54 epidemiological studies. *Lancet.* 1996;347:1713-1727.

9. Melbye M, Wohlfahrt J, Olsen JH, et al. Induced abortion and the risk of breast cancer. *N Engl J Med.* 1997;336:81-85.

10. Erlandsson G, Montgomery SM, Cnattingius S, Ekbom A. Abortions and breast cancer: record-based case-control study. *Int J Cancer.* 2003;103:676-679.

11. Paoletti X, Clavel-Chapelon F. Induced and spontaneous abortion and breast cancer risk: results from the E3N cohort study. *Int J Cancer.* 2003;106:270-276.

12. National Cancer Institute. Early Reproductive Events and Breast Cancer Workshop: Summary Report. Available at: http://www.cancer.gov/cancerinfo/ere-workshop-report. Accessed December 12, 2005.

13. Willett WC, Rockhill B, Hankinson SE, et al. Epidemiology and nongenetic causes of breast cancer. In: Harris JR, Lippman ME, Morrow M, Osborne CK, eds. *Diseases of the Breast.* 3rd ed. Philadelphia, Pa: Lippincott Williams & Wilkins; 2000:175.

14. Peto J, Mack TM. High constant incidence in twins and other relatives of women with breast cancer. *Nat Genet.* 2000;26:411-414.

15. Pike MC, Spicer DV, Dahmoush L, Press MF. Estrogens, progestogens, normal breast cell proliferation and breast cancer risk. *Epidemiol Rev.* 1993;15:17-35.

16. Collaborative Group on Hormonal Factors in Breast Cancer. Breast cancer and breast-feeding: collaborative reanalysis of individual data from 47 epidemiological studies in 30 countries, including 50,302 women with breast cancer and 96,973 women without the disease. *Lancet.* 2002;360:187-195.

17. Harris JR, Lippman ME, Veronesi U, Willett W. Breast cancer (1). *N Engl J Med.* 1992;327:319-328.

18. McTiernan A. Behavioral risk factors for breast cancer: can risk be modified? *Oncologist.* 2003;8:326-334.

19. Chang SC, Ziegler RG, Dunn B, et al. Association of energy intake and energy balance with postmenopausal breast cancer in the prostate, lung, colorectal, and ovarian cancer screening trial. *Cancer Epidemiol Biomarkers Prev.* 2006;15:334-341.

20. Adams SA, Matthews CE, Hebert JR, et al. Association of physical activity with hormone receptor status: the Shanghai Breast Cancer Study. *Cancer Epidemiol Biomarkers Prev.* 2006;15:1170-1178.

21. Key T, Appleby P, Barnes I, Reeves G, for the Endogenous Hormones and Breast Cancer Collaborative Group. Endogenous sex hormones and breast cancer in postmenopausal women: reanalysis of nine prospective studies. *J Natl Cancer Inst.* 2002;94:606-616.

22. Lippman ME, Krueger KA, Eckert S, et al. Indicators of lifetime estrogen exposure: effect on breast cancer incidence and interaction with raloxifene therapy in the multiple outcomes of raloxifene evaluation study participants. *J Clin Oncol.* 2001;19:3111-3116.

23. Fisher B, Dignam J, Wolmark N, et al. Tamoxifen in treatment of intraductal breast cancer: National surgical adjuvant breast and bowel project B-24 randomized controlled trial. *Lancet.* 1999;353:1993-2000.

24. Chlebowski RT, Hendrix SL, Langer RD, et al. Influence of estrogen plus progestin on breast cancer and mammography in healthy postmenopausal women: The Women's Health Initiative Randomized Trial. *JAMA.* 2003;289:3243-3253.

25. Li CI, Anderson BO, Daling JR, Moe RE. Trends in incidence rates of invasive lobular and ductal breast carcinoma. *JAMA.* 2003;289:1421-1424.

26. Verkooijen HM, Fioretta G, Vlastos G, et al. Important increase of invasive lobular breast cancer incidence in Geneva, Switzerland. *Int J Cancer.* 2003;104:778-781.

27. Michels KB, Solomon CG, Hu FB. Type 2 diabetes and subsequent incidence of breast cancer in the Nurses' Health Study. *Diabetes Care.* 2003;26:1752-1758.

28. Lawlor DA, Smith GD, Ebrahim S. Hyperinsulinaemia and increased risk of breast cancer: findings from the British Women's Heart and Health Study. *Cancer Causes Control.* 2004;15:267-275.

29. Muti P, Quattrin T, Grant BJ, et al. Fasting glucose is a risk factor for breast cancer: a prospective study. *Cancer Epidemiol Biomarkers Prev.* 2002;11:1361-1368.

30. Garland CF, Gorham ED, Mohr SB, et al. Vitamin D and prevention of breast cancer: pooled analysis. *J Steroid Biochem Mol Biol.* 2007;103:708-711.

31. Michels KB, Xue F. Role of birthweight in the etiology of breast cancer. *Int J Cancer.* 2006;119:2007-2025.

32. Fisher B, Costantino JP, Wickerham DL, et al. Tamoxifen for the prevention of breast cancer: report of the National Surgical Adjuvant Breast and Bowel Project P-1 study. *J Natl Cancer Inst.* 1998;90:1371-1388.

33. Hirose K, Takezaki T, Hamajima N, Miura S, Tajima K. Insulin, insulin-like growth factor-I and breast cancer risk in Japanese women. *Asian Pac J Cancer Prev.* 2003;4:239-246.

34. Trichopoulou A, Lagiou P, Kuper H, Trichopoulos D. Cancer and Mediterranean dietary traditions. *Cancer Epidemiol Biomarkers Prev.* 2000;9:869-873.

35. Prieto-Ramos F, Serra-Majem L, La Vecchia C, Ramon JM, Tresserras R, Salleras L. Mortality trends and past and current dietary factors of breast cancer in Spain. *Eur J Epidemiol.* 1996;12:141-148.

36. Hanf V, Gonder U. Nutrition and primary prevention of breast cancer: foods, nutrients and breast cancer risk. *Eur J Obstet Gynecol Reprod Biol.* 2005;123:139-149.

37. Wu AH, Pike MC, Stram DO. Meta-analysis: dietary fat intake, serum estrogen levels, and the risk of breast cancer. *J Natl Cancer Inst.* 1999;91:529-534.

38. Kasim-Karakas SE, Almario RU, Gregory L, et al. Effects of prune consumption on the ratio of 2-hydroxyestrone to 16alpha-hydroxyestrone. *Am J Clin Nutr.* 2002;76:1422-1427.

39. Morimoto LM, White E, Chen Z, et al. Obesity, body size, and risk of postmenopausal breast cancer: the Women's Health Initiative (United States). *Cancer Causes Control.* 2002;13:741-751.

40. Suzuki R, Rylander-Rudqvist T, Ye W, Saji S, Wolk A. Body weight and postmenopausal breast cancer risk defined by estrogen and progesterone receptor status among Swedish women: A prospective cohort study. *Int J Cancer.* 2006;119:1683-1689.

41. Smith-Warner SA, Spiegelman D, Yuan SS, et al. Alcohol and breast cancer in women: a pooled analysis of cohort studies. *JAMA*. 1998;279:535.

42. Longnecker MP. Alcoholic beverage consumption in relation to risk of breast cancer: meta-analysis and review. *Cancer Causes Control*. 1994;5:73-82.

43. Singletary KW, Gapstur SM. Alcohol and breast cancer: review of epidemiologic and experimental evidence and potential mechanisms. *JAMA*. 2001;286:2143-2151.

44. Boyd NF, Stone J, Vogt KN, Connelly BS, Martin LJ, Minkin S. Dietary fat and breast cancer risk revisited: a meta-analysis of the published literature. *Br J Cancer*. 2003;89:1672-1685.

45. Cho E, Spiegelman D, Hunter DJ, et al. Premenopausal fat intake and risk of breast cancer. *J Natl Cancer Inst*. 2003;95:1079-1085.

46. Henderson BE, Bernstein L. The international variation in breast cancer rates: an epidemiological assessment. Breast Cancer Res Treat. 1991;18(suppl 1):S11-S17.

47. Go VL, Wong DA, Butrum R. Diet, nutrition and cancer prevention: where are we going from here? *J Nutr*. 2001;131(suppl 11):3121S-3126S.

48. Cho E, Chen WY, Hunter DJ, et al. Red Meat Intake and Risk of Breast Cancer Among Premenopausal Women. *Arch Int Med*. 2006;166:2252-2259.

49. Taylor EF, Burley VJ, Greenwood DC, Cade JE. Meat consumption and risk of breast cancer in the UK Women's Cohort Study. *Br J Cancer*. 2007;96:1139-1146.

50. Prentice RL, Kakar F, Hursting S, Sheppard L, Klein R, Kushi LH. Aspects of the rationale for the Women's Health Trial. *J Natl Cancer Inst*. 1988;80:802-814.

51. Kim EH, Willett WC, Colditz GA, et al. Dietary Fat and Risk of Postmenopausal Breast Cancer in a 20-year Follow-up. *Am J Epidemiol*. 2006;164:990-997.

52. Thiebaut AC, Kipnis V, Chang SC, et al. Dietary fat and postmenopausal invasive breast cancer in the National Institutes of Health-AARP Diet and Health Study cohort. *J Natl Cancer Inst*. 2007;99:451-462.

53. Althuis MD, Fergenbaum JH, Garcia-Closas M, Brinton LA, Madigan MP, Sherman ME. Etiology of hormone receptor-defined breast cancer: a systematic review of the literature. *Cancer Epidemiol Biomarkers Prev*. 2004;13:1558-1568.

54. Allen NE, Appleby PN, Davey GK, Kaaks R, Rinaldi S, Key TJ. The associations of diet with serum insulin-like growth factor I and its main binding proteins in 292 women meat-eaters, vegetarians, and vegans. *Cancer Epidemiol Biomarkers Prev*. 2002;11:1441-1448.

55. dos Santos Silva I, Johnson N, De Stavola B, et al. The insulin-like growth factor system and mammographic features in premenopausal and postmenopausal women. *Cancer Epidemiol Biomarkers Prev*. 2006;15:449-455.

56. Wakai K, Tamakoshi K, Date C, et al. Dietary intakes of fat and fatty acids and risk of breast cancer: a prospective study in Japan. *Cancer Sci*. 2005;96:590-599.

57. Garcia Rodriguez LA, Gonzalez-Perez A. Risk of breast cancer among users of aspirin and other anti-inflammatory drugs. *Br J Cancer*. 2004;91:525-529.

58. Terry MB, Gammon MD, Zhang FF, et al. Association of frequency and duration of aspirin use and hormone receptor status with breast cancer risk. *JAMA*. 2004; 291:2433-2440.

59. Prentice RI, Caan B, Chlebowski RT, et al. Low-fat dietary pattern and risk of invasive breast cancer: The Women's Health Initiative randomized controlled Dietary Modification Trial. *JAMA*. 2006;295.629-642.

60. Institute of Medicine. Dietary Reference Intakes for Energy, Carbohydrate, Fiber, Fat, Fatty Acids, Cholesterol, Protein, and Amino Acids (Macronutrients). Washington, D.C.: National Academies Press, 2005.

61. Rock CL, Flatt SW, Thomson CA, et al. Effects of a high-fiber, low-fat diet intervention on serum concentrations of reproductive steroid hormones in women with a history of breast cancer. *J Clin Oncol.* 2004;22:2379-2387.

62. Mattisson I, Wirfalt E, Johansson U, Gullberg B, Olsson H, Berglund G. Intakes of plant foods, fiber and fat and risk of breast cancer- a prospective study in the Malmo Diet and Cancer cohort. *Br J Cancer.* 2004;90:122-127.

63. Duncan AM. The role of nutrition in the prevention of breast cancer. *AACN Clin Issues.* 2004;15:119-135.

64. van Gils CH, Peeters PHM, Bueno-de-Mesquita B, et al. Consumption of vegetables and fruits and risk of breast cancer. *JAMA.* 2005;293:183–193.

65. Fung TT, Hu FB, McCullough ML, Newby PK, Willett WC, Holmes MD. Diet quality is associated with the risk of estrogen receptor-negative breast cancer in postmenopausal women. *J Nutr.* 2006;136:466-472.

66. Yamamoto S, Sobue T, Kobayashi M, et al. Soy, isoflavones, and breast cancer risk in Japan. *J Natl Cancer Inst.* 2003;95:906-913.

67. Trock BJ, Hilakivi-Clarke L, Clarke R. Meta-analysis of soy intake and breast cancer risk. *JNCI.* 2006;98:459-471.

68. Adebamowo CA, Cho E, Sampson L, et al. Dietary flavonols and flavonol-rich foods intake and the risk of breast cancer. *Int J Cancer.* 2005;114:628-633.

69. Newman SC, Miller AB, Howe GR. A study of the effect of weight and dietary fat on breast cancer survival time. *Am J Epidemiol.* 1986;123:767-774.

70. Le Marchand L. Ethnic variation in breast cancer survival: a review. *Breast Cancer Res Treat.* 1991;18(suppl 1):S119-S126.

71. Kroenke CH, Chen WY, Rosner B, Holmes MD. Weight, weight gain, and survival after breast cancer diagnosis. *J Clin Oncol.* 2005;23:1370-1378.

72. Tao MH, Shu XO, Ruan ZX, Gao YT, Zheng W. Association of overweight with breast cancer survival. *Am J Epidemiol.* 2006;163:101-107.

73. Kato I, Tominaga S, Kuroishi T. Relationship between westernization of dietary habits and mortality from breast and ovarian cancers in Japan. *Jpn J Cancer Res.* 1987;78:349-357.

74. Borugian MJ, Sheps SB, Kim-Sing C, et al. Insulin, macronutrient intake, and physical activity: are potential indicators of insulin resistance associated with mortality from breast cancer? *Cancer Epidemiol Biomarkers Prev.* 2004;13:1163-1172.

75. Gregorio DI, Emrich LJ, Graham S, Marshall JR, Nemoto T. Dietary fat consumption and survival among women with breast cancer. *J Natl Cancer Inst.* 1985;75:37-41.

76. Chlebowski R. Low-fat diet may reduce risk of breast cancer relapse. American Society of Clinical Oncology annual meeting: Summary of clinical trial results. Available at: http://www.cancer.gov/clinicaltrials/results/low-fat-diet0505. Accessed December 12, 2005.

77. Rock CL, Demark-Wahnefried W. Nutrition and survival after the diagnosis of breast cancer: a review of the evidence. *J Clin Oncol.* 2002;20:3302-3316.

78. Rock CL, Flatt SW, Natarajan L, et al. Plasma carotenoids and recurrence-free survival in women with a history of breast cancer. *J Clin Oncol.* 2005;23:6631-6638.

79. Rock CL, Flatt SW, Thomson CA, et al. Effects of a high-fiber, low-fat diet intervention on serum concentrations of reproductive steroid hormones in women with a history of breast cancer. *J Clin Oncol.* 2004;12:2379-2387.

80. Pierce JP, Stefanick ML, Flatt SW, et al. Greater survival after breast cancer in physically active women with high vegetable-fruit intake regardless of obesity. *J Clin Oncol.* 2007;25:2345-2351.

81. Pierce JP, Natarajan L, Caan BJ, et al. Influence of a diet very high in vegetables, fruit, and fiber and low in fat on prognosis following treatment for breast cancer: The Women's Healthy Eating and Living (WHEL) randomized trial. *JAMA.* 2007;298:289-298.

82. Fink BN, Gaudet MM, Britton JA, et al. Fruits, vegetables, and micronutrient intake in relation to breast cancer survival. *Breast Cancer Res Treat.* 2006;98:199-208.

83. Jain M, Miller AB, To T. Premorbid diet and the prognosis of women with breast cancer. *J Natl Cancer Inst.* 1994;86:1390-1397.

24. Ovarian Cancer

Ovarian cancer is the second most common gynecologic cancer (after cervical cancer) and the leading cause of death from gynecologic cancer in the United States. It generally affects women aged 40 to 65.

The ovary is composed of epithelial cells along the surface, germ (egg-producing) cells, and surrounding connective tissue. Each of these cell types has the potential for malignant transformation. In addition, breast and gastrointestinal cancers commonly metastasize to the ovaries. The most common ovarian malignancy is epithelial carcinoma (approximately 90% of cases), which is the focus of this chapter.

In the early stages, ovarian cancer usually causes subtle and nonspecific symptoms that rarely prompt a woman to seek medical attention. More severe symptoms, often associated with ovarian torsion or rupture, are rare. As a result, only about 20% of cases are diagnosed at an early stage.

Nonspecific symptoms may include:

- Anorexia and fatigue.
- Low abdominal discomfort (eg, pressure, swelling, cramps, bloating, flatus).
- Low back pain.
- Early satiety and maldigestion.
- Nausea, diarrhea, and constipation.

- Frequent urination.

- Weight gain or loss.

- Irregular or abnormal vaginal bleeding, and dyspareunia.

- Unilateral or bilateral lower extremity edema.

Risk Factors

Possible risk factors are listed below, although the exact mechanisms of induction are not clearly understood.

Nulliparity or infertility.

Age. Most ovarian cancers occur in women over 50 years, with the highest risk for those over 60.

Family history. Women who have relatives with ovarian cancer have an approximately 3-fold increased risk, with multiple affected relatives raising the risk further.

BRCA gene mutation. Women with a BRCA1 or BRCA2 mutation have a 25% to 45% lifetime risk of ovarian malignancy, with BRCA1 generally presenting a higher risk.

Race. White women have higher rates of ovarian cancer than black women.[1]

Previous cancer. Women with a history of breast cancer or colon cancer may have an increased risk.

Endometriosis.

Diet. See Nutritional Considerations below.

In addition, estrogen-replacement therapy, smoking, and obesity may be risk factors. Breast-feeding, previous pregnancy (and especially multiparity), oral contraceptive use, tubal ligation, and hysterectomy may reduce risk for ovarian cancer.

Diagnosis

A careful history may reveal multiple, frequent symptoms with a relatively acute onset and severity but is unlikely to distinguish between benign and malignant disease.

Physical examination may reveal no pertinent findings, as an early tumor is often not palpable. However, as the tumor enlarges, a lower abdominal mass may be felt. Pelvic examination may reveal an asymptomatic, irregular, and fixed adnexal mass. Although not pathognomonic for ovarian cancer, especially in premenopausal women, a pelvic or abdominal mass should prompt further evaluation through imaging and/or laboratory testing.

Ultrasound helps to distinguish benign from malignant masses. In cases where ultrasound reveals an apparently benign mass, continued observation may be prudent. However, if a malignant mass is a possibility, most women should undergo surgical biopsy to determine a histologic diagnosis. Ultrasound may also serve as an annual screening tool in women with the BRCA gene mutation.

CT scan and MRI are not helpful for the diagnosis of a known pelvic mass, but they may reveal extraovarian primary tumors or serve to quantify the extent of metastases prior to surgery.

Tumor markers, such as CA-125, are not helpful for screening or diagnosis because they can be elevated in benign conditions (eg, endometriosis), particularly in premenopausal women, and also in nonovarian malignancies. CA-125 is also not always positive in early stages of ovarian cancer. However, in postmenopausal women, the test has a positive predictive value of 97%.[2] The CA-125 marker is used to monitor treatment of ovarian cancer, comparing presurgery and posttreatment levels.

Treatment

The preferred treatment depends on histology and surgical tumor staging:

- **Stage I** is limited to the ovary or ovaries.
- **Stage II** includes pelvic extension.
- **Stage III** includes extrapelvic peritoneal spread and/or inguinal or retroperitoneal lymph node involvement.
- **Stage IV** involves distant metastases.

In early stages, treatment involves surgical resection, along with abdominal hysterectomy, bilateral salpingo-oophorectomy, omentectomy, and selective lymphadenectomy. With more advanced disease, surgical removal and postoperative chemotherapy are indicated.

Nutritional Considerations

Epidemiologic investigations have revealed important clues to etiological factors in ovarian cancer. Mortality in both the Mediterranean region[3] and Asia[4] is associated with consumption of meat, milk, and animal fat. These associations have not yet been tested in randomized clinical trials. Nonetheless, they suggest important hypotheses regarding possible means to reduce risk.

Diet and Prevention of Ovarian Cancer

The following factors are under investigation for a possible role in reducing ovarian cancer risk:

Avoiding or reducing meat and saturated fat. A high intake of fat is associated with an approximately 25% increase in risk for ovarian cancer, and most of this risk is attributed to saturated fat intake.[5] Various food sources of saturated fat have been implicated, including meat,[6,7] eggs,[8] and whole milk.[9] An analysis of pooled data from studies involving more than 523,000 women found a roughly 30% greater risk for ovarian cancer in women consuming the most saturated fat, compared with those consuming the lowest amount, although total fat was not associated with risk.[10] Animal fat and meat influence estrogen activity and increase blood concentrations of insulin-like growth factor-1 (IGF-1),[11] a polypeptide implicated in several cancers, including ovarian cancer.[12] However, German investigators found no association between animal food consumption and ovarian cancer.[13]

Avoiding milk. Studies of dairy products and ovarian cancer risk have produced conflicting results and are a subject of some controversy. Although some studies have not revealed a relationship, a meta-analysis of prospective study data concluded that each glass of milk consumed daily raised the risk for ovarian cancer by 13%, on average.[14] In addition, a pooled analysis of 12 prospective cohort studies including 553,217 women concluded that consumption of 3 dairy servings per day was associated with a 20% increased risk for this cancer, compared with 1 serving per day.[15]

Saturated fat aside, even consumption of small amounts of skim or low-fat milk (1 or more servings daily) has been associated with an increased risk for ovarian cancer. This has been attributed to galactose-related oocyte toxicity and/or elevation of gonadotropin concentrations.[16,17] Milk consumption also elevates IGF-1 blood concentrations. Some researchers have suggested this is due to the fact that cow's milk contains IGF-1 that is identical to the growth factor produced by humans.[18] However, milk's macronutrients also stimulate IGF-1 production within the human body.

Increased fruit and vegetable intake. A protective effect of fruits and vegetables remains uncertain. Some studies found that women eating 3 or more vegetable servings per day had a 39% lower risk for ovarian cancer, compared with women eating 1 or fewer servings per day.[17] However, these benefits may relate only to fruit and vegetable intake during adolescence.[19] Further, both the European Prospective Investigation into Cancer and Nutrition (EPIC) study (involving more than 325,000 women)[20] and the Netherlands Cohort Study on Diet and Cancer (involving more than 62,000 women)[21] failed to show a protective effect of high fruit and vegetable intakes.

Avoidance of obesity. Obesity in adolescence or early adulthood increases later risk for ovarian cancer by 1.5 to 2 times that of women with normal body mass index (BMI).[22,23]

Tea and alcohol intake. The Swedish Mammography Cohort[24] found an inverse association of tea drinking with ovarian cancer, while the Iowa Women's Health Study suggested a roughly 50% lower risk with weekly tea consumption (<1 cup/d).[25] These effects may be attributed to the ability of tea to reduce estradiol levels in women.[26]

Alcohol intake may be protective against ovarian cancer.[27] However, this may be contingent upon a relatively high folate intake (eg, >360 µg/d compared with <250 µg/d),[28] concentrations of which become depleted by alcohol use. Nonetheless, this association is not a reason to initiate or maintain alcohol consumption, given that alcohol contributes to risk of breast cancer and other chronic health problems.

Diet and Survival After Ovarian Cancer Diagnosis

The preceding studies relate to risk of developing ovarian cancer. Some studies suggest that diet may also play a role after diagnosis. The following foods are under study:

Vegetables. Women with ovarian cancer who consume vegetable-rich diets tend to have enhanced survival. In a population-based, case-controlled study, women who consumed the most vegetables had a 25% lower mortality risk, compared with women consuming the least. A similar association was found in these women for the intake of cruciferous vegetables (including broccoli, cauliflower, and cabbage), and survival was inversely associated with intake of red meat, white meat, and total protein.[29]

Green tea. In a study of 254 women with histopathologically confirmed ovarian cancer followed for 3 years or more, a dose-response relationship was observed between tea intake and survival. Drinking 1 cup or more of green tea per day was associated with a 57% lower mortality.[30] Although green tea is known to inhibit cancer growth through a variety of mechanisms in vitro and in vivo,[31] further study is needed to assess the benefit of green tea for promoting cancer survival.

Orders

See Basic Diet Orders chapter.

Weight loss, as appropriate. See Obesity chapter.

Smoking cessation.

What to Tell the Family

Risk of developing ovarian cancer or of succumbing to it may be reduced through healthy diet and lifestyle practices, along with timely screening and early intervention. Family members may support the patient and improve their own health by adopting the same changes. Smoking cessation, maintenance of a healthy weight, and breast-feeding should all be encouraged.

References

1. Mink PJ, Sherman ME, Devesa SS. Incidence patterns of invasive and borderline ovarian tumors among white women and black women in the United States. *Cancer.* 2002;95:2380-2389.

2. American College of Obstetricians and Gynecologists. ACOG Committee Opinion Number 280: The role of the generalist obstetrician-gynecologist in the early detection of ovarian cancer. *Obstet Gynecol.* 2002;100:1413-1416.

3. Serra-Majem L, La Vecchia C, Ribas-Barba L, et al. Changes in diet and mortality from selected cancers in southern Mediterranean countries, 1960-1989. *Eur J Clin Nutr.* 1993;47(suppl 1):S25-S34.

4. Kato I, Tominaga S, Kuroishi T. Relationship between westernization of dietary habits and mortality from breast and ovarian cancers in Japan. *Jpn J Cancer Res.* 1987;78:349-357.

5. Huncharek M, Kupelnick B. Dietary fat intake and risk of epithelial ovarian cancer: a meta-analysis of 6,689 subjects from 8 observational studies. *Nutr Cancer.* 2001;40:87-91.

6. Mori M, Miyake H. Dietary and other risk factors of ovarian cancer among elderly women. *Jpn J Cancer Res.* 1988;79:997-1004.

7. La Vecchia C, Decarli A, Negri E, et al. Dietary factors and the risk of epithelial ovarian cancer. *J Natl Cancer Inst.* 1987;79:663-669.

8. Risch HA, Jain M, Marrett LD, Howe GR. Dietary fat intake and risk of epithelial ovarian cancer. *J Natl Cancer Inst.* 1994;86:1409-1415.

9. Mettlin CJ, Piver MS. A case-control study of milk-drinking and ovarian cancer risk. *Am J Epidemiol.* 1990;132:871-876.

10. Genkinger JM, Hunter DJ, Spiegelman D, et al. A pooled analysis of 12 cohort studies of dietary fat, cholesterol and egg intake and ovarian cancer. *Cancer Causes Control.* 2006;17:273-285.

11. Heald AH, Cade JE, Cruickshank JK, Anderson S, White A, Gibson JM. The influence of dietary intake on the insulin-like growth factor (IGF) system across three ethnic groups: a population-based study. *Public Health Nutr.* 2003;6:175-180.

12. Druckmann R, Rohr UD. IGF-1 in gynecology and obstetrics: update 2002. *Maturitas.* 2002;41(suppl 1):S65-S83.

13. Schulz M, Nothlings U, Allen N, et al. No association of consumption of animal foods with risk of ovarian cancer. *Cancer Epidemiol Biomarkers Prev.* 2007;16:852-855.

14. Larsson SC, Orsini N, Wolk A. Milk, milk products and lactose intake and ovarian cancer risk: a meta-analysis of epidemiological studies. *Int J Cancer.* 2006;118:431-441.

15. Genkinger JM, Hunter DJ, Spiegelman D, et al. Dairy products and ovarian cancer: a pooled analysis of 12 cohort studies. *Cancer Epidemiol Biomarkers Prev.* 2006;15:364-372.

16. Fairfield KM, Hunter DJ, Colditz GA, et al. A prospective study of dietary lactose and ovarian cancer. *Int J Cancer.* 2004;110:271-277.

17. Larsson SC, Bergkvist L, Wolk A. Milk and lactose intakes and ovarian cancer risk in the Swedish Mammography Cohort. *Am J Clin Nutr.* 2004;80:1353-1357.

18. Allen NE, Appleby PN, Davey GK, Kaaks R, Rinaldi S, Key TJ. The associations of diet with serum insulin-like growth factor I and its main binding proteins in 292 women meat-eaters, vegetarians and vegans. *Cancer Epidemiol Biomarkers Prev.* 2002;11:1441-1448.

19. Fairfield KM, Hankinson SE, Rosner BA, Hunter DJ, Colditz GA, Willett WC. Risk of ovarian carcinoma and consumption of vitamins A, C, and E and specific carotenoids: a prospective analysis. *Cancer.* 2001;92:2318-2326.

20. Schulz M, Lahmann PH, Boeing H, et al. Fruit and vegetable consumption and risk of epithelial ovarian cancer: the European Prospective Investigation into Cancer and Nutrition. *Cancer Epidemiol Biomarkers Prev.* 2005;14(pt 1):2531-2535.

21. Mommers M, Schouten LJ, Goldbohm RA, van den Brandt PA. Consumption of vegetables and fruits and risk of ovarian carcinoma. *Cancer.* 2005;104:1512-1519.

22. Engeland A, Tretli S, Bjorge T. Height, body mass index, and ovarian cancer: a follow-up of 1.1 million Norwegian women. *J Natl Cancer Inst.* 2003;95:1244-1248.

23. Fairfield KM, Willett WC, Rosner BA, Manson JE, Speizer FE, Hankinson SE. Obesity, weight gain, and ovarian cancer. *Obstet Gynecol.* 2002;100:288-296.

24. Larsson SC, Wolk A. Tea consumption and ovarian cancer risk in a population-based cohort. *Arch Intern Med.* 2005;165:2683-2686.

25. Zheng W, Doyle TJ, Kushi LH, Sellers TA, Hong CP, Folsom AR. Tea consumption and cancer incidence in a prospective cohort study of postmenopausal women. *Am J Epidemiol.* 1996;144:175-182.

26. Kapiszewska M, Miskiewicz M, Ellison PT, Thune I, Jasienska G. High tea consumption diminishes salivary 17beta-estradiol concentration in Polish women. *Br J Nutr.* 2006;95:989-995.

27. Kushi LH, Mink PJ, Folsom AR, et al. Prospective study of diet and ovarian cancer. *Am J Epidemiol.* 1999;149:21-31.

28. Navarro Silvera SA, Jain M, Howe GR, Miller AB, Rohan TE. Dietary folate consumption and risk of ovarian cancer: a prospective cohort study. *Eur J Cancer Prev.* 2006;15:511-515.

29. Nagle CM, Purdie DM, Webb PM, Green A, Harvey PW, Bain CJ. Dietary influences on survival after ovarian cancer. *Int J Cancer*. 2003;106:264-269.

30. Zhang M, Lee AH, Binns CW, Xie X. Green tea consumption enhances survival of epithelial ovarian cancer. *Int J Cancer*. 2004;112:465-469.

31. Chung FL, Schwartz J, Herzog CR, Yang YM. Tea and cancer prevention: studies in animals and humans. *J Nutr*. 2003;133:3268S-3274S.

25. Endometrial Cancer

Cancer of the endometrium, the mucous membrane lining of the uterus, accounts for 90% of uterine cancers. With nearly 40,000 new cases annually, it is the most common gynecologic cancer in the United States and the fourth most common cancer found in women. It occurs most frequently after menopause.

Epithelial and muscle cells of the uterus have potential for malignant transformation and constitute the 2 main histologic subtypes of uterine cancer: adenocarcinoma and sarcoma. Adenocarcinoma, the most common uterine malignancy, is the focus of this chapter.

Abnormal vaginal bleeding is the most common symptom of endometrial cancer, but a woman may also experience discharge, weight loss, abdominal or pelvic pain, dysuria, and/or dyspareunia. Vaginal bleeding in any postmenopausal woman should be considered uterine cancer until proven otherwise.

Most endometrial cancers are slow-growing and are discovered at an early stage. These cases can be successfully treated, usually by hysterectomy, with better than 90% cure rates. Advanced cases that spread beyond the uterus are often fatal.

The underlying cause is unknown, but estrogen likely plays a central role. Type 1 endometrial carcinomas demonstrate a response to estrogen, whereas type 2 carcinomas do not. Because type 2 tumors lack well-identified risk factors, the following risk factors relate to type 1 endometrial carcinoma.

Risk Factors

Although endometrial cancer is more common in whites, blacks often have worse outcomes from the disease.[1]

The following factors are also associated with risk:

Obesity. A majority of patients diagnosed with endometrial cancer at a young age are obese.[2] The European Prospective Investigation into Cancer and Nutrition (EPIC) study including over 220,000 women found a nearly 80% greater risk for obese women, compared with those of normal weight. Risk increased by 300% in women who were morbidly obese (BMI ≥40).[3] Other studies have reached similar conclusions.[4-6] The relationship between obesity and cancer may be explained by obesity-related elevations in sex steroid hormones and growth factors.[7] Peripheral conversion of androgens to estrogen in adipose tissue leads to greater endogenous estrogen concentrations in obese persons.

Age. Risk increases with age, and the disease generally affects women over 50 years.

Menopausal Estrogen Therapy. Unopposed estrogen increases risk, but the combined use of estrogen and progestin is not associated with increased risk.

Diabetes.

Hypertension.

Physical inactivity.

Polycystic ovary syndrome (PCOS). Anovulation from PCOS or other causes results in persistent exposure to unopposed endogenous estrogen.

Prolonged exposure to estrogen. Early menarche, late menopause, and nulliparity (especially when due to anovulation) may increase the risk.

Genetics. A family history of hereditary nonpolyposis colorectal cancer greatly increases the risk.

Estrogen-secreting tumors or history of estrogen-responsive cancer.

Decreased sex-hormone binding globulin levels.

Tamoxifen use. There is an increased risk in women using tamoxifen as therapy for breast cancer.

Oral contraceptive use, multiparity, and exercise are considered protective.

Diagnosis

The patient's medical history may reveal abnormal vaginal bleeding or discharge in addition to nonspecific findings, such as lower abdominal pain, dysuria, and dyspareunia. Pelvic exam may reveal uterine enlargement but cannot distinguish whether it is benign or malignant. An incidental Pap smear finding of either normal or atypical endometrial cells increases the chance of a uterine cancer diagnosis. However, a normal Pap result does not rule out endometrial cancer.

Endometrial biopsy is indicated in any postmenopausal woman with vaginal bleeding and should follow any Pap smear that shows endometrial cells, whether normal or atypical, because the mere presence of endometrial cells may be a sign of endometrial pathology. Biopsy may not be necessary in asymptomatic premenopausal women. Annual endometrial biopsy may be used to screen women with a personal or family history of hereditary nonpolyposis colorectal cancer gene mutations or an extensive family history of colon cancer.

Hysteroscopy or dilation and curettage can also provide endometrial tissue samples, but these procedures are far more invasive, require anesthesia, and have more frequent complications compared with endometrial biopsy. Although it is the preferred procedure for diagnosis, hysteroscopy can be reserved for cases in which endometrial biopsy is inconclusive, but the pre-test probability for cancer is high.

Transvaginal ultrasound can measure the endometrial thickness, which should be less than 4 mm in a postmenopausal woman. Sonohysterography, which involves infusion of fluid into the uterus, may also help distinguish normal from abnormal endometrium.

Treatment

Endometrial cancer staging requires hysterectomy and bilateral salpingo-oophorectomy. Perioperative inspection of the opened uterus, along with clinical history, helps determine whether lymphadenectomy is required. Selective lymphadenectomy reduces associated morbidity and mortality. Peritoneal fluid cytology should be obtained during surgery for purposes of staging.

Surgical cytoreduction, radiation, hormone therapy, and chemotherapy may all be part of a treatment regimen. Progestin therapy without hysterectomy may be used in women with the lowest stage or grade of disease who would like to preserve their fertility.

The International Federation of Gynecology and Obstetrics defines the following stages of endometrial cancer:

I. Cancer only in body of uterus.

II. Cancer spread from uterus to cervix.

III. Cancer spread outside the uterus but inside the pelvis; bladder and rectum are not affected; lymph nodes may be positive.

IV. Cancer involves bladder, rectum, or organ outside pelvis.

Cancer antigen (CA)-125 measured preoperatively helps predict whether the cancer has spread beyond the uterus. However, it cannot be used as a screening tool or as a substitute for surgical staging.

Nutritional Considerations

As with many cancers, the risk for uterine cancers appears to be associated with greater intakes of foods found in Western diets (animal products, refined carbohydrates). Risk may be lower among women whose diets are high in fruits, vegetables, whole grains, and legumes. The lower risk in persons eating plant-based diets may be related to a reduced amount of free hormones circulating in the blood or to a protective effect of micronutrients found in these diets.

The following factors are under study for possible protective effects:

Eating less meat and fat. One study found a 50% greater risk of endometrial cancer among women who consumed the greatest amount of processed meat and fish.[8] Another found that consumption of red meat and eggs is also associated with greater endometrial cancer risk.[9] Overall, case-control studies have identified increased risk of endometrial cancer associated with intake of meat, particularly red meat, a finding not reflected in most prospective studies.[10]

Higher intake of fat, particularly saturated fat, is associated with elevations of endometrial cancer risk of approximately 60% to 80%.[9,11] Some evidence indicates that this association is due to the influence of dietary fat on adiposity and, consequently, on circulating estrogens.

Fruits, vegetables, whole grains, and legumes. Available evidence suggests that vegetables, fruits, and the nutrients these foods contain (ie, vitamin C, various carotenoids, folate, phytosterols) may be associated with reduced risk of endometrial cancer. The hypothesized risk reduction may be as high as 50% to 60%.[12,13] In the American Cancer Society's Cancer Prevention Study II Nutrition Cohort of over 41,000 women, protective effects of vegetables and fruits (20% and 25% lower risk, respectively) were identified only in women who had both never used hormone therapy and were consuming the largest amounts of these foods.[14]

An inverse association between whole grain intake and endometrial cancer has been observed, although some data suggest that this benefit may be restricted to women who have never used hormones.[15] Higher intakes of soy and other legumes may also decrease risk.[9]

Some whole grains and most legumes have a low glycemic index (a ranking of carbohydrate-containing foods based on the food's effect on blood sugar compared with a standard reference food's effect). Women whose diets had the most high–glycemic index foods had a roughly 50% greater risk for endometrial cancer than those whose diets had the lowest amount of these foods. Among obese women (BMI >30), the risk for endometrial cancer in those eating the most high–glycemic index foods was increased by roughly 90%.[16] Among nondiabetic women, those whose diets were highest in glycemic load (glycemic index of a food times the number of grams of carbohydrates in the food serving) had a roughly 45% greater risk for endometrial cancer.[17]

Moderating alcohol consumption. Studies on alcohol intake and risk for uterine cancer have produced conflicting results, with various studies finding no association, a protective effect, or increased risk. The Multiethnic Cohort Study of 41,574 women found a significantly greater risk (twice that of non-drinkers) in those having 2 or more alcoholic beverages daily.[18] However, the Netherlands Cohort Study of 62,573 women found no evidence of increased risk associated with alcohol use.[19]

Orders

See Basic Diet Orders chapter.

What to Tell the Family

The 5-year survival rate for uterine cancers is high, particularly with early detection and treatment. The family may support the patient's adherence to diet and exercise recommendations by adopting the same practices, which are likely to improve their health as well. Some evidence suggests that following a low-fat, plant-based diet, maintaining a healthy weight, and getting regular exercise may reduce the risk of this disease.

References

1. Connell PP, Rotmensch J, Waggoner SE, Mundt AJ. Race and clinical outcome in endometrial carcinoma. *Obstet Gynecol.* 1999;94:713-720.

2. Soliman PT, Oh JC, Schmeler KM, et al. Risk factors for young premenopausal women with endometrial cancer. *Obstet Gynecol.* 2005;105:575-580.

3. Friedenreich C, Cust A, Lahmann PH, et al. Anthropometric factors and risk of endometrial cancer: the European prospective investigation into cancer and nutrition. *Cancer Causes Control*. 2007;18:399-413.

4. Schouten LJ, Goldbohm RA, van den Brandt PA. Anthropometry, physical activity, and endometrial cancer risk: results from the Netherlands Cohort Study. *J Natl Cancer Inst*. 2004;96:1635-1638.

5. Reeves GK, Pirie K, Beral V, Green J, Spencer E, Bull D; Million Women Study Collaboration. Cancer incidence and mortality in relation to body mass index in the Million Women Study: cohort study. *BMJ*. 2007;335:1134-1146.

6. Chang SC, Lacey JV Jr, Brinton LA, et al. Lifetime weight history and endometrial cancer risk by type of menopausal hormone use in the NIH-AARP diet and health study. *Cancer Epidemiol Biomarkers Prev*. 2007;16:723-730.

7. Kaaks R, Lukanova A, Kurzer MS. Obesity, endogenous hormones, and endometrial cancer risk: a synthetic review. *Cancer Epidemiol Biomarkers Prev*. 2002;11:1531-1543.

8. Zheng W, Kushi LH, Potter JD, et al. Dietary intake of energy and animal foods and endometrial cancer incidence. The Iowa women's health study. *Am J Epidemiol*. 1995;142:388-394.

9. Goodman MT, Hankin JH, Wilkens LR, et al. Diet, body size, physical activity, and the risk of endometrial cancer. *Cancer Res*. 1997;57:5077-5085.

10. Bandera EV, Kushi LH, Moore DF, Gifkins DM, McCullough ML. Consumption of animal foods and endometrial cancer risk: a systematic literature review and meta-analysis. *Cancer Causes Control*. 2007;18:967-988.

11. Littman AJ, Beresford SA, White E. The association of dietary fat and plant foods with endometrial cancer (United States). *Cancer Causes Control*. 2001;12:691-702.

12. McCann SE, Freudenheim JL, Marshall JR, Brasure JR, Swanson MK, Graham S. Diet in the epidemiology of endometrial cancer in western New York (United States). *Cancer Causes Control*. 2000;11:965-974.

13. Barbone F, Austin H, Partridge EE. Diet and endometrial cancer: a case-control study. *Am J Epidemiol*. 1993;137:393-403.

14. McCullough ML, Bandera EV, Patel R, et al. A prospective study of fruits, vegetables, and risk of endometrial cancer. *Am J Epidemiol*. 2007;166:902-911.

15. Kasum CM, Nicodemus K, Harnack LJ, et al. Whole grain intake and incident endometrial cancer: the Iowa Women's Health Study. *Nutr Cancer*. 2001;39:180-186.

16. Silvera SA, Rohan TE, Jain M, Terry PD, Howe GR, Miller AB. Glycaemic index, glycaemic load and risk of endometrial cancer: a prospective cohort study. *Public Health Nutr*. 2005;8:912-919.

17. Folsom AR, Demissie Z, Harnack L, and the Iowa Women's Health Study. Glycemic index, glycemic load, and incidence of endometrial cancer: the Iowa Women's Health study. *Nutr Cancer*. 2003;46:119-124.

18. Setiawan VW, Monroe KR, Goodman MT, Kolonel LN, Pike MC, Henderson BE. Alcohol consumption and endometrial cancer risk: the multiethnic cohort. *Int J Cancer*. 2008;122:634-638.

19. Loerbroks A, Schouten LJ, Goldbohm RA, van den Brandt PA. Alcohol consumption, cigarette smoking, and endometrial cancer risk: results from the Netherlands Cohort Study. *Cancer Causes Control*. 2007;18:551-560.

26. Cervical Cancer

Cervical cancer occurs primarily in 2 varieties: squamous cell carcinoma (about 80% of cases) and adenocarcinoma (about 15%). Adenosquamous carcinoma makes up most of the remaining cases, and this type may have a poorer outcome. Since the inception of annual Pap smear screening, there has been a marked decline in cervical cancer incidence. The majority of cases now occur in women who have not been adequately screened.[1,2] Due in part to the success of such screening programs, cervical cancer only accounts for about 1% of all cancer deaths in developed countries. Cervical cancer is age-related; incidence is extremely low in women under 20 and peaks in women aged 45 to 49.[3]

Symptoms are absent in many cases, but abnormal vaginal discharge or bleeding often occurs. Advanced disease may also cause pain in the low back and pelvis with radiation into the posterior legs, as well as bowel or urinary symptoms, such as passage of blood and a sensation of pressure.

In 2006, the FDA approved Gardasil, a recombinant vaccine that protects against 4 strains of the human papillomavirus (HPV 6, 11, 16, and 18) that are implicated in up to 70% of cases of cervical intraepithelial neoplasia, a precursor to cervical cancer, and 90% of cases of female genital warts. However, the vaccine does not protect against cervical cancer among those already infected with HPV, and it does not influence risk of cases not due to these HPV strains.[4]

Risk Factors

Women in developing nations have much higher mortality (nearly 50%), compared with those in developed nations due to the scarcity of screening programs. Other risk factors include:

Human papillomavirus (HPV) infection. This virus has many subtypes and not all cause cancer, but most cervical cancers involve HPV. High-risk HPV includes types 16, 18, 31, 33, 35, 39, and 45.

Sexual factors. Early sexual intercourse, history of multiple sexual partners (or a partner with multiple partners), history of sexually transmitted disease, sexual relationship with a person who has exposure to HPV, and intercourse with an uncircumcised man are associated with increased risk. Uncircumcised men and their sexual partners have an elevated rate of HPV infection.[5]

Smoking.

History of genital squamous dysplasia.

High parity. Women with 7 or more full-term pregnancies have a 2 to 4 times greater risk for squamous cell cervical cancer than do women who have 0 to 2 babies.[6]

Oral contraceptives. The proportion of adenocarcinoma increases with the duration of oral contraception.

Immunosuppression.

Diagnosis

Due to the frequent asymptomatic presentation of cervical cancer, diagnosis may be incidental on routine pelvic examination. A cervical lesion is often visible with invasive disease, and cancer is confirmed via biopsy. However, cytology from a Pap smear may be negative in up to 50% of cases involving invasive disease.[7] In addition, the Pap smear commonly shows severe inflammation in malignant disease. If such cases are clinically suspected, further testing is required.

An abnormal Pap smear requires further evaluation, which may include colposcopy with directed biopsy of abnormal cervical tissue or conization.

A histologic diagnosis is followed by a full clinical staging workup via clinical examination; radiography; blood work, which may include tumor markers; and endoscopy (in presumed advanced disease).

Treatment

Cervical cancer is staged using the system established by the International Federation of Gynecology and Obstetrics (FIGO) through clinical (as opposed to pathological or surgical) evaluation. The following stages include multiple subtypes that further classify the cervical cancer:

Stage 0: Carcinoma remains in situ.

Stage I: Carcinoma is limited to the uterus.

Stage II: Carcinoma has spread from the uterus but does not include the lower third of the vagina or pelvic wall.

Stage III: Carcinoma has spread to the lower third of the vagina or pelvic wall or causes hydronephrosis.

Stage IV: Carcinoma has spread to the bladder or rectum or to distant organs beyond the pelvic area.

In general, squamous cell carcinoma, adenocarcinoma, and adeno-squamous cervical cancers are treated similarly with either radical hysterectomy (with regional lymphadenectomy) or radiation plus chemotherapy. Radiation and chemotherapy may also be administered after surgery in women at high risk of recurrence (eg, positive surgical margins or lymph nodes, or parametrial invasion).

Surgery preserves the ovaries and may be preferable to radiation and chemotherapy for premenopausal women. In addition to causing hormone-deficient vaginal stenosis, radiation and chemotherapy may damage the vagina, which could lead to dyspareunia in sexually active women.

Women with early cervical cancer who want to retain fertility may select a conization procedure or other surgical options that remove the cancerous lesion but permit pregnancy.

Nutritional Considerations

Epidemiologic studies suggest that dietary factors may influence risk for cervical cancer. Part of the effect of diet may be attributable to the suppressive action of certain micronutrients on HPV infection, particularly carotenoids (both vitamin A and non-vitamin A precursors), folate, and vitamins C and E. The following factors have been associated with reduced risk:

Fruits and vegetables. A systematic review of evidence linking fruits, vegetables, and some of their bioactive components to protection against cervical cancer graded the evidence as "possible" for vegetables, vitamin C, and many carotenoids (eg, alpha-carotene, beta-carotene, lycopene, lutein/zeaxanthin, and cryptoxanthin). A possible protective effect against HPV persistence was also determined for the intake of fruits, vegetables, vitamins C and E, and the carotenoids mentioned above. Evidence was also noted as "probable" for retinol and vitamin E, as well as for the roles of folate and homocysteine, in cervical neoplasia (see below).[8]

Folic acid and other B vitamins. Interactions appear to exist between folate status, mutations in the folate-dependent enzyme methylene-tetrahydrofolate reductase (MTHFR), plasma homocysteine, and HPV that may reduce cervical cancer risk. Lower red blood cell levels of folate have been associated with a 5-fold greater risk for HPV-related cervical dysplasia.[9] A combination of factors that increase folate requirement (MTHFR polymorphism and pregnancy) was associated with a 23-fold greater risk for cervical intraepithelial neoplasia, compared with the risk in nulliparous women with the normal MTHFR genotype.[10]

Blood levels of homocysteine may increase with the MTHFR genotype, and hyperhomocysteinemia is associated with a 2.5-to-3 times greater risk for invasive cervical cancer.[11] HPV increases the risk for cervical neoplasia almost 5-fold, above a homocysteine level of roughly 9 umol/L.[12] Other studies showed that circulating levels of vitamin B_{12} were inversely associated with HPV persistence,[13] and that B_{12} supplements were inversely associated with high-grade squamous intraepithelial lesions of the cervix.[14]

Food sources of vitamin E. The review cited above describes evidence of a protective effect of high blood levels of vitamin E as "possible" for HPV persistence and "probable" for cervical neoplasia.[8]

In addition, obese women appear to have a modestly higher risk for cervical adenocarcinoma, which represents 15% of cervical cancers. Mortality from cervical cancer overall is also increased in obese patients.[15]

While an important body of research on diet and cervical cancer risk exists, there has been little research on the role of diet in survival after diagnosis.

Orders

See Basic Diet Orders chapter.

Smoking cessation.

What to Tell the Family

Cervical cancer is fairly easily treated if detected early. For this reason, Pap smear evaluations should be conducted regularly. Cervical cancer risk is closely tied to cancer-causing forms of the human papillomavirus (HPV). HPV infection may be chronic or transient, and it is affected by diet, tobacco use, and genetic factors. Men can also be screened for HPV. Risk of cervical cancer is reduced by avoiding multiple sexual partners and maintaining a diet of fruits and vegetables especially high in carotenoids and foods high in folic acid (legumes, whole grains, fruits, and vegetables).

References

1. Hildesheim A, Hadjimichael O, Schwartz PE, et al. Risk factors for rapid-onset cervical cancer. *Am J Obstet Gynecol.* 1999;180(pt 1):571-577.

2. Janerich DT, Hadjimichael O, Schwartz PE, et al. The screening histories of women with invasive cervical cancer, Connecticut. *Am J Public Health.* 1995;85:791-794.

3. National Cancer Institute. SEER Cancer Statistics Review 1973-1999. Available at: http://seer.cancer.gov/csr/1973_1999/overview/overview14.pdf. Accessed September 7, 2005.

4. Garland SM, Hernandez-Avila M, Wheeler CM, et al. Quadrivalent vaccine against human papillomavirus to prevent human anogenital disease. *N Engl J Med.* 2007;356:1928-1943.

5. Castellsague X, Bosch X, Munoz N, et al. Male circumcision, penile human papillomavirus infection, and cervical cancer in female partners. *N Engl J Med.* 2002;346:1105-1112.

6. Munoz N, Franceschi S, Bosetti C, et al. Role of parity and human papillomavirus in cervical cancer: the IARC multicenter case-control study. *Lancet.* 2002;359:1093-1101.

7. Sasieni PD, Cuzick J, Lynch-Farmery E. Estimating the efficacy of screening by auditing smear histories of women with and without cervical cancer. The National Co-ordinating Network for Cervical Screening Working Group. *Br J Cancer.* 1996;73:1001-1005.

8. Garcia-Closas R, Castellsague X, Bosch X, Gonzalez CA. The role of diet and nutrition in cervical carcinogenesis: a review of recent evidence. *Int J Cancer.* 2005;117:629-637.

9. Butterworth CE Jr, Hatch KD, Macaluso M, et al. Folate deficiency and cervical dysplasia. *JAMA.* 1992;267:528-533.

10. Piyathilake CJ, Macaluso M, Johanning GL, et al. Methylenetetrahydrofolate reductase (MTHFR) polymorphism increases the risk of cervical intraepithelial neoplasia. *Anticancer Res.* 2000;20:1751-1757.

11. Weinstein SJ, Ziegler RG, Selhub J, et al. Elevated serum homocysteine levels and increased risk of invasive cervical cancer in US women. *Cancer Causes Control.* 2001;12:317-324.

12. Thomson SW, Heimburger DC, Cornwell PE, et al. Effect of total plasma homocysteine on cervical dysplasia risk. *Nutr Cancer.* 2000;37:128-133.

13. Sedjo RL, Papenfuss MR, Craft NE, Giuliano AR. Effect of plasma micronutrients on clearance of oncogenic human papillomavirus (HPV) infection (United States). *Cancer Causes Control.* 2003;14:319-326.

14. Hernandez BY, McDuffie K, Wilkens LR, et al. Diet and premalignant lesions of the cervix: evidence of a protective role for folate, riboflavin, thiamin, and vitamin B_{12}. *Cancer Causes Control.* 2003;14:859-870.

15. Modesitt SC, van Nagell JR Jr. The impact of obesity on the incidence and treatment of gynecologic cancers: a review. *Obstet Gynecol Surv.* 2005;60:683-692.

27. Prostate Cancer

Prostate cancer is the second most common malignancy in men in the United States; only skin cancer occurs more frequently. Although most cases progress slowly and may never become clinically apparent, the disease is the second-leading cause of cancer death in men and the most common cause of cancer death in male nonsmokers. Further, because of the disease's strong association with age, the number of new cases and deaths from prostate cancer is expected to increase with the aging of the population.

Nearly all prostate cancer cases are adenocarcinomas; less than 3% are transitional cell carcinomas. Hormonal factors are important in the etiology of prostate cancer. Research studies have shown strong associations with testosterone and insulin-like growth factor I (IGF-I).

Symptoms often include dysuria, difficulty voiding, urinary frequency and retention, and hematuria. However, more than 80% of cases are asymptomatic and present with only an elevated prostate-specific antigen (PSA) level or firm nodule on digital rectal examination.

The most common sites of metastasis are lymph nodes and bone. A small number of cases present with symptoms of metastatic disease, such as vertebral back pain, renal failure due to ureteral obstruction, or weight loss.

Risk Factors

Age. Prevalence increases rapidly after middle age. The condition rarely occurs before age 45, whereas most men over 70 years show microscopic evidence of malignant cells.

Race. African American men have the highest incidence of and mortality from prostate cancer of any demographic group. They also tend to have higher serum PSA levels and more advanced disease at diagnosis.

Family history. Prostate cancer is likely influenced by several genetic factors. Men who have a first-degree relative with prostate cancer are twice as likely to develop the disease themselves. Early onset of prostate cancer in a first-degree family member further increases the risk.

Genetics. A smaller number of CAG repeats in the gene coding for the androgen receptor has been associated with increased risk. The incidence of prostate cancer is higher in families with breast cancer, and patients with *BRCA1* or *BRCA2* mutations appear to have a 2-fold to 5-fold increased risk.

Obesity. In the Cancer Prevention Study II Nutrition Cohort that included 69,991 men, the risk for fatal prostate cancer was roughly 55% greater in men whose body mass indices (BMI) fell between 30 and 35, compared with men at a BMI below 25.[1] In men treated with prostatectomy, obesity was also significantly associated with treatment failure.[2] Obesity-related diseases (eg, insulin resistance syndrome) appear to double the risk for prostate cancer.[3]

High blood concentrations of IGF-I. IGF-I concentrations are associated with cancer risk and are influenced by both body weight and certain dietary intakes, as described in Nutritional Considerations below.

Lack of physical activity. In men aged 65 or older, a higher risk of advanced and fatal prostate cancer was found in those who were sedentary compared with those who were physically active.[4] Other studies have concluded that a sedentary lifestyle is not associated with prostate cancer risk overall, but it may increase the risk for developing aggressive prostate cancer.[5]

Diagnosis

The presence of an indurated area of the prostate, gland asymmetry, or a palpable nodule detected during digital rectal examination is suggestive, but malignancy may be present even with a normal prostate exam.

Most cases are detected by PSA screening. PSA is a very sensitive but nonspecific test. Most elevated PSA results are false-positive for cancer and reflect chronic prostatitis or benign prostatic hyperplasia. This has led to considerable controversy about the meaning of an elevated PSA reading. Higher PSA velocity or shorter doubling time may help distinguish elevated PSA due to prostate cancer from that due to benign prostatic conditions. PSA also reliably reflects the effectiveness of treatment and disease activity after recurrence.

Prostate biopsy, usually via transrectal ultrasound, is necessary for definitive diagnosis.

Tumors are staged according to the TNM (tumor, node, metastasis) classification, Whitmore-Jewett system, or surgical staging. Metastatic survey may include bone scan, CT scan of the abdomen and pelvis, and ProstaScint scan (using monoclonal antibodies specific for prostate-specific membrane antigen).

Treatment

Due to the indolent nature of most cases of prostate cancer, active surveillance (careful monitoring of tumor growth without active treatment) can often be an acceptable option, particularly for older patients or those with low-grade disease.

Treatments for localized disease include radical prostatectomy, external beam radiation, internal radiation (brachytherapy), and cryotherapy. Radical prostatectomy and, to a lesser extent, external beam radiation often result in some degree of urinary incontinence and impotence. Brachytherapy tends to be associated with irritative voiding symptoms.

Gonadotropin-releasing hormone (GnRH) agonists (eg, leuprolide), androgen receptor antagonists (eg, flutamide, bicalutamide), and, to a lesser extent, orchiectomy are used as androgen-deprivation therapies to reduce circulating testosterone or minimize the stimulation of testosterone on the prostate. These treatments may be used as primary or adjuvant therapy for localized disease but are most commonly used as a primary therapy for advanced disease or for palliation of symptoms from metastatic disease.

Chemotherapy is sometimes used for hormone-refractory prostate cancer and is under investigation as a treatment option for earlier stages of the disease.

Nutritional Considerations

Prostate cancer risk appears to be increasing worldwide, a trend that may be due in part to the globalization of Western eating habits. Prostate cancer risk has been associated with higher meat[6] and dairy intake[7] and with diets that are high in processed foods and low in fiber (including processed meat, red meat, refined grains and vegetable oils, and soft drinks).[8] Conversely, evidence is accumulating that a low-fat, vegetarian diet may help prevent prostate cancer[9] and possibly play a role in its treatment.[10-12] The following principal issues have emerged in research on diet and prostate cancer.

Animal Products and Increased Risk

Populations consuming meat-based diets have higher risk of prostate cancer, compared with those following largely plant-based diets. In some studies, risk is associated with specific products or with a particular component of animal-derived products. For example, epidemiologic evidence suggests that prostate cancer risk increases with animal fat[13] or saturated fat[14] intake. High intakes of red meat and dairy products were shown to be associated with twice the risk for metastatic prostate cancer compared with the lowest intakes.[15]

Not all studies have indicated strong associations between red meat and prostate cancer risk. Some have suggested that risk relates to processed meat only[16] and that risk may be identified only in certain groups (eg, black, rather than white, individuals).[17]

Several mechanisms have been proposed to explain these associations:

Androgenic effects. High-fat, low-fiber diets are associated with elevated blood testosterone concentrations, presumably as a result of either increased production or decreased excretion.[18,19] In turn, higher testosterone concentrations are associated with increased risk of prostate cancer.[20] Men who adopt low-fat, high-fiber diets show about a 15% reduction in testosterone concentrations.[18,19]

Insulin-like growth factor. The association between animal product intake and prostate cancer risk may also be mediated by insulin-like growth factor I (IGF-I), a peptide with hormonal actions that increases with animal fat and animal protein consumption.[21]

Carcinogens produced by cooking. Carcinogenic heterocyclic amines and polycyclic aromatic hydrocarbons tend to form as meat is cooked at high temperatures, and these are associated with increased risk of prostate cancer.[22]

Dairy Product Intake and Increased Risk

Dairy products may play a role in prostate cancer risk that is distinct from that of other animal products. Two large Harvard University cohort studies (the Physicians' Health Study and the Health Professionals Follow-Up Study), among several other epidemiologic studies, have shown significant increases in prostate cancer risk among the highest consumers of dairy products, independent of fat content.[23,24] Similarly, in the Alpha-Tocopherol, Beta-Carotene (ATBC) Cancer Prevention Study of 29,133 male smokers, the highest dairy consumers had a 26% higher risk compared with those consuming the least dairy products.[25] Two mechanisms have been proposed to explain this association:

Hormonal effects of dairy products. Dairy products contain a variety of hormonally active compounds and may elevate blood concentrations of IGF-I.[26]

Calcium's ability to suppress vitamin D activation. Compared with men who have the lowest calcium intakes, those with the highest intakes appear to have as much as double the risk for developing prostate cancer.[27-29] In the Health Professionals Follow-Up Study of approximately 48,000 men, those with calcium intakes between 1500 and 1999 mg/d had an 85% greater risk, and those with intakes above 2,000 mg/d had a roughly 245% greater risk, compared with those who had calcium intakes between 500 and 749 mg/d.[29] Not all studies, however, have shown an association between calcium and prostate cancer.[30]

The association between calcium and prostate cancer may be related to calcium's tendency to suppress the activation of vitamin D from its prohormone form. Among vitamin D's biological actions is maintenance of cellular differentiation within the prostate.[31] In a sample of the Health Professionals Follow-Up Study cohort, higher calcium intake was associated with lower circulating 1,25(OH)2 vitamin D levels.[29]

Fruit and Vegetable Intake and Reduced Risk

High intake of certain fruits and vegetables is associated with reduced risk of prostate cancer. Lycopene is a carotenoid antioxidant that imparts a bright red color to tomatoes, watermelon, pink grapefruit, and other foods. Intake of lycopene-containing foods has been associated with a lower risk of prostate cancer.[32,33] Not all studies support this finding, however. A prospective investigation involving over 29,000 subjects casts doubt on this association, with the possible exception of a protective effect in men with a family history of prostate cancer.[34] Nevertheless, clinical trials have found evidence of benefit.

In a study of men with high-grade prostatic intraepithelial neoplasia, lycopene supplementation (4 mg/d) was associated with a reduction in the number who developed occult prostate cancer, compared with a control group on low-lycopene diets.[35] Lycopene may interfere with IGF-I and other mediators of prostate cancer risk, such as androgen signaling, oxidative stress, and interleukin-6.[36]

Supplementation with lycopene has been associated with biochemical and clinical improvement in men with existing prostate cancer.[37,38] However, caution regarding supplementation is warranted. Evidence indicates that other constituents of tomatoes, rather than lycopene alone, may be responsible for the apparent oncostatic effect[39] seen in humans in one small clinical trial.[40] Additional studies are needed to determine the degree to which tomato products, lycopene, or both are useful for the prevention and treatment of prostate cancer.

Intake of cruciferous vegetables (eg, broccoli, cabbage, cauliflower, and Brussels sprouts) is also associated with reduced risk for prostate cancer,[41,42] perhaps because these foods can induce phase II detoxification enzymes, as well as cell-cycle arrest and apoptosis in prostate cancer cells.[43]

Regular intake of allium vegetables (eg, onions, leeks, scallions, and garlic) has also been associated with a decreased risk of prostate cancer. In one study, allium vegetable intake was strongly associated with decreased prostate cancer mortality.[44] In another study, risk of developing prostate cancer was 71% lower in daily consumers of onions, compared with nonconsumers.[45] It has been suggested that the possible anticancer effects of allium vegetables may involve immune stimulation and resultant release of interleukin-2, tumor necrosis factor, and interferon, and enhanced natural killer cell activity.[46]

Additional Diet-Related Factors

Selenium. In epidemiologic studies, men who consumed higher levels of selenium or had higher levels of selenium in their body tissues were about half as likely to develop prostate cancer, compared with those who had the lowest intakes.[47] Preliminary data suggest that selenium supplements (200 μg/d) may reduce prostate cancer risk.[48]

Alcohol. A large prospective cohort study found that alcohol was a minor factor in prostate cancer risk, except in men who tend to binge. Compared with abstainers, men who drank 105 grams of alcohol (equivalent to 8 to 9 drinks) or more per week but who drank only 1 to 2 days each week had a 60% higher risk.[49] Although some evidence suggests that liquor consumption increases risk more than beer or wine,[50] other evidence indicates that risk increases with any type of alcohol.[51]

Diet and Prognosis

A limited number of studies have addressed diet's possible influence on survival after diagnosis. Overall, evidence suggests that low-fat, plant-based diets may be helpful.[12]

Observational studies show that higher saturated fat intakes are associated with a 3-fold higher prostate cancer mortality, compared with the lowest intake.[52,53] Prospective studies have found an inverse association with monounsaturated fat intake.[54] In the Health Professionals Follow-Up Study, prostate cancer patients with the highest intakes of tomato sauce had a 45% lower risk for disease progression, compared with individuals having the lowest intakes.[55]

Limited evidence suggests a substantial improvement in prostate cancer survival with diets that emphasize whole grain, legumes, and vegetables and avoid dairy products and meats.[56] In a small clinical trial, diet treatment increased PSA doubling time from 6.5 months to 17 months.[11] Similarly, in a randomized clinical trial using a vegan diet and stress reduction in 93 men with early prostate cancer who had elected not to undergo other treatment, the intervention group experienced a mean PSA reduction of 4%, compared with a 6% increase in the control group. None of the experimental-group patients required medical treatment during the trial, but 6 control-group patients required conventional treatment, due to rising PSA concentrations or evidence of disease progression on magnetic resonance imaging.[10]

Other investigators have found that a plant-based diet can significantly decrease the rate of PSA rise (or lead to a PSA reduction) in patients with recurrent prostate cancer.[57,58]

Growing evidence indicates that obese men treated for prostate cancer are at greater risk of recurrence compared with those nearer normal weight.[59] As noted above, obesity (BMI ≥ 30 kg/m^2) was significantly associated with treatment failure in one study.[2] Studies also suggest that higher body mass index (BMI) is associated with more aggressive cancer progression (ie, high-grade disease, positive surgical margins, extraprostatic extension, and lymph node metastasis).[60] See the Obesity chapter for healthful weight control measures.

The benefits of a low-fat, plant-based diet and exercise take on particular significance in light of the fact that cardiovascular disease remains a leading cause of death in prostate cancer patients.[61] (See Coronary Heart Disease chapter.)

Orders

See Basic Diet Orders chapter.

Moderate physical activity and stress reduction may be beneficial.

Limit alcohol to 0 to 2 drinks per day.

What to Tell the Family

Prostate cancer is increasingly common. Diet and lifestyle factors may influence the risk of developing the disease, particularly in its more aggressive and invasive forms. Cancer risk is not limited to the identified patient, however. A low-fat, plant-based diet and regular exercise habits, adopted early in life, may reduce cancer risk and improve the overall health of the entire family.

References

1. Rodriguez C, Freedland SJ, Deka A, et al. Body mass index, weight change, and risk of prostate cancer in the Cancer Prevention Study II Nutrition Cohort. *Cancer Epidemiol Biomarkers Prev.* 2007;16:63-69.

2. Strom SS, Wang X, Pettaway CA, et al. Obesity, weight gain, and risk of biochemical failure among prostate cancer patients following prostatectomy. *Clin Cancer Res.* 2005;11:6889-6894.

3. Laukkanen JA, Laaksonen DE, Niskanen L, Pukkala E, Hakkarainen A, Salonen JT. Metabolic syndrome and the risk of prostate cancer in Finnish men: a population-based study. *Cancer Epidemiol Biomarkers Prev.* 2004;13:1646-1650.

4. Giovannucci EL, Liu Y, Leitzmann MF, Stampfer MJ, Willett WC. A prospective study of physical activity and incident and fatal prostate cancer. *Arch Intern Med.* 2005;165:1005-1010.

5. Patel AV, Rodriguez C, Jacobs EJ, Solomon L, Thun MJ, Calle EE. Recreational physical activity and risk of prostate cancer in a large cohort of US men. *Cancer Epidemiol Biomarkers Prev.* 2005;14:275-279.

6. Koo LC, Mang OW, Ho JH. An ecological study of trends in cancer incidence and dietary changes in Hong Kong. *Nutr Cancer.* 1997;28:289-301.

7. Qin LQ, Xu JY, Wang PY, Kaneko T, Hoshi K, Sato A. Milk consumption is a risk factor for prostate cancer: meta-analysis of case-control studies. *Nutr Cancer.* 2004;48:22-27.

8. Walker M, Aronson KJ, King W, et al. Dietary patterns and risk of prostate cancer in Ontario, Canada. *Int J Cancer.* 2005;116:592-598.

9. Chen YC, Chiang CI, Lin RS, Pu YS, Lai MK, Sung FC. Diet, vegetarian food and prostate carcinoma among men in Taiwan. *Br J Cancer.* 2005;93:1057-1061.

10. Ornish D, Weidner G, Fair WR, et al. Intensive lifestyle changes may affect the progression of prostate cancer. *J Urol.* 2005;174:1065-1069.

11. Saxe GA, Hebert JR, Carmody JF, et al. Can diet in conjunction with stress reduction affect the rate of increase in prostate specific antigen after biochemical recurrence of prostate cancer? *J Urol.* 2001;166:2202-2207.

12. Berkow SE, Barnard ND, Saxe GA, Ankerberg-Nobis T. Diet and survival after prostate cancer diagnosis. *Nutr Rev.* 2007;65:391-403.

13. Willett WC. Specific fatty acids and risks of breast and prostate cancer: dietary intake. *Am J Clin Nutr.* 1997;66(suppl 6):S1557-S1563.

14. Chan JM, Gann PH, Giovannucci EL. Role of diet in prostate cancer development and progression. *J Clin Oncol.* 2005;23:8152-8160.

15. Michaud DS, Augustsson K, Rimm EB, Stampfer MJ, Willett WC, Giovannucci E. A prospective study on intake of animal products and risk of prostate cancer. *Cancer Causes Control.* 2001;12:557-567.

16. Rohrmann S, Platz EA, Kavanaugh CJ, Thuita L, Hoffman SC, Helzlsouer KJ. Meat and dairy consumption and subsequent risk of prostate cancer in a US cohort study. *Cancer Causes Control.* 2007;18:41-50.

17. Rodriguez C, McCullough ML, Mondul AM, et al. Meat consumption among Black and White men and risk of prostate cancer in the Cancer Prevention Study II Nutrition Cohort. *Cancer Epidemiol Biomarkers Prev.* 2006;15:211-216.

18. Dorgan JF, Judd JT, Longcope C, et al. Effects of dietary fat and fiber on plasma and urine androgens and estrogens in men: a controlled feeding study. *Am J Clin Nutr.* 1996;64:850-855.

19. Hamalainen E, Adlercreutz H, Puska P, Pietinen P. Diet and serum sex hormones in healthy men. *J Steroid Biochem.* 1984;20:459-464.

20. Ross RK, Henderson BE. Do diet and androgens alter prostate cancer risk via a common etiologic pathway? *J Natl Cancer Inst.* 1994;86:252-254.

21. Gunnell D, Oliver SE, Peters TJ, et al. Are diet-prostate cancer associations mediated by the IGF axis? A cross-sectional analysis of diet, IGF-I and IGFBP-3 in healthy middle-aged men. *Br J Cancer.* 2003;88:1682-1686.

22. Cross AJ, Peters U, Kirsh VA, et al. A prospective study of meat and meat mutagens and prostate cancer risk. *Cancer Res.* 2005;65:11779-11884.

23. Giovannucci E, Rimm EB, Wolk A, et al. Calcium and fructose intake in relation to risk of prostate cancer. *Cancer Res.* 1998;58:442-447.

24. Chan JM, Stampfer MJ, Ma J, Gann PH, Gaziano JM, Giovannucci E. Dairy products, calcium, and prostate cancer risk in the Physicians' Health Study. *Am J Clin Nutr.* 2001;74:549-554.

25. Mitrou PN, Albanes D, Weinstein SJ, et al. A prospective study of dietary calcium, dairy products and prostate cancer risk (Finland). *Int J Cancer.* 2007;120:2466-2473.

26. Heaney RP, McCarron DA, Dawson-Hughes B, et al. Dietary changes favorably affect bone remodeling in older adults. *J Am Dietetic Assoc.* 1999;99:1228-1233.

27. Tseng M, Breslow RA, Graubard BI, Ziegler RG. Dairy, calcium, and vitamin D intakes and prostate cancer risk in the National Health and Nutrition Examination Epidemiologic Follow-up Study cohort. *Am J Clin Nutr.* 2005;81:1147-1154.

28. Berndt SI, Carter HB, Landis PK, et al. Calcium intake and prostate cancer risk in a long-term aging study: the Baltimore Longitudinal Study of Aging. *Urology.* 2002;60:1118-1123.

29. Giovannucci E, Liu Y, Stampfer MJ, Willett WC. A prospective study of calcium intake and incident and fatal prostate cancer. *Cancer Epidemiol Biomarkers Prev.* 2006;15:203-210.

30. Baron JA, Beach M, Wallace K, et al. Risk of prostate cancer in a randomized clinical trial of calcium supplementation. *Cancer Epidemiol Biomarkers Prev.* 2005;14:586-589.

31. Tseng M, Breslow RA, DeVellis RF, Ziegler RG. Dietary patterns and prostate cancer risk in the National Health and Nutrition Examination Survey Epidemiological Follow-up Study cohort. *Cancer Epidemiol Biomarkers Prev.* 2004;13:71-77.

32. Giovannucci E, Rimm EB, Liu Y, Stampfer MJ, Willett WC. A prospective study of tomato products, lycopene, and prostate cancer risk. *J Natl Cancer Inst.* 2002;94:391-398.

33. Gann PH, Ma J, Giovannucci E, et al. Lower prostate cancer risk in men with elevated plasma lycopene levels: results of a prospective analysis. *Cancer Res.* 1999;59:1225-1230.

34. Kirsh VA, Mayne ST, Peters U, et al. A prospective study of lycopene and tomato product intake and risk of prostate cancer. *Cancer Epidemiol Biomarkers Prev.* 2006;15:92-98.

35. Mohanty NK, Saxena S, Singh UP, Goyal NK, Arora RP. Lycopene as a chemopreventive agent in the treatment of high-grade prostate intraepithelial neoplasia. *Urol Oncol.* 2005;23:383-385.

36. Wertz K, Siler U, Goralczyk R. Lycopene: modes of action to promote prostate health. *Arch Biochem Biophys.* 2004;430:127-134.

37. Kucuk O, Sarkar FH, Djuric Z, et al. Effects of lycopene supplementation in patients with localized prostate cancer. *Exp Biol Med* (Maywood). 2002;227:881-885.

38. Kucuk O, Sarkar FH, Sakr W, et al. Phase II randomized clinical trial of lycopene supplementation before radical prostatectomy. *Cancer Epidemiol Biomarkers Prev.* 2001;10:861-868.

39. Boileau TW, Liao Z, Kim S, Lemeshow S, Erdman JW Jr, Clinton SK. Prostate carcinogenesis in N-methyl-N-nitrosourea (NMU)-testosterone-treated rats fed tomato powder, lycopene, or energy-restricted diets. *J Natl Cancer Inst.* 2003;95:1578-1586.

40. Kim HS, Bowen P, Chen L, et al. Effects of tomato sauce consumption on apoptotic cell death in prostate benign hyperplasia and carcinoma. *Nutr Cancer.* 2003;47:40-47.

41. Cohen JH, Kristal AR, Stanford JL. Fruit and vegetable intakes and prostate cancer risk. *J Natl Cancer Inst.* 2000;92:61-68.

42. Kolonel LN, Hankin JH, Whittemore AS, et al. Vegetables, fruits, legumes and prostate cancer: a multiethnic case-control study. *Cancer Epidemiol Biomarkers Prev.* 2000;9:795-804.

43. Sarkar FH, Li Y. Indole-3-carbinol and prostate cancer. *J Nutr.* 2004;134(suppl 12):S3493-S3498.

44. Colli JL, Colli A. International comparisons of prostate cancer mortality rates with dietary practices and sunlight levels. *Urol Oncol.* 2006;24:184-194.

45. Galeone C, Pelucchi C, Levi F, et al. Onion and garlic use and human cancer. *Am J Clin Nutr.* 2006;84:1027-1032.

46. Lamm DL, Riggs DR. Enhanced immunocompetence by garlic: role in bladder cancer and other malignancies. *J Nutr.* 2001;131(suppl 3):1067S-1070S.

47. Yoshizawa K, Willett WC, Morris SJ, et al. Study of prediagnostic selenium level in toenails and the risk of advanced prostate cancer. *J Natl Cancer Inst.* 1998;90:1219-1224.

48. Duffield-Lillico AJ, Dalkin BL, Reid ME, et al. Selenium supplementation, baseline plasma selenium status and incidence of prostate cancer: an analysis of the complete treatment period of the Nutritional Prevention of Cancer Trial. *BJU Int.* 2003;91:608-612.

49. Platz EA, Leitzmann MF, Rimm EB, Willett WC, Giovannucci E. Alcohol intake, drinking patterns, and risk of prostate cancer in a large prospective cohort study. *Am J Epidemiol.* 2004;159:444-453.

50. Sesso HD, Paffenbarger RS Jr, Lee IM. Alcohol consumption and risk of prostate cancer: The Harvard Alumni Health Study. *Int J Epidemiol.* 2001;30:749-755.

51. Putnam SD, Cerhan JR, Parker AS, et al. Lifestyle and anthropometric risk factors for prostate cancer in a cohort of Iowa men. *Ann Epidemiol.* 2000;10:361-369.

52. Fradet Y, Meyer F, Bairati I, Shadmani R, Moore L. Dietary fat and prostate cancer progression and survival. *Eur Urol.* 1999;35:388-391.

53. Meyer F, Bairati I, Shadmani R, Fradet Y, Moore L. Dietary fat and prostate cancer survival. *Cancer Causes Control.* 1999;10:245-251.

54. Kim DJ, Gallagher RP, Hislop TG, et al. Premorbid diet in relation to survival from prostate cancer (Canada). *Cancer Causes Control.* 2000;11:65-77.

55. Chan JM, Holick CN, Leitzmann MF, et al. Diet after diagnosis and the risk of prostate cancer progression, recurrence, and death (United States). *Cancer Causes Control.* 2006;17:199-208.

56. Carter JP, Saxe GP, Newbold V, Peres CE, Campeau RJ, Bernal-Green L. Hypothesis: dietary management may improve survival from nutritionally linked cancers based on analysis of representative cases. *J Am Coll Nutr.* 1993;12:209-226.

57. Nguyen JY, Major JM, Knott CJ, Freeman KM, Downs TM, Saxe GA. Adoption of a plant-based diet by patients with recurrent prostate cancer. *Integr Cancer Ther.* 2006;5:214-223.

58. Saxe GA, Major JM, Nguyen JY, Freeman KM, Downs TM, Salem CE. Potential attenuation of disease progression in recurrent prostate cancer with plant-based diet and stress reduction. *Integr Cancer Ther.* 2006;5:206-213.

59. Amling CL, Riffenburgh RH, Sun L, et al. Pathologic variables and recurrence rates as related to obesity and race in men with prostate cancer undergoing radical prostatectomy. *J Clin Oncol.* 2004;22:439-445.

60. Freedland SJ, Grubb KA, Yiu SK, et al. Obesity and risk of biochemical progression following radical prostatectomy at a tertiary care referral center. *J Urol.* 2005;174:919-922.

61. Moyad MA. Dietary fat reduction to reduce prostate cancer risk: controlled enthusiasm, learning a lesson from breast or other cancers, and the big picture. *Urology.* 2002;59(suppl 1):51-62.

28. Leukemia

Leukemias are malignancies of hematopoietic stem cells in the bone marrow. There are many varieties of leukemia, and they can be distinguished by the affected cell type. Among them, four predominant categories are recognized. These are acute myeloid leukemia (AML), acute lymphoid leukemia (ALL), chronic myeloid leukemia (CML), and chronic lymphoid leukemia (CLL).

About 30,000 new cases of leukemia are diagnosed in the United States each year. The acute leukemias have a rapid clinical onset and are nearly uniformly fatal within months without treatment. Chronic leukemias often have a subacute onset of symptoms with an average survival of 4 to 5 years after diagnosis for CML, and 8 to 12 years for CLL. Over time, chronic leukemias typically transform into a more aggressive disease with a terminal blast phase that resembles acute leukemia.

Acute Leukemias

ALL is a proliferation of lymphoid precursors, primarily of B-cell origin. AML is characterized by proliferations of myeloid precursors, called blasts. Untreated, acute leukemias are uniformly fatal.

ALL accounts for about 12% of all leukemias in the United States but represents 60% of leukemias in persons younger than 20 years. With intensive chemotherapy regimens, about 80% of children and 40% of adults with ALL will be cured.

In contrast, AML is particularly common in older adults, with a median age at diagnosis of 68. Intensive chemotherapy, including stem cell transplants in selected patients, results in about a 50% long-term, disease-free survival.

Chronic Leukemias

Chronic leukemias more commonly affect older patients. They are, in general, more indolent than acute leukemias. However, many cases ultimately lead to a terminal phase that resembles acute leukemia.

CLL is a malignancy of mature B cells. It is the most common adult leukemia, with more than 80% of cases occurring in patients over the age of 60. Worldwide incidence is highly variable; North America has the highest rate, while CLL is rare in Southeast Asia.

CML is characterized by uncontrolled production of neutrophils, eosinophils, and basophils. It accounts for only 5% of childhood leukemia and has a peak incidence around age 53. CML is identified by a typical translocation, called the Philadelphia chromosome, which results in a fusion protein (BCR-ABL) that releases controls on stem cell proliferation and blocks apoptosis.

Clinical symptoms of chronic leukemia are generally nonspecific and often occur due to proliferation of the affected cell line or to decreased production of other blood cells. Common presentations include anemia (pallor, fatigue, palpitations), thrombocytopenia (epistaxis, menorrhagia, bleeding, bruising), and leukopenia (fever, frequent infections). Weight loss, lymphadenopathy, splenomegaly, gingival hypertrophy, and bone pain may also occur. Many patients with chronic leukemia remain asymptomatic, with discovery of the disease occurring during routine blood tests.

Risk Factors

Age. ALL occurs mostly in children, with a peak age range of 3 to 5 years. AML incidence increases with age, peaking at about age 60. CLL and CML are also both diseases of adults, with onset most common in patients older than 50.

Gender. ALL, AML, and CLL are more common in males.

Race/Ethnicity. AML is more common in white populations, and CLL is more common in Eastern European Jews.

Viral exposure. Exposure to human T-cell lymphoma/leukemia virus (HTLV-1) and Epstein-Barr virus may increase the risk of some ALL subtypes.

Radiation exposure has been associated with ALL. Ionizing radiation is associated with increased risk for AML, and exposure to ionizing radiation is the only known risk factor for CML.

Tobacco. For AML, tobacco use is a strong risk factor, accounting for about 1 in 5 cases.

Chemicals. Exposure to benzene, petroleum products, and pesticides is associated with increased risk for AML. Prior chemotherapy is also a risk factor and accounts for up to 10% of AML cases. Some studies suggest that herbicides (including Agent Orange) and insecticides may increase risk for CLL.

Family history. For CLL, risk is increased in first-degree relatives of affected patients.

Down syndrome. Children with Down syndrome are at increased risk for both AML and ALL.

Diagnosis

Complete blood count with white blood cell (WBC) differential can give a presumptive diagnosis. For acute leukemias, the WBC count is usually above 15,000 (and may exceed 100,000), with blast cells usually evident. However, a significant minority of patients will present with a decreased WBC count. Anemia and thrombocytopenia are usually present. Auer rods (azurophilic, rod-shaped inclusions in the cytoplasm of blasts) are almost diagnostic for AML.

The classic diagnosis for CLL requires an absolute lymphocyte count higher than 5,000 without another known cause for the lymphocytosis. Anemia or thrombocytopenia at presentation is correlated with a more aggressive clinical course.

In CML, the peripheral blood shows an increased WBC count with a significant left shift that includes cells usually seen only in the bone marrow. An increased number of basophils is almost always seen and can substantially predate an increase in WBCs. Thrombocytosis occurs in at least half of cases at presentation.

Bone marrow biopsy is often necessary for definitive diagnosis and staging. For CLL and CML, flow cytometry on peripheral blood can be diagnostic. For CML, polymerase chain reaction (PCR) on peripheral blood can demonstrate the presence of the Philadelphia chromosome.

Upon diagnosis, the following tests are typically indicated:

- Laboratory testing, which includes electrolytes, magnesium, phosphorous, renal function tests (blood urea nitrogen, creatinine), liver function tests (transaminases, alkaline phosphatase, bilirubin, lactate dehydrogenase), and coagulation studies (prothrombin time, partial thromboplastin time).

- Chest x-ray.

- HLA typing of the patient and siblings in potential transplant patients.

- Herpes simplex and cytomegalovirus serology.

Treatment

Acute leukemias are treated with chemotherapy, the goal being complete remission and cure of the disease. Stem cell transplantation is an option for some patients.

In CML, imatinib, a tyrosine kinase inhibitor, is currently the treatment of choice at diagnosis. Allogeneic stem cell transplant is appropriate (except in elderly patients) when imatinib cannot sustain a complete remission. Standard chemotherapy is currently used only in palliative efforts after progression.

Many patients with CLL can be observed without immediate treatment (up to one-third never require treatment). When initiated, treatment consists of chemotherapy and/or monoclonal antibody therapy. Allogeneic bone marrow transplantation is a potentially curative treatment for CLL in younger patients, but it is not yet considered standard therapy. Radiation therapy may be indicated for palliation in patients with large, bulky masses that cause compression symptoms.

Nutritional Considerations

The body of scientific literature addressing the role of diet in leukemia risk is considerably smaller than for solid tumors. Epidemiologic evidence suggests that the following factors are associated with reduced risk, although all require further study.

Reducing or Eliminating Meat Consumption

In a study of children below 10 years of age, those eating more than 12 hot dogs per month had 9 times the usual risk of developing childhood leukemia. Increased risk for childhood leukemia was also found for children whose fathers eat 12 or more hot dogs per month.[1] A higher-than-average meat intake was also found in a study of over 13,000 male

Iowa farmers who experienced a 25% greater risk for leukemia, compared with individuals who were not farmers and consumed less meat.[2] The risk for leukemia attributable to meat, particularly processed meat, may be related to the intake of nitrates used as preservatives, which are metabolized to highly carcinogenic N-nitroso compounds in the gut.

High Vegetable and Fruit Intake

In the Iowa Women's Health Study of more than 35,000 women, the risk of leukemia was inversely associated with vegetable intake.[3] In a study of 131 children with leukemia, higher maternal intake of fruits and vegetables was associated with a roughly 25% lower risk for ALL.[4] Similarly, the Northern California Leukemia Study involving 138 children found an inverse association between maternal fruit and vegetable intake and ALL.[5] This study also found that regular childhood intake of oranges, orange juice, and bananas was associated with roughly a 50% reduction in leukemia risk among children 2 to 14 years old.[6]

Breast-Feeding

Evidence regarding the effect of breast-feeding on leukemia risk is mixed. A meta-analysis of 14 case-control studies concluded that breast-feeding was associated with a 15% to 24% reduction in risk for both childhood ALL and AML.[7] However, a later case-control study found no effect of breast-feeding on risk of childhood ALL.[8]

Healthy Body Weight

Women who are overweight or obese have a 61% to 90% greater risk for leukemia than women of normal weight.[9,10] The obesity-leukemia relationship may be due to excess energy intake.[2,11] Among the hypothesized mechanisms are genetic polymorphisms in enzymes that reduce the oxidative stress brought on by excess calorie intake.[12] Avoidance of obesity may be especially important for pregnant women, because excess maternal weight gain is a known risk factor for macrosomia, a condition associated with a greater risk for infant leukemia.[13] Being overweight or underweight also reduces survival in children with acute myelocytic leukemia.[14]

Avoiding Alcohol

Maternal alcohol intake during pregnancy raises the risk of both ALL and AML in children.[15,16]

Orders

See Basic Diet Orders chapter.

What to Tell the Family

The role of the family is mainly to support the patient during diagnosis and treatment, which can often be difficult. Leukemias make up a family of blood cancers that have highly variable courses and treatment. Acute leukemias are rapidly fatal without treatment but may be curable with aggressive treatment. Chronic leukemias can be slow-growing; CLL may not need initial treatment, and CML can usually be controlled with oral therapy for years. Bone marrow transplantation is often considered for patients younger than 55 years.

The role of diet in causing leukemia or influencing its course is not as clear as it is for solid tumors. Further research is required before specific dietary recommendations can be made.

References

1. Peters JM, Preston-Martin S, London SJ, Bowman JD, Buckley JD, Thomas DC. Processed meats and risk of childhood leukemia (California, USA). *Cancer Causes Control.* 1994;5:195-202.

2. Cerhan JR, Cantor KP, Williamson K, Lynch CF, Torner JC, Burmeister LF. Cancer mortality among Iowa farmers: recent results, time trends, and lifestyle factors (United States). *Cancer Causes Control.* 1998;9:311-319.

3. Ross JA, Kasum CM, Davies SM, Jacobs DR, Folsom AR, Potter JD. Diet and risk of leukemia in the Iowa Women's Health Study. *Cancer Epidemiol Biomarkers Prev.* 2002;11:777-781.

4. Petridou E, Ntouvelis E, Dessypris N, et al. Maternal diet and acute lymphoblastic leukemia in young children. *Cancer Epidemiol Biomarkers Prev.* 2005;14:1935-1939.

5. Jensen CD, Block G, Buffler P, Ma X, Selvin S, Month S. Maternal dietary risk factors in childhood acute lymphoblastic leukemia (United States). *Cancer Causes Control.* 2004;15:559-570.

6. Kwan ML, Block G, Selvin S, Month S, Buffler PA. Food consumption by children and the risk of childhood acute leukemia. *Am J Epidemiol.* 2004;160:1098-1107.

7. Kwan ML, Buffler PA, Abrams B, Kiley VA. Breast-feeding and the risk of childhood leukemia: a meta-analysis. *Public Health Rep.* 2004;119:521-535.

8. Kwan ML, Buffler PA, Wiemels JL, et al. Breastfeeding patterns and risk of childhood acute lymphoblastic leukaemia. *Br J Cancer.* 2005;93:379-384.

9. Pan SY, Johnson KC, Ugnat AM, Wen SW, Mao Y, and the Canadian Cancer Registries Epidemiology Research Group. Association of obesity and cancer risk in Canada. *Am J Epidemiol.* 2004;159:259-268.

10. Ross JA, Parker E, Blair CK, Cerhan JR, Folsom AR. Body mass index and risk of leukemia in older women. *Cancer Epidemiol Biomarkers Prev.* 2004;13:1810-1813.

11. Hursting SD, Margolin BH, Switzer BR. Diet and human leukemia: an analysis of international data. *Prev Med.* 1993;22:409-422.

12. Smith MT, Wang Y, Kane E, et al. Low NAD(P)H:quinone oxidoreductase 1 activity is associated with increased risk of acute leukemia in adults. *Blood.* 2001;97:1422-1426.

13. Hjalgrim LL, Westergaard T, Rostgaard K, et al. Birth weight as a risk factor for childhood leukemia: a meta-analysis of 18 epidemiologic studies. *Am J Epidemiol.* 2003;158:724-735.

14. Lange BJ, Gerbing RB, Feusner J, et al. Mortality in overweight and underweight children with acute myeloid leukemia. *JAMA.* 2005;293:203-211.

15. Shu XO, Ross JA, Pendergrass TW, Reaman GH, Lampkin B, Robison LL. Parental alcohol consumption, cigarette smoking, and risk of infant leukemia: a Children's Cancer Group study. *J Natl Cancer Inst.* 1996;88:24-31.

16. van Duijn CM, van Steensel-Moll HA, Coebergh JW, van Zanen GE. Risk factors for childhood acute non-lymphocytic leukemia: an association with maternal alcohol consumption during pregnancy? *Cancer Epidemiol Biomarkers Prev.* 1994;3:457-460.

29. Lymphoma

Lymphomas are a group of malignancies of lymphoid tissue. They are classified as either Hodgkin or non-Hodgkin lymphoma. While lymphomas generally affect lymph nodes or lymphoid tissue, such as the spleen, they can also affect extranodal tissue, such as the lung, liver, or gastrointestinal tract.

Non-Hodgkin lymphomas are the sixth most common cause of cancer-related death in the United States. Since 1950, the age-adjusted death rate has more than doubled. These cancers are characterized as B-cell (90%) or T-cell lymphomas, depending on the lymphoid cell of origin. The classification of non-Hodgkin lymphoma has more than 40 separate diagnoses. Untreated, the most aggressive forms have an extremely poor prognosis, with survival rates measured in weeks or months. However, with appropriate treatment, many of the aggressive types are curable. On the other hand, the less aggressive types may not need immediate treatment, but they are generally not considered curable.

Hodgkin lymphoma is characterized by the histologic presence of the Reed-Sternberg cell. There are 5 types of Hodgkin lymphoma, differentiated by histologic appearance:

1. Nodular sclerosing

2. Mixed cellularity

3. Lymphocyte depletion

4. Lymphocyte-rich (classical Hodgkin disease)

5. Nodular lymphocyte-predominant

Overall, Hodgkin lymphoma currently has a cure rate of more than 85%. The different types are generally treated similarly and have comparable outcomes.

Presenting symptoms of both categories of lymphoma include painless lymphadenopathy; constitutional symptoms (eg, fever, night sweats, weight loss, fatigue); pruritis; and symptoms of localized compression, such as coughing and chest discomfort. However, indolent lymphomas are often asymptomatic at presentation.

Risk Factors

Non-Hodgkin Lymphoma

Increasing age. Although the disease occurs in all age groups, incidence rises dramatically after age 50.

Family history. Individuals with one or more affected first-degree relatives have twice the usual risk.

Exposure history. Herbicides and other organic chemicals have been linked to an increased risk.

Immunodeficiency disorders. These include immune deficiency states, chronic immunosuppression, and auto-immune diseases.

Infectious agents. Viral (eg, HIV, Epstein-Barr virus, human T-cell lymphotropic virus type I, human herpes virus type 8) and bacterial (*H pylori*) infections have been associated with an increased risk of specific types of lymphoma.

Hodgkin Lymphoma

Age. There is a bimodal age distribution with peak incidence in young adults (ages 15-35) and in individuals older than 50.

Male gender. The condition is more prevalent in males, especially in children and younger adults.

Geography. Incidence increases in areas with high industrial development.

Genetics. There is nearly a 100-fold increased risk in monozygotic twins of individuals with Hodgkin disease and, at least among young patients, a 7-fold increased risk among siblings of Hodgkin disease patients. Although associations between certain *HLA* haplotypes and risk of Hodgkin disease have been identified, it remains unclear whether the increased familial risk is due to a genetic susceptibility or common environmental exposures.

Infectious agents. Several associations have suggested a link between Epstein-Barr virus and Hodgkin disease. Other infectious etiologies may also play a role.

Breast-feeding. In several studies, breast-feeding has been associated with reduced risk of Hodgkin disease.

Diagnosis

Biopsy of a lymph node or extranodal site of involvement is diagnostic. Histologic findings determine the type and classification of lymphoma.

Following diagnosis, staging is done to determine the extent of disease. Necessary laboratory testing includes a complete blood count (CBC), chemistry panel, lactate dehydrogenase, uric acid, C-reactive protein, serum protein electrophoresis, and β_2 microglobulin. Computed tomography (CT) scans of the thorax, abdomen, and pelvis are used to document both lymphadenopathy and extranodal involvement.

In many cases, a bone marrow biopsy will be performed to assess marrow involvement. Positron emission tomography (PET) scans are increasingly being used for both initial staging and assessment of treatment response.

Treatment

Radiation and/or chemotherapy are the mainstays of treatment. Rituximab, a monoclonal antibody that targets CD20+ cells, is administered with chemotherapy.

Aggressive non-Hodgkin lymphoma types and advanced Hodgkin lymphoma require combination chemotherapy. In cases of bulky disease, radiation therapy to the affected area may be considered. Localized Hodgkin lymphoma is treated with radiation therapy to the affected area.

As the cure rate of Hodgkin disease has improved, research has focused on decreasing the toxicity and long-term consequences of treatment, especially second malignancies.

Observation alone without specific treatment is common in asymptomatic non-Hodgkin lymphoma patients with indolent histologies.

Bone marrow transplantation is an option for some patients.

Nutritional Considerations

Only a limited number of research studies have addressed associations between diet and risk for lymphoma. The following factors have been under study for possible roles in reducing risk:

Reducing or avoiding intake of animal products. Compared with individuals who eat beef, pork, or lamb less than once per week, those who eat these foods daily had more than twice the risk for non-Hodgkin lymphoma.[1] Intake of foods high in saturated fat, particularly hamburger and other red meats, was also associated with roughly twice the risk for this cancer.[2] Lymphoma risk associated with milk intake was 1.5 times greater for persons who drank the most milk, compared with those who drank the least.[3] Individuals who drank more than 2 glasses of milk per day had 3 times the lymphoma risk of those who drank less than 1 glass per day.[4]

Reducing intake of fats, particularly trans fats. In a case-control study of diet and non-Hodgkin lymphoma, individuals in the highest tertiles of total, saturated, and monounsaturated fat intake had approximately 50% higher risk, compared with those in the lowest tertile.[5] In the Nurses' Health Study, women in the highest quintile of trans fat consumption had 2.4 times the risk of non-Hodgkin lymphoma, compared with those in the lowest quintile.[1]

Increasing intake of fruits and vegetables. Compared with women eating 3 daily servings of fruits and vegetables, those who ate 6 or more servings per day had a 40% lower risk for non-Hodgkin lymphoma.[6] Cruciferous vegetables may be particularly protective: Women consuming them 2 or more times a week had a 30% lower risk for non-Hodgkin lymphoma, compared with women who ate these vegetables less than twice per month.[7]

A high-fiber diet. Individuals consuming the largest amount of whole grains or dietary fiber from fruits and vegetables had roughly half the risk for non-Hodgkin lymphoma, compared with those eating the least amount from these food categories.[6-8]

A gluten-free diet for individuals with celiac disease. Patients with celiac disease have a higher risk for several types of cancer, and their risk for non-Hodgkin lymphoma is 9 times that of the general population. The risk for cancer overall is reduced considerably with a gluten-free diet. However, the risk for non-Hodgkin lymphoma in these patients is still 6 times that of the general population.[9] Patients with dermatitis herpetiformis, a condition often experienced by individuals with celiac disease, also more frequently develop lymphomas of both the B-cell and T-cell varieties, although this risk is reduced by following a gluten-free diet.[10]

Maintenance of a healthy weight. Studies suggest that being significantly overweight or obese may increase the risk for non-Hodgkin lymphoma. The odds of developing non-Hodgkin lymphoma were found to be increased by 50% in persons with a body mass index (BMI) >30 kg/m^2 and were 200% greater in those with a BMI of >35 kg/m^2, compared with individuals having a BMI of <25 kg/m^2.[11,12]

Orders

See Basic Diet Orders chapter.

What to Tell the Family

Lymphoma is a complex group of over 40 diseases with widely differing treatments and prognoses. In general, lymphomas are highly treatable, and most patients survive beyond 5 years. Limited evidence suggests that low-fat, plant-based diets may reduce the risk of this disease. It is not yet known whether dietary factors can influence its course.

References

1. Zhang S, Hunter DJ, Rosner BA, et al. Dietary fat and protein in relation to risk of non-Hodgkin's lymphoma among women. *J Natl Cancer Inst.* 1999;91:1751-1758.

2. Chiu BC, Cerhan JR, Folsom AR, et al. Diet and risk of non-Hodgkin's lymphoma in older women. *JAMA.* 1996;275:1315-1321.

3. Chang ET, Smedby KE, Zhang SM, et al. Dietary factors and risk of non-Hodgkin's lymphoma in men and women. *Cancer Epidemiol Biomarkers Prev.* 2005;14:512-520.

4. Ursin G, Bjelke E, Heuch I, Vollset SE. Milk consumption and cancer incidence: a Norwegian prospective study. *Br J Cancer.* 1990;61:456-459.

5. Purdue MP, Bassani DG, Klar NS, Sloan M, Kreiger N, and the Canadian Cancer Registries Epidemiology Research Group. Dietary factors and risk of non-Hodgkin's lymphoma by histologic subtype: a case-control analysis. *Cancer Epidemiol Biomarkers Prev.* 2004;13:1665-1676.

6. Zhang SM, Hunter DJ, Rosner BA, et al. Intakes of fruits, vegetables, and related nutrients and the risk of non-Hodgkin's lymphoma among women. *Cancer Epidemiol Biomarkers Prev.* 2000;9:477-485.

7. Zheng T, Holford TR, Leaderer B, et al. Diet and nutrient intakes and risk of non-Hodgkin's lymphoma in Connecticut women. *Am J Epidemiol.* 2004;159:454-466.

8. Chatenoud L, Tavani A, La Vecchia C, et al. Whole grain food intake and cancer risk. *Int J Cancer.* 1998;77:24-28.

9. Green PH, Fleischauer AT, Bhagat G, Goyal R, Jabri B, Neugut AI. Risk of malignancy in patients with celiac disease. *Am J Med.* 2003;115:191-195.

10. Hervonen K, Vornanen M, Kautiainen H, Collin P, Reunala T. Lymphoma in patients with dermatitis herpetiformis and their first-degree relatives. *Br J Dermatol.* 2005;152:82-86.

11. Pan SY, Mao Y, Ugnat AM, and the Canadian Cancer Registries Epidemiology Research Group. Physical activity, obesity, energy intake, and the risk of non-Hodgkin's lymphoma: a population-based case-control study. *Am J Epidemiol.* 2005;162:1162-1173.

12. Cerhan JR, Bernstein L, Severson RK, et al. Anthropometrics, physical activity, related medical conditions, and the risk of non-Hodgkin lymphoma. *Cancer Causes Control.* 2005;16:1203-1214.

SECTION VI: INFECTIOUS DISEASES

30. Human Immunodeficiency Virus

Human immunodeficiency virus (HIV) is a retrovirus that infects and destroys specific lymphocytes (T-helper cells) and monocytes, ultimately disabling cell-mediated immunity cells containing the CD4+ antigen, particularly CD4+ T-helper cells. The virus enters the body through disrupted mucosal barriers and via contact with body fluids. Over time, morbidity and mortality occur due to opportunistic infections and malignancies that result from compromised immunity. Worldwide, approximately 60 million people are infected with HIV. About 40,000 new infections occur yearly in the United States.

Acquired immunodeficiency syndrome (AIDS) is defined as (1) a CD4 count of less than 200 cells/μL (the normal range is greater than 400 cells/μL) in an HIV-infected individual, or (2) the presence of an opportunistic infection resulting in an AIDS-defining illness. An opportunistic infection occurs when pathogens, such as bacteria, fungi, parasites, or atypical mycobacteria that would normally be controlled by a healthy immune system, flourish in patients with impaired immune systems.

Examples of opportunistic infections include: candidiasis of the esophagus or vagina; cryptosporidiosis with persistent diarrhea; cytomegalovirus (commonly as retinitis); herpes simplex infections of the esophagus, oropharynx, genitalia, or skin; Kaposi sarcoma; *Mycobacterium avium* complex infection; *Pneumocystis jiroveci* pneumonia (formerly known as *Pneumocystis carinii*); and toxoplasmosis of the brain. A complete listing is available at http://aidsinfo.nih.gov/.

HIV transmission occurs by sexual (including oral) intercourse, intravenous drug use with shared needles, vertical transmission through the placenta, breast-feeding, blood products, and open wound-fluid interchange. Perinatal infection can occur if the mother's viral load is not suppressed and the baby is born vaginally. Transmissibility rises in direct proportion to the HIV viral load.

Acute HIV seroconversion is often asymptomatic, although patients may manifest nonspecific symptoms that can be difficult to differentiate from other viral infections. For example, the initial presentation may be a flu-like or mononucleosis-like syndrome (headache, fever, chills, cough, myalgias, adenopathy) with a rash that occurs within 4 to 14 days of infection and lasts less than 3 weeks. Patients may also have aseptic meningitis that appears to be of viral origin on spinal fluid examination. Patients then return to their baseline state of health for 2 to 10 or more years, while the virus replicates within T cells and the CD4+ cell count declines.

As the number of CD4+ T cells declines, patients become more susceptible to infection and neoplasm. Once the CD4+ cells are sufficiently depleted, patients experience multiple opportunistic infections and malignancies that may affect any organ system. These include:

Pulmonary: *Pneumocystis* pneumonia, tuberculosis, pulmonary Kaposi sarcoma or fungal pulmonary disease (eg, coccidiomycosis or histoplasmosis).

Neurologic: Bell palsy, dementia, meningitis (aseptic and cryptococcal), syphilis, histoplasmosis, coccidiomycosis, cerebritis, spinal cord dysfunction (due to syphilis or viral infections such as cytomegalovirus), peripheral neuropathy.

Gastrointestinal: Esophagitis due to candidiasis, herpes simplex, or aphthous ulcerations; diarrhea due to parasites, including cryptosporidiosis and *Giardia lamblia;* liver disease due to hepatitis C coinfection, HIV-associated biliary tract disease, or cholangiopathy due to pneumocystis, cryptosporidiosis, cytomegalovirus, or *Mycobacterium avium* complex.

Rheumatologic: Arthritis.

Dermatologic: Kaposi sarcoma (due to herpesvirus 8), herpetic lesions, molluscum contagiosum caused by the poxvirus.

Hematologic: B-cell lymphomas, thrombocytopenia.

Risk Factors

High-risk sexual intercourse. This includes both heterosexual and homosexual contact. Approximately 90% of cases occur through heterosexual transmission.[1] Condom use reduces, but does not eliminate, the risk. Factors associated with increased risk of transmission include male-male sexual intercourse, lack of circumcision (female-to-male transmission),[2] and sexual intercourse during menses (female-to-male transmission).

Injection drug use. Drug injection is a particularly important source of the HIV epidemics in Eastern Europe, Asia, and the Middle East. For this reason, needle exchange programs have been implemented in several countries, resulting in decreased HIV transmission.

Perinatal transmission. Children are at risk in utero, during delivery (especially during vaginal delivery), and during breast-feeding. Prior to the initiation of antiretroviral therapy during pregnancy, transmission rates were as high as 25% and cesarean sections were recommended. However, through suppression of the HIV viral load with antiretroviral therapy during pregnancy, transmission rates have markedly declined and elective cesarean deliveries are no longer recommended. Avoidance of breast-feeding in HIV-positive mothers is recommended.

Occupational exposure. Risk of transmission after an accidental needle stick exposure is less than 1%. Hollow-bore needles have a greater risk of transmitting HIV, compared with solid-bore needles, which are used for suturing, piercing, etc.

Blood transfusion. Since 1985 the screening of blood products has significantly decreased the HIV transmission rate. The risk of transmission due to blood transfusion is now about 1 in 2 million.

Diagnosis

Early diagnosis is important, because early antiretroviral treatment enhances immunologic responses to HIV and likely delays progression to AIDS.

Several tests are available to identify HIV infection:

HIV RNA viral load is the most sensitive test for identifying primary HIV infection and is also used to follow disease progression. During acute infection, the viral load can be greater than 500,000, but it then falls significantly.

HIV enzyme-linked immunosorbent assay (ELISA) is positive in 95% of cases within 6 weeks of infection.

Western blot to identify HIV viral proteins has better than 99% specificity for HIV infection and is generally used for confirmation of a positive ELISA test.

Assay for the p24 antigen is rarely used because it is less sensitive than testing for HIV RNA.

CD4+ count is used to monitor the progression of HIV infection: the lower the value, the greater the risk for opportunistic infections. For example, *Pneumocystis* pneumonia is more likely to occur with a CD4+ count of <200 cells/μL, while cytomegalovirus infections occur with CD4+ counts <75 cells/μL. Abnormal complete blood count (CBC) is common and may reveal leukopenia, lymphocytosis, thrombocytopenia, and/or anemia.

After diagnosis, the CD4+ count and viral load are followed every 3 to 6 months to evaluate the progression of infection and the need for prophylaxis of opportunistic infections.

It is important to screen for other sexually transmitted diseases, including gonorrhea, chlamydia, syphilis, herpes, and hepatitis A, B, and C. Tuberculosis and toxoplasmosis screening are also done at the initial visit.

HIV genotyping and phenotyping should be done to assess drug resistance. Up to 25% of persons receiving antiretroviral therapy can still transmit resistant HIV.

Routine follow-up is important, with CBC, creatinine, renal function tests, and liver function tests to evaluate for medication side effects.

Other diagnostic tests are indicated, as necessary, for diagnosis of opportunistic infections (eg, chest x-ray, viral titers).

Treatment

Antiretroviral therapy has significantly improved the prognosis for HIV, reducing progression to AIDS, opportunistic infections, hospitalizations, and death. Most patients will achieve full viral suppression within several months of beginning therapy. The timing for initiation of antiretroviral therapy is controversial. Some clinicians initiate therapy at the time of HIV diagnosis, irrespective of the CD4+ count, while others wait for the CD4+ count to drop to the 300 to 350 cells/μL range. Some evidence suggests that early initiation of antiretroviral therapy (within 1 year of seroconversion) regardless of CD4+ count delays the onset of AIDS; this possibility is currently under investigation. Physicians and patients may consider enrollment in a clinical trial to take advantage of experimental therapies.

Antiretrovirals

Common classes of antiretroviral agents include:

Nucleoside reverse transcriptase inhibitors (eg, zidovudine, tenofovir, didanosine, lamivudine, emtricitabine, stavudine, abacavir).

Non-nucleoside reverse transcriptase inhibitors (eg, efavirenz, nevirapine, and delavirdine). Etravirine is currently available on a compassionate-use basis.

Protease inhibitors (eg, indinivir, lopinavir/ritonavir, atazanavir, fosamprenavir, darunavir).

A regimen combining three antiretroviral medications—known as highly active antiretroviral therapy (HAART) or "triple therapy"—is used to avoid or delay drug resistance. Strict adherence is essential to avoid resistance.

Once antiviral therapy begins, the CD4+ count and viral load should be assessed every 3 to 6 months, along with medication resistance studies if there is evidence of viral progression. Progression despite therapy adherence should lead to HIV genotyping and/or phenotyping, if not done previously, to help select alternative medicines.

Enfuvirtide is a fusion inhibitor, administered by injection. Its use may be indicated for patients who have failed typical HAART therapy, although studies have also suggested its use as part of an initial regimen. Enfuvirtide is typically used with an HAART regimen that is modified in an effort to overcome viral resistance.

Additional antiretroviral classes include **entry inhibitors** that act at various stages of viral entry into the CD4 cell and **integrase inhibitors**, which inhibit the viral integrase enzyme involved in several important steps in the HIV life cycle.

Prophylaxis

Antimicrobial prophylaxis for opportunistic infections is based on following the CD4+ count to anticipate risk. These infections are typically reactivations of indolent infections, rather than new infections.

Pneumocystis jiroveci **pneumonia:** Prophylaxis is usually indicated when the CD4+ count falls below 200 cells/μL. Agents include trimethoprim-sulfamethoxazole, dapsone, and aerosolized pentamidine.

Mycobacterium avium **complex:** Prophylaxis is usually indicated when CD4+ count falls below 100 cells/μL. Agents include clarithromycin and azithromycin.

Long-Term Antimicrobial Suppression

If *Pneumocystis jiroveci* pneumonia or cytomegalovirus retinitis develops, antimicrobial suppression should occur until the CD4+ count is above 200 cells/μL (in the case of pneumocystis) or above 75 cells/μL (in the case of cytomegalovirus) for over 6 months.

Exercise

Regular exercise can reduce some side effects of antiretroviral treatment. Aerobic exercise can help reduce total body and visceral fat and normalize lipid profiles in HIV-infected patients.[3] Combinations of aerobic exercise and progressive resistive exercise (done for at least 20 minutes ≥3 times per week) may also lead to significant reductions in depressive symptoms and improvements in cardiopulmonary fitness.[4]

Psychological Treatment

Psychological approaches can provide benefits for persons with HIV. Although further research is needed to confirm initial findings, available evidence suggests that excessive psychosocial stress can reduce resistance to opportunistic infections in HIV-positive persons. In women with HIV, higher indications of psychosocial stress increased the odds of developing progressive, persistent HPV-related squamous intraepithelial neoplasia 7-fold, compared with women experiencing the least life stress.[5] Greater stress also accounted for 46% of the variance in recurrence of genital herpes lesions.[6] Various psychological approaches are significantly associated with decreased viral load,[7] higher CD4+ cell counts,[8] and greater adherence to antiretroviral therapy.[9] HIV-positive men assigned to cognitive-behavioral stress management or active coping interventions were shown to have greater numbers of CD4+ cells.[10]

Nutritional Considerations

Nutritional issues in HIV infection relate to macronutrient and energy needs, lipid disorders, and micronutrient adequacy.

Macronutrient and Energy Needs

HIV infection can trigger a chronic-inflammation, wasting syndrome with increases in protein turnover and energy requirements. Studies of asymptomatic HIV-infected men showed elevated protein breakdown, protein synthesis, and resting energy expenditure, compared with non-HIV-infected individuals. Compensatory increased energy intake can help prevent wasting. Nonetheless, wasting is common, despite HAART.[11]

Protein intake is associated with decreased lean body mass, loss of which is strongly associated with disease progression and death in HIV-positive persons.[12] A review of available evidence noted that protein requirements of 1.0 to 1.4 grams/kg are indicated for maintenance of lean mass, and 1.5 to 2.0 grams/kg for anabolism.[13]

Protein supplementation with amino acids (L-arginine, L-glutamine) and related compounds (eg, beta-hydroxy beta-methylbutyrate, a metabolite of leucine) has a significant anticatabolic effect in HIV-positive persons.[14-17] However, additional clinical trials are required before these supplements can be routinely recommended.

Unless they are obese, patients should not be encouraged to lose significant amounts of weight. Studies have consistently shown that HIV-infected patients with a body mass index (BMI) of >25 have higher CD4+ cell counts, decreased risk of viral progression, and decreased mortality compared with their thinner (BMI <25) counterparts. This relationship may be explained by the elevated leptin production in heavier persons, which supports CD4+ cell proliferation.[18] Loss of excess weight may be helpful, however, for overweight patients on HAART whose risk factors for heart disease and diabetes have been elevated by the therapy.[19]

Diet and Lipid Disorders

A diet that addresses cardiovascular risk factors is appropriate for patients with HIV. Individuals with HIV were observed to have disturbances in lipid metabolism and insulin resistance prior to the advent of protease inhibitors. However, these medications appear to exacerbate this tendency, even in those without HIV infection. Medication-related decreases in the catabolism of both apoB and nuclear sterol regulatory element binding proteins in the liver and adipocytes bring about increases in fatty acid and cholesterol biosynthesis, insulin resistance, and lipodystrophy. As a result, 10% to 50% of patients on protease inhibitors have hypercholesterolemia, and 40% to 80% of these individuals have hypertriglyceridemia. Although prospective studies do not indicate that this situation leads to increased cardiovascular risk, retrospective analyses found significantly greater risk for myocardial infarction in users of protease inhibitors. Substitution with reverse transcriptase inhibitors does not appear to provide lipid-lowering benefits.[20]

Micronutrient Adequacy

Preliminary evidence suggests that higher intakes of fruits, vegetables, and juices increase T cell proliferation[21] or reduce CD38+/CD8+ count, a marker of disease progression.[22] Fruits and vegetables also provide many nutrients that are deficient in persons with HIV and help reduce the oxidative stress that may occur as a side effect of HAART.[23]

Low blood concentrations of many micronutrients are common in HIV-positive individuals and are associated with disease progression and increased mortality.[24] However, reviews have reached differing conclusions as to whether multivitamin supplements reduce morbidity and mortality.[24,25] Micronutrient supplements have been shown to be helpful for raising CD4 count.[26] Preliminary evidence suggested that selenium supplementation (200 μg/d) reduced the need for hospitalization by lowering the frequency of opportunistic infections,[27] and another study found that a 200 μg/d selenium supplement resulted in an increase in CD4 count and no increase in viral load over a 9-month period, while placebo-treated subjects experienced the opposite effects.[28]

Magnesium deficiency has been found in roughly 60% of HIV-infected individuals.[29] However, routine magnesium supplementation is not recommended except for persons on foscarnet, which frequently causes hypomagnesemia.[30] Future clinical trials may determine the impact of micronutrient supplementation on HIV and disease outcome.

Orders

See Coronary Heart Disease chapter.

Nutrition consultation to assess protein requirements.

Exercise prescription.

What to Tell the Family

HIV infection is not currently curable, but progressive immunosuppression and life-threatening, opportunistic infections can be greatly diminished through a combination of medications and a healthful diet. Emotional support from family, friends, and community, and also psychotherapeutic treatments, may provide additional immune benefits for persons with HIV. Family members can encourage healthy lifestyle changes through diet, regular exercise, and abstinence from tobacco and alcohol.

References

1. National Institute of Allergy and Infectious Diseases. HIV Infection in Women. May 2006. Available at: http://www.niaid.nih.gov/factsheets/womenhiv.htm. Accessed January 17, 2008.

2. Moses S, Plummer FA, Bradley JE, Ndinya-Achola JO, Nagelkerke NJ, Ronald AR. The association between lack of male circumcision and risk for HIV infection: a review of the epidemiological data. *Sex Transm Dis.* 1994;21:201-210.

3. Malita FM, Karelis AD, Toma E, Rabasa-Lhoret R. Effects of different types of exercise on body composition and fat distribution in HIV-infected patients: a brief review. *Can J Appl Physiol.* 2005;30:233-245.

4. Nixon S, O'Brien K, Glazier RH, Tynan AM. Aerobic exercise interventions for adults living with HIV/AIDS. *Cochrane Database Syst Rev.* 2005;(2):CD001796.

5. Pereira DB, Antoni MH, Danielson A, et al. Life stress and cervical squamous intraepithelial lesions in women with human papillomavirus and human immunodeficiency virus. *Psychosom Med.* 2003;65:427-434.

6. Pereira DB, Antoni MH, Danielson A, et al. Stress as a predictor of symptomatic genital herpes virus recurrence in women with human immunodeficiency virus. *J Psychosom Res.* 2003;54:237-244.

7. Ironson G, Weiss S, Lydston D, et al. The impact of improved self-efficacy on HIV viral load and distress in culturally diverse women living with AIDS: the SMART/EST Women's Project. *AIDS Care.* 2005;17:222-236.

8. Antoni MH, Cruess DG, Klimas N, et al. Stress management and immune system reconstitution in symptomatic HIV-infected gay men over time: effects on transitional naive T cells (CD4(+)CD45RA(+)CD29(+). *Am J Psychiatry.* 2002;159:143-145.

9. Weber R, Christen L, Christen S, et al. Effect of individual cognitive behaviour intervention on adherence to antiretroviral therapy: prospective randomized trial. *Antivir Ther.* 2004;9:85-95.

10. Antoni MH. Stress management effects on psychological, endocrinological, and immune functioning in men with HIV infection: empirical support for a psychoneuroimmunological model. *Stress.* 2003;6:173-188.

11. Crenn P, Rakotoanbinina B, Raynaud JJ, Thuillier F, Messing B, Melchior JC. Hyperphagia contributes to the normal body composition and protein-energy balance in HIV-infected asymptomatic men. *J Nutr.* 2004;134:2301-2306.

12. Williams SB, Bartsch G, Muurahainen N, Collins G, Raghavan SS, Wheeler D. Protein intake is positively associated with body cell mass in weight-stable HIV-infected men. *J Nutr.* 2003;133:1143-1146.

13. Coyne-Meyers K, Trombley LE. A review of nutrition in human immunodeficiency virus infection in the era of highly active antiretroviral therapy. *Nutr Clin Pract.* 2004;19:340-355.

14. Rathmacher JA, Nissen S, Panton L, et al. Supplementation with a combination of beta-hydroxy-beta-methylbutyrate (HMB), arginine, and glutamine is safe and could improve hematological parameters. *J Parenter Enteral Nutr.* 2004;28:65-75.

15. Schon T, Elias D, Moges F, et al. Arginine as an adjuvant to chemotherapy improves clinical outcome in active tuberculosis. *Eur Respir J.* 2003;21:483-488.

16. Clark RH, Feleke G, Din M, et al. Nutritional treatment for acquired immunodeficiency virus-associated wasting using beta-hydroxy beta-methylbutyrate, glutamine, and

arginine: a randomized, double-blind, placebo-controlled study. *J Parenter Enteral Nutr.* 2000;24:133-139.

17. Shabert JK, Winslow C, Lacey JM, Wilmore DW. Glutamine-antioxidant supplementation increases body cell mass in AIDS patients with weight loss: a randomized, double-blind controlled trial. *Nutrition.* 1999;15:860-864.

18. Jones CY, Hogan JW, Snyder B, et al. Overweight and human immunodeficiency virus (HIV) progression in women: associations [between] HIV disease progression and changes in body mass index in women in the HIV epidemiology research study cohort. *Clin Infect Dis.* 2003;37(suppl 2):S69-S80.

19. Gerrior JL, Neff LM. Nutrition assessment in HIV infection. *Nutr Clin Care.* 2005;8:6-15.

20. Calza L, Manfredi R, Chiodo F. Dyslipidaemia associated with antiretroviral therapy in HIV-infected patients. *J Antimicrob Chemother.* 2004;53:10-14.

21. Winkler P, Ellinger S, Boetzer AM, et al. Lymphocyte proliferation and apoptosis in HIV-seropositive and healthy subjects during long-term ingestion of fruit juices or a fruit-vegetable-concentrate rich in polyphenols and antioxidant vitamins. *Eur J Clin Nutr.* 2004;58:317-325.

22. Gil L, Lewis L, Martinez G, et al. Effect of increase of dietary micronutrient intake on oxidative stress indicators in HIV/AIDS patients. *Int J Vitam Nutr Res.* 2005;75:19-27.

23. Tang AM, Lanzillotti J, Hendricks K, et al. Micronutrients: current issues for HIV care providers. *AIDS.* 2005;19:847-861.

24. Lanzillotti JS, Tang AM. Micronutrients and HIV disease: a review pre- and post-HAART. *Nutr Clin Care.* 2005;8:16-23.

25. Irlam JH, Visser ME, Rollins N, Siegfried N. Micronutrient supplementation in children and adults with HIV infection. *Cochrane Database Syst Rev.* 2005;(4):CD003650.

26. Kaiser JD, Campa AM, Ondercin JP, Leoung GS, Pless RF, Baum MK. Micronutrient supplementation increases CD4 count in HIV-infected individuals on highly-active antiretroviral therapy: a prospective, double-blinded, placebo-controlled trial. *J Acquir Immune Defic Syndr.* 2006;42:523-528.

27. Burbano X, Miguez-Burbano MJ, McCollister K, et al. Impact of a selenium chemoprevention clinical trial on hospital admissions of HIV-infected participants. *HIV Clin Trials.* 2002;3:483-491.

28. Hurwitz BE, Klaus JR, Llabre MM, et al. Suppression of Human Immunodeficiency Virus Type 1 Viral Load With Selenium Supplementation: A Randomized Controlled Trial. *Arch Intern Med.* 2007;167:148-154.

29. Singhal N, Austin J. A clinical review of micronutrients in HIV infection. *J Int Assoc Physicians AIDS Care* (Chicago, Ill). 2002;1:63-75.

30. Huycke MM, Naguib MT, Stroemmel MM, et al. A double-blind placebo-controlled crossover trial of intravenous magnesium sulfate for foscarnet-induced ionized hypocalcemia and hypomagnesemia in patients with AIDS and cytomegalovirus infection. *Antimicrob Agents Chemother.* 2000;44:2143-2148.

31. Upper Respiratory Infection

Upper respiratory infections (URIs), or colds, can be caused by many families of viruses, such as rhinovirus (which has at least 100 serotypes), coronavirus, and respiratory syncytial virus. URIs are the most common acute illnesses in the industrial world.

Cold symptoms include:

- Rhinitis (sneezing, nasal congestion, and postnasal drip).

- Pharyngitis.

- Cough, usually dry.

- Fatigue and myalgias.

- Mild fever.

- Conjunctivitis.

Risk Factors

Direct contact with individuals who have an upper respiratory infection permits viral transfer. In particular, closed settings such as homes and schools have higher attack rates than work settings. Seasonal variations occur for some viral families. However, cold climates are not necessarily a risk factor for disease occurrence or severity.[1]

Touching is the most effective mode of transmission. Typically, a person with a cold rubs his or her eyes or nose and then shakes hands or touches objects that others touch later. Saliva is not an effective mode of transmission.

Diagnosis

Common cold symptoms are listed above. Colds and influenza typically have few physical findings and often cannot be distinguished reliably in clinical settings. If a definitive diagnosis of influenza is important, certain tests may be useful (see Influenza chapter). Patients with symptoms or signs of lower respiratory infection, such as dyspnea or rales, should be evaluated for pneumonia or exacerbation of chronic lung disease. URIs do not cause signs of systemic inflammatory response; patients who appear seriously ill may require antibiotics or hospital admission. Severe or persistent cough or paroxysms of coughing in adults or adolescents should raise the question of pertusis, a highly infectious URI caused by *Bordetella pertussis*.

Prevention and Treatment

Covering the mouth and nose when coughing and sneezing, washing hands appropriately, and avoiding touching one's eyes and nose are the most effective preventive strategies.

Moderation in exercise may help immunity. There is a high incidence of upper respiratory infection in endurance athletes, which some have attributed to impairments in neutrophil function, reductions in serum and mucosal immunoglobulin production, and, possibly, impaired natural killer cell cytotoxicity. In contrast, some evidence suggests that moderate physical activity has a stimulant effect on these parameters. Further study is needed.[2]

Individuals who have more frequent or long-lasting periods of psychological stress are at greater risk for upper respiratory infection. In this population, studies have shown an increase in certain proinflammatory cytokines (eg, interleukin-6)[3] or a reduction in mucosal production of secretory immunoglobulin A (sIgA).[4] Although further research is required, some studies have found that stress management techniques (cognitive-behavioral therapy, progressive muscle relaxation, focused breathing, relaxation, guided imagery) increase the production of sIgA and reduce the number of sick days.[4,5]

When cold symptoms occur, only symptomatic treatment is beneficial. There are no specific treatments for URIs, such as antibiotics. Heated and humidified air may improve symptoms.[6] The following agents may also be helpful:

Decongestants. A brief course of pseudoephedrine may be of benefit, as may topical nasal decongestant sprays. However, topical agents should only be used for 2 to 3 days, as they cause tachyphylaxis, and extended use of pseudoephedrine is unlikely to be helpful. In general, it is best to avoid nasal sprays, except perhaps for sleep. Pseudoephedrine taken with an antihistamine is more effective than when taken alone. Data are lacking on decongestant use in children.[7]

Intranasal cromolyn sodium and **ipratropium bromide** may reduce the severity of cold symptoms. Cromolyn sodium can also be inhaled.

Antihistamines. Clemastine fumarate improves sneezing and rhinorrhea,[8] and **diphenhydramine** may also be effective. Both drugs cause sedation and anticholinergic effects and should be used with caution in elderly patients or in individuals taking other anticholinergic agents. Several other antihistamines are also available without a prescription.

Analgesics. Acetaminophen, aspirin, and **ibuprofen** may improve sore throat symptoms and myalgias. Their use for mild fever is unnecessary. Aspirin should not be used in children with an acute viral illness, due to the risk of Reye syndrome.

Evidence supporting **mucolytics**, such as **guaifenesin**, and **antitussives**, such as **dextromethorphan** and **codeine**, is varied and inconclusive.[9] Their use may benefit certain patients, but more research is needed to make global recommendations. Caution: Codeine may be habit-forming.

Antibiotics should be considered or used only for specific bacterial infections, such as sinusitis, streptococcal pharyngitis, otitis media, and bronchitis. In the case of bronchitis, they should not be used unless the cough is persistent or the patient has underlying lung disease. Not all cases of otitis media and sinusitis require antibiotics. Unnecessary prescribing increases the likelihood of antibiotic resistance.

Antibacterial cleaning products do not affect disease transmission, and they may cause bacterial resistance. Phenol/acetate sprays for household use do have virucidal properties.

Complications of upper respiratory illness include sinusitis, asthma exacerbation, otitis media, and other respiratory illnesses. See the chapters on these conditions for more information.

Nutritional Considerations

Upper respiratory infections are caused not simply by the presence of an invading microorganism, but also by the failure of the immune system to eliminate the intruder. Diet is a significant modulator of immunity. Notably, high-fat diets are immunosuppressive, while certain micronutrients play important roles in immune function. Unfortunately, many Americans regularly consume too much fat, and up to 50% get less than half the Recommended Dietary Allowance for many micronutrients.[10] Deficiencies of these nutrients are known to impair immune function.[11]

Although diet changes (eg, increasing the intake of carotenoid-containing foods or reducing fat intake) have been found to stimulate immune function,[12,13] these improvements have mainly been identified in clinical trials of nutrient supplements, rather than in trials of therapeutic diets. Clinical trials comparing the immune-enhancing effects of various diets (eg, high-fat vs. low-fat, omnivore vs. vegetarian) are not yet available, so potential benefits of dietary alterations for the treatment or prevention of colds remain speculative.

The role of certain micronutrients in the prevention or treatment of URIs is discussed below.

Vitamin mineral supplements. Older individuals are often deficient in a number of vitamins and minerals, predisposing them to a blunting of the innate and the adaptive immune responses.[14,15] Some studies suggest that multiple vitamin-mineral supplements may reduce sick days and antibiotic use. The trace elements zinc and selenium, known to be important in immune function, may be responsible for this effect.[14]

Zinc. The potential of zinc lozenges to reduce the duration of common colds is controversial. Zinc ions inhibit rhinoviruses through several mechanisms: prevention of viral replication;[16] potentiation of the antiviral action of native human interferon; and stimulation of T-cells.[17] Zinc lozenges have significantly reduced the duration of colds in some studies[18-20] but not in others,[21] and meta-analyses of controlled trials have not confirmed the effectiveness of this treatment.[22] These discrepancies may be due to the formulation of zinc lozenges, which seems to influence their effectiveness. Many (zinc aspartate, zinc glycinate, zinc orotate) bind zinc tightly and do not release the positively charged zinc ions that are the active principle, or they release negatively charged zinc ions that may actually increase the duration of colds. In comparison, studies using other forms of zinc (eg, zinc gluconate, zinc acetate) have found them to be an effective treatment.[16,18,23] Patients should be cautioned that irritation of the oral mucosa and mild gastrointestinal complaints are common with zinc lozenges, while nasal irritation occurs more frequently with gel and spray forms. In addition, zinc lozenges are maximally effective only when used every 2 hours. Nasal gel/spray formulations are most effective when used every 4 hours. Zinc nasal preparations have been implicated as a possible cause of the loss of sense of smell. Patients should be appropriately cautioned prior to use.

Vitamin C. The utility of vitamin C for preventing or treating colds is widely accepted in the general population. However, most evidence supports the efficacy of megadoses for upper respiratory infections only for individuals who are under significant physical or environmental stress, such as marathon runners, skiers, soldiers, and people exposed to severe cold.[24,25] In these persons, the relative risk for developing colds was reduced by 50% when they took vitamin C supplements, compared with the risk in individuals not using supplements.[24] Among the same groups, those taking vitamin C had 80% to 100% reductions in pneumonia incidence, compared with persons given placebo.[25]

Vitamin E. In pharmacologic amounts, vitamin E reduces the production by cyclooxygenase of prostaglandin E2, a suppressor of T-cell function, and enhances lymphocyte proliferation and interleukin-2 production.[26] In elderly nursing home residents, 200 IU of vitamin E per day significantly reduced the incidence of common colds and the number of persons who got colds.[27] Further research is required to determine whether vitamin E can reduce the incidence of infections in younger populations.

Vitamin E supplementation may have the opposite effect in persons with established respiratory infections. Supplements of 200 mg/day caused longer illness duration, more symptoms, and higher fever frequency.[26]

Echinacea. Anecdotal reports support the effectiveness of the common botanical echinacea, but clinical trials to date have been negative or inconclusive. A lack of standardization of purportedly active ingredients is another stumbling block that must be overcome before echinacea can be recommended for URIs.[28]

Excessive alcohol intake can increase susceptibility to infection. Although small amounts (1-2 drinks per day) do not appear to adversely affect immunity,[29,30] alcohol abuse increases the incidence of infectious diseases through depleting circulating lymphocyte populations and suppressing production of cytokines important in antimicrobial immunity.[29]

Orders

See Basic Diet Orders chapter.

What to Tell the Family

The common cold is easily transmitted within the household. Family members should be encouraged to cover their mouths and noses while coughing and sneezing and to promptly wash their hands, taking care not to contaminate handles and light switches. Refraining from touching the eyes and nose may also help prevent respiratory infections. Vitamins and other supplements may be beneficial in some, but not all, individuals.

References

1. Warshauer DM, Dick EC, Mandel AD, Flynn TC, Jerde RS. Rhinovirus infections in an isolated Antarctic station. Transmission of the viruses and susceptibility of the population. *Am J Epidemiol.* 1989;129:319-340.

2. Mackinnon LT. Chronic exercise training effects on immune function. *Med Sci Sports Exerc.* 2000;32(suppl 7):S369-S376.

3. Cohen S. Keynote Presentation at the Eight International Congress of Behavioral Medicine: the Pittsburgh common cold studies: psychosocial predictors of susceptibility to respiratory infectious illness. *Int J Behav Med.* 2005;12:123-131.

4. Reid MR, Mackinnon LT, Drummond PD. The effects of stress management on symptoms of upper respiratory tract infection, secretory immunoglobulin A, and mood in young adults. *J Psychosom Res.* 2001;51:721-728.

5. Hewson-Bower B, Drummond PD. Psychological treatment for recurrent symptoms of colds and flu in children. *J Psychosom Res.* 2001;51:369-377.

6. Singh M. Heated, humidified air for the common cold. *Cochrane Database Syst Rev.* 2004;(2):CD001728.

7. Taverner D, Latte J, Draper M. Nasal decongestants for the common cold. *Cochrane Database Syst Rev.* 2004;(3):CD001953.

8. Turner RB, Sperber SJ, Sorrentino JV, et al. Effectiveness of clemastine fumarate for treatment of rhinorrhea and sneezing associated with the common cold. *Clin Infect Dis.* 1997;25:824-830.

9. Schroeder K, Fahey T. Over-the-counter medications for acute cough in children and adults in ambulatory settings. *Cochrane Database Syst Rev.* 2004;(4):CD001831.

10. Ames BN, Wakimoto P. Are vitamin and mineral deficiencies a major cancer risk? *Nat Rev Cancer.* 2002;2:694-704.

11. Cunningham-Rundles S, McNeeley DF, Moon A. Mechanisms of nutrient modulation of the immune response. *J Allergy Clin Immunol.* 2005;115:1119-1128.

12. Kelley DS. Modulation of human immune and inflammatory responses by dietary fatty acids. *Nutrition.* 2001;17:669-673.

13. Watzl B, Bub A, Brandstetter BR, Rechkemmer G. Modulation of human T-lymphocyte functions by the consumption of carotenoid-rich vegetables. *Br J Nutr.* 1999;82:383-389.

14. High KP. Nutritional strategies to boost immunity and prevent infection in elderly individuals. *Clin Infect Dis.* 2001;33:1892-1900.

15. El-Kadiki A, Sutton AJ. Role of multivitamins and mineral supplements in preventing infections in elderly people: systematic review and meta-analysis of randomised controlled trials. *BMJ.* 2005;330:871-874.

16. Hulisz D. Efficacy of zinc against common cold viruses: an overview. *J Am Pharm Assoc.* 2004;44:594-603.

17. Mossad SB. Effect of zincum gluconicum nasal gel on the duration and symptom severity of the common cold in otherwise healthy adults. *QJM.* 2003;96:35-43.

18. Eby GA. Zinc lozenges: cold cure or candy? Solution chemistry determinations. *Biosci Rep.* 2004;24:23-39.

19. Kurugol Z, Akilli M, Bayram N, Koturoglu G. The prophylactic and therapeutic effectiveness of zinc sulphate on common cold in children. *Acta Paediatr.* 2006;95:1175-1181.

20. McElroy BH, Miller SP. An open-label, single-center, phase IV clinical study of the effectiveness of zinc gluconate glycine lozenges (Cold-Eeze) in reducing the duration and symptoms of the common cold in school-aged subjects. *Am J Ther.* 2003;10:324-329.

21. Turner RB; Cetnarowski WE. Effect of treatment with zinc gluconate or zinc acetate on experimental and natural colds. *Clin Infect Dis.* 2000;31:1202-1208.

22. Marshall I. Zinc for the common cold. *Cochrane Database Syst Rev.* 2000;(2):CD001364.

23. Mossad SB, Macknin ML, Medendorp SV, Mason P. Zinc gluconate lozenges for treating the common cold. A randomized, double-blind, placebo-controlled study. *Ann Intern Med.* 1996;125:81-88.

24. Douglas RM, Hemila H, D'Souza R, Chalker EB, Treacy B. Vitamin C for preventing and treating the common cold. *Cochrane Database Syst Rev.* 2004;(4):CD000980.

25. Hemila H. Vitamin C supplementation and respiratory infections: a systematic review. *Mil Med.* 2004;169:920-925.

26. Graat JM, Schouten EG, Kok FJ. Effect of daily vitamin E and multivitamin-mineral supplementation on acute respiratory tract infections in elderly persons: a randomized controlled trial. *JAMA.* 2002;288:715-721.

27. Meydani SN, Leka LS, Fine BC, et al. Vitamin E and respiratory tract infections in elderly nursing home residents: a randomized controlled trial. *JAMA.* 2004;292:828-836.

28. Caruso TJ, Gwaltney JM Jr. Treatment of the common cold with echinacea: a structured review. *Clin Infect Dis.* 2005;40:807-810.

29. Friedman H, Newton C, Klein TW. Microbial infections, immunomodulation, and drugs of abuse. *Clin Microbiol Rev.* 2003;16:209-219.

30. Takkouche B, Regueira-Mendez C, Garcia-Closas R, Figueiras A, Gestal-Otero JJ, Hernan MA. Intake of wine, beer, and spirits and the risk of clinical common cold. *Am J Epidemiol.* 2002; 55:853-858.

32. Influenza

Influenza viruses A and B cause acute respiratory infection. Influenza may present with symptoms similar to the common cold (see Upper Respiratory Infection chapter) but also often causes more severe systemic symptoms, such as high fever, myalgias, weakness, and severe pulmonary involvement.

Symptoms typically begin abruptly after a 1- to 4-day incubation. An infected person can pass the virus to others for up to 24 hours before symptoms begin and for approximately 1 week after symptom onset. Uncomplicated influenza is self-limiting. In high-risk populations, however, influenza can cause significant morbidity and mortality.

Influenza has become a matter of increasing concern due to outbreaks of H5N1 avian influenza and the confirmation that the pandemic of 1918, which killed up to 50 million people, was caused by an avian virus with properties similar to those of H5N1.[1,2] Wild birds may carry influenza viruses in their digestive tracts and are believed to pass them to domesticated birds, typically in poultry farms, where viruses may replicate and be transmitted to humans. H5N1 has proven fatal to nearly 100% of infected chickens and about 50% of infected humans.[3]

At present, however, the greatest threat is seasonal influenza, which kills approximately 36,000 persons in the United States every year.[4]

Risk Factors

Contact with infected individuals. Direct contact with persons who have an upper respiratory infection permits viral transfer. Coughing or sneezing aerosolizes respiratory droplets containing influenza virus. The droplets commonly make contact with hands and household surfaces and can be easily transmitted to uninfected persons. They can also be directly inhaled. Saliva, however, is not an effective mode of transmission.

Closed settings. Homes and schools have higher transmission rates, compared with typical work settings.

Immunocompromise. Persons with compromised immune systems, including those with malnutrition, diabetes, and chronic respiratory disease, generally have a higher risk of mortality if they are infected by influenza. However, the influenza pandemic of 1918 and the recent H5N1 outbreaks led to unexpectedly high mortality rates in young, otherwise healthy persons.

Winter season. Influenza infections more commonly occur in the winter, but cold climates are not necessarily a risk factor.

Contact with infected birds. Risk for H5N1 influenza is principally related to contact with infected domesticated birds or bird feces, secretions, and products.

Diagnosis

Influenza typically has few physical findings and in mild cases may be indistinguishable from common colds.

Patients with symptoms or signs of lower-respiratory infection, such as dyspnea and rales, should be evaluated for pneumonia or exacerbation of chronic lung disease. Persons who appear seriously ill may require hospitalization and antibiotic treatment when bacterial pneumonia or systemic infection is suspected.

Rapid influenza tests that distinguish influenza A and B are valuable diagnostic tools when influenza is suspected in the clinic and when antiviral therapy could shorten the course and reduce symptoms. Rapid tests may not be useful or cost-effective during outbreaks, when the probability of flu is high. Most individuals who present with flu-like illnesses during an outbreak can be treated accordingly without further testing. Clinical judgment is paramount in these situations.[5]

Diagnostic testing can help track the specific strains of viruses circulating in a certain region or during a particular season, but it is not helpful clinically.

Prevention and Treatment

Covering the mouth and nose when coughing and sneezing, washing hands appropriately, and avoiding touching one's eyes and nose are the most effective preventive strategies to avoid infection.

Vaccines, when well matched to the circulating strains, are approximately 75% effective in preventing influenza.[6] Vaccines may also reduce hospitalization and pneumonia related to influenza as well as all-cause mortality in the elderly.[7] Current vaccines will not protect against emerging strains of avian influenza; however, annual vaccines could help avert epidemics by reducing the risk of coinfection. Each influenza viron contains 2 copies of its genetic code. It is therefore possible for a person infected simultaneously with seasonal and avian influenza to produce a new influenza viron that is both highly virulent (avian influenza) and highly transmissible (annual influenza).

Exercise appears to improve vaccine response, particularly in the elderly. The efficacy of influenza vaccine is reduced in older people, partly because of immunosenescence.[8] Moderate exercise (>20 minutes, 3 times/week) significantly improved antibody response to influenza vaccine in studies in this population.[8,9]

In older individuals, levels of perceived stress have been shown to affect certain immune responses to flu vaccine (eg, production of antibodies and interleukin-2).[8,10] A limited body of evidence suggests that stress-management interventions can produce significant increases in antibody titer after flu vaccination.[11] However, further research is required before such interventions can be recommended universally.

Treatment

Influenza is a self-limited illness, except in high-risk individuals or when a highly pathogenic strain is involved. In general, symptoms can be prevented or reduced in duration with antivirals if started within 36 hours, although drugs are most effective when started within 12 to 24 hours of exposure or symptom development. It is not clear whether these drugs prevent complications or are effective in high-risk populations.[12] Because of its high cost, preventive drug therapy may be reserved for high-risk populations. Vaccination remains the most effective mode of prevention, even when some individuals within a group are not immunized, a phenomenon referred to as "herd immunity."

The following antivirals may reduce symptoms and shorten the course of disease:

Oseltamivir (Tamiflu) and zanamivir (Relenza). These neuraminidase inhibitors are generally effective for prevention and treatment of influenza A and B, but only oseltamivir is approved for prevention. Most H5N1 infections have been sensitive to oseltamivir, although resistance has been reported.[13,14] Oseltamivir is generally well-tolerated, but zanamivir may cause respiratory side effects, including bronchospasm, in those with respiratory problems.

Probenecid. This gout medication, when taken simultaneously with one-half the normal oseltamivir dose, may provide an effective serum concentration for influenza treatment, thus extending the supply of a potentially scarce medicine.[15] This is an off-label use of probenecid.

Amantadine and rimantadine (M2 ion channel blockers). These drugs are only effective against influenza A, but even when they are used for influenza A, resistance is common. Rimantadine may have fewer central nervous system side effects. However, if one drug is ineffective, the other drug is also ineffective. Current H5N1 avian influenza strains are resistant to these drugs. The CDC has recommended that these drugs not be used for prevention or treatment of influenza until broader susceptibility of influenza A viruses is verified.

Acetaminophen, aspirin, and ibuprofen. These common medications may improve myalgias. Their use for mild fever is unnecessary. Aspirin should not be used in children with an acute viral illness, due to the risk of Reye syndrome. When cold symptoms occur, only symptomatic treatment is beneficial (see Upper Respiratory Infection chapter).

The most common complication of influenza is viral and/or bacterial pneumonia. Rare extrapulmonary complications include myositis, rhabdomyolysis, pericarditis, myocarditis, Reye syndrome, Guillain-Barré syndrome, and toxic shock syndrome due to coinfection with *S aureus*. All of these require specialized treatment.

Nutritional Considerations

The nutritional status of the host can affect immunity in a variety of ways, and deficiencies of most micronutrients can impair immunity, including antibody response.[16] However, in one study, the immune response to vaccination in older patients was not associated with plasma levels of several micronutrients believed to affect immunity, such as retinol and zinc.[17] Similarly, another study showed that immune response was not improved by supplementation with a combination multiple vitamin/trace element formula.[18]

A botanical extract may be of benefit. The berries of black elder contain high levels of naturally occurring flavonoids that have been shown to markedly stimulate proinflammatory cytokine production.[19] These flavonoids may also act against herpes simplex virus type 1, respiratory syncytial virus, and the parainfluenza and influenza viruses,[20] and studies have found that black elderberry extract reduced the duration of influenza by >50%.[20] Further research is necessary to confirm its effectiveness.

Orders

See Basic Diet Orders chapter.

What to Tell the Family

Influenza is easily transmitted within households or closed living environments, such as nursing homes. Covering one's mouth and nose while coughing and sneezing and prompt hand washing should be encouraged. Refraining from touching the eyes and nose may also help prevent respiratory infections. A flu vaccine is important for persons over the age of 50; pregnant women; children aged 6 months to 5 years; people living in long-term care facilities; anyone with a chronic disease, such as diabetes, HIV infection, or asthma; household contacts of persons at high risk; and health care workers. When flu occurs in the family, prescription medicines may be effective for treatment or prevention if received within 48 hours of symptom onset.

References

1. Taubenberger JK, Reid AH, Lourens RM, Wang R, Jin G, Fanning TG. Characterization of the 1918 influenza virus polymerase genes. *Nature*. 2005;437:889-893.

2. Belshe RB. The origins of the pandemic influenza—lessons from the 1918 virus. *N Engl J Med*. 2005;353:2209-2211.

3. World Health Organization. Epidemic and Pandemic Alert and Response (EPR): Avian influenza. Available at: http://www.who.int/csr/disease/avian_influenza/en/index.html. Accessed February 3, 2006.

4. Centers for Disease Control and Prevention. Influenza: The Disease. Available at: http://www.cdc.gov/flu/about/disease.htm. Accessed August 18, 2007.

5. Rothberg MB, Fisher D, Kelly B, Rose DN. Management of influenza symptoms in healthy children: cost-effectiveness of rapid testing and antiviral therapy. *Arch Pediatr Adolesc Med*. 2005;159:1055-1062.

6. Edwards KM, Dupont WD, Westrich MK, Plummer WD Jr, Palmer PS, Wright PF. A randomized controlled trial of cold-adapted and inactivated vaccines for the prevention of influenza A disease. *J Infect Dis*. 1994;169:68-76.

7. Fedson DS, Wajda A, Nicol JP, Hammond GW, Kaiser DL, Roos LL. Clinical effectiveness of influenza vaccination in Manitoba. *JAMA*. 1993;270:1956-1961.

8. Kohut ML, Cooper MM, Nickolaus MS, Russell DR, Cunnick JE. Exercise and psychosocial factors modulate immunity to influenza vaccine in elderly individuals. *J Gerontol A Biol Sci Med Sci*. 2002;57:M557-M562.

9. Kohut ML, Arntson BA, Lee W, et al. Moderate exercise improves antibody response to influenza immunization in older adults. *Vaccine*. 2004;22:2298-2306.

10. Moynihan JA, Larson MR, Treanor J, et al. Psychosocial factors and the response to influenza vaccination in older adults. *Psychosom Med*. 2004;66:950-953.

11. Vedhara K, Bennett PD, Clark S. Enhancement of antibody responses to influenza vaccination in the elderly following a cognitive-behavioural stress management intervention. *Psychother Psychosom*. 2003;72:245-252.

12. Centers for Disease Control and Prevention. Prevention and control of influenza: recommendations of the Advisory Committee on Immunization Practices (ACIP). *MMWR Recomm Rep*. 2004;53:1-40.

13. Le QM, Kiso M, Someya K, et al. Avian flu: isolation of drug-resistant H5N1 virus. *Nature*. 2005;437:1108.

14. Hatakeyama S, Sugaya N, Ito M, et al. Emergence of influenza B viruses with reduced sensitivity to neuraminidase inhibitors. *JAMA*. 2007;297:1435-1442.

15. Butler D. Wartime tactic doubles power of scarce bird-flu drug. *Nature*. 2005;438:6.

16. Cunningham-Rundles S, McNeeley DF, Moon A. Mechanisms of nutrient modulation of the immune response. *J Allergy Clin Immunol*. 2005;115:1119-1128.

17. Gardner EM, Bernstein ED, Popoff KA, Abrutyn E, Gross P, Murasko DM. Immune response to influenza vaccine in healthy elderly: lack of association with plasma beta-carotene, retinol, alpha-tocopherol, or zinc. *Mech Ageing Dev*. 2000;117:29-45.

18. Allsup SJ, Shenkin A, Gosney MA, et al. Difficulties of recruitment for a randomized controlled trial involving influenza vaccination in healthy older people. *Gerontology*. 2002;48:170-173.

19. Barak V, Halperin T, Kalickman I. The effect of Sambucol, a black elderberry-based, natural product, on the production of human cytokines: I. Inflammatory cytokines. *Eur Cytokine Netw*. 2001;12:290-296.

20. Zakay-Rones Z, Thom E, Wollan T, Wadstein J. Randomized study of the efficacy and safety of oral elderberry extract in the treatment of influenza A and B virus infections. *J Int Med Res*. 2004;32:132-140.

SECTION VII: CARDIOVASCULAR DISEASES

33. Coronary Heart Disease

Coronary heart disease (CHD) is the most common cause of death for both men and women in Western countries and is increasingly prevalent in developing countries. Also called coronary artery disease, this atherosclerotic process includes injury to arterial endothelium, fatty streaks due to macrophage ingestion of oxidized LDL cholesterol at the damaged site, platelet aggregation, and fibrosis. These events contribute to plaque formation in the intimal layer of medium and large arteries. Progressive arterial narrowing causes ischemia, which occurs initially with exertion but may eventually occur at rest.

Atherosclerosis commonly begins in childhood and slowly progresses throughout life. However, rapid progression may occur by the third decade of life. Symptoms often do not present until late stages. Angina pectoris is frequently the main presenting symptom. It results from ischemia due to the narrowing of one or more coronary arteries. Angina is typically described as substernal pressure, and it can radiate to the neck, arms, back, and upper abdomen. Stable angina tends to occur regularly or predictably with exertion, whereas unstable angina occurs unpredictably, often with minimal exertion or at rest.

When atherosclerotic plaques rupture, vasoconstriction and clot formation can lead to complete occlusion of a coronary artery, causing myocardial infarction (MI). MI may be silent, or it may be signaled by prolonged pain or discomfort similar to that associated with simple angina. Compared with men (who are more likely to experience crushing substernal chest pain), women are more likely to experience shortness of breath, jaw or back pain, and nausea/vomiting. Further, care is sometimes delayed for women because caregivers and patients may believe that women are not at significant risk for cardiac disease.

Atherosclerosis of the extremities—ie, peripheral vascular disease—often presents as claudication, in which calf, thigh, or hip pain is associated with activity and relieved with rest. Other signs of peripheral vascular disease include underdeveloped calf muscles, hairless shiny skin on the lower extremities, dystrophic toenails, bruits over the femoral, iliac, or popliteal arteries, and decreased peripheral pulses.

Risk Factors

Increasing age.

Diabetes. Hyperinsulinemia or impaired glucose tolerance, without a diagnosis of diabetes, also raises the risk for CHD.

Dyslipidemia.

Cigarette smoking.

Hypertension.

Family history. First-degree relatives with myocardial infarction before age 55 (men), or 65 (women).

Male gender.

Obesity. Excess weight is associated with several risk factors for CHD (see Obesity chapter).

The metabolic syndrome. The presence of the metabolic syndrome predicts CHD more strongly than do its individual components:[1] (See Obesity chapter.)

Chronic kidney disease and **microalbuminuria.**

Sedentary lifestyle.

Inflammation. Elevated inflammatory markers, such as CRP, are associated with risk of CHD.

Stress. Some evidence suggests that psychological stress is associated with CHD risk. Socioeconomic status has also been associated with risk, perhaps through its contribution to stress.

Diagnosis

Diagnosis of atherosclerosis and CHD is based on a patient's individual risk factors, along with a careful medical history, physical exam, and diagnostic tests. Stress tests and imaging studies are generally not advised for asymptomatic individuals, except when certain or multiple CHD risk factors exist, or when vigorous exercise is planned.

Blood Tests

No blood test can definitively diagnose atherosclerosis. However, epidemiological studies have found fibrinogen,[2] white blood cell counts,[3] cholesterol, C-reactive protein, and homocysteine concentrations to be associated with plaque formation and heart disease risk. For MI, a number of laboratory tests are available, but none is completely sensitive or specific. Correlation with patient symptoms, electrocardiograms, and angiographic studies is crucial.

Creatine kinase-MB fraction (CK-MB). CK-MB is a specific marker for acute myocardial injury. The serum concentration rises within 2 to 8 hours of the onset of acute MI. Serial measurements every 2 to 4 hours (for about 12 hours) help determine the extent and time frame of myocardial injury. CK-MB is also useful for the determination of reinfarction, or extension of myocardial injury. Concentrations normally decrease after 1 to 3 days, so subsequent elevations or plateaus indicate another myocardial infarction.

Troponins. These proteins combine with calcium to facilitate cardiac muscle cell contraction through actin-myosin interaction. Troponins are released into the bloodstream during myocardial injury. Troponin T lacks specificity for myocardial injury because it is also present in skeletal muscle cells. Troponin I is more specific for myocardial injury than troponin T or CK-MB.

Levels of both troponin I and CK-MB increase during the early course of a myocardial infarction. Because troponin I remains elevated for 5 to 14 days, it has greater sensitivity than CK-MB and LDH as a marker for diagnosing recent MI. However, this prolonged elevation may mask reinfarction or extension of infarction in the early days after an initial event.

Cholesterol. Elevated total and low-density lipoprotein (LDL) cholesterol concentrations, and low high-density lipoprotein (HDL) cholesterol concentrations (less than 50 mg/dL in women and 40 mg/dL in men), increase the risks for atherosclerosis and CHD events. Although the National Cholesterol Education Program defines elevated total cholesterol concentration as above 200 mg/dL and elevated LDL cholesterol concentration as above 100 mg/dL (with higher thresholds for some groups), evidence indicates a significant benefit for maintaining lower levels.[4] In epidemiologic studies and clinical trials, CHD event risk continually decreases until total cholesterol is below about 150 mg/dL. Many experts now call for LDL cholesterol concentrations below 70 mg/dL for high-risk patients or for secondary prevention, and CHD risk continuously decreases until LDL is below 40 mg/dL.[5]

Low HDL levels are common in populations that follow low-fat, plant-based diets and have low coronary risk, and they appear to be the result of decreased transport rather than an increase in HDL catabolism common to individuals eating a high-fat Western diet.[6] The ratio of total cholesterol:HDL and LDL:HDL is favorable in individuals following diets low in fat and high in fiber, while the ability of HDL to exert an antiinflammatory effect (ie, to reduce LDL oxidation) actually increases.[7]

Triglycerides. Elevated concentrations (above 150 mg/dL) increase risk for heart disease.

Homocysteine. Elevated levels may cause damage to arterial walls, thus increasing the risk for plaque formation. Men normally have a slightly higher homocysteine concentration than women. Levels tend to increase with age. Although homocysteine levels have been correlated with CHD risk, neither a cause-effect relationship nor a treatment outcome benefit has been established in clinical trials.[8]

C-reactive protein (CRP). CRP is an acute phase marker of inflammation. High sensitivity-CRP (hs-CRP) has been found to be associated with increased risk of cardiac events, with levels greater than 3 mg/dL associated with greatest risk.[9] However, hs-CRP has not reliably been shown to have a cause-effect relationship or a treatment outcome benefit in cardiovascular disease. The usefulness of CRP and many other inflammatory and acute phase reactants as screening measures or therapeutic targets in cardiovascular disease remains unproven,[10-13] pending the results of additional clinical trials. The Atherosclerosis Risk in Communities Study (ARIC) concluded that routine measurement of CRP, homocysteine, and 17 other novel risk markers is not warranted and reinforced the utility of standard risk factor assessment and management.[14] The Centers for Disease Control and Prevention and the American Heart Association have issued a statement that patients considered to be at intermediate risk for CHD, based on Framingham scores, could be further risk-stratified based on CRP levels, if treating physicians deem it appropriate.[9]

Noninvasive Tests

EKG. Findings may include ST elevation (acute myocardial injury or infarction) or depression (myocardial ischemia), T wave inversion (myocardial ischemia or MI), and ventricular premature complexes.

Stress tests. Methods include treadmill or bicycle exercise stress tests (EST), and EST or pharmacologic stress tests combined with nuclear imaging or echocardiography. These tests may be used for CHD diagnosis, risk stratification, and prognosis, and they often help determine the advisability for cardiac catheterization and revascularization.

EKG changes and symptoms (eg, exertional chest pain) are monitored during stress tests, providing both determinants of CHD presence and severity and indications for test termination. Pharmacologic stress modalities are typically used when an exercise stress test is inappropriate or inconclusive. Pharmacologic stress agents include coronary vasodilators, such as dipyridamole and adenosine, and cardiac inotropes, such as dobutamine and (less commonly) arbutamine.

Other Imaging Tests

Cardiac catheterization with coronary angiography. A catheter is inserted into a peripheral artery (usually a femoral artery) and advanced under fluoroscopic guidance to the coronary artery ostia. A radiopaque dye is then injected to identify the locations and severities of coronary blockages. This invasive procedure is performed when coronary artery stenosis is known or suspected, and the need for coronary artery angioplasty, stent placement, or bypass surgery is anticipated.

Intravascular ultrasound (IVUS). IVUS is highly sensitive to the presence and composition of coronary artery plaques. Its 3 major uses currently are to clarify the severity of stenoses identified on angiography, to characterize the composition and stability of plaques,[15] and to assess the deployment of coronary artery stents.

Computed tomography (CT). Electron beam tomography (EBT) accurately identifies and quantifies coronary artery calcification. This test has several applications in CHD, including diagnosis, disease distribution, risk stratification, prognosis, and treatment decisions. EBT is a helpful screening method in specific patient populations but has limited value for low-risk, asymptomatic patients.

CT angiography (CTA) uses intravenous contrast to obtain noninvasive coronary angiograms. Technical advances such as 64-slice scanners can produce angiograms that rival invasive coronary angiography, and the entire approach to CHD diagnosis and risk stratification may change as this technology continues to improve.

Magnetic resonance imaging (MRI). Cardiac MRI has historically been best suited for evaluation of cardiac chambers, pericardium, thoracic vessels, and congenital heart disease. However, technical advances to minimize the effects of cardiac motion have expanded MRI applications to include CHD evaluation. Such applications overlap substantially with CTA, and the role for MRI in CHD remains uncertain.

Treatment

Diet and lifestyle changes to modify risk factors (eg, smoking, obesity, hypertension, lack of physical activity, and dyslipidemia) are the cornerstone of treatment, with medications playing an adjunctive role. Unfortunately, counseling of patients regarding the importance of diet and exercise in the prevention of heart disease remains suboptimal.[16]

Prevention Strategies

Important preventive steps include the following:

Blood pressure control. (See Hypertension chapter.)

Reduction of plasma lipids. (See Dyslipidemias chapter.)

Smoking cessation.

Dietary change. (See Nutritional Considerations below.)

Physical activity.

Pharmacologic Agents

Drugs are used to reduce the symptoms of angina, as well to control specific risk factors.

Nitrates (sublingual nitroglycerin vs. oral forms) are vasodilators and provide greatest benefit through decreased preload (venodilation).

Beta-blockers (eg, propranolol, atenolol, metoprolol) decrease myocardial oxygen demand by decreasing contractility and heart rate.

Calcium-channel blockers (diltiazem, verapamil, nifedipine, amlodipine) relax arterial smooth muscle, resulting in decreased afterload.

Antiplatelet therapy. For those who can tolerate aspirin, 81 mg to 325 mg daily is prescribed to decrease CHD event risk. Clopidogrel (75 mg daily) is an alternative for persons unable to tolerate aspirin, or for those who have had CHD events despite aspirin. Clopidogrel may also be combined with low-dose aspirin (81 mg daily) for high-risk patients and aspirin failures, and after stent placement.

Lipid-lowering agents, such as the following, may also be prescribed. (See Dyslipidemias chapter.)

HMG CoA reductase inhibitors (statins).

Cholesterol absorption inhibitors (ezetimibe, colesevelam).

Bile acid sequestrants (cholestyramine, colestipol).

Fibrinates (gemfibrozil, fenofibrate).

Nicotinic acid.

Surgery and Other Mechanical Interventions

For high-risk CHD patients, including those with prominent symptoms, severe multivessel coronary artery disease (CAD), acute coronary syndromes, or MI, coronary revascularization may be achieved with percutaneous transluminal coronary angioplasty, intracoronary stent placement, or coronary artery bypass graft (CABG) surgery. For most categories of patients, stenting and CABG have similar success rates for relief of symptoms and control of CHD event risk. The need for subsequent revascularization is usually lower after CABG than after angioplasty or stent placement.

The Role of Exercise

Regular exercise reduces cardiovascular mortality in patients with established coronary heart disease,[17] particularly if the activity is sufficiently intense.[18] Current recommendations suggest a minimum of 30 minutes of moderately vigorous physical activity every day. Although aerobic exercise has well-established benefits, studies indicate that resistance exercise may reduce CHD risk by lowering blood pressure, reducing body fat, and improving insulin resistance.[19] Before a CHD patient starts an exercise regimen, however, a physical examination is essential.

Nutritional Considerations

The role of diet in coronary heart disease is evident from its pathological process, which involves the formation of arterial plaques, alterations in endothelial function (which, in turn, influence blood pressure), heightened risk for thrombosis, and inflammatory processes. Diet plays a role through the regulation of blood lipids and by influencing endothelial function and the underlying inflammation that causes disease progression.

Diets promoting cardiovascular health should begin early because the atherosclerosis that contributes to coronary artery disease begins in childhood.[20]

A modified diet, particularly if combined with regular exercise, can prevent, delay, or reverse the progression of atherosclerosis and development of CHD, with subsequent reduction in cardiovascular events.

The primary goals of dietary intervention are described below.

Controlling Blood Lipid Concentrations

Saturated fats, trans fats, and cholesterol in the diet increase concentrations of blood lipids, particularly LDL cholesterol, while soluble fiber tends to reduce them. Controlling blood lipoprotein concentrations with a combination of diet, exercise, and medication, if necessary, is a cornerstone of treatment for most CHD patients, as described in more detail in the Dyslipidemias chapter.

Improving Antioxidant Status and Endothelial Function

Dietary antioxidants, folate, magnesium, and other substances in foods may reduce the burden of oxidized LDL and improve endothelial function through increased availability of nitric oxide. Endothelial dysfunction, represented by an increase in blood levels of asymmetric dimethylarginine (ADMA), is a strong predictor of coronary events and coronary mortality. [21] ADMA increases after high-fat meals. [22]

Reducing Inflammation

The role of inflammatory processes in atherosclerosis is increasingly apparent. Loss of excess body fat reduces C-reactive protein,[23] an indicator of inflammation.

The following dietary steps help patients in achieving these goals:

Decreasing dietary saturated fat and cholesterol. Following diets low in saturated fat and cholesterol can help reduce progression of atherosclerosis.[24] The National Cholesterol Education Program has recommended moderate reductions in total fat (≤30% of energy), saturated fat (≤7% of energy), and cholesterol (<200 mg/d) intake. In clinical trials, such changes reduce plasma LDL cholesterol concentration about 5%.[25]

Studies suggest that low-fat vegetarian and vegan regimens are significantly more effective, reducing LDL cholesterol approximately 15% to 30%.[6,26] Because such regimens have also been shown to reduce body weight and blood pressure and to be useful in programs for reversing atherosclerosis, they may be preferable to many patients, provided they are prescribed along with basic diet instruction. [27] Combining daily aerobic exercise with a healthful diets adds to its benefit, particularly with regard to weight and blood glucose control.[28]

Trans fatty acids,[29] found in partially hydrogenated oils used in processed foods and margarines, increase LDL cholesterol and tend to reduce HDL cholesterol.[30] Trans fatty acids also have pro-inflammatory effects similar to those of saturated fat and adversely affect vascular reactivity, reducing arterial flow-mediated dilation (a direct measure of vascular endothelial function) by 29% on diets containing 8% of calories from trans fat.[31] The balance of dietary fats can be altered by the elimination of animal products, tropical oils (the leading sources of saturated fats), and partially hydrogenated vegetable oils (trans fats).

Some investigators have further adjusted this balance in clinical studies by the addition of omega-3 fatty acids in either foods or supplements. Several researchers have found an anti-atherosclerotic effect from both alpha-linolenic acid[32] and long-chain omega-3 fats.[33] Cardioprotective properties of these fatty acids include reduction of blood viscosity and triglyceride-lowering, antiplatelet, antidysrhythmic, and anti-inflammatory effects.[34]

There are 3 important caveats to such studies. First, benefits of omega-3 fatty acids have generally been demonstrated in individuals following less than optimal diets, rather than in vegetarians or individuals following very low-fat diets. Second, while many studies have used fish oils, some evidence indicates that diets rich in plant sources of omega-3 fatty acids are associated with a similar reduction in heart disease risk.[35] Walnuts, flaxseed, flaxseed oil, and canola oil are rich sources of alpha-linolenic acid and lack the cholesterol of nonplant sources of omega-3 fatty acids. Third, fats or oils that provide omega-3 fatty acids are as energy dense as any other fats and are mixtures of various fat types. Fish oils, for example, include significant amounts of saturated fat (15% to 30% of total fat content) and cholesterol. Patients who include fatty fish in their diets as a means of increasing omega-3 intake will also increase total and saturated fat intake and may experience elevated cholesterol and weight gain.

Increasing dietary fiber. Soluble fiber, as is found in oats, barley, and beans, is particularly helpful in this regard. (See Dyslipidemias chapter for more information.) Sources of soluble dietary fiber and pectin, found mainly in fruits and vegetables, have also reduced atherosclerotic progression.[36]

Consuming soy products. Both epidemiologic[37] and clinical[38] studies have shown that soy products (eg, soymilk and meat substitutes) may reduce CHD risk. In addition to reducing blood lipids, soy has cardioprotective effects, such as lowering oxidized LDL, homocysteine, and blood pressure.

Clinical trials have combined these dietary lipid-lowering strategies. A vegetarian diet emphasizing cholesterol-lowering foods (including oats, soy foods, nuts, and sterol/stanol margarines) appears to be particularly effective, lowering LDL cholesterol concentration approximately 30%, an effect similar to that of treatment with lovastatin.[38]

Increasing fruits and vegetables. Fruits and vegetables can help reduce atherosclerosis and lower risk for CHD, particularly if the diet is low in saturated fat.[39] However, the benefits of these foods go beyond their having no cholesterol, very little saturated fat, and abundant fiber. Among their active components are vitamin C,[40] antioxidant flavonoids,[41] and folic acid.[42]

Several studies have shown that higher dietary intakes of carotenoid-containing fruits and vegetables are associated with a decreased risk of coronary artery disease.[43] Others have found an inverse relationship between lower blood levels of carotenoids and higher risk for cardiovascular events.[44]

In addition to the above considerations, evidence suggests that other dietary factors may be helpful, as described below.

In epidemiological studies, whole grain consumption is associated with a lower risk of heart disease,[45] as is frequent consumption of nuts.[46] In addition to providing the lipid-lowering benefit of dietary fiber, these foods provide magnesium and vitamin E, both of which are inversely related to coronary heart disease occurrence or mortality.[47,48] Nuts are high in fat and calories, however, and may influence body weight.

The role of alcohol remains controversial. No controlled clinical trials have examined the effect of alcohol intake on cardiovascular endpoints. Nevertheless, moderate alcohol consumption (1-2 drinks/day) may reduce cardiovascular disease risk through several mechanisms: increasing blood concentrations of HDL cholesterol, plasminogen, and tissue plasminogen activator; improving endothelial function; and decreasing platelet aggregation, fibrinogen, and lipoprotein (a).[49] However, regular alcohol consumption also contributes to several medical conditions, including serious diseases of the liver, pancreas, central nervous system, and cardiovascular system. Alcohol also increases the risks for some cancers, notably gastrointestinal and breast cancers.[50]

Caution with coffee and other sources of caffeine. The Health Professionals Study, which included nearly 129,000 men and women, did not find evidence that coffee increases the risk for CHD, although an association between nonfiltered coffee (ie, the percolated variety, which has been found to raise serum cholesterol) and CHD risk was not ruled out.[51] However, in persons who are slow caffeine metabolizers, the risk appears greater, and there are two groups affected. One is obese individuals, who do not clear caffeine from the blood as efficiently as do persons at a healthy body weight.[52] The other is persons who possess the CYP1A2*1F polymorphism, in whom risk for MI rises incrementally as coffee increases from 1 cup to more than 4 cups per day, compared with rapid caffeine metabolizers who possess the CYP1A21A allele.[53] Individuals with pre-existing coronary artery disease should also consider avoiding caffeine.[54]

Moderation in alcohol consumption. Individuals who have one or two drinks per day have reduced risk of myocardial infarction compared with teetotalers. Possible mechanisms include alcohol's ability to increase plasma HDL concentrations and to interfere with blood clotting. More than moderate drinking, however, is associated with increased cardiac mortality.[55]

Survival and Prognosis after Coronary Events

A low-fat vegetarian diet reduces the risk for repeated coronary events. Individuals who adhered to a low-fat (<10% of energy) vegetarian diet as part of treatment for pre-existing heart disease had an absence of coronary events in a 12-year study.[26] Diet interventions that have also included exercise, stress reduction, and smoking cessation appear to cause regression of atherosclerotic lesions.[6]

Mediterranean-style diets also decrease the risk for repeated cardiovascular events. The combination of known protective nutrients found in the plant-based Mediterranean diet significantly reduced cardiac death, nonfatal MI, unstable angina, stroke, heart failure, and pulmonary or peripheral embolism when compared with a Western diet.[56] However, Mediterranean diets are higher in fat (25%-35%) than low-fat vegetarian diets and are therefore not likely to be as effective for weight loss or regression of atherosclerotic lesions.

Orders

Vegetarian diet, nondairy, low-fat.

Nutrition consultation to advise patient regarding the above diet and arrange follow-up.

Smoking cessation.

Exercise prescription: Patient must be screened to ensure safe initiation of an exercise program and slowly work toward a goal of 30 minutes daily of aerobic semivigorous activity. Exercise physiology and physical therapy consultation as appropriate.

What to Tell the Family

Atherosclerosis and coronary heart disease are preventable, treatable, and in some cases possibly reversible. Diet therapy and exercise are fundamental for these aims, and many patients are eventually able to reduce or eliminate previously required medications. Vegetarian diets are particularly effective and appear to be as acceptable to patients as other regimens. Because such diets usually require learning new cooking techniques and acquiring new tastes, families play an important role in joining the patient in the process of dietary change. Family members can support the heart disease patient by following a similar diet and exercise regimen, which will likely benefit their health as well.

References

1. McNeill AM, Rosamond WD, Girman CJ, et al. The metabolic syndrome and 11-year risk of incident cardiovascular disease in the Atherosclerosis Risk in Communities Study. *Diabetes Care.* 2005;28:385-390.

2. Kannel WB, D'Agostino RB, Belanger AJ. Update on fibrinogen as a cardiovascular risk factor. *Ann Epidemiol.* 1992;2:457-466.

3. Kannel WB, Anderson K, Wilson PW. White blood cell count and cardiovascular disease. Insights from the Framingham Study. *JAMA.* 1992;267:1253-1256.

4. National Heart, Lung, and Blood Institute, National Institutes of Health. Third report of the National Cholesterol Education Program (NCEP) expert panel on detection, evaluation, and treatment of high blood cholesterol in adults. Washington, DC: US Dept. of Health and Human Services; 2002. NIH Publication No. 02-5215.

5. Grundy SM, Cleeman JI, Merz JB, et al. Implications of recent clinical trials for the National Cholesterol Education Program Adult Treatment Panel III guidelines. J Am Coll Cardiol. 2004;44:720-732.

6. Ornish D, Scherwitz LW, Billings JH, et al. Intensive lifestyle changes for reversal of coronary heart disease. *JAMA.*1998;280:2001-2007.

7. Roberts CK, Ng C, Hama S, Eliseo AJ, Barnard RJ. Effect of a Diet and Exercise Intervention on Inflammatory/Anti-inflammatory Properties of HDL in Men with Cardiovascular Risk Factors. *J Appl Physiol.* 2006;101:1727-1732.

8. Loscalzo J. Homocysteine trials; clear outcomes for complex reasons. *N Engl J Med.* 2006;354:1629-1632.

9. Pearson TA, Mensah GA, Alexander RW, et al. Markers of inflammation and cardiovascular disease: application to clinical and public health practice. A statement for healthcare professionals from the Centers for Disease Control and Prevention and the American Heart Association. *Circulation.* 2003;107:499–511.

10. Hansson GK. Inflammation, atherosclerosis, and coronary artery disease [Mechanics of Disease]. *N Engl J Med*. 2005;352:1685-1695.

11. Tall AR. C-reactive protein reassessed. *N Engl J Med*. 2004;350:1450-1453.

12. Blankenberg S, McQueen MJ, Smieja M, et al. Comparative impact of multiple biomarkers and n-terminal pro-brain natriuretic peptide in the context of conventional risk factors for the prediction of recurrent cardiovascular events in the Heart Outcomes Prevention Evaluation (HOPE) Study. *Circulation*. 2006;114:201-208.

13. Miller M, Zhan M, Havas S. High attributable risk of elevated C-reactive protein to conventional coronary heart disease risk factors: the Third National Health and Nutrition Examination Survey. *Arch Intern Med*. 2005;165:2063-2068.

14. Folsom AR, Chambless LE, Ballantyne CM, et al. An assessment of incremental coronary risk prediction using C-reactive protein and other novel risk markers: the Atherosclerosis Risk in Communities Study. *Arch Intern Med*. 2006;166:1368-1373

15. Nair A, Kuban BD, Tuzcu EM, Schoenhagen P, Nissen SE, Vince DG. Coronary Plaque Classification with Intravascular Ultrasound Radiofrequency Data Analysis. *Circulation*. 2002;106:2200-2206.

16. Ma J, Urizar GG Jr, Alehegn T, Stafford RS. Diet and physical activity counseling during ambulatory care visits in the United States. *Prev Med*. 2004;39:815-822.

17. Thompson PD, Lim V. Physical activity in the prevention of atherosclerotic coronary heart disease. *Curr Treat Options Cardiovasc Med*. 2003;5:279-285.

18. Tanasescu M, Leitzmann MF, Rimm EB, Willett WC, Stampfer MJ, Hu FB. Exercise type and intensity in relation to coronary heart disease in men. *JAMA*. 2002;288:1994-2000.

19. Braith RW, Stewart KJ. Resistance exercise training: its role in the prevention of cardiovascular disease. *Circulation*. 2006;113:2642-2650.

20. Zieske AW, Malcom GT, Strong JP. Natural history and risk factors of atherosclerosis in children and youth: the PDAY study. *Pediatr Pathol Mol Med*. 2002;21:213-237.

21. Schulze F, Lenzen H, Hanefeld C, et al. Asymmetric dimethylarginine is an independent risk factor for coronary heart disease: results from the multicenter Coronary Artery Risk Determination investigating the Influence of ADMA Concentration (CARDIAC) study. *Am Heart J*. 2006;152:493.e1-8.

22. Stuhlinger MC, Abbasi F, Chu AW, et al. Relationship between insulin resistance and an endogenous nitric oxide synthase inhibitor. *JAMA*. 2002;287:1420-1426.

23. Clifton JM, Keogh JB, Foster PR, Noakes M. Effect of weight loss on inflammatory and endothelial markers and FMD using two low-fat diets. *Int J Obes* (Lond). 2005;29:1445-1451.

24. Bemelmans WJ, Lefrandt JD, Feskens EJ, et al. Change in saturated fat intake is associated with progression of carotid and femoral intima-media thickness, and with levels of soluble intercellular adhesion molecule-1. *Atherosclerosis*. 2002;163:113-120.

25. Hunninghake DB, Stein EA, Dujovne CA, et al. The efficacy of intensive dietary therapy, alone or combined with lovastatin, in outpatients with hypercholesterolemia. *N Engl J Med*. 1993;328:1213-1219.

26. Esselstyn CB Jr. Updating a 12-year experience with arrest and reversal therapy for coronary heart disease (an overdue requiem for palliative cardiology). *Am J Cardiol*. 1999;84:339-341, A8.

27. Barnard ND, Scialli AR, Turner-McGrievy G, Lanou AJ. Acceptability of a low-fat vegan diet compares favorably to a step II diet in a randomized, controlled trial. *J Cardiopulm Rehabil*. 2004;24:229-235.

28. Roberts CK, Won D, Pruthi S, et al. Effect of a short-term diet and exercise intervention on oxidative stress, inflammation, MMP-9, and monocyte chemotactic activity in men with metabolic syndrome factors. *J Appl Physiol*. 2006;100:1657-1665.

29. Dyerberg J, Christensen JH, Eskesen D, Astrup A, Stender S. Trans, and n-3 polyunsaturated fatty acids and vascular function—a yin yang situation? *Atheroscler Suppl*. 2006;7:33-35.

30. Ascherio A, Willett WC. Health effects of trans fatty acids. *Am J Clin Nutr*. 1997;66(suppl 4):1006S-1010S.

31. Mozaffarian D. Trans fatty acids—effects on systemic inflammation and endothelial function. *Atheroscler Suppl*. 2006;7:29-32.

32. Djousse L, Folsom AR, Province MA, Hunt SC, Ellison RC, and the National Heart, Lung, and Blood Institute Family Heart Study. Dietary linolenic acid and carotid atherosclerosis: the National Heart, Lung, and Blood Institute Family Heart Study. *Am J Clin Nutr*. 2003;77:819-825.

33. De Caterina R, Zampolli A. n-3 fatty acids: antiatherosclerotic effects. *Lipids*. 2001;36:S69-S78.

34. Harris WS. Are omega-3 fatty acids the most important nutritional modulators of coronary heart disease risk? *Curr Atheroscler Rep*. 2004;6:447-452.

35. Erkkila AT, Lehto S, Pyorala K, Uusitupa MI. n-3 fatty acids and 5-year risks of death and cardiovascular disease events in patients with coronary artery disease. *Am J Clin Nutr*. 2003;78:65-71.

36. Wu H, Dwyer KM, Fan Z, Shircore A, Fan J, Dwyer JH. Dietary fiber and progression of atherosclerosis: the Los Angeles Atherosclerosis Study. *Am J Clin Nutr*. 2003;78:1085-1091.

37. Zhang X, Shu XO, Gao YT, et al. Soy food consumption is associated with lower risk of coronary heart disease in Chinese women. *J Nutr*. 2003;133:2874-2878.

38. Jenkins DJ, Kendall CW, Marchie A, et al. Effects of a dietary portfolio of cholesterol-lowering foods vs lovastatin on serum lipids and C-reactive protein. *JAMA*. 2003;290:502-510.

39. Tucker KL, Hallfrisch J, Qiao N, Muller D, Andres R, Fleg JL. The combination of high fruit and vegetable and low saturated fat intakes is more protective against mortality in aging men than is either alone: the Baltimore Longitudinal Study of Aging. *J Nutr*. 2005;135:556-561.

40. Joshipura KJ, Hu FB, Manson JE, et al. The effect of fruit and vegetable intake on risk for coronary heart disease. *Ann Intern Med*. 2001;134:1106-1114.

41. Hirvonen T, Pietinen P, Virtanen M, et al. Intake of flavonols and flavones and risk of coronary heart disease in male smokers. *Epidemiology*. 2001;12:62-67.

42. Voutilainen S, Rissanen TH, Virtanen J, Lakka TA, Salonen JT. Low dietary folate intake is associated with an excess incidence of acute coronary events: The Kuopio Ischemic Heart Disease Risk Factor Study. *Circulation*. 2001;103:2674-2680.

43. Osganian SK, Stampfer MJ, Rimm E, Spiegelman D, Manson JE, Willett WC. Dietary carotenoids and risk of coronary artery disease in women. *Am J Clin Nutr*. 2003;77:1390-1399.

44. Rissanen TH, Voutilainen S, Nyyssonen K, et al. Low serum lycopene concentration is associated with an excess incidence of acute coronary events and stroke: the Kuopio Ischaemic Heart Disease Risk Factor Study. *Br J Nutr.* 2001;85:749-754.

45. Mozaffarian D, Kumanyika SK, Lemaitre RN, Olson JL, Burke GL, Siscovick DS. Cereal, fruit, and vegetable fiber intake and the risk of cardiovascular disease in elderly individuals. *JAMA.* 2003;289:1659-1666.

46. Ellsworth JL, Kushi LH, Folsom AR. Frequent nut intake and risk of death from coronary heart disease and all causes in postmenopausal women: the Iowa Women's Health Study. *Nutr Metab Cardiovasc Dis.* 2001;11:372-377.

47. Al-Delaimy WK, Rimm EB, Willett WC, Stampfer MJ, Hu FB. Magnesium intake and risk of coronary heart disease among men. *J Am Coll Nutr.* 2004;23:63-70.

48. Kushi LH, Folsom AR, Prineas RJ, Mink PJ, Wu Y, Bostick RM. Dietary antioxidant vitamins and death from coronary heart disease in postmenopausal women. *N Engl J Med.* 1996;334:1156-1162.

49. Vogel RA. Alcohol, heart disease, and mortality: a review. *Rev Cardiovasc Med.* 2002;3:7-13.

50. Room R, Babor T, Rehm J. Alcohol and public health. *Lancet.* 2005;365:519-530.

51. Lopez-Garcia E, van Dam RM, Willett WC, et al. Coffee consumption and coronary heart disease risk in men and women. A prospective cohort study. *Circulation.* 2006;113:2045-2053.

52. Carillo JA, Benitez J. Clinically significant pharmacokinetic interactions between dietary caffeine and medications. *Clin Pharmacokinet.* 2000;39:127-153.

53. Cornelis MC, El-Sohemy A, Kabagambe EK, Campos H. Coffee, CYP1A2 genotype, and risk of myocardial infarction. *JAMA.* 2006;295:1135-1141.

54. de Vreede-Swagemakers, Gorgels AP, Weijenberg AP, et al. Risk indicators for out-of-hospital cardiac arrest in patients with coronary artery disease. *J Clin Epidemiol.* 1999;52:601-607.

55. O'Keefe JH, Bybee KA, Lavie CJ. Alcohol and cardiovascular health: the razor-sharp double-edged sword. *J Am Coll Cardiol.* 2007;50:1009-1014.

56. de Lorgeril M, Salen P, Martin JL, Monjaud I, Delaye J, Mamelle N. Mediterranean diet, traditional risk factors, and the rate of cardiovascular complications after myocardial infarction: final report of the Lyon Diet Heart Study. *Circulation.* 1999;99:779-785.

34. Dyslipidemias

Dyslipidemias are characterized by abnormal concentrations of circulating lipids, increasing the risk of atherosclerosis and other serious conditions. Specific classes of dyslipidemias include elevated very low-density lipoprotein (VLDL) and low-density lipoprotein (LDL) levels, hypercholesterolemia, hypertriglyceridemia, and low concentrations of high-density lipoprotein (HDL).

Dyslipidemias are typically asymptomatic and are frequently detected during routine screening. Occasionally, xanthelasmas and xanthomas are present. These are fatty deposits under the skin surface commonly found in patients with genetic disorders such as familial hypercholesterolemia.

Hyperlipidemia often results from delayed or defective hepatic clearance, or overproduction of VLDL by the liver. VLDL is subsequently transformed into LDL. Familial hypercholesterolemia involves defective hepatic and nonhepatic LDL receptors. Excess intake of saturated fats increases the liver's production of VLDL and triglycerides via a molecular mechanism involving protein activators.[1] Saturated fats are found in animal products, such as meat, dairy products (milk, cream, cheese), and butter, and tropical oils (palm, palm kernel, and coconut).

High total and LDL cholesterol concentrations and low HDL cholesterol concentrations predict cardiovascular risk in both men and women. High triglyceride concentrations (>150 mg/dL) are also associated with increased risk, particularly for women. The risk of cardiovascular disease increases by an average of 2% for each corresponding 1% rise in total cholesterol.

Risk Factors

Although dyslipidemias are a frequent finding in all demographic groups that follow Western diets, they occur somewhat more commonly in men. Additional risk factors may include:

Diets high in total fat, saturated fat, and cholesterol (see Nutritional Considerations below).

Smoking. Cigarette smoking lowers HDL levels and is an independent risk factor for cardiovascular disease.

Obesity. Obesity is associated with increased total cholesterol, LDL, VLDL, and triglycerides, as well as with decreased levels of HDL.

Diabetes mellitus and the metabolic syndrome. Hyperinsulinemia is associated with low HDL levels and hypertriglyceridemia.

Physical inactivity. A lack of regular exercise is associated with low HDL concentrations.

Nephrotic syndrome. This condition is usually associated with elevated cholesterol and triglyceride concentrations. Decreased vascular oncotic pressure due to proteinuria leads to increased lipoprotein production by the liver.

Chronic kidney disease. Hypertriglyceridemia is common.

Hypothyroidism. Total and LDL concentrations may be elevated.

Alcoholism. While moderate intake may increase HDL levels, more than moderate use leads to hypertriglyceridemia and may contribute to hypertension.

Family history.

Drugs. Estrogen-progestin contraceptives, oral estrogens, tamoxifen, beta-blockers, atypical antipsychotics, and steroids may raise triglyceride levels. Protease inhibitors and other drugs may also adversely affect lipid profiles.

Pregnancy. Triglyceride concentrations may increase.

Diagnosis

The National Cholesterol Education Program (NCEP) recommends routine blood lipid assessment every 5 years beginning at age 20.[2] More frequent screening may be performed when borderline values and/or coronary artery disease risk factors are present.

The patient's medical and lifestyle history must be taken into account when assessing the lipid profile. Ideally, the patient should be in a steady state (no significant weight change or acute illness). Medications should be noted, since some drugs may interfere with lipid metabolism. Improvement of the conditions listed above that lead to hyperlipidemia may also improve the lipid profile. Hypothyroidism, chronic kidney disease, and insulin resistance should be considered in the diagnostic evaluation, as they may contribute to secondary dyslipidemia.

Laboratory Testing

Patients should fast for about 12 hours before blood sampling, because chylomicron clearance can take up to 10 hours. However, a fasting sample is not required for routine cholesterol (without hypertriglyceridemia) screening.

Common laboratory assays measure total plasma cholesterol, HDL, and triglycerides directly. VLDL cholesterol levels are calculated by dividing the triglyceride value by 5. LDL cholesterol is calculated by subtracting HDL cholesterol and VLDL cholesterol from total cholesterol. When triglycerides are above 400 mg/dL, LDL calculation is inaccurate, and LDL must be measured directly.

Classification of Lipid Concentrations

Total cholesterol. According to NCEP guidelines, total cholesterol concentrations below 200 mg/dL are desirable. A borderline high concentration is 200 to 239 mg/dL, and hypercholesterolemia is defined as greater than 240 mg/dL. However, epidemiologic evidence suggests that stricter standards may be appropriate. Risk of cardiac events decreases as total cholesterol levels fall until plateauing at a total cholesterol of approximately 150 mg/dL.[3] For children, total cholesterol should be less than 180 mg/dL.

Triglyceride. Normal triglyceride concentration is less than 150 mg/dL. Borderline is 150 to 199 mg/dL, and high is 200 to 499 mg/dL. A meta-analysis of 26 studies including over 96,000 individuals showed that those in the top 20% for triglyceride concentrations had an 80% higher risk for fatal or nonfatal CHD when compared with those in the lowest quintile.[4]

HDL cholesterol. Concentrations of 60 mg/dL or higher are optimal. In general, an HDL concentration below 40 mg/dL is considered a major risk factor for coronary heart disease (CHD), although women's risk of CHD increases marginally with HDL cholesterol <50.[2] However, HDL is often interpreted in the context of total cholesterol and LDL concentrations and may be less significant when LDL is low or when the ratio of total cholesterol to HDL, or LDL to HDL, is favorable.

LDL cholesterol. According to the NCEP, LDL cholesterol concentrations below 100 mg/dL are considered optimal. A range of 100 to129 mg/dL is near optimal. Borderline is 130 to 159 mg/dL. High is 160 to 189 mg/dL. However, increasing evidence supports stricter standards, including reductions below 70 mg/dL for very high-risk patients. Studies of hunter-gatherer populations and normal neonates have modified the concept of "normal" cholesterol levels.[5] Normal human LDL cholesterol concentration may be as low as 50 to 70 mg/dL, approximately half the US adult population mean. Coronary heart disease risk decreases as LDL cholesterol concentration decreases, reaching a nadir at approximately 40 mg/dL.[6]

Treatment

The mainstay of treatment for hyperlipidemia is dietary and lifestyle modification, followed by drug therapy, as necessary. Hyperlipidemia should not be considered refractory to dietary treatment if the therapeutic regimen includes animal products or more than minimal amounts of vegetable oils. Such diets do not lower LDL cholesterol concentrations as effectively as high-fiber, low-fat diets that exclude animal products (see Nutritional Considerations below).

Regular exercise can improve lipid concentrations. Low to moderate amounts of physical activity such as walking lower triglyceride concentrations by an average of 10 mg/dL, while raising HDL by 5 mg/dL (these numbers are means drawn from large groups). More strenuous activity may have greater effects.[7]

Patients with familial hypercholesterolemia typically require medication starting in early childhood.

HMG CoA reductase inhibitors (statins) decrease cholesterol production in the liver and are first-line agents in the treatment of elevated LDL cholesterol. Statins also have important effects on cardiovascular risk aside from their ability to reduce lipid concentrations, and they may be indicated for high-risk patients even when lipid targets can be achieved without drug therapy. Potential side effects include myopathy, hepatotoxicity, and memory loss. Statin therapy may also reduce HDL to a below-goal level.

When statin therapy is insufficient, the addition of other medications may further reduce LDL concentrations. It is not clear that this leads to improvements in clinical outcomes.

Bile acid sequestrants (eg, cholestyramine, colestipol, colesevelam) are second-line agents for LDL reduction. They inhibit bile acid resorption from the intestine and further reduce plasma LDL through other mechanisms. They can produce gastrointestinal distress, constipation, and impaired absorption of other drugs.

Fibrates (eg, gemfibrozil, fenofibrate) are first-line treatments for elevated triglyceride concentrations and may be prescribed in combination with the above drug classes. They also raise HDL concentrations. Gallstones, dyspepsia, and myopathy may occur. Myopathy risk may be particularly high when fibrates are combined with statins.

Nicotinic acid (niacin) is a second-line therapy for all lipid disorders. Niacin is often combined with statins, as it raises HDL levels at low doses. LDL lowering occurs at higher doses, which unfortunately often cause side effects, including skin itching or burning. GI distress, flushing, hepatotoxicity, hyperglycemia, and gout may also occur.

Ezetimibe decreases GI cholesterol absorption and is a favored second-line therapy (followed by colesevelam) due to effectiveness, safety, and relative rarity of side effects. It lowers LDL and is particularly effective when combined with statins. In combination, lipid targets may be met with lower statin doses, and Framingham risk scores may be decreased more than typically occurs with statin therapy alone,[8] but clinical outcomes comparing statin monotherapy with combined ezetimibe therapy are not well characterized.

Nutritional Considerations

Elevated concentrations of blood lipids, particularly LDL cholesterol, are a significant risk factor for atherosclerosis and coronary heart disease (see Coronary Heart Disease chapter). Reducing saturated fat and cholesterol intake decreases these concentrations. Cholesterol is present only in foods of animal origin, and these products are often the primary source of saturated fat. Thus, a diet that reduces or eliminates animal products lowers total and LDL cholesterol and triglycerides.

Many individuals present a mixed dyslipidemia consisting of high LDL, low HDL, and elevated TG concentrations, each of which is associated with increased CHD risk. Dietary strategies to address these dyslipidemias are discussed below.

Minimizing saturated fat and cholesterol. A diet low in saturated fat and cholesterol reduces cholesterol production and blood lipid concentrations. The NCEP recommends "Therapeutic Lifestyle Changes," which include a diet deriving ≤7% of calories from saturated fat and ≤200 mg/day of cholesterol. In outpatients, such a diet typically lowers LDL by about 5%,[9] which may not be enough to achieve blood lipid goals.

More substantial diet changes appear to produce better results. Diets that eliminate cholesterol and animal fat (ie, vegetarian and vegan diets) reduce LDL cholesterol by 17% to 40%, with the strongest effects seen when the diet is combined with exercise.[10,11] Reducing total fat, saturated fat, and cholesterol intake also lowers triglyceride levels by approximately 20%.[12]

Partially hydrogenated oils (trans fatty acids) are similar to saturated fats in their effect on LDL cholesterol concentrations, and they also tend to reduce HDL.[13]

Although some authorities recommend replacing saturated fat and/ or trans fatty acids with monounsaturated and polyunsaturated fats, it is important to remember that all oils are mixtures containing varying amounts of saturated fat. For example, olive oil is approximately 13% saturated fat, and fish oils range from 15% to 30% saturated fat. Therefore, many individuals may need to reduce total fat intake, rather than just replace one type of fat with another, in order to attain desirable lipid levels. In addition, greater fat intake often leads to weight gain,[14] and many patients with dyslipidemia need to lose excess weight to prevent or effectively treat cardiovascular disease. Diets very low in fat are an essential component of interventions that may reverse atherosclerotic lesions.[15]

Diets that are low in saturated fat also tend to reduce HDL; however, they generally improve the cholesterol:HDL ratio.[13]

For individuals who need to maintain a higher calorie intake because of the presence of certain diseases (eg, COPD, sickle cell disease, or cystic fibrosis), unsaturated fats can help provide needed calories while keeping cholesterol and triglyceride levels within normal limits. Certain types of unsaturated fats may be better than others for this purpose. For example, individuals in the National Heart, Lung and Blood Institute Family Heart Study who consumed the highest amount of the omega-3 polyunsaturated fat linolenic acid had triglyceride levels that were 12% lower than those of persons with the lowest intakes.[16] Unsaturated fats consumed in foods (eg, nuts) may be preferable to using oils because of the potentially cardioprotective nutrients found in these foods (eg, magnesium, fiber, vitamin E, and flavonoids).

Soluble fiber. Soluble fiber (found in oats, barley, legumes, and many fruits and vegetables) reduces cholesterol concentrations chiefly through binding of bile acids, leading to increased cholesterol excretion, although several other mechanisms have also been suggested.[17] Soluble fiber appears to be most effective in the context of a diet low in saturated fat.[17] At an intake of 8 grams per day, soluble fiber lowers total cholesterol and lowers the LDL:HDL cholesterol ratio.[18]

In the National Heart, Lung and Blood Institute Family Heart Study, men and women who ate an average of 5.5 fruit and vegetable servings per day had LDL concentrations that were 6% and 7% lower, respectively, than for individuals who only ate roughly 1.5 servings each day.[16] Dietary supplementation with psyllium seed (a source of soluble fiber) was found to lower total and LDL cholesterol by roughly 5% and 7% respectively and enabled patients taking either bile acid binding resins or statins to reduce these medications by 50% yet still attain the same degree of lipid lowering.[19]

Soy protein reduces hepatic cholesterol synthesis and may increase the hepatic LDL receptor uptake of cholesterol. In clinical tests, soy protein decreased total cholesterol by 9%, LDL by 13%, and triglycerides by 10%.[20] Isoflavones in soybeans have a lipid-modulating effect independent of that of soy protein. In a meta-analysis, isoflavones were shown to reduce total cholesterol by approximately 2% and LDL cholesterol by approximately 4%, with larger reductions among hypercholesterolemic individuals.[21]

Nuts (almonds, peanuts, pecans, and walnuts) appear to have hypolipidemic effects, apparently due to their fiber or plant sterol content.[22] The effects of nuts on lipids are highly variable. A systematic review of clinical trials reported that almonds, peanuts, pecan nuts, or walnuts reduced cholesterol by 2% to 16% and LDL by 2% to 19% when compared with an NCEP Step I diet, Mediterranean diets, low-fat diets, or habitual intake (ie, controls).[23] However, most studies used portions (ie, 1 to 3 ounces/day, equal to ~175 to ~525 calories/day) that might impede efforts to lose weight.

Plant sterols and stanols (often in the form of specialized margarines) reduce LDL cholesterol concentrations by roughly 10% by inhibiting cholesterol absorption.[24]

A regimen combining the effects of a vegetarian diet, soluble fiber, soy protein, nuts, and plant sterols has been shown to lower LDL by nearly 30% in short-term clinical trials,[25] an effect similar to that of statins. Although each of these foods alone contributes to lowering lipids, their effects are complementary when the foods are combined.

Avoiding boiled coffee. A majority of studies have indicated a strong relationship between boiled, unfiltered coffee consumption and elevated cholesterol levels.[26] Coffee may be undesirable for many patients with hyperlipidemia for other reasons (see Coronary Heart Disease chapter).

Nutritional Effects on HDL and Triglycerides

Diet influences HDL and triglyceride concentrations. Factors under study include the following:

Reducing dietary fat. Diets that are low in total and saturated fat tend to lower HDL. However, they tend to reduce LDL to a greater degree, reducing the total cholesterol:HDL ratio.[13]

In persons with very high triglycerides, **fish oil** (4 g per day) lowers triglycerides by 25% to 30%.[27] Adding fish oils to a statin regimen further reduces triglycerides by 28% to 40%, when compared with the effect of statins alone.[28] The effect of fish oils has not been compared with that of the vegetarian or vegan diets used for reversal of coronary disease.

Increased fiber and unrefined carbohydrate. Diets rich in refined carbohydrate may lower HDL and raise triglyceride concentrations, at least transiently.[29] However, in a meta-analysis, diets high in both carbohydrate (≥60%) and fiber (≥20 g/1000 kcal) reduced HDL nonsignificantly (6%) while reducing triglycerides by 13%.[30]

Limiting alcohol. Alcohol increases HDL. Consuming ~1 drink per day causes an average rise of 6%[31] but raises triglycerides by 5 to 10 mg/dL.[7,32] Restricting alcohol consumption joins diet, exercise, and weight loss as cornerstones of treatment for patients with elevated triglyceride levels.[33]

Minerals. Chromium supplementation (usually 200 µg/d) increases HDL, decreases TG, or both.[34] High-dose zinc supplementation (over 50 mg daily) lowers HDL significantly (ie, by 11% to 25%).[35]

Orders

Diet: Vegetarian, low-fat, nondairy, high in soluble fiber. Avoid trans fats.

Nutrition consultation to advise patient in above diet and arrange follow-up.

Smoking cessation.

Exercise prescription (patient-specific).

Alcohol restriction for hypertriglyceridemia.

Avoid oral contraceptives, if relevant.

What to Tell the Family

Dyslipidemias are common contributors to atherosclerosis. However, cholesterol and triglyceride concentrations can be reduced through restriction of saturated fat, cholesterol, trans fatty acids, and total fat. Increasing dietary fiber, soy foods, and exercise can make these measures more effective. The patient's family may also be at risk for lipid disorders and other cardiovascular problems. Their adoption of the same diet and lifestyle changes being made by the patient, including smoking cessation, will encourage patient adherence and improve family members' health.

References

1. Lin J, Yang R, Tarr PT, et al. Hyperlipidemic effects of dietary saturated fats mediated through PGC-1β coactivation of SREBP. *Cell.* 2005;120:261-273.

2. National Cholesterol Education Program. Third Report of the National Cholesterol Education Program (NCEP) Expert Panel on Detection, Evaluation, and Treatment of High Blood Cholesterol in Adults (Adult Treatment Panel III) final report. *Circulation.* 2002;106:3143-3421.

3. Stamler J, Wentworth D, Neaton JD. Is relationship between serum cholesterol and risk of premature death from coronary heart disease continuous and graded? Findings in 356,222 primary screenees of the Multiple Risk Factor Intervention Trial (MRFIT). *JAMA.* 1986;256:2823-2828.

4. Asia Pacific Cohort Studies Collaboration. Serum triglycerides as a risk factor for cardiovascular diseases in the Asia-Pacific region. *Circulation.* 2004;110:2678-2686.

5. O'Keefe JH Jr, Cordain L, Harris WH, Moe RM, Vogel R. Optimal low-density lipoprotein is 50 to 70 mg/dL: lower is better and physiologically normal. *J Am Coll Cardiol.* 2004;43:2142-2146.

6. Grundy SM, Cleeman JI, Merz CN, et al. Implications of recent clinical trials for the National Cholesterol Education Program Adult Treatment Panel III guidelines. *Circulation.* 2004;110:227-239.

7. Hata Y, Nakajima K. Life-style and serum lipids and lipoproteins. *J Atheroscler Thromb.* 2000;7:177-197.

8. Davies GM, Cook JR, Erbey J, Alemao E, Veltri EP. Projected coronary heart disease risk benefit with ezetimibe. *Atherosclerosis.* 2005;179:375-378.

9. Hunninghake DB, Stein EA, Dujovne CA, et al. The efficacy of intensive dietary therapy alone or combined with lovastatin in outpatients with hypercholesterolemia. *N Engl J Med.* 1993;328:1213-1219.

10. Ornish D, Scherwitz LW, Billings JH, et al. Intensive lifestyle changes for reversal of coronary heart disease. *JAMA.* 1998;280:2001-2007.

11. Barnard ND, Scialli AR, Bertron P, Hurlock D, Edmonds K, Talev L. Effectiveness of a low-fat vegetarian diet in altering serum lipids in healthy premenopausal women. *Am J Cardiol.* 2000;85:969-972.

12. Pelkman CL, Fishell VK, Maddox DH, Pearson TA, Mauger DT, Kris-Etherton PM. Effects of moderate-fat (from monounsaturated fat) and low-fat weight-loss diets on the serum lipid profile in overweight and obese men and women. *Am J Clin Nutr.* 2004;79:204-212.

13. Lichtenstein A. Thematic review series: patient-oriented research. Dietary fat, carbohydrate, and protein: effects on plasma lipoprotein patterns. *J Lipid Res.* 2006;47:1661-1667.

14. Peters JC. Dietary fat and body weight control. *Lipids.* 2003;38:123-127.

15. Ornish D, Brown SE, Scherwitz LW, et al. Can lifestyle changes reverse coronary heart disease? The Lifestyle Heart Trial. *Lancet.* 1990;336:129-133.

16. Djousse L, Arnett DK, Coon H, Province MA, Moore LL, Ellison RC. Fruit and vegetable consumption and LDL cholesterol: the National Heart, Lung, and Blood Institute Family Heart Study. *Am J Clin Nutr.* 2004;79:213-217.

17. Brown L, Rosner B, Willett WW, Sacks FM. Cholesterol-lowering effects of dietary fiber: a meta-analysis. *Am J Clin Nutr.* 1999;69:30-42.

18. Jenkins DJ, Kendall CW, Vuksan V, et al. Soluble fiber intake at a dose approved by the US Food and Drug Administration for a claim of health benefits: serum lipid risk factors for cardiovascular disease assessed in a randomized controlled crossover trial. *Am J Clin Nutr.* 2002;75:834-839.

19. Moreyra AE, Wilson AC, Koraym A. Effect of combining psyllium fiber with simvastatin in lowering cholesterol. *Arch Intern Med.* 2005;165:1161-1166.

20. Anderson JW, Johnstone BM, Cook-Newell ME. Meta-analysis of the effects of soy protein intake on serum lipids. *N Engl J Med.* 1995;333:276-282.

21. Taku K, Umegaki K, Sato Y, Taki Y, Endoh K, Watanabe S. Soy isoflavones lower serum total and LDL cholesterol in humans: a meta-analysis of 11 randomized controlled trials. *Am J Clin Nutr.* 2007;85:1148-1156.

22. Kris-Etherton PM, Yu-Poth S, Sabate J, Ratcliffe HE, Zhao G, Etherton TD. Nuts and their bioactive constituents: effects on serum lipids and other factors that affect disease risk. *Am J Clin Nutr.* 1999;70:504S-511S.

23. Mukuddem-Petersen J, Oosthuizen W, Jerling JC. A systematic review of the effects of nuts on blood lipid profiles in humans. *J Nutr.* 2005;135:2082-2089.

24. Katan MB, Grundy SM, Jones P, et al. Efficacy and safety of plant stanols and sterols in the management of blood cholesterol levels. *Mayo Clin Proc.* 2003;78:965-978.

25. Jenkins DJ, Kendall CW, Marchie A, et al. Effects of a dietary portfolio of cholesterol-lowering foods vs lovastatin on serum lipids and C-reactive protein. *JAMA.* 2003;290:502-510.

26. Rodrigues IM, Klein LC. Boiled or filtered coffee? Effects of coffee and caffeine on cholesterol, fibrinogen and C-reactive protein. *Toxicol Rev.* 2006;25:55-69.

27. Din JN, Newby DE, Flapan AD. Omega 3 fatty acids and cardiovascular disease--fishing for a natural treatment. *BMJ.* 2004; 328:30-35.

28. Nambi V, Ballantyne CM. Combination therapy with statins and omega-3 fatty acids. *Am J Cardiol.* 2006;98:34i-38i.

29. Ma Y, Olendzki BC, Hafner AR et al. Low-carbohydrate and high-fat intake among adult patients with poorly controlled type 2 diabetes mellitus. *Nutrition.* 2006;22:1129-1136.

30. Anderson JW, Randles KM, Kendall CW, Jenkins DJ. Carbohydrate and fiber recommendations for individuals with diabetes: a quantitative assessment and meta-analysis of the evidence. *J Am Coll Nutr.* 2004;23:5-17.

31. Ashen MD, Blumenthal RS. Clinical practice. Low HDL cholesterol levels. *N Engl J Med.* 2005;353:1252-1260.

32. Rimm EB, Williams P, Fosher K, Criqui M, Stampfer MJ. Moderate alcohol intake and lower risk of coronary heart disease: meta-analysis of effects on lipids and haemostatic factors. *BMJ.* 1999;319:1523-1528.

33. Malloy MJ, Kane JP. A risk factor for atherosclerosis: triglyceride-rich lipoproteins. *Adv Intern Med.* 2001;47:111-136.

34. Cefalu WT, Hu FB. Role of chromium in human health and in diabetes. *Diabetes Care.* 2004;27:2741-2751.

35. Hughes S, Samman S. The effect of zinc supplementation in humans on plasma lipids, antioxidant status and thrombogenesis. *J Am Coll Nutr.* 2006;25:285-291.

35. Hypertension

Hypertension is a major risk factor for cardiovascular disease, including coronary heart disease and stroke, as well as for end-stage renal disease and peripheral vascular disease. The World Health Organization has identified hypertension as one of the most important preventable causes of premature death in developed countries.[1] Hypertension, obesity, insulin resistance, and lipid abnormalities (hypertriglyceridemia and low HDL-cholesterol levels) make up the metabolic syndrome, a particularly virulent risk profile for cardiovascular disease.

About 65 million people in the United States have hypertension. Because it is typically asymptomatic, affected individuals often do not know they have the condition. In fact, one-third of hypertensive persons are unaware of their disease, and only about half of those who are aware achieve adequate blood pressure control.[2]

The vast majority of cases are primary or "essential" (ie, no specific cause has been identified). Approximately 5% to 10% of cases are due to renal or endocrine disease (eg, renovascular disease, obesity, thyroid disease, chronic steroid therapy, Cushing disease, or pheochromocytoma).

Hypertension usually is without signs or symptoms. When hypertension is severe, it may cause headache, vision changes, and nausea and vomiting.

Risk Factors

African Americans have a higher prevalence of hypertension compared with African blacks and North American whites (including Latinos).

The following factors increase the likelihood of developing hypertension:

Age. About two-thirds of Americans over age 65 have high blood pressure.

Family history.

Obesity. The prevalence of hypertension in obese adults is doubled, compared with individuals near their ideal weight. In addition, sleep apnea, which is often due to overweight, is also associated with increased risk but maintains this association even in thinner individuals.

Lack of exercise. In Western populations, physical inactivity contributes an estimated 5% to 13% of the risk for hypertension.[3]

Dietary factors are discussed in Nutritional Considerations below.

Renovascular/kidney disease.

Endocrine disease. Hyperaldosteronism, thyroid disorders, hyperparathyroidism, Cushing syndrome, and pheochromocytoma (rare) are among the endocrine causes of hypertension.

Alcohol excess.

Medications. Corticosteroids, nonsteroidal anti-inflammatory drugs (NSAIDs), antihistamines, diet pills, oral contraceptives, and some antidepressants can increase blood pressure.

Diagnosis

Sustained and untreated high blood pressure may lead to end-organ damage, including coronary heart disease and left ventricular hypertrophy, heart failure (hypertension is the leading cause in developed countries), stroke, retinopathy, and kidney disease. Therefore, early diagnosis and treatment are important.

The Seventh Report of the Joint National Committee on Prevention, Detection, Evaluation, and Treatment of High Blood Pressure defines normal blood pressure as less than 120/80 mm Hg.[2] *Prehypertension* is defined as a blood pressure between 120/80 and 139/89 mm Hg. Prehypertension indicates increased risk for progression to hypertension and requires regular monitoring. Hypertension is defined as an average seated blood pressure measurement of 140/90 mm Hg or greater during at least three office visits. Stage 1 hypertension is defined as a systolic blood pressure measurement of 140 to 159 mm Hg or a diastolic measurement of 90 to 99 mm Hg. Stage 2 hypertension is defined as a systolic measurement greater than 160 mm Hg or a diastolic measurement greater than 100 mm Hg. Although the above categories are defined by the higher systolic or diastolic measurement, systolic pressures correlate more strongly with coronary heart disease risk.

Malignant hypertension causing retinal damage—papilledema, exudates, or hemorrhages—usually involves a diastolic pressure ≥120 mm Hg. Individuals with similar blood pressures but without symptoms or end-organ damage are considered hypertensive *urgencies*, and they require blood pressure reduction in an outpatient setting over 1 to 2 days.[4]

Elevated blood pressure accompanied by acute or chronic end-organ damage is a hypertensive *emergency* and requires blood pressure reduction within minutes to hours.[4] Diastolic pressures ≥100 can cause encephalopathy in patients with previously normal blood pressure.

Diagnostic evaluation should consider possible causes of hypertension and its sequelae. Abnormal history or physical examination findings should guide cost-effective testing. Routine laboratory testing and procedures include an electrocardiogram, lipid profile, urinalysis, hematocrit, and a basic metabolic panel. Lipid goals are based on a cardiovascular risk factor assessment.

Children with hypertension should be evaluated for coarctation of the aorta.

Treatment

Goal blood pressure for persons with hypertension is less than 140/90 mm Hg or less than 130/80 mm Hg for patients with diabetes or chronic kidney disease. Some data also support more aggressive lowering of systolic pressures. However, in individuals with renal disease, systolic pressure should not go below 110.

Prehypertension usually does not require drug therapy unless the patient has coronary heart disease, diabetes, heart failure, chronic kidney disease, history of stroke, or other end-organ damage. Lifestyle interventions should be instituted for prehypertension, and the patient should monitor blood pressure at regular intervals.

Lifestyle modifications are an integral initial step in the treatment of hypertension. These may include a low-sodium, low-fat diet (particularly a vegetarian diet), maintenance of appropriate body weight, reduction in alcohol use, increased physical activity, and possibly stress reduction (eg, through meditation or yoga). Energy expenditure in the form of vigorous activity[5] or even walking and leisure-time physical activity also lowers the risk for developing hypertension.[6] Smoking cessation does not treat hypertension but should be encouraged for cardiovascular and other health-risk reduction.

Pharmacologic therapy includes several drug choices. Individuals with inadequate response to single-drug treatment often respond to another drug class. However, most patients require at least 2 drugs to achieve target blood pressure, and the use of 3 or more drugs is common.

A **thiazide** diuretic is usually prescribed as first-line pharmacotherapy and is particularly beneficial for patients with diabetes and systolic heart failure. Thiazides are inexpensive. They tend to reduce calciuria, an effect that may be beneficial for those at risk for osteoporosis and calcium stones.

Other drug classes that can be used alone (for specific protective functions) or in combination include the following:

- **Angiotensin-converting enzyme (ACE) inhibitors** are advantageous in patients after myocardial infarction and in those who have proteinuria or systolic heart failure. They may also be advantageous in diabetes. Side effects include cough, hyperkalemia and, rarely, angioedema. ACE inhibitors are contraindicated in pregnant women.

- **Beta-blockers** serve as optimal treatment after myocardial infarction. They also are used for systolic heart failure, atrial fibrillation, and angina, and they are safe in pregnancy. However, beta-blockers should be avoided in patients with reactive airway disease or second-degree or third-degree heart block. Erectile dysfunction is a common side effect.

- **Angiotensin receptor blockers (ARBs)** have benefits similar to those of ACE inhibitors. Patients with side effects from ACE inhibitors may be switched to ARBs, and the two classes may be combined for additional benefit. The combination may also be indicated in cases of severe proteinuria. Like ACE inhibitors, ARBs may cause hyperkalemia and are contraindicated in pregnancy.

- **Calcium channel blockers** help protect against angina. Nondihydropyridine calcium channel blockers may be used for heart rate control. Calcium channel blockers may cause pedal edema and/or conduction abnormalities.

- **Alpha-adrenergic blockers** (eg, methyldopa) are indicated in patients with concomitant benign prostatic hyperplasia because of their vasodilatory action on both blood vessels and prostatic smooth muscle. They are associated with risk of postural hypotension but are safe in pregnancy.

- **Arterial vasodilators** include specific drugs that have noteworthy side effects. Hydralazine may cause lupus syndrome, but it is safe in pregnancy.

- **Minoxidil** may cause sodium (ie, water) retention. It can also cause some degree of hair regrowth, which may be advantageous in balding men.

- **Potassium-sparing diuretics** are optimal for patients at risk of hypokalemia. However, close monitoring of potassium levels is required.

People with hypertension often have lower melatonin levels, compared with those with normal blood pressure,[7] and some fail to experience the normal nocturnal decrease in blood pressure.[8] In limited studies, melatonin supplements (2.5 mg at bedtime) lowered nocturnal blood pressure significantly (6 mm Hg and 4 mm Hg for systolic and diastolic, respectively) in men with high blood pressure.[9] An assessment of melatonin's clinical value awaits further studies.

Nutritional Considerations

Nutritional factors play a large role not only in reducing the risk that hypertension will occur, but also in managing the condition after it has been diagnosed. The Dietary Approaches to Stop Hypertension (DASH) study showed that diets rich in fruits and vegetables and reduced in saturated fat can both lower the risk for high blood pressure and assist with blood pressure control in hypertensive persons.[10,11] The DASH study was predicated on the observation that vegetarian diets are associated with markedly reduced risk of hypertension. Vegetables and fruits accounted for approximately half of the blood-pressure-lowering effect of the diet.

Restricting sodium intake enhanced the blood-pressure-lowering effect. While the DASH diet reduced systolic blood pressure by 5 to 6 mm, individuals eating the DASH diet in combination with the lowest sodium intake (1200 mg/day) had a further blood pressure decrease of 5 to 8 mm Hg.[12]

Some investigators have carried these observations a step further. Vegetarian and vegan diets reduce blood pressure in both normotensive and hypertensive individuals and have the potential to reduce or eliminate medication use in some patients.[13] Possible mechanisms underlying these results may include a combination of the following:

Weight loss reduces blood pressure. A meta-analysis of 105 randomized controlled trials showed that weight-reduction diets lowered blood pressure by 5.0 mm Hg systolic and 4.0 mm Hg diastolic on average.[14] Although a reduction in plasma volume is the most likely reason, this effect may also be attributed to a 15% lower activity of angiotensin-converting enzyme (ACE) after weight loss.[15] However, weight loss is clearly not the only reason for the effect of such a diet on blood pressure, as vegetarian diets reduce blood pressure even in the absence of weight loss.

Reducing or eliminating meat may influence blood viscosity. Numerous studies have linked beef, veal, lamb, poultry, and animal fat to high blood pressure.[16-19] Saturated fat appears to influence blood viscosity.[20] A higher proportional intake of fatty acids from polyunsaturated sources (linoleic acid and alpha-linolenic acids), compared with saturated fats, is associated with a lower risk for developing hypertension.[21]

Vegetables and fruits are rich in potassium, which influences blood pressure. Potassium, from either food or supplements, reduces blood pressure and stroke risk.[22] Fruits and vegetables are rich potassium sources. Some evidence also suggests that fruits and vegetables may lower blood pressure by providing antioxidant flavonoids that upregulate endothelial nitric oxide production[23,24] and by suppressing enzymes involved in the generation of superoxide radicals that are known to reduce nitric oxide availability.[25]

Plant-based foods are low in sodium.[26] Hypertension is rare in societies whose dietary sodium intake is very low.[27] A 2004 meta-analysis of contributors to hypertension in Finland, Italy, the Netherlands, the United Kingdom, and the United States found that 9% to17% of the risk for hypertension was attributable to dietary sodium alone.[28] In a recent meta-analysis, sodium restriction reduced systolic blood pressure by 3.6 mm Hg.[14] The principal sources of sodium are canned foods, snack foods, discretionary use of salt in food preparation or consumption, and dairy products. In their natural state, vegetables, fruits, grains, and legumes are very low in sodium.

Replacing animal protein with soy and other plant proteins may help lower blood pressure. Plant proteins are higher in L-arginine (an amino acid involved in production of nitric oxide) compared with animal protein, and intake of vegetable (not animal) protein is inversely related to blood pressure.[29] A number of studies have found that soy protein supplementation reduced blood pressure significantly (~5–8 mm Hg systolic, ~2.5–5.0 mm Hg diastolic) in both normal and hypertensive individuals.[30]

Additional considerations in preventing or controlling hypertension include:

Limiting alcohol. In excess of moderate consumption (1-2 drinks/day), alcohol intake raises the risk for developing hypertension.[28] Avoiding alcohol reduces systolic blood pressure.[14] The relationship between moderate alcohol intake and hypertension is complicated, however. Studies have found a lower risk for hypertension-related mortality in moderate drinkers, even in those with hypertension, compared with persons who rarely or never drink alcohol.[31,32]

Folic acid. The Nurses' Health Study found that women consuming the highest amounts of folate from diet and supplements (>1000 μg per day) had only one-third the risk for developing hypertension, compared with women consuming less than 200 μg per day.[33] One possible explanation is that folate is an important cofactor for nitric oxide synthase and subsequent nitric oxide generation.

Vitamin C. A diet that meets the Dietary Reference Intake (DRI) for vitamin C may not be adequate in persons at risk for hypertension. Studies show that blood pressure rises as vitamin C depletion occurs in humans,[34] and higher vitamin C intakes are associated with lower blood pressure.[35] However, there do not appear to be any additional blood pressure-lowering effects of vitamin C over an intake of 500 mg per day.[36]

Vitamin D. The Nurses' Health Study and the Health Professionals Study reported that plasma concentrations of 25-hydroxy vitamin D were inversely associated with the risk for incident hypertension.[37] Similarly, the National Health and Nutrition Examination Survey (NHANES) found that serum concentrations of 25-hydroxy vitamin D were inversely associated with blood pressure.[38] Vitamin D supplementation is inversely related to plasma renin activity,[39] and clinical as well as epidemiological evidence indicates that it may reduce blood pressure in humans.[40] Additional evidence from clinical trials is needed to establish whether this vitamin has significant blood pressure-lowering effects.

Magnesium. Many studies have shown that magnesium intake is inversely associated with blood pressure.[41] The Women's Health Study of over 28,000 women found that the highest magnesium intakes (434 mg/day) were associated with a 7% lower risk for developing hypertension, compared with intakes of 256 mg/day.[42]

Other factors. Curiously, a meta-analysis of controlled clinical trials has shown that a daily intake of cocoa (consumed as 3 ounces of dark chocolate) lowers systolic blood pressure by 4.7 mm Hg and lowers diastolic blood pressure by 2.8 mm Hg.[43] This quantity of chocolate provides roughly 450 kilocalories. Also, some studies have shown that omega-3 supplements reduce systolic pressure by approximately 2 mm Hg and diastolic pressure by 1.5 mm Hg in omnivores whose baseline diets were generally high in omega-6 fatty acids.[44] These benefits have not been demonstrated in individuals already following low-fat, vegetarian diets, nor have they been shown with alpha-linolenic acid.[45]

Orders

Vegetarian diet, low-fat. Foods rich in vitamin C and potassium should be encouraged.

Sodium less than 2 g daily.

See Basic Diet Orders chapter.

Smoking cessation and alcohol restriction, if applicable.

Individualized exercise prescription, as appropriate.

What to Tell the Family

Hypertension usually has no symptoms but can be deadly. It is important for the patient and the family to have their blood pressure checked regularly and to adhere to the prescribed treatment plan. A good-quality home blood pressure monitor provides a convenient means of tracking hypertension and progress with treatment.

Hypertension is not treated with medication alone. Dietary and lifestyle changes can help reduce blood pressure and can reduce, sometimes even eliminate, the need for medication. The family can support and enhance the patient's adherence to the recommended diet. Because weight problems and hypertension often run in families, it is important for the entire family to shift to healthier eating and exercise patterns. Smoking cessation and alcohol restriction should be encouraged.

References

1. Ezzati M, Lopez AD, Rodgers A, Vander Hoorn S, Murray CJ. Selected major risk factors and global and regional burden of disease. *Lancet.* 2002;360:1347-1360.

2. Chobanian AV, Bakris GL, Black HR, et al. The Seventh Report of the Joint National Committee on Prevention, Detection, Evaluation, and Treatment of High Blood Pressure: The JNC 7 Report. *JAMA.* 2003;289:2560-2572.

3. Geleijnse JM, Kok FJ, Grobbee DE. Impact of dietary and lifestyle factors on the prevalence of hypertension in Western populations. *Eur J Public Health.* 2004;14:235-239.

4. Bales A. Hypertensive crisis. How to tell if it's an emergency or urgency. *Postgrad Med.* 1999;105:119-126,130.

5. Hernelahti M, Kujala U, Kaprio J. Stability and change of volume and intensity of physical activity as predictors of hypertension. *Scand J Public Health.* 2004;32:303-309.

6. Nakanishi N, Suzuki K. Daily life activity and the risk of developing hypertension in middle-aged Japanese men. *Arch Intern Med.* 2005;165:214-220.

7. Sewerynek E. Melatonin and the cardiovascular system. *Neuro Endocrinol Lett.* 2002;23(suppl 1):79-83.

8. Jonas M, Garfinkel D, Zisapel N, Laudon M, Grossman E. Impaired nocturnal melatonin secretion in non-dipper hypertensive patients. *Blood Press.* 2003;12:19-24.

9. Scheer FA, Van Montfrans GA, van Someren EJ, Mairuhu G, Buijs RM. Daily nighttime melatonin reduces blood pressure in male patients with essential hypertension. *Hypertension*. 2004;43:192-197.

10. Appel LJ, Champagne CM, Harsha DW, Cooper LS, Obarzanek E, Elmer PJ. Effects of comprehensive lifestyle modification on blood pressure control: main results of the PREMIER clinical trial. *JAMA*. 2003;289:2083-2093.

11. Svetkey LP, Simons-Morton D, Vollmer WM, et al. Effects of dietary patterns on blood pressure: subgroup analysis of the Dietary Approaches to Stop Hypertension (DASH) randomized clinical trial. *Arch Intern Med*. 1999;159:285-293.

12. Sacks FM, Svetkey LP, Vollmer WM, et al. Effects on blood pressure of reduced dietary sodium and the Dietary Approaches to Stop Hypertension (DASH) diet. DASH-Sodium Collaborative Research Group. *N Engl J Med*. 2001;344:3-10.

13. Berkow SE, Barnard ND. Blood pressure regulation and vegetarian diets. *Nutr Rev*. 2005;63:1-8.

14. Dickinson HO, Mason JM, Nicolson DJ, et al. Lifestyle interventions to reduce raised blood pressure: a systematic review of randomized controlled trials. *J Hypertens*. 2006;24:215-233.

15. Harp JB, Henry SA, DiGirolamo M. Dietary weight loss decreases serum angiotensin-converting enzyme activity in obese adults. *Obes Res*. 2002;10:985-990.

16. Bener A, Al-Suwaidi J, Al-Jaber K, Al-Marri S, Dagash MH, Elbagi IE. The prevalence of hypertension and its associated risk factors in a newly developed country. *Saudi Med J*. 2004;25:918-922.

17. Miura K, Greenland P, Stamler J, Liu K, Daviglus ML, Nakagawa H. Relation Miura K, Greenland P, Stamler J, Liu K, Daviglus ML, Nakagawa H. Relation of vegetable, fruit, and meat intake to 7-year blood pressure change in middle-aged men: the Chicago Western Electric Study. *Am J Epidemiol*. 2004;159:572-580.

18. Beegom R, Singh RB. Association of higher saturated fat intake with higher risk of hypertension in an urban population of Trivandrum in south India. *Int J Cardiol*. 1997;58:63-70.

19. Ascherio A, Hennekens C, Willett WC, et al. Prospective study of nutritional factors, blood pressure, and hypertension among U.S. women. *Hypertension*. 1996;27:1065-1072.

20. Ernst E, Pietsch L, Matrai A, Eisenberg J. Blood rheology in vegetarians. *Br J Nutr*. 1986;56:555-560.

21. Djousse L, Arnett DK, Pankow JS, Hopkins PN, Province MA, Ellison RC. Dietary linolenic acid is associated with a lower prevalence of hypertension in the NHLBI Family Heart Study. *Hypertension*. 2005;45:368-373.

22. Whelton PK, He J, Appel LJ, et al. Primary prevention of hypertension: clinical and public health advisory from the National High Blood Pressure Education Program. *JAMA*. 2002;288:1882-1888.

23. Xu JW, Ikeda K, Yamori Y. Upregulation of endothelial nitric oxide synthase by cyanidin-3-glucoside, a typical anthocyanin pigment. *Hypertension*. 2004;44:217-222.

24. Achike FI, Kwan CY. Nitric oxide, human diseases and the herbal products that affect the nitric oxide signaling pathway. *Clin Exp Pharmacol Physiol*. 2003;30:605-615.

25. Tauber AI, Fay JR, Marletta MA. Flavonoid inhibition of the human neutrophil NADPH-oxidase. *Biochem Pharmacol*. 1984;33:1367-1369.

26. He J, Whelton PK. What is the role of dietary sodium and potassium in hypertension and target organ injury? *Am J Med Sci.* 1999;317:152-159.

27. Adrogue HJ, Wesson DE. Role of dietary factors in the hypertension of African Americans. *Semin Nephrol.* 1996;16:94-101.

28. Witteman JC, Willett WC, Stampfer MJ, et al. Relation of moderate alcohol consumption and risk of systemic hypertension in women. *Am J Cardiol.* 1990;65:633-637.

29. Elliott P, Stamler J, Dyer AR, et al. Association between protein intake and blood pressure: the INTERMAP Study. *Arch Intern Med.* 2006;166:79-87.

30. He J, Gu D, Wu X, et al. Effect of soybean protein on blood pressure: a randomized, controlled trial. *Ann Intern Med.* 2005;143:1-9.

31. Malinski MK, Sesso HD, Lopez-Jimenez F, Buring JE, Gaziano JM. Alcohol consumption and cardiovascular disease mortality in hypertensive men. *Arch Intern Med.* 2004;164:623-628.

32. Renaud SC, Gueguen R, Conard P, Lanzmann-Petithory D, Orgogozo JM, Henry O. Moderate wine drinkers have lower hypertension-related mortality: a prospective cohort study in French men. *Am J Clin Nutr.* 2004;80:621-625.

33. Forman JP, Rimm EB, Stampfer MJ, Curhan GC. Folate intake and the risk of incident hypertension among U.S. women. *JAMA.* 2005;293:320-329.

34. Block G. Ascorbic acid, blood pressure, and the American diet. *Ann NY Acad Sci.* 2002;959:180-187.

35. Chen J, He J, Hamm L, Batuman V, Whelton PK. Serum antioxidant vitamins and blood pressure in the United States population. *Hypertension.* 2002;40:810-816.

36. Hajjar IM, George V, Sasse EA, Kochar MS. A randomized, double-blind, controlled trial of vitamin C in the management of hypertension and lipids. *Am J Ther.* 2002;9:289-293.

37. Forman JP, Giovannucci E, Holmes MD, et al. Plasma 25-hydroxyvitamin D levels and risk of incident hypertension. *Hypertension.* 2007;49:1063-1069.

38. Scragg R, Sowers M, Bell C. Serum 25-hydroxyvitamin D, Ethnicity, and Blood Pressure in the Third National Health and Nutrition Examination Survey. *Am J Hypertens.* 2007;20:713-719.

39. Sigmund CD. Regulation of renin expression and blood pressure by vitamin D3. *J Clin Invest.* 2002;110:155–156.

40. Richart T, Li Y, Staessen JA. Renal versus extrarenal activation of vitamin D in relation to atherosclerosis, arterial stiffening, and hypertension. *Am J Hypertens.* 2007;20:1007-1015.

41. Mizushima S, Cappuccio FP, Nichols R, Elliott P. Dietary magnesium intake and blood pressure: a qualitative overview of the observational studies. *J Hum Hypertens.* 1998;12:447-453.

42. Song Y, Sesso HD, Manson JE, Cook NR, Buring JE, Liu S. Dietary magnesium intake and risk of incident hypertension among middle-aged and older US women in a 10-year follow-up study. *Am J Cardiol.* 2006;98:1616-1621.

43. Taubert D, Roesen R, Schomig E. Effect of cocoa and tea intake on blood pressure: a meta-analysis. *Arch Intern Med.* 2007;167:626-634.

44. Robinson JG, Stone NJ. Antiatherosclerotic and antithrombotic effects of omega-3 fatty acids. *Am J Cardiol.* 2006;98(4A):39i-49i.

45. Wendland E, Farmer A, Glasziou P, Neil A. Effect of alpha linolenic acid on cardiovascular risk markers: a systematic review. *Heart.* 2006;92:166-169.

36. Heart Failure

Heart failure is the inability to pump blood adequately to meet the body's needs. This condition may lead to inadequate perfusion to the body's peripheral tissues as well as to pulmonary edema (left heart failure), build-up of pressure in the venous system (right heart failure), or both. Primarily a disease of elderly persons, heart failure likely affects more than 5 million Americans. It can develop in anyone with a history of hypertension, myocardial infarction (MI), coronary heart disease (CHD), valvular heart disease, or diabetes, among other disorders.

Heart failure may be right-sided or left-sided. Signs and symptoms of right-sided failure include increased jugular venous pressure, right upper quadrant or abdominal discomfort, hepatomegaly, ascites and/or jaundice, and peripheral edema. Left-sided failure is characterized by dyspnea, orthopnea, and paroxysmal nocturnal dyspnea, attributable to elevated pulmonary pressure with or without pulmonary edema or effusion. Acute heart failure often causes prominent dyspnea, diaphoresis, tachycardia, and pale, cold extremities.

Low-output heart failure is marked by decreased cardiac output and is most often caused by hypertension, myocardial infarction, or chronic coronary artery disease. High-output heart failure is often caused by anemia or hyperthyroidism.

The most common proximate cause of heart failure is left ventricular systolic dysfunction, which is marked by reduced myocardial contractility, resulting in low stroke volume. Diastolic dysfunction (myocardial stiffness and impaired relaxation) produces heart failure due to elevated ventricular filling pressure. It is usually due to hypertension and often occurs without associated systolic dysfunction. Diastolic dysfunction accounts for approximately half of heart failure diagnoses. It is more common in women.

Complications of heart failure include activity-limiting symptoms, syncope, dysrhythmias (which may be lethal), progressive systolic or diastolic dysfunction, thromboembolism (usually strokes), and circulatory collapse.

Risk Factors

Compared with white Americans, African Americans are more commonly affected and are at greater risk of morbidity and mortality.

Other risk factors include:

Age. The likelihood of heart failure and left-ventricular dysfunction increases with age.

History of MI or CHD. Left ventricular dysfunction often results from ischemic injury to the myocardium.

History of cardiomyopathy. Family or personal history of dilated, hypertrophic, or restrictive cardiomyopathy.

Diabetes. Diabetic cardiomyopathy causes left ventricular dysfunction and aggravates the effects of other contributors to heart failure.

Use of thiazoladinediones. Rosiglitazone and pioglitazone raise the risk of heart failure in diabetes patients. Rosiglitazone is also associated with other cardiac risks.[1,2]

Smoking. Smoking dramatically raises risk for CHD and thus heart failure.

History of rheumatic fever or valvular heart disease.

Hypertension. Pulmonary hypertension generally leads to right-sided heart failure, whereas systemic hypertension leads to left-sided heart failure.

Alcohol abuse. Alcohol toxicity may lead to dilated cardiomyopathy.

Pericardial disease.

Obesity. Hypertension and left ventricular hypertrophy are commonly found in obese patients. Surprisingly, however, BMI appears to have an inverse association with CHF-related mortality in most studies.[3] In a study of more than 7,500 individuals, a linear increase in CHF mortality has been found to occur with a BMI below 30 kg/m². Persons with a BMI of 25 to 29.9, 22.5 to 24.9, and <22.5 had a mortality risk approximately 120%, 145%, and 170% greater than those with a BMI >30 kg/m².[3]

Diagnosis

The New York Heart Association classification system describes the functional limitations of heart failure:[4]

Class I: Symptoms (eg, fatigue, dyspnea, and palpitations) are experienced on heavy exertion.

Class II: Symptoms occur with mild to moderate levels of exertion.

Class III: Symptoms occur with less than ordinary exertion.

Class IV: Symptoms occur with any exertion or at rest.

Diagnostic Tools

2-D and Doppler echocardiogram is the most common imaging modality for assessing cardiac function. Echocardiography can evaluate left and right ventricular systolic function, diastolic function, valvular structure and function, and cardiac chamber sizes. It also identifies possible heart failure etiologies, such as MI, valvular disease, and cardiomyopathies.

Chest x-ray can identify intrinsic pulmonary disease, pulmonary edema, and pleural effusions. It can also estimate the degree of cardiac enlargement but is much less accurate than echocardiography.

Electrocardiogram may reveal MI, dysrhythmias, conduction abnormalities, or left ventricular hypertrophy.

Measurement of circulating concentrations of **brain natriuretic peptide (BNP)**, which is produced by the heart, is increasingly used to diagnose and assess the degree of heart failure and monitor treatment effects.

Additional blood tests, such as a complete blood count and comprehensive metabolic panel, are usually standard. Additional tests should be ordered when clinically appropriate to help determine the etiology. Heart failure without an identifiable cause usually requires an evaluation for coronary heart disease, such as exercise stress testing, noninvasive imaging, or cardiac catheterization.

Treatment[5]

Treatment of heart failure should target the underlying disorder: hypertension, coronary artery disease, diabetes, etc. See relevant chapters for specific information. Certain medications (ie, drugs for erectile dysfunction, NSAIDs, metformin, and thiazolidinediones) are contraindicated. Thiazolidinediones may exacerbate heart failure by causing pulmonary and peripheral edema. Metformin increases the risk of lactic acidosis.

Diastolic heart failure (with preserved systolic function) is not well codified. Treatment strategies overlap with systolic failure in some cases (ie, treatment of hypertension, diuretic use for pulmonary symptoms, rate control in atrial fibrillation, and treatment of ischemic CHD), but other treatment strategies need further study. [5]

Oral Drugs

Diuretics are first-line therapy for heart failure patients with fluid retention and systolic heart failure, but they are less useful (and may be contraindicated) for diastolic heart failure. Loop diuretics (eg, furosemide) are most commonly used, prevent volume overload, and have favorable vascular effects.

Angiotensin-converting enzyme inhibitors (ACEI) (eg, enalapril, lisinopril) are first-line heart failure treatments. They decrease mortality in a broad range of heart failure patients by decreasing afterload.

Beta-blockers are a first-line treatment for all categories of heart failure and are not limited to patients with coronary artery disease or hypertension. Carvedilol, metoprolol succinate, and bisoprolol have all been shown to decrease heart failure mortality.[6]

Angiotensin II receptor blockers (ARB) (eg, losartan, candesartan, irbesartan) are generally equivalent to ACEIs and often used if side effects (usually cough) limit ACEI use. Some patients benefit from combined use of ACEIs and ARBs, which more completely blocks the effects of angiotensin II.

Nitrates reduce cardiac preload through venous dilation.

Aldosterone blockers (eg, spironolactone, eplerenone) have been shown to decrease heart failure mortality when added to usual therapy[7,8] but may be associated with risk for hyperkalemia. They should not generally be used when both ACEIs and ARBs are already prescribed for systolic failure.

Hydralazine. Evidence suggests that black patients may respond particularly well to the addition of hydralazine and nitrates when initial therapy is not successful.

Calcium channel blockers (eg, verapamil, amlodipine) may be used to treat angina and hypertension but are not usual therapies for heart failure patients and are contraindicated for patients with significant systolic dysfunction.

Anticoagulants (eg, warfarin) can be used to prevent thromboembolism in heart failure, especially if the patient has a history of thromboembolism, if systolic dysfunction is severe, and/or if sinus rhythm is absent. Benefit has not been clearly established for patients with less severe heart failure and sinus rhythm.

Digoxin is an oral inotropic agent that provides symptomatic relief in patients with decompensated heart failure. Its therapeutic window is narrow, and low (yet therapeutic) serum digoxin concentration may be associated with greater survival, while high serum digoxin concentration may increase mortality.[9] It may be useful for patients who remain symptomatic despite optimal treatment with diuretics, ACEI or ARB, and beta-blockers, especially if atrial fibrillation is present. Digoxin is not useful for diastolic dysfunction. Dosage must be adjusted for older patients and those with renal dysfunction, as well as in the presence of many drugs that influence digoxin levels.

Intravenous Medications

In general, intravenous therapies for heart failure decompensation are intended to relieve symptoms and facilitate hospital discharge. They are not generally used for prolonging survival beyond the short term. The following drugs are used for treatment of decompensation:

Nesiritide is administered intravenously for decompensated heart failure, often in an emergency or intensive care setting. Nesiritide has not been shown to improve 1-month or 6-month survival and is very expensive.

Dobutamine is an inotropic and vasoactive agent administered intravenously for symptom relief and systolic function improvement. It requires close monitoring, as it may produce dysrhythmias or abrupt blood pressure changes. It is sometimes used for home infusions after demonstrated acute efficacy to relieve symptoms and decrease the need for hospitalization.

Phosphodiesterase inhibitors (eg, amrinone, milrinone) increase contractility by modulating calcium influx into cardiac cells. They also facilitate both arterial and venous dilation, reducing preload and afterload. They are not used for chronic therapy, as this has resulted in increased mortality for heart failure patients.

Surgical Procedures

Implantable cardioverter-defibrillator (ICD) use has been shown to decrease mortality from lethal dysrhythmias for high-risk patients, particularly those with documented dysrhythmias and/or severe systolic dysfunction.

Intra-aortic balloon pump (IABP) is used to treat acute heart failure decompensation. IABP assists the heart by decreasing afterload and improving cardiac output. After insertion into the aorta via catheter, the balloon inflates at the beginning of diastole to enhance coronary perfusion. It deflates at the beginning of systole, thereby increasing cardiac output.

Cardiac transplant may be necessary for patients with end-stage heart failure. Left ventricular assist devices (LVAD) are used in extraordinary cases to bridge a severely ill patient to cardiac transplantation.

Other Treatments

Exercise conditioning, which should be approved by a physician and overseen by an exercise physiologist.

Leg elevation above the heart should be done during rest.

Compression stockings may help control leg edema and improve fluid removal. Results are variable, and a therapeutic trial will help determine usefulness for individual heart failure patients.

Nutritional Considerations

Diet therapy for congestive heart failure chiefly involves restriction of excess sodium and fluid, which can overburden an already reduced ability to handle plasma volume due to weakening of the heart muscle. Because the condition is usually the result of long-term cardiovascular disease, treatment should also include diet therapy for CHD (see Coronary Heart Disease chapter), along with adequate calories to prevent the excessive weight loss that may accompany this condition. However, there is emerging evidence that minimizing saturated fat and eliminating trans fatty acids may be of benefit in patients with CHF.[10,11] The primary nutritional considerations are as follows:

Sodium reduction. A higher intake of dietary sodium is a strong and independent risk factor for heart failure in overweight persons.[12] In patients with heart failure, sodium restriction is an important part of treatment and may reduce the need for diuretic therapy.[13] Restriction of sodium to 2000 to 2400 mg per day, along with fluid restriction to 1.5 liters daily, improves functional class and reduces edema.[14] The most commonly recommended limit is 2000 mg of sodium daily.[15] Moderation in sodium intake is also important for the control and treatment of hypertension (see Hypertension chapter), which increases risk for heart failure.[16]

Maintaining magnesium adequacy. About 30% of heart failure patients have magnesium deficiency, which can cause a positive sodium balance and negative potassium balance and is associated with a poorer prognosis.[17]

Thiamine supplements for patients treated with diuretics. Evidence of vitamin B$_1$ deficiency has been found in 57% to 98% of patients treated with diuretics; the risk increases in a dose-related manner.[18] Supplementation with high-dose thiamine (200 mg/day) improves both biochemical indicators of deficiency and left ventricular function.[19,20]

Avoiding saturated and trans fatty acids. Preliminary evidence suggests that minimizing saturated fat[10] and avoiding trans fatty acids[11] may reduce signs of CHF as well as CHF mortality. Further research is required to determine if these changes are an effective intervention strategy.

Moderation in alcohol consumption. Although heavy alcohol consumption has been associated with CHF-related parameters (eg, left ventricular dysfunction and dilated cardiomyopathy), several studies have revealed a lower risk for CHF with moderate consumption (eg, 1 serving/day).[21] In a study of 21,601 participants in the Physicians' Health Study, having a minimum of 1 drink per day was associated with a nearly 40% lower risk for developing CHF. This effect was attributed to the benefit of alcohol on coronary artery disease.[21]

Dietary supplements as adjunctive treatments. A meta-analysis of controlled clinical trials with coenzyme Q10 found significant improvements in stroke volume, cardiac output, cardiac index, and end-diastolic volume in patients with heart failure, regardless of etiology (eg, idiopathic, dilated, ischemic, hypertension, valvular heart disease, and congenital heart disease).[22] Amounts typically used range from 150 mg to 300 mg per day as a supplement to conventional treatment. Other supplements, including L-carnitine, taurine, and the herb crataegus oxycantha L, are under investigation for possible roles in heart failure treatment.[23-31] None of these is yet established as safe and effective.

Orders

Diet: Sodium less than 2 grams daily. When heart failure is the result of heart disease, a cardiovascular-specific diet should be ordered (see Coronary Heart Disease chapter).

Fluid restriction as appropriate.

Nutrition consultation to help the patient adjust to the above diet.

Exercise physiologist, physical therapist, and occupational therapist consultations to prescribe exercise regimen and provide appropriate support for activities of daily living.

What to Tell the Family

Heart failure is usually progressive. However, patients may be able to prolong survival, improve heart function, ameliorate chronic symptoms, avoid repeated episodes of decompensation, and decrease the need for hospitalization by following a low-sodium diet, restricting fluids, and taking medications as prescribed. Exercise conditioning is also important, as it can help improve exercise tolerance and oxygen uptake. The family may need to provide physical support as the patient attempts to recondition and help the patient comply with diet changes.

References

1. Singh S, Loke YK, Furberg CD. Long-term risk of cardiovascular events with rosiglitazone: a meta-analysis. *JAMA.* 2007;298:1189-1195.

2. Lincoff AM, Wolski K, Nicholls SJ, Nissen SE. Pioglitazone and risk of cardiovascular events in patients with type 2 diabetes mellitus: a meta-analysis of randomized trials. *JAMA.* 2007;298:1180-1188.

3. Kenchaiah S, Pocock SJ, Wang D, et al. Body mass index and prognosis in patients with chronic heart failure: insights from the Candesartan in Heart failure: Assessment of Reduction in Mortality and morbidity (CHARM) program. *Circulation.* 2007;116:627-636.

4. Hunt SA, Baker DW, Chin MH, et al. ACC/AHA guidelines for the evaluation and management of chronic heart failure in the adult: executive summary. A report of the American College of Cardiology/American Heart Association Task Force on Practice Guidelines (Committee to Revise the 1995 Guidelines for the Evaluation and Management of Heart Failure). *Circulation.* 2001;104:2996-3007.

5. Hunt SA, Abraham WT, Chin MH, et al. ACC/AHA 2005 guideline update for the diagnosis and management of chronic heart failure in the adult: a report of the American College of Cardiology/American Heart Association Task Force on Practice Guidelines (Writing Committee to Update the 2001 Guidelines for the Evaluation and Management of Heart Failure): developed in collaboration with the American College of Chest Physicians and the International Society for Heart and Lung Transplantation: endorsed by the Heart Rhythm Society. *Circulation.* 2005;112:e154-e235.

6. Patel M, Gattis W. Which β-blocker for heart failure? *Am Heart J.* 2004;147:238.

7. Pitt B, Zannad F, Remme WJ, et al. The effect of spironolactone on morbidity and mortality in patients with severe heart failure. *N Engl J Med.* 1999;341:709-717.

8. Pitt B, Remme W, Zannad F. Eplerenone, a selective aldosterone blocker, in patients with left ventricular dysfunction after myocardial infarction. *N Engl J Med.* 2003;348:1309-1321.

9. Rathore SS, Curtis JP, Wang Y, Bristow MR, Krumholz HM. Association of serum digoxin concentration and outcomes in patients with heart failure. *JAMA.* 2003;289:871-878.

10. Lennie TA, Chung ML, Habash DL, Moser DK. Dietary fat intake and proinflammatory cytokine levels in patients with heart failure. *J Card Fail.* 2005;11:613-618.

11. Mozaffarian D, Rimm EB, King IB, Lawler RL, McDonald GB, Levy WC. trans fatty acids and systemic inflammation in heart failure. *Am J Clin Nutr.* 2004;80:1521-1525.

12. He J, Ogden LG, Bazzano LA, Vupputuri S, Loria C, Whelton PK. Dietary sodium intake and incidence of congestive heart failure in overweight U.S. men and women: first

National Health and Nutrition Examination Survey Epidemiologic Follow-up Study. *Arch Intern Med.* 2002;162:1619-1624.

13. Futterman LG, Lemberg L. Heart failure: update on treatment and prognosis. *Am J Crit Care.* 2001;10:285-293.

14. Colin Ramirez E, Castillo Martinez L, Orea Tejeda A, Rebollar Gonzalez V, Narvaez David R, Asensio Lafuente E. Effects of a nutritional intervention on body composition, clinical status, and quality of life in patients with heart failure. *Nutrition.* 2004;20:890-895.

15. Chavey WE II, Blaum CS, Bleske BE, Harrison RV, Kesterson S, Nicklas JM, and the American Heart Association. Guideline for the management of heart failure caused by systolic dysfunction: part II. Treatment. *Am Fam Physician.* 2001;64:1045-1054.

16. Haider AW, Larson MG, Franklin SS, Levy D, for the Framingham Heart Study. Systolic blood pressure, diastolic blood pressure, and pulse pressure as predictors of risk for congestive heart failure in the Framingham Heart Study. *Ann Intern Med.* 2003;138:10-16.

17. Witte KK, Clark AL, Cleland JG. Chronic heart failure and micronutrients. *J Am Coll Cardiol.* 2001;37:1765-1774.

18. Zenuk C, Healey J, Donnelly J, Vaillancourt R, Almalki Y, Smith S. Thiamine deficiency in congestive heart failure patients receiving long-term furosemide therapy. *Can J Clin Pharmacol.* 2003;10:184-188.

19. Shimon I, Almog S, Vered Z, et al. Improved left ventricular function after thiamine supplementation in patients with congestive heart failure receiving long-term furosemide therapy. *Am J Med.* 1995;98:485-490.

20. Seligmann H, Halkin H, Rauchfleisch S, et al. Thiamine deficiency in patients with congestive heart failure receiving long-term furosemide therapy: a pilot study. *Am J Med.* 1991;91:151-155.

21. Djousse L, Gaziano JM. Alcohol consumption and risk of heart failure in the Physicians' Health Study I. *Circulation.* 2007;115:34-39.

22. Bhagavan HN, Chopra RK. Potential role of ubiquinone (coenzyme Q10) in pediatric cardiomyopathy. *Clin Nutr.* 2005;24:331-338.

23. Rizos I. Three-year survival of patients with heart failure caused by dilated cardiomyopathy and L-carnitine administration. *Am Heart J.* 2000;139(pt 3):S120-S123.

24. Anand I, Chandrashekhan Y, De Giuli F, et al. Acute and chronic effects of propionyl-L-carnitine on the hemodynamics, exercise capacity, and hormones in patients with congestive heart failure. *Cardiovasc Drugs Ther.* 1998;12:291-299.

25. Kobayashi A, Masumura Y, Yamazaki N. L-carnitine treatment for congestive heart failure-experimental and clinical study. *Jpn Circ J.* 1992;56:86-94.

26. Azuma J, Sawamura A, Awata N. Usefulness of taurine in chronic congestive heart failure and its prospective application. *Jpn Circ J.* 1992;56:95-99.

27. Azuma J, Sawamura A, Awata N, et al. Therapeutic effect of taurine in congestive heart failure: a double-blind crossover trial. *Clin Cardiol.* 1985;8:276-282.

28. Azuma J, Hasegawa H, Sawamura A, Awata N, Ogura K, Harada H. Therapy of congestive heart failure with orally administered taurine. *Clin Ther.* 1983;5:398-408.

29. Pittler MH, Schmidt K, Ernst E. Hawthorn extract for treating chronic heart failure: meta-analysis of randomized trials. *Am J Med.* 2003;114:665-674.

30. Degenring FH, Suter A, Weber M, Saller R. A randomised double blind placebo controlled clinical trial of a standardised extract of fresh Crataegus berries (Crataegisan)

in the treatment of patients with congestive heart failure NYHA II. *Phytomedicine.* 2003;10:363-369.

31. Tauchert M. Efficacy and safety of crataegus extract WS 1442 in comparison with placebo in patients with chronic stable New York Heart Association class-III heart failure. *Am Heart J.* 2002;143:910-915.

37. Deep Venous Thrombosis

Deep venous thrombosis (DVT) leads to an estimated 300,000 hospitalizations per year in the United States. Although it most often occurs in the lower extremities, DVT can also develop in the upper extremities, especially in patients with indwelling central venous catheters. DVT most commonly affects the iliac, popliteal, and femoral veins.

Pulmonary embolus (PE), due to embolization of a DVT, is the second-leading preventable cause of hospital mortality. Symptoms of a PE may include dyspnea, chest pain, palpitations, sweating, and hemoptysis. Collectively, DVT and PE are the common forms of venous thrombo-embolism (VTE).

While DVT is often asymptomatic in the absence of PE, signs and symptoms may include swelling, tenderness, increased warmth and erythema in the affected area of the limb, and a palpable venous cord. Cyanosis of the limb, which indicates deoxygenated hemoglobin trapped in nonfunctioning veins, may occur.

Risk Factors

Race and Ethnicity. A higher risk for VTE may occur in blacks,[1] and a lower risk in Asian-Pacific Islanders and Latinos,[2] compared with whites.

Prior DVT or PE. A previous history is a major indicator of risk.

Age. Risk increases with age, due in part to increased comorbidities.

Surgery. Major surgeries (eg, orthopedic, thoracic, abdominal, and genitourinary) pose the greatest risk, but individualized risk assessments should be done to determine if minor surgeries also require prophylaxis.

Trauma. Examples include fracture of the spine, pelvis, femur, or tibia.

Heritable coagulopathies. Factor V Leiden and prothrombin gene mutations cause about 50% of inherited coagulopathies. Deficiencies of antithrombin and proteins C/S, elevated fibrinogen levels, and other clotting disorders also raise risk.

Neoplasm and myeloproliferative disorders.

Prolonged immobilization. Venous stasis occurs in postoperative convalescence, nonambulatory patients, and extended air travel.

Indwelling central venous catheter.

Pregnancy and exogenous hormones. Fibrinolysis may be impaired during pregnancy and postpartum and with oral contraceptives and hormone replacement therapy. Patients older than 35 who use oral contraceptives and smoke are at even greater risk.

Gender. DVT more commonly affects men.

Sickle cell disease, heart failure, inflammatory bowel disease, lupus anticoagulant, elevated antiphospholipid antibodies, nephrotic syndrome, obesity, atherosclerosis, winter months, and hyperhomocysteinemia also raise DVT risk.

Diagnosis

Diagnostic procedures must differentiate DVT from other disorders that cause similar symptoms. Included in the differential diagnosis are venous insufficiency, muscle strain or rupture, ruptured popliteal cyst, cellulitis, lymphedema, traumatic injuries and fractures, and idiopathic etiology.

Imaging

Duplex venous ultrasonography is the most common initial diagnostic method for DVT. A thrombus can be detected by direct visualization or by inference when the vein fails to collapse when compressed.

Magnetic resonance imaging offers high sensitivity and specificity for suspected thromboses of the venae cavae or pelvic veins, conditions that other imaging modalities often miss. MRI and magnetic resonance angiography (MRA) also may detect PE.

Impedance plethysmography measures changes in venous capacity during movement or compression. Venous obstruction alters the venous capacity that occurs following inflation or deflation of the cuff. This test can help identify obstruction in areas typically missed by ultrasound (eg, inferior vena cava).

Venography works by injecting contrast medium into a superficial vein of the foot and moving it to the deep veins by a system of tourniquets.

A filling defect or the absence of filling in the deep veins is required to make the diagnosis. Because venography is uncomfortable and time-consuming and requires technical expertise, it is generally reserved for cases in which noninvasive methods yield equivocal or inconsistent findings. For patients with contrast allergy, magnetic resonance venography is an alternative.

Ventilation-perfusion (V/Q) scan is a validated method to identify PE. However, it has relatively poor sensitivity in most clinical situations. Other imaging modalities, such as spiral CT pulmonary angiography and MRA, are replacing V/Q scans in many situations. Invasive pulmonary angiography is the most definitive method, but it carries the greatest risks.

2D echocardiogram is a rapid and simple procedure for PE diagnosis. Occasionally, the embolus may be seen in transit through the right ventricle or in the proximal pulmonary arteries, and not uncommonly signs of acute right ventricular overload will greatly assist diagnosis and risk stratification. Echocardiography also may identify other etiologies for patient symptoms.

Electrocardiogram (ECG) and chest x-ray (CXR) have limited sensitivity and specificity for PE and are mainly used to exclude other causes of symptoms.

Blood Tests

D-dimer is an end product of the degradation of fibrin clots. A positive result suggests DVT or PE, but the test has poor specificity (about 50%). Sensitivity is up to 98% but is lower in populations at high risk for VTE. Combination screening with D-dimer and at least one imaging modality may be most effective.[3,4]

Arterial blood gas determination is not sensitive or specific for PE, but severe hypoxemia may indicate massive embolism and affect treatment decisions.

Treatment

For reduction in VTE-related mortality, prevention of VTE is far more effective than treatment. Patient education (regarding adequate circulation) and prophylaxis for those at high risk are of paramount importance.

Patients with DVT should be initially treated with intravenous heparin in the hospital, or with subcutaneous low-molecular-weight heparin (LMWH) in an outpatient setting, along with warfarin. Warfarin initially reduces protein C and S, thus inducing a hypercoagulable state that is countered by the simultaneous use of heparin. Partial thromboplastin time (PTT) should be closely monitored when using IV heparin but not LMWH. Osteoporosis may occur in individuals receiving heparin therapy for more than 6 months, and thrombocytopenia is a possible early heparin-induced side effect. Protamine sulfate reverses heparin's effects in the case of bleeding or other complications.

Oral anticoagulation with warfarin should be overlapped with heparin until a therapeutic International Normalized Ratio (INR) is reached, and heparin or LMWH can be safely discontinued. Uncomplicated DVT patients are generally treated for 3 to 6 months. Patients with multiple DVT episodes, high recurrence risk, associated PE, cancer, or coagulopathies may require prolonged or even lifetime warfarin anticoagulation.

Recommended nonpharmaceutical treatments for DVT include elevation of the affected limb and application of warm compresses to the affected area.

If anticoagulation therapy is not viable (eg, patient has active hemorrhage), external compression devices are a mechanical alternative for DVT prophylaxis and treatment.

Patients are often admitted to the hospital for suspected PE, presence of concomitant illness, morbid obesity, noncompliance with or poor response to oral anticoagulation, or lack of a caretaker.[6]

Surgical procedures for treatment of extensive DVT or PE include balloon or direct thrombectomy and insertion of inferior vena cava filters. Treatment with inferior vena cava filters is also indicated for patients with contraindications or poor response to anticoagulation, and for prophylaxis in high-risk patients.

Nonsteroidal anti-inflammatory drugs are contraindicated for DVT and PE because they may mask the symptoms of a new thrombus. Aspirin therapy is not adequate for preventing DVT formation or PE.

Nutritional Considerations

DVT is rare in societies in which diets are primarily based on unrefined plant foods rather than on animal products or highly refined foods and, as a result, are lower in fat and higher in dietary fiber.[5,6] The reasons for this association are unclear. However, dietary intake influences factor VIIc, factor VIIIc, and von Willebrand factor, all of which are, in turn, related to the risk for venous thromboembolism.[7]

In addition, low fiber intake is associated with higher activity of plasminogen activator inhibitor-1 (PAI-1), the body's main inhibitor of fibrinolysis.[8] Low-fat, high-fiber diets, combined with exercise, improve fibrinolysis[9,10] and may thereby help reduce DVT risk. Some researchers have hypothesized that individuals on low-fiber diets often strain to pass stools, raising intravenous pressures and damaging the valves that facilitate blood return.[5] High-fiber diets help prevent this problem.

The following nutritional factors are associated with reduced risk of DVT:

Avoiding red and processed meats. In the Atherosclerosis Risk in Communities Study (ARIC) involving nearly 15,000 individuals, those who ate 1.5 servings or more per day of red and processed meat had twice the risk for venous thromboembolism, compared with those who ate less than 0.5 servings per day.[7]

Low-fat, high-fiber diets. Elevated blood cholesterol concentrations are associated with DVT risk.[11] Some evidence suggests that simultaneously elevated cholesterol and triglycerides increase this risk.[12] Greatly reducing dietary cholesterol and saturated fat and increasing dietary fiber have a major effect on blood lipids. Low-fat, vegetarian, and vegan diets are particularly effective for achieving this goal (see Dyslipidemia chapter). Elevated fibrinogen levels, which is another risk factor for DVT,[13] are lower in persons following vegetarian diets.[14,15]

Fruits and vegetable intake. Also in the ARIC Study, persons consuming roughly 5 servings of fruits and vegetables each day had about half the risk for venous thromboembolism (DVT or pulmonary embolism) compared with those eating less than 2.5 servings per day.[7]

Weight control. Obesity increases the risk for developing DVT.[16,17] The risk may be due to an obesity-related increase in PAI-1[18] or to associated elevation of venous pressure. See the Obesity chapter for a discussion of weight-control techniques.

In addition, constancy of vitamin K intake is important for patients using warfarin anticoagulation. For this population, even small increases in dietary vitamin K appear capable of reducing INR to subtherapeutic levels.[19] Conversely, decreased vitamin K may result in prolonged INR and increased bleeding risk. Food sources of vitamin K (mainly green vegetables) need not be eliminated, but vegetable intake should be consistent from day to day to avoid excessively low or high intakes. Patients should not take a vitamin K supplement without physician approval.

Orders

See Basic Diet Orders and Dyslipidemia chapters.

Individualized exercise prescription to avoid extended periods of immobility.

What to Tell the Family

Some evidence suggests that a health-promoting diet, regular exercise, and maintenance of a healthy weight may reduce the risk of DVT. Persons who are on medication to prevent DVT recurrence should follow similar diet and exercise measures, along with maintaining consistency in intake of vitamin K-containing foods. Family members will help adherence and improve their own health by adopting similar diet and exercise routines.

References

1. Tsai AW, Cushman M, Rosamond WD, Heckbert SR, Polak JF, Folsom AR. Cardiovascular risk factors and venous thromboembolism incidence: the longitudinal investigation of thromboembolism etiology. *Arch Intern Med.* 2002;162:1182-1189.

2. White RH. The Epidemiology of Venous Thromboembolism. *Circulation.* 2003;107:4-8.

3. Perrier A, Roy PM, Sanchez O, et al. D-dimer, multidetector-row CT may be sufficient to screen for pulmonary embolism. *N Engl J Med.* 2005;352:1760-1768, 1812-1814.

4. Elias A, Cazanave A, Elias M, et al. Diagnostic management of pulmonary embolism using clinical assessment, plasma D-dimer assay, complete lower limb venous ultrasound, and helical computed tomography of pulmonary arteries. A multicenter clinical outcome study. *Thromb Haemost.* 2005;93:982-988.

5. Burkitt DP, Walker AR, Painter NS. Dietary fiber and disease. *JAMA.* 1974;229:1068-1074.

6. Burkitt DP. Varicose veins, deep vein thrombosis, and hemorrhoids: epidemiology and suggested etiology. *Br Med J.* 1972;2:556-561.

7. Steffen LM, Folsom AR, Cushman M, Jacobs DR Jr, Rosamond WD. Greater fish, fruit, and vegetable intakes are related to lower incidence of venous thromboembolism: the Longitudinal Investigation of Thromboembolism Etiology. *Circulation.* 2007;115:188-195.

8. Boman K, Hellsten G, Bruce A, Hallmans G, Nilsson TK. Endurance physical activity, diet, and fibrinolysis. *Atherosclerosis.* 1994;106:65-74.

9. Lindahl B, Nilsson TK, Jansson JH, Asplund K, Hallmans G. Improved fibrinolysis by intense lifestyle intervention. A randomized trial in subjects with impaired glucose tolerance. *J Intern Med.* 1999;246:105-112.

10. Marckmann P, Sandstrom B, Jespersen J. Low-fat, high-fiber diet favorably affects several independent risk markers of ischemic heart disease: observations on blood lipids, coagulation, and fibrinolysis from a trial of middle-aged Danes. *Am J Clin Nutr.* 1994;59:935-939.

11. Vaya A, Mira Y, Ferrando F, et al. Hyperlipidemia and venous thromboembolism in patients lacking thrombophilic risk factors. *Br J Haematol.* 2002;118:255-259.

12. Kawasaki T, Kambayashi J, Ariyoshi H, Sakon M, Suehisa E, Monden M. Hypercholesterolemia as a risk factor for deep-vein thrombosis. *Thromb Res.* 1997;88:67-73.

13. Vaya A, Mira Y, Martinez M, et al. Biological risk factors for deep vein thrombosis. *Clin Hemorheol Microcirc.* 2002;26:41-53.

14. Famodu AA, Osilesi O, Makinde YO, et al. The influence of a vegetarian diet on haemostatic risk factors for cardiovascular disease in Africans. *Thromb Res.* 1999;95:31-36.

15. Mezzano D, Munoz X, Martinez C, et al. Vegetarians and cardiovascular risk factors: hemostasis, inflammatory markers and plasma homocysteine. *Thromb Haemost.* 1999;81:913-917.

16. Goldhaber SZ, Tapson VF, and the DVT FREE Steering Committee. A prospective registry of 5,451 patients with ultrasound-confirmed deep vein thrombosis. *Am J Cardiol.* 2004;93:259-262.

17. Abdollahi M, Cushman M, Rosendaal FR. Obesity: risk of venous thrombosis and the interaction with coagulation factor levels and oral contraceptive use. *Thromb Haemost.* 2003;89:493-498.

18. Skurk T, Hauner H. Obesity and impaired fibrinolysis: role of adipose production of plasminogen activator inhibitor-1. *Int J Obes Relat Metab Disord.* 2004;28:1357-1364.

19. Kurnik D, Loebstein R, Rabinovitz H, Austerweil N, Halkin H, Almog S. Over-the-counter vitamin K1-containing multivitamin supplements disrupt warfarin anticoagulation in vitamin K1-depleted patients. A prospective, controlled trial. *Thromb Haemost.* 2004;92:1018-1024.

38. Venous Insufficiency and Varicosities

Chronic venous insufficiency is a common clinical problem, whose presentation ranges from mildly unsightly veins to recurrent cellulitis and ulceration requiring frequent hospitalizations. An estimated 20% of the US adult population has some degree of varicose veins, and up to 5% have advanced chronic venous insufficiency and venous ulceration.

The venous system of the lower extremities is composed of deep veins that lie within the muscular compartments and superficial veins that lie outside the deep fascia and muscles. Venous insufficiency is a disorder of the deep veins, whereas varicose veins, the most common manifestation of chronic venous disease, are a disorder of the superficial veins.

Although the underlying etiology is not fully understood (genetic, hormonal, and environmental factors have been postulated), these disorders result from chronic venous hypertension, which can be caused by incompetence of the venous valves, obstruction to venous flow, and/or failure of the muscular "venous pump" (the pumping effect that occurs upon contraction of leg muscles during walking and other activities).

Most cases of varicose veins are asymptomatic. However, clinical symptoms may include swelling, aching, tension, leg fatigue, burning, and pruritis, which may be relieved with recumbency or leg elevation. As venous insufficiency progresses, skin pigmentation and induration occur. In severe cases, recurrent cellulitis and ulceration can develop, which may be limb- or life-threatening.

Risk Factors

The following factors are associated with increased risk of varicose veins:

Family history. There is as much as a 90% risk of developing varicose veins if both parents have varicose veins, but less than a 20% risk if neither parent is affected.

Female gender. Varicose veins occur up to twice as often in women.

Increasing height.

Increasing age.

History of leg injury, phlebitis, or deep venous thrombosis raises the risk for venous insufficiency.

Lifestyle factors. Prolonged standing,[1] sedentary lifestyle, and pregnancy are suspected risk factors for the development of varicose veins, and obesity raises risk for both venous disorders. Physical inactivity is associated with risk for chronic venous insufficiency and varicose veins in some,[2,3] although not all,[4] studies.

Klippel-Trenaunay-Weber syndrome. This condition occurs due to an abnormal or absent deep venous system and results in a triad of extensive unilateral varicose veins, limb hypertrophy, and a port-wine stain.

Diagnosis

A thorough history and physical examination are usually sufficient for diagnosis. Additional testing is generally reserved for severe cases or when intervention is planned.

Doppler venous ultrasound gives information about the anatomy and flow patterns of the venous system. It accurately maps the veins of the leg and identifies the location and severity of valvular incompetence. In addition, it evaluates for deep venous thrombosis, which is fairly common in these patients. Ankle-brachial index (ankle-to-brachial blood pressure ratio) is calculated in conjunction with Doppler ultrasound to assess the presence of concurrent arterial disease, which is common in patients with venous disease.

Venography is an invasive method for evaluating the venous system. It is rarely used due to the safety and accuracy of Doppler ultrasound. However, venography is useful in some patients, particularly those who will undergo vascular surgery.

Treatment

Bed rest, leg elevation, and compression stockings or bandages are the initial therapy in most patients. Compression stockings act by decreasing venous pressure and reflux. They should be able to exert 20 to 30 mm Hg at the ankle with a decreasing pressure gradient toward the knee (note that compression stockings are different from the "anti-embolism" stockings used in hospitals for DVT prevention, which exert less than 10 mm Hg).

Intermittent pneumatic compression pumps can be used for several hours daily and may be more effective than compression stockings or bandages.

Several drug therapies have been used. Diuretics may be used in patients with severe edema. Aspirin and oral antibiotics may be used to accelerate the healing of venous ulcers.

Venous ablation by injection sclerotherapy is useful in some patients with varicose veins for whom conservative therapies have failed.

Several surgical options are available and have high success rates. These include venous ligation with or without stripping, endovenous catheter ablation, and valvular reconstruction.

Nutritional Considerations

Chronic venous insufficiency and varicose veins appear to be related to an obesity-promoting Western lifestyle poor in dietary fiber and low in physical activity. Evidence suggests that avoidance of these risk factors may reduce the incidence of venous disorders. In persons with established venous insufficiency and varicose veins, the therapeutic applications of flavonoid-containing botanicals may strengthen blood vessels by increasing collagen cross-linking in the vascular endothelium.[5]

In observational studies, the following factors are associated with reduced risk of venous disorders:

High-Fiber Diets

Denis Burkitt, known for the identification and treatment of Burkitt's lymphoma, hypothesized that varicose veins result from a fiber-poor diet, resulting in constipation-induced straining during defecation.[6] This straining may raise intra-abdominal pressure, causing transmission of pressure to the major venous trunks draining the leg veins. (Dr. Burkitt hypothesized a similar mechanism for the pathogenesis of hemorrhoids.) The resulting retrograde blood flow to these veins may in turn result in a dilation of the proximal segment of the veins and failure of the valves in a sequential manner. Further abdominal straining and the presence of unsupported blood in the veins cause a deterioration in vascular integrity.[1,6]

Although this hypothesis has not been proven,[7] epidemiological evidence supports a relationship between a lack of fiber and the prevalence of varicose veins. The presence of varicose veins in some developing regions is associated both with increases in refined (fiber-poor) carbohydrate and decreases in stool weight.[8] Straining during defecation resulted in an almost 3-fold higher risk for the prevalence of both mild and severe trunk varices, but this was observed in men only.[9] Subjects with trunk varicose veins and those with chronic venous insufficiency had higher levels of haemostatic factors (fibrinogen, tissue plasminogen activator [tPA], and von Willebrand factor) compared with those without trunk varices or chronic venous insufficiency.[10] Although additional studies are needed to investigate the role of a high-fiber diet in varicose vein prevention, low-fat, high-fiber diet interventions have reduced tPA and increased fibrinolysis,[11,12] indicating their possible utility in this condition.

Avoidance of Overweight

Obesity has not been consistently associated with chronic venous insufficiency. However, most studies have shown that overweight and obese women are more likely to develop varicose veins. Women who are moderately overweight (BMI=25.0–29.9 kg/m^2) have a 1.5-fold increased risk of varicose veins, compared with nonoverweight women. Women with a BMI ≥30 have a 3-fold greater risk.[13] Obesity prevention appears to be more effective than obesity treatment. Obesity surgery was not effective for improvement of venous insufficiency.[14] For details on dietary contributors to and treatments for obesity, see the Obesity chapter.

Botanical Treatments

Certain botanical treatments have demonstrated promise for treating chronic venous insufficiency in limited clinical trials. These include the following:

Horse chestnut seed. Systematic reviews have concluded that extracts of horse chestnut seed (*Aesculus hippocastanum*, 50 mg twice a day) reduce leg pain, leg volume, edema, and itching.[15,16] The active ingredient (aescin) appears to inhibit elastase and hyaluronidase, slowing the degradation of the capillary endothelium and extravascular matrix and normalizing capillary permeability.[1]

Diosmin-hesperidin combination. Long-term controlled clinical trials have revealed that this combination (Daflon 500 mg twice daily) of flavonoids increases venous tone, improves lymphatic drainage, and reduces capillary hyperpermeability, with resultant changes in chronic venous insufficiency and associated venous conditions. These improvements included significant decreases in ankle and calf circumferences, functional discomfort (nocturnal cramps and sensations of leg heaviness, swelling, or heat), and plethysmographic parameters, such as venous capacitance, distensibility, and emptying.[1,17] A recent meta-analysis of controlled clinical trials indicated that adding Daflon 500 mg twice daily increased the likelihood of healing venous leg ulcers by 32%, compared with conventional therapy alone.[18]

Butcher's broom. Extracts of *Ruscus aculeatus* (150 mg 2 to 3 times/day) improve venous insufficiency through inhibition of the permeability-inducing effect of histamine, bradykinin, and leukotriene B4.[1] It is particularly effective when combined with another flavonoid (hesperidin) and vitamin C.[19] Benefits include improved venous emptying; decreased capillary filtration rate; reduction of pain severity, cramps, heaviness, paresthesia, venous capacity, and severity of edema; and decreases in calf and ankle circumference.[1,19,20]

Orders

See Basic Diet Orders chapter.

Exercise prescription.

What to Tell the Family

Some evidence suggests that venous insufficiency and varicose veins may be, in part, preventable through a high-fiber, low-fat diet, regular exercise, and maintenance of normal body weight. Medical, surgical, and botanical approaches are available for treatment.

References

1. MacKay D. Hemorrhoids and varicose veins: a review of treatment options. *Altern Med Rev.* 2001;6:126-140.

2. Jawien A. The influence of environmental factors in chronic venous insufficiency. *Angiology.* 2003;54(suppl 1):S19-S31.

3. Brand FN, Dannenberg AL, Abbott RD, et al. The epidemiology of varicose veins: the Framingham Study. *Am J Prev Med.* 1988;4:96-101.

4. Lee AJ, Evans CJ, Allan PL, Ruckley CV, Fowkes FG. Lifestyle factors and the risk of varicose veins: Edinburgh Vein Study. *J Clin Epidemiol.* 2003;56:171-179.

5. Miller AL. Botanical influences on cardiovascular disease. *Altern Med Rev.* 1998;3: 422-431.

6. Burkitt DP. The protective properties of dietary fiber. *N C Med J.* 1981;42:467-471.

7. Fowkes FG, Lee AJ, Evans CJ, Allan PL, Bradbury AW, Ruckley CV. Lifestyle risk factors for lower limb venous reflux in the general population: Edinburgh Vein Study. *Int J Epidemiol.* 2001;30:846-852.

8. Richardson JB, Dixon M. Varicose veins in tropical Africa. *Lancet.* 1977;1:791-792.

9. Lee AJ, Evans CJ, Hau CM, Fowkes FG. Fiber intake, constipation, and risk of varicose veins in the general population: Edinburgh Vein Study. *J Clin Epidemiol.* 2001;54:423-429.

10. Lee AJ, Lowe GD, Rumley A, Ruckley CV, Fowkes FG. Haemostatic factors and risk of varicose veins and chronic venous insufficiency: Edinburgh Vein Study. *Blood Coagul Fibrinolysis.* 2000;11:775-781.

11. Lindahl B, Nilsson TK, Jansson JH, et al. Improved fibrinolysis by intense lifestyle intervention. A randomized trial in subjects with impaired glucose tolerance. *J Intern Med.* 1999;246:105-112.

12. Marckmann P, Sandstrom B, Jespersen J. Low-fat, high-fiber diet favorably affects several independent risk markers of ischemic heart disease: observations on blood lipids, coagulation, and fibrinolysis from a trial of middle-aged Danes. *Am J Clin Nutr.* 1994;59:935-939.

13. Beebe-Dimmer JL, Pfeifer JR, Engle JS, Schottenfeld D. The epidemiology of chronic venous insufficiency and varicose veins. *Ann Epidemiol.* 2005;15:175-184.

14. Raftopoulos I, Ercole J, Udekwu AO, Luketich JD, Courcoulas AP. Outcomes of Roux-en-Y gastric bypass stratified by a body mass index of 70 kg/m2: a comparative analysis of 825 procedures. *J Gastrointest Surg.* 2005;9:44-52.

15. Pittler MH, Ernst E. Horse chestnut seed extract for chronic venous insufficiency. *Cochrane Database Syst Rev.* 2006;(1):CD003230.

16. Siebert U, Brach M, Sroczynski G, Berla K. Efficacy, routine effectiveness, and safety of horse chestnut seed extract in the treatment of chronic venous insufficiency. A meta-analysis of randomized controlled trials and large observational studies. *Int Angiol.* 2002;21:305-315.

17. Lyseng-Williamson KA, Perry CM. Micronised purified flavonoid fraction: a review of its use in chronic venous insufficiency, venous ulcers, and hemorrhoids. *Drugs.* 2003;63:71-100.

18. Smith PC. Daflon 500 mg and venous leg ulcer: new results from a meta-analysis. *Angiology.* 2005;56(suppl 1):S33-S39.

19. Boyle P, Diehm C, Robertson C. Meta-analysis of clinical trials of Cyclo 3 Fort in the treatment of chronic venous insufficiency. *Int Angiol.* 2003;22:250-262.

20. Vanscheidt W, Jost V, Wolna P, et al. Efficacy and safety of a Butcher's broom preparation (Ruscus aculeatus L. extract) compared to placebo in patients suffering from chronic venous insufficiency. *Arzneimittelforschung.* 2002;52:243-250.

SECTION VIII: RESPIRATORY DISEASES

39. Asthma

Asthma is a chronic respiratory disease in which bronchial obstruction and bronchospasm lead to dyspnea, wheezing, chest tightness, and/or cough. Inflammation of the airways is key to its pathogenesis. Inflammatory cells—including mast cells, eosinophils, T lymphocytes, plasma cells, and basophils—release histamine, various kinins, leukotrienes, prostaglandins, lipid mediators, tumor necrosis factor α (TNF-α), neuropeptides, substance P, and a host of other inflammatory mediators. Other features are smooth muscle hypertrophy, edema, basement membrane thickening, and mucous accumulation in airways.

The inflammatory process is triggered by allergens, which play a central role in approximately 60% of asthma patients. Other triggers include respiratory infections; inhaled irritants (particularly tobacco smoke and occupational exposures); gastroesophageal reflux, stress; exercise; cold temperatures; and medications such as aspirin, nonsteroidal anti-inflammatory drugs (NSAIDs), and beta-blockers. Asthma is also caused by agents to which a person has specific sensitivity, such as aspirin and tartrazine, which is a petroleum-derived colorant (FD & C Yellow #5).[1]

The prevalence of asthma in the United States is approximately 5%. Although the disease commonly begins in childhood, up to 40% of patients develop asthma as adults. Among adult patients, 10% to 20% have occupational asthma. An increase in the global prevalence of asthma over the past 30 years has been attributed to climate change, allergen exposure, urbanization, and air pollution, among other factors, but the precise pathogenesis of the observed increase is not clear. Asthma is more prevalent in affluent countries, leading to the question of whether overuse of antibiotics has led to reduced bacterial antigen exposure and a shift of the immune system to a more atopic phenotype. Air pollution's direct contribution to asthma is not clear; certain components may exacerbate asthma.

Risk Factors

In children, asthma occurs more commonly in boys. Among adults, however, the disease is most prevalent in women over 40. Both mortality and morbidity are greater in African Americans, compared with whites. These differences are attributed in part to socioeconomic factors.[2]

Other risk factors include:

Atopy.

Family history. About 75% of children with 2 asthmatic parents also have asthma.

Environmental and occupational factors. These factors include tobacco smoke, animal dander, dust mites, cockroach allergens,[3] plants, pollen, mold, enzymes, chemicals, and metals.

Some (though not all) studies have suggested that obesity may be associated with asthma or with a worse clinical course in individuals with asthma. The Nurses' Health Study II revealed a linear relationship between body mass index (BMI) and asthma risk, with a relative risk of 2.7 for the most obese group.[4] This association does not, however, indicate that obesity causes asthma. Some evidence suggests improvement in objective measures of asthma severity and control after weight loss.[5]

Diagnosis

A characteristic history of periodic bronchospasm and variable airflow obstruction, occurring with or without stimuli that provoke an attack, is usually present. During acute attacks, symptoms such as tachypnea, chest tightness, wheezing, shortness of breath, and cough, with or without sputum production, are common. Difficulty taking deep breaths, difficulty finishing sentences, and/or lethargy indicate greater severity, and, possibly, status asthmaticus.

Physical examination often reveals use of accessory respiratory muscle, a prolonged expiratory phase with diffuse wheezing, and sometimes hyper-resonant lung fields with diminished breath sounds due to air trapping. Severe attacks may have less wheezing (due to reduced air flow), cyanosis, and signs of mental obtundation.

Peak expiratory flow rate (PEFR) can suggest a diagnosis of asthma when below-normal values respond to bronchodilators. In addition, PEFR may be used to diagnose exacerbations.

Routine pulmonary function tests during asymptomatic periods may be entirely normal. During exacerbations or in patients who have had asthma for many years, spirometry typically shows reduced FEV1 (forced expiratory volume in 1 second), a reduced FEV1/FVC (forced vital capacity) ratio, and/or reduced peak flows, and may also demonstrate increased total lung capacity (TLC), residual volume (RV), and functional residual capacity (FRC).

Blood testing may reveal eosinophilia and elevated serum IgE levels in asthma patients with atopy.

Skin testing can identify allergens that may be environmentally controlled.

Medicines, such as beta-blockers, NSAIDs, and aspirin, may reveal an underlying asthma diagnosis if symptoms are triggered after ingestion.

Treatment

With optimal asthma management, patients should not have symptoms, exercise limitations, exacerbations, or any need for oral steroids or albuterol. Overall, medications and side effects should be minimal.

Types of Asthma

Mild intermittent asthma is treated on an as-needed basis with inhaled beta-2-selective agonists, such as albuterol. Beta-adrenergic medications are bronchodilators and can be used before exercise or when symptoms occur; these are sometimes called "rescue medications".[6] Alternatives for exercise-induced asthma are cromolyn and nedocromil (mast cell stabilizers) taken just before exercise.

Mild persistent asthma usually requires daily inhalation of a corticosteroid, along with a short-acting beta-agonist for breakthrough symptoms. Inhaled corticosteroids decrease the risk of exacerbations and reduce the need for rescue medication. Common steroid preparations include budesonide, fluticasone, triamcinalone, beclomethasone, and flunisolide.

Moderate persistent asthma calls for an increased dose of inhaled corticosteroid and/or the addition of a long-acting beta-agonist or leukotriene antagonist. Examples of leukotriene antagonists are zileuton, montelukast, pranlukast, and zafirlukast. Sustained-release theophylline and cromolyn are alternatives. Failure to control symptoms with the use of two of the above medications suggests the patient may have severe asthma or perhaps another diagnosis.

Severe asthma requires high-dose inhaled corticosteroids or oral corticosteroids, along with other controller medicines.

Other Considerations

Leukotriene antagonists are no substitute for inhaled corticosteroids,[7] but in patients who make an excess of leukotrienes, leukotriene antagonists may complement the above therapies. Patients with exercise-induced bronchoconstriction, nasal polyposis, and aspirin sensitivity (triad asthma) tend to respond well to leukotriene antagonists.

Long-acting beta-agonists, such as salmeterol and formoterol, are not to be used as monotherapy,[8] as they have no significant anti-inflammatory effects. Indeed, they cause prolonged bronchodilation, which may mask a progressive inflammatory process that could eventually lead to a severe attack.

A recent study showed a small increase in risk of death among patients, particularly for African Americans, using salmeterol in addition to typical asthma drugs.[9]

Cromolyn and theophylline are rarely considered as first-line agents. However, in combination with inhaled corticosteroids, they may be beneficial.

Omalizumab is a new monoclonoal antibody directed to human IgE for use in asthma patients with a positive skin test or in-vitro reactivity to a perennial aeroallergen. For atopic patients with refractory asthma or those for whom inhaled and/or oral steroids cause major side effects, anti-IgE therapy may reduce steroid requirements and side effects and provide improved control.

Emergency Treatment

Immediate bronchodilation with inhaled albuterol is the mainstay of emergency treatment. In the emergency room, the delivery method for albuterol is most often continuous nebulization (approximately 10 mg/hr), or 2.5 mg every 20 minutes for 3 doses. However, data show that using a metered-dose inhaler (with a spacer) for 4 to 6 successive inhalations is approximately equal to 1 nebulizer. The metered-dose method has the advantages of reducing the total amount of albuterol administered and shortening the length of stay in the emergency department, without increasing hospital admissions.[10]

Systemic corticosteroids, such as prednisone, prednisolone, and methylprednisolone, should be started concurrently in a patient who does not adequately respond to albuterol therapy. Their effect is often delayed up to 6 hours. Inhaled ipratropium bromide (an anticholinergic agent) is indicated if a person has moderate to severe airway obstruction that is unresponsive to beta agonists alone.

Heliox can benefit patients with severe airflow obstruction and mild hypoxemia in the acute setting. In patients with severe hypoxemia, the helium concentration should be decreased to a level less than what has been shown to be effective for improving airflow obstruction (70%-80% helium) in order to deliver oxygen concentrations needed to maintain normoxia. Therefore, heliox is contraindicated in severe hypoxemia.

Magnesium sulfate, given intravenously, may be tried when a patient does not respond to bronchodilators, but further study is needed, especially in children.

Nutritional Considerations

The following factors are under investigation for their roles in asthma:

Maintenance of ideal body weight. Studies have found that a higher body weight increases the risk of asthma in both children and adults.[11]

Modifying fatty acid intake. Recent reviews[12] and prospective studies[13,14] have implicated omega-6 fatty acids (found in animal products and in margarine and other vegetable oils) as a possible risk factor for asthma. Consumption of these fatty acids has increased in Westernized societies along with a rise in asthma incidence, possibly due to their being precursors of leukotrienes with bronchoconstrictive effects. Studies have implicated margarine consumption as a risk factor for current asthma in both young adults[15] and an older adult population.[16] Also, a high ratio of omega-6 to omega-3 fatty acid intake was significantly associated with the risk for asthma in a pediatric population.[13]

Clinical interventions have not convincingly demonstrated a benefit of adjustment in fatty acid intake in asthmatic patients. Increasing dietary intake of the omega-6 fat linoleic acid did not result in asthma exacerbation in one study.[17] Although fish intake has been associated with a lower risk for childhood asthma in some studies,[18] others have found the reverse—greater fish intake was associated with increased asthma risk.[19,20] In spite of some data suggesting improvement in exercise-induced asthma symptoms in individuals given omega-3 fatty acid supplements,[21] intervention trials have not yet definitively established the benefit of this approach.[22]

Avoidance of salty foods. Pulmonary function improves with low-salt diets.[23] In persons with exercise-induced asthma, following a low-salt diet (1,500 mg/day sodium restriction, equivalent to about 3.7 g NaCl/day) reduces post-exercise asthma severity to below the diagnostic limit of a 10% fall in FEV1.[24]

Fruits, vegetables, and other foods high in antioxidants. Several studies have found relationships between higher fruit and vegetable intakes and reduced risk for asthma.[12,25] In some studies, patients with asthma were found to have lower dietary intakes or blood levels of antioxidants.[26,27] Elevated levels of lipid peroxides indicative of oxidative stress have been found in these patients[28] and appear to correlate with symptom severity.[29] The Nurses' Health Study, a prospective study in adults, found that women in the highest quintile of vitamin E intake from food (not from supplements) had a 47% lower risk of adult-onset asthma than those in the lowest quintile. Studies have also found that supplemental antioxidants in the form of carotenoids (high-dose beta-carotene, lycopene, and other carotenoids) or combinations of vitamin C and vitamin E significantly improved exercise-induced asthma.[24]

Avoidance of allergenic foods, beverages, and preservatives. Food-induced bronchospasm occurs with the intake of certain foods in 2% to 24% of persons with asthma. Foods implicated most often as a cause include peanuts, milk, eggs, tree nuts, soy, wheat, legumes, beans, and turkey.[30] The presence of histamine in wine may aggravate asthma,[31] and several studies have found that asthma may be induced by green tea.[32] Double-blind, controlled studies have demonstrated that sulfite-containing beverages and foods can cause potentially life-threatening asthmatic reactions in as many as 5% of the asthmatic population.[33,34] Most sulfite-sensitive persons with asthma are steroid-dependent. Avoidance is the most beneficial approach to sulfite sensitivity.[31]

Further evidence that food allergy is a risk factor for life-threatening asthma is demonstrated by a substantially higher rate of food allergy in children requiring intubation for asthma compared with controls.[35]

Avoidance of trigger foods improves peak expiratory flow rate in asthmatic children.[36,37] When dairy products are omitted from the diet, calcium may be obtained from calcium-fortified soymilk or juices, green leafy vegetables, beans, and calcium-precipitated tofu.

Allergy testing should be considered in patients who appear to experience exacerbation of asthma in relation to certain foods or food groups. Alternatively, patients can attempt to determine if a food triggers asthma by eliminating all common potentially allergenic foods and then reintroducing them one at a time. Patients should keep careful records of food intake and any change in symptom frequency to confirm that a given food is provoking an exacerbation of asthma.

Vegetarian and vegan diets. In a study of 27,766 Seventh-day Adventists,[38] vegetarian women reported a lower incidence of asthma, compared with women on nonvegetarian diets.[38] The theoretical basis for the value of vegan diets is the absence of potential triggers, particularly dairy products and eggs, as well as a relative lack of arachidonic acid. Observational studies have produced conflicting results, including some that suggest a protective effect of dairy product use in relation to asthma.[39] However, in a clinical trial of a vegan diet, 22 of 24 asthma patients noted significant improvements in vital capacity, FEV1, and physical working capacity after 1 year on a vegan diet.[40] Additional clinical trials are required to investigate the role of vegetarian and vegan diets.

Preventive measures. Measures recommended to decrease the risk for developing asthma include breast-feeding for the first 4 to 6 months of life and avoiding the following foods until children reach the specified ages: dairy products until at least 1 year old; eggs until at least 2 years old; and peanuts, nuts, and fish until at least 3 years old.[41]

Orders

Smoking cessation.

Avoid allergenic foods per patient history.

Vegetarian diet, nondairy, may be tried on a prospective basis.

What to Tell the Family

Asthma can generally be well managed with diet and medications. Family members can help by encouraging a diet high in fruits, vegetables, and whole grains, and by minimizing fats and oils. Adopting such a diet themselves may help protect family members from later health problems, as well as make it easier for the patient to adhere to the dietary changes.

References

1. Ardern KD, Ram FS. Tartrazine exclusion for allergic asthma. *Cochrane Database Syst Rev.* 2001;(4):CD000460.

2. Weiss KB, Gergen PJ, Crain EF. Inner-city asthma: the epidemiology of an emerging US public health concern. *Chest.* 1992;101:362S-367S.

3. Rosenstreich DL, Eggleston P, Kattan M, et al. The role of cockroach allergy and exposure to cockroach allergen in causing morbidity among inner-city children with asthma. *N Engl J Med.* 1997;336:1356.

4. Camargo CA Jr, Weiss ST, Zhang S, Willett WC, Speizer FE. Prospective study of body mass index, weight change, and risk of adult-onset asthma in women. *Arch Intern Med.* 1999;159:2582-2588.

5. Stenius-Aarniala B, Poussa T, Kvarnstrom J, Gronlund EL, Ylikahri M, Mustajoki P. Immediate and long-term effects of weight reduction in obese people with asthma: randomized controlled study. *BMJ.* 2000;320:827-832.

6. Nelson HS. Beta-adrenergic bronchodilators. *N Engl J Med.* 1995;333:499-506.

7. Bleecker ER, Welch MJ, Weinstein SF, et al. Low-dose inhaled fluticasone propionate versus oral zafirlukast in the treatment of persistent asthma. *J Allergy Clin Immunol.* 2000;105:1123-1129.

8. Verberne AA, Frost C, Roorda RJ, van der Laag H, Kerrebijn KF. One-year treatment with salmeterol compared with beclomethasone in children with asthma. *Am J Respir Crit Care Med.* 1997;156:688-695.

9. Nelson HS, Weiss ST, Bleecker ER, Yancey SW, Dorinsky PM, and the SMART Study Group. The Salmeterol Multicenter Asthma Research Trial: a comparison of usual pharmacotherapy for asthma or usual pharmacotherapy plus salmeterol. *Chest.* 2006;129:15-26.

10. Newman KB, Milne S, Hamilton C, Hall K. A comparison of albuterol administered by metered-dose inhaler and spacer with albuterol by nebulizer in adults presenting to an urban emergency department with acute asthma. *Chest.* 2002;121:1036-1041.

11. King ME, Mannino DM, Holguin F. Risk factors for asthma incidence. A review of recent prospective evidence. *Panminerva Med.* 2004;46:97-110.

12. McKeever TM, Britton J. Diet and asthma. *Am J Respir Crit Care Med.* 2004;170:725-729.

13. Oddy WH, de Klerk NH, Kendall GE, Mihrshahi S, Peat JK. Ratio of omega-6 to omega-3 fatty acids and childhood asthma. *J Asthma.* 2004;41:319-326.

14. Huang SL, Pan WH. Dietary fats and asthma in teenagers: analyses of the first Nutrition and Health Survey in Taiwan (NAHSIT). *Clin Exp Allergy.* 2001;31:1875-1880.

15. Bolte G, Winkler G, Holscher B, Thefeld W, Weiland SK, Heinrich J. Margarine consumption, asthma, and allergy in young adults: results of the German National Health Survey 1998. *Ann Epidemiol.* 2005;15:207-213.

16. Nagel G, Linseisen J. Dietary intake of fatty acids, antioxidants and selected food groups and asthma in adults. *Eur J Clin Nutr.* 2005;59:8-15.

17. Morris A, Noakes M, Clifton PM. The role of n-6 polyunsaturated fat in stable asthmatics. *J Asthma.* 2001;38:311-319.

18. Mellis CM. Is asthma prevention possible with dietary manipulation? *Med J Aust.* 2002;177:S78-S80.

19. Takemura Y, Sakurai Y, Honjo S, et al. The relationship between fish intake and the prevalence of asthma: the Tokorozawa childhood asthma and pollinosis study. *Prev Med.* 2002;34:221-225.

20. Huang SL, Lin KC, Pan WH. Dietary factors associated with physician-diagnosed asthma and allergic rhinitis in teenagers: analyses of the first Nutrition and Health Survey in Taiwan. *Clin Exp Allergy.* 2001;31:259-264.

21. Mickleborough TD, Rundell KW. Dietary polyunsaturated fatty acids in asthma- and exercise-induced bronchoconstriction. *Eur J Clin Nutr.* 2005;59:1335-1346.

22. Schachter HM, Reisman J, Tran K, et al. Health effects of omega-3 fatty acids on asthma. *Evid Rep Technol Assess* (Summ). 2004;91:1-7.

23. Ram FS, Ardern KD. Dietary salt reduction or exclusion for allergic asthma. *Cochrane Database Syst Rev.* 2004;(3):CD000436.

24. Mickleborough T, Gotshall R. Dietary components with demonstrated effectiveness in decreasing the severity of exercise-induced asthma. *Sports Med.* 2003;33:671-681.

25. Chen R, Hu Z, Seaton A. Eating more vegetables might explain reduced asthma symptoms. *BMJ.* 2004;328:1380.

26. Harik-Khan RI, Muller DC, Wise RA. Serum vitamin levels and the risk of asthma in children. *Am J Epidemiol.* 2004;159:351-357.

27. Gilliland FD, Berhane KT, Li YF, Gauderman WJ, McConnell R, Peters J. Children's lung function and antioxidant vitamin, fruit, juice, and vegetable intake. *Am J Epidemiol.* 2003;158:576-584.

28. Wood LG, Fitzgerald DA, Gibson PG, Cooper DM, Garg ML. Lipid peroxidation as determined by plasma isoprostanes is related to disease severity in mild asthma. *Lipids.* 2000;35:967-974.

29. Hartert TV, Peebles RS. Dietary antioxidants and adult asthma. *Curr Opin Allergy Clin Immunol.* 2001;1:421-429.

30. Roberts G, Lack G. Food allergy and asthma--what is the link? *Paediatr Respir Rev.* 2003;4:205-212.

31. Vally H, Thompson PJ. Allergic and asthmatic reactions to alcoholic drinks. *Addict Biol.* 2003;8:3-11.

32. Shirai T, Reshad K, Yoshitomi A, Chida K, Nakamura H, Taniguchi M. Green tea-induced asthma: relationship between immunological reactivity, specific and nonspecific bronchial responsiveness. *Clin Exp Allergy.* 2003;33:1252-1255.

33. Bush RK, Taylor SL, Holden K, et al. Prevalence of sensitivity to sulfiting agents in asthmatic patients. *Am J Med.* 1986;81:816.

34. Buckley R, Saltzman HA, Sieker, HO. The prevalence and degree of sensitivity to ingested sulfites. *J Allergy Clin Immunol.* 1985;77:144.

35. Roberts G, Patel N, Levi-Schaffer F, et al. Food allergy as a risk factor for life-threatening asthma in childhood: a case-controlled study. *J Allergy Clin Immunol.* 2003;112:168.

36. Yusoff NA, Hampton SM, Dickerson JW, Morgan JB. The effects of exclusion of dietary egg and milk in the management of asthmatic children: a pilot study. *J R Soc Health.* 2004;124:74-80.

37. Yazicioglu M, Baspinar I, Ones U, Pala O, Kiziler U. Egg and milk allergy in asthmatic children: assessment by immulite allergy food panel, skin prick tests, and double-blind placebo-controlled food challenges. *Allergol Immunopathol (Madr).*1999;27:287-293.

38. Knutsen SF. Lifestyle and the use of health services. *Am J Clin Nutr.* 1994;59:1171S-1175S.

39. Woods RK, Walters EH, Raven JM, et al. Food and nutrient intakes and asthma risk in young adults. *Am J Clin Nutr.* 2003;78:414-421.

40. Lindahl O, Lindwall L, Spangberg A, Stenram A, Ockerman PA. Vegan regimen with reduced medication in the treatment of bronchial asthma. *J Asthma.* 1985;22:45-55.

41. Stanaland BE. Therapeutic measures for prevention of allergic rhinitis/asthma development. *Allergy Asthma Proc.* 2004;25:11-15.

40. Chronic Obstructive Pulmonary Disease

Chronic obstructive pulmonary disease (COPD) is a progressive and irreversible airway disorder usually caused by smoking. It is characterized by diminished inspiratory and expiratory lung capacity, airflow obstruction, and impaired gas exchange. COPD is the fourth most common cause of death in the United States and the fifth most common cause of death worldwide. Its incidence and mortality rate are rising due to increasing worldwide cigarette use and air pollution.

COPD pathophysiology involves chronic bronchitis and/or emphysema and sometimes asthma (reversible airway hyperreactivity). Chronic bronchitis is characterized by airway inflammation and defined by the presence of a productive cough that lasts at least 3 months and occurs in more than 2 successive years. Emphysema entails enlargement of air spaces and destruction of the lung parenchyma, resulting in closure of small airways and loss of lung elasticity.

Risk Factors

Smoking. Cigarette smoking is the most important risk factor for COPD, causing more than 90% of cases. Secondhand smoke also contributes to COPD. However, relatively few smokers (<15%) develop COPD.

Genetics. There is a clear genetic role in the development of COPD. It is unclear whether genetic predisposition is requisite for COPD to occur.

α_1-antitrypsin deficiency. α_1-antitrypsin is an inhibitor of the elastase enzyme. This inherited disorder predisposes affected individuals to emphysema due to the uncontrolled action of elastase, which destroys the lung parenchyma.

Airway hyperresponsivity.

Allergy.

Occupation. Certain occupational exposures (eg, mining and agriculture) are linked to COPD.

Air pollution. The role of pollutants in the pathogenesis of COPD is unclear. However, the incidence of COPD and the frequency of acute exacerbations are significantly increased in areas of heavy air pollution.

Diagnosis

Pulmonary function testing showing an obstructive pattern is the most reliable indicator for diagnosis. This would be a ratio of forced expiratory volume in 1 second to the forced vital capacity of less than 70% (FEV_1/FVC ratio <70%).

Chest x-rays may reveal hyperinflation of the lungs—flattening of the diaphragm and radiolucency of the lung fields. However, x-rays may appear normal until the emphysema component is quite advanced. CT scans are more sensitive.

Hematocrit levels may be elevated due to chronic hypoxia.

Arterial blood gas concentration may reveal hypoxemia and hypercapnia.

Treatment

Quitting smoking is essential at any stage of the disease. Although lung damage will not be reversed (especially in advanced cases), smoking cessation will lead to improvements in pulmonary function.

Physical exercise, as part of a pulmonary rehabilitation program, can improve functional status in COPD. Exercise programs do not necessarily increase lung function, but they should increase patients' ability to perform activities of daily living. Inspiratory muscle training in particular is associated with significant improvements in pulmonary capacity, endurance, exercise capacity, and dyspnea.[1] As with other forms of exercise, benefits are lost if patients do not maintain their efforts.[2]

Respiratory therapy and pulmonary rehabilitation improve quality of life and exercise capacity.

Continuous or nighttime supplemental oxygen provides symptomatic relief and improves mortality in patients with chronic hypoxemia.

Bronchodilators, including anticholinergics (eg, **ipratropium bromide**) and β_2-adrenergic agents (eg, **albuterol**), may alleviate symptoms by reducing bronchial tone. Patients with spirometry that does not respond to bronchodilators may still have long-term improvement in symptoms with regular use. Anticholinergics, such as the long-acting agent **tiotropium**, may be combined with beta-agonists.

Methylxanthines (eg, theophylline) are a controversial treatment. They may be beneficial by augmenting the action of the diaphragm during exhalation, improving gas exchange, and increasing airway caliber.

The role of **corticosteroids** is still under investigation. Inhaled steroids, although often prescribed, have not been beneficial in most patients. Systemic steroids may help hospitalized patients with acute exacerbations.

Antibiotics may help in exacerbations but should not be used prophylactically.

Surgical intervention may be helpful in a minority of advanced cases. Lung-volume-reduction surgery may benefit selected end-stage patients by increasing elastic recoil, improving expiratory airflow, and improving the function of the diaphragm and intercostal muscles. Lung transplantation may also be considered.

Emergency Treatments

Acute exacerbations of COPD must be treated emergently. It is important to identify and treat the cause of the exacerbation (eg, infection, excessive sedation); administer bronchodilator therapy (eg, beta-agonists) and supplemental oxygen; ensure clearance of pulmonary secretions; and closely monitor for signs of respiratory failure. Caution is required for oxygen administration, as excessive oxygenation may cause a lethal hypercapnia.

If respiratory failure occurs, intubation may be necessary. Noninvasive positive pressure ventilation (BiPAP) is often used in deteriorating patients, as it may eliminate the need for intubation.

New treatment options for reducing inflammation and for blocking certain enzymes are under investigation.

Nutritional Considerations

While the mechanism by which cigarette smoke causes COPD in some persons is unclear, a growing body of evidence supports the hypothesis that COPD is influenced by oxidative stress, inflammation, and an imbalance between protease and antiprotease activity.[3] Antioxidants and fatty acids influence these processes and thus have theoretical roles in the prevention and treatment of COPD. However, most studies of specific nutrients and foods relate to COPD prevention, rather than treatment, and further research is necessary to establish their value. Of course, nutritional interventions, if shown to be clinically useful, must be used along with avoidance of smoking or other causative agents and with appropriate treatment.

The following dietary factors are under investigation for their possible roles in preventing COPD or affecting its course:

Avoiding Western Diets

Studies in both men and women have shown that people following a Western dietary pattern, high in refined grains, cured and red meats, desserts, and french fries, have a greater risk for developing COPD, while those following largely plant-based diets have a lower risk.[4,5]

Avoiding Cured Meats

The Third National Health and Nutrition Examination Survey (NHANES III) found an almost 80% greater risk for COPD in those who consumed the highest intake of cured meats, such as bacon, sausage, and hot dogs ($\geq$14 times per month), compared with individuals who avoided these meats.[6] Similarly, the Health Professionals Study of more than 42,000 men found that those who ate cured meats daily had more than 2.5 times the risk for COPD, compared with individuals who rarely ate these products.[7] Nitrites found in cured meats are pro-oxidants, and the subsequent nitrative/nitrosative reactions may result in damage to the extracellular matrix that is characteristic of emphysema.[6]

Fruits and Vegetables

Although cause and effect cannot be established from existing evidence, a number of studies have associated higher intakes of fruits and vegetables with a lower risk for COPD. In a population of smokers, eating at least 4 ounces of fruit and 3 ounces of vegetables daily was associated with a 50% lower COPD risk, compared with eating the least amounts of these foods.[8] Similarly, a slower rate of decline in lung function (FEV_1) was found in a general population with higher average intake of foods containing vitamin C.[9]

However, benefits of higher fruit and vegetable intakes on COPD risk were not apparent in a study of both smokers and nonsmokers.[10] A British study found no association between average fruit intake and FEV_1, but it did find a decline in FEV_1 in individuals whose fruit intakes decreased over time.[11]

The putative protective effects of these foods may be partly related to the antioxidant effects of carotenoids[12] and flavonoids[13] and to replacement of the vitamin C that COPD patients lose as a result of a systemic oxidant/antioxidant imbalance.[14] However, these mechanisms and effects are speculative only, and the effect of diets high in fruits or vegetables on the incidence or progression of COPD remains to be assessed in clinical trials.

Omega-3 Fatty Acids

In human subjects with COPD, supplementation with an omega-3-containing calorie supplement (400 cals/day) for 2 years significantly improved dyspnea and reduced the rate of decline in arterial oxygen saturation, compared with a group given an isocaloric supplement containing omega-6 fatty acids.[15] Other evidence indicates benefits of omega-3 fatty acid supplements on exercise capacity in patients with COPD, in comparison with those on placebo.[16] Additional controlled clinical trials are needed to determine if omega-3 fats reduce the incidence or progression of COPD.

If omega-3 fatty acids influence COPD, the mechanism may relate to their anti-inflammatory effects. Through competition for the lipoxygenase pathway, omega-3 fatty acids interfere with production of omega-6 fat-derived leukotrienes (eg, LTB4), which have proinflammatory, bronchoconstrictive effects.[17]

Vitamin E

Some observational studies have found protective effects of dietary (not supplementary) vitamin E intake on lung function.[10] However, in the Alpha-Tocopherol Beta-Carotene Cancer Prevention Study involving over 29,000 subjects, neither alpha-tocopherol (50 mg/d) nor beta carotene (20 mg/d) supplements lessened COPD symptoms, although high baseline blood levels of vitamin E were associated with a lower risk for COPD and dyspnea in smokers, compared with individuals who had the lowest levels.[12] Clinical trials have not yet assessed the value of diets high in vitamin E for reducing COPD risk or decreasing its rate of progression.

The association between certain antioxidants and COPD derives some theoretical support from the fact that a deficiency of alpha-1 protease inhibitor leads to lung tissue breakdown and pulmonary emphysema. Blood vitamin E concentrations correlate positively with serum alpha-1 protease inhibitor levels in smokers.[18]

Attainment or Maintenance of a Healthy Body Weight

By some estimates, almost 1 in 4 patients with COPD is malnourished.[19] Lower-than-ideal bodyweight is associated with a greater risk for death from COPD,[20,21] and a loss of fat-free mass appeared to be an independent predictor of mortality.[22]

The issue of caloric supplementation in underweight persons with COPD is controversial. A review of existing evidence concluded that supplementation has no significant effect on anthropometric measures, lung function, or exercise capacity in COPD patients.[23] However, a joint statement published by the American Thoracic and European Respiratory Societies suggests that caloric supplementation should be considered in persons with a BMI less than 21 kg/m2, involuntary weight loss of >5% in the past month or >10% over a 6-month period, or depletion in fat-free and/or lean body mass. Although a lack of weight gain from calorie supplements was noted by the expert panel, it was attributed to other nutritional variables and the presence of systemic inflammation. Pairing such supplementation with supervised exercise was deemed an effective strategy for promoting gain of lean body mass and weight.[21]

In contrast to low body weight, the effect of obesity on pulmonary mechanics in COPD patients presents an obvious disadvantage as well. Loss of excess weight often results in improved functional status.[21]

Orders

See Basic Diet Orders chapter.

Nutritional supplements, if indicated and per recommendation of registered dietitian.

What to Tell the Family

COPD is preventable in most cases by not smoking or by quitting smoking early. The family can play an important role in preventing COPD by encouraging smokers in the family to quit and by following healthful diets.

When a family member has COPD, he or she may require medications to reduce lung inflammation, dilate the bronchi, and reduce airway obstruction. Eventually, supplemental oxygen becomes necessary.

References

1. Geddes EL, Reid WD, Crowe J, O'Brien K, Brooks D. Inspiratory muscle training in adults with chronic obstructive pulmonary disease: a systematic review. *Respir Med.* 2005;99:1440-1458.

2. Weiner P, Magadle R, Beckerman M, Weiner M, Berar-Yanay N. Maintenance of inspiratory muscle training in COPD patients: one-year follow-up. *Eur Respir J.* 2004;23:61-65.

3. Golpon HA, Coldren CD, Zamora MR, et al. Emphysema lung tissue gene expression profiling. *Am J Respir Cell Mol Biol.* 2004;31:595-600.

4. Varraso R, Fung TT, Hu FB, Willett W, Camargo CA Jr. Prospective study of dietary patterns and chronic obstructive pulmonary disease among US men. *Thorax.* 2007;62:785-790.

5. Varraso R, Fung TT, Barr RG, Hu FB, Willett W, Camargo CA Jr. Prospective study of dietary patterns and chronic obstructive pulmonary disease among US women. *Am J Clin Nutr.* 2007;86:488-495.

6. Jiang R, Paik DC, Hankinson JL, Barr RG. Cured meat consumption, lung function, and chronic pulmonary disease among United States adults. *Am J Respir Crit Care Med.* 2007;175:798-804.

7. Varraso R, Jiang R, Barr RG, Willett W, Camargo CA Jr. Prospective study of cured meats consumption and risk of chronic obstructive pulmonary disease in men. *Am J Epidemiology.* 2007;166:1438-1445.

8. Watson L, Margetts B, Howart P, Dorward M, Thompson R, Little P. The association between diet and chronic obstructive pulmonary disease in subjects selected from general practice. *Eur Respir J.* 2002;20:313-318.

9. McKeever TM, Scrivener S, Broadfield E, Jones Z, Britton J, Lewis SA. Prospective study of diet and decline in lung function in a general population. *Am J Respir Crit Care Med.* 2002;165:1299-1303.

10. Butland BK, Fehily AM, Elwood PC. Diet, lung function, and lung function decline in a cohort of 2,512 middle aged men. *Thorax.* 2000;55:102-108.

11. Carey IM, Strachan DP, Cook DG. Effects of changes in fresh fruit consumption on ventilatory function in healthy British adults. *Am J Respir Crit Care Med.* 1998;158:728-733.

12. Rautalahti M, Virtamo J, Haukka J, et al. The effect of alpha-tocopherol and beta-carotene supplementation on COPD symptoms. *Am J Respir Crit Care Med.* 1997;156:1447-1452.

13. Tabak C, Arts ICW, Smit HA, Heederik D, Kromhout D. Chronic obstructive pulmonary disease and intake of catechins, flavonols, and flavones. *Am J Respir Crit Care Med.* 2001;164:61-64.

14. Calikoglu M, Unlu A, Tamer L, Ercan B, Bugdayci R, Atik U. The levels of serum vitamin C, malonyldialdehyde, and erythrocyte reduced glutathione in chronic obstructive pulmonary disease and in healthy smokers. *Clin Chem Lab Med.* 2002;40:1028-1031.

15. Matsuyama W, Mitsuyama H, Watanabe M, et al. Effects of omega-3 polyunsaturated fatty acids on inflammatory markers in COPD. *Chest.* 2005;128:3817-3827.

16. Broekhuizen R, Wouters EF, Creutzberg EC, Weling-Scheepers CA, Schols AM. Polyunsaturated fatty acids improve exercise capacity in chronic obstructive pulmonary disease. *Thorax.* 2005;60:376-382.

17. Kostikas K, Gaga M, Papatheodorou G, Karamanis T, Orphanidou D, Loukides S. Leukotriene B4 in exhaled breath condensate and sputum supernatant in patients with COPD and asthma. *Chest.* 2005;127:1553-1559.

18. van Antwerpen VL, Theron AJ, Richards GA, et al. Vitamin E, pulmonary functions, and phagocyte-mediated oxidative stress in smokers and nonsmokers. *Free Radic Biol Med.* 1995;18:935-941.

19. Cochrane WJ, Afolabi OA. Investigation into the nutritional status, dietary intake, and smoking habits of patients with chronic obstructive pulmonary disease. *J Hum Nutr Diet.* 2004;17:3-11, quiz 13-15.

20. Meyer PA, Mannino DM, Redd SC, Olson DR. Characteristics of adults dying with COPD. *Chest.* 2002;122:2003-2008.

21. Nici L, Donner C, Wouters E, et al. American Thoracic Society/European Respiratory Society statement on pulmonary rehabilitation. *Am J Respir Crit Care Med.* 2006;173:1390-1413.

22. Schols AM, Broekhuizen R, Weling-Scheepers CA, Wouters EF. Body composition and mortality in chronic obstructive pulmonary disease. *Am J Clin Nutr.* 2005;82:53-59.

23. Ferreira IM, Brooks D, Lacasse Y, Goldstein RS, White J. Nutritional supplementation for stable chronic obstructive pulmonary disease. *Cochrane Database Syst Rev.* 2005;(2):CD000998.

41. Cystic Fibrosis

Cystic fibrosis (CF) is a systemic disease of the exocrine glands characterized by a progressive obstructive lung disease (bronchiectasis) and exocrine pancreatic insufficiency. The sweat glands, vas deferens, and other organs are also affected to varying degrees.

CF is the most common inherited genetic disorder in North America. In the United States, 30,000 individuals have the condition, and about 12 million people are carriers. Cystic fibrosis is also the most common cause of pancreatic insufficiency in children. Because normal absorption and digestion of nutrients, especially fat, are altered by pancreatic insufficiency, failure to thrive, malnutrition, diabetes, and growth problems are common clinical features in the absence of treatment. Altered fatty acid metabolism produces excess arachidonic acid and leads to inflammatory complications in multiple systems. The median age of survival is approximately 35 years.

CF is caused by mutations of the cystic fibrosis transmembrane conductance regulator (CFTR) gene, which controls the concentration of sodium and chloride across certain epithelial cell membranes. Its disruption causes excessive sodium and chloride resorption. Water, in turn, follows the abnormal movement of sodium and chloride into the epithelial cell layer. This dehydrates airway surfaces produces thick mucus, and impedes mucociliary transport, which renders lungs susceptible to bacterial infections. Destruction of the pancreas is common, resulting in the absence of digestive enzymes normally released into the digestive tract; 85% to 90% of patients with CF have pancreatic exocrine insufficiency. Over 1,000 mutations of this gene have been identified; the most common is the ΔF508 mutation.

Risk Factors

Genetics. CF is an autosomal recessive condition. If both parents are carriers, a child has a 25% chance of having the disease and a 50%

chance of also being a carrier. One in 25 whites is a carrier. A family history of cystic fibrosis and unexplained infant death are also risk factors.

Race. The prevalence of CF is approximately 1 in 2,500 for whites, 1 in 15,000 for blacks, and 1 in 30,000 for Asian Americans.

Diagnosis

Signs and symptoms of cystic fibrosis reflect sinopulmonary, hepatic, endocrine, and intestinal involvement.

Respiratory problems include:

Recurrent respiratory infections, which are associated with *Haemophilus influenza* and *Staphylococcus aureus* in the first decade of life. Teenage and adult years are characterized by infections with mucoid *Pseudomonas aeruginosa*, and *S aureus*, which quickly acquire multiple drug resistance. Any sputum culture growing *P aeruginosa* should prompt an evaluation for bronchiectasis, and, if present, a workup for cystic fibrosis.

Acute exacerbations of respiratory chronic bacterial colonization usually present with increased green-colored sputum, malaise, fatigue, wheezing, dyspnea, pneumothorax, and hemoptysis, due to increased inflammation in the airway. A decline in pulmonary status typically manifests with worse spirometry (particularly FEV1) and may be accompanied by hypoxia and chest x-ray changes.

Concurrent sinus disease, including chronic sinusitis and nasal polyposis, is relatively common and may contribute to progressive lung decline.

Intestinal involvement may lead to:

Bowel obstruction, with meconium ileus and intussusception, is particularly common at birth. Other digestive symptoms are steatorrhea, abdominal cramping and constipation, rectal prolapse, liver disease, and cystic fibrosis-related diabetes.

Malabsorption, which causes failure to thrive, retarded growth, and fatigue.

Male infertility is also a symptom. Men nearly always have azoospermia due to congenital bilateral absence of the vas deferens.

Women may have some abnormalities of the cervical mucus, but fertility does not appear to be significantly reduced in the absence of severe malnutrition.

Cystic fibrosis is diagnosed by a sweat test (which can be done as early as 48 hours of age). Mandatory newborn screening is now instituted in at least 10 states. A positive sweat test (see below) combined with pulmonary and/or gastrointestinal symptoms establishes the classic diagnosis in nearly all cases. CF mutations, identified through genetic testing, can also confirm diagnosis, or they can be used to make the diagnosis in patients with mild forms of the disease.

A patient with the symptoms and/or signs presented above may require the following tests (additional tests are available if the diagnosis remains in doubt):

Sweat test. Most patients with CF have chloride values between 60 and 110 mEq/L.

Genetic testing. Patients who exhibit signs and symptoms but do not have a positive sweat test should have a genetic test. Prenatal testing and newborn screening may be used. Early detection renders a better clinical course.

Stool tests. Fecal fat analysis can be used to confirm pancreatic insufficiency.

Bone density evaluation may reveal osteopenia or osteoporosis.

Treatment

The cornerstones of treatment for CF patients are antibiotics, airway clearance, and nutritional support. A standard treatment regimen includes airway clearance and exercise, mucolytic agents, bronchodilators, antiinflammatory agents, supplemental oxygen, and nutritional support. CF patients should be cared for at a comprehensive cystic fibrosis care center by a multidisciplinary health care team that includes a physician, nurse, respiratory therapist, dietitian, and social worker. A consensus statement detailing the current evidence-based approach to the care of CF patients has recently been published.[1]

Pulmonary

The pulmonary status of patients should be regularly monitored by an assessment of symptoms, a physical examination, and spirometry. Percent predicted forced expiratory volume in 1 second (FEV_1) is accepted as the single most useful objective measure of pulmonary status. Oxygen saturation at rest, during exercise, and/or during sleep should be measured routinely in patients with moderate-to-severe pulmonary disease to assess the need for supplemental oxygen.

Participation in **regular exercise** may help preserve pulmonary function. A review of exercise benefits indicated that, over 3 years of physical training, the mean annual rate of decline in forced vital capacity was significantly greater in the control group compared with the exercise group.[2] Both aerobic exercise and resistance exercise appear to benefit CF patients. Children who received aerobic training had significantly better peak aerobic capacity, whereas those who received resistance training had better weight gain, lung function, and leg strength than children who received aerobic training.[3]

Antibiotics are used both for pulmonary exacerbations and chronic suppressive therapy, although the latter is under study for its role in antibiotic resistance. During acute exacerbations of chronic infections, therapy is typically aggressive, frequently using 2 combined intravenous antipseudomonal antibiotics (depending on sputum culture sensitivities) over 2 to 3 weeks. A complete microbiologic assessment of expectorated sputum, including antibiotic susceptibility testing, should be performed at least once a year. Over 80% of CF patients are chronically infected by *P aeruginosa* by adulthood, and this represents the most significant cause of infection over the life of the patient.

Chest physiotherapy may be administered through a number of techniques and should be performed daily to assist with clearing airway mucus. The method prescribed should be individualized, based on efficacy and compliance. Patient assistance with expensive modalities such as mechanical vests may be available through the Cystic Fibrosis Foundation.

CF is an obstructive airway disease. **Bronchodilators** (see Asthma chapter) are used by the great majority of patients.

Inhaled recombinant human **DNase I** decreases sputum viscosity by degrading extracellular DNA into smaller pieces, and it demonstrated 6% improvement in FEV_1 in Phase III trials.[4]

Inhaled **hypertonic saline** allows for hydration of dehydrated airways. In a large randomized clinical trial, its use led to improvements in FEV_1 and a 56% relative risk reduction for acute exacerbations.[5]

Azithromycin used three times a week in patients chronically colonized with *P aeruginosa* led to improvements in FEV_1, reduction in acute exacerbations (hazard ratio 0.65), and weight gain—without increases in *S aureus* or *P aeruginosa* resistance or atypical mycobacterial colonization.[6]

Inhaled **tobramycin** is a cornerstone of standard CF care. In a clinical trial, inhaled tobramycin (TOBI) 300 mg twice daily led to a 12% improvement in FEV_1. Treatment is given every other month in order to avoid antibiotic resistance.[7]

In advanced disease, when FEV_1 drops below 30% of predicted values, **bilateral lung transplant** is an option, but an imperfect one at best. Thorough risk/benefit evaluation is required.

Corticosteroids are generally reserved for treatment of asthma in CF because of their poor side-effect profile.

Many other therapies are under investigation.

Pancreatic

Exogenous pancreatic enzyme replacement therapy allows for the digestion of lipids and prevents symptoms of steatorrhea.

A significant percentage of patients develop CF-related diabetes mellitus (CFRD). An oral glucose tolerance test should be done yearly and treatment instituted when 2-hour glucose levels surpass 200 mg/dL. Frequently, A1c levels are normal. CF-related diabetes is typically preceded by decline in lung function several years prior to CFRD diagnosis. CF patients should not automatically be placed on diabetic diets (due to high caloric needs). Instead, insulin therapy should be increased to achieve optimal glycemic control.

Gastrointestinal

In the absence of steatorrhea, constipation can occur. This can be avoided and/or treated with an osmotic laxative, such as polyethylene glycol electrolyte solution (eg, MiraLax or Golytely).

Primary biliary cirrhosis can be treated with ursodeoxycholic acid, which improves biliary excretion and bile acid composition, even in asymptomatic or minimally symptomatic patients.

Bone

Proper nutrition (see below) and exercise may help prevent decreased bone density. Bisphosphonates are effective when indicated.

Nutritional Considerations

Nutritional management has a dramatic effect on growth and survival in patients with CF, but it is often challenging due to malabsorption. Survival is markedly poorer in patients who are underweight for their height. Thus, a high-energy diet is commonly recommended, along with nutritional supplements.[8]

Energy Intake

Maintenance of a high-calorie diet is a cornerstone of therapy. A study of adults with CF found that 60% failed to meet recommended calorie needs, and 72% failed to meet recommendations for both protein and energy.[9] Patients with CF are susceptible to weight loss for several reasons, including ongoing steatorrhea and azotorrhea (despite enzyme therapy); a 10% to 30% increase in elevated resting energy expenditure (REE), particularly during pulmonary exacerbations; treatment with bronchodilators (which cause an 8% to 20% increase in REE)[10]; infection-related anorexia; gastrointestinal disturbances; and clinical depression.[8]

With proper nutrition therapy, including an energy intake of 120% to 150% of the Recommended Dietary Allowance (RDA), patients with CF may grow normally. Although nutritional supplements have been used in an attempt to attain this goal, research does not support their efficacy.[11] Instead, high-fat diets have typically been used,[8] although this approach may increase the susceptibility of CF patients to oxidative stress.[12] The kind of fat that should be given is also under debate (see below).

Provision of a diet high in essential fatty acids helps with weight maintenance and prevention of deficiency symptoms. Biochemical evidence of deficiency of both the essential omega-6 fatty acid linoleic acid and docosahexanoic acid, a derivative of the essential omega-3 fatty acid alpha-linolenic acid, is common in patients with CF, although clinical signs and symptoms are rare.[13]

Although a diet high in fat (including animal fat) is often recommended, it has disadvantages for patients with CF. The omega-6 fatty acid arachidonic acid found in these foods may adversely affect CF patients by contributing to oxidative stress and a proinflammatory effect in lung tissue through an increase in leukotriene B4.[12] Omega-3 fats, however, appear to be of clinical benefit in patients with CF. Reduction of sputum volume, improved lung function, and a decrease in leukotriene B4 and in use of antibiotics have been observed in patients given supplements of eicosapentanoic and docosahexanoic acids.[8,14] Increasing the intake of plant sources of omega-3 fats (alpha-linolenic acid) and monounsaturated fats has been suggested as an alternative approach to improving fatty acid nutrition in CF patients.[8] The Cystic Fibrosis Foundation consensus panel has made similar recommendations, suggesting that oils rich in both omega-3 and monounsaturated fats (eg, flax, canola, soy) benefit CF patients.[13]

Nutritional Adequacy

Patients should be monitored for evidence of vitamin deficiency and treated accordingly. Patients with CF require supplemental nutrients for various reasons. The fat-soluble vitamins A, D, E, and K are a priority, mainly because pancreatic enzyme insufficiency often results in malabsorption of these nutrients. Current vitamin supplementation recommendations include: Vitamin A, 500 to 1000 IU/d; Vitamin E, 400 to 800 IU/d; Vitamin D, 400 to 800 IU/d and adequate sunlight exposure; and Vitamin K, 2.5 to 5 mg/wk. Commercially available vitamins containing A, D, E, and K that are specially formulated for CF patients are sufficient for most adult patients when 2 per day are taken. Occasionally, patients require additional supplementation, most commonly with vitamin D.

Oxidative stress occurs to a greater degree in patients with CF than in healthy controls.[12] Consequently, deficiencies of antioxidants (eg, vitamin C) and low concentrations of antioxidant enzymes (eg, glutathione peroxidase) have been found in patients with CF, along with poor selenium and zinc status.[8] The amounts of vitamins required in supplements follow.

Vitamin D. Vitamin D deficiency is common among individuals with CF, especially at northern latitudes.[15] Lack of vitamin D aggravates the already greater risk for osteoporosis and fractures seen in CF patients.[13] Low concentrations of vitamin D have been found in persons with CF taking 1000 IU of vitamin D per day,[8] and the deficiency appears not to be corrected even with megadoses of the vitamin.[15] For increasing calcium absorption and bone density and decreasing markers of bone resorption, the active hormone (D_3) form of vitamin D and vitamin D analogues appear more effective than vitamin D_2.[16]

Vitamin K. Vitamin K deficiency is also common in CF. Supplements in the range of 0.1 to 0.3 mg/d may not be sufficient; a dose of 1 mg/d may be necessary for normalization of vitamin K status.[17,18]

Orders

Nutrition consultation to assess nutrient status, advise patient in dietary change, and arrange follow-up. The diet should be individualized based on clinical status.

Exercise prescription: Patient-specific aerobic and resistance training.

What to Tell the Family

Cystic fibrosis is an inherited disease that frequently causes respiratory tract infection, resulting in poor appetite and weight loss. Poor absorption of nutrients is also common, requiring pancreatic enzyme replacement and supplements of fat-soluble (and possibly water-soluble) vitamins. Patients with CF should follow a high-calorie, high-fat, nutrient-dense diet to help meet needs for energy, growth, and vitamins and minerals. Additional supplementation with fatty acids and minerals may be required if clinical examination or laboratory studies indicate a state of deficiency or insufficiency. Long-term complications of CF that may be delayed through proper diet, exercise, and medical care include osteoporosis, diabetes, and accelerated loss of pulmonary capacity. Care of patients in close consultation with an accredited CF center is recommended.

References

1. Yankaskas JR, Marshall BC, Sufian B, Simon RH, Rodman D. Cystic fibrosis adult care: consensus conference report. *Chest.* 2004;125(suppl 1):1S-39S.

2. Bradley J, Moran F. Physical training for cystic fibrosis. *Cochrane Database Syst Rev.* 2002;(2):CD002768.

3. Selvadurai HC, Blimkie CJ, Meyers N, et al. Randomized controlled study of in-hospital exercise training programs in children with cystic fibrosis. *Pediatr Pulmonol.* 2002;33:194-200.

4. Fuchs HJ, Borowitz DS, Christiansen DH, et al. Effect of aerosolized recombinant human DNase on exacerbations of respiratory symptoms and on pulmonary function in patients with cystic fibrosis. The Pulmozyme Study Group. *N Engl J Med.* 1994;331:637-642.

5. Elkins MR, Robinson M, Rose BR, et al. A controlled trial of long-term inhaled hypertonic saline in patients with cystic fibrosis. *N Engl J Med.* 2006;354:229-240.

6. Saiman L, Marshall BC, Mayer-Hamblett N, et al. Azithromycin in patients with cystic fibrosis chronically infected with Pseudomonas aeruginosa: a randomized controlled trial. *JAMA.* 2003;290:1749-1756.

7. Ramsey BW, Pepe MS, Quan JM, et al, for the Cystic Fibrosis Inhaled Tobramycin Study Group. Intermittent administration of inhaled tobramycin in patients with cystic fibrosis. *N Engl J Med.* 1999;340:23-30.

8. Wood LG, Gibson PG, Garg ML. Circulating markers to assess nutritional therapy in cystic fibrosis. *Clin Chim Acta.* 2005;353:13-29.

9. White H, Morton AM, Peckham DG, Conway SP. Dietary intakes in adult patients with cystic fibrosis-do they achieve guidelines? *J Cyst Fibros.* 2004;3:1-7.

10. Schols A. Nutritional modulation as part of the integrated management of chronic obstructive pulmonary disease. *Proc Nutr Soc.* 2003;62:783-791.

11. Poustie VJ, Watling RM, Smyth RL. Oral protein-energy supplements for children with chronic disease: systematic review. *Proc Nutr Soc.* 2003;62:801-806.

12. Wood LG, Fitzgerald DA, Lee AK, et al. Improved antioxidant and fatty acid status of patients with cystic fibrosis after antioxidant supplementation is linked to improved lung function. *Am J Clin Nutr.* 2003;77:150-159.

13. Borowitz D, Baker RD, Stallings V. Consensus report on nutrition for pediatric patients with cystic fibrosis. *J Pediatr Gastroenterol Nutr.* 2002;35:246-259.

14. Cawood AL, Carroll MP, Wootton SA, et al. Is there a case for n-3 fatty acid supplementation in cystic fibrosis? *Curr Opin Clin Nutr Metab Care.* 2005;8:153-159.

15. Boyle MP, Noschese ML, Watts SL, et al. Failure of high-dose ergocalciferol to correct vitamin D deficiency in adults with cystic fibrosis. *Am J Respir Crit Care Med.* 2005;172:212-217.

16. Aris R, Lester G, Ontjes D. Treatment of bone disease in cystic fibrosis. *Curr Opin Pulm Med.* 2004;10:524-530.

17. Wilson DC, Rashid M, Durie PR, et al. Treatment of vitamin K deficiency in cystic fibrosis: Effectiveness of a daily fat-soluble vitamin combination. *J Pediatr.* 2001;138:851-855.

18. van Hoorn JH, Hendriks JJ, Vermeer C, Forget PP. Vitamin K supplementation in cystic fibrosis. *Arch Dis Child.* 2003;88:974-975.

SECTION IX: RENAL AND GENITOURINARY DISEASES

42. Chronic Kidney Disease

Chronic kidney disease (CKD) is a progressive syndrome of renal insufficiency and failure in which the kidneys lose their ability to filter blood, concentrate the urine, excrete wastes, and maintain electrolyte balance. Formerly called chronic renal failure, CKD is an important public health issue that has been increasing in incidence and prevalence worldwide and consumes disproportionate healthcare resources in the United States. CKD is also a major independent risk factor for cardiovascular mortality.

About 75% of CKD cases are due to diabetes mellitus and/or hypertension. Other common etiologies include glomerulonephritis, renal cystic disease, congenital urologic disorders, urinary obstruction, multiple myeloma, amyloidosis, analgesic abuse, and atheroemboli.

While biochemical and hormonal abnormalities occur early, few symptoms occur until about 75% of kidney function has been lost. Initial presentation includes fluid retention, hypertension, anemia, and electrolyte disturbances. As kidney function is further compromised, overt signs of uremia occur: shortness of breath, nausea, vomiting, anorexia, weight loss, encephalopathy, asterixis, pruritis, and pericarditis.

Risk Factors

African Americans have a significantly higher rate of CKD than other racial groups. This is partly due to higher rates of hypertension in this group. Non-Hispanic whites generally have the lowest risk. Other factors associated with increased risk include:

Older age.

Family history.

Urinary tract disorders that may increase the risk of kidney damage: urinary tract infections, urolithiasis, urinary tract obstruction.

Systemic medical disorders that may increase the risk of kidney damage: diabetes mellitus, hypertension, autoimmune disorders (eg, systemic lupus erythematosus), systemic infections.

Nephrotoxic medications (eg, nonsteroidal antiinflammatory drugs, contrast dye).

Tobacco smoking.

Diagnosis

The National Kidney Foundation has developed guidelines for classifying chronic kidney disease based on glomerular filtration rate (GFR):

Stage 1: Normal GFR (>90 ml/min/1.73 m^2 for adults) with persistent albuminuria or structural abnormalities.

Stage 2: GFR between 60 and 89 ml/min/1.73 m^2 with persistent albuminuria or structural abnormalities.

Stage 3: GFR between 30 and 59 ml/min/1.73 m^2.

Stage 4: GFR between 15 and 29 ml/min/1.73 m^2.

Stage 5 (end-stage renal failure): GFR <15 ml/min/1.73 m^2.

Further testing to determine the underlying etiology may include urinalysis; renal imaging, including ultrasound and CT scan; and renal biopsy.

Because the kidneys are essential to regulating electrolyte and acid-base balance, CKD leads to chemistry disorders such as hyperkalemia, hyperphosphatemia, hypocalcemia, and metabolic acidosis.

Treatment

Treatment for CKD aims to reduce the high cardiovascular mortality rate in this high-risk population and to slow disease progression. It is also important to address the underlying etiology, treat related conditions to reduce cardiovascular risk, and replace lost kidney function via dialysis or transplant when uremia develops.

In patients with diabetes mellitus or hypertension, control of blood glucose and blood pressure is very important. The rate of fall of GFR can be reduced or even halted with aggressive blood pressure and glucose control. **Angiotensin-converting enzyme (ACE) inhibitors** and **angiotensin-receptor blockers (ARBs)** are especially helpful blood pressure medications for diabetic patients, because they are kidney-protective.

Specific treatments for underlying disorders should be applied. In some cases, addressing the underlying etiology will retard or halt the loss of kidney function.

Sodium restriction and/or **diuretics** are usually needed to combat fluid retention. Anemia is common in CKD patients due to the loss of renal erythropoietin production and should be treated with **supplemental iron** (if iron deficiency is also present) and **synthetic erythropoietin** to reach a target hemoglobin of 11 to 12 g/dL. **Phosphate binders** and dietary **phosphorus restriction** are indicated to keep phosphate <4.5 mg/dL.

Exercise can benefit patients with CKD. Resistance training in particular helps reduce the catabolic effects of a **low-protein** (0.6g/kg/d) **diet**,[1] whereas aerobic exercise may help control blood pressure and lipid levels.[2]

Ultimately, **dialysis or kidney transplantation** will be necessary for patients who progress to end-stage kidney failure.

Nutritional Considerations

Managing CKD presents a nutritional challenge. Patients with CKD frequently have risk factors for atherosclerosis (hypertension, insulin resistance, and dyslipidemia), which would benefit from a fat-, sodium-, and sugar-restricted (but high-fiber) diet. These patients also commonly present with malnutrition,[3] which calls for a less restricted meal plan. The right kind of diet, as described below, can help control blood pressure, cholesterol, and the buildup of nitrogenous waste products in the blood, and may prevent cardiovascular events. Dietary changes can also slow progression to end-stage kidney disease. The following dietary factors may be clinically important.

Low Total and Animal Protein

A prolonged high-protein intake is accompanied by an increase in GFR,[4] which in turn may cause intraglomerular hypertension and eventual loss of renal function.[5] In women with mild renal insufficiency, those with the highest protein intake had a 3.5-fold greater risk for developing a ≥15% decrease in GFR, compared with those eating the least protein. This effect was attributed to nondairy animal (not vegetable) sources of protein.[5]

Some studies suggest that restricting protein intake to 0.6 to 0.75 g/kg/d may delay the need for renal replacement therapy.[6,7] A meta-analysis of five studies, including the Modification of Diet in Renal Disease (MDRD) Study, reported a roughly 35% lower risk for renal failure or death on a low-protein diet.[8] The MDRD Study showed that protein restriction to less than 0.6 g protein/kg body weight improved the metabolic acidosis known to promote muscle catabolism and bone calcium loss in patients with CKD.[9] A more recent review, based on 8 prior trials, indicated that reducing protein intake may reduce mortality from CKD by 31%, compared with higher or unrestricted protein intake.[10] The degree of protein restriction may be crucial in accomplishing these benefits. This conclusion was reached in a study that provided graded reductions in protein intake from ≥0.8 g down to 0.3 g protein/kg body weight. Suppression of renal dysfunction progression and reductions in mortality occurred only when protein intake was no more than 0.5 mg/kg of body weight; importantly, this effect was achieved without signs of malnutrition.[11] Diets even lower in protein (0.3 g vegetable protein/kg/d, supplemented with essential amino acids and keto analogs) have been found to correct metabolic acidosis, secondary hyperparathyroidism, resistance to insulin, and decreased Na^+-K^+-ATPase activity.[12] Despite these studies, evidence for the benefit of a low-protein diet is not conclusive. The MDRD Study did not reveal significant benefit of protein restriction on progression of renal disease in all patients,[13] and a recent review based on 2 clinical trials found that, in children with CRF, protein restriction did not reduce disease progression.[14]

Sodium Restriction

Patients with CKD are often salt-sensitive, responding to elevated intakes of sodium chloride with increases in glomerular filtration and proteinuria.[15] Blood pressure is a known determinant of CKD progression, and sodium restriction is an important part of blood pressure control in kidney disease.[16] Although additional clinical trials are required, evidence indicates that patients with CKD who adhere to low-salt diets have half the rate of decline in GFR as those who follow high-sodium diets.[17]

Water-Soluble Vitamins

Low-protein diets may increase the risk for deficiency of thiamine, riboflavin, and especially pyridoxine, and vitamin C levels are also often low in CKD patients. In those patients not on dialysis, 5 mg per day of pyridoxine and 30 to 50 mg per day of vitamin C have been suggested.[18] No standard recommendations for amounts of thiamine or riboflavin exist for this group of patients.

Vitamin D Supplementation

Vitamin D deficiency is present early in the course of CKD, and correction may prevent activation of key pathogenic mechanisms in cardiovascular disease (eg, inflammation, myocardial cell hypertrophy and proliferation, and the renin-angiotensin system).[19] Although vitamin D analogues are usually given intravenously in vitamin D-deficient patients, an oral form (vitamin D_2, ergocalciferol) is recommended by the National Kidney Foundation Kidney

Disease Outcomes Quality Initiative (NKF-K/DOQI) Workgroup guidelines for stage 3 to 4 CKD patients with vitamin D deficiency and concomitant elevation in PTH.[20]

A Diet High in Fiber and Low in Saturated Fat and Cholesterol

Most individuals with chronic kidney disease die from cardiovascular causes before developing end-stage renal disease.[21] In a significant number of patients, pharmacologic (ie, statin-based) reduction of serum lipids preserves GFR and reduces proteinuria.[22] Studies show that a vegetarian diet has similar effects on lipids and also decreases proteinuria.[23,24]

Dietary and supplemental sources of fiber may be helpful for reducing the buildup of nitrogenous waste products in the blood that cause many symptoms of uremia. Fiber may act through several mechanisms, including the adsorption and excretion of metabolic wastes, as well as stimulation of colonic bacterial proliferation and subsequent incorporation of excess nitrogenous compounds.[25]

High-fiber diets have been shown to reduce blood urea concentrations by roughly 20 percent.[26-28] Although further clinical trials are needed, preliminary data indicate that high-fiber diets[26] and fiber-supplemented diets[27] both cause fecal nitrogen loss. Decreases in serum urea equal to 17% and 19% after 8 and 12 weeks of fiber supplementation, respectively, have been found with certain types of fiber, such as ispaghula husk.[27] A more recent randomized crossover study with a fermentable carbohydrate supplement found a 23% decrease in plasma urea concentration in CRF patients restricted to 0.8 g/kg protein/d.[28]

A High-Calorie Diet

Protein-calorie malnutrition in CKD may result from loss of appetite and poor food intake. In turn, these may be caused by uremia, unpalatable therapeutic diets, lack of adequate dialysis, psychosocial or economic factors, and leptin-induced anorexia and metabolic acidosis.[18] Malnutrition-related consequences of metabolic acidosis include proteolysis; negative nitrogen balance; impairments of insulin activity, glucose utilization, and albumin synthesis; and a reduction in insulin-like growth factors (eg, IGF-1).[18] Protein-energy deficit is associated with poor clinical outcome and mortality in CKD, and the low albumin concentration that is a marker for this condition is a strong predictor of mortality. Nutritional assessment is essential in these patients.

Fatty Acid Supplements

Omega-3 fatty acid supplements are under study for their role in treatment of a form of primary glomerulonephritis called immunoglobulin A nephropathy. Some results have been encouraging, at least for some patient subgroups.[29] Nevertheless, more study is required.

Avoiding Star Fruit

Several reports have noted the toxic effects of *Averrhoa carambola* in patients with both CKD and end-stage renal failure on dialysis. The primary symptoms are neurological[30] and include hiccoughing, vomiting, asthenia, paresis, muscle twitching, insomnia, mental confusion, convulsion, and coma. The outcome is fatal in some cases despite hemodialysis.[31] The exact cause has not been elucidated, although some have suggested a role for oxalate, which is more concentrated in carambola than in other foods.[30]

Orders

Low-protein (0.3 to 0.6 g/kg ideal body weight, and dependent on residual kidney function), low-sodium, high-fiber, low-saturated-fat, and low-cholesterol diet.

Nutrition consultation by registered dietitian to determine appropriate energy and protein requirements.

Exercise prescription.

Smoking cessation.

What to Tell the Family

CKD increases the risk for heart problems and further loss of kidney function. The family can help the patient make the dietary changes that will help preserve health. These include limiting sodium, restricting total and animal protein intake and following a high-fiber diet. If the patient smokes cigarettes, the family can help with the quitting process. Family members can also encourage regular exercise. All of these lifestyle changes are good for everyone involved.

When necessary, family members can also monitor medication use, to be sure that conditions such as high blood pressure and diabetes are well controlled.

References

1. Castaneda C, Gordon PL, Uhlin KL, et al. Resistance training to counteract the catabolism of a low-protein diet in patients with chronic renal insufficiency. A randomized, controlled trial. *Ann Intern Med.* 2001;135:965-976.

2. Johansen, KL. Exercise and chronic kidney disease: current recommendations. *Sports Med.* 2005;35:485-499.

3. Shoji T, Nishizawa Y. Chronic kidney disease as a metabolic syndrome with malnutrition-need for strict control of risk factors. *Intern Med.* 2005;44:179-187.

4. Schaap GH, Bilo HJ, Alferink TH, et al. The effect of a high protein intake on renal function of patients with chronic renal insufficiency. *Nephron.* 1987;47:1-6.

5. Knight EL, Stampfer MJ, Hankinson SE, et al. The impact of protein intake on renal function decline in women with normal renal function or mild renal insufficiency. *Ann Intern Med.* 2003;138:460-467.

6. Lentine K, Wrone EM. New insights into protein intake and progression of renal disease. *Curr Opin Nephrol Hypertens.* 2004;13:333-336.

7. Aparicio M, Chauveau P, Combe C. Low protein diets and outcome of renal patients. *J Nephrol.* 2001;14:433-439.

8. Pedrini MT, Levey AS, Lau J, Chalmers TC, Wang PH. The effect of dietary protein restriction on the progression of diabetic and nondiabetic renal diseases: a meta-analysis. *Ann Intern Med.* 1996;124:627-632.

9. Gennari FJ, Hood VL, Greene T, Wang X, Levey AS. Effect of dietary protein intake on serum total CO_2 concentration in chronic kidney disease: Modification of Diet in Renal Disease study findings. *Clin J Am Soc Nephrol.* 2006;1:52-57.

10. Fouque D, Laville M, Boisselle JP. Low protein diets for chronic kidney disease in non diabetic adults. *Cochrane Database Syst Rev.* 2006;(2):CD001892.

11. Ideura T, Shimazui M, Morita H, Yoshimura A. Protein intake of more than 0.5 g/kg BW/day is not effective in suppressing the progression of chronic renal failure. *Contrib Nephrol.* 2007;155:40-49.

12. Aparicio M, Chauveau P, Combe C. Are supplemented low-protein diets nutritionally safe? *Am J Kidney Dis.* 2001;37:S71-S76.

13. Levey AS, Greene T, Beck GJ, et al. Dietary protein restriction and the progression of chronic renal disease: what have all of the results of the MDRD study shown? Modification of Diet in Renal Disease Study group. *J Am Soc Nephrol.* 1999;10:2426-2439.

14. Chaturvedi S, Jones C. Protein restriction for children with chronic renal failure. *Cochrane Database Syst Rev.* 2007;(4):CD006863.

15. Weir MR, Fink JC. Salt intake and progression of chronic kidney disease: an overlooked modifiable exposure? A commentary. *Am J Kidney Dis.* 2005;45:176-188.

16. Flack JM, Peters R, Shafi T, et al. Prevention of hypertension and its complications: theoretical basis and guidelines for treatment. *J Am Soc Nephrol.* 2003;14:S92-S98.

17. Cianciaruso B, Bellizzi V, Minutolo R, et al. Salt intake and renal outcome in patients with progressive renal disease. *Miner Electrolyte Metab.* 1998;24:296-301.

18. Toigo G, Aparicio M, Attman PO, et al. Expert Working Group report on nutrition in adult patients with renal insufficiency (pt 1 of 2). *Clin Nutr.* 2000;19:197-207.

19. Levin A, Li YC. Vitamin D and its analogues: do they protect against cardiovascular disease in patients with kidney disease? *Kidney Int.* 2005;68:1973-1981.

20. Joy MS, Karagiannis PC, Peyerl FW. Outcomes of secondary hyperparathyroidism in chronic kidney disease and the direct costs of treatment. *J Manag Care Pharm.* 2007;13:397-411.

21. Chan CM. Hyperlipidemia in chronic kidney disease. *Ann Acad Med Singapore.* 2005;34:31-35.

22. Fried LF, Orchard TJ, Kasiske BL. Effect of lipid reduction on the progression of renal disease: a meta-analysis. *Kidney Int.* 2001;59:260-269.

23. Azadbakht L, Shakerhosseini R, Atabak S, et al. Beneficiary effect of dietary soy protein on lowering plasma levels of lipid and improving kidney function in type II diabetes with nephropathy. *Eur J Clin Nutr.* 2003;57:1292-1294.

24. Jibani MM, Bloodworth LL, Foden E, et al. Predominantly vegetarian diet in patients with incipient and early clinical diabetic nephropathy: effects on albumin excretion rate and nutritional status. *Diabet Med.* 1991;8:949-953.

25. Bliss DZ. Dietary fiber in conservative management of chronic renal failure. *Pediatr Nephrol.* 2004;19:1069-1070.

26. Parillo M, Riccardi G, Pacioni D, et al. Metabolic consequences of feeding a high-carbohydrate, high-fiber diet to diabetic patients with chronic kidney failure. *Am J Clin Nutr.* 1988;48:255-259.

27. Bliss DZ, Stein TP, Schleifer CR, et al. Supplementation with gum arabic fiber increases fecal nitrogen excretion and lowers serum urea nitrogen concentration in chronic renal failure patients consuming a low-protein diet. *Am J Clin Nutr.* 1996;63:392-398.

28. Younes H, Egret N, Hadj-Abdelkader M, et al. Fermentable carbohydrate supplementation alters nitrogen excretion in chronic renal failure. *J Ren Nutr.* 2006;16:67-74.

29. Appel GB, Waldman M. The IgA nephropathy treatment dilemma. *Kidney Int.* 2006;69:1939-1944.

30. Chen LL, Fang JT, Lin JL. Chronic renal disease patients with severe star fruit poisoning: hemoperfusion may be an effective alternative therapy. *Clin Toxicol* (Phila). 2005;43:197-199.

31. Tse KC, Yip PS, Lam MF, et al. Star fruit intoxication in uraemic patients: case series and review of the literature. *Int Med J.* 2003;33:314–316.

43. End-Stage Renal Disease

Chronic kidney disease (CKD) is a progressive syndrome in which the kidneys lose their ability to filter blood, concentrate urine, excrete wastes, and maintain electrolyte balance. End-stage renal disease (ESRD) is the end result of many forms of CKD. It is characterized by severely limited kidney function that is insufficient to maintain life. Thus, patients with ESRD require renal replacement therapy via dialysis or kidney transplantation.

The term *uremia* refers to the constellation of ESRD sequelae that include shortness of breath, nausea, vomiting, anorexia, weight loss, lethargy, encephalopathy, asterixis, pruritis, pericarditis, seizures, and coma. Further, more than half of patients with ESRD are malnourished, which is associated with increased mortality.

Life expectancy for ESRD patients has improved since the advent of dialysis in the 1960s. Nonetheless, the 5-year survival is less than 50%.

Risk Factors

African Americans have a significantly higher prevalence of CKD compared with other racial groups, due, in part, to higher rates of hypertension. Non-Hispanic whites generally have the lowest risk. Other risk factors for CKD and ESRD include:

Older age.

Family history of CKD.

Urinary tract disorders: urolithiasis and urinary tract obstruction.

Systemic medical disorders: diabetes mellitus, hypertension, autoimmune disorders (eg, systemic lupus erythematosus), and systemic infections.

Nephrotoxic medications; for example, NSAIDs and contrast dye.

Tobacco use.

Diagnosis

ESRD is defined by a glomerular filtration rate that is less than 15 mL/min/1.73 m^2 and the need for replacement therapy.

Creatinine and blood urea nitrogen (BUN) are significantly elevated.

Testing to determine the underlying etiology may include urinalysis, renal imaging such as ultrasound and CT scan, and renal biopsy.

Due to the kidneys' importance in regulating electrolyte and acid-base balance, ESRD leads to hyperkalemia, hyperphosphatemia, often hypocalcemia, and anion gap metabolic acidosis. Vitamin D deficiency is also common.

Treatment

In general, once CKD has degenerated to ESRD over the course of years, it is irreversible. Treatment is aimed at treating complications and replacing renal function via dialysis or transplantation.

Referral to a nephrologist should occur once GFR reaches 30 mL/min/1.73 m^2 in progressive CKD, and otherwise as early as possible in order to plan for long-term therapy. Kidney transplantation is the treatment of choice for appropriate candidates, and it requires considerable preparation and planning. Avoiding dialysis prior to transplant may reduce morbidity and mortality. In patients who require dialysis prior to transplant, or those ineligible for transplant, there are 2 options for maintenance dialysis. Hemodialysis involves the creation of an arterovenous fistula and dialysis graft, usually in the arm, and treatment at a dialysis center, typically 3 times weekly. Peritoneal dialysis involves inserting the dialysate into the patient's abdomen and allowing dialysis to occur continuously or intermittently without requiring the patient to travel regularly to a dialysis center. Both methods have advantages and disadvantages, and outcomes are similar.

Complications

It is essential to treat ESRD complications that may arise. When remaining kidney function is markedly reduced, these treatments often are used in conjunction with dialysis therapy:

- **Volume overload and hypertension** (treated with a dietary sodium restriction).

- **Hyperkalemia** (treated with a low-potassium diet and, acutely, with kayexalate).

- **Hypocalcemia** (treated with calcitriol or other vitamin D analogues).

- **Metabolic acidosis** (treated with alkali therapy, such as sodium bicarbonate).

- **Hyperphosphatemia** (treated with dietary phosphate restriction and phosphate binders).

- **Anemia** (treated with erythropoietin).

Psychiatric Interventions

Psychiatric disorders are common and can interfere with treatment. Adherence to recommended diet and fluid restrictions increases life expectancy and can reduce the risk of medical complications and treatment side effects, as well as improve quality of life.[1] However, psychiatric disorders may interfere with treatment compliance, causing significantly higher interdialytic weight gain.[2] Depression is the most common psychiatric problem in ESRD patients and is associated with both mortality and morbidity.[3] Antidepressant treatment (pharmacologic and psychotherapy combined) is not only effective in improving mood, but also improves biochemical indicators of nutritional status in hemodialysis patients.[4] Psychological interventions have improved adherence to fluid restriction and related interdialytic weight gain.[5]

Exercise

Exercise should be encouraged in ESRD patients. Exercise training in patients with ESRD and hypertension reduces blood pressure and has other cardiovascular benefits, such as reducing the incidence of cardiac arrhythmias and improving left ventricular function and heart rate variability.[6,7] Exercise also reduces depression in ESRD patients.[8]

Nutritional Considerations

Nutrition-related concerns include maintenance of acceptable weight and serum proteins (eg, albumin), prevention of renal osteodystrophy, and reduction of cardiovascular risk.

Weight Maintenance and Protein Requirements

Protein needs are higher in patients with ESRD due to losses that occur during dialysis. The recommended dietary protein intake for clinically stable maintenance hemodialysis patients is 1.2 g/kg body weight/d, and 1.2 to 1.3 g/kg body weight/d for individuals on peritoneal dialysis, 50% of which should come from sources high in biological value.[9]

Nutritional status should be assessed, and every patient with ESRD should receive a diet plan. ESRD patients on dialysis may spontaneously reduce protein and calorie intake as a result of uremic toxins, elevations in leptin and other cytokines, and delayed gastric emptying.[10] The average energy intake of patients with ESRD is lower than the recommended 30 to 35 kcal/kg,[11] and 50% of patients reveal evidence of malnutrition.[12]

To prevent malnutrition-related morbidity and mortality, ESRD patients on dialysis should have periodic nutrition screening, consisting of laboratory measures (eg, albumin), comparison of initial weight with both usual body weight and percent of ideal body weight, subjective global assessment, and dietary interviews with review of food diaries. Nutrition counseling should be intensive initially and provided every 1 or 2 months thereafter. If nutrient intake appears inadequate, malnutrition is apparent, or adverse events or illnesses threaten nutritional status, counseling should be increased. If protein-calorie needs cannot be met with the usual diet, patients should be offered dietary supplements or, if necessary, tube feeding or parenteral nutrition to approximate protein and calorie requirements.[9]

Sodium and Potassium Balance

ESRD patients should avoid high-sodium foods. Hypertension in dialysis patients is largely attributed to positive sodium balance and volume expansion.[13] While many patients on dialysis can effectively control blood pressure without drugs on a low-sodium (2 g) diet and a low-sodium (130 mmol) dialysate,[14] current practice is such that almost 70% of dialysis patients require antihypertensive medications. Although many patients may not achieve a therapeutic degree of sodium restriction, those who do can effectively control blood pressure and reverse left ventricular hypertrophy.[15]

A high-potassium diet is normally desirable to control blood pressure and reduce risk for stroke. However, individuals with ESRD on hemodialysis cannot to excrete potassium. Therefore, ESRD patients may need to avoid such foods as bananas, melon, legumes, potatoes, tomatoes, pumpkin, winter squash, sweet potatoes, spinach, orange juice, milk, and bran cereal to prevent life-threatening hyperkalemia-induced arrhythmia. Evidence indicates that the vast majority of patients comply with potassium restriction.[1] In patients on peritoneal dialysis, hyperkalemia tolerate this diet because they are unable is significantly less likely, and hypokalemia has been reported in some patients, at times requiring an increase in potassium-containing foods and even potassium supplementation.[16]

Fluid Restriction

It is essential that ESRD patients restrict their fluid intake. Without adherence to a specified fluid allowance, patients are more likely to have poorly controlled blood pressure[17] and risk congestive heart failure. The typical fluid allowance for patients on dialysis is 700 to 1000 mL/d, plus urine output.

Phosphorus

Elevated blood phosphorus concentrations are associated with increased mortality in ESRD patients[12] and increase the risk for cardiovascular events, at least in part by contributing to vascular calcification.[18] Excess phosphorus also causes secondary hyperparathyroidism, triggering the release of calcium from the bone matrix, and osteodystrophy.[12] Management of hyperphosphatemia and renal osteodystrophy has improved with phosphate binders, particularly sevelamer hydrochloride (Renagel), which also helps prevent hypercalcemia-related vascular calcification.[19] Long-acting nicotinic acid or niacin is also effective in lowering serum phosphorus while increasing plasma high-density lipoprotein concentrations. However, certain factors continue to confound adequate control of phosphorus levels. These include covert phosphate intake from processed foods,[20] treatment with high doses of vitamin D analogues, and the high protein needs of ESRD patients. Protein intake over 50 grams/d causes positive phosphate balance, in spite of phosphate binder therapy.[12,21]

Micronutrient Supplements

Micronutrient supplements are essential for ESRD patients. Individuals on dialysis commonly suffer from deficiencies of vitamin C, folate, vitamin B_6, calcium, vitamin D, iron, zinc, and possibly selenium, which can contribute to an antioxidant-deficient state.[22] The National Kidney Foundation clinical practice guidelines for nutrition in chronic renal failure suggest that patients achieve 100% of the Dietary Reference Intakes (DRI) for vitamins A, C, E, K, B_1, B_2, B_6, B_{12}, and folic acid, as well as 100% of the DRI for copper and zinc.[9] As a result of restricted intake of many foods and losses of water-soluble vitamins during dialysis, patients are usually given specially formulated vitamins. Intravenous forms of vitamin D analogues and iron are typically given to patients. While oral iron supplements may not be needed, oral vitamin D (ergocalciferol) may be beneficial. A deficiency of this vitamin may be a risk factor for early mortality in ESRD patients, and vitamin D supplementation may improve survival.[23]

Certain other dietary supplements may be helpful. Supplementation with L-carnitine has been approved by the US Food and Drug Administration to treat carnitine depletion in dialysis patients. In small studies, L-carnitine has been shown to improve lipid metabolism, protein nutrition, antioxidant status, and anemia.[24] Carnitine treatment in the amount of 1 gram or greater during each dialysis session for 10 or more sessions per month was associated with reduced need for future hospitalization in one study.[25] However, some large studies have not confirmed carnitine's benefits. Therefore, evidence remains inadequate to support the routine use of carnitine in patients who do not have signs of deficiency.[26] Both vitamin C (250 mg/d) and vitamin E (400 IU/d) have proven effective in some patients for treating painful muscle cramps, and they provide a less toxic alternative to quinine therapy.[27,28] However, additional clinical trials are required before these can be used as standard therapy.

Saturated Fat and Cholesterol

Dialysis patients should follow a diet low in saturated fat and cholesterol. These patients are at very high risk for coronary artery disease. They often have increases in serum triglycerides and low high-density lipoprotein (HDL) cholesterol.[29] Although they must eat a relatively high-calorie diet to spare protein, patients on dialysis should avoid foods that raise triglycerides and cholesterol concentrations (see Dyslipidemias chapter).

The relationship between total cholesterol and cardiovascular mortality is clearly evident in ESRD patients,[30] although this relationship may be obscured in those with elevated markers of inflammation or malnutrition, preexisting cardiovascular disease, diabetes, or advanced age.

Orders

2-gram sodium, 2-gram potassium, phosphate-restricted diet, low in saturated fat and cholesterol.

Nutrition consultation to assess calorie and protein requirements and instruct patient in above dietary recommendations.

B-complex with small doses of vitamin C, 1 tablet daily by mouth. Consider supplemental ergocalciferol or cholecalciferol.

What to Tell the Family

End-stage renal disease is often preventable with proper control of blood pressure, blood lipids, and blood glucose, in combination with appropriate medications. Family members can help ESRD patients maintain a healthful diet, regular physical activity, and appropriate medication regimens.

References

1. Durose CL, Holdsworth M, Watson V, et al. Knowledge of dietary restrictions and the medical consequences of noncompliance by patients on hemodialysis are not predictive of dietary compliance. *J Am Diet Assoc.* 2004;104:35-41.

2. Taskapan H, Ates F, Kaya B, et al. Psychiatric disorders and large interdialytic weight gain in patients on chronic haemodialysis. *Nephrology* (Carlton). 2005;10:15-20.

3. Wuerth D, Finkelstein SH, Kliger AS, et al. Chronic peritoneal dialysis patients diagnosed with clinical depression: results of pharmacologic therapy. *Semin Dial.* 2003;16:424-427.

4. Koo JR, Yoon JY, Joo MH, et al. Treatment of depression and effect of antidepression treatment on nutritional status in chronic hemodialysis patients. *Am J Med Sci.* 2005;329:1-5.

5. Sharp J, Wild MR, Gumley AI. A systematic review of psychological interventions for the treatment of nonadherence to fluid-intake restrictions in people receiving hemodialysis. *Am J Kidney Dis.* 2005;45:15-27.

6. Kouidi EJ. Central and peripheral adaptations to physical training in patients with end-stage renal disease. *Sports Med.* 2001;31:651-665.

7. Deligiannis A, Kouidi E, Tourkantonis A. Effects of physical training on heart rate variability in patients on hemodialysis. *Am J Cardiol.* 1999;84:197-202.

8. Levendoglu F, Altintepe L, Okudan N, et al. A twelve week exercise program improves the psychological status, quality of life and work capacity in hemodialysis patients. *J Nephrol.* 2004;17:826-832.

9. National Kidney Foundation. Clinical practice guidelines for nutrition in chronic renal failure. K/DOQI, National Kidney Foundation. *Am J Kidney Dis.* 2000;35(suppl 2):S1-S140.

10. Mehrotra R, Kopple JD. Nutritional management of maintenance dialysis patients: why aren't we doing better? *Annu Rev Nutr.* 2001;21:343-379.

11. Cuppari L, Avesani CM. Energy requirements in patients with chronic kidney disease. *J Ren Nutr.* 2004;14:121-126.

12. Ritz E. The clinical management of hyperphosphatemia. *J Nephrol.* 2005;18:221-228.

13. Wang X, Axelsson J, Lindholm B, et al. Volume status and blood pressure in continuous ambulatory peritoneal dialysis patients. *Blood Purif.* 2005;23:373-378.

14. Krautzig S, Janssen U, Koch KM, Granolleras C, Shaldon S. Dietary salt restriction and reduction of dialysate sodium to control hypertension in maintenance hemodialysis patients. *Nephrol Dial Transplant.* 1998;13:552-553.

15. Ozkahaya M, Toz H, Ozerkan F, et al. Impact of volume control on left ventricular hypertrophy in dialysis patients. *J Nephrol.* 2002;15:655-660.

16. Newman LN, Weiss MF, Berger J, Priester A, Negrea LA, Cacho CP. The law of unintended consequences in action: increase in incidence of hypokalemia with improved adequacy of dialysis. *Adv Perit Dial.* 2000;16:134-137.

17. Rahman M, Fu P, Sehgal AR, et al. Interdialytic weight gain, compliance with dialysis regimen, and age are independent predictors of blood pressure in hemodialysis patients. *Am J Kidney Dis.* 2000;35:257-265.

18. Cozzolino M, Brancaccio D, Gallieni M, et al. Pathogenesis of vascular calcification in chronic kidney disease. *Kidney Int.* 2005;68:429-436.

19. Klemmer PJ. Calcium loading, calcium accumulation, and associated cardiovascular risks in dialysis patients. *Blood Purif.* 2005;23(suppl 1):12-19.

20. Uribarri J, Calvo MS. Hidden sources of phosphorus in the typical American diet: does it matter in nephrology? *Semin Dial.* 2003;16:186-188.

21. Rufino M, de Bonis E, Martin M, et al. Is it possible to control hyperphosphataemia with diet, without inducing protein malnutrition? *Nephrol Dial Transplant.* 1998;13(suppl 3):65-67.

22. Kalantar-Zadeh K, Kopple JD. Trace elements and vitamins in maintenance dialysis patients. *Adv Ren Replace Ther.* 2003;10:170-182.

23. Wolf M, Shah A, Gutierrez O, et al. Vitamin D levels and early mortality among incident hemodialysis patients. *Kidney Int.* 2007;72:1004-1013.

24. Bellinghieri G, Santoro D, Calvani M, et al. Carnitine and hemodialysis. *Am J Kidney Dis.* 2003;41(suppl 1):S116-S122.

25. Weinhandl ED, Rao M, Gilbertson DT, Collins AJ, Pereira BJ. Protective effect of intravenous levocarnitine on subsequent-month hospitalization among prevalent hemodialysis patients, 1998 to 2003. *Am J Kidney Dis.* 2007;50:803-812.

26. Steinman TI, Nissenson AR, Glassock RJ, et al. L-carnitine use in dialysis patients: is national coverage for supplementation justified? What were CMS regulators thinking--or were they? *Nephrol News Issues.* 2003;17:28-30, 32-34, 36.

27. Khajehdehi P, Mojerlou M, Behzadi S, et al. A randomized, double-blind, placebo-controlled trial of supplementary vitamins E, C and their combination for treatment of haemodialysis cramps. *Nephrol Dial Transplant.* 2001;16:1448-1451.

28. Roca AO, Jarjoura D, Blend D, et al. Dialysis leg cramps. Efficacy of quinine versus vitamin E. *ASAIO J.* 1992;38:M481-M485.

29. Wanner C, Krane V, Metzger T, et al. Lipid changes and statins in chronic renal insufficiency and dialysis. *J Nephrol.* 2001;14(suppl 4):S76-S80.

30. Wan RK, Mark PB, Jardine AG. The cholesterol paradox is flawed; cholesterol must be lowered in dialysis patients. *Semin Dial.* 2007;20:504-509.

44. Nephrolithiasis

Nephrolithiasis is characterized by the formation of crystalline aggregates ("kidney stones") that can develop anywhere along the urinary tract. Kidney stones are common in Western societies; nearly 10% of Americans will develop a symptomatic kidney stone during their lifetime. The rate of recurrence is >50%.

The 5 major stone compositions are calcium oxalate, calcium phosphate, magnesium ammonium phosphate (struvite), uric acid, and cystine. Calcium-based stones are the most common, causing more than 75% of cases, and calcium oxalate is the most common type of stone overall.

Most often, stones are due to increased concentrations of stone-forming material in the urine, either from increased excretion or decreased urinary volume. Stone formation occurs when a stone-forming material becomes supersaturated in the urine and begins the process of crystal formation.

Severe flank pain, known as renal colic, occurs with stones that become lodged in the ureter. It may radiate to the lower abdomen, groin, testicles, or perineum. Lower urinary tract symptoms, including dysuria, urgency, and frequency, occur with stones that become lodged at the ureterovesical junction. Nausea, vomiting, hematuria (gross and/or microscopic), and costovertebral angle tenderness may also be present, even in the absence of pain.

Risk Factors

Whites have a greater risk than Asian Americans, Latinos, and blacks.

Age. Risk increases with increasing age.

Male gender. Males are more likely to develop stones than females.

History of nephrolithiasis. Individuals who have developed a kidney stone have a ≈50% chance of recurrence within 10 years.

Geography. Areas of elevated temperatures and high humidity appear to have an increased incidence of stone disease.

Nationality. Developed countries have a much higher risk of nephrolithiasis compared with developing countries. This is presumably due to dietary factors.

Obesity. Compared with persons at or near ideal body weight (BMI = 21 to 23), obese men (BMI ≥30) have a 33% greater risk for stone formation, while obese women have a 200% greater risk.[1] Patients who have had bariatric surgery are at risk for hyperoxaluria, which increases risk for kidney stones and kidney failure.[2]

Diabetes.

Diet (See below).

Family history. A family history of nephrolithiasis raises risk 2 to 3 times.

Cystinuria. A history of cystinuria, an autosomal recessive disorder, increases risk of cystine stone formation.

Urinary stasis (eg, bladder outlet obstruction), **chronic urinary tract infections**, **dehydration** (eg, diarrhea or malabsorption), and certain **antiviral medications** (eg, indinavir, acyclovir) may also raise risk of nephrolithiasis. In addition, a guaifenesin metabolite may bind with calcium to form stones.

Diagnosis

Clinical presentation is highly specific for kidney stones, especially in patients with a history of the condition.

Noncontrast abdominal CT scan is the preferred means for detecting stones and urinary tract obstructions. Abdominal (kidney-ureter-bladder) x-ray will identify many radiopaque stones but cannot detect small or radiolucent (uric acid and proteinaceous) stones or obstructions. The intravenous pyelogram has been largely replaced by the more rapid abdominal CT intravenous pyelogram or by noncontrast CT with abdominal x-ray. X-rays permit an assessment of radiolucence of stones.

Ultrasound is used in patients who should avoid radiation (eg, pregnant women). Doppler ultrasonography may also aid the diagnosis of obstruction.

Urinalysis will usually reveal hematuria. Sediment examination may reveal pathognomonic crystals, and pH may give clues about etiology. Twenty-four–hour urine collections (for creatinine, calcium, phosphorus, oxalate, uric acid, cystine, citrate) on 2 occasions, after complete resolution and recovery from the acute event and resultant treatments, can aid diagnosis.

A chemistry panel that includes calcium and uric acid may help reveal etiology (eg, hyperuricemia and hyperparathyroidism).

If a stone is passed, it should be sent to the laboratory for analysis.

Treatment

Immediate urologic attention is necessary for patients who present with fever, renal failure, intractable pain, persistent nausea, or urinary tract infections.

Small (<5 mm) stones often pass spontaneously. Increased fluid intake facilitates passage.

Selective alpha-blockers (eg, tamsulosin) or **calcium channel blockers** also may facilitate stone passage when used in combination with **steroids**.

Nonsteroidal anti-inflammatory drugs (eg, indomethacin, ketorolac) and/or **narcotics** may be administered for pain. However, NSAIDs may increase bleeding risk following ureteroscopy or shock wave lithotripsy.

About 10% to 20% of stones require surgical removal. Minimally invasive surgical techniques include shock wave lithotripsy, percutaneous nephrolithotomy, and ureteroscopy. Open renal and ureteral surgery is necessary in about 1% of cases.

Extracorporeal shock wave lithotripsy is the treatment of choice for most renal calculi. Percutaneous nephrostolithotomy is as effective as open surgery and is generally indicated for large or complex stones and cystine or monohydrate calcium stones, which are relatively resistant to lithotripsy. Ureterorenoscopy with holmium laser lithotripsy is the treatment of choice for ureteral stones and stones that failed lithotripsy.

Stone-specific treatment may be necessary in some cases.

For stones caused by indinavir antiretroviral therapy, hydration and temporary interruption of therapy (1 to 3 days) may decrease recurrence.[3]

Nutritional Considerations

The incidence of kidney stones increases with animal protein intake, obesity, and poor fluid intake. Oxalates appear to be problematic primarily in persons with low calcium intake, and a vegetarian diet may offer significant protection against stone formation. However, because recurrence is common, treatment lends itself to dietary modification.

In observational studies, the following factors are associated with reduced risk:

Reducing Intake of Animal Protein and Sodium

A high animal protein intake causes a significant increase in the urinary excretion of calcium, oxalate, and uric acid, 3 of the 6 main urinary risk factors for calcium stone formation.[4] Compared with individuals eating 50 grams or less of animal protein per day, those eating the most (77 g or more) have a 33% higher risk for kidney stones.[5] A diet restricted in animal protein and sodium, when compared with a standard (low-calcium) diet used for prevention of calcium oxalate stone formation, reduces the risk for stone recurrence by half.[6]

Limiting Oxalates

Although calcium intake was previously considered a culprit, current evidence indicates that urinary oxalate is the most important determinant of calcium oxalate crystallization.[7] Individuals who tend to form stones of this type experience a significant increase in urinary oxalate excretion with even small increases in oxalate intake, whereas persons who do not form these stones do not experience a similar increase in urinary oxalate excretion with increased oxalate intake.[8] Patients should be advised to avoid high-oxalate foods, such as rhubarb, spinach, strawberries, chocolate (especially dark), wheat bran, nuts, beets, and lea. Alternatively, certain food preparation methods may be used to reduce oxalate content. Boiling, for example, reduces soluble oxalate content by 30% to 87%, compared with steaming, which achieves a 5% to 53% reduction.[9]

Calcium at Mealtime

Calcium intake from foods lowers the risk for calcium oxalate stones,[10] presumably because calcium binds oxalates within the intestinal tract. Oxalate absorption decreases as calcium intakes increase over a range of 200 to 1200 mg per day.[11] Individuals consuming the greatest amount of calcium from foods have about a 30% lower risk for stone formation compared with persons consuming the lowest amounts.[12] Research findings are mixed regarding the potential for calcium supplements to affect risk for urolithiasis. In the Nurses' Health Study, women taking calcium supplements experienced a 20% increase in risk for stone formation compared with their risk when not using supplements.[10] However, individuals taking doses of >500 mg per day have been associated with decreased risk.[13] Whether taking calcium supplements contributes to stone formation may depend on timing, with between-meal dosing associated with the risk for stone formation, while supplements taken with meals may reduce risk by binding dietary oxalates in the digestive tract.[10]

Limiting Colas, Coffee, and Tea

Although further research is required, evidence indicates that cola consumption significantly increases urinary calcium[14] and oxalate excretion.[15] Patients who avoid colas and other phosphoric acid–containing beverages have been found to have a 15% lower rate of stone recurrence than those who continue to consume these beverages.[16] The association of coffee and tea intake with risk for stone formation appears to be less controversial, with findings of an inverse association with risk.[17,18] Overall fluid consumption appears to be most important. Individuals who consume the highest amount of fluid each day (~2.6 L) have a 30% to 40% lower risk for stone formation than those consuming the least amount (~1.4 L).[5,17]

Vegetarian Diets

Vegetarian diets are associated with low excretion of calcium, oxalate, and uric acid[4] and may lower the risk for urolithiasis in a number of ways. These include the absence of animal protein and provision of higher amounts of magnesium and potassium, both of which are associated with lower risk for stone formation.[13,19] Vegetarian diets also provide ample amounts of whole grains high in phytic acid, a plant constituent that is associated with about a 40% lower risk for stone formation in persons eating the most (about 900 mg/d) compared with those eating the least amount (about 600 mg/d).[20] Nationwide surveys have determined that the risk for stone formation is 40% to 60% lower in individuals following vegetarian diets.[21] Compared with individuals following self-selected or Western diets, those on a vegetarian diet also have a decreased risk for uric acid crystallization.[22]

Avoidance of high-dose vitamin C. The association between high-dose vitamin C supplements and stone formation is controversial. Clinical studies with high-dose vitamin C supplements (2000 mg/d) have found that both stone formers and non-stone formers have an increase in oxalate absorption and endogenous synthesis that could contribute to stone formation.[23] In the Health Professionals Study of more than 45,000 men, consumption of vitamin C up to and over 1500 mg per day had no association with stone formation.[24] However, a longer follow-up period of these subjects indicated that those who consumed ≥1000 mg of vitamin C per day had a roughly 40% greater risk for kidney stone formation compared with those who consumed less than the recommended dietary allowance of 90 mg/d.[12] By comparison, there was no association between high-dose vitamin C and stone risk for women in the Nurses' Health Study.[25]

Magnesium. In the Health Professionals Study of more than 45,000 men, those with the highest magnesium intakes had a roughly 30% lower risk for kidney stone than those consuming the least magnesium.[12] Controlled clinical trials with magnesium supplements have not indicated a significant protective effect.[26]

Dietary citrates. Citrates inhibit the formation of calcium oxalate stones by binding to calcium and interfering with calcium oxalate crystallization. However, hypocitraturia is common, found in 20% of stone formers, and increases the risk of stones.[27] Citrate supplementation (eg, potassium citrate or potassium-magnesium citrate) is commonly prescribed for these patients. Gastrointestinal disturbances may limit compliance and benefit.[28,29]

Dietary citrates in the form of fruit juices (eg, orange, grapefruit, apple, lemon) have been investigated for their potential to prevent stone formation. Of these, only lemon juice has been found to both increase urinary citrate and significantly reduce stone recurrence,[29] and additional confirmation from controlled trials is needed before lemon juice can be considered a mainstay of therapy in hypocitraturic patients.

Wine. In a prospective study, each 8-oz serving of wine decreased the risk for stone formation by 39% to 59%.[17,18] However, the potent diuretic effects of alcohol give it the potential to cause dehydration and increase stone risk if adequate consumption of other fluids is not maintained.

Orders

See Basic Diet Orders chapter.

For patients with suspected or documented oxalate stones, consult with registered dietitian for instructions on how to follow a low-oxalate, high-magnesium diet. Avoid vitamin C supplements over 1000 mg/d.

Consume ≥2.5 L of fluid per day.

What to Tell the Family

The risk of kidney stones is influenced by dietary factors, particularly high intake of animal protein and salt, along with low fluid consumption. Family members can help the patient in making diet changes, and may benefit from these changes themselves. It is helpful to avoid animal protein and oxalate-containing foods, get adequate intake of calcium-rich foods at mealtime to reduce oxalate absorption, and drink adequate fluids.

References

1. Taylor EN, Stampfer MJ, Curhan GC. Obesity, weight gain, and the risk of kidney stones. *JAMA*. 2005;293:455-462.

2. Asplin JR, Coe FL. Hyperoxaluria in kidney stone formers treated with modern bariatric surgery. *J Urol*. 2007;177:565-569.

3. Condra JH, Schleif WA, Blahy OM, et al. In vivo emergence of HIV-1 variants resistant to multiple protease inhibitors. *Nature*.1995;374:569-571.

4. Robertson WG, Peacock M, Heyburn PJ, et al. Should recurrent calcium oxalate stone formers become vegetarians? *Br J Urol*. 1979;51:427-431.

5. Curhan GC, Willett WC, Rimm EB, et al. A prospective study of dietary calcium and other nutrients and the risk of symptomatic kidney stones. *N Engl J Med*. 1993;328:833-838.

6. Borghi L, Schianchi T, Meschi T, et al. Comparison of two diets for the prevention of recurrent stones in idiopathic hypercalciuria. *N Engl J Med*. 2002;346:77-84.

7. Lewandowski S, Rodgers AL. Idiopathic calcium oxalate urolithiasis: risk factors and conservative treatment. *Clin Chim Acta*. 2004;345:17-34.

8. de O G Mendonca C, Martini LA, Baxmann AC, et al. Effects of an oxalate load on urinary oxalate excretion in calcium stone formers. *J Ren Nutr*. 2003;13:39-46.

9. Chai W, Liebman M. Effect of different cooking methods on vegetable oxalate content. *J Agric Food Chem.* 2005;53:3027-3030.

10. Curhan GC, Willett WC, Speizer FE, et al. Comparison of dietary calcium with supplemental calcium and other nutrients as factors affecting the risk for kidney stones in women. *Ann Intern Med.* 1997;126:497-504.

11. von Unruh GE, Voss S, Sauerbruch T, et al. Dependence of oxalate absorption on the daily calcium intake. *J Am Soc Nephrol.* 2004;15:1567-1573.

12. Taylor EN, Stampfer MJ, Curhan GC. Dietary factors and the risk of incident kidney stones in men: new insights after 14 years of follow-up. *J Am Soc Nephrol.* 2004;15:3225-3232.

13. Hall WD, Pettinger M, Oberman A, et al. Risk factors for kidney stones in older women in the southern United States. *Am J Med Sci.* 2001;322:12-18.

14. Iguchi M, Umekawa T, Takamura C, et al. Glucose metabolism in renal stone patients. *Urol Int.* 1993;51:185-190.

15. Rodgers A. Effect of cola consumption on urinary biochemical and physicochemical risk factors associated with calcium oxalate urolithiasis. *Urol Res.* 1999;27:77-81.

16. Shuster J, Jenkins A, Logan C, et al. Soft drink consumption and urinary stone recurrence: a randomized prevention trial. *J Clin Epidemiol.* 1992;45:911-916.

17. Curhan GC, Willett WC, Speizer FE, et al. Beverage use and risk for kidney stones in women. *Ann Intern Med.* 1998;128:534-540.

18. Curhan GC, Willett WC, Rimm EB, et al. Prospective study of beverage use and the risk of kidney stones. *Am J Epidemiol.* 1996;143:240-247.

19. Hirvonen T, Pietinen P, Virtanen M, Albanes D, Virtamo J. Nutrient intake and use of beverages and the risk of kidney stones among male smokers. *Am J Epidemiol.* 1999;150:187-194.

20. Curhan GC, Willett WC, Knight EL, et al. Dietary factors and the risk of incident kidney stones in younger women: Nurses' Health Study II. *Arch Intern Med.* 2004;164:885-891.

21. Robertson WG, Peacock M, Marshall DH. Prevalence of urinary stone disease in vegetarians. *Eur Urol.* 1982;8:334-339.

22. Siener R, Hesse A. The effect of a vegetarian and different omnivorous diets on urinary risk factors for uric acid stone formation. *Eur J Nutr.* 2003;42:332-337.

23. Massey LK, Liebman M, Kynast-Gales SA. Ascorbate increases human oxaluria and kidney stone risk. *J Nutr.* 2005;135:1673-1677.

24. Curhan GC, Willett WC, Rimm EB, Stampfer MJ. A prospective study of the intake of vitamins C and B6, and the risk of kidney stones in men. *J Urol.* 1996;155:1847-1851.

25. Curhan GC, Willett WC, Speizer FE, Stampfer MJ. Intake of vitamins B6 and C and the risk of kidney stones. *J Am Soc Nephrol.* 1999;10:840-845.

26. Massey L. Magnesium therapy for nephrolithiasis. *Magnes Res.* 2005;18:123-126.

27. Reynolds TM. ACP Best Practice No 181: Chemical pathology clinical investigation and management of nephrolithiasis. *J Clin Pathol.* 2005;58:134-140.

28. Kang DE, Sur RL, Haleblian GE, Fitzsimons NJ, Borawski KM, Preminger GM. Long-term lemonade based dietary manipulation in patients with hypocitraturic nephrolithiasis. *J Urol.* 2007;177:1358-1362.

29. Jendle-Bengten C, Tiselius HG. Long-term follow-up of stone formers treated with a low dose of sodium potassium citrate. *Scand J Urol Nephrol.* 2000;34:36-41.

45. Benign Prostatic Hyperplasia

Benign prostatic hyperplasia (BPH) is the most common benign neoplasm of men. The stromal and, to a lesser degree, epithelial cells of the prostate become hyperplastic, causing the prostate to enlarge. The prevalence of BPH increases with age, rising from about 8% in the third decade of life to greater than 90% in the ninth decade. The etiology is multifactorial and not well understood. Family history, age, and hormone concentrations appear to play a role in BPH development. Testosterone and dihydrotestosterone, while necessary for BPH to occur, are not alone adequate to cause the condition. The role of estrogen in BPH remains unclear. Symptoms are related to obstruction of the urethra and include hesitancy, reduced urine flow rate, dribbling, urgency, frequency, and nocturia.

Risk Factors

The following factors are associated with increased risk of BPH:

Aging. BPH occurs more commonly with advancing age.

Family history. Data suggest an autosomal dominant genetic pattern.[1]

Androgen. Higher androgen concentrations are associated with BPH.

Obesity. Excessive overweight may make detection more difficult via digital rectal examination (DRE). In addition, obesity, particularly abdominal obesity, may increase risk for BPH, presumably due to resultant hyperinsulinemia.[2,3] Elevated levels of estrogens secondary to conversion from testosterone in adipose tissues may also play a role.

Physical inactivity. The Health Professionals Study and Massachusetts Male Aging Study found lower levels of physical activity to be associated with increased risk for BPH.[4,5]

Diagnosis

DRE will typically detect prostate enlargement. The surface of the prostate should be smooth and is usually symmetrical; asymmetry or induration suggests malignancy. Some men with large prostates have no obstructive symptoms, while men with small prostates may have obstructive symptoms.

Prostate biopsy, ultrasound, and/or the prostate-specific antigen (PSA) blood test help rule out malignancy and confirm a diagnosis of BPH. Other tests are available to evaluate bladder and urethral function.

Treatment

The purpose of BPH treatment is to improve the patient's quality of life.

Observation alone ("watchful waiting") is appropriate if symptoms are mild.

Medical treatment includes use of **alpha-adrenergic antagonists**, such as prazosin, terazosin, doxazosin, tamsulosin, and alfuzosin, which relax smooth muscle. Tamsulosin and alfuzosin are more specific for the alpha 1a prostate receptor, causing fewer systemic side effects, compared with other medications.[6]

In cases of moderate or greater prostate enlargement, **5-alpha-reductase inhibitors**, such as finasteride, can be administered to block the conversion of testosterone to dihydrotestosterone. A combination of an alpha-adrenergic antagonist and finasteride appears to improve long-term outcomes.[7]

Plant extracts from saw palmetto (*Serenoa repens*), *Pygeum africanum*, and *Secale cereale*, along with concentrated beta-sitosterol (a plant sterol), may play treatment roles, but need further investigation.

Surgical options for severe refractory symptoms include transurethral resection of the prostate (TURP), transurethral incision of the prostate, open prostatectomy, laser prostatectomy (or photovaporization), microwave therapy, and transurethral needle ablation, among others.

Nutritional Considerations

Research studies have examined the relationship between dietary factors and the risk of BPH. The following factors are associated with reduced risk in epidemiologic studies:

Limiting or avoiding animal products and vegetable oils. Several studies have implicated high total meat and animal product intake in BPH, particularly beef and dairy products.[8-11] The Health Professionals Follow-Up Study found that higher intakes of total protein, animal protein, and polyunsaturated fatty acids, including eicosapentanoic acid (EPA), docosahexanoic acid (DHA), and vegetable oils, were all associated with BPH.[12]

Soy product intake. Epidemiologic evidence shows that Asian men have a lower risk for prostate disease, compared with their Western counterparts; some have suggested that the difference may be partly attributable to a higher intake of isoflavones in Asian diets.[13,14]

Isoflavones in soy foods may inhibit 5-alpha reductase and aromatase, which, in turn, reduces the age-related increase in estrogen's effect on prostate stromal cell proliferation.[13]

Lower energy intake. Some studies have shown an association between higher caloric intake and a greater risk for BPH. The Health Professionals Follow-Up Study reported a 50% increase in risk for BPH in men in the highest decile of calorie intake compared with those in the lowest decile, as well as a 70% higher risk for moderate-to-severe lower urinary tract symptoms in men consuming the most calories.[12]

Fruit and vegetable intake. The Health Professionals Study found that consumption of fruits and vegetables rich in beta-carotene, lutein, and vitamin C was inversely related to BPH.[15] Examples of these foods are carrots, spinach, broccoli, collard greens, corn, oranges, melon, and kiwi.

Orders

See Basic Diet Orders chapter.

Low-fat diet.

Exercise prescription.

What to Tell the Family

BPH is not necessarily a symptom of old age. Rather, it is a problem that has dietary and lifestyle components. Patients should consider following a reduced-fat diet that is low in or free from animal products and includes regular consumption of soy foods. Effective medications are available with minimal side effects. Severe obstructive symptoms (eg, urinary retention and bladder stones) should be treated with surgery to avoid permanent bladder failure.

References

1. Sanda MG, Beaty TH, Stutzman RE, et al. Genetic susceptibility of benign prostatic hyperplasia. *J Urol.* 1994;152:115-119.

2. Dahle SE, Chokkalingam AP, Gao YT, Deng J, Stanczyk FZ, Hsing AW. Body size and serum levels of insulin and leptin in relation to the risk of benign prostatic hyperplasia. *J Urol.* 2002;168:599-604.

3. Hammarsten J, Hogstedt B, Holthuis N, Mellstrom D. Components of the metabolic syndrome-risk factors for the development of benign prostatic hyperplasia. *Prostate Cancer Prostatic Dis.* 1998;1:157-162.

4. Meigs JB, Mohr B, Barry MJ, Collins MM, McKinlay JB. Risk factors for clinical benign prostatic hyperplasia in a community-based population of healthy aging men. *J Clin Epidemiol.* 2001;54:935-944.

5. Platz EA, Kawachi I, Rimm EB, et al. Physical activity and benign prostatic hyperplasia. *Arch Intern Med.* 1998;158:2349-2356.

6. Wilt TJ, Mac Donald R, Rutks I. Tamsulosin for benign prostatic hyperplasia. Cochrane Database Syst Rev. 2003;(1):CD002081.

7. McConnell JD, Roehrborn CG, Bautista OM, et al. The long-term effect of doxazosin, finasteride, and combination therapy on the clinical progression of benign prostatic hyperplasia. *N Engl J Med.* 2003;349:2387-2398.

8. Koskimaki J, Hakama M, Huhtala H, Tammela TL. Association of dietary elements and lower urinary tract symptoms. *Scand J Urol Nephrol.* 2000;34:46-50.

9. Lagiou P, Wuu J, Trichopoulou A, Hsieh C-C, Adami H-O, Trichopoulos D. Diet and benign prostatic hyperplasia: a study in Greece. *Urology.* 1999;54:284-290.

10. Chyou PH, Nomura AM, Stemmermann GN, Hankin JH. A prospective study of alcohol, diet, and other lifestyle factors in relation to obstructive uropathy. *Prostate.* 1993;22:253-264.

11. Araki H, Watanabe H, Mishina T, Nakao M. High-risk group for benign prostatic hypertrophy. *Prostate.* 1983;4:253-264.

12. Suzuki S, Platz EA, Kawachi I, Willett WC, Giovannucci E. Intakes of energy and macronutrients and the risk of benign prostatic hyperplasia. *Am J Clin Nutr.* 2002;75:689-697.

13. Gaynor ML. Isoflavones and the prevention and treatment of prostate disease: Is there a role? *Cleveland Clinic J Med.* 2003;70:203-216.

14. Denis L, Morton MS, Griffiths K. Diet and its preventive role in prostatic disease. *Eur Urol.* 1999;35:377-387.

15. Rohrmann S, Giovannucci E, Willett WC, Platz EA. Fruit and vegetable consumption, intake of micronutrients, and benign prostatic hyperplasia in US men. *Am J Clin Nutr.* 2007;85:523-529.

46. Urinary Tract Infection

Urinary tract infection (UTI) occurs when pathogenic bacteria enter the urethra and cause infection and inflammation. The urethra alone may be affected (urethritis), but more commonly the infection reaches the bladder (cystitis). The kidneys may also be involved (pyelonephritis), sometimes leading to complicated UTI, stone formation, and/or sepsis. The remainder of this chapter focuses primarily on acute, uncomplicated cystitis.

UTIs are the most common bacterial infection in all age groups. The bacterial pathogens originate from the fecal flora. *Escherichia coli* (*E coli*) are the most common (≈85%). *Staphylococcus saprophyticus*, *Klebsiella, Proteus,* and *enterococcus* may also cause infection.

Cystitis is generally a clinical diagnosis, and radiologic investigation is not usually required except in certain cases involving children (eg, when febrile, when known risk factors are present, or in males). The usual symptoms of cystitis are dysuria, urinary frequency, and urinary urgency. However, urinary tract infections are frequently asymptomatic, particularly in the elderly. Pain in the suprapubic region may be reported, and hematuria and cloudy urine may occur as well. Patients with pyelonephritis typically present with fever spikes, nausea/vomiting, and costovertebral pain.

In elderly persons, confusion and other mental status changes may be the only signs of a urinary tract infection. Among children, symptoms typically include irritability, changes in eating habits, incontinence, and diarrhea. Vomiting or sensation of incomplete voiding may be the only symptom in young girls.

Risk Factors

Gender. Females have UTIs more frequently, compared with males, due to a shorter urethra that is in closer proximity to the perineum. More than 50% of women will have a urinary tract infection during their lifetime,[1] with 20% of these women experiencing 2 or more infections. In men, UTIs are rare (less than 0.1%), except in cases of anatomic abnormalities.

Sexual intercourse. A young woman's risk of infection is associated with frequency of intercourse. In addition, a new sexual partner and spermicide use are risk factors.

Bladder catheterization.

Urinary tract obstruction. Prostatic enlargement (benign prostatic hyperplasia or cancer) or inflammation, nephrolithiasis, and other obstructions raise UTI risk.

Anatomic abnormalities. These may include ureterovesical reflux.

Diabetes mellitus. Hyperglycemia and neurogenic bladder predispose to infection.

Menopause. Atrophic urogenital changes after menopause increase risk.

Diagnosis

The diagnosis of acute cystitis can usually be made by history. Acute onset of dysuria, urinary frequency, and absence of vaginal symptoms usually warrant empiric treatment. A urine dip or urinalysis (of a sample collected midstream) is an inexpensive way to help confirm suspicion, where leukocytes, red blood cells, and/or nitrites may be noted. False-positive and false-negative tests are frequent.

Urine culture is not indicated in an uncomplicated bladder infection, unless resistance to standard antibiotic therapies is likely. In complicated and recurrent infections, a urine culture and sensitivity should be done. Standard urine cultures may be negative in urethritis caused by chlamydia. Blood cultures should be performed if pyelonephritis is suspected; bacteremia is present in about one-third of cases.

Persons with recurrent or refractory infections may need diagnostic testing for anatomic abnormalities. This may require ultrasound, a spiral CT scan for kidney stones, intravenous pyelogram, cystogram, and cystoscopy.

Cigarette smokers with UTI, hematuria, and irritation during voiding should be evaluated for malignancy (transitional cell carcinoma) with CT intravenous pyelogram, cystoscopy, and urine cytology.

Treatment

Asymptomatic bacteriuria does not necessarily require treatment. However, therapy is advisable in the context of advanced age, pregnancy, male gender, immunocompromise, structural abnormalities, kidney stones, or pyelonephritis.

Uncomplicated cases of urinary tract infection usually require a 3- to 7-day course of antibiotic therapy. A longer course of antibiotics may be necessary for patients with a history of UTI, immunocompromise, diabetes, or prolonged symptoms. For chronic UTI, treatment lasting 6 months or more, along with prophylactic antibiotics, may be needed.

Empiric Treatment for Uncomplicated UTI

Trimethoprim/sulfamethoxazole (TMP/SMX) combinations are appropriate for empirical therapy (3-day course), but prevalence of resistant bacteria is increasing.

Nitrofurantoin, used for 7 days, is an effective treatment, and bacterial resistance is rare. The longer course may affect compliance.

Fluoroquinolones are less appropriate for empiric therapy because of their broad spectrum of bacterial coverage. In TMP/SMX-resistant bacteria, resistance to fluoroquinolones occurs more frequently than to nitrofurantoin.[2]

Uncomplicated UTI

Treatment based on culture and sensitivity will likely include one of the above drug classes. Cost-effective therapy with the narrowest-spectrum agent should be used.

Other possible antibiotics include sulfonamides, trimethoprim, and cephalosporins.

Complicated UTI

Fluoroquinolones (except for moxifloxacin) are first-line empiric agents.

Nitrofurantoin is not an appropriate empiric therapy.

Treatment usually is needed for 1 to 2 weeks and may require hospitalization and pathogen-focused drugs.

Pyelonephritis

Uncomplicated pyelonephritis is best treated with TMP/SMX for 14 days, if resistance is not likely. Ciprofloxacin for 7-14 days is also a good option.

Complicated pyelonephritis will require hospitalization and pathogen-focused IV antibiotics. These include ampicillin and gentamicin, TMP/SMX, fluoroquinolones, and third-generation cephalosporins.

Other

In men, all UTIs should be considered complicated. Fluoroquinolones should be used as first-line agents for at least a 7-day course. TMP/SMX may also be considered.

Various prophylactic regimens, such as TMP/SMX, nitrofurantoin, and cranberry or other supplements, may help recurrent UTIs.[3] Voiding after intercourse may also reduce risk for women.

Phenazopyridine (Pyridium) is an analgesic that can be used for severe dysuria. It may turn the urine orange or red, and give a false-positive nitrite test because of the discolored urine.

Amoxicillin and doxycycline are used to treat sexually transmitted urethritis. Sexual partners should be treated as well.

Nutritional Considerations

The role of diet in the prevention and treatment of urinary tract infection remains unsettled. Some nutritional strategies with anecdotal support (vitamin C, high intake of fluids) have not demonstrated clinical effectiveness. Others, such as cranberry juice, have proven effective in clinical trials.[4] Still others, such as probiotic treatment and high-fiber diets, await further evaluation. In epidemiologic or clinical studies, the following factors are associated with reduced risk:

Breast-feeding. Secretory immunoglobulin A (sIgA) in breast milk prevents the translocation of intestinal bacteria across the gut mucosa by blocking interactions between bacteria and the epithelial lining of the gut. Breast-feeding also alters the colonization of the gut, achieving a reduced presence of the P-fimbriated type of *E coli* associated with higher risk for UTI.[5] Nonbreast-fed babies had, on average, twice the risk for urinary tract infection, compared with breast-fed infants.[6] The difference in risk between breast-fed and nonbreast-fed infants is particularly large in girls.

Flavonoid-containing juices. Certain classes of flavonoids (eg, epicatechin) block adhesion of *E coli* fimbria to uroepithelial cells. They may also prevent UTI by other mechanisms, such as the down-regulation of genes in *E coli* responsible for fimbrial expression. Epidemiologic and clinical studies show that women who consume cranberry or cranberry-lingonberry juices have a 20% lower risk for UTI compared with those not drinking juice, a finding comparable to that of continuous low-dose antimicrobial prophylaxis.[4,7]

Lactobacilli. Limited evidence suggests that women who consume probiotic lactobacilli have a significantly (80% lower) decreased risk for UTI.[8] However, this research requires confirmation. Lactobacilli can be purchased over the counter in many health food stores and pharmacies.

High-fiber diets. Constipation is a risk factor for UTI and recurrent UTI,[9] although the reasons are unclear.[10] Clinical trials have not yet established the usefulness of dietary fiber for UTI prevention, but increasing high-fiber foods in persons with low-fiber diets is a potentially beneficial strategy.

Orders

See Basic Diet Orders chapter.

Breast-feeding for at least 6 months, and longer if possible, is recommended.

For adults wishing to use flavonoid-containing juices as a preventive measure, cranberry juice consumed 3 times daily with meals would be appropriate.

What to Tell the Family

Urinary tract infection is often a combined result of a decreased ability to prevent opportunistic infection and the presence of a common (*E coli*) bacterial strain that travels from the gastrointestinal tract into the urethral opening. Useful preventive measures include careful personal hygiene and daily cranberry juice. Infections are generally treated by antibiotics to prevent kidney damage. Timed voiding may help (ie, emptying bladder every 3-4 hours), along with drinking plenty of water (~80 oz daily in adults).

References

1. Foxman B. Epidemiology of urinary tract infections: incidence, morbidity, and economic costs. *Am J Med.* 2002;113(suppl 1A):5S-13S.

2. Karlowsky JA, Thornsberry C, Jones ME, Sahm DF. Susceptibility of antimicrobial-resistant urinary Escherichia coli isolates to fluoroquinolones and nitrofurantoin. *Clin Infect Dis.* 2003;36:183-187.

3. Kontiokari T, Sundqvist K, Nuutinen M, Pokka T, Koskela M, Uhari M. Randomised trial of cranberry-lingonberry juice and Lactobacillus GG drink for the prevention of urinary tract infections in women. *BMJ.* 2001;322:1571.

4. Kontiokari T, Nuutinen M, Uhari M. Dietary factors affecting susceptibility to urinary tract infection. *Pediatr Nephrol.* 2004;19:378-383.

5. Wold AE, Adlerberth I. Breast feeding and the intestinal microflora of the infant—implications for protection against infectious diseases. *Adv Exp Med Biol.* 2000;478:77-93.

6. Marild S, Hansson S, Jodal U, et al. Protective effect of breast-feeding against urinary tract infection. *Acta Paediatr.* 2004;93:164-168.

7. Avorn J, Monane M, Gurwitz JH. Reduction of bacteriuria and pyuria after ingestion of cranberry juice. *JAMA.* 1994;271:751-754.

8. Kontiokari T, Laitinen J, Jarvi L, et al. Dietary factors protecting women from urinary tract infection. *Am J Clin Nutr.* 2003;77:600-604.

9. Hari P, Mantan M, Bagga A. Management of urinary tract infections. *Indian J Pediatr.* 2003;70:235-239.

10. Issenman RM, Filmer RB, Gorski PA. A review of bowel and bladder control development in children: how gastrointestinal and urologic conditions relate to problems in toilet training. *Pediatrics.* 1999;103:1346-1352.

47. Erectile Dysfunction

Erectile dysfunction (ED) is the inability to acquire or sustain an erection of sufficient rigidity for sexual intercourse. The condition affects 15 million to 30 million men in the United States. Related disorders include abnormal curvature of the penis during erection (Peyronie disease), decreased libido, anejaculation or retrograde ejaculation, and premature ejaculation. Any disorder that impairs blood flow to the penis (eg, atherosclerosis) or causes injury to the penile nerves, smooth muscle, or fibrous tissue has the potential to cause ED. At least 25% of cases are related to reversible etiologies, including psychogenic causes, endocrine abnormalities, and drugs (eg, sympathetic blockers, antidepressants, and antihypertensives). Prostate surgery usually leads to ED that improves over the first 18 months after surgery (if nerve-sparing techniques are used). However, irreversible ED is still common after prostate surgery.

Changes in erectile function are common and normal with increasing age. Erections may take longer to develop, be less rigid, or require more direct stimulation. Orgasms may be less intense, the volume of ejaculate frequently decreases, and the refractory period increases. Further, emotional disturbances may result in erectile difficulties in the absence of organic pathology. However, ED is not an inevitable consequence of aging. Most cases are treatable, and occasional episodes are considered normal.

Risk Factors

Age. Erectile dysfunction is most common in men older than 65. About 5% of 40-year-old men and 15% to 25% of 65-year-old men experience some degree of erectile dysfunction.

Vascular disease. Atherosclerosis causes a reduction in blood flow and accounts for 50% to 60% of cases. Hypertension also raises risk of ED and vascular disease.

Diabetes mellitus. At least half of patients with long-standing diabetes experience ED, due to damage of small blood vessels and nerves.

Neurologic conditions. Several neurologic conditions result in ED, including spinal cord and brain injuries, multiple sclerosis, Parkinson disease, and Alzheimer disease.

Hormone imbalance. Thyroid disorders, testosterone deficiency (eg, pituitary tumor and kidney or liver disease), and hyperprolactinemia can result in loss of libido and ED.

Surgery. Colon, prostate, bladder, and rectum surgery may damage erectile nerves and blood vessels. Nerve-sparing techniques decrease impotence incidence to ~50%. Cryotherapy of the prostate causes ED in >90% of men.

Radiation therapy. Radiation treatment for prostate or bladder cancer causes ED in ~50% of treated men. The use of brachytherapy may reduce this number.

Medications. More than 200 commonly prescribed drugs result in ED as a prominent side effect. These include thiazides, antihistamines, antidepressants, tranquilizers, ketoconazole, and appetite suppressants.

Substance abuse. Excessive use of alcohol, tobacco, marijuana, 3,4-methylenedioxymethamphetamine (MDMA, better known as Ecstasy), and other recreational drugs can cause ED, which may be irreversible in some cases. For example, excessive tobacco use can permanently damage penile arteries.

Obesity. Excess body fat weight contributes to ED by increasing estrogen activity and aggravating diabetes and lipid disorders.

Diagnosis

A careful medical and sexual history is essential for diagnosis. Sexual history should include onset of symptoms, presence of spontaneous erections (ie, morning erections), and risk factors. A psychiatric interview and questionnaire may reveal psychological factors, such as depression and anxiety. In some cases, it may be helpful to interview the patient's sexual partner.

Physical examination can provide clues to systemic problems, such as neurologic abnormalities (eg, visual field defects that occur with pituitary tumor), vascular abnormalities (eg, decreased peripheral pulses), developmental abnormalities (eg, abnormal secondary sex characteristics, penile curvature, gynecomastia), and primary testicular failure (bilaterally small, absent, or undescended testes).

Laboratory evaluation may include serum testosterone, prolactin, and thyroid function tests to evaluate for hormonal abnormalities, particularly if libido is poor. Nocturnal penile tumescence testing can help rule out psychological etiologies, but it is rarely performed because of the ready availability of ED medications. Doppler ultrasound or angiography of the penile arteries may be used to identify arterial occlusion or venous leak, but neither is likely to alter the choice of therapy.

Treatment

Treatment is aimed at restoring the ability to acquire and sustain erections and reactivating the libido.

The most commonly used class of medications is **phosphodiesterase-5 inhibitors** (eg, sildenafil, vardenafil, tadalafil). These medications are contraindicated in men taking nitrates and are less likely to be effective in men with diabetes or those who have had prostatectomy.

Hormonal therapy with **testosterone** may be effective but is only recommended in a small number of patients with documented hypogonadism.

Yohimbine may improve erections and increase libido by stimulating the parasympathetic nervous system,[1] especially in psychogenic ED. (See Nutritional Considerations.)

Treatment of **comorbid psychiatric disorders** may improve sexual functioning. Between 20% and 50% of men with impotence have symptoms of depression, which may contribute to erectile dysfunction. Self-esteem may also suffer as a result of erectile dysfunction. Individual or couples psychotherapy may be a helpful part of impotence treatment.[2]

Vacuum devices, intraurethral therapies (alprostadil), and vasodilating **penile injections** may be beneficial.

Surgical interventions include implantable prostheses and correction of penile curvature.

Nutritional Considerations

Impotence is often the result of vascular disease, and risk factors for cardiovascular disease are commonly found in patients with erectile dysfunction. These include obesity, elevated cholesterol and triglyceride levels, smoking, inactivity, endothelial dysfunction, elevated C-reactive protein concentration, and the metabolic syndrome.[3-6] Moreover, impotence should be viewed as a sign that other cardiovascular problems may manifest in the future, and that diet and lifestyle changes to help prevent these problems are essential.

Although the evidence on nutritional treatment is limited, interventions that reduce cardiovascular risk factors or improve blood vessel reactivity (diet, exercise, and certain botanical agents) may improve impotence symptoms. In one study, a low-fat, low-cholesterol diet combined with exercise resulted in normal sexual function in 31% of impotent men, compared with about 5% in a control group. This combination also significantly reduced several vascular risk factors, including obesity, high blood pressure, elevated serum lipids, and elevated blood glucose and insulin concentrations.[7] See Coronary Heart Disease chapter for dietary factors to prevent or treat cardiovascular disease.

Dietary supplements are not a substitute for a healthful diet and lifestyle because they do not address the cause of vascular disorders. Nonetheless, 2 dietary supplements, L-arginine and ginseng, have proven effective in treating erectile dysfunction in clinical trials. These appear to work by enhancing nitric oxide release and increasing cyclic guanosine monophosphate (cGMP), which allows penile arterial relaxation and engorgement.

L-arginine is a precursor to nitric oxide. It was shown to be effective in 30% to 40% of patients taking 3 to 5 grams per day, compared with placebo.[8,9] Combinations of arginine and yohimbine hydrochloride[10] or arginine and flavonoids that stimulate production of nitric oxide synthase (eg, oligomeric proanthocyanidins) increase the percentage of individuals responding to L-arginine to more than 90%.[11] However, not all trials of L-arginine have been adequately controlled, and further study is necessary.

Panax ginseng contains active ingredients (ginsenosides) that increase the release of nitric oxide. Controlled clinical studies have found that mean scores on the International Index of Erectile Function were significantly higher in patients treated with ginseng than in those who received placebo.[12] The studies also found that the number of patients treated with ginseng who experienced improvement in erectile parameters was double that of placebo-treated patients.[13] Additional controlled clinical studies are needed to definitively establish a role for ginseng in ED treatment.

Dietary supplements should be used only under medical supervision, due to the possibility of medication interactions.

Orders

See Basic Diet Orders and Coronary Heart Disease chapters.

Smoking cessation.

Exercise prescription.

Referral for psychiatric evaluation, as appropriate.

What to Tell the Family

Discussion with family members regarding the patient's medical problems should only be done with permission from the patient, particularly in the case of sensitive diagnoses, such as erectile dysfunction. With the patient's permission, however, the sexual partner may be included in discussions of treatment options.

Patients with impotence are commonly at risk for other cardiovascular problems. Dietary changes, especially a low-fat, vegetarian diet, along with smoking cessation and exercise, can alter these risk factors. To the extent that the entire family adopts such a diet, patient adherence is facilitated, and the patient and family are all likely to benefit.

References

1. Weber R. Erectile Dysfunction. *Clinical Evidence*. 2003;63:1003-1011.

2. Althof SE, Wieder M. Psychotherapy for erectile dysfunction: now more relevant than ever. *Endocrine*. 2004;23:131-134.

3. Fung MM, Bettencourt R, Barrett-Connor E. Heart disease risk factors predict erectile dysfunction 25 years later: the Rancho Bernardo Study. *J Am Coll Cardiol*. 2004;43:1405-1411.

4. Giugliano F, Esposito K, Di Palo C, et al. Erectile dysfunction associates with endothelial dysfunction and raised proinflammatory cytokine levels in obese men. *J Endocrinol Invest*. 2004;27:665-669.

5. Gunduz MI, Gumus BH, Sekuri C. Relationship between metabolic syndrome and erectile dysfunction. *Asian J Androl*. 2004;6:355-358.

6. Bacon CG, Mittleman MA, Kawachi I, et al. Sexual function in men older than 50 years of age: results from the health professionals follow-up study. *Ann Intern Med*. 2003;139:161-168.

7. Esposito K, Giugliano F, Di Palo C, et al. Effect of lifestyle changes on erectile dysfunction in obese men: a randomized controlled trial. *JAMA*. 2004;291:2978-2984.

8. McKay D. Nutrients and botanicals for erectile dysfunction: examining the evidence. *Altern Med Rev*. 2004;9:4-16.

9. Chen J, Wollman Y, Chernichovsky T, et al. Effect of oral administration of high-dose nitric oxide donor L-arginine in men with organic erectile dysfunction: results of a double-blind, randomized, placebo-controlled study. *BJU Int*. 1999;83:269-273.

10. Lebret T, Herve JM, Gorny P, Worcel M, Botto H. Efficacy and safety of a novel combination of L-arginine glutamate and yohimbine hydrochloride: a new oral therapy for erectile dysfunction. *Eur Urol*. 2002;41:608-613.

11. Stanislavov R, Nikolova V. Treatment of erectile dysfunction with pycnogenol and L-arginine. *J Sex Marital Ther*. 2003;29:207-213.

12. Hong B, Ji YH, Hong JH, et al. A double-blind crossover study evaluating the efficacy of Korean red ginseng in patients with erectile dysfunction: a preliminary report. *J Urol*. 2002;168:2070-2073.

13. Choi HK, Seong DH, Rha KH. Clinical efficacy of Korean red ginseng for erectile dysfunction. *Int J Impot Res*. 1995;7:181-186.

SECTION X: GASTROINTESTINAL DISORDERS

48. Infantile Colic

Infantile colic refers to excessive and persistent crying in a baby less than 3 months old. Although the condition is sometimes attributed to psychosocial causes, this chapter will focus solely on digestive contributors. Criteria developed by pediatrician Morris Wessel in 1954 and used as a diagnostic standard ever since define colic as crying that occurs in an otherwise healthy baby for 3 or more hours a day on 3 or more days a week for 3 or more weeks. These criteria are somewhat controversial in that they may not adequately distinguish abnormal crying from normal behavior that occurs around 6 weeks of age.

Colic episodes are usually characterized by abrupt onset and conclusion of intense and irregular crying that borders on screaming, hypertonicity, and general inconsolability.

Symptoms of colic may include flushing, constipation, tense abdominal distention, loss of appetite, and persistent crying and irritability.

Risk Factors

Risk factors for infantile colic are poorly understood. The condition does not appear to be related to gender or gestational age at birth. The following list identifies possible risk factors that have emerged in research studies, but whose validity has yet to be established:

Parental smoking.

Stressful home environment, including maternal prenatal anxiety and depression.

White race.

Residence in developed nations and/or locations farther from the equator.

Certain feeding behaviors, including swallowing of air, excessive feeding, and underfeeding.

First-born birth order.

Possible nutritional contributors are described in Nutritional Considerations (see below).

Diagnosis

A detailed history is important, along with questions to determine the social factors at play with the parents and how they respond to their crying baby. It is essential to consider the possibility of parental abuse.

A complete physical examination should be performed. Colic is often considered a diagnosis of exclusion; definitive testing is not available. In addition to Wessel's "rule of 3's" discussed above, the Rome III clinical diagnostic criteria are also used to characterize colic and other functional gastrointestinal disorders.

If malabsorption, intussusception, bowel obstruction, or gastroesophageal reflux are possible, consider laboratory testing, stool samples, and imaging, as appropriate.

Treatment

Colic is self-limiting and will resolve with time. Offering reassurance to the family is helpful, and all interventions should be individualized to the family's needs. In addition to dietary factors described below, the following interventions may help decrease the severity and length of illness, although most evidence is inconclusive.

Parental counseling and support may be an effective strategy for reducing parental anxiety and infant crying.[1]

Feeding techniques that reduce air-swallowing include breast-feeding at one breast, rather than equal feeding time at each breast;[2] using a curved bottle with a plastic bag when feeding with formula or pumped breast milk; and keeping the infant in an upright position during feeding.

Reduction of stimulation may be helpful. Neurobehavioral assessments have shown that infants with the greatest responsiveness to external stimuli are more likely to be colicky, compared with other infants.[3] This may explain the finding of a systematic review that stimulation reduction was a beneficial strategy for colicky infants.[4]

Recent evidence suggests that some cases of colic may result from altered colonic flora and can be corrected with probiotics.[5] A new formula composed of a partial hydrolysate with a probiotic and palmitic acid has been shown to be effective in reducing colic.[6]

Lactose intolerance is not thought to be a cause. However, transient lactose intolerance may contribute to symptoms, and treatment of lactose-containing formula with lactase may decrease symptoms.[7]

Simethicone has not generally been shown to be helpful. Sucrose is not sufficiently calming to justify its use.

Dicyclomine and other antispasmodics should not be used to treat infantile colic due to lack of proven efficacy and risk of serious adverse effects, including seizures and death.

Nutritional Considerations

Links between diet and infantile colic should be regarded as tentative, pending further research. Nevertheless, some evidence indicates that replacement of cow's milk and cow's milk-based formula with hypoallergenic formula or elimination of cow's milk products from a breast-feeding mother's diet may be helpful for certain patients. Also, in some cases, the maternal diet may influence colic as a result of the transmission of offending proteins or other compounds through breast milk. The key nutritional issues include:

Cow's milk proteins. Several lines of evidence support the possibility that cow's milk proteins may elicit colic symptoms. The first is the observation that colic symptoms often improve in infants who are either given formula free of cow's milk proteins or who are breast-fed by mothers who avoid cow's milk.[8,9] In addition, many infants experience colic symptoms after ingestion of breast milk subsequent to maternal ingestion of whey capsules.[9]

In spite of the belief that the maternal intestinal wall provides a barrier to large molecules, it has been shown that cow's milk (and other) proteins are absorbed from the maternal gastrointestinal tract into the circulation and subsequently pass into breast milk. Passing on these proteins when breast-feeding is a suspected cause of colic.[10]

Disaccharidase deficiency or galactosemia may also cause colic symptoms.[11] A 1-week trial of a hypoallergenic formula may be recommended for colicky infants,[4,12] although this is not a proven strategy for reducing colic symptoms.

Allergy-causing and gas-producing foods. A breast-feeding mother who eats a hypoallergenic diet may improve her infant's colic.[13] Breast-feeding mothers with atopy may find that colic symptoms increase on days that dairy products are consumed.[14] A survey of breast-feeding women revealed that the foods mothers found to be most strongly linked to colic in their infants were cruciferous vegetables (broccoli, cabbage, cauliflower), onions, and chocolate.[15]

However, evidence that many other foods may exacerbate colic is increasing. In a randomized controlled trial in which many of these foods (eg, cow's milk, eggs, peanuts, tree nuts, wheat, soy, and fish) were excluded from the diets of breast-feeding women with colicky infants, a reduction in colic symptoms was observed, compared with women who continued eating these foods.[16]

Fructose malabsorption. Rarely, patients with colic may have isolated fructose malabsorption.[17] A study of colicky infants found carbohydrate malabsorption revealed by increased breath hydrogen excretion.[18] Excluding sweetened juices and other fructose-containing products may reduce colic symptoms in these infants.[17]

Orders

For breast-feeding mothers. see Basic Diet Orders chapter.

Parental smoking cessation.

Nutrition consultation to advise breast-feeding mothers in the use of a dairy-free or hypoallergenic diet, as appropriate, and arrange follow-up.

Social work consultation to assess the home environment and arrange follow-up to evaluate the possibility of ill feelings toward the infant, care provider burnout, and maternal depression or anxiety.

What to Tell the Family

In the absence of other medical issues, colic typically resolves within 4 months and is always self-limited. Reassurance of the family is important. Dietary changes, including a dairy-free or hypoallergenic diet for breast-feeding mothers or the use of a nondairy or hypoallergenic formula, may be given a therapeutic trial. If switching to a soy-based formula, it is essential to use a baby formula, not common soymilk sold in grocery stores.

All household smokers should stop smoking for the present and future health of the baby and other family members.

Caregivers should understand that they may not be able to console the infant on every occasion and that caring for a colicky baby is very stressful. They should be encouraged to ask for help if anxiety, depression, or feelings of frustration or anger toward the baby arise. Reducing stimulation, including the stimulation of a family's repeated efforts to console the baby, may result in decreased colic symptoms.

References

1. Taubman, B. Parental counseling compared with elimination of cow's milk or soy milk protein for the treatment of infant colic syndrome: a randomized trial. *Pediatrics.* 1988;81:756-761.

2. Evans K, Evans R, Simmer K. Effect of the method of breast feeding on breast engorgement, mastitis and infantile colic. *Acta Paediatr.* 1995;84:849-852.

3. St James-Roberts I, Goodwin J, Peter B, et al. Individual differences in responsivity to a neurobehavioral examination predict crying patterns of 1-week-old infants at home. *Dev Med Child Neurol.* 2003;45:400-407.

4. Lucassen PL, Assendelft WJ, Gubbels JW, et al. Effectiveness of treatments for infantile colic: systematic review. *BMJ.* 1998;316:1563-1569.

5. Savino F, Pelle E, Palumeri E, Oggero R, Miniero R. *Latobacillus reuteri* (American Type Culture Collection Strain 55730) versus simethicone in the treatment of infantile colic: a prospective randomized study. *Pediatrics.* 2007;119:e124-e130.

6. Savino F, Palumeri E, Castagno E, et al. Reduction of crying episodes owing to infantile colic: A randomized controlled study on the efficacy of a new infant formula. *Eur J Clin Nutr.* 2006;60:1304-1310.

7. Kanabar D, Randhawa M, Clayton P. Improvement of symptoms in infant colic following reduction of lactose load with lactase. *J Hum Nutr Diet.* 2001;14:359-363.

8. Jakobsson I, Lindberg T. Cow's milk as a cause of infantile colic in breast-fed infants. *Lancet.* 1978;312:437-439.

9. Jakobsson I, Lindberg T. Cow's milk proteins cause infantile colic in breast-fed infants: a double-blind crossover study. *Pediatrics.* 1983;71:268-271.

10. Clyne PS, Kulczycki A Jr. Human breast milk contains bovine IgG. Relationship to infant colic? *Pediatrics.* 1991;87:439-444.

11. Kerner JA Jr. Formula allergy and intolerance. *Gastroenterol Clin North Am.* 1995;24:1-25.

12. Sicherer SH. Clinical aspects of gastrointestinal food allergy in childhood. *Pediatrics.* 2003;111:1609-1616.

13. Garrison MM, Christakis DA. A systematic review of treatments for infant colic. *Pediatrics.* 2000;106(pt 2):184-190.

14. Evans RW, Fergusson DM, Allardyce RA, Taylor B. Maternal diet and infantile colic in breast-fed infants. *Lancet.* 1981;1:1340-1342.

15. Lust KD, Brown JE, Thomas W. Maternal intake of cruciferous vegetables and other foods and colic symptoms in exclusively breast-fed infants. *J Am Diet Assoc.* 1996;96:46-48.

16. Hill DJ, Roy N, Heine RG, et al. Effect of a low-allergen maternal diet on colic among breastfed infants: a randomized, controlled trial. *Pediatrics.* 2005;116:e709-e715.

17. Wales JK, Primhak RA, Rattenbury J, Taylor CJ. Isolated fructose malabsorption. *Arch Dis Child.* 1990;65:227-229.

18. Duro D, Rising R, Cedillo M, Lifshitz F. Association between infantile colic and carbohydrate malabsorption from fruit juices in infancy. *Pediatrics*. 2002;109:797-805.

49. Gastroesophageal Reflux Disease

Gastroesophageal reflux disease (GERD) is a syndrome of inappropriate backflow of gastric acid into the esophagus, which can result in inflammation and erosion of the esophageal mucosa. It is the most common upper gastrointestinal tract disorder in Western nations, affecting approximately 10% of Americans.

The pathophysiology involves defective lower esophageal sphincter function, due to inappropriate sphincter relaxation. This condition may be exacerbated by alcohol intake, smoking, fatty foods, caffeine, chocolate, various medications (eg, anticholinergics, calcium channel blockers), inadequate sphincter size or function, or abnormal sphincter position.

Symptoms include heartburn, dysphagia, hoarseness, regurgitation, and a persistent, nonproductive cough. Because the characteristic heartburn may mimic cardiac chest pain, it is useful to characterize the heartburn pain to distinguish it from cardiac ischemia. The pain associated with reflux is of a burning quality and may radiate to the back. It usually occurs within 30 minutes after ingesting specific foods and is often exacerbated by recumbency and relieved by antacids. The symptoms of reflux, unlike those of cardiac chest pain, are not related to exertion and are not associated with shortness of breath, nausea, diaphoresis, or pain radiation to the jaw or arms. Pain is generally referred to as "burning" rather than the "crushing" pain associated with ischemic cardiac disease.

Chronic reflux can result in severe sequelae, including erosion, ulceration, scarring, or stricture of the esophageal mucosa. Furthermore, a possible complication of chronic reflux is the development of Barrett esophagus, in which metaplasia of the lower esophageal mucosa results in replacement of the squamous epithelium with columnar epithelium. Patients with Barrett's esophagus are at high risk for developing esophageal adenocarcinoma.

Risk Factors

Disorders and conditions that cause increased gastric pressure. Pregnancy and obesity (see Nutritional Considerations below) cause increased intra-abdominal pressure that is translated to the stomach. A meta-analysis involving more than 18,000 individuals revealed that overweight persons (body mass index of 25 to 29.9) had more than 50% greater risk for GERD, compared with those whose BMI was below 25. Obese individuals (BMI over 30) were at more than twice the risk.[1]

Diets high in refined carbohydrate. Diets high in refined carbohydrates (white bread and sweets) were associated with greater risk for GERD symptoms in a study of 7,124 participants in the German National Health Interview and Examination Survey.[2] Additional dietary factors are noted in Nutritional Considerations, below.

Diabetes. Diabetes mellitus can cause prolonged gastric emptying, resulting in increased gastric contents and gastric pressure. The increased pressure exerts abnormally high pressure on the lower esophageal sphincter and predisposes to reflux.

Hiatal hernia. In this syndrome, the stomach herniates upward through the diaphragm, displacing the lower esophageal sphincter from its anatomic position. As a result, the sphincter is often not functionally competent.

Disorders that result in esophageal dysmotility. Such disorders, which include scleroderma and Parkinson disease, can impair esophageal clearance of refluxed gastric acid. Raynaud phenomenon can be an early sign of scleroderma and is often complicated by reflux. When the two are present, scleroderma is the likely diagnosis.

Diagnosis

Initial assessment should include a thorough history and physical examination to rule out a cardiac source of chest pain. Focused diagnostic testing may be necessary, including an EKG, chest x-ray, and blood tests that include cardiac enzymes.

In many cases, diagnosis can be made on the basis of the patient's clinical response to a therapeutic trial using a proton pump inhibitor (eg, omeprazole). A therapeutic trial of lifestyle changes (see Treatment, below), antacids, or H2 (Histamine-2) receptor blockers (eg, ranitidine) may also be attempted, but these methods are less reliable for diagnostic purposes.

Upper GI endoscopy is the test of choice to diagnose esophagitis. It permits direct inspection of the inflamed mucosa and biopsy to rule out Barrett's esophagus, malignancy, and infection. However, a negative examination does not distinguish between nonerosive GERD and functional dyspepsia.

Further diagnostic testing may include the following:

Barium esophagram evaluates anatomical causes (eg, hiatal hernia) and complications (eg, strictures) of gastroesophageal reflux disease.

24-hour pH monitoring correlates esophageal pH with symptom onset in order to diagnose reflux.

Esophageal manometry measures pressure within the esophagus to evaluate esophageal sphincter function and esophageal dysmotility. This method is not sufficiently sensitive to establish a diagnosis of GERD.

Treatment

Lifestyle modification is often the initial therapy for mild-to-moderate disease. Weight loss, as described below, is an effective treatment, as is elevating the head of the patient's bed by 6 to 8 inches.[3] Other commonly prescribed lifestyle changes have, as yet, little evidence to support their efficacy. These include dietary changes (see below), smoking cessation, avoiding postprandial recumbency, and avoidance of tight-fitting clothing that increases intra-abdominal pressure.

Medications are usually effective for symptomatic relief. **Oral antacids** or **H2 receptor blockers** (eg, ranitidine) are used for mild and intermittent symptoms. Medications that decrease esophageal sphincter tone, such as calcium channel blockers, should be avoided.

Proton pump inhibitors (eg, omeprazole) are generally reserved for severe or recurrent symptoms.

Severe reflux may require surgical **fundoplication**, which involves wrapping the distal end of the esophagus with the fundus of the stomach to restore the competence of the lower esophageal sphincter.

Patients with Barrett esophagus require regular screening endoscopies to monitor for esophageal carcinoma.

Attaining or maintaining a healthy body weight may be helpful. As noted above, overweight individuals have a significantly increased risk for gastroesophageal reflux disease.[4] Available evidence is limited but suggests that weight loss may provide symptomatic improvement.[5,6]

In addition, psychological distress, caused by either major life events[7,8] or overt psychiatric disease,[9] is associated with GERD symptoms.

Limited evidence suggests that stress-reduction techniques (eg, relaxation training) may reduce symptoms in many persons.[10]

Nutritional Considerations

The role of dietary factors in GERD remains unsettled. It is noteworthy, however, that cultural differences are associated with differences in prevalence, suggesting a role for diet. The incidence of gastroesophageal reflux disease is lower in China (approximately 5%) and certain other countries than in Western countries,[11] which may reflect differences in eating styles, food choices, and body weight. The following factors appear to be associated with reduced GERD symptoms. Note, however, that the potential of these interventions is suggested only by observational studies; they have not yet been tested in clinical trials.

Weight loss. As noted above, obesity is associated with a markedly increased risk of GERD.

Eating more fiber. Persons eating the most fiber have a 30% lower risk for GERD, compared with those who eat the least.[12] High-fiber bread in particular has been associated with reduced risk.[13]

Avoiding irritating foods. Although research is not abundant, available evidence indicates that fried, fatty, or spicy foods, raw onions, chocolate, peppermint, fatty foods, and drinks with high titratable acidity, such as citrus drinks and juices, may be associated with reflux and heartburn.[14-17]

Eliminating coffee. Coffee reduces lower esophageal sphincter pressure, permitting gastroesophageal reflux.[18] Although studies have repeatedly shown that caffeine itself is not responsible for GERD, some evidence does indicate that decaffeination of coffee significantly reduces reflux.[19,20] In addition, other compounds in coffee may trigger reflux.[21]

Avoiding alcohol. Compared with nondrinkers, alcohol consumers have at least double the risk of gastroesophageal reflux disease.[22]

Eating smaller meals. The total amount of food consumed during a meal appears to be related to reflux symptoms, perhaps because gastric distention triggers GERD symptoms.[23] Reducing meal size may therefore be a reasonable preventive strategy,[24,25] particularly for patients who frequently experience delayed gastric emptying.[26]

Thickened feedings. Thickened feedings for children under 2 years of age reduce regurgitation severity and emesis frequency, although this does not lower the reflux index.[27]

Orders

See Basic Diet Orders chapter.

Avoid patient-specific food triggers, or eliminate potential triggers (as described above) prospectively.

Smoking cessation.

Alcohol restriction.

Stress reduction.

What to Tell the Family

Gastroesophageal reflux disease is a common disorder that may be prevented or managed by maintaining a healthy weight, avoiding mealtime overeating, and avoiding caffeine and irritating foods. In chronic cases, treatment may also involve antacid medications (eg, proton pump inhibitors) and occasionally even surgery to prevent erosive esophagitis.

References

1. Corley DA, Kubo A. Body Mass Index and Gastroesophageal Reflux Disease: A Systematic Review and Meta-Analysis. *Am J Gastroenterol.* 2006;101:2619–2628.

2. Nocon M, Labenz J, Willich SN. Lifestyle factors and symptoms of gastro-oesophageal reflux--a population-based study. *Aliment Pharmacol Ther.* 2006;23:169-174.

3. Kaltenback T, Crockett S, Gerson LB. Are lifestyle measures effective in patients with gastroesophageal reflux disease? An evidence-based approach. *Arch Intern Med.* 2006;166:965-971.

4. Hampel H, Abraham NS, El-Serag HB. Meta-analysis: obesity and the risk for gastroesophageal reflux disease and its complications. *Ann Intern Med.* 2005;143:199-211.

5. Mathus-Vliegen EM, Tygat GN. Gastro-oesophageal reflux in obese subjects: influence of overweight, weight loss and chronic gastric balloon distension. *Scand J Gastroenterol.* 2002;37:1246-1252.

6. Fraser-Moodie CA, Norton B, Gornall C, et al. Weight loss has an independent beneficial effect on symptoms of gastro-oesophageal reflux in patients who are overweight. *Scand J Gastroenterol.* 1999;34:337-340.

7. Naliboff BD, Mayer M, Fass R, et al. The effect of life stress on symptoms of heartburn. *Psychosom Med.* 2004;66:426-434.

8. Stanghellini V. Relationship between upper gastrointestinal symptoms and lifestyle, psychosocial factors and comorbidity in the general population: results from the Domestic/International Gastroenterology Surveillance Study (DIGEST). *Scand J Gastroenterol Suppl.* 1999;231:29-37.

9. Avidan B, Sonnenberg A, Giblovich H, et al. Reflux symptoms are associated with psychiatric disease. *Aliment Pharmacol Ther.* 2001;15:1907-1912.

10. McDonald-Haile J, Bradley LA, Bailey MA, et al. Relaxation training reduces symptom reports and acid exposure in patients with gastroesophageal reflux disease. *Gastroenterology.* 1994;107:61-69.

11. Chang CS, Poon SK, Lien HC, et al. The incidence of reflux esophagitis among the Chinese. *Am J Gastroenterol.* 1997;92:668-671.

12. El-Serag HB, Satia JA, Rabeneck L, et al. Dietary intake and the risk of gastro-oesophageal reflux disease: a cross sectional study in volunteers. *Gut.* 2005;54:11-17.

13. Nilsson M, Johnsen R, Ye W, et al. Lifestyle related risk factors in the aetiology of gastro-oesophageal reflux. *Gut.* 2004;53:1730-1735.

14. Rodriguez-Stanley S, Collings KL, Robinson M, et al. The effects of capsaicin on reflux, gastric emptying and dyspepsia. *Aliment Pharmacol Ther.* 2000;14:129-134.

15. Rodriguez S, Miner P, Robinson M, et al. Meal type affects heartburn severity. *Dig Dis Sci.* 1998;43:485-490.

16. Feldman M, Barnett C. Relationships between the acidity and osmolality of popular beverages and reported postprandial heartburn. *Gastroenterology.* 1995;108:125-131.

17. Nebel OT, Fornes MF, Castell DO. Symptomatic gastroesophageal reflux: incidence and precipitating factors. *Am J Dig Dis.* 1976;21:953-956.

18. Thomas FB, Steinbaugh JT, Fromkes JJ, Mekhjian HS, Caldwell JH. Inhibitory effect of coffee on lower esophageal sphincter pressure. *Gastroenterology.* 1980;79:1262-1266.

19. Pehl C, Pfeiffer A, Wendl B, et al. The effect of decaffeination of coffee on gastro-oesophageal reflux in patients with reflux disease. *Aliment Pharmacol Ther.* 1997;11:483-486.

20. Wendl B, Pfeiffer A, Pehl C, et al. Effect of decaffeination of coffee or tea on gastro-oesophageal reflux. *Aliment Pharmacol Ther.* 1994;8:283-287.

21. DiBaise JK. A randomized, double-blind comparison of two different coffee-roasting processes on development of heartburn and dyspepsia in coffee-sensitive individuals. *Dig Dis Sci.* 2003;48:652-656.

22. Rosaida MS, Goh KL. Gastro-oesophageal reflux disease, reflux oesophagitis and non-erosive reflux disease in a multiracial Asian population: a prospective, endoscopy based study. *Eur J Gastroenterol Hepatol.* 2004;16:495-501.

23. Holloway RH, Hongo M, Berger K, et al. Gastric distention: a mechanism for postprandial gastroesophageal reflux. *Gastroenterology.* 1985;89:779-784.

24. Emerenziani S, Zhang X, Blondeau K, et al. Gastric fullness, physical activity, and proximal extent of gastroesophageal reflux. *Am J Gastroenterol.* 2005;100:1251-1256.

25. Colombo P, Mangano M, Bianchi PA, et al. Effect of calories and fat on postprandial gastro-oesophageal reflux. *Scand J Gastroenterol.* 2002;37:3-5.

26. McCallum RW, Berkowitz DM, Lerner E. Gastric emptying in patients with gastroesophageal reflux. *Gastroenterology.* 1981;80:285-291.

27. Craig WR, Hanlon-Dearman A, Sinclair C, et al. Metoclopramide, thickened feedings, and positioning for gastro-oesophageal reflux in children under two years. *Cochrane Database Syst Rev.* 2004;(4):CD003502.

50. Gastritis and Peptic Ulcer Disease

Gastritis and peptic ulcer disease (PUD) affect up to 50% of adult populations in Westernized countries. Gastritis is a superficial erosion and inflammation of the gastric mucosa. Peptic ulcers are deeper erosions and ulcerations that extend through the muscularis layer of the gastric or duodenal mucosa.

These disorders result from a disrupted balance between formation of caustic gastric acid and maintenance of the protective mucosal barrier that depends on secretion of bicarbonate, prostaglandins, and mucosal growth factors. In general, gastritis and gastric ulcers are associated with insufficient mucosal protection, whereas duodenal ulcers are associated with excess acid secretion.

Helicobacter pylori infection may be responsible for up to 95% of duodenal ulcers and 85% of gastric ulcers worldwide. The bacteria disrupt the mucosal protective barrier, making it more vulnerable to acid damage and inciting an inflammatory response. The bacteria also reduce somatostatin production, leading to increased gastrin secretion and action. In the United States, *H pylori* infection is a less prevalent cause of ulcers; nonsteroidal anti-inflammatory drugs (NSAIDs) are the most common cause of gastric ulcers in the United States. Other etiologies include irritants such as aspirin and steroids; severe physiologic stress, including burns, sepsis, trauma, and major surgery; local trauma, such as nasogastric tube placement; and hypersensitivity and autoimmune reactions.

These disorders are often asymptomatic. When symptoms occur, they may include:

Gnawing epigastric or **right-upper-quadrant abdominal pain** that may radiate to the back.

Nausea and vomiting.

Weight loss/anorexia.

Dyspepsia.

Gastrointestinal bleeding that may present as hematemesis, melena, guiac-positive stools, and/or anemia.

Whereas eating may relieve or exacerbate the pain of gastritis and gastric ulcers, duodenal ulcer pain is relieved by eating but increases 2 to 3 hours after meals.

The sudden onset of severe pain (or significant worsening of existing pain) or peritoneal signs (abdominal rigidity, guarding, rebound tenderness) may signify a perforation, which is a surgical emergency.

Risk Factors

Increasing age. Gastric ulcers typically occur in patients over 40 years old, and the incidence of duodenal ulcers peaks at around age 60.

H pylori **infection.** One in 6 patients exposed to *H pylori* will develop an ulcer. Ulcers recur much less often when *H pylori* is eradicated.

NSAIDs. NSAIDs suppress prostaglandin formation in the mucosa, which is normally a part of the protective mechanism of the mucosal barrier. NSAIDs and aspirin are the major causes of PUD not associated with *H pylori* infection.

Tobacco use. Nicotine increases acid secretion and reduces mucosal blood flow in the stomach and duodenum. Smoking is known to delay healing of gastric ulcers, but its role in the pathogenesis of ulcers is unclear.

Alcohol use. Alcohol can cause gastritis by stimulating acid secretion and damaging the mucosal barrier. However, no evidence for a role in ulcer formation has been found.

Major surgery or severe illness. Prophylaxis for gastritis and ulcers may be administered in hospitalized patients, especially those on mechanical ventilation or those undergoing major surgery. Although some reports have argued for prophylaxis in all hospitalized patients, this claim is not backed by rigorous data.

Family history. More than 25% of ulcer patients have a family history of ulcers, compared with 5% of non-ulcer patients.

Diagnosis

Upper gastrointestinal endoscopy is diagnostic for gastritis and peptic ulcer disease. This test permits direct visualization of the mucosa and biopsy to evaluate for *H pylori* infection and rule out carcinoma.

Barium swallow with upper gastrointestinal x-ray series may also be used for diagnosis. This test is less invasive and less expensive than endoscopy but has lower sensitivity and does not allow for biopsy.

Patients with known PUD should be tested for *H pylori* infection; however, despite the high prevalence of *H pylori* infection in PUD patients, routine screening in asymptomatic patients is not advised. Immuno-globin G (IgG) and immunoglobin A (IgA) serologies may be used in patients who have not previously been treated for *H pylori*. Because IgG remains positive after therapy, it is not a useful test to follow the effectiveness of treatment. Patients who have previously been treated require urease breath testing or endoscopic biopsy to evaluate for active infection.

Depending on the patient's history, laboratory procedures may include complete blood count, amylase and lipase, liver function tests, electrocardiogram, cardiac enzymes to rule out cardiac ischemia, and a urine pregnancy test.

If perforation is suspected, an upright chest x-ray may reveal free air under the diaphragm; however, CT scan may also be necessary to diagnose a perforation. Endoscopy and barium swallow are contraindicated if perforation is suspected.

Treatment

Patients should avoid agents known to exacerbate the symptoms of gastritis or PUD. These include tobacco, alcohol, NSAIDs, aspirin, and steroids.

Antacid therapy to reduce acid production includes histamine-2 (H2) receptor blockers (eg, ranitidine) and proton pump inhibitors (eg, omeprazole). Oral antacids and sucralfate, a mucosal protective agent that binds to ulcers and forms a protective barrier against acid, may also be used.

It is important to treat *H pylori* infection, if present. Eradication of *H pylori* decreases the annual ulcer recurrence risk from 50% to 80% to less than 10% and reduces the likelihood of complications such as bleeding. Several "triple therapy" regimens, which are usually administered for 2 weeks, are available (eg, omeprazole, clarithromycin, and amoxicillin; bismuth, metronidazole, and tetracycline).

Ulcer disease tends to be more severe in the absence of *H pylori* infection. Patients in this situation are treated with high-dose proton pump inhibitor therapy. Further, *H pylori*–negative ulcers appear to have a worse outcome when treated empirically with antibiotics.[1] Thus, *H pylori* infection should be documented prior to antibiotic treatment, except in settings where the prevalence of *H pylori* is greater than 90%.[2]

Emergent surgical intervention is necessary for perforated ulcers and intractable bleeding.

Exercise has been hypothesized to influence the risk for ulcer disease or gastritis through reductions in basal or meal-stimulated acid secretion. Some evidence suggests that exercise significantly decreases the risk of duodenal ulcer[3] and of severe gastrointestinal hemorrhage in persons with gastritis or duodenal ulcer.[4] However, controlled clinical studies have not confirmed the ability of exercise to prevent or ameliorate gastritis. In fact, some have shown that certain kinds of exercise (eg, long-distance running) actually increase the risk for this condition.[5] Approximately 20% of long-distance runners experience GI bleeding, confirmed by endoscopy. [6] Exercise-induced ischemia and acid secretion have been postulated as mechanisms by which runners may develop erosive gastritis, hemorrhagic gastritis, or gastric ulcer. [5]

Nutritional Considerations

For decades, doctors have recommended dietary adjustments aimed at preventing or treating symptoms of gastritis and PUD. Common suggestions have included avoiding spicy foods, coffee, and alcohol, and increasing consumption of bland foods and milk. While these suggestions seem reasonable, some have not stood up well in controlled investigations. For example, milk ingestion tends to increase gastric acid secretion.[7] Although certain spices (black pepper, chili powder, red pepper) may cause dyspepsia,[7] they have not been shown to contribute to either gastritis or peptic ulcer.

Diet may moderate the risk for gastritis or peptic ulcer through acting on *H pylori,* among other effects.[8] In turn, *H pylori* infection can affect nutritional status and may specifically interfere with vitamin C, folate, and vitamin B_{12} absorption. It is unknown if diets higher in these nutrients can offset the effects of *H pylori*–induced malabsorption.

The following factors have been associated with reduced risk of gastritis or ulcer disease in epidemiologic studies:

High-fiber diets. A large cohort study at the Harvard School of Public Health found that high-fiber diets were associated with reduced risk for developing duodenal ulcer. Over a 6-year period, the risk was 45% lower for those with the highest fiber intake, compared with those with the lowest. Food sources of soluble fiber (found in oats, legumes, barley, and certain fruits and vegetables) were especially protective, resulting in a 60% lower risk for this group.[9] However, supplementation with dietary fiber in the form of wheat bran had no effect on ulcer recurrence.[10]

Similarly, high-fiber diets did not appear to increase ulcer healing rates, compared with diets low in fiber.[11]

Diets high in vitamin A. In the same Harvard cohort study, total vitamin A intake (from food and supplements) was associated with lower risk. The risk was 54% lower among persons consuming the most vitamin A, compared with those consuming the least.[12]

Green tea. Several studies show that regular green tea consumption is associated with a 40% to 50% lower risk for gastritis.[13] Cellular tests suggest that the catechins in green tea (eg, epigallocatechin-3-gallate, EGCG) may suppress *H pylori*–induced gastritis through antioxidant and antibacterial actions.[14] However, current evidence is not yet sufficient for recommending green tea for prevention of gastritis.

Avoiding alcohol. The relationship between alcohol and gastritis and peptic ulcer is complex and may be related to amounts consumed. Chronic alcohol abuse favors *H pylori* infection, and the ammonia produced by this organism contributes to gastritis.[15] Alcohol may also slow the rate of healing in established ulcers,[16] although this has not been demonstrated in patients on proton pump inhibitors.

However, studies have also found an inverse association between moderate alcohol consumption and *H pylori* infection. Alcohol may have bactericidal effects on *H pylori*,[17] and it may prevent infection and associated gastritis through an adaptive cytoprotective response (eg, endogenous release of prostaglandins with protective effects on gastric mucosa).[18] But, while moderate consumption is associated with the lowest odds for infection, higher intakes are associated with greater risk.[19] The protective effect of moderate alcohol consumption for gastritis and PUD is not evident among smokers; in combination with smoking, alcohol increases the risk for duodenal ulcer.[20]

In addition, the following are under study for their role in managing gastritis and PUD:

Avoiding coffee. Coffee, either in its caffeinated or decaffeinated forms, stimulates acid secretion,[9] and some studies have suggested a correlation between coffee intake and symptoms in patients with duodenal ulcer.[21]

Coffee consumption may also mediate the relationship between *H pylori* infection and ulcer, although studies have variously found coffee consumption to be associated with both increased and decreased risk for *H pylori* infection.[22-24] Overall, there is no current evidence implicating coffee consumption in the susceptibility to, treatment of, or recovery from gastritis.

Probiotics. Probiotics (eg, *Lactobacillus caseii*) interfere with *H pylori* adhesion to epithelial cells, attenuate *H pylori*-induced gastritis,[25] and inhibit growth of *H pylori* in humans, in addition to reducing the side effects of eradication treatment.[26] Combining probiotic treatment with omeprazole, amoxicillin, and clarithromycin in *H pylori*-infected children significantly improved the treatment effectiveness, compared with drug treatment alone.[27] Further study is needed to determine if probiotic treatment results in the prevention of initial infection, reduction of gastritis symptoms, prevention of ulcer occurrence, and improved healing of gastric lesions.

Orders

See Basic Diet Orders chapter.

Alcohol restriction.

Smoking cessation.

Stress reduction.

Exercise prescription.

What to Tell the Family

Bacterial infection plays a significant role in peptic ulcer disease, and testing and treatment for *H pylori* are important. Family members can help by encouraging a patient who is suffering from symptoms of gastritis or ulcer to get appropriate testing and treatment.

In addition, the risk for developing gastritis and ulcer disease may be reduced by following a healthy diet and exercise regimen, something that family members can support and take part in.

Caution should be used when considering the use of aspirin and NSAIDs. In patients with existing disease, these treatments should be used along with medications to reduce acid secretion, speed ulcer healing, and eradicate the bacteria that often cause this disease. For individuals having difficulty managing their medications, attentive family members can be helpful.

References

1. Bytzer P, Teglbjaerg PS. *Helicobacter pylori*-negative duodenal ulcers: Prevalence, clinical characteristics, and prognosis—results from a randomized trial with 2-year follow-up. *Am J Gastroenterol*. 2001;96:1409-1416.

2. Borody TJ, George LL, Brandl S, et al. Helicobacter pylori-negative duodenal ulcer. Am J Gastroenterol. 1991;86:1154-1157.

3. Cheng Y, Macera CA, Davis DR, et al. Does physical activity reduce the risk of developing peptic ulcers? Br J Sports Med. 2000;34:116-121.

4. Pahor M, Guralnik JM, Salive ME, et al. Physical activity and risk of gastrointestinal hemorrhage in older persons. JAMA. 1994;272:595-599.

5. Choi SJ, Kim YS, Chae JR, et al. Effects of ranitidine for exercise induced gastric mucosal changes and bleeding. World J Gastroenterol. 2006;12:2579-2583.

6. Schwartz AE, Vanagunas A, Kamel PL. Endoscopy to evaluate gastrointestinal bleeding in marathon runners. Ann Intern Med. 1990;113:632-633.

7. Marotta RB, Floch MH. Diet and nutrition in ulcer disease. Med Clin North Am. 1991;75:967-979.

8. Levenstein S. Stress and peptic ulcer: life beyond Helicobacter. BMJ. 1998;316:538-541.

9. Aldoori WH, Giovannucci EL, Stampfer MJ, et al. Prospective study of diet and the risk of duodenal ulcer in men. Am J Epidemiol. 1997;145:42-50.

10. Rydning A, Borkje B, Lange O, et al. Effect of wheat fibre supplements on duodenal ulcer recurrence. Scand J Gastroenterol. 1993;28:1051-1054.

11. Rydning A, Weberg R, Lange O, Berstad A. Healing of benign gastric ulcer with low-dose antacids and fiber diet. Gastroenterology. 1986;91:56-61.

12. Aldoori WH, Giovannucci EL, Stampfer MJ, Rimm EB, Wing AL, Willett WC. A prospective study of alcohol, smoking, caffeine, and the risk of duodenal ulcer in men. Epidemiology. 1997;8:420-424.

13. Setiawan VW, Zhang ZF, Yu GP, et al. Protective effect of green tea on the risks of chronic gastritis and stomach cancer. Int J Cancer. 2001;92:600-604.

14. Lee KM, Yeo M, Choue JS, et al. Protective mechanism of epigallocatechin-3-gallate against Helicobacter pylori-induced gastric epithelial cytotoxicity via the blockage of TLR-4 signaling. Helicobacter. 2004;9:632-642.

15. Lieber CS. Gastric ethanol metabolism and gastritis: interactions with other drugs, Helicobacter pylori, and antibiotic therapy (1957-1997)—a review. Alcohol Clin Exp Res. 1997;21:1360-1366.

16. Battaglia G, Di Mario F, Dotto P, et al. Markers of slow-healing peptic ulcer in the elderly. A study on 1,052 ranitidine-treated patients. Dig Dis Sci. 1993;38:1414-1421.

17. Bujanda L. The effects of alcohol consumption upon the gastrointestinal tract. Am J Gastroenterol. 2000;95:3374-3382.

18. Tursi A, Cammarota G, Papa A, et al. Effect of adequate alcohol intake, with or without cigarette smoking, on the risk of Helicobacter pylori infection. Hepatogastroenterology. 1998;45:1892-1895.

19. Brenner H, Bode G, Adler G, Hoffmeister A, Koenig W, Rothenbacher D. Alcohol as a gastric disinfectant? The complex relationship between alcohol consumption and current Helicobacter pylori infection. Epidemiology. 2001;12:209-214.

20. Piper DW, Nasiry R, McIntosh J, et al. Smoking, alcohol, analgesics, and chronic duodenal ulcer. A controlled study of habits before first symptoms and before diagnosis. Scand J Gastroenterol. 1984;19:1015-1021.

21. Eisig JN, Zaterka S, Massuda HK, Bettarello A. Coffee drinking in patients with duodenal ulcer and a control population. Scand J Gastroenterol. 1989;24:796-798.

22. Brenner H, Rothenbacher D, Bode G, Adler G. Relation of smoking and alcohol and coffee consumption to active *Helicobacter pylori* infection: cross sectional study. *BMJ.* 1997;315:1489-1492.

23. Moayyedi P, Axon AT, Feltbower R, et al. Relation of adult lifestyle and socioeconomic factors to the prevalence of *Helicobacter pylori* infection. *Int J Epidemiol.* 2002;31:624-631.

24. Bode G, Hoffmeister A, Koenig W, Brenner H, Rothenbacher D. Characteristics of differences in Helicobacter pylori serology and - 13C-urea breath-testing in an asymptomatic sample of blood donors. *Scand J Clin Lab Invest.* 2001;61:603-608.

25. Felley C, Michetti P. Probiotics and *Helicobacter pylori*. *Best Pract Res Clin Gastroenterol.* 2003;17:785-791.

26. Tursi A, Brandimarte G, Giorgetti GM, Modeo ME. Effect of *Lactobacillus casei* supplementation on the effectiveness and tolerability of a new second-line 10-day quadruple therapy after failure of a first attempt to cure *Helicobacter pylori* infection. *Med Sci Monit.* 2004;10:CR662-CR666.

27. Sykora J, Valeckova K, Amlerova J, et al. Effects of a specially designed fermented milk product containing probiotic *Lactobacillus casei* DN-114 001 and the eradication of *H. pylori* in children: a prospective randomized double-blind study. *J Clin Gastroenterol.* 2005;39:692-698.

51. Celiac Sprue

Celiac sprue, also known as celiac disease, gluten-sensitive enteropathy, and nontropical sprue, is an immune-mediated disorder of the small intestine in which patients are sensitive to gluten, a protein contained in wheat, barley, and rye. Gluten acts as a foreign antigen, causing an immune response that damages the lining of the small intestine, resulting in malabsorption of fat, calcium, iron, folate, and other nutrients.

Classically, signs and symptoms initially appear upon the introduction of wheat into a child's diet (usually at age 6 months to 12 months). However, the disease may not present until later in life, typically between the ages of 10 and 40. In children, the presentation may include failure to thrive, delayed growth, irritability, vomiting, constipation, large stools, peripheral edema, clubbing, and frequent respiratory infections. In adults, many cases are asymptomatic, but some patients may have diarrhea, weight loss, abdominal swelling, and bloating.

Patients may also have nonintestinal symptoms. Malabsorption of vitamin D and calcium may result in rickets, osteoporosis, and bone fractures. Iron malabsorption can result in anemia. Amenorrhea, infertility, dermatitis herpetiformis, and neurologic symptoms (eg, peripheral neuropathy, ataxia, seizures) may occur.

Risk Factors

Celiac sprue occurs in people of all ages and ethnicities but appears to be most common in Caucasians of Northern European descent. Other risk factors include:

Genetics. More than 95% of affected patients have HLA-DQ2 and/or HLA-DQ8 mutations. Celiac sprue occurs in 10% of first-degree relatives of affected patients.

Immune disorders. Patients with a history of immune disorders (eg, IgA deficiency, autoimmune thyroid disease, type 1 diabetes mellitus) are at increased risk. About 5% of patients with type 1 diabetes mellitus have concurrent celiac disease.

Dermatitis herpetiform.

Down syndrome. Patients with Down syndrome have double the risk of celiac disease, compared with the general population.

Diagnosis

Diagnosis in infants is suggested by a constellation of diarrhea, failure to thrive, and irritability.

Serologic testing with IgA antitissue transglutaminase or antiendomysial antibody is used to screen for celiac disease. Antigliadin antibody testing is no longer routinely used.

Small intestine biopsy establishes the diagnosis and should be done in most cases.[1,2] In equivocal cases, HLA haplotype testing may be useful. HLA testing may also be done to determine susceptibility in offspring. Rarely, a follow-up biopsy may be performed for comparison after the patient has followed a gluten-free diet for 3 to 6 months.

It may also be advisable to assess hematologic indices to check for iron deficiency anemia.

Treatment

The cornerstone of treatment is dietary adjustment to avoid gluten (see Nutritional Considerations below). In addition to easing symptoms, dietary adjustment may decrease the risk of esophageal carcinoma, small bowel carcinoma, and B-cell lymphoma, which occur in greater frequency in these patients. In addition, immunosuppressant therapy with corticosteroids may be necessary for patients who do not respond to gluten avoidance. Dapsone has been used to treat associated dermatitis herpetiformis.

Nutritional Considerations

Nutritional adjustments are essential in the management of celiac disease. The key aspects of treatment are as follows:

Gluten-Free Diet

A gluten-free diet eliminates wheat, barley, rye, and other gluten-containing foods. Patients should consult with an experienced dietitian to identify these foods and ensure adequate nutrient balance.

Although gluten is also found in oats, some studies suggest that pure oat flour can be tolerated without disease recurrence. Thus, once the disease has become quiescent, many gastroenterologists will introduce oats to the diet (less than 2 g/d), and patients may eventually be able to tolerate 40 to 60 grams per day. However, some patients are sensitive to oats, a sensitivity confirmed by the presence of oat-specific intestinal T cells. Further caution regarding oats is justified, as commercial oat products may be contaminated with other gluten-containing grains.[3]

Patients should be aware that 100% gluten avoidance is impossible. Even naturally gluten-free products may contain 20 to 200 mg gluten/kg. Evidence supports setting the threshold for gluten-contamination at 100 mg/kg; the intake of gluten-free flour up to 300 g/d provides 30 mg of gluten, which is within the range found to allow for mucosal recovery in clinical and challenge studies.[4]

Addressing Nutrient Deficiencies

Celiac disease patients' diets and gluten-free products are often low in B vitamins, calcium, vitamin D, iron, zinc, magnesium, and fiber.[5] Consequently, newly diagnosed or inadequately treated patients often have low bone-mineral density, low fiber intake, and micronutrient deficiencies, despite increased obesity in this population.[5] Patients who have been managed on gluten-free diets sometimes reveal signs of poor nutrient status[6,7] and impaired calcium absorption.[8] Patient counseling regarding healthful sources of micronutrients is recommended. These may include, but are not limited to, fortified soy milk for calcium and vitamin D, and legumes for magnesium and iron.

The prevalence of vitamin B-complex deficiency is between 5% and 7% of persons with undiagnosed celiac disease, compared with 1% to 2% in a control population.[9] About 5% of patients diagnosed with iron and/or folate deficiency were found to have histologically confirmed celiac disease after endoscopy and biopsy.[10] In patients following a gluten-free diet for 10 years, 37% had low blood levels of folate, and 20% had low blood levels of vitamin B_6.[11] Between 20% and 40% of untreated celiac patients appear to have poor vitamin B_{12} status.[6,11]

Nutritional deficiencies of fat-soluble vitamins, occurring as a result of malabsorption, are not uncommon. Cases of myopathy and vitamin D deficiency in celiac disease have been reported, and low levels of vitamin E have been implicated in neurologic complications of celiac disease. Vitamin E supplementation and a gluten-free diet reverse the resulting myopathy.[12] Malabsorption of vitamin K in untreated celiac disease may also prolong the prothrombin time, requiring parenteral administration of this vitamin.[13]

Orders

Gluten-free diet.

Nutrition consultation to assist patient with diet changes, with outpatient follow-up as needed.

What to Tell the Family

Family members can help the identified patient avoid gluten-containing foods, recognizing that it is important to avoid them completely. It is important to read food labels carefully.

The following organizations provide recipes, lists of gluten-free commercial products, and information on the gluten content of medications:

- Celiac Sprue Association (*www.csaceliacs.org*)
- Gluten Intolerance Group of North American (*www.gluten.net*)
- Celiac Disease Foundation (*www.celiac.org*)
- Coeliac Society of the United Kingdom (*www.coeliac.co.uk*)
- Canadian Celiac Association (*www.celiac.ca*)
- National Foundation for Celiac Awareness (www.celiaccentral.org)

References

1. Hill ID, Dirks MH, Liptak GS, et al. Guideline for the diagnosis and treatment of celiac disease in children: Recommendations of the North American Society for Pediatric Gastroenterology, Hepatology, and Nutrition. *J Pediatr Gastroenterol Nutr.* 2005;40:1.

2. Richter JC, Netzer P, Cottagnoud P, Stuckt A. Testing strategies and follow-up for celiac disease in a general internal medicine outpatient department from 2000 to 2005. *Swiss Med Wkly.* 2006;136:732-738.

3. Alaedini A, Green PH. Narrative review: celiac disease: understanding a complex autoimmune disorder. *Ann Intern Med.* 2005;142:289-298.

4. Collin P, Thorell L, Kaukinen K, Maki M. The safe threshold for gluten contamination in gluten-free products. Can trace amounts be accepted in the treatment of coeliac disease? *Aliment Pharmacol Ther.* 2004;19:1277-1283.

5. Kupper C. Dietary guidelines and implementation for celiac disease. *Gastroenterology.* 2005;128(suppl 1):S121-S127.

6. Dickey W. Low serum vitamin B12 is common in coeliac disease and is not due to autoimmune gastritis. *Eur J Gastroenterol Hepatol.* 2002;14:425-427.

7. Hallert C, Grant C, Grehn S, et al. Evidence of poor vitamin status in coeliac patients on a gluten-free diet for 10 years. *Aliment Pharmacol Ther.* 2002;16:1333-1339.

8. Pazianas M, Butcher GP, Subhani JM, et al. Calcium absorption and bone mineral density in celiacs after long term treatment with gluten-free diet and adequate calcium intake. *Osteoporos Int.* 2005;16:56-63.

9. Delco F, El-Serag HB, Sonnenberg A. Celiac sprue among US military veterans: associated disorders and clinical manifestations. *Dig Dis Sci.* 1999;44:966-972.

10. Howard MR, Turnbull AJ, Morley P, Hollier P, Webb R, Clarke A. A prospective study of the prevalence of undiagnosed coeliac disease in laboratory defined iron and folate deficiency. *J Clin Pathol.* 2002;55:754-757.

11. Dahele A, Ghosh S. Vitamin B12 deficiency in untreated celiac disease. *Am J Gastroenterol.* 2001;96:745-750.

12. Kleopa KA, Kyriacou K, Zamba-Papanicolaou E, Kyriakides T. Reversible inflammatory and vacuolar myopathy with vitamin E deficiency in celiac disease. *Muscle Nerve.* 2005;31:260-265.

13. Cavallaro R, Iovino P, Castiglione F, et al. Prevalence and clinical associations of prolonged prothrombin time in adult untreated coeliac disease. *Eur J Gastroenterol Hepatol.* 2004;16:219-223.

52. Constipation

The term "constipation" refers to the difficult or infrequent passage of stool. A common definition of constipation is fewer than 3 spontaneous, complete bowel movements per week. It is the most common gastrointestinal complaint in the United States, with an adult prevalence of about 15% to 20%.

Constipation is also a common pediatric condition. Many cases are related to behavioral issues. However, the condition can result from dietary causes, including fiber deficiencies, dehydration, and dairy intolerance.[1] Constipation also results from numerous disorders, such as cystic fibrosis and lead poisoning.

The most common primary cause of constipation is slow transit of stool through the colon, which accounts for 95% of cases. Less common primary causes include pelvic-floor dysfunction and anismus.

Other common identifiable causes in adults include medications (eg, narcotics, antacids, calcium channel blockers, tricyclic antidepressants, and many other drugs), particularly in older adults; smoking cessation (constipation is a temporary result of nicotine withdrawal[2]); Parkinson disease; anatomical obstructions (eg, tumor, stricture, third-trimester pregnancy, anal canal disease), hemorrhoids, abscesses, fistulae, and fissures, which can decrease the desire to defecate due to pain; diet (see Nutritional Considerations below); and hormonal factors (eg, hypothyroidism).

Symptoms and signs of constipation include:

Complaints of hard, dry stool that is difficult to pass or leaves the sensation of incomplete evacuation.

Infrequent bowel movements.

Bloating and abdominal discomfort. These symptoms are more common in irritable bowel syndrome (IBS) than in simple constipation. IBS can be differentiated from simple constipation by the presence of discomfort or pain that occurs prior to defecation (see Irritable Bowel Syndrome chapter).

Lower back pain. Pain is uncommon in idiopathic chronic constipation.

Rectal bleeding (eg, stercoral ulcerations/erosions).

Hemorrhoids or, uncommonly, **headaches** due to straining in adults.

Risk Factors

The highest reported prevalence of constipation occurs in persons over 60 years of age, followed by children under age 10. The association with age is largely attributable to other factors, such as medication, diet, and exercise. For unclear reasons, whites report constipation less frequently than do other racial groups, and women are affected approximately twice as often as men. The condition is more common in individuals with relatively low income and less education.

Additional possible risk factors include:

- Family history.
- Pelvic floor dysfunction.

- Pelvic and abdominal surgery.
- Childbirth.
- Anorectal problems.[3,4]

Diagnosis

Careful history and rectal examination can establish the diagnosis, and physical examination may help identify causes of secondary constipation.

Identification of drug side effects in adults, including those from the use of over-the-counter products such as antacids and iron supplements, does not negate the need for further evaluation. Drugs may make evident a problem that had not previously been apparent.

A **detailed bowel habits diary**, submitted by a patient or parent, may be helpful. Many people misjudge normal bowel function as abnormal.

Laboratory evaluation is indicated if hypothyroidism, anorexia, hypercalcemia, or diabetes is suspected. These conditions may also apply in children, as may celiac disease, lead poisoning, cystic fibrosis, and urinary tract infection.

Plain film imaging of the abdomen can detect megacolon or megarectum (eg, as seen with Hirschsprung's disease in children) and assist in monitoring progress in a hospitalized patient. However, in cases of intra-abdominal bowel distention, plain films often cannot distinguish ileus from mechanical obstruction.

If history and physical examination are normal, **colonoscopy** or **barium enema** can help rule out obstruction. **Gastrografin** should be used if perforation or partial obstruction is suspected. Barium can become desiccated behind a partial obstruction.

Final diagnostic steps may include:

Marker studies to determine normality of colon transit.

Anorectal manometry to assess the appropriateness of internal and external anal sphincter tone and intrarectal pressure during defecation.

Treatment

Treatment of any identified cause should be attempted before medications are considered. Unfortunately, most constipation treatments are not well supported by clinical trials.

For idiopathic constipation, the most effective treatment is to increase fiber intake and fluids stepwise, consume foods that reduce transit time (see Nutritional Considerations below), and take advantage of the body's normal rhythms of colonic motility, which occur after meals, especially in the morning.

Biofeedback and behavioral changes may be helpful in outlet dysfunction, especially in children.

Severe constipation may require a multidimensional approach that includes manual disimpaction.

Drug Therapy

Many of the following drugs can be used in children, but doses must be adjusted accordingly. Many of these remedies are available in oral form and as rectal suppositories and enemas.

Simple therapies, including supplemental corn syrup, fruit juices with sorbitol (for infants already eating solid foods), and those therapies mentioned above, should be tried first. Enemas and stimulant laxatives should not be used in infants.

Laxatives are not generally recommended, because they prevent the bowel from recovering normal function and often need to be continued indefinitely. Although they are generally well tolerated, laxatives may cause abdominal distention, nausea, anorexia, cramps, gas, and (rarely) diarrhea severe enough to produce malabsorption or dangerous electrolyte imbalances, which may worsen with continual use. Laxative abuse is common and often hidden. Clinicians should try to wean patients from laxatives for these reasons.

Bulk-forming agents (eg, oral fiber supplements such as **psyllium**, **methylcellulose**, and **polycarbophil**) hold water in the intestinal contents, making them easier to pass. However, they can also worsen symptoms of constipation, and patients should be warned of this possibility prior to initiating supplements.

Emollients, such as **docusate** and **mineral oil**, soften stools but are not always very effective.

Hyperosmolar agents, which cannot be absorbed, produce diarrhea through an osmotic fluid shift.

Magnesium salts are effective for rapid emptying and intended for one-time use. Hypermagnesemia can occur with frequent use.

Lactulose works more slowly than salts and may be used for long-term treatment when diet therapy is not possible or ineffective. It may cause gas.

Sorbitol is less expensive than lactulose and functions similarly.

Glycerin is available as a suppository.

Polyethylene glycol formulations (Colyte or MiraLax) have varying electrolyte compositions. Although these are still relatively expensive, they may produce less gas than sorbitol and lactulose.

Stimulants or contact irritants increase peristalsis. They include **senna**, **bisacodyl**, and **castor oil**. These agents are not for chronic use, as they may cause electrolyte abnormalities.

Additional Treatments for Adult Patients

Drugs that act as prokinetics may be helpful (an exception is metoclopramide, which has not been shown to be helpful for severe constipation). Effective agents include:

Misoprostol[5] and **colchicine**.[6]

Tegaserod, a serotonin agonist (5-HT4), had been approved for chronic constipation but has since been withdrawn from the U.S. market.[7]

Lubiprostone is a chloride channel agonist that improves constipation, but it produces nausea in one-third of patients.

Patients with refractory slow-transit constipation may be considered for **colectomy with ileorectostomy**. However, this procedure is experimental and currently can only be recommended as part of a research protocol. Long-term outcome data are not available.

If slow transit is not present, the patient may have pelvic floor dysfunction, which may respond to **pelvic floor exercises** or **biofeedback**.[8] The value of exercise is not limited to such patients; individuals who report daily physical activity have roughly half the risk for constipation, compared with those who are least active. When higher levels of both activity and fiber intake are paired, the risk for constipation drops roughly 70%, compared with that of individuals who are least active and eat the least fiber.[9]

The rationale for biofeedback treatment is based on the observation that inappropriate (paradoxical) contraction or a failed relaxation of the puborectal muscle and of the external anal sphincter often occurs during attempts to defecate and is considered a form of maladaptive learning.[10] Although additional long-term studies are required, the available evidence indicates that biofeedback training provides a significantly higher probability of successful outcome in treatment of functional constipation and functional fecal incontinence than does standard medical care.[11]

Nutritional Considerations

Constipation is common in developed countries. According to most estimates, 20% of North Americans are affected, which is similar to the percentage of people affected in other Westernized cultures.[12,13] The most common association is with a diet low in fiber, which is found only in plant-derived foods such as beans, vegetables, fruits, and whole grains. Americans eat an average of 5 to 14 grams of fiber daily,[14] far less than individuals residing in developing countries. In persons eating more traditional, higher-fiber diets, constipation is rare.[15-17] The following considerations are important in preventing or alleviating constipation:

Increasing intake of high-fiber foods. A lower intake of dietary fiber differentiates children with chronic constipation from those with regular bowel habits.[18,19] Increasing dietary fiber improves constipation and significantly reduces the need for laxatives in children,[20] the elderly,[21] and postsurgery patients.[22]

Although high-fiber foods should generally be the first choice, there may be a role for fiber supplements in some individuals (eg, edentulous patients or those with dysphagia). Evidence indicates that fiber supplements permit discontinuation of laxatives in about 70% of constipated patients.[23] Several types of fiber supplements have been shown to be effective for constipation relief, including psyllium (Metamucil),[24] methylcellulose (Citrucel),[25] and Japanese konjac root (glucomannan).[26]

Increasing fluid intake. A hypohydrated or dehydrated state contributes to constipation.[27] Poor fluid intake is often found in constipated children.[18] A combination of 25 grams of fiber and 1.5 to 2.0 liters of fluid daily was more effective for constipation relief than fiber intake alone in patients with functional chronic constipation.[28]

Avoiding cow's milk. Many children with chronic constipation are allergic to cow's milk, manifesting IgE antibodies to cow's milk antigens. Cow's milk consumption is also significantly higher in infants and children with constipation and anal fissure than in those without these disorders.[29] In roughly half of constipated, cow's milk-allergic children and adolescents who have had a colonoscopy, lymphoid nodular hyperplasia was found, compared with 20% of controls. In one-third of all cow's milk–allergic individuals, a significantly higher number of intraepithelial T cells was also found, indicating an enhancement of local immune responses against food antigens.[30] Immune activation is known to affect gastric motility,[31] possibly indicating a role for an immune response to food antigens in constipation. Roughly one-third to two-thirds of constipated children with cow's milk sensitivity improve on milk-free diets.[30,32] A controlled clinical trial found that constipation returned within 5 to 10 days of reintroduction of cow's milk.[33] When calcium adequacy is in question, calcium-fortified soymilk, rice milk, or juices may be substituted for cow's milk.

Orders

See Basic Diet Orders chapter.

What to Tell the Family

Constipation is a common disorder that is usually preventable with a diet high in minimally processed, high-fiber foods; consumption of ≥1.5 to 2.0 liters of fluid per day; and regular exercise. Health practitioners can provide helpful information about dietary approaches to prevention and treatment. Most patients and their families are not fully aware of the best sources of dietary fiber (beans and other legumes, vegetables, fruits, and whole grains) or of the absence of fiber in animal-derived or heavily processed food products. They may also have been inappropriately influenced by advertisements for over-the-counter treatments or specific foods, such as breakfast cereals and snack bars. Children with milk sensitivity may respond to the removal of dairy products from their diet. Laxatives should be the treatment of last resort because they prevent normal bowel function. Biofeedback training is an option for patients, especially children who do not respond well to other treatments.

References

1. Heine RG, Elsayed S, Hosking CS, Hill DJ. Cow's milk allergy in infancy. *Curr Opin Allergy Clin Immunol.* 2002;2:217-225.

2. Hajek P, Gillison F, McRobbie H. Stopping smoking can cause constipation. *Addiction.* 2003;98:1563-1567.

3. Sandler RS, Jordan MC, Shelton BJ. Demographic and dietary determinants of constipation in the U.S. population. *Am J Public Health.* 1990;80:185-189.

4. Sonnenberg A, Koch TR. Physician visits in the United States for constipation: 1958-1986. *Dig Dis Sci.* 1989;34:606-611.

5. Roarty TP, Weber F, Soykan I, McCallum RW. Misoprostol in the treatment of chronic refractory constipation: results of a long-term open label trial. *Aliment Pharmacol Ther.* 1997;11:1059-1066.

6. Verne GN, Davis RH, Robinson ME, Gordon JM. Treatment of chronic constipation with colchicine: a randomized, double-blind, placebo-controlled crossover trial. *Am J Gastroenterol.* 2003;98:1112-1116.

7. Kamm MA, Muller-Lissner S, Talley NJ, et al. Tegaserod for the treatment of chronic constipation: a randomized, double-blind, placebo-controlled multinational study. *Am J Gastroenterol.* 2005;100:362-372.

8. Chiarioni G, Salandini L, Whitehead WE. Biofeedback benefits only patients with outlet dysfunction, not patients with isolated slow transit constipation. *Gastroenterology.* 2005;129:86-97.

9. Dukas L, Willett WC, Giovannucci EL. Association between physical activity, fiber intake, and other lifestyle variables and constipation in a study of women. *Am J Gastroenterol.* 2003;98:1790-1796.

10. Bassotti G, Chistolini F, Sietchiping-Nzepa F, et al. Biofeedback for pelvic floor dysfunction in constipation. *BMJ.* 2004;328:393-396.

11. Palsson OS, Heymen S, Whitehead WE. Biofeedback treatment for functional anorectal disorders: a comprehensive efficacy review. *Appl Psychophysiol Biofeedback.* 2004;29:153-174.

12. Higgins PD, Johanson JF. Epidemiology of constipation in North America: a systematic review. *Am J Gastroenterol.* 2004;99:750-759.

13. Chiarelli P, Brown W, McElduff P. Constipation in Australian women: prevalence and associated factors. *Int Urogynecol J Pelvic Floor Dysfunct.* 2000;11:71-78.

14. Bialostosky K, Wright JD, Kennedy-Stephenson J, McDowell M, Johnson CL. Dietary intake of macronutrients, micronutrients, and other dietary constituents: United States, 1988-94. *Vital Health Stat.* 2002;11:1-158.

15. Burkitt DP, Walker AR, Painter NS. Effect of dietary fibre on stools and the transit-times, and its role in the causation of disease. *Lancet.* 1972;2:1408-1412.

16. Khoshbaten M, Hekmatdoost A, Ghasemi H, Entezariasl M. Prevalence of gastrointestinal symptoms and signs in northwestern Tabriz, Iran. *Indian J Gastroenterol.* 2004;23:168-170.

17. Ho KY, Kang JY, Seow A. Prevalence of gastrointestinal symptoms in a multiracial Asian population, with particular reference to reflux-type symptoms. *Am J Gastroenterol.* 1998;93:1816-1822.

18. Comas Vives A, Polanco Allue I, Grupo de Trabajo Espanol para el Estudio del Estrenimiento en la Poblacion Infantil. Case-control study of risk factors associated with constipation. The FREI Study. *An Pediatr* (Barc). 2005;62:340-345.

19. Morais MB, Vitolo MR, Aguirre AN, Fagundes-Neto U. Measurement of low dietary fiber intake as a risk factor for chronic constipation in children. *J Pediatr Gastroenterol Nutr.* 1999;29:132-135.

20. Tse PW, Leung SS, Chan T, Sien A, Chan AK. Dietary fibre intake and constipation in children with severe developmental disabilities. *J Paediatr Child Health.* 2000;36:236-239.

21. Howard LV, West D, Ossip-Klein DJ. Chronic constipation management for institutionalized older adults. *Geriatr Nurs.* 2000;21:78-82.

22. Griffenberg L, Morris M, Atkinson N, Levenback C. The effect of dietary fiber on bowel function following radical hysterectomy: a randomized trial. *Gynecol Oncol.* 1997;66:417-424.

23. Khaja M, Thakur CS, Bharathan T, Baccash E, Goldenberg G. 'Fiber 7' supplement as an alternative to laxatives in a nursing home. *Gerodontology.* 2005;22:106-108.

24. Ramkumar D, Rao SS. Efficacy and safety of traditional medical therapies for chronic constipation: systematic review. *Am J Gastroenterol.* 2005;100:936-971.

25. Wong PW, Kadakia S. How to deal with chronic constipation: a stepwise method of establishing and treating the source of the problem. *Postgrad Med.* 1999;106:199-200, 203-204, 207-210.

26. Loening-Baucke V, Miele E, Staiano A. Fiber (glucomannan) is beneficial in the treatment of childhood constipation. *Pediatrics.* 2004;113:259-264.

27. Arnaud MJ. Mild dehydration: a risk factor of constipation? *Eur J Clin Nutr.* 2003;57(suppl 2):S88-S95.

28. Anti M, Pignataro G, Armuzzi A, et al. Water supplementation enhances the effect of high-fiber diet on stool frequency and laxative consumption in adult patients with functional constipation. *Hepatogastroenterology.* 1998;45:727-732.

29. Andiran F, Dayi S, Mete E. Cow's milk consumption in constipation and anal fissure in infants and young children. *J Paediatr Child Health.* 2003;39:329-331.

30. Turunen S, Karttunen TJ, Kokkonen J. Lymphoid nodular hyperplasia and cow's milk hypersensitivity in children with chronic constipation. *J Pediatr.* 2004;145:606-611.

31. Hermann GE, Tovar CA, Rogers RC. Induction of endogenous tumor necrosis factor-alpha: suppression of centrally stimulated gastric motility. *Am J Physiol.* 1999;276(pt 2):R59-R68.

32. Carroccio A, Scalici C, Maresi E, et al. Chronic constipation and food intolerance: a model of proctitis causing constipation. *Scand J Gastroenterol.* 2005;40:33-42.

33. Iacono G, Cavataio F, Montalto G, et al. Intolerance of cow's milk and chronic constipation in children. *N Engl J Med.* 1998;339:1100-1104.

53. Diverticular Disease

Diverticula are herniations, or "outpouchings," of the colonic mucosa and submucosa through the muscularis layer. They occur at susceptible sites in the colonic wall, most commonly in areas where intramural blood vessels penetrate and weaken the muscular layer.

Diverticulosis indicates the presence of diverticula. When uncomplicated, the condition is asymptomatic. When colonic bacteria breach the diverticula and inflammation occurs either outside the diverticulum or within the bowel wall, the clinical syndrome of diverticulitis occurs. Among diverticulosis patients, 10% to 20% develop either diverticulitis or bleeding, which results when an adjacent blood vessel ruptures into a diverticulum. Diverticular bleeding is the most common cause of lower gastrointestinal bleeding in the elderly.

Diverticulosis is usually asymptomatic, although patients may give a history of mild lower abdominal pain, cramping, bloating, constipation, and/or diarrhea. The discomfort is often relieved by bowel movements. Diverticulitis presents with fever, severe lower abdominal pain and tenderness, nausea, and vomiting. Diverticular bleeding may present as guiac-positive stools, iron-deficiency anemia, melena, or frank hematochezia.

As described below, the development of diverticula has been associated with a low-fiber diet. It is hypothesized that a lack of fiber renders the stool dry and low in bulk, requiring increased pressure to be generated by colonic contraction to propel the stool through the colon. Over time, this increased pressure is thought to result in the formation of diverticula. In contrast, high fiber intake results in stool that is of appropriate bulk and consistency, which may make the stools easier to pass.

Risk Factors

Advancing age. Diverticula are present in nearly half of Americans by age 60, and more than two-thirds of Americans over age 80 are affected. In contrast, less than 5% of people under age 40 are affected.

Geographic area. Industrialized countries have a much higher incidence of diverticular disease than developing nations. Some Western nations have prevalence rates that approach 40% of the population, whereas developing countries in Asia and Africa have prevalence well below 1%. Further, developing nations that adopt a more Western lifestyle have increased rates of diverticulosis.

Inadequate dietary fiber intake. Several studies have linked low fiber intake to the development of diverticular disease (see Nutritional Considerations).

Total fat and red meat intake. High intake of total fat and red meat has also been correlated with a higher risk for diverticular disease, independent of fiber intake.[1]

Sedentary lifestyle.

Diagnosis

Asymptomatic diverticulosis is often incidentally identified on colonoscopy, abdominal CT scan, or barium enema.

If diverticular bleeding is suspected, a colonoscopy may identify the site of bleeding and confirm the presence of diverticula. Upper GI endoscopy should also be considered to rule out upper GI bleeding.

The triad of left lower abdominal pain, fever, and leukocytosis suggests diverticulitis. Abdominal CT scan is the diagnostic test of choice.

Colonoscopy and barium enema may increase the risk of colonic perforation and are contraindicated in acute diverticulitis.

Colonoscopy with biopsy to rule out colon cancer should be performed after the initial event has subsided.

Treatment

Nutrition is the primary consideration for prevention and treatment of diverticulosis. Increasing fiber intake, either through high-fiber foods or psyllium-based fiber supplements, along with other diet changes, may reduce the risk of developing diverticula (see Nutritional Considerations below).

Uncomplicated diverticulitis is treated with bowel rest (no oral intake of food, drink, or medications) and intravenous antibiotics.

Patients with acute diverticulitis have a 40% risk of recurrence and 80% risk of recurrence following the second episode. Thus, recurrent cases of diverticulitis often require resection of the involved colon.

Diverticulitis complicated by fistula formation, colonic perforation, or bowel obstruction is treated emergently with resection of the involved portion of the colon and colostomy formation.

Diverticular bleeding, if severe or recurrent, may require immediate fluid resuscitation and blood transfusion, along with resection of the involved area of the colon.

Nutritional Considerations

Diverticular disease is associated with a fiber-poor diet, ie, a diet low in fruits, vegetables, whole grains, and legumes but high in animal products and/or refined foods. The following factors have been associated with a reduced risk of diverticular disease in epidemiologic studies:

A high-fiber diet. Fiber-poor diets result in diverticular formation.[2] Fiber may protect against colonic perforation by increasing stool weight and water content, resulting in a decreased fecal transit time and reduction of colonic segmentation pressures.[3] Individuals eating generous amounts of insoluble fiber (eg, wheat bran, legumes, skin of fruit, nuts, and seeds) have roughly a 40% lower risk of diverticular disease, compared with those consuming little dietary fiber.[4] Not surprisingly, omnivores have a high (33%) incidence of diverticular disease, while vegetarians have a much lower incidence by comparison (12%).[5]

Avoiding meat. Eating a diet low in fiber and high in meat is associated with a 3-fold increased risk for symptomatic diverticular disease.[1] In persons eating the largest amount of meat, the risk for right-sided diverticulosis in particular is roughly 25 times that of persons eating the least.[6] It should be noted that fiber intake and meat intake are not entirely independent variables; like all animal products, meat contains no fiber.

During symptomatic episodes, avoiding solid foods and staying hydrated on a liquid diet or intravenous fluids in combination with antibiotics is helpful.[7]

It should also be noted that high levels of physical activity may have a protective effect against diverticular disease. Constipation is a known risk factor for diverticulitis and is related to inactivity.[8] While moderate physical activity has little protective effect, more intense activity, such as jogging or running, reduces risk by about 40%.[9]

Orders

See Basic Diet Orders chapter.

Exercise prescription.

What to Tell the Family

Diverticula are outpouchings of the lining of the gut caused by pressure building up from with the intestinal tract. This pressure appears to result from low-fiber diets and may be preventable by a high-fiber diet. Family members can help by serving plenty of high-fiber vegetables, fruits, beans, and whole grains at home and eating these foods themselves. Diet changes are much more likely to be permanent when the whole family joins in.

References

1. Aldoori WH, Giovannucci EL, Rimm EB, et al. A prospective study of diet and the risk of symptomatic diverticular disease in men. *Am J Clin Nutr.* 1994;60:757-764.

2. Floch MH, Bina I. The natural history of diverticulitis: fact and theory. *J Clin Gastroenterol.* 2004;38(suppl 1):S2-S7.

3. Morris CR, Harvey IM, Stebbings WSL, et al. Epidemiology of perforated colonic diverticular disease. *Postgrad Med J.* 2002;78:654-658.

4. Aldoori WH, Giovannucci EL, Rockett HR, Sampson L, Rimm EB, Willett WC. A prospective study of dietary fiber types and symptomatic diverticular disease in men. *J Nutr.* 1998;128:714-719.

5. Gear JS, Ware A, Fursdon P, et al. Symptomless diverticular disease and intake of dietary fibre. *Lancet.* 1979;1:511-514.

6. Lin OS, Soon MS, Wu SS, et al. Dietary habits and right-sided colonic diverticulosis. *Dis Colon Rectum.* 2000;43:1412-1418.

7. Petrakis I, Sakellaris G, Kogerakis N, et al. New perspectives in the management of sigmoid diverticulitis. *Panminerva Med.* 2001;43:289-293.

8. Simren M. Physical activity and the gastrointestinal tract. *Eur J Gastroenterol Hepatol.* 2002;14:1053-1056.

9. Aldoori WH, Giovannucci EL, Rimm EB, et al. Prospective study of physical activity and the risk of symptomatic diverticular disease in men. *Gut.* 1995;36:276-282.

54. Irritable Bowel Syndrome

Irritable bowel syndrome (IBS) is characterized by chronic abdominal pain and altered bowel habits without an identifiable organic cause. It affects 10% to 15% of the US population and represents up to 50% of all referrals to gastroenterologists.

The pathophysiology is unclear. To date, no physiologic or psychological etiology has been identified. Investigation has centered on abnormal gastrointestinal motility, hypersensitivity of gastrointestinal nerves, microscopic inflammation, infection, carbohydrate or bile acid malabsorption, and emotional stress, but clinical studies thus far are inconclusive.

Abdominal pain is the predominant symptom that causes patients to seek medical advice. Altered bowel habits are also often present and may occur as diarrhea, constipation, or alternating diarrhea and constipation. Other symptoms include bloating, incomplete evacuation, nausea, dyspepsia, dysphagia, reflux, and heartburn. The condition may also be accompanied by comorbid somatic conditions (eg, dysmenorrhea, urinary frequency and urgency, sexual dysfunction, or fibromyalgia and other pain syndromes) and psychiatric disorders (eg, somatization, depression, anxiety).

Risk Factors

At least half of cases present in patients less than 35 years of age. In Western societies women are affected twice as often as men.

Diagnosis

A careful history and physical examination are essential to avoid unnecessary and costly diagnostic testing. The examining physician should attempt to identify foods, nutrients or additives (eg, lactose, sorbitol, saccharin, sucralose), and medications (eg, antacids, calcium channel blockers, anticholinergics) that are related to symptoms. It is also important to look for factors that suggest organic disease and require further diagnostic testing to rule it out. Examples include hematochezia, weight loss greater than 10 pounds, family history of colon cancer, recurring fever, anemia, and severe diarrhea.

The Rome II criteria have been designed to create a standardized system for diagnosis, but the utility of these criteria has not been fully established. The criteria include:

*   At least 12 weeks of continuous recurrent abdominal pain that is relieved by defecation, and/or a change in the consistency, frequency, or form of stool.

*   Abnormal stool passage (straining, urgency, or feeling of incomplete evacuation).

*   Passage of mucus.

*   Bloating or abdominal distention.

In appropriate patients, laboratory studies may include complete blood count (CBC), chemistry panel, thyroid function tests, 24-hour stool collection, and stool testing for ova and parasites.

Colonoscopy may be useful to rule out inflammatory bowel disease and colon cancer, especially in patients over 50. In younger patients with symptoms of IBS, colonoscopy is not usually necessary.

Treatment

There is no specific curative treatment. The therapeutic regimen should focus on relieving symptoms and reassuring the patient that a serious illness is not present. The following nutritional interventions and several medications have been used with varying success:

*   Avoid possible food triggers, including lactose and artificial sweeteners (eg, sorbitol, saccharin, sucralose).

*   Diarrheal symptoms can be treated with loperamide, cholestyramine, or other antidiarrheal medications.

- Constipation can be treated with fiber supplementation or osmotic laxatives.

- Abdominal pain may respond to antispasmodic agents (eg, mebeverine, dicyclomine, hyoscyamine) or tricyclic antidepressants (eg, amitriptyline).

- Recent studies suggest that antibiotic therapy (eg, rifaximin) can be useful in certain cases, especially in patients with bacterial overgrowth and diarrhea.

Individuals with irritable bowel syndrome may have enhanced autonomic, neuroendocrine, attentional, and pain-modulatory responses to stimuli.[1] Brain imaging studies have demonstrated increased activation of the anterior mid-cingulate cortex that is linked to fear and psychological distress, and repression of descending opiate-mediated inhibitory pathways originating in the anterior cingulated gyrus of the limbic system.[2] Sympathetic activity is increased at rest.[3]

Psychological interventions should also be considered and are often necessary. Psychological distress, major depression, anxiety, panic disorder and agoraphobia, somatization, and hypochondriasis are more common in persons with IBS, compared with other patients.[4,5] A recent review of randomized, controlled trials of psychological treatments found that 8 out of 12 treatments showed positive responses, mainly reductions in pain and diarrhea, with no effect on constipation.[6] Treatment guidelines published by the American Gastroenterology Association suggest that cognitive-behavioral treatment, dynamic (interpersonal) psychotherapy, hypnosis, and stress management/relaxation are effective in reducing abdominal pain and diarrhea.[7] Hypnotherapy may also be effective in some individuals,[8,9] although a recent review suggests caution due to the poor methodological quality and small size of most studies.[10]

Nutritional Considerations

Irritable bowel syndrome appears to have both nutrition- and stress-related etiologies. As with some other intestinal diseases, it may be more common in individuals consuming Western diets than in persons consuming the high-fiber, low-fat diets that are traditional in developing societies.[11] Both diet and psychological interventions have resulted in symptomatic improvements, and it is likely that patients will benefit most from a combination of medical, nutritional, and behavioral approaches. The following measures may be helpful:

Increased insoluble fiber. The rationale for treatment with increased fiber is the assumption that symptoms are caused by an increase in intraluminal pressure,[12] which is relieved by a bulking agent such as wheat bran. Several studies have revealed that adding bran fiber decreases bloating, constipation, and diarrhea in patients with irritable bowel syndrome. However, a placebo effect appears to account for some of these benefits, and a subpopulation of patients experiences an exacerbation of symptoms (eg, bloating) with bran treatment.[13]

Other investigations have indicated that fiber types other than wheat bran (eg, partially hydrolyzed guar gum) are more effective for this purpose.[12] Additional controlled clinical trials are needed to compare the efficacy of different types of fiber.

Elimination diets for patients with adverse food reactions. Elimination diets help roughly half of IBS patients.[14] Salicylates, amines, and glutamates in foods are suspected of causing symptoms in some individuals. Among the foods that contain these compounds are milk, eggs, and wheat, the 3 foods most frequently cited in IBS exacerbations.[15,16] Other studies have found that IgG4 antibodies to milk, eggs, wheat, beef, pork, and lamb were commonly elevated in individuals with IBS.[17] In a controlled trial, a diet excluding foods to which patients had raised IgG antibodies resulted in greater symptom improvement, compared with a sham diet.[18] Another intervention in which beef, wheat, and dairy products were eliminated significantly reduced total symptom scores, an effect attributed to a dramatic decrease in gas (hydrogen and methane) production.[19]

Probiotic therapy. A number of studies have indicated differences in intestinal microbial populations between individuals with IBS and others, suggesting that antibiotic treatments may play a causative role. Repopulating the intestinal tract with "friendly" bacteria may be helpful. Most studies have suggested a benefit from probiotic treatment with *Lactobacillus plantarum, Bifidobacterium breve, Streptococcus faecium,* and combinations of these with other organisms.[13,14] Double-blind, placebo-controlled studies indicate significant relief of IBS symptoms with the use of probiotics in adults[20] and in children.[21] However, studies have not yet specifically indicated the strain selection, dose, and viability needed to consistently produce symptom relief in IBS patients.[22]

Peppermint oil. Enteric-coated peppermint oil capsules have been evaluated in controlled clinical trials and found helpful in reducing the symptoms of irritable bowel syndrome in more than half of patients overall and in 75% of children.[23-25] Proposed mechanisms for its effects include local calcium channel blockade causing smooth muscle relaxation and a direct antimicrobial effect against symptom-inducing bacterial overgrowth in the small intestine.[26]

Orders

See Basic Diet Orders chapter.

What to Tell the Family

Irritable bowel syndrome is a complex illness that is frequently exacerbated by stress and, possibly, by poor diet. Patients may benefit from taking medications, making diet changes that increase insoluble fiber (bran cereal, whole grain breads), and eliminating suspected offending foods. Stress reduction techniques and hypnotherapy may also be helpful.

References

1. Mayer EA, Naliboff BD, Chang L, Coutinho SV. Stress and irritable bowel syndrome. *Am J Physiol Gastrointest Liver Physiol.* 2001;280:G519-G524.

2. Ringel Y, Sperber AD, Drossman DA. Irritable bowel syndrome. *Annu Rev Med.* 2001;52:319-338.

3. Adeyemi EO, Desai KD, Towsey M, Ghista D. Characterization of autonomic dysfunction in patients with irritable bowel syndrome by means of heart rate

variability studies. *Am J Gastroenterol.* 1999;94:816-823.

4. Kumano H, Kaiya H, Yoshiuchi K, Yamanaka G, Sasaki T, Kuboki T. Comorbidity of irritable bowel syndrome, panic disorder, and agoraphobia in a Japanese representative sample. *Am J Gastroenterol.* 2004;99:370-376.

5. Locke GR III, Weaver AL, Melton LJ III, Talley NJ. Psychosocial factors are linked to functional gastrointestinal disorders: a population based nested case-control study. *Am J Gastroenterol.* 2004;99:350-357.

6. Mertz H. Psychotherapeutics and serotonin agonists and antagonists. *J Clin Gastroenterol.* 2005;39(suppl 3):S247-S250.

7. Drossman DA, Camilleri M, Mayer EA, Whitehead WE. AGA technical review on irritable bowel syndrome. *Gastroenterology.* 2002;123:2108-2131.

8. Gonsalkorale WM, Whorwell PJ. Hypnotherapy in the treatment of irritable bowel syndrome. *Eur J Gastroenterol Hepatol.* 2005;17:15-20.

9. Vlieger AM, Menko-Frankenhuis C, Wolfkamp SC, Tromp E, Benninga MA. Hypnotherapy for children with functional abdominal pain or irritable bowel syndrome: a randomized controlled trial. *Gastroenterology.* 2007;133:1430-1436.

10. Webb AN, Kukuruzovic RH, Catto-Smith AG, Sawyer SM. Hypnotherapy for treatment of irritable bowel syndrome. *Cochrane Database Syst Rev.* 2007;(4):CD005110.

11. Walker AR, Segal I. Epidemiology of noninfective intestinal diseases in various ethnic groups in South Africa. *Isr J Med Sci.* 1979;15:309-313.

12. Parisi GC, Zilli M, Miani MP, et al. High-fiber diet supplementation in patients with irritable bowel syndrome (IBS): a multicenter, randomized, open trial comparison between wheat bran diet and partially hydrolyzed guar gum (PHGG). *Dig Dis Sci.* 2002;47:1697-1704.

13. Floch MH. Use of diet and probiotic therapy in the irritable bowel syndrome: analysis of the literature. *J Clin Gastroenterol.* 2005;39(suppl):S243-S246.

14. O'Mahony L, McCarthy J, Kelly P, et al. Lactobacillus and bifidobacterium in irritable bowel syndrome: symptom responses and relationship to cytokine profiles. *Gastroenterology.* 2005;128:541-551.

15. Spanier JA, Howden CW, Jones MP. A systematic review of alternative therapies in the irritable bowel syndrome. *Arch Intern Med.* 2003;163:265-274.

16. Niec AM, Frankum B, Talley NJ. Are adverse food reactions linked to irritable bowel syndrome? *Am J Gastroenterol.* 1998;93:2184-2190.

17. Zar S, Mincher L, Benson MJ, Kumar D. Food-specific IgG4 antibody-guided exclusion diet improves symptoms and rectal compliance in irritable bowel syndrome. *Scand J Gastroenterol.* 2005;40:800-807.

18. Atkinson W, Sheldon TA, Shaath N, Whorwell PJ. Food elimination based on IgG antibodies in irritable bowel syndrome: a randomised controlled trial. *Gut.* 2004;53:1459-1464.

19. King TS, Elia M, Hunter JO. Abnormal colonic fermentation in irritable bowel syndrome. *Lancet.* 1998;352:1187-1189.

20. Guyonnet D, Chassany O, Ducrotte P, et al. Effect of a fermented milk containing Bifidobacterium animalis DN-173 010 on the health-related quality of life and symptoms in irritable bowel syndrome in adults in primary care: a multicentre, randomized, double-blind, controlled trial. *Aliment Pharmacol Ther.* 2007;26:475-486.

21. Gawronska A, Dziechciarz P, Horvath A, Szajewska H. A randomized double-blind placebo-controlled trial of Lactobacillus GG for abdominal pain disorders in children. *Aliment Pharmacol Ther.* 2007;25:177-184.

22. Quigley EM, Flourie B. Probiotics and irritable bowel syndrome: a rationale for their use and an assessment of the evidence to date. *Neurogastroenterol Motil.* 2007;19:166-172.

23. Grigoleit HG, Grigoleit P. Peppermint oil in irritable bowel syndrome. *Phytomedicine.* 2005;12:601-606.

24. Kline RM, Kline JJ, Di Palma J, Barbero GJ. Enteric-coated, pH-dependent peppermint oil capsules for the treatment of irritable bowel syndrome in children. *J Pediatr.* 2001;138:125-128.

25. Cappello G, Spezzaferro M, Grossi L, Manzoli L, Marzio L. Peppermint oil (Mintoil) in the treatment of irritable bowel syndrome: a prospective double blind placebo-controlled randomized trial. *Dig Liver Dis.* 2007;39:530-536.

26. Logan AC, Beaulne TM. The treatment of small intestinal bacterial overgrowth with enteric-coated peppermint oil: a case report. *Altern Med Rev.* 2002;7:410-417.

55. Inflammatory Bowel Disease

The most prevalent chronic inflammatory disorders of the digestive tract are ulcerative colitis and Crohn disease, referred to collectively as inflammatory bowel disease (IBD). Approximately 1 million Americans have some form of IBD. Although the disorders share some clinical and pathologic features, each is a distinct condition. Crohn disease can affect any part of the gastrointestinal tract from the mouth to the anus, often invading the deep layers of affected tissues, whereas ulcerative colitis affects the mucosa of the colon and rectum.

Causes of IBD have not been fully established, but the disorder is believed to be caused by abnormal immune system activation, which results in chronic inflammation and ulceration. Individuals with ulcerative colitis or pancolitis have a higher risk of colon cancer, chronic active hepatitis, cirrhosis, arthritis, and nutritional deficiencies.

Risk Factors

Genetics. There are numerous well-described genes related to the development of Crohn disease.[1] In particular, *NOD2* gene mutations are present in a significant percentage of patients with Crohn disease.[2]

Environment. IBD is more common in developed countries, urban areas, and colder climates, as well as among people of high socioeconomic status. Incidence also increases in populations that migrate from low-risk to high-risk areas.

Age. Onset usually occurs in people between the ages of 15 and 35.

Race. Whites have the highest risk. Also, Ashkenazi Jews have up to an 8-fold greater risk of developing IBD, compared with the general population. Non-Hispanic whites and African Americans are more likely to have IBD, compared with Hispanics and Asian Americans. Recently, however, Crohn disease has become as frequent in Japan as in the United States, likely due to westernized lifestyle, including diet, increasing urbanization, and industrialization.

Family history. People with an affected relative have a 10-fold greater risk of having IBD. If the relative is first-degree, the risk is 20 to 35 times greater.

NSAIDs. Use of nonsteroidal antiinflammatory drugs may trigger or cause relapse of IBD. Large intestinal ulcers, bleeding, strictures, and perforation are occasionally due to NSAIDs.[3]

Additional possible risk factors that require further study include the following:

Smoking. Studies on smoking and IBD risk, including those evaluating maternal smoking during pregnancy and risk to the child for future IBD, show conflicting results. Overall, smoking appears to be associated with increased risk for Crohn disease and reduced risk for ulcerative colitis.[4]

Lack of breast-feeding. Some evidence suggests that breast-feeding may reduce risk, but more studies are needed to assess this possibility. See Nutritional Considerations for more information.

Diagnosis

Crohn disease and ulcerative colitis have many common symptoms, ranging from mild to severe, which may develop rapidly or gradually. These include:

Persistent diarrhea, which may be bloody and lead to dehydration.

Abdominal pain is much more common in Crohn disease than in ulcerative colitis.

Loss of appetite and subsequent weight loss. Children with IBD, particularly Crohn disease, often fail to develop and grow normally.

Fever, which is a common sign in severe IBD cases.

Chronic inflammation, which may result in fissures, ulcers, fistulas, scarring, and strictures.

In severe cases of ulcerative colitis, **toxic megacolon** may result, with an increased danger of colon perforation.

Extraintestinal manifestations include arthritis (more common in Crohn disease); eye inflammations (conjunctivitis/uveitis); skin lesions (eg, erythema nodosum, pyoderma gangrenosum, and aphthous stomatitis), which occur more often in Crohn disease; anemia (primarily due to rectal bleeding); and liver disorders (mainly primary sclerosing cholangitis).

Diagnostic Tests

The following methods are often used to diagnose or evaluate IBD. Test selection depends on the type and severity of symptoms and previous test results. Invasive testing increases perforation risk and is not appropriate for patients with severe disease.

Endoscopic procedures, with or without biopsy, are recommended depending on the area of the digestive tract affected. Sigmoidoscopy, colonoscopy, esophagogastroduodenoscopy (EGD), endoscopic retrograde cholangiopancreatography (ERCP), and capsule "minicamera" endoscopy can be used to diagnose and observe the extent of IBD. These tests can also rule out other diseases that may mimic IBD, such as cancer and hemorrhoids.

Radiologic tests provide important information that cannot be obtained through endoscopy alone. Plain abdominal x-ray can detect small-bowel obstruction in Crohn disease or toxic megacolon in ulcerative colitis. Barium swallow or enema can reveal strictures or intestinal fistula. However, neither one should be performed in cases of recent obstruction or severe inflammation.

CT scan may rule out complications of IBD (eg, intra-abdominal abscess, stricture, small-bowel obstruction, fistula, and bowel perforation), narrow the differential, and aid in abscess drainage.

Laboratory Tests

Complete blood count is used to check for anemia.

Tests for electrolytes and carotenoid concentrations assess the possible consequences of malabsorption. Serum albumin may be used as a measure of disease severity.

A diagnosis of colitis may be supported by testing for **perinuclear antineutrophil cytoplasmic antibody** (P-ANCA) in ulcerative colitis and **anti-Saccharomyces cerevisiae antibody**, which typically indicates Crohn disease.

Stool culture may be useful, because treatable bacterial infections, particularly *Clostridium difficile*, can trigger an IBD flare.

Treatment

The goal of treatment is to reduce the inflammation that triggers signs and symptoms and to induce remission. Treatment involves medication in mild to moderate cases, or surgery in severe and refractory cases. The following medications are commonly prescribed for patients with IBD:

Aminosalicylates. Sulfasalazine can be administered orally, in enema formulations, or as suppositories. However, it has numerous common side effects, which include infertility in men. Oral mesalamine has significantly fewer side effects for people who cannot tolerate sulfasalazine.

Corticosteroids. Prednisone, methylprednisolone, and hydrocortisone control inflammation in moderate to severe cases of IBD, but they all have numerous short-term and long-term side effects. Budesonide, however, is designed to be released specifically in the ileum and ascending colon, where Crohn disease typically is most active. It is effective and is rapidly metabolized and quickly cleared from the blood with relatively few side effects.

Broad-spectrum antibiotics. Ciprofloxacin, metronidazole, and ampicillin can be used as first-line therapy when purulent perianal disease is present, but they are only adjunctive therapies in flares of colonic Crohn disease, in severe ulcerative colitis, in Crohn disease unresponsive to other medical therapy, and in patients with severe side effects from other medications. These agents alter the bacterial composition of the intestines and suppress the intestine's immune system.[5] Ciprofloxacin is preferred to metronidazole, which causes peripheral neuropathy when used chronically.

Immunomodulators. Azathioprine and mercaptopurine reduce the steroid dosage needed, aid in healing fistulas, and help maintain disease remission. Cyclosporine A is used in acute flares of ulcerative colitis resistant to other medications. These drugs are used in refractory disease, having greater toxicity than corticosteroids, including the possibility of causing kidney damage, hepatitis, hypertension, seizures, and immunosuppression and increasing the risk of lymphoma.

Biologic therapy (proteins, genes, and antibodies). These agents are used in patients who have not responded to conventional therapy. Infliximab is a chimeric monoclonal antibody that blocks the immune system's production of tumor necrosis factor-α. Adalizumab appears to have efficacy similar to that of infliximab. Natalizumab, an antibody that prevents leukocyte trafficking to tissues, also is effective in treating Crohn disease.

Symptomatic Treatment

The following treatments may be used for symptomatic relief:

Antidiarrheals, such as loperamide, may be effective.

Increased fiber intake should be encouraged when constipation occurs and stricture is not present.

Iron supplements are used when chronic intestinal bleeding leads to iron-deficient anemia (see Nutritional Considerations). When anemia is the result of chronic inflammation, erythropoietin may be required, in addition to iron supplements.

Vitamin B$_{12}$ injections, high-dose oral administration, or nasal sprays are needed in cases in which persistent diarrhea impairs B$_{12}$ absorption, or when the terminal ileum is affected in Crohn disease. In either case, evidence for decreased body stores of vitamin B$_{12}$ is usually indicated before starting lifelong replacement therapy. The vitamin also promotes normal growth and development in children.

Exercise. IBD patients can benefit from exercise. Although only limited evidence suggests that exercise reduces risk for the onset of IBD, benefits of regular activity include improvement of psychological symptoms; improvements in muscle strength and bone health, which are often impaired with glucocorticoid therapy; and a reduced risk for colon cancer that may result from long-standing IBD.[6]

Bacterial flora. The bacterial flora of affected individuals differs from that of healthy individuals.

Surgery. Total colectomy may be necessary in severe cases of ulcerative colitis. Bowel resection is indicated in Crohn disease when severe complications occur, including bleeding, strictures, and fistulas. However, in Crohn disease, surgery is not usually curative. Postsurgery relapses can be reduced by continuous preventive treatment with 6-mercaptopurine or azathioprine and possibly with aminosalicylates or metronidazole.

Nutritional Considerations

Western diets high in animal protein and fat and low in fruit, vegetables, and fiber have been associated with the onset of IBD.[7,8] Dietary changes may modify the risk for IBD or act as an adjunct to the antiinflammatory treatments used to control disease activity.

Research studies have adduced several factors that may play a role in the risk of developing IBD:

Absence of breast-feeding. Breast-feeding may protect against IBD by protecting against gastrointestinal infection during infancy; by stimulating the early development, maturation, and immunologic competence of the gastrointestinal mucosa; and by delaying exposure to cow's milk (see below).[9] A meta-analysis found that the risk for ulcerative colitis was 25% lower and the risk for Crohn disease 35% lower in individuals who were breast-fed.[10]

Western dietary pattern. Western diets that are relatively high in meat, dairy products, and sugar, and low in fiber and other plant constituents, compared with diets that are traditional in other regions of the world, have been associated with a higher risk of IBD. It is difficult to identify which aspects of the diet are responsible for this pattern. Candidates that have been studied are discussed below. However, it may be that interventions to reduce risk need to address the overall dietary pattern, rather than its components.

Animal protein. Dietary data from Japan suggest that the westernization of traditional Asian diets is associated with increased risk for IBD. When the incidence of Crohn disease and the daily intake of various dietary components were compared annually from 1966 to 1985, animal protein intake emerged as the strongest independent risk factor.[11]

Animal protein contributes significantly to the colonic sulfur pool, resulting in the generation of hydrogen sulfide. Hydrogen sulfide may increase disease activity in ulcerative colitis through a direct toxic effect on intestinal mucosa and by interfering with butyrate oxidation, an important antiinflammatory fatty acid produced from dietary fiber.[12]

Among patients with ulcerative colitis, meat intake per se more than triples the rate of relapse. Consumption of the highest, compared with the lowest, intake of red meat and processed meat (172 g/d, compared with 124 g/d) increases the rate of relapse more than 5-fold.[13] Conversely, a pilot study restricting animal protein and other dietary sources of sulfur resulted in a complete absence of IBD relapse, compared with an expected relapse rate of 22% to 26% with medication alone.[14] Further studies are needed to confirm these effects.

On diets that provide vegetable sources of protein, fecal sulfide content is much lower than that of meat-based diets.[15] This may help explain why epidemiologic studies have found an inverse relationship between Crohn disease prevalence and vegetable protein intake.[11]

Dairy products. Individuals with IBD reveal symptoms of sensitivity to cow's milk far more often than controls do, and those who had documented cow's milk allergy developed ulcerative colitis at an earlier age than did people with this disease who were free of milk allergy. Patients with IBD have antibodies to cow's milk protein, and these correlate with disease activity in Crohn disease.[9] Studies also indicate that cow's milk increases both intestinal permeability and production of proinflammatory cytokines, both of which are involved in IBD.[16] Preliminary data indicate that allergies to foods other than dairy products might be involved in IBD,[17] but further study is required before hypoallergenic diets are established as an effective IBD treatment.

Some evidence suggests that a milk-borne pathogen may play an etiologic role in Crohn disease. *Mycobacterium avium subsp. paratuberculosis* (MAP) is commonly found in milk products, survives pasteurization, and causes a Crohn-like illness (Johne disease) in dairy cows and other ruminants. MAP has been found with far greater frequency in patients with Crohn disease than in those with ulcerative colitis or controls.[18] However, the pathogen has not yet been proven to be a causative agent in Crohn disease, and the benefit of eradicating MAP with antibiotic therapy has not been established.[18]

High-fat diet. Fat intake may affect IBD through conversion of omega-6 fatty acids (found in animal products and vegetable oils, such as corn, safflower, and sunflower oil) to proinflammatory eicosanoids (eg, leukotriene B4).[19] Diets that are high in fat, particularly animal fat, and cholesterol have been associated with significant increases in the risk for IBD.[7,8] The intake of foods containing partially hydrogenated fats is also associated with IBD risk. In countries where margarine consumption has increased, a rise in the rate of Crohn disease followed.[9] Persons eating fast foods (ie, foods high in hydrogenated oils) at least twice per week had 3 times the risk for Crohn disease and 4 times the risk for ulcerative colitis compared with those who avoided these foods.[20]

Low-fiber diet. Compared with persons consuming small amounts of fiber, those eating 15 grams or more per day had half the risk for developing Crohn disease.[20] Fruit intake in particular appears more strongly associated with reduced risk of IBD compared with cereals.[9] Individuals eating high-fiber diets were more likely to remain in remission, or had significantly fewer and shorter hospitalizations and required less intestinal surgery, than a control group.[21]

In addition to their fiber content, vegetables and fruits also provide antioxidant vitamins, minerals, carotenoids, and flavonoids. These compounds help limit oxidative stress, a condition found in individuals with IBD as a result of intestinal inflammation,[22] even in persons with low indices of disease activity while taking medication.[23] This is not a reason for supplementation, however. These compounds are easily obtained from dietary sources; their role in IBD management has yet to be established.

High sugar intake. Studies have consistently found an association between higher intakes of sugars and the development of IBD.[7,9] However, these associations may merely reflect lifestyle patterns common in populations with IBD. A biological mechanism has not been established for sugar's effect in IBD, and larger clinical trials have not documented significant benefits of a diet low in refined carbohydrates. Further studies are required to determine if such a diet helps to prevent or treat IBD.

In addition, the following dietary factors may play a role in clinical treatment:

Dietary supplements. Some patients with IBD may have significant malabsorption of nutrients. Others may have an increased need for certain antioxidants due to oxidative stress. Serum concentrations of several nutrients (beta-carotene, vitamin C, vitamin E, selenium, and zinc) have been found to be significantly lower or outright deficient in IBD patients, as are antioxidant status and serum concentrations of magnesium and vitamin D.[21,24] These deficiencies indicate a need for micronutrient-dense foods and a multiple vitamin-mineral supplement.

However, oral forms of iron may be contraindicated. Although iron-deficiency anemia is common in patients with IBD due to gastrointestinal blood loss, oral iron supplements have been found to exacerbate disease, while intravenous iron did not.[25] Other types of dietary supplements, including fatty acids, botanicals, and probiotics, appear to be promising adjunctive approaches to IBD. Clinicians should consider prescribing the following nutrients for individuals with IBD:

B-vitamin supplements and plasma homocysteine. Many individuals with IBD have elevated levels of plasma homocysteine. In turn, recent evidence indicates that homocysteine plays a pathogenic, proinflammatory role in IBD.[26] Lower levels of folate,[27,28] vitamin B$_{12}$,[29,30] and vitamin B$_6$[31] have been found in patients with IBD and elevated homocysteine. Clinical trials to assess benefits of lowering homocysteine levels with B vitamins in IBD have not yet been published. However, the folate-depleting effects of sulfasalazine may be involved in intestinal dysplasia, an abnormality preventable by folate supplementation.[22]

Vitamin K status is often poor in patients with Crohn disease and is associated with higher levels of uncarboxylated osteocalcin and a greater rate of bone turnover.[32,33] No evidence currently indicates that supplementation with vitamin K improves these indices. However, a high intake of vegetables containing vitamin K (eg, green leafy vegetables) is advised.

Omega-3 fatty acids. Some investigators have speculated that long-chain omega-3 fatty acids may decrease disease activity in IBD by reducing leukotriene B4 (LTB4) and other indices of immune overreactivity.[21,22] Studies have suggested advantages of omega-3 supplementation in patients with ulcerative colitis,[34] for reducing the rate of relapse in Crohn disease[35] or as an adjunct to mesalazine for maintaining remission in pediatric patients with Crohn disease.[36] However, a review of studies on supplementation of omega-3 fatty acids found insufficient evidence to support conclusions about their effects on clinical, endoscopic, or histologic scores, or on remission or relapse rates.[37]

Orders

See Basic Diet Orders chapter.

What to Tell the Family

The role of dietary factors in IBD has not been fully elucidated. Some evidence suggests that Western diets, high in animal protein, animal fat, hydrogenated oils, and sugar, may increase the risk of IBD. While the role of dietary changes in modifying the course of IBD is under investigation, individuals with inflammatory bowel diseases may wish to make dietary changes as described above. Their families can assist them in doing so and may benefit themselves from these same diet adjustments.

References

1. Biank V, Broeckel U, Kugathasan S. Pediatric inflammatory bowel disease: clinical and molecular genetics. *Inflammatory Bowel Diseases*. 2007;13:1430-1438.

2. Hugot JP, Zaccaria I, Cavanaugh J, et al. Prevalence of CARD15/NOD2 Mutations in Caucasian Healthy People. *Am J Gastroenterol*. 2007;102:1259-1267.

3. Beaugerie L, Thiefin G. Gastrointestinal complications related to NSAIDs [in French]. *Gastroenterol Clin Biol*. 2004;28(spec 3):C62-C72.

4. Bamias G, Nyce MR, De La Rue SA, Cominelli F. New concepts in the pathophysiology of inflammatory bowel disease. *Annals Internal Medicine*. 2005;143:895-904.

5. Sartor RB. Therapeutic manipulation of the enteric microflora in inflammatory bowel diseases: antibiotics, probiotics, and prebiotics. *Gastroenterology*. 2004;126:1620-1633.

6. Peters HP, De Vries WR, Vanberge-Henegouwen GP, Akkermans LM. Potential benefits and hazards of physical activity and exercise on the gastrointestinal tract. *Gut*. 2001;48:435-439.

7. Sakamoto N, Kono S, Wakai K, et al. Dietary risk factors for inflammatory bowel disease: a multicenter case-control study in Japan. *Inflamm Bowel Dis*. 2005;11:154-163.

8. Reif S, Klein I, Lubin F, Farbstein M, Hallak A, Gilat T. Pre-illness dietary factors in inflammatory bowel disease. *Gut*. 1997;40:754-760.

9. Cashman KD, Shanahan F. Is nutrition an aetiological factor for inflammatory bowel disease? *Eur J Gastroenterol Hepatol*. 2003;15:607-613.

10. Klement E, Cohen RV, Boxman J, Joseph A, Reif S. Breastfeeding and risk of inflammatory bowel disease: a systematic review with meta-analysis. *Am J Clin Nutr.* 2004;80:1342-1352.

11. Shoda R, Matsueda K, Yamato S, Umeda N. Epidemiologic analysis of Crohn disease in Japan: increased dietary intake of n-6 polyunsaturated fatty acids and animal protein relates to the increased incidence of Crohn disease in Japan. *Am J Clin Nutr.* 1996;63:741-745.

12. Tilg H, Kaser A. Diet and relapsing ulcerative colitis: take off the meat? *Gut.* 2004;53:1399-1401.

13. Jowett SL, Seal CJ, Pearce MS, et al. Influence of dietary factors on the clinical course of ulcerative colitis: a prospective cohort study. *Gut.* 2004;53:1479-1484.

14. Roediger WE. Decreased sulphur amino acid intake in ulcerative colitis. *Lancet.* 1998;351:1555.

15. Magee EA, Richardson CJ, Hughes R, Cummings JH. Contribution of dietary protein to sulfide production in the large intestine: an in vitro and a controlled feeding study in humans. *Am J Clin Nutr.* 2000;72:1488-1494.

16. DeMeo MT, Mutlu EA, Keshavarzian A, Tobin MC. Intestinal permeation and gastrointestinal disease. *J Clin Gastroenterol.* 2002;34:385-396.

17. Van Den Bogaerde J, Cahill J, Emmanuel AV, et al. Gut mucosal response to food antigens in Crohn's disease. *Aliment Pharmacol Ther.* 2002;16:1903-1915.

18. Sartor RB. Does Mycobacterium avium subspecies paratuberculosis cause Crohn's disease? *Gut.* 2005;54:896-898.

19. Calder PC. Polyunsaturated fatty acids, inflammation, and immunity. *Lipids.* 2001;36:1007-1024.

20. Persson PG, Ahlbom A, Hellers G. Diet and inflammatory bowel disease: a case-control study. *Epidemiology.* 1992;3:47-52.

21. Head K, Jurenka JS. Inflammatory bowel disease. Part II: Crohn's disease--pathophysiology and conventional and alternative treatment options. *Altern Med Rev.* 2004;9:360-401.

22. Head KA, Jurenka JS. Inflammatory bowel disease Part 1: ulcerative colitis--pathophysiology and conventional and alternative treatment options. *Altern Med Rev.* 2003;8:247-283.

23. Wendland BE, Aghdassi E, Tam C, et al. Lipid peroxidation and plasma antioxidant micronutrients in Crohn disease. *Am J Clin Nutr.* 2001;74:259-264.

24. Geerling BJ, Badart-Smook A, Stockbrugger RW, Brummer RJ. Comprehensive nutritional status in patients with long-standing Crohn disease currently in remission. *Am J Clin Nutr.* 1998;67:919-926.

25. Seril DN, Liao J, West AB, Yang GY. High-iron diet: foe or feat in ulcerative colitis and ulcerative colitis-associated carcinogenesis. *J Clin Gastroenterol.* 2006;40:391-397.

26. Danese S, Sgambato A, Papa A, et al. Homocysteine triggers mucosal microvascular activation in inflammatory bowel disease. *Am J Gastroenterol.* 2005;100:886-895.

27. Papa A, De Stefano V, Danese S, Gasbarrini A, Gasbarrini G. Thrombotic complications in inflammatory bowel disease: a multifactorial etiology. *Am J Gastroenterol.* 2001;96:1301-1302.

28. Chowers Y, Sela BA, Holland R, Fidder H, Simoni FB, Bar-Meir S. Increased levels of homocysteine in patients with Crohn's disease are related to folate levels. *Am J Gastroenterol.* 2000;95:3498-3502.

29. Mahmood A, Needham J, Prosser J, et al. Prevalence of hyperhomocysteinemia, activated protein C resistance and prothrombin gene mutation in inflammatory bowel disease. *Eur J Gastroenterol Hepatol.* 2005;17:739-744.

30. Romagnuolo J, Fedorak RN, Dias VC, Bamforth F, Teltscher M. Hyperhomocysteinemia and inflammatory bowel disease: prevalence and predictors in a cross-sectional study. *Am J Gastroenterol.* 2001;96:2143-2149.

31. Saibeni S, Cattaneo M, Vecchi M, et al. Low vitamin B(6) plasma levels, a risk factor for thrombosis, in inflammatory bowel disease: role of inflammation and correlation with acute phase reactants. *Am J Gastroenterol.* 2003;98:112-117.

32. Duggan P, O'Brien M, Kiely M, McCarthy J, Shanaham F, Cashman KD. Vitamin K status in patients with Crohn's disease and relationship to bone turnover. *Am J Gastroenterol.* 2004;99:2178-2185.

33. Schoon EJ, Muller MC, Vermeer C, Schurgers LJ, Brummer RJ, Stockbrugger, RW. Low serum and bone vitamin K status in patients with longstanding Crohn's disease: another pathogenetic factor of osteoporosis in Crohn's disease? *Gut.* 2001;48:473-477.

34. Lorenz R, Weber PC, Szimnau P, Heldwein W, Strasser T, Loeschke K. Supplementation with n-3 fatty acids from fish oil in chronic inflammatory bowel disease--a randomized, placebo-controlled, double-blind cross-over trial. *J Intern Med Suppl.* 1989;731:225-232.

35. Belluzzi A, Brignola C, Campieri M, Pera A, Boschi S, Miglioli M. Effect of an enteric-coated fish-oil preparation on relapses in Crohn's disease. *N Engl J Med.* 1996;334:1557-1560.

36. Romano C, Cucchiara S, Barabino A, Annese V, Sferlazzas C. Usefulness of omega-3 fatty acid supplementation in addition to mesalazine in maintaining remission in pediatric Crohn's disease: a double-blind, randomized, placebo-controlled study. *World J Gastroenterol.* 2005;11:7118-7121.

37. MacLean CH, Mojica WA, Newberry SJ, et al. Systematic review of the effects of n-3 fatty acids in inflammatory bowel disease. *Am J Clin Nutr.* 2005;82:611-619.

56. Cirrhosis

Cirrhosis is a chronic, irreversible liver disease that results from prolonged hepatocellular injury. Ultimately, regenerating hepatocytes and increased fibrosis destroy the liver architecture, and the organ's synthetic and metabolic functions are progressively decreased.

The majority of cases are due to chronic alcohol use or viral hepatitis, especially hepatitis C. However, any chronic liver disease that destroys the underlying hepatic structure (eg, hemochromatosis, Wilson disease, sclerosing cholangitis, autoimmune hepatitis) can result in cirrhosis.

Affected individuals may initially be asymptomatic. When symptoms occur, they can be nonspecific, including weight loss, anorexia, fatigue, weakness, nausea, dull abdominal pain, and constipation or diarrhea. As the disease progresses, clinical features become progressively more prominent. These include jaundice, spider angiomata, palmar erythema, gynecomastia, testicular atrophy, bruising, and hypocoagulation. Portal hypertension occurs as the liver architecture is obliterated, resulting in ascites, edema, splenomegaly, and esophageal varices.

Complications of advanced disease can be fatal. Hepatic encephalopathy can result in lethargy, confusion, slurred speech, hallucinations, asterixis, obtundation, and coma. Hemorrhage from esophageal varices occurs in up to 40% of cirrhosis patients, resulting in massive hematemesis and high mortality. Other complications include spontaneous bacterial peritonitis, acute renal failure (hepatorenal syndrome), and hepatocellular carcinoma.

Risk Factors

Chronic alcohol abuse. Alcoholic liver disease results in 12,000 deaths per year in the United States. Unfortunately, many patients become symptomatic only after severe liver disease is present. Daily alcohol intake as low as 20 grams (two drinks) per day for women and 40 grams (4 drinks) per day for men can result in liver disease over the course of 10 years. However, a somewhat higher amount, perhaps 80 grams daily or more, may be necessary to significantly predispose an individual to cirrhosis.

Unprotected intercourse. Hepatitis B and, less commonly, hepatitis C infections are transmitted through unprotected sexual intercourse.

Intravenous drug use. Hepatitis B and C transmission is also common through intravenous drug use.

Inherited or acquired chronic liver disease. Hemochromatosis, Wilson disease, and autoimmune hepatitis can lead to cirrhosis.

Toxins. Chronic toxic exposures can lead to chronic hepatic injury, although it is not yet clear if toxin exposures other than alcohol lead to cirrhosis.

Diagnosis

History and physical examination should include a special focus on alcohol use, exposure to toxins, intravenous drug abuse, blood transfusion, multiple viral infections, the presence of tattoos, and the characteristic presentation of cirrhosis. Additional investigations are:

Abdominal CT scan and **ultrasound** can provide evidence of abnormal liver architecture to define the extent of cirrhosis. They can also identify ascites and other hepatic and abdominal pathology, such as hepatocellular carcinoma and portal hypertension.

Percutaneous liver biopsy can be diagnostic and may suggest the underlying cause of cirrhosis. Because the biopsy sample represents only about 1/10,000 of the liver tissue, the patterns of cirrhosis may be missed. Biopsy may not be necessary when portal hypertension is present and when the diagnosis is clearly established by clinical, laboratory, and radiologic findings.

Liver function tests can be normal early in the disease, but they become abnormal as the liver is destroyed. Transaminase levels reflect hepatocellular injury; alkaline phosphatase reflects cholestasis; and albumin reflects hepatic synthetic activity.

Metabolic and **electrolyte abnormalities** are common, including hypoalbuminemia, hypocholesterolemia, decreased coagulation factors, decreased nitrogen, elevated ammonia, anemia, thrombocytopenia, and leukopenia.

Upper gastrointestinal (GI) endoscopy may be used to diagnose esophageal varices.

Treatment

Treatment is aimed at slowing or reversing disease progression (if the underlying disease is treatable), preventing and treating complications, and, if possible, providing a cure through liver transplantation.

It is essential to address the underlying etiology. Required measures include avoiding alcohol and hepatotoxic medications, treating viral hepatitis with appropriate antiviral regimens (eg, alpha interferon plus ribavirin), and treating autoimmune hepatitis or severe alcoholic hepatitis with steroids or immunosuppressive agents.

Also critical are prevention and treatment of cirrhosis complications. Esophageal varices can be treated with a beta-blocker to decrease the risk of bleeding. Bleeding varices can be treated with endoscopic rubber banding, sclerotherapy, intravenous vasopressin or somatostatin, or balloon tamponade.

Lactulose decreases ammonia absorption from the gut, thereby decreasing the risk of hepatic encephalopathy.

Ascites can be managed with sodium restriction and diuretics. For severe or recurrent symptomatic ascites, slow removal of ascitic fluid via paracentesis is indicated. Ascites complicated by bacterial infection (spontaneous bacterial peritonitis) requires intravenous antibiotics.

Patients can be screened for the development of hepatocellular carcinoma by serum α-fetoprotein (AFP) concentration and right-upper-quadrant ultrasound.

Ultimately, liver transplantation is the only potential cure. Transplantation is an option for appropriate patients with advanced disease and severe complications, including variceal hemorrhage, hepatic encephalopathy, and hepatorenal syndrome. Transplantation is contraindicated in patients who continue to use alcohol or drugs. It is also contraindicated in patients who are unsuitable for surgery due to cardiopulmonary disease.

Nutritional Considerations

Malnutrition, a common complication in liver cirrhosis, is associated with poor outcome. However, cachexia and muscle wasting are seen frequently in advanced cirrhosis, and there is no evidence that increasing nutrient intake can reverse these findings. Thus, the wasting is likely due to the underlying disease process. However, decreased nutrient intake can accompany cirrhosis or any chronic illness, and the patient should be encouraged to ingest a diet with calories, protein, and fluid appropriate for his or her age and (dry) weight and the degree of protein encephalopathy and fluid retention. This recommendation can be challenging in cirrhotic patients and should be the major goal of nutrition support, rather than attempting to provide an increased level of nutrient provision. It is also reasonable to provide essential vitamins and minerals in the form of a supplement.

If the underlying illness is partially reversed by disease-specific therapy, the recommended energy and protein intake will be adequate to cause a gradual regain of dry weight. Attempts to cause rapid regain of weight are rarely, if ever, indicated. Adverse results of such a program might include excessive fluid retention, refeeding syndrome, and/or glucose intolerance.

The typical management of cirrhosis involves medications (eg, lactulose) that loosen stools and thus decrease the absorption of ammonia, a compound that is a main cause of hepatic encephalopathy. Dietary changes, such as the use of vegetable protein instead of animal protein, may also lower blood ammonia levels.[1,2] Probiotic treatments may have a similar effect. Nutrition therapy, particularly with branched-chain amino acids, can also help support patients who are losing weight due to poor appetite and may improve survival.

A sodium-restricted diet is standard treatment for patients with ascites.[3] A 2000 mg sodium-restricted diet, when combined with diuretic therapy, is effective for controlling fluid overload in 90% of patients with cirrhosis and ascites.[4]

In addition, the following interventions are under investigation for a possible role in cirrhosis prevention or management:

Low-fat diets. Mortality from cirrhosis in many countries is greater than what per capita alcohol consumption would predict.[5] Several investigations have concluded that excess dietary fat may encourage cirrhosis progression. High intakes of total fat,[6] saturated fat,[7] and polyunsaturated fat[5] have been implicated.

Vegetarian diets. Plant-based diets have theoretical advantages in the management of liver disease. Such diets are typically high in fiber, which may reduce ammonia-related encephalopathy in two ways: first, by enhancing the use of nitrogen by colonic bacteria; and second, by facilitating nitrogen removal from the body by speeding food remnants through the intestines.[2] Vegetable protein sources are also higher in arginine, an amino acid that decreases blood ammonia levels through increasing urea synthesis. They are also lower in methionine and tryptophan, amino acids that exacerbate encephalopathy through gut conversion to neurotoxic metabolites (mercaptans and oxyphenol, respectively). Clinical studies show that vegetarian diets improve the results of standard tests (eg, number connection score), improve nitrogen balance and electroencephalogram (EEG) results, and lower blood ammonia concentrations.[2]

However, the efficacy of vegetarian diets in patients with cirrhosis remains to be adequately tested.

Antioxidants and B vitamins. Cirrhotic patients have significant reductions in antioxidant enzymes and lower blood levels of certain antioxidant nutrients, such as carotenoids, vitamin E, and zinc.[8-10] Low circulating plasma proteins account for a large part of these abnormal laboratory values and do not necessarily reflect decreased body stores of these nutrients. However, this is a theoretically important consideration because oxidative stress contributes significantly to liver damage.[11] Poor folate status is also found in persons with cirrhosis,[12] and an estimated 50% have increased blood homocysteine concentrations.[13] Elevated homocysteine is associated with liver fibrosis and cirrhosis, particularly if individuals possess the common *MTHFR C677T* polymorphism.[14,15] Although folate and vitamin B_6 supplements improve post-load (but not basal) blood concentrations of homocysteine,[13] no data show that supplementation with B vitamins and antioxidants alters the clinical course in cirrhosis patients. Due to a reduction in food intake and documented deficiencies of several nutrients in cirrhosis,[8] patients should take at least a multiple vitamin with minerals that meets 100% of the dietary allowance for all vitamins and minerals.

Coffee consumption. Some observational studies have suggested that coffee consumers have a lower risk for liver disease, compared with nonconsumers. Among individuals consuming large amounts of alcohol, an inverse relationship has been observed between coffee intake and serum levels of gamma-glutamyltransferase.[16] In a study of more than 125,000 individuals without known liver disease at baseline, those consuming 1 to 4 or more cups of coffee daily had a 30% to 80% lower risk for developing alcoholic (not nonalcoholic) cirrhosis.[17] One possible explanation involves coffee's phenolic acids, which are strong antioxidants that inhibit inflammation and enhance the expression of both antioxidant and phase 2 detoxifying enzymes.[18]

Vitamin D deficiency. The American Gastroenterological Association (AGA) recommends that individuals with cirrhosis receive at least 400 to 800 IU of vitamin D daily, in addition to 1000 to 1200 mg of elemental calcium.[19] AGA further suggests that vitamin D deficiency should be corrected by increasing serum 25-hydroxyvitamin D levels to at least 25 to 30 mg/mL.[19]

Branched-chain amino acids and enteral feeding for malnourished patients. Protein-energy malnutrition is common, occurring in 65% to 90% of patients with cirrhosis. Blood concentrations of branched-chain amino acids serve as both indicators of nutritional status and predictors of survival.[20] Branched-chain amino acids, at doses of 12 to 14 grams per day, exert significant antianorectic and anticachectic effects in individuals with cirrhosis,[21] presumably by interfering with brain serotonergic activity and inhibiting the overexpression of critical muscular proteolytic pathways. In a multicenter randomized trial of 646 patients with decompensated cirrhosis, the ingestion of 12 g/day of branched-chain amino acids over 2 years was associated with decreased mortality of roughly 35%, compared with nutrition support from diet alone.[22]

However, some data suggest that branched-chain amino acid therapy may be indicated only for the most decompensated patients with encephalopathy.[23] Enteral feeding is the recommended route for artificial nutrition in cirrhosis and is associated with improved liver function and a lower hospital mortality rate.[24]

Probiotic treatment. An imbalance in gut flora and bacterial translocation in cirrhosis patients contributes significantly to ammonia production, resulting in varying degrees of encephalopathy.[25] Providing these patients with supplemental combinations of probiotics reduces blood concentrations of ammonia and endotoxin;[25,26] reduces proinflammatory cytokine production, markers of lipid peroxidation; and improves liver function tests.[27] Patients with liver disease treated with a combination of probiotics (*Lactobacillus plantarum*) and fiber also had a lower rate of postoperative bacterial infections than those treated with selective intestinal decontamination, indicating a beneficial effect on the prevention of bacterial translocation. Additional controlled clinical trials are needed to confirm these findings.

Orders

See Basic Diet Orders chapter.

Provide small, frequent meals with adequate energy, protein, and fluid.

Sodium less than 2 grams daily.

Nutrition assessment by a registered dietitian.

Daily multivitamin with minerals.

What to Tell the Family

Cirrhosis of the liver is a life-threatening chronic illness, which is ultimately terminal without transplantation. However, the management of some cirrhosis cases may be improved with diet, thorough compliance with prescribed medications, and abstinence from alcohol.

References

1. Gheorghe L, Iacob R, Vadan R, Iacob S, Gheorghe C. Improvement of hepatic encephalopathy using a modified high-calorie high-protein diet. *Rom J Gastroenterol.* 2005;14:231-238.

2. Amodio P, Caregaro L, Patteno E, Marcon M, Del Piccolo F, Gatta A. Vegetarian diets in hepatic encephalopathy: facts or fantasies? *Dig Liver Dis.* 2001;33:492-500.

3. Heidelbaugh JJ, Sherbondy M. Cirrhosis and chronic liver failure: Part II. Complications and treatment. *Am Fam Phys.* 2006;74:767-776.

4. Runyon BA. Management of adult patients with ascites caused by cirrhosis. *Hepatology*. 1998;27:264-272.

5. Nanji AA, French SW. Dietary factors and alcoholic cirrhosis. *Alcohol Clin Exp Res*. 1986;10:271-273.

6. Rotily M, Durbec JP, Berthezene P, Sarles H. Diet and alcohol in liver cirrhosis: a case-control study. *Eur J Clin Nutr*. 1990;44:595-603.

7. Corrao G, Ferrari PA, Galatola G. Exploring the role of diet in modifying the effect of known disease determinants: application to risk factors of liver cirrhosis. *Am J Epidemiol*. 1995;142:1136-1146.

8. Leevy CM, Moroianu SA. Nutritional aspects of alcoholic liver disease. *Clin Liver Dis*. 2005;9:67-81.

9. Chari S, Gupta M. Status of blood antioxidant enzymes in alcoholic cirrhosis. *Indian J Physiol Pharmacol*. 2003;47:343-346.

10. Van de Casteele M, Zaman Z, Zeegers M, Servaes R, Fevery J, Nevens F. Blood antioxidant levels in patients with alcoholic liver disease correlate with the degree of liver impairment and are not specific to alcoholic liver injury itself. *Aliment Pharmacol Ther*. 2002;16:985-992.

11. Yadav D, Hertan HI, Schweitzer P, Norkus EP, Pitchumoni CS. Serum and liver micronutrient antioxidants and serum oxidative stress in patients with chronic hepatitis C. *Am J Gastroenterol*. 2002;97:2634-2639.

12. Halifeoglu I, Gur B, Aydin S, Ozturk A. Plasma trace elements, vitamin B_{12}, folate, and homocysteine levels in cirrhotic patients compared with healthy controls. *Biochemistry* (Mosc). 2004;69:693-696.

13. Bosy-Westphal A, Ruschmeyer M, Czech N, et al. Determinants of hyperhomocysteinemia in patients with chronic liver disease and after orthotopic liver transplantation. *Am J Clin Nutr*. 2003;77:1269-1277.

14. Adinolfi LE, Ingrosso D, Cesaro G, et al. Hyperhomocysteinemia and the *MTHFR C677T* polymorphism promote steatosis and fibrosis in chronic hepatitis C patients. *Hepatology*. 2005;41:995-1003.

15. Ventura P, Rosa MC, Abbati G, et al. Hyperhomocysteinaemia in chronic liver diseases: role of disease stage, vitamin status and methylenetetrahydrofolate reductase genetics. *Liver Int*. 2005;25:49-56.

16. Homan DJ, Mobarhan S. Coffee: good, bad, or just fun? A critical review of coffee's effects on liver enzymes. *Nutr Rev*. 2006;64:43-46.

17. Klatsky AL, Morton C, Udaltsova N, Friedman GD. Coffee, cirrhosis, and transaminase enzymes. *Arch Intern Med*. 2006;166:1190-1195.

18. Vinson JA. Coffee and cirrhosis: active ingredients? *Arch Intern Med*. 2006;166:2404-2405.

19. American Gastroenterological Association. American Gastroenterological Association medical position statement: osteoporosis in hepatic disorders. *Gastroenterology*. 2003;125:937–940.

20. Moriwaki H, Miwa Y, Tajika M, Kato M, Fukushima H, Shiraki M. Branched-chain amino acids as a protein- and energy-source in liver cirrhosis. *Biochem Biophys Res Commun*. 2004;313:405-409.

21. Laviano A, Muscaritoli M, Cascino A, et al. Branched-chain amino acids: the best compromise to achieve anabolism? *Curr Opin Clin Nutr Metab Care*. 2005;8:408-414.

22. Muto Y, Sato S, Watanabe A, et al. Effects of oral branched-chain amino acid granules on event-free survival in patients with liver cirrhosis. *Clin Gastroenterol Hepatol.* 2005;3:705-713.

23. Fabbri A, Magrini N, Bianchi G, Zoli M, Marchesini G. Overview of randomized clinical trials of oral branched-chain amino acid treatment in chronic hepatic encephalopathy. *JPEN.* 1996;20:159-164.

24. Cabre E, Gassull MA. Nutritional aspects of liver disease and transplantation. *Curr Opin Clin Nutr Metab Care.* 2001;4:581-589.

25. Liu Q, Duan ZP, Ha da K, Bengmark S, Kurtovic J, Riordan SM. Synbiotic modulation of gut flora: effect on minimal hepatic encephalopathy in patients with cirrhosis. *Hepatology.* 2004;39:1441-1449.

26. Zhao HY, Wang HJ, Lu Z, Xu SZ. Intestinal microflora in patients with liver cirrhosis. *Chin J Dig Dis.* 2004;5:64-67.

27. Loguercio C, Federico A, Tuccillo C, et al. Beneficial effects of a probiotic VSL#3 on parameters of liver dysfunction in chronic liver diseases. *J Clin Gastroenterol.* 2005;39:540-543.

57. Viral Hepatitis

Hepatitis is an inflammation of the liver that results in diffuse hepatic cell death and may lead to areas of liver necrosis. It can be acute or chronic (lasting >6 months) and may progress to fulminant liver failure, cirrhosis, and/or hepatocellular carcinoma. The most common causes of hepatitis in the United States are alcohol abuse and viral infection.

Viral hepatitis can be caused by dozens of viral infections, most commonly the hepatitis viruses (especially hepatitis A, hepatitis B, and hepatitis C) and the herpes viruses (cytomegalovirus, Epstein-Barr virus, varicella-zoster virus, herpes simplex virus).

Most cases are subclinical and asymptomatic. In clinically apparent disease, common symptoms include fever, nausea, vomiting, fatigue, jaundice, right-upper-quadrant abdominal tenderness, and dark urine and pale stools. Extrahepatic manifestations may occur, particularly with chronic hepatitis. These include amenorrhea, arthritis, skin rash, vasculitis, thyroiditis, gynecomastia, glomerulonephritis, polyarteritis nodosa, and Sjögren's syndrome. Complications of chronic hepatitis include cirrhosis, progressive liver failure, and hepatocellular carcinoma.

Hepatitis A is a self-limited cause of acute hepatitis and does not result in a carrier state or chronic disease. Transmission occurs via the fecal-oral route and most commonly results from poor hygienic practices and inadequate sanitation. Disease is usually mild and self-limited, and patients may be asymptomatic. However, fulminant liver failure may occur in patients with underlying liver disease, especially hepatitis C.

Hepatitis B generally causes a mild or subclinical acute hepatitis but may result in chronic hepatitis or an asymptomatic carrier state. Progression to chronic hepatitis is most common in perinatal infections and young children. Transmission occurs via blood and body fluids (eg, unprotected sex, intravenous drug use, blood transfusions, tattoos, and body piercing). Sexual contact is the most common mode of transmission in the United States, whereas perinatal transmission is common in developing countries.

Hepatitis C is the most common cause of chronic hepatitis in the United States and is the most common indication for liver transplantation. Acute hepatitis is usually asymptomatic, but many cases will progress to chronic hepatitis. Hepatitis C patients usually do well for 20 to 25 years before developing cirrhosis, which occurs in about 20% to 30% of chronic cases. Although transmission can occur via blood products, this route is much less common since universal blood screening for hepatitis was initiated in 1990. Intravenous drug use in adults and vertical transmission in infants are the most common causes of hepatitis C today. Transmission rate is higher in patients with concomitant HIV.

Hepatitis D is dependent on co-infection with the hepatitis B virus. If hepatitis D acquired at the same time as hepatitis B, complete recovery can be expected. However, hepatitis D occurring as a superinfection in a hepatitis B patient can cause a syndrome of accelerated hepatitis, with progression to chronic hepatitis within weeks. Transmission occurs via blood and body fluids.

Hepatitis E usually causes a self-limited and mild acute hepatitis. However, the disease may be severe in pregnant women, in whom it may progress to acute onset of liver failure, with mortality as high as 25%. The virus is most commonly spread by fecally contaminated water in endemic areas. No chronic disease state exists for hepatitis E.

Risk Factors

Exposure to blood or body fluids (eg, intravenous drug use, high-risk sexual intercourse, tattoos, body piercing, blood transfusion, occupational needlestick exposure). Transmission via blood transfusion is now rare due to universal screening.

Contact with an infected person (hepatitis A).

Poor hygiene and inadequate sanitation (hepatitis A and hepatitis E).

Underlying liver disease. Patients with underlying liver disease (eg, autoimmune hepatitis, hemochromatosis, Wilson's disease, alpha-1 antitrypsin deficiency) are at increased risk of developing symptomatic hepatitis.

Alcohol use, smoking, HIV infection, and fatty liver are risk factors for progression of hepatitis.

Diagnosis

Abnormal liver function tests are common in viral hepatitis patients, especially during the acute phases of infection. Transaminases (aspartate aminotransferase [AST] and alanine aminotransferase [ALT]), bilirubin, and alkaline phosphatase are generally elevated. Coagulation studies, such as prothrombin time (PT) and partial thromboplastin time (PTT), and albumin are often normal, except in severe disease.

Hepatitis Virus Serology

- **Hepatitis A:** Antihepatitis A virus IgM reflects acute infection. IgG reflects past exposure or vaccination and confers lifelong immunity.

- **Hepatitis B:** Surface antigen and core antibody reflect acute infection. Hepatitis B envelope antigen indicates high infectivity. Be sure to test for superinfection with hepatitis D virus.

- **Hepatitis C:** Testing includes serology, PCR, and genotyping.

- **Hepatitis D:** Antihepatitis D virus IgM or IgG is consistent with infection.

- **Hepatitis E:** Antihepatitis E virus IgM or IgG is consistent with infection.

Biopsy may be indicated to evaluate for etiology and staging of disease.

Right-upper-quadrant ultrasound is usually indicated to evaluate the biliary system and rule out cholelithiasis and biliary obstruction.

X-ray, CT scan, MRI, and/or endoscopic retrograde cholangiopancreatography (ERCP) may be necessary to rule out other abdominal pathology (eg, pancreatitis, cholecystitis, malignancy).

Treatment

Initial treatment includes supportive fluids and electrolyte management, monitoring of nutrition status, and avoidance of hepatotoxic substances (eg, alcohol, acetaminophen, statins). Abstinence from alcohol is mandatory (see Nutritional Considerations below).

In addition to the above measures, treatment targets the underlying hepatitis virus as follows:

- **Hepatitis A:** Most cases are self-limited. Hepatitis A immunoglobin may be given.

- **Hepatitis B:** Hepatitis B immunoglobin is given for postexposure prophylaxis. Chronic hepatitis B is treated with interferon alpha. Lamivudine and ribavirin may also be used.

- **Hepatitis C:** Chronic disease is treated with interferon alpha and ribavirin for 6 months to 1 year.

- **Hepatitis D:** Interferon alpha is given for at least 1 year.

- **Hepatitis E:** The disease is usually self-limited. Prevention via clean water sources is essential.

Vaccination is available for hepatitis A and hepatitis B. All patients with chronic hepatitis B should be vaccinated for hepatitis A, and patients with hepatitis C should be vaccinated for both hepatitis A and hepatitis B.

Acute complications of liver failure are treated as necessary (eg, lactulose to reduce serum ammonia concentration in patients with hepatic encephalopathy; fresh-frozen plasma for coagulopathy).

End-stage liver failure may require liver transplantation.

Nutritional Considerations

The following nutrition considerations apply to prevention and treatment of viral hepatitis:

Hygiene and sanitation. Persons who travel internationally or who are in areas of the United States where contamination occurs should be aware of an increased risk for hepatitis A. Uncooked food, water, and ice can increase the risk for hepatitis A transmission. Drinking bottled water, making sure food is prepared hygienically, and careful washing of hands and dishes can help prevent virus spread.[1]

Avoiding contaminated shellfish. Shellfish are often taken from wastewater-polluted areas of the sea and can concentrate the microbial pathogens in seawater. Those taken from near the shoreline (eg, clams and oysters) are particularly likely to be pathogenic. An estimated 4 million cases of infectious hepatitis A and hepatitis E occur each year globally as a result of consumption of raw or partially cooked filter-feeding shellfish/mollusks taken from polluted coastal waters.[2]

Abstinence from alcohol. In persons with hepatitis C, alcohol appears to have undesirable effects on immune function, viral replication, and hepatic regeneration, while contributing to increased hepatic iron content and negating the effects of drug (ie, interferon) treatment. Alcohol and the hepatitis C virus also act in an additive and possibly synergistic fashion to promote the development and progression of liver damage.[3] A review of studies indicates significantly worse outcomes for alcohol users who have hepatitis C.[4]

Orders

See Basic Diet Orders chapter.

What to Tell the Family

Viral hepatitis may be relatively mild and self-limiting, or it may become chronic, depending on the virus involved and success of treatment. In cases of hepatitis A, family members may protect themselves by avoiding direct contact with the affected member and by practicing safe hygiene. In patients with chronic hepatitis B or the more common hepatitis C, the family can help keep the patient well nourished.

References

1. Wilson TR. The ABCs of hepatitis. *Nurse Pract.* 2005;30:12-21.

2. Shuval H. Estimating the global burden of thalassogenic diseases: human infectious diseases caused by wastewater pollution of the marine environment. *J Water Health.* 2003;1:53-64.

3. Riley TR III, Bhatti AM. Preventive strategies in chronic liver disease: part I. Alcohol, vaccines, toxic medications and supplements, diet and exercise. *Am Fam Physician.* 2001;64:1555-1560.

4. Hutchinson SJ, Bird SM, Goldberg DJ. Influence of alcohol on the progression of hepatitis C virus infection: a meta-analysis. *Clin Gastroenterol Hepatol.* 2005;3:1150-1159.

58. Alcoholic and Toxic Liver Disease

The liver is responsible for concentrating and metabolizing most drugs and toxins. Because of this function, toxic insults to the liver are common. Drug- or alcohol-related hepatotoxicity is the most common cause of fulminant liver failure. Alcohol-related liver disease alone accounts for more than 12,000 deaths yearly in the United States, and alcohol abuse is the most common cause of cirrhosis.

Alcohol is the most frequently abused drug worldwide. Its major metabolite, acetaldehyde, is directly toxic to the liver. Abuse results in a broad spectrum of liver disease, including asymptomatic fatty liver, alcoholic hepatitis, cirrhosis, and end-stage liver failure. Many alcoholics become symptomatic only when severe, life-threatening liver disease is already present.

Virtually any drug can cause some degree of hepatotoxicity, although certain drugs are more toxic than others. In some cases (eg, sulfonamides), substances are directly toxic to the liver. In others, liver damage occurs by immune-mediated hypersensitivity. Some common hepatotoxic substances include acetaminophen, tetracycline, aspirin, phenytoin, methyldopa, isoniazid, methotrexate (when combined with alcohol), HMG-CoA reductase inhibitors ("statins"), and valproic acid. In high doses, vitamin A, arsenic, iron, and copper can be hepatotoxic. Further, hepatotoxicity may be the most common adverse effect of herbal supplements. Known hepatotoxic herbs include kava, pennyroyal oil, Ma-huang (*Ephedra sinica*), valerian, mistletoe, comfrey, chaparral, sassafras, borage, and germander.

The presentation and severity of liver disease vary widely. Some patients remain asymptomatic despite significant liver damage, while others present with a severe, acute illness. Nausea, vomiting, malaise, and diaphoresis are common symptoms. A syndrome similar to viral hepatitis may occur, including fever, headache, jaundice, and right-upper-quadrant pain.

Because of the liver's regenerative ability, withdrawal of or abstinence from offending substances can result in significant reversal of liver damage, even in cases of advanced liver disease, as long as cirrhosis is not yet established.

Risk Factors

Sustained alcohol intake exceeding 80 grams per day in men is strongly associated with progression to hepatic fibrosis, cirrhosis, and liver failure. However, about half of chronic alcohol abusers do not develop severe liver disease, a fact that suggests the importance of other risk factors. Additional contributors to risk include:

Gender. Females have an increased risk of liver disease for a given amount and duration of alcohol use, and liver disease in women tends to progress more rapidly than in men.

Genetics. There appear to be genetic predispositions to alcohol abuse and alcoholic liver disease. However, specific genes have yet to be definitely identified.

Viral hepatitis. Concurrent infection with hepatitis B virus or hepatitis C virus is strongly associated with risk of accelerated liver disease in alcoholic patients.

Obesity.

Malnutrition. Inadequate nutritional intake in chronic alcohol abusers may worsen the severity of liver disease.

Asian race. Asians have a relative deficiency of the mitochondrial aldehyde dehydrogenase-2 (ALDH2) enzyme, which results in flushing upon alcohol intake and may create an aversion to alcohol use in these populations.

Acetaminophen. The combination of alcohol and acetaminophen should be avoided, as acetaminophen toxicity is greatly increased with the concomitant ingestion of alcohol.

Drug dosages. Toxicity due to medications is typically dose-related.

Nutritional supplements. High doses of preformed vitamin A can be hepatotoxic, as can certain botanicals. See Nutritional Considerations below.

Diagnosis

The diagnosis of drug- and toxin-induced liver injury is often difficult. A detailed history and physical examination are essential and should include an investigation for accidental, environmental, and intentional exposures.

Liver Function Tests

Elevations of the aminotransferases aspartate aminotransferase (AST) and alanine aminotransferase (ALT) are common and signify hepatocellular injury. A ratio of AST-to-ALT greater than 2 suggests alcoholic hepatitis.

Elevation of alkaline phosphatase or bilirubin out of proportion to the aminotransferases suggests cholestasis.

Low albumin concentration and extended prothrombin time (due to impaired synthesis of coagulation factors, primarily factor VII) reflect impaired hepatic synthetic function.

Bilirubin can be elevated due to either hepatocellular injury or cholestasis.

In suspected cases of alcoholism, a careful history and the CAGE criteria, below, may be used to establish the diagnosis. A positive response to at least 2 of the following questions is seen in the majority of patients with alcoholism and provides 93% sensitivity and 76% specificity.[1] Over 80% of nonalcoholics answer negatively to all 4 of the questions:

1. Have you felt the need to **C**ut down drinking?

2. Have you ever felt **A**nnoyed by criticism of drinking?

3. Have you had **G**uilty feelings about drinking?

4. Do you ever take a morning **E**ye opener?

Hematologic abnormalities may be present in patients with alcoholic liver disease, including macrocytosis, leukocytosis, thrombocytopenia, and folate deficiency.

Liver biopsy is useful in ruling out viral hepatitis and other specific causes of liver disease, but it is often not diagnostic for drug-induced toxicity. The presence of eosinophils can be suggestive. Biopsy can grade the severity of toxic liver disease and exclude coexisting liver diseases, but it may not be necessary when the clinical presentation is clear (eg, the chronic use of a single drug associated with hepatotoxicity).

Right-upper-quadrant ultrasound, abdominal x-ray, CT scan, MRI, and/or endoscopic retrograde cholangiopancreatography (ERCP) may be indicated to rule out other liver and abdominal pathology, such as cholecystitis, pancreatitis, and malignancy.

Treatment

Suspected drugs or toxins should be discontinued immediately. Recovery often occurs after withdrawal of the offending substance.

Abstinence from alcohol is essential. Patients should be appropriately counseled on alcohol cessation, including referral to Alcoholics Anonymous, psychotherapy, or similar programs.

Weight reduction is a requirement for overweight patients.

Acetaminophen overdose is treated with activated charcoal and n-acetylcysteine.

Other than treatment for acute acetaminophen toxicity, specific therapies are generally not available. In cases of hypersensitivity reactions (eg, penicillin, procainamide) or alcoholic hepatitis, corticosteroids may be useful.

Supportive treatments in cases of liver failure include nutritional changes (see Nutritional Considerations below), vitamin K for coagulopathy, and correction of micronutrient deficiencies (eg, folate). Secondary complications (eg, hepatic encephalopathy) should be addressed as necessary.

Liver transplantation may be required in patients with severe acute liver failure or chronic liver disease.

Nutritional Considerations

High doses of preformed vitamin A and other supplements with potential or suspected hepatotoxicity should be avoided. Most cases of chronic hypervitaminosis A are the result of self-administration of preformed vitamin A (ie, retinol, not provitamin A carotenoids).[2] Hepatotoxicity can occur with doses of more than 100,000 IU per day. However, rare cases have occurred with dosages of 25,000 IU per day, and alcohol potentiates the hepatotoxicity of vitamin A. Steatosis, perisinusoidal fibrosis, chronic hepatitis, and cirrhosis may result from chronic overadministration.[3] Niacin also has hepatotoxic potential, although this may be limited to sustained-release preparations.[4]

Several botanical supplements are sources of hepatotoxic pyrrolizidine alkaloids (eg, comfrey). Kava, a botanical used for anxiolytic effects, was withdrawn from the market after suggestions of hepatotoxicity. Certain herbal products that are freely available to consumers (eg, pennyroyal, skullcap, and chaparral) and Chinese herbal formulas that are not commercially distributed are associated with hepatotoxic effects. The U.S. Food and Drug Administration has issued warnings regarding the hepatotoxicity of certain formulas touted for weight loss, such as LipoKinetix, although the active hepatotoxins in this product have not yet been identified.[5] A surprising number of patients with acute hepatitis or acute liver failure have no identifiable cause of illness other than the use of herbal weight-loss products, particularly those containing hepatotoxins such as usnic acid, a lichen alkaloid. Ephedra alkaloids, which are also used for weight loss by millions of people, are associated with development of severe hepatic dysfunction and even fulminant hepatic failure.[6]

Dietary supplements that contain extracts of *Camellia sinensis* (green tea) have been reported to cause hepatotoxicity[7] and even acute liver failure.[8] The mechanism of toxicity has not been elucidated, and the effect has not been seen with green tea in liquid form, which is associated with numerous health benefits.[9]

A botanical extract called milk thistle has shown promise, but it has yet to be proven effective in clinical trials. Silymarin, the active principle of milk thistle, has antioxidant, radical-scavenging, anti-inflammatory, and liver-regenerative effects that have partly validated its history of use for toxic liver disorders. Treatment was associated with decreased levels of gamma-glutamyl transferase (GGT) activity and procollagen III peptide, and with normalization of serum bilirubin, AST, and ALT levels.[10] However, there are several reasons to be cautious with silymarin. First, the majority of previously published studies are limited by a lack of high-quality evidence.[10,11] Second, isolated compounds from milk thistle, such as silymarin, may not have the same effect as the full mixture of flavanolignans found in the milk thistle plant.[10]

Orders

See Basic Diet Orders chapter.

What to Tell the Family

Liver damage most often results from excessive habitual alcohol intake. However, it can also be caused by several prescription medications, in addition to self-medication with over-the-counter (OTC) supplements. The family can support patients by providing an environment that discourages alcohol consumption, by making sure medications are taken only as directed, and by checking with qualified healthcare personnel, such as a physician and a pharmacist, before allowing the use of OTC supplements.

References

1. Mayfield D, McLeod G, Hall P. The CAGE questionnaire. Validation of a new alcoholism screening instrument. *Am J Psychiatry*. 1974;131:1121-1123.

2. Scherl S, Goldberg NS, Volpe L, Juster F. Overdosage of vitamin A supplements in a child. *Cutis*. 1992;50:209-210.

3. Riley TR III, Bhatti AM. Preventive strategies in chronic liver disease: part I. Alcohol, vaccines, toxic medications and supplements, diet and exercise. *Am Fam Physician*. 2001;64:1555-1560.

4. Pieper JA. Overview of niacin formulations: differences in pharmacokinetics, efficacy, and safety. *Am J Health Syst Pharm.* 2003;60(suppl 2):S9-S14; quiz S25.

5. Willett KL, Roth RA, Walker L. Workshop overview: Hepatotoxicity assessment for botanical dietary supplements. *Toxicol Sci.* 2004;79:4-9.

6. Neff GW, Reddy KR, Durazo FA, Meyer D, Marrero R, Kaplowitz N. Severe hepatotoxicity associated with the use of weight loss diet supplements containing ma huang or usnic acid. *J Hepatol.* 2004;41:1062-1064.

7. Bonkovsky HL. Hepatotoxicity associated with supplements containing Chinese green tea (Camellia sinensis). *Ann Intern Med.* 2006;144:68-71.

8. Molinari M, Watt KD, Kruszyna T, et al. Acute liver failure induced by green tea extracts: case report and review of the literature. *Liver Transpl.* 2006;12:1892-1895.

9. Cabrera C, Artacho R, Gimenez R. Beneficial effects of green tea--a review. *J Am Coll Nutr.* 2006;25:79-99.

10. Ball KR, Kowdley KV. A review of *Silybum marianum* (milk thistle) as a treatment for alcoholic liver disease. *J Clin Gastroenterol.* 2005;39:520-528.

11. Rambaldi A, Jacobs BP, Iaquinto G, Gluud C. Milk thistle for alcoholic and/or hepatitis B or C virus liver diseases. *Cochrane Database Syst Rev.* 2005;(2):CD003620.

59. Nonalcoholic Fatty Liver Disease

Nonalcoholic fatty liver disease (NAFLD) comprises a spectrum of conditions characterized by hepatic fat accumulation in the absence of alcohol abuse, with fat making up at least 10% of the liver tissue (steatosis). Nonalcoholic steatohepatitis (NASH), in which fat accumulation is accompanied by inflammation, is the most common type of NAFLD and the most common form of liver disease in the United States.[1] Clinically, NASH may be indistinguishable from alcoholic hepatitis, but it is most often a subclinical disease.

The progressive accumulation of triglycerides in hepatic tissue results from increased delivery of fatty acids to the liver, decreased export of fatty acids from the liver, or impaired oxidation of fatty acids within the liver. Insulin resistance is thought to play a key role in disease development by causing alterations in lipid metabolism, leading to increased uptake of fatty acids by the liver and increased oxidation of lipids within it.

Most patients remain asymptomatic, although nonspecific symptoms, such as fatigue, malaise, and tenderness of the upper-right abdomen, may occur. In more serious cases, the pathologic features resemble those of alcoholic liver disease and may include fibrosis, inflammation, necrosis, and cirrhosis.

Risk Factors

Fatty liver disease is particularly prevalent among Latin Americans. Other risk factors include:

Obesity, especially abdominal obesity.

States of insulin resistance (typically related to obesity, diabetes mellitus, and the metabolic syndrome).

Hyperlipidemia, especially hypertriglyceridemia.

Severe or **rapid weight loss.**

Total parenteral nutrition.

Drugs (eg, glucocorticoids, synthetic estrogens, and certain pesticides).

Pregnancy. Rarely, fatty liver occurs during pregnancy.

Diagnosis

Laboratory studies include complete blood count (CBC), blood chemistry, liver function tests, and coagulation studies. It may also be useful to evaluate ammonia level for hepatic encephalopathy.

Alcoholic liver disease should be ruled out by history, physical examination, and laboratory testing, as necessary. NASH differs from alcoholic hepatitis in that the alanine aminotransferase (ALT) is generally greater than the aspartate aminotransferase (AST), and alkaline phosphatase and bilirubin are not generally elevated. However, liver function testing is not sufficient to make the diagnosis.

Ultrasound, CT scan, and MRI may be diagnostic. These tests can identify fatty liver and evaluate for other disorders, including biliary tract disease.

Liver biopsy may be useful if the cause of fatty liver is unclear. Biopsy will also reveal the grade and stage of disease to guide management and estimate prognosis.

Treatment

Weight loss is essential for overweight patients with NAFLD. Even modest weight loss (~5% of body weight) may have significant beneficial effects by alleviating diabetes and hypertension.

Exercise may be beneficial, with or without associated weight loss. Use of pharmacologic weight loss agents may be beneficial, although this treatment has not yet been adequately studied. Morbidly obese patients (BMI >35 kg/m²) may consider surgical options, such as gastric bypass.

Diabetes mellitus in NAFLD patients should be treated as appropriate. Insulin-sensitizing drugs (eg, metformin, pioglitazone) may be especially useful and are also under investigation for use in nondiabetic patients with fatty liver, as they may reduce steatosis. Treatment of hyperlipidemia may decrease the progression of disease.

Rarely, patients with advanced disease may require liver transplantation.

Nutritional Considerations

Obesity, diabetes, and insulin resistance syndrome are implicated in the genesis of nonalcoholic fatty liver diseases. These conditions involve steatosis and oxidative stress, both of which can be modulated by diet. Preliminary research suggests that weight reduction on a low-fat, high-fiber diet may be an effective treatment for NAFLD. Although further clinical trials are needed to establish the role of diet in treating these conditions, key nutritional issues are as follows:

Weight Loss

Loss of excess weight may reduce the risk for developing NAFLD and effectively treat hepatic steatosis and NASH. Compared with a rate of 20% in the general population, NAFLD affects up to 75% of obese individuals.[2] Gradual, moderate weight loss (~10% of body weight) usually reduces steatosis and may lead to improvement in liver function tests and histology.[3] However, rapid weight loss exceeding ~1 lb per week in children and ~3.5 lbs per week in adults may result in necroinflammation, portal fibrosis, steatohepatitis, and bile stasis, along with worsening fibrosis.[1] Nevertheless, rapid weight loss resulting from bariatric surgery reduces disease progression in patients with NAFLD.[4]

Plant-based diets may be particularly helpful for both prevention and treatment of certain characteristic traits of NAFLD. Clinical trials have not yet evaluated the effect of low-fat, high-fiber vegetarian diets on NAFLD, as they have for cardiovascular disease and diabetes. However, these diets typically cause weight loss[5] and can lower the concentrations of blood fats (eg, triglycerides) that contribute to nonalcoholic fatty liver disease.[6] Such diets are also associated with reduced insulin resistance, another precursor of NAFLD,[7] and greater antioxidant protection, compared with omnivorous diets.[8,9]

In addition, iron accumulation aggravates insulin resistance and oxidative stress. Plant-based diets have somewhat less iron bioavailability, and vegetarians have lower body-iron stores.[10]

Alcohol Avoidance

Alcohol intake strongly predicts blood triglyceride concentrations, and dyslipidemias (including elevated triglycerides) are present in a majority of individuals with nonalcoholic fatty liver disease.[11] Some evidence indicates that steatosis correlates directly with alcohol intake.[12] Consumption of more than 40 grams of alcohol per day doubles the risk of fatty liver[13] and other liver diseases. Women may be affected at even lower levels of intake (eg, 20 to 30 g/d).

Two other nutritional issues merit mention:

Balanced Glucose and Lipid in Total Parenteral Nutrition

Patients receiving total parenteral nutrition should receive a proper ratio of glucose and lipid. Excess glucose administration (>400 g/d for a 70-kg male) may cause steatosis through excessive hepatic lipogenesis. Patients receiving total parenteral nutrition should receive two-thirds of nonprotein calories as glucose and one-third as either long-chain triglycerides or a mixture of medium-chain and long-chain triglycerides.[14]

Orders

See Basic Diet Orders chapter.

What to Tell the Family

In many cases fatty liver disease is responsive to diet changes, along with medications that address the elevations in weight, blood fats, and insulin resistance associated with this condition. Family members can assist the patient by participating in and encouraging a low-fat, high-fiber diet suitable for safe and gradual weight loss, along with appropriate exercise. These measures may help the patient avoid more serious liver damage. See Obesity chapter.

References

1. Patrick L. Nonalcoholic fatty liver disease: relationship to insulin sensitivity and oxidative stress. Treatment approaches using vitamin E, magnesium, and betaine. *Altern Med Rev*. 2002;7:276-291.

2. Cortez-Pinto H, Camilo ME. Non-alcoholic fatty liver disease/non-alcoholic ste
atitis (NAFLD/NASH): diagnosis and clinical course. *Best Pract Res Clin Gastroe*.
2004;18:1089-1104.

3. Sass DA, Chang P, Chopra KB. Nonalcoholic fatty liver disease: a clinical review. *D*.
Dis Sci. 2005;50:171-180.

4. Zivkovic AM, German JB, Sanyal AJ. Comparative review of diets for the metabolic syndrome: implications for nonalcoholic fatty liver disease. *Am J Clin Nutr*. 2007;86:285-300.

5. Barnard ND, Scialli AR, Turner-McGrievy G, Lanou AJ, Glass J. The effects of a low-
fat, plant-based dietary intervention on body weight, metabolism, and insulin sensitivity.
Am J Med. 2005;118:991-997.

6. Mach T. Fatty liver--current look at the old disease. *Med Sci Monit*. 2000;6:209-216.

7. Kuo CS, Lai NS, Ho LT, Lin CL. Insulin sensitivity in Chinese ovo-lactovegetarians
compared with omnivores. *Eur J Clin Nutr*. 2004;58:312-316.

8. Szeto YT, Kwok TC, Benzie IF. Effects of a long-term vegetarian diet on biomarkers of
antioxidant status and cardiovascular disease risk. *Nutrition*. 2004;20:863-866.

9. Gawrieh S, Opara EC, Koch TR. Oxidative stress in nonalcoholic fatty liver disease:
pathogenesis and antioxidant therapies. *J Investig Med*. 2004;52:506-514.

10. Hua NW, Stoohs RA, Facchini FS. Low iron status and enhanced insulin sensitivity in
lacto-ovo vegetarians. *Br J Nutr*. 2001;86:515-519.

11. Friis-Liby I, Aldenborg F, Jerlstad P, Rundstrom K, Bjornsson E. High prevalence of
metabolic complications in patients with non-alcoholic fatty liver disease. *Scand J Gastroenterol*. 2004;39:864-869.

12. Kondili LA, Tosti ME, Szklo M, et al. The relationships of chronic hepatitis and cirrhosis to alcohol intake, hepatitis B and C, and delta virus infection: a case-control study
in Albania. *Epidemiol Infect*. 1998;121:391-395.

13. Pares A, Tresserras R, Nunez I, et al. Prevalence and factors associated to the presence of fatty liver in apparently healthy adult men. *Med Clin* (Barc). 2000;11:561-565.

14. Paquot N, Delwaide J. Fatty liver in the intensive care unit. *Curr Opin Clin Nutr Metab
Care*. 2005;8:183-187.

60. Cholelithiasis

Cholelithiasis, or gallstones, is a common syndrome in which hard
stones composed of cholesterol or bile pigments form in the gallbladder.
If stones are present in the common bile duct, the condition is called
choledocholithiasis. The syndrome occurs in up to 20% of women and
8% of men worldwide.

Most stones are composed of cholesterol. In bile, cholesterol is in equilibrium with bile salts and with phosphatidylcholine. When the concer
tration of cholesterol rises to the point of supersaturation, crystallizati

. A sludge containing cholesterol, mucin, calcium salts, and bili-
. forms, and, ultimately, stones develop.

ost gallstones are asymptomatic. Some result in biliary colic, in
which stones intermittently obstruct the neck of the gallbladder and/
or the common bile duct and cause episodic right-upper-quadrant pain.
Chronic obstruction may result in cholecystitis (infection and inflammation of the gallbladder) or cholangitis (infection and inflammation of the
common bile duct). Both syndromes are serious and, if untreated, may
result in sepsis, shock, and death.

Presenting symptoms include episodic right-upper-quadrant or epigastric pain, which generally occurs in the middle of the night after eating a
large meal and may radiate to the back, right scapula, or right shoulder.
Nausea, vomiting, dyspepsia, burping, and food intolerance (especially
to fatty, greasy, or fried foods; meats; and cheeses) are common. More
severe symptoms, including fever and jaundice, may signify cholecystitis or cholangitis.

Risk Factors

Family history. Gallstones are more than twice as common in first-
degree relatives of patients with gallstones.

Increasing age. Gallstones are most common in individuals over age 40.

Female gender. Females are more likely to develop gallstones in all
age groups, probably due to the effects of estrogens. This increased
risk is particularly striking in young women, who are affected 3 to 4
times more often than men of the same age.

Elevated estrogen and progesterone. During pregnancy, oral contraceptive use, or hormone replacement therapy, estrogen and progesterone induce changes in the biliary system that predispose to gallstones.

Obesity. Obesity is a significant risk factor for the development of cholesterol gallstones due to enhanced cholesterol synthesis and secretion.

apid weight loss. Bariatric surgery and very-low-calorie diets in-
ease risk of gallstone formation, possibly due to gallbladder stasis
increased concentrations of bile constituents.

ladder stasis. When bile remains in the gallbladder for an ex-
period, supersaturation can occur, resulting in gallstones. Gall-
stasis is associated with diabetes mellitus, total parenteral

nutrition (probably due to lack of enteral stimulation), postvagotomy, rapid weight loss, celiac sprue, and spinal cord injury.

Cirrhosis. Cirrhosis results in as much as a 10-fold increased risk of gallstones.

Ileal disease or resection (as in Crohn disease). Altered enterohepatic cycling of bile salts increases risk of gallstone formation.

Hemolytic states. The rapid destruction of red blood cells in sickle cell disease and other hemolytic conditions causes the release of bilirubin, which in turn increases the risk of pigment gallstones.

Medications. Drugs implicated in the development of cholelithiasis include clofibrate, octreotide, and ceftriaxone.

Physical inactivity. The Health Professionals Follow-up Study suggested that many cases of symptomatic cholelithiasis could be prevented by 30 minutes of daily aerobic exercise. Young or middle-aged men (65 years or younger) who were the most physically active had half the risk for developing gallstones, compared with those who were least active. In older men, physical activity cut risk by 25%.[1] Physical activity also protects against gallstones in women.[2]

Diagnosis

Right-upper-quadrant ultrasound will directly reveal the presence of gallstones and show evidence of cholecystitis, if present.

Hydroxy iminodiacetic acid (HIDA) scan is sometimes indicated to rule out cystic duct obstruction and acute cholecystitis.

Endoscopic retrograde cholangiopancreatography (ERCP) or **magnetic resonance cholangiopancreatography (MRCP)** assesses the presence of gallstones within the bile ducts. ERCP can also be used to extract stones when they are found, avoiding the need for surgery.

Laboratory tests include complete blood count (CBC), liver function tests, amylase, and lipase.

Treatment

Asymptomatic gallstones are generally not treated. Cholecystectomy is the treatment of choice for symptomatic disease. Lithotripsy, which breaks up stones, and oral bile acids (eg, ursodeoxycholic acid), which dissolve small stones and stone fragments, are indicated for patients who are not surgical candidates.

It is helpful to avoid large meals, as a large caloric load is the most likely trigger for biliary colic symptoms.

Nutritional Considerations

Gallstones are strongly related to a high-fat, low-fiber diet. They are uncommon in Asian and African populations that follow traditional, largely plant-based diets, and they become more common with a shift toward Westernized diets.[3] A surplus of animal protein and animal fat, a lack of dietary fiber, and the consumption of fat from saturated rather than unsaturated sources appear to be the main nutritional risk factors for gallstone development. The following factors are associated with reduced risk of gallstones:

Plant-based diets. Both animal fat and animal protein may contribute to the formation of gallstones. In most Western populations, an estimated 80% of gallstones are cholesterol stones,[4] suggesting the possibility that dietary changes (eg, reducing dietary saturated fat and cholesterol and increasing soluble fiber) may reduce the risk of gallstone formation.

Vegetarian women have a lower risk for gallstones, compared with non-vegetarian women.[5] This may relate to the fact that vegetarian diets are often high in fiber and provide fat mainly in unsaturated form. However, vegetarian women may also be more health-conscious in general, compared with omnivores, and may be more physically active (see Treatment section). Fruit and vegetable intake may account for part of this protection; consuming roughly 7 servings of fruits and vegetables per day was associated with a 20% lower risk for cholecystectomy, compared with women who ate less than 3.5 servings per day.[6] Vitamin C, another nutrient found in higher amounts in vegetarian diets than in nonvegetarian diets, affects the rate-limiting step in the catabolism of cholesterol to bile acids and is inversely related to the risk of gallstones in women.[7]

Women consuming the most vegetable protein had a 20% to 30% lower risk than those consuming the least.[8,9] Similarly, women and men whose fat intake comes primarily from plant sources have a reduced risk of developing gallstones.[10] An exception is trans fatty acids—the partially hydrogenated vegetable oils often used in snack foods—which are associated with increased gallstone risk.[11]

Replacement of sugars and refined starches with high-fiber carbohydrates. The cholesterol saturation index of bile, a known risk factor for gallstone formation,[12] is higher with diets that provide carbohydrates in a refined, as opposed to unrefined, form.[13] Individuals consuming the most refined carbohydrates had a 60% greater risk for developing gallstones, compared with those who consumed the least.[14] Conversely, individuals eating the most fiber (particularly insoluble fiber) have a 15% lower risk for gallstones compared with those eating the least.[15,16] However, no intervention trial has tested whether a diet that is low in sugar and high in unrefined starches reduces gallstone risk.

Avoidance of overweight and a healthful approach to weight control. Obese women with a BMI of 30 kg/m^2 or more have at least double the risk for gallstone disease, compared with women of normal weight (BMI < 25 kg/m^2). The same degree of risk exists for men with a BMI of at least 25 kg/m^2, compared with males with a BMI of <22.5 kg/m^2. With more severe obesity (ie, BMI 30 to 45 kg/m^2), the risk for women is 3.7 to 7.4 times that of women with a BMI of less than 24 kg/m^2.[17]

Weight cycling (repeatedly losing and regaining weight) increases the likelihood of cholelithiasis. In women, the risk increased from 20% in "light" cyclers (those who lost and regained 5 to 9 lbs) to 70% in "severe" cyclers (those who lost and regained ≥20 lbs).[18] A similar pattern has been shown in men.[19]

Very-low-calorie diets increase the risk of gallstones. Gallbladder stasis and bile cholesterol saturation index occur during rapid weight loss, accounting for a greater risk of gallstone development. Including a small amount of fat (10 g/day) provides maximal gallbladder emptying and prevents gallstone formation in calorie-restricted dieters.[20] Such observations support weight control efforts based on low-fat, plant-based diets, which typically cause healthful and sustained weight control, rather than those based on very-low-calorie formula diets.

Moderate alcohol intake. Compared with infrequent consumption or abstinence, moderate alcohol intake was found to be inversely associated with the risk for gallstones.[21,22] However, given the current epidemic of nonalcoholic fatty liver disease in 50% to 75% of obese persons[23] and other health risks (eg, breast cancer) due to alcohol consumption, caution regarding alcohol use is warranted.

Orders

See Basic Diet Orders chapter.

Exercise prescription.

What to Tell the Family

Several studies suggest that the risk of gallstones is lower among individuals following high-fiber diets, particularly vegetarian diets, and that patients are well advised to avoid foods high in saturated fat (eg, animal products) and trans fat (eg, processed foods). Family members can help the patient by serving high-fiber, vegetarian meals at home and encouraging similar eating habits at restaurants. Diet changes are easiest when the whole family changes together.

References

1. Leitzmann MF, Giovannucci EL, Rimm EB, et al. The relation of physical activity to risk for symptomatic gallstone disease in men. *Ann Intern Med*. 1998;128:417-425.

2. Leitzmann MF, Rimm EB, Willett WC, et al. Recreational Physical Activity and the Risk of Cholecystectomy in Women. *N Engl J Med*. 1999;341:777-784.

3. Burkitt DP. The protective properties of dietary fiber. *N C Med J*. 1981;42:467-471.

4. Friedman GD, Kannel WB, Dawber TR. The epidemiology of gallbladder disease: observations in the Framingham Study. *J Chronic Dis*. 1966;19:273-292.

5. Pixley F, Wilson D, McPherson K, Mann J. Effect of vegetarianism on development of gallstones in women. *BMJ*. 1985;291:11-12.

6. Tsai CJ, Leitzmann MF, Willett WC, Giovannucci EL. Fruit and vegetable consumption and risk of cholecystectomy in women. *Am J Med*. 2006;119:760-767.

7. Simon JA, Hudes ES. Serum ascorbic acid and gallbladder disease prevalence among US adults: the Third National Health and Nutrition Examination Survey (NHANES III). *Arch Intern Med*. 2000;160:931-936.

8. Tsai CJ, Leitzmann MF, Willett WC, et al. Dietary protein and the risk of cholecystectomy in a cohort of US women: the Nurses' Health Study. *Am J Epidemiol*. 2004;60:11-18.

9. Maclure KM, Hayes KC, Colditz GA, et al. Dietary predictors of symptom-associated gallstones in middle-aged women. *Am J Clin Nutr*. 1990;52:916-922.

10. Tsai CJ, Leitzmann MF, Willett WC, Giovannucci EL. The effect of long-term intake of cis unsaturated fats on the risk for gallstone disease in men: a prospective cohort study. *Ann Intern Med*. 2004;141:514-522.

11. Tsai CJ, Leitzmann MF, Willett WC, et al. Long-term intake of trans-fatty acids and risk of gallstone disease in men. *Arch Intern Med*. 2005;165:1011-1015.

12. Erlinger S. Gallstones in obesity and weight loss. *Eur J Gastroenterol Hepatol*. 2000;12:1347-1352.

13. Thornton JR, Emmett PM, Heaton KW. Diet and gall stones: effects of refined and unrefined carbohydrate diets on bile cholesterol saturation and bile acid metabolism. *Gut*. 1983;24:2-6.

14. Tsai CJ, Leitzmann MF, Willett WC, et al. Dietary carbohydrates and glycaemic load and the incidence of symptomatic gall stone disease in men. *Gut*. 2005;54:823-828.

15. Tsai CJ, Leitzmann MF, Willett WC, et al. Long-term intake of dietary fiber and decreased risk of cholecystectomy in women. *Am J Gastroenterol*. 2004;99:1364-1370.

16. Attlll AF, Scafato E, Marchioli R, et al. Diet and gallstones in Italy: the cross-sectional MICOL results. *Hepatology.* 1998;27:1492-1498.

17. Everhart JE. Contributions of obesity and weight loss to gallstone disease. *Ann Intern Med.* 1993;119:1029-1035.

18. Syngal S, Coakley EH, Willett WC, et al. Long-term weight patterns and risk for cholecystectomy in women. *Ann Intern Med.* 1999;130:471-477.

19. Tsai CJ, Leitzmann MF, Willett WC, Giovannucci EL. Weight cycling and risk of gallstone disease in men. *Arch Intern Med.* 2006 ;166:2369-2374.

20. Gebhard RL, Prigge WF, Ansel HJ, et al. The role of gallbladder emptying in gallstone formation during diet-induced rapid weight loss. *Hepatology.* 1996;24:544-548.

21. Leitzmann MF, Giovannucci EL, Stampfer MJ, et al. Prospective study of alcohol consumption patterns in relation to symptomatic gallstone disease in men. *Alcohol Clin Exp Res.* 1999;23:835-841.

22. de Lorimier AA. Alcohol, wine, and health. *Am J Surg.* 2000;180:357-361.

23. Patrick L. Nonalcoholic fatty liver disease: relationship to insulin sensitivity and oxidative stress. Treatment approaches using vitamin E, magnesium, and betaine. *Altern Med Rev.* 2002;7:276-291.

---

61. Pancreatitis

Pancreatitis is an inflammation of the pancreas caused by inappropriate activation of pancreatic enzymes (proteases, lipase, amylase) within and surrounding the pancreas, resulting in autodigestion of pancreatic tissue, necrosis, edema, and possibly hemorrhage.

About 80% of acute pancreatitis cases result from excessive intake of alcohol, which is directly toxic to pancreatic tissue, or from gallstones, which block the flow of pancreatic digestive enzymes. Less common etiologies include severe hypertriglyceridemia, hypercalcemia, mumps, abdominal trauma, and medications such as azathioprine, ACE inhibitors, valproic acid, thiazides, diuretics, and steroids. Pancreatitis also occurs as a transient complication of endoscopic retrograde cholangiopancreatography (ERCP) and may manifest only by elevated amylase levels. About 10% of cases are idiopathic.

Acute pancreatitis represents an exacerbation of chronic, underlying inflammation. It varies from a mild, self-limited condition to a severe pathological process with hemorrhagic necrosis leading to systemic multi-organ failure and death. Clinical presentation includes steady, severe epigastric pain and tenderness that generally follow a large meal or alcohol intake. The pain often persists for hours, radiates to the back, and may be relieved by leaning forward. Further symptoms include abdominal distention, nausea, vomiting, fever, tachycardia, diaphoresis, and jaundice. Severe cases may present with signs of peritonitis (guarding, rebound tenderness, fever), dehydration, and shock.

The clinical syndrome of chronic pancreatitis results from a slowly progressive destruction of pancreatic tissue that occurs over several years due to persistent inflammation and fibrosis. As many as 80% to 90% of cases result from long-standing alcohol abuse, but the condition can also be caused by cystic fibrosis, severe malnutrition, and hyperparathyroidism. Presentation may be similar to acute pancreatitis, with epigastric pain that often radiates to the back, nausea, vomiting, food intolerance, steatorrhea, jaundice, and glucose intolerance. However, chronic pancreatitis may be asymptomatic.

Risk Factors

The annual incidence of pancreatitis in the United States is 4 per 100,000 in Native Americans, 5.7 per 100,000 in Caucasians, and 20.7 per 100,000 in African Americans. The risk among African Americans aged 35 to 64 is 10 times greater than for any other demographic group. Whether the increased incidence is related to genetics or to environmental and lifestyle factors is unclear.

Alcohol use. About 10% of chronic alcoholics will develop acute pancreatitis. From 70% to 80% of heavy alcohol users will develop chronic pancreatitis.

Gallstones. Gallstones increase risk of acute pancreatitis. The higher prevalence of gallstones in women accounts for the higher incidence of acute pancreatitis among women, compared with men.

Genetics. Five mutations in cationic trypsinogen have been found in patients with hereditary pancreatitis.[1]

Diagnosis

Initial laboratory studies include complete blood count (CBC), liver function tests, blood alcohol level, amylase, lipase, and lipid panel. Radiographic scans also play an important role.

Lipase and amylase are generally elevated in acute pancreatitis, although the degrees of elevation do not correlate with disease severity. In chronic pancreatitis, lipase and amylase are usually not elevated.

Hypokalemia, hypocalcemia, and leukocytosis are often present in acute disease.

Elevated liver enzymes, bilirubin, and LDH may be present, especially if biliary disease is the etiology of pancreatitis. Liver enzymes may also be elevated due to compression of the common bile duct by an edematous pancreatic head.

Severe hypertriglyceridemia (>1000 mg/dL) may be the cause of pancreatitis in a small number of cases.

Patients are often hypoxemic, especially in severe disease.

Abdominal films, CT scan, and ultrasound evaluate for gallstone-related blockages, pancreatic necrosis or edema, and abscess or pseudocyst formation, and rule out nonpancreatic etiologies of abdominal pain.

Endoscopic retrograde cholangiopancreatography (ERCP) reveals the structure of the common bile duct and pancreatic duct and can be used to repair strictures and remove gallstones. However, many specialists are now using magnetic resonance cholangiopancreatography (MRCP) or endoscopic ultrasound more commonly than ERCP.

Treatment

Supportive care is the mainstay of treatment. This includes aggressive IV fluid administration to maintain blood pressure; bowel rest (no oral intake; insert nasogastric tube if patient is vomiting); IV medications for pain control; antiemetics to relieve nausea or vomiting; insulin administration for glucose intolerance; and monitoring and correcting electrolyte abnormalities, especially calcium. In advanced cases, admission to an intensive care unit (ICU) may be indicated.

Addressing the underlying etiology is another treatment priority. For example, the patient should avoid alcohol and fatty foods. Cholecystectomy for gallstone pancreatitis should be delayed until the acute event resolves. Endoscopic or surgical intervention may be necessary in select cases.

Nutritional Considerations

Alcohol use, smoking, body weight, diet, genetic factors, and medications all affect the risk of developing pancreatitis. Diet may also have an important role after diagnosis. Dietary recommendations differ, depending on whether the condition is acute or chronic.

Acute Pancreatitis

Maintain a healthy body weight. Obesity appears to be a risk factor for the development of pancreatitis[2] and for an increased severity when it occurs.[3] Gallstones are a risk factor for acute pancreatitis, one that occurs more frequently in obese persons. Diets low in fat and high in fiber are helpful for gallstone prevention and for obesity prevention and management (see Cholelithiasis and Obesity chapters).

Control triglyceride levels in patients with hypertriglyceridemia. To reduce triglycerides, a fat-restricted diet is advised[4] (see Dyslipidemias chapter). The only exception may be the therapeutic use of high doses of omega-3 fatty acids, which may reduce triglycerides by 30% to 50%.[5] Foods with a high glycemic index, particularly sucrose (table sugar) and high fructose corn syrup, also tend to raise triglycerides.[6,7] Patients with triglyceridemia-related pancreatitis may be well-advised to choose carbohydrates that do not raise triglyceride levels; ie, ones that are rich in fiber and have a low glycemic index.[8]

Chronic Pancreatitis

Oxidative stress, defined as a disturbance in the balance between pro-oxidants and antioxidants leading to cellular damage, is a frequent finding in patients with chronic pancreatitis. A known source of this imbalance is the metabolism of xenobiotics, resulting in glutathione depletion and subsequent damage to pancreatic acinar cells.[9] Patients with chronic pancreatitis have demonstrably low tissue levels of antioxidant enzymes.[10] These patients also have lower blood concentrations of several antioxidants, including selenium (a glutathione precursor), vitamin A, vitamin E, and several carotenoids, compared with patients who have acute pancreatitis and with controls.[11] Some studies have suggested that antioxidant supplements (combinations of either selenium, beta carotene, and vitamins C and E or methionine, vitamin C, and selenium) may ameliorate the pain associated with chronic (not acute) pancreatitis, diminish the frequency of acute exacerbations, and reduce the need for pancreatic surgery.[9,12] Studies have not provided conclusive evidence of the benefit of antioxidant supplementation in critically ill patients.

Avoidance of alcohol reduces the risk of both acute and chronic pancreatitis.[13] The risk for chronic pancreatitis in particular is exacerbated by the combination of smoking and alcohol intake.[14]

Orders

See Basic Diet Orders and Obesity chapters for general recommendations.

What to Tell the Family

Pancreatitis is usually caused by alcohol abuse. Although the contribution of alcohol to accidents and behavioral problems is better known, family members should be alerted to this dangerous complication. They can help the patient maintain sobriety. They can also help the patient adopt a low-fat, high-fiber diet in order to prevent gallstones and to reduce triglycerides.

Family members can help the patient manage medications, taking care to alert physicians to any that may elevate risk to the pancreas. These drugs include atypical antipsychotics (clozapine, olanzapine, and risperidone);[15] protease inhibitors;[16] and hormone replacement therapy.[17]

References

1. Hirota M, Ohmuraya M, Baba H. Genetic background of pancreatitis. *Postgrad Med J.* 2006;82:775-778.

2. Patterson RE, Frank LL, Kristal AR, et al. A comprehensive examination of health conditions associated with obesity in older adults. *Am J Prev Med.* 2004;27:385-390.

3. Martinez J, Sanchez-Paya J, Palazon JM, et al. Is obesity a risk factor in acute pancreatitis? A meta-analysis. *Pancreatology.* 2004;4:42-48.

4. Yadav D, Pitchumoni CS. Issues in hyperlipidemic pancreatitis. *J Clin Gastroenterol.* 2003;36:54-62.

5. O'Keefe JH Jr, Harris WS. From Inuit to implementation: omega-3 fatty acids come of age. *Mayo Clin Proc.* 2000;75:607-614.

6. Hellerstein MK. Carbohydrate-induced hypertriglyceridemia: modifying factors and implications for cardiovascular risk. *Curr Opin Lipidol.* 2002;13:33-40.

7. Parks EJ, Hellerstein MK. Carbohydrate-induced hypertriacylglycerolemia: historical perspective and review of biological mechanisms. *Am J Clin Nutr.* 2000;71:412-433.

8. Riccardi G, Rivellese AA. Dietary treatment of the metabolic syndrome--the optimal diet. *Br J Nutr.* 2000;83(suppl 1):S143-S148.

9. McCloy R. Chronic pancreatitis at Manchester, UK. Focus on antioxidant therapy. *Digestion.* 1998;59(suppl 4):36-48.

10. Cullen JJ, Mitros FA, Oberley LW. Expression of antioxidant enzymes in diseases of the human pancreas: another link between chronic pancreatitis and pancreatic cancer. *Pancreas.* 2003;26:23-27.

11. Morris-Stiff GJ, Bowrey DJ, Oleesky D, et al. The antioxidant profiles of patients with recurrent acute and chronic pancreatitis. *Am J Gastroenterol.* 1999;94:2135-2140.

12. Bowrey DJ, Morris-Stiff GJ, Puntis MC. Selenium deficiency and chronic pancreatitis: disease mechanism and potential for therapy. *HPB Surg.* 1999;11:207-216.

13. Corrao G, Bagnardi V, Zambon A, et al. A meta-analysis of alcohol consumption and the risk of 15 diseases. *Prev Med.* 2004;38:613-619.

14. Morton C, Klatsky AL, Udaltsova N. Smoking, coffee, and pancreatitis. *Am J Gastroenterol.* 2004;99:731-738.

15. Koller EA, Cross JT, Doraiswamy PM, et al. Pancreatitis associated with atypical antipsychotics: from the Food and Drug Administration's MedWatch surveillance system and published reports. *Pharmacotherapy.* 2003;23:1123-1130.

16. Mantel-Teeuwisse AK, Kloosterman JM, Maitland-van der Zee AH, et al. Drug-Induced lipid changes: a review of the unintended effects of some commonly used drugs on serum lipid levels. *Drug Safety.* 2001;24:443-456.

17. Barrett-Connor E. Postmenopausal estrogen therapy and selected (less-often-considered) disease outcomes. *Menopause.* 1999;6:14-20.

SECTION XI: GYNECOLOGY AND OBSTETRICS

62. Dysmenorrhea

Dysmenorrhea refers to pain and cramping during menses that interfere with normal functioning. It is the most common gynecologic complaint, affecting at least 50% of menstruating women; about 15% of women experience severe, sometimes incapacitating symptoms.

Primary dysmenorrhea (menstrual pain that occurs in the absence of underlying pelvic pathology) is thought to be related to the release of prostaglandins during menstruation, which can cause excessive and prolonged uterine contractions and subsequent ischemia. The pain is most severe at menses onset and lasts 12 to 72 hours. It is wavelike and cramping in nature and may radiate to the back. Accompanying symptoms (related to prostaglandin-induced sequelae) may include nausea, vomiting, diarrhea, fatigue, headache, and respiratory difficulties. It typically begins within 2 years of menarche.

Secondary dysmenorrhea is caused by pelvic disease, such as endometriosis, uterine fibroids, pelvic inflammatory disease, pelvic adhesions, and cervical stenosis. The pain of secondary dysmenorrhea usually begins earlier in the menstrual cycle and continues beyond the end of menses. Further symptoms may be present depending on the underlying pathology. It typically begins well after menarche, often as late as the fourth or fifth decade of life.

Risk Factors

The following factors are associated with risk for primary dysmenorrhea. Further studies are needed to firmly establish these risk factors, due to the presence of confounding variables and possible selection bias.[1] Risk factors for secondary dysmenorrhea depend on the underlying pelvic pathology.

Age. The most intense symptoms occur during adolescence and typically decrease with age.

Body mass index less than 20.

Heavy, prolonged, or irregular menses.

History of sexual abuse or assault.

In addition to the above factors, psychological factors, miscarriage, pelvic inflammatory disease, premenstrual syndrome, sterilization, female genital cutting ("female circumcision"), and work in cold environments[2,3] may also be associated with risk. Smoking is associated with increased risk. Oral contraceptives and previous pregnancy are considered protective, but available studies on these factors may have been subject to publication bias. Younger age at birth of first child and fish intake may reduce risk. More studies are needed to clarify these factors.

Diagnosis

Primary dysmenorrhea is a diagnosis of exclusion. A complete history, including menstrual, gynecologic, psychosocial, and dietary histories, and physical examination are necessary for all patients. Abdominal, pelvic, and rectal examinations may reveal underlying disorders. More extensive evaluation may not be necessary in many cases, particularly when the history and physical support the diagnosis of primary dysmenorrhea and the pain responds to nonsteroidal anti-inflammatory drugs.

Laboratory testing may include pregnancy testing, Pap smear, urinalysis, and complete blood count.

Cultures for gonorrhea and chlamydia are generally indicated, but negative cultures do not exclude pelvic infection.

Imaging studies may include pelvic and vaginal ultrasound.

Laparoscopy may be indicated for the diagnosis and removal of fibroids, endometriosis, adhesions, ovarian cysts, and other abdominal or pelvic pathologies. However, laparoscopy has not been shown to be superior to medical therapy for the relief of pain.

Treatment

Primary Dysmenorrhea

Primary dysmenorrhea is best treated with a multidisciplinary approach that may include medical, lifestyle, and nutritional interventions.

Nonpharmacologic Therapies

Nutritional interventions, such as a low-fat vegan diet, vitamin E, magnesium, and other supplements, are described below (see Nutritional Considerations).

Regular exercise decreases blood estrogen concentrations,[4] which would be expected to decrease the risk of dysmenorrhea. In unblinded trials, women who exercise appear to have less severe menstrual symptoms, compared with women who do not exercise.[5]

Smoking cessation may be helpful.

Heat applied to the lower abdomen may be as effective as acetaminophen and ibuprofen.[6,7]

Acupuncture[8] and **transcutaneous electrical nerve stimulation** (TENS)[9] may be beneficial. Limited evidence from controlled trials indicates that acupuncture produces significantly better pain relief compared with sham acupuncture and decreases the use of pain medications. Acupressure provides pain relief similar to that of nonsteroidal anti-inflammatory drugs (NSAIDs) when compared with sham acupressure treatment.[10]

Other therapies, such as yoga, are also under investigation.

Medical Therapies

NSAIDs (ibuprofen, naproxen) and **aspirin** are often effective in treating the pain of primary (and occasionally secondary) dysmenorrhea. Treatment is more effective if begun prior to the expected onset of symptoms and continued throughout menses.

Oral contraceptives are often effective and are commonly used for pain that is refractory to NSAID therapy.

Intrauterine devices with levonorgestrel are also helpful, although devices without hormones may aggravate symptoms.

Calcium channel blockers, nitroglycerin, and **nitric oxide,** agents that block uterine contractions, and other pharmaceuticals are under investigation.

Women who do not respond to therapy should be considered for empiric treatment for endometriosis (see Endometriosis chapter), or laparoscopy.

Secondary Dysmenorrhea

Treatment is based on the underlying pathology. NSAIDs and oral contraceptive pills may be useful in some patients.

Nutritional Considerations

Diet therapies have not been extensively studied. However, evidence supports a role for diet changes that alter estrogen concentrations or estrogen activity. These interventions may also involve the inhibition of prostaglandins (eg, PGE2) that cause the uterine muscle contraction and ischemia.[11]

A low-fat, vegan diet may reduce dysmenorrhea symptoms. High-fiber, plant-based diets are associated with reduced blood estrogen concentrations. In a placebo-controlled, crossover trial, a low-fat, vegan diet was shown to increase serum concentrations of sex-hormone-binding globulin and reduce duration and severity of menstrual pain.[12] Another hypothesized protective aspect of these diets is their content of phytoestrogens, which compete with other estrogens for receptor binding. Low-fat, vegan diets may also have a higher ratio of omega-3 to omega-6 fatty acids, which reduces pro-inflammatory prostaglandin formation.[13-15] Omega-6 fatty acids (found in animal products and vegetable oils) are precursors of proinflammatory eicosanoids. A systematic review of studies on diet and dysmenorrhea concluded from observational and clinical trials that a higher dietary ratio of omega-3 to omega-6 fatty acids and supplementation with omega-3 fatty acids are protective against dysmenorrhea.[16]

Certain dietary supplements may be helpful for dysmenorrhea. A Cochrane Library review determined that some evidence supports the use of thiamine, magnesium, and vitamin E in treatment of dysmenorrhea.[17] A recent controlled trial of vitamin E came to similar conclusions.[18]

Orders

Vegetarian diet, low-fat, nondairy. See Basic Diet Orders chapter.

Exercise prescription.

Smoking cessation.

What to Tell the Family

A patient making diet changes to improve symptoms of dysmenorrhea will benefit from the support of family members, who are likely to find that the same diet changes help them with weight control and other health issues.

References

1. Latthe P, Mignini L, Gray R, Hills R, Khan K. Factors predisposing women to chronic pelvic pain: systematic review. *BMJ*. 2006;332:749-755.

2. Christiani DC, Niu T, Xu X. Occupational Stress and Dysmenorrhea in Women Working in Cotton Textile Mills. *Int J Occup Environ Health*. 1995;1:9-15.

3. Messing K, Saurel-Cubizolles MJ, Bourgine M, Kaminski M. Factors associated with dysmenorrhea among workers in French poultry slaughterhouses and canneries. *J Occup Med.* 1993;35:493-500.

4. McTiernan A, Tworoger SS, Rajan KB, et al. Effect of exercise on serum androgens in postmenopausal women: a 12-month randomized clinical trial. *Cancer Epidemiol Biomarkers Prev.* 2004;13:1099-1105.

5. Fugh-Berman A, Kronenberg F. Complementary and alternative medicine (CAM) in reproductive-age women: a review of randomized controlled trials. *Reprod Toxicol.* 2003;17:137-152.

6. Akin MD, Weingand KW, Hengehold DA, Goodale MB, Hinkle RT, Smith RP. Continuous low-level topical heat in the treatment of dysmenorrhea. *Obstet Gynecol.* 2001;97:343-349.

7. Akin MD, Price W, Rodriguez G Jr, Erasala G, Hurley G, Smith RP. Continuous, low-level, topical heat wrap therapy as compared to acetaminophen for primary dysmenorrhea. *J Reprod Med.* 2004;49:739-745.

8. Helms JM. Acupuncture for the management of primary dysmenorrhea. *Obstet Gynecol.*1987;69:51-56.

9. Proctor ML, Smith CA, Farquhar CM, Stones RW. Transcutaneous electrical nerve stimulation and acupuncture for primary dysmenorrhoea (Cochrane Review). *Cochrane Database Syst Rev.* 2002;(1):CD002123.

10. French L. Dysmenorrhea. *Am Fam Physician.* 2005;71:285-291.

11. Saldeen P, Saldeen T. Women and omega-3 Fatty acids. *Obstet Gynecol Surv.* 2004;59:722-730.

12. Barnard ND, Scialli AR, Hurlock D, Bertron P. Diet and sex-hormone binding globulin, dysmenorrhea, and premenstrual symptoms. *Obstet Gynecol.* 2000;95:245-250.

13. Deutch B. Menstrual pain in Danish women correlated with low n-3 polyunsaturated fatty acid intake. *Eur J Clin Nutr.* 1995;49:508-516.

14. Sampalis F, Bunea R, Pelland MF, Kowalski O, Duguet N, Dupuis S. Evaluation of the effects of Neptune Krill Oil on the management of premenstrual syndrome and dysmenorrhea. *Altern Med Rev.* 2003;8:171-179.

15. Harel Z, Biro FM, Kottenhahn RK, Rosenthal SL. Supplementation with omega-3 polyunsaturated fatty acids in the management of dysmenorrhea in adolescents. *Am J Obstet Gynecol.* 1996;174:1335-1338.

16. Fjerbaek A, Knudsen UB. Endometriosis, dysmenorrhea and diet--What is the evidence? *Eur J Obstet Gynecol Reprod Biol.* 2007;132:140-147.

17. Wilson ML, Murphy PA. Herbal and dietary therapies for primary and secondary dysmenorrhoea. *Cochrane Database Syst Rev.* 2001;(3):CD002124.

18. Ziaei S, Zakeri M, Kazemnejad A. A randomised controlled trial of vitamin E in the treatment of primary dysmenorrhoea. *BJOG.* 2005;12:466-469.

63. Endometriosis

Endometriosis is a common condition in which implants of endometrial tissue appear outside of the uterine cavity, usually within the pelvis. It is a frequent cause of dysmenorrhea and pelvic pain, and it may cause infertility. The pathogenesis is unknown but is thought to be associated with retrograde menstruation, in which menstrual tissue flows through the fallopian tubes and into the pelvic and abdominal peritoneum. Other hypotheses suggest the condition may result from displacement of endometrial tissue through surgical processes (eg, cesarean section, episiotomy), transport of cells through blood or lymph to distant locations, and differentiation of peritoneal cells to become endometrial cells.

Endometriosis is largely dependent upon active menstruation. The disease rarely occurs prior to menarche or after menopause. The most commonly involved locations are the peritoneal surface of the ovaries, anterior and posterior cul-de-sac, and the pelvic ligaments. In the gastrointestinal tract, the sigmoid colon and the appendix are most commonly affected. In some cases, the vagina and urinary system can be involved.

The severity of the condition varies greatly. It can be asymptomatic, or severe and even debilitating. Symptoms are often nonspecific and do not always correlate with the severity of disease. Common symptoms include pelvic, abdominal, or low-back pain occurring in the premenstrual or perimenstrual period; abnormal uterine bleeding; dyspareunia; and infertility. Further symptoms occur based on the location of ectopic endometrial tissue (eg, rectal bleeding or pain with defecation if colonic lesions are present, suprapubic pain upon urination if bladder lesions are present). Most women with endometriosis have no symptoms, and many women with severe pain have minimal visible endometriosis, suggesting that the body's response to the implants is more important than the presence of the implants themselves.

Risk Factors

The risk factors for endometriosis are not well understood. It is most commonly diagnosed in women in their late 20s and early 30s, and the occurrence is increased by about 7% in first-degree relatives. Dietary factors may play a role and are discussed in Nutritional Considerations below.

Diagnosis

Endometriosis is usually suspected from the history, although tender nodules and masses may be palpable or visible on the vagina or cervix during pelvic examination.

Many gynecologists believe that definitive diagnosis can be made only by laparoscopic visualization of lesions and/or biopsy. Endometrial implants may appear in various colors (black, red, yellow, white, blue, or clear). If a visual diagnosis is in question, a biopsy that reveals endometrial glands and stroma is considered diagnostic. As most endometriosis is asymptomatic and many women with typical endometriosis symptoms have no visible disease, an alternative view is that endometriosis is better diagnosed by history, physical examination, and response to therapy than by surgical visualization.

Endoscopy of the colon or **cystoscopy** may reveal implants of the sigmoid or proximal colon and bladder.

Elevated serum CA-125 concentration suggests the presence of the condition (but is not specific), and higher values may correspond with advanced disease.

Imaging studies are not usually helpful, although an ultrasound may be used to detect bulky disease such as endometriomas, which may benefit from surgical removal.

Treatment

The treatment strategy depends upon the severity of disease, proximity to menopause, and whether the patient hopes to become pregnant. After menopause, symptoms will likely improve dramatically, even in severe disease.

Analgesics (eg, NSAIDs) and **oral contraceptive** pills are indicated for pain relief. Oral contraceptives may also reduce the risk of ovarian cancer.[1]

Gonadotropin-releasing hormone (GnRH) analogues, danazol, or **progestins** (eg, norethindrone acetate, intrauterine levonorgestrel) may be very helpful. GnRH analogs (eg, nasal nafarelin, leuprolide injections, goserelin implants) decrease ovarian estrogen production, preventing the pain-inducing stimulation of ectopic endometrial tissue. Treatment usually lasts at least 6 months. GnRH analogues cause a temporary decrease in bone density that has not been shown to be clinically important. Supplemental estrogen or norethindrone acetate may minimize the side effects of hot flashes and bone mineral loss.

Aromatase inhibitors are under investigation.

Medical therapy affords long-term relief in about 50% of patients. Surgery is often used for severe or intractable disease, although it has not been proven superior to medical therapy. Laser ablation or electrocautery of endometrial implants and adhesions may treat the pain, decrease the rate of recurrence, and restore fertility. If there is no desire for future pregnancy, definitive treatment is total abdominal hysterectomy with bilateral salpingo-oophorectomy. However, most patients can be managed effectively without such extreme measures.

Exercise. Women who exercise have a much lower risk for endometriosis, and those who engage in frequent strenuous exercise have at least 75% lower risk for endometriosis, compared with those who do not engage in high-intensity activity.[2]

Nutritional Considerations

Endometriosis is an estrogen-dependent disorder,[3] and some studies have suggested that oxidative stress may contribute to the disease process.[4] These observations may explain the apparent value of diet and exercise interventions, which can improve both hormone levels and antioxidant status. Conversely, alcohol may increase the risk for endometriosis through its documented tendency to increase both estrogen level and oxidative stress. The following factors have been shown in epidemiologic studies to be associated with reduced risk of endometriosis:

A high-fiber, plant-based diet. Although research on the effectiveness of dietary approaches is limited, several lines of evidence support the use of plant-based diets. First, case-control studies have suggested that frequent red meat and ham consumption is associated with endometriosis risk, while fruit and vegetable intake appears to be protective. In an Italian population including 504 cases and an equal number of matched controls, women who ate at least 7 servings of red meat per week had twice the risk of endometriosis compared with those who ate fewer than 3 servings of red meat weekly. Women having 13 or more servings per week of green vegetables had a 70% lower risk of endometriosis compared with those who ate fewer than 6 servings per week. And those eating 14 or more servings of fruit per week had a 20% lower risk compared with women having fewer than 6 servings per week.[5]

Plant-based diets tend to reduce blood estrogen concentrations and increase sex-hormone binding globulin concentration, effects that may be attributable to a reduction in fat intake, an increase in fiber intake, or the weight loss that typically results from these diet changes.[6-8] (See Dysmenorrhea chapter.)

Avoiding alcohol. Data on alcohol intake in relation to endometriosis are sparse. However, some evidence suggests that greater alcohol intake may be associated with increased risk of endometriosis.[9,10]

Orders

See Basic Diet Orders chapter.

Exercise prescription.

Alcohol restriction.

What to Tell the Family

Endometriosis is a painful disorder that will often respond to available medical therapies. Regular exercise may improve symptoms. Alcohol consumption should be minimized. A low-fat, vegan diet, which is helpful for functional menstrual pain, has not been tested for endometriosis. To the extent patients seek to make lifestyle changes, family members can help by supporting these changes.

References

1. Zullo F, Palomba S, Zupi E, et al. Effectiveness of presacral neurectomy in women with severe dysmenorrhea caused by endometriosis who were treated with laparoscopic conservative surgery: A 1-year prospective randomized double-blind controlled trial. *Am J Obstet Gynecol.* 2003;189:5-10.

2. Dhillon PK, Holt VL. Recreational physical activity and endometrioma risk. *Am J Epidemiol.* 2003;158:156-164.

3. Giudice LC, Kao LC. Endometriosis. *Lancet.* 2004;364:1789-1799.

4. Van Langendonckt A, Casanas-Roux F, Donnez J. Oxidative stress and peritoneal endometriosis. *Fertil Steril.* 2002;77:861-870.

5. Parazzini F, Chiaffarino F, Surace M, et al. Selected food intake and risk of endometriosis. *Hum Reprod.* 2004;19:1755-1759.

6. Goldin BR, Woods MN, Spiegelman DL, et al. The effect of dietary fat and fiber on serum estrogen concentrations in premenopausal women under controlled dietary conditions. *Cancer.* 1994;74(suppl 3):1125-1131.

7. Bagga D, Ashley JM, Geffrey SP, et al. Effects of a very low fat, high fiber diet on serum hormones and menstrual function: Implications for breast cancer prevention. *Cancer.* 1995;76:2491-2496.

8. Barnard ND, Scialli AR, Hurlock D, Bertron P. Diet and sex-hormone binding globulin, dysmenorrhea, and premenstrual symptoms. *Obstet Gynecol.* 2000;95:245-250.

9. Perper MM, Breitkopf LJ, Breitstein R, Cody RP, Manowitz P. MAST scores, alcohol consumption, and gynecological symptoms in endometriosis patients. *Alcohol Clin Exp Res.* 1993;17:272-278.

10. Grodstein F, Goldman MB, Cramer DW. Infertility in women and moderate alcohol use. *Am J Public Health.* 1994;84:1429-1432.

64. Uterine Fibroids

Uterine leiomyomas, or fibroids, are benign tumors of the uterus composed of smooth muscle and connective tissue. Fibroids are very common, present in at least one-quarter of women by the age of 40.

Fibroids are classified by anatomic location as intramural (within the myometrium), submucosal (underlying the endometrium), or subserosal (underlying the uterine serosa). There is no identifiable cause of uterine fibroids. However, estrogen is necessary for their growth; many grow during pregnancy and then recede at menopause. Further, higher parity and low-dose oral contraceptive use have been shown to decrease the risk of fibroid formation.

Most uterine fibroid cases are asymptomatic. However, symptoms may include uterine bleeding, resulting in prolonged or heavy menstrual flow and possibly anemia; dysmenorrhea; urinary frequency and urgency; constipation; dyspareunia; and abdominal tenderness. Complications of pregnancy may be more common in women with fibroids, including miscarriage, placental abruption, and premature labor.

Risk Factors

African American women are up to 3 times more likely to have fibroids compared with white women and often have more severe disease at a younger age.[1,2]

Age. Fibroids occur during the reproductive years, most commonly becoming clinically apparent during the fourth and fifth decades of life. They do not occur in prepubescent girls and usually shrink at menopause.

Genetics. Monozygotic twins have a 2 to 3 times greater risk of fibroids than dizygotic twins when one twin is affected.[3]

Pregnancy. Parity appears to decrease the risk of fibroids.

Oral contraceptive pills. Although these appear to be protective, the Nurses' Health Study showed an increased risk in women who used oral contraceptive pills at ages 13 to 16. Low-dose oral contraceptives and menopausal hormone therapy are not contraindicated in women with fibroids.

Some evidence suggests that cigarette smoking may decrease the risk of fibroids. Of course, the health risks of smoking far outweigh this potential benefit.

Diagnosis

Fibroids may be suspected from the patient history, and a bimanual pelvic exam often confirms the diagnosis. The uterus is generally enlarged, mobile, and asymmetric. Extremely large fibroids may cause a palpable uterus on abdominal exam. Imaging studies can be used for confirmation, but are not essential.

Transvaginal ultrasound can be used to detect and localize fibroids. However, for women with large uteri or more than 4 fibroids, it is less precise than MRI.[4]

Sonohysterography can better characterize submucosal fibroids than transvaginal ultrasound.

Pelvic MRI best localizes all types of fibroids, accurately assesses their size, and distinguishes fibroids from other growths (eg, ovarian tumors). However, expense should be taken into consideration.

Hysterosalpingography is best reserved for fertility evaluations. It defines the contour of the endometrium and patency of the fallopian tubes.

Hysteroscopy provides direct visualization inside the uterus and can diagnose submucosal fibroids.

Treatment

Most uterine fibroids are asymptomatic and need not be treated. Intervention depends upon a number of factors, including age (women approaching menopause may not require therapy, as fibroids typically regress spontaneously), fertility concerns, and the location and size of the fibroids.

Surgery

Myomectomy, via hysteroscopy, laparoscopy, or laparotomy, preserves childbearing potential, but is at least as difficult for the surgeon and patient as hysterectomy. Hysteroscopy is best for submucosal fibroids. Laparotomy may be indicated for large or multiple fibroids.

Hysterectomy is a definitive treatment that offers clear symptomatic improvement in approximately 90% of fibroid patients who undergo it. The primary indication for hysterectomy is uncontrollable bleeding.

Other options for women who do not desire pregnancy include endometrial ablation via hysteroscopic myomectomy, cryotherapy, uterine artery embolization, or magnetic resonance-guided ultrasonic ablation.

Pharmacologic Interventions

Gonadotropin-releasing hormone (GnRH) analogs (eg, leuprolide) can shrink fibroids prior to surgical removal. Symptoms will usually return with discontinuation of therapy. GnRH analogs are generally not recommended for long-term management (an off-label use) due to cost.

Low-dose combined oral contraceptive pills (OCPs) may be useful in controlling menstrual bleeding and may give sufficient symptom relief. OCPs generally do not affect the size of the fibroids.

GnRH antagonists (ie, mifepristone and androgens) are under investigation for treating fibroids.

Pain can be treated with **nonsteroidal anti-inflammatory drugs**.

Raloxiphene appears to benefit postmenopausal women,[5] but further trials are needed to establish its effect for premenopausal women.

Lifestyle Modification

Exercise may reduce risk of developing fibroids. Women who were physically active for ≥7 hours per week were 40% less likely to develop fibroids than those whose activity was <2 hours each week. [6]

Nutritional Considerations

Evidence for a direct effect of diet on fibroid risk or progression is very limited. However, the excessive production of certain growth factors (insulin-like growth factor I, epidermal growth factor) is a risk factor for fibroid growth,[7] and evidence indicates that these may be the effectors of estrogen- and progesterone-mediated fibroid growth.[8] Diets low in fat and high in fiber (eg, vegetarian diets) have the ability to modulate blood hormone concentration and activity[9] and reduce levels of growth factors.[10] These effects may underlie the results of studies that have found higher risk for fibroids in women who eat red meat more often than do others, and in those who are overweight, as described below. However, this does not necessarily mean that a diet change, even if effective, will alleviate symptoms rapidly enough to obviate other treatments.

Epidemiologic studies indicate that the following factors are associated with reduced risk of fibroids:

Avoiding red meat. Available evidence suggests that women who eat more than one serving per day of red meat have a 70% greater risk for uterine myoma, compared with women who eat the least red meat.[11] A hypothesized mechanism may be the tendency of fatty, low-fiber foods to increase estrogen concentrations or activity.

Increasing vegetable intake. Frequent intake of green vegetables was associated with a 50% reduction in the risk for developing fibroids, compared with less frequent intake of these vegetables.[11] Further research is needed to substantiate this relationship.

Weight control. A greater number of women with fibroids are obese, compared with the general population.[12] In the Black Women's Health Study, compared with the thinnest women (body mass index [BMI] <20 kg/m²), risk appears to increase gradually in women with a BMI of 20 to 22.4 (34% increased risk), to a maximum risk in women with a BMI of 27.5 to 29.9 (47% increased risk), before falling in the most obese group (20% increased risk).[13]

Limiting alcohol. Alcohol appears to increase the risk for fibroids. This risk is positively correlated with the number of years of alcohol intake and specifically with beer consumption. Compared with women who abstained from alcohol, those who drank one or more beers per day had a greater than 50% increased risk for leiomyomata.[14]

Orders

See Basic Diet Orders chapter.

Avoid alcohol.

What to Tell the Family

Dietary contributors to fibroids are still under investigation. However, the changes that appear to be helpful—limiting meat and alcohol and increasing vegetables—can be beneficial for the whole family, and are most sustainable when the family makes these changes together.

References

1. Marshall LM, Spiegelman D, Barbieri RL, et al. Variation in the incidence of uterine leiomyoma among premenopausal women by age and race. *Obstet Gynecol.* 1997;90:967-973.

2. Kjerulff KH, Langenberg P, Seidman JD, Stolley PD, Guzinski GM. Uterine leiomyomas. Racial differences in severity, symptoms and age at diagnosis. *J Reprod Med.* 1996;41:483-490.

3. Treloar SA, Martin NG, Dennerstein L, Raphael B, Heath AC. Pathways to hysterectomy: insights from longitudinal twin research. *Am J Obstet Gynecol.* 1992;167:82-88.

4. Dueholm M, Lundorf E, Hansen ES, Ledertoug S, Olesen F. Accuracy of MRI and transvaginal ultrasonography in the diagnosis, mapping, and measurement of uterine myomas. *Am J Obstet Gynecol.* 2002;186:409-415.

5. Palomba S, Sammartino A, Di Carlo C, Affinito P, Zullo F, Nappi C. Effects of raloxifene treatment on uterine leiomyomas in postmenopausal women. *Fertil Steril.* 2001;76:38-43.

6. Baird DD, Dunson DB, Hill MC, Cousins D, Schectman JM. Association of physical activity with development of uterine leiomyoma. *Am J Epidemiol.* 2007;165:157-163.

7. Lethaby A, Vollenhoven B. Fibroids (uterine myomatosis, leiomyomas). *Am Fam Physician.* 2005;71:1753-1756.

8. Flake GP, Andersen J, Dixon D. Etiology and pathogenesis of uterine leiomyomas: a review. *Environ Health Perspect.* 2003;111:1037-1054.

9. Barnard ND, Scialli AR, Hurlock D, Bertron P. Diet and sex-hormone binding globulin, dysmenorrhea, and premenstrual symptoms. *Obstet Gynecol.* 2000;95:245-250.

10. Allen NE, Appleby PN, Davey GK, Kaaks R, Rinaldi S, Key TJ. The associations of diet with serum insulin-like growth factor I and its main binding proteins in 292 women meat-eaters, vegetarians, and vegans. *Cancer Epidemiol Biomarkers Prev.* 2002;11:1441-1448.

11. Chiaffarino F, Parazzini F, La Vecchia C, Chatenoud L, Di Cintio E, Marsico S. Diet and uterine myomas. *Obstet Gynecol.* 1999;94:395-398.

12. Shikora SA, Niloff JM, Bistrian BR, Forse RA, Blackburn GL. Relationship between obesity and uterine leiomyomata. *Nutrition.* 1991;7:251-255.

13. Wise LA, Palmer JR, Spiegelman D, et al. Influence of body size and body fat distribution on risk of uterine leiomyomata in U.S. black women. *Epidemiology.* 2005;16:346-354.

14. Wise LA, Palmer JR, Harlow BL, et al. Risk of uterine leiomyomata in relation to tobacco, alcohol and caffeine consumption in the Black Women's Health Study. *Hum Reprod.* 2004;19:1746-1754.

65. Polycystic Ovarian Syndrome

Polycystic ovarian syndrome (PCOS) is a disorder involving excessive androgen production by the ovaries and adrenal cortices. PCOS affects approximately 5% of women in the United States. The etiology is unknown, but the fundamental problem appears to be resistance to insulin activity. Increased circulating insulin decreases the concentration of sex hormone-binding globulins, thereby increasing the concentration of unbound free testosterone.

The classic presentation is a triad of hirsutism, anovulation, and obesity, with onset during the peripubertal years. However, it has been recognized in recent years that many women with PCOS are not obese or hirsute and present only with anovulation and androgenizing effects. Affected women generally have multiple ovarian cysts and may be infertile. They are believed to have insulin resistance and are at risk for type 2 diabetes and the metabolic syndrome. Women with PCOS often have acne but rarely have more virilizing signs such as male-pattern baldness. Adolescents may also present with precocious puberty or acanthosis nigricans.

Although PCOS is not curable, weight loss (when applicable) and symptomatic treatment usually control most symptoms.

Risk Factors

Obesity. Obesity, particularly abdominal obesity, increases risk of PCOS.

Epilepsy. Both epilepsy and anti-seizure medications increase the risk of PCOS.[1]

Family History. Approximately 40% of first-degree relatives are affected.[2]

Diagnosis

Diagnosis of PCOS can be difficult, as presentation may be atypical.

For diagnosis, according to the Rotterdam Consensus Group criteria, 2 of the following 3 points should be met, and other diseases with similar clinical presentation should be ruled out:[3]

1. **Menstrual irregularity.** Anovulation, oligo-ovulation, amenorrhea, oligomenorrhea, or irregular bleeding.

2. **Signs of hyperandrogenism.** Hirsutism, acne, male-pattern baldness, or elevated serum free testosterone concentration.

3. **Polycystic ovaries, visible on transvaginal ultrasound**. An isolated finding of polycystic ovaries in the absence of clinical hyperandrogenism is common and does not indicate PCOS.

Laboratory studies may include measurements of prolactin, blood glucose, and insulin. A **glucose tolerance test** is indicated in most cases.

Because coronary artery disease is common in patients with PCOS, **cardiovascular risk factors** should be evaluated (eg, hypercholesterolemia, hypertriglyceridemia). Smoking should also be discouraged.

Testing for **sleep apnea** (sleep questionnaire, overnight polysomnography) may be indicated, because women with PCOS are at increased risk.

Treatment

In obese women, aggressive but sustainable weight-loss strategies can be considered first, as many PCOS sequelae improve with weight loss.

Weight loss, physical activity, and insulin-sensitizing agents (eg, metformin, thiazolidinediones) are usually necessary to reduce insulin resistance.

Oral contraceptives are used to regulate the menstrual cycle and protect the endometrium in women who are not interested in becoming pregnant.

Hirsutism is usually treated by hair removal (eg, electrolysis, laser treatment), oral contraceptive pills (often combined with an anti-androgen medication, such as spironolactone), or other pharmacologic agents.

Acne is treated with topical or oral agents.

Treatment of infertility is often necessary if the patient desires pregnancy.

- Weight loss and exercise may be beneficial; even small weight reductions may improve fertility.

- Clomiphene and metformin are initial choices to induce ovulation.

- Assisted reproductive technologies (eg, in-vitro fertilization) may be necessary.

Nutritional Considerations

PCOS appears to be related to diet and lifestyle factors, particularly insofar as they influence body weight and insulin resistance. Although weight loss is an accepted treatment, even relatively lean women may develop PCOS, suggesting that diet may affect the outcome of this disorder even in the absence of weight change.

A diet that addresses cardiovascular risk factors is appropriate for women with PCOS. Roughly half of women with PCOS are obese,[4] and losing as little as 5% to 10% of weight results in resumption of menses and decrease in blood androgen levels.[4,5] The composition of the therapeutic diet is a matter of controversy. However, there are several reasons why a diet low in fat and high in fibrous carbohydrates is superior to other weight-loss treatments.

Such a diet helps reverse insulin resistance, which affects 50% to 70% of women with PCOS.[4,6] This is particularly important because of insulin's tendency to reduce sex hormone-binding globulin (SHBG) and increase free testosterone concentrations.[7] Low-fat, high-fiber diets also reduce body weight and effectively address dyslipidemia (elevated triglycerides, low HDL), elevations of C-reactive protein and homocysteine, and oxidative stress.[4] Low-fat, high-fiber diets reduce circulating androgens and increase SHBG.[4,8]

A diet that emphasizes whole grain intake, as opposed to refined carbohydrates, may improve metabolic defects in PCOS by providing fiber and inositol. Inositol has been repeatedly found in clinical trials to improve insulin action, decrease androgen levels, and improve ovulatory function in both lean and obese women with PCOS.[9-11] The benefits of metformin in PCOS appear at least partly due to increasing inositol availability.[12]

Orders

See Basic Diet Orders chapter.

What to Tell the Family

PCOS can often be effectively treated through weight loss, dietary changes, and medical therapies. Diets that are low in fat and high in fiber are likely to achieve the best results, particularly when coupled with exercise. Families of affected patients would do well to adopt a similar diet and increased exercise to facilitate the patient's adherence and for their own health benefits.

References

1. Bilo L, Meo R, Valentino R, Di Carlo C, Striano S, Nappi C. Characterization of reproductive endocrine disorders in women with epilepsy. *J Clin Endocrinol Metab.* 2001;86:2950-2956.

2. Azziz R, Kashar-Miller MD. Family history as a risk factor for the polycystic ovary syndrome. *J Pediatr Endocrinol Metab.* 2000;13(suppl 5):1303-1306.

3. The Rotterdam ESHRE/ASRM-Sponsored PCOS consensus workshop group. Revised 2003 consensus on diagnostic criteria and long-term health risks related to polycystic ovary syndrome. *Hum Reprod.* 2004;19:41-47.

4. Marsh K, Brand-Miller J. The optimal diet for women with polycystic ovary syndrome? *Br J Nutr.* 2005;94:154-165.

5. Stamets K, Taylor DS, Kunselman A, Demers LM, Pelkman CL, Legro RS. A randomized trial of the effects of two types of short-term hypocaloric diets on weight loss in women with polycystic ovary syndrome. *Fertil Steril.* 2004;81:630-637.

6. Hahn S, Tan S, Elsenbruch S, et al. Clinical and biochemical characterization of women with polycystic ovary syndrome in North Rhine-Westphalia. *Horm Metab Res.* 2005;37:438-444.

7. Holte J. Polycystic ovary syndrome and insulin resistance: thrifty genes struggling with over-feeding and sedentary life style? *J Endocrinol Invest.* 1998;21:589-601.

8. Berrino F, Bellati C, Secreto G, et al. Reducing bioavailable sex hormones through a comprehensive change in diet: the diet and androgens (DIANA) randomized trial. *Cancer Epidemiol Biomarkers Prev.* 2001;10:25-33.

9. Nestler JE, Jakubowicz DJ, Reamer P, Gunn RD, Allan G. Ovulatory and metabolic effects of D-chiro-inositol in the polycystic ovary syndrome. *N Engl J Med.* 1999;340:1314-1320.

10. Iuorno MJ, Jakubowicz DJ, Baillargeon JP, et al. Effects of d-chiro-inositol in lean women with the polycystic ovary syndrome. *Endocr Pract.* 2002;8:417-423.

11. Gerli S, Mignosa M, Di Renzo GC. Effects of inositol on ovarian function and metabolic factors in women with PCOS: a randomized double blind placebo-controlled trial. *Eur Rev Med Pharmacol Sci.* 2003;7:151-159.

12. Baillargeon JP, Jakubowicz DJ, Iuorno MJ, Jakubowicz S, Nestler JE. Effects of metformin and rosiglitazone, alone and in combination, in nonobese women with polycystic ovary syndrome and normal indices of insulin sensitivity. *Fertil Steril.* 2004;82:893-902.

66. Menopausal Symptoms

At menopause, a woman's ovaries stop producing eggs; her body produces less estrogen and progesterone; and menstrual periods become less frequent, eventually stopping altogether. The mean age of menopause in normal women in the United States is 51. Menopause that occurs beyond age 56 is considered late menopause.

A perimenopausal transition generally occurs for several years prior to the cessation of menstruation. During this time, the ovulatory cycle is often erratic, resulting in irregular menses, heavy breakthrough bleeding, hot flashes, and vaginal dryness.

Upon cessation of ovarian follicular function, production of estrogen declines and production of gonadotropin (follicle-stimulating hormone, luteinizing hormone) rises. The decrease in circulating estrogen results in the clinical symptoms of menopause.

Hot flashes are the most common initial menopause symptom, occurring in up to two-thirds of North American women. This phenomenon may be due to estrogen withdrawal and consequent bursts of gonadotropin-releasing hormone from the hypothalamus, which can affect the nearby thermoregulatory center in the brain. A sensation of heat and perspiration may last several minutes and is often preceded or followed by chills and shivering. In some cases, palpitations accompany these symptoms.

Vaginal dryness, due to the decrease in estrogen stimulation of the vagina and urethra, is common and may cause dyspareunia.

Psychological distress may occur, including depression, anxiety, irritability, fatigue, and difficulty concentrating. These symptoms may reflect the contributions of hormonal shifts and the sleep disturbances associated with hot flashes, which can be improved by any measures that improve sleep.

Risk Factors

About 40% of North American women seek treatment for menopausal symptoms. There are some suggestions that African American women are less likely to report symptoms compared with whites. Risk factors for the development of menopausal symptoms are poorly defined but are likely related to a combination of environmental, lifestyle, and social factors. No consistent evidence has linked weight, health status, and hysterectomy with vascular symptoms of menopause. Symptoms appear to be significantly less common in Asia, compared with North America, a difference that has been attributed to diet.

Assessment

If the menopausal status is in doubt (eg, in a young woman with amenorrhea), testing for serum follicle-stimulating hormone (FSH) concentration may be helpful. A low value suggests hypothalamic amenorrhea, and an elevated value suggests premature ovarian failure. During the early years of normal menopause, however, FSH levels fluctuate widely, and measuring levels gives little information on menopausal status.

For women at risk for osteoporosis, evaluation with dual-energy x-ray absorptiometry (DEXA) scan may be used to measure bone density. An initial examination at age 65 is reasonable; earlier screening has been suggested for women who smoke or have family histories of early-onset fragility fractures.

Women with risk factors for coronary artery disease should be followed regularly and treated as necessary for prevention, including treatment for hypertension, hyperlipidemia, and other cardiovascular complications (see Cardiovascular section). This and other screening recommendations (eg, for breast cancer and colon cancer) are related to a woman's age and not to her menopausal status.

Treatment

Menopause is a normal part of life, and no treatment is typically required. Symptoms, when they occur, are usually tolerable and eventually pass. However, for women with particularly bothersome symptoms, the following considerations may be helpful.

Oral hormone therapy is highly effective for menopausal symptoms, but women considering this therapy should be counseled that it has been associated with an increased risk of stroke, breast cancer, and endometrial cancer. Other effective treatments for hot flashes include some antidepressant medications (eg, venlafaxine), clonidine, and gabapentin.

Over-the-counter moisturizers may be used for vaginal dryness. If vaginal moisturizers are of insufficient benefit, **topical estrogens** may be used (at lower doses than for oral therapy). The vehicle for disbursement (eg, cream, ring, pessary, tablet) is not important. Systemic symptoms are generally not improved by local therapy, but systemic side effects also rarely occur. Progestins may be necessary when using standard dose topical estrogens to decrease the risk of endometrial stimulation.

Nutritional therapies may be useful (see Nutritional Considerations).

Women should be counseled on adequate dietary or supplement intake of **calcium** and **vitamin D**.

Exercise may reduce vasomotor symptoms. Physically active women reported approximately 50% fewer (and less severe) hot flashes, compared with sedentary women, although strenuous exercise may also trigger these episodes. Randomized, controlled trials have not examined the efficacy of exercise in managing hot flashes, and not all studies have reported benefits.[1] Exercise is also important for stimulating bone formation and decreasing resorption, as well as for cardiovascular health.

Antiresorptive medications can be considered for patients with low bone-mineral density.

Stress management techniques appear to reduce hot flashes and improve other menopausal symptoms. Several studies have found significant decreases (30% to 100%) in hot flashes with the use of relaxation and paced respiration (slow deep breathing) and with the use of coping-skills training in cognitive-behavioral interventions.[2] Because norepinephrine release plays a role in the physiology of hot flashes, some have suggested that the benefit of relaxation and other stress management techniques may stem from decreased central nervous system adrenergic tone.[3]

Nutritional Considerations

Dietary approaches to menopausal symptoms have been of interest to women and their physicians for many years. Epidemiologic studies have shown that symptoms occur more commonly in parts of the world where Western dietary habits prevail, and clinical studies have found that dietary factors (fiber and perhaps fat) influence hormone concentrations and activity. However, clinical trials of nutritional interventions for menopausal symptoms have been limited. The following approaches may be considered:

Soy products are popularly prescribed for menopausal symptoms. Asian populations that frequently use soy products have a much lower prevalence of menopausal symptoms, compared with their Western counterparts, leading to the speculation that phytoestrogens in soy (isoflavones) may be acting as estrogens.

However, Asian diets and lifestyles vary from Western diets in many other respects (eg, less intake of meat and dairy products and greater intake of grains and vegetables), making it difficult to attribute this difference to soy. A review of clinical studies that examined the effect of soy on menopausal symptoms found some benefit, though not enough to recommend using soy to treat hot flashes.[4] Other reviewers concluded that the effect of soy foods on reduction of hot flashes is modest and disappears after 6 weeks.[5]

Red clover contains isoflavones as well, and studies in postmenopausal women have found increases in high-density lipoprotein (HDL), arterial compliance, bone density, and cognitive function in women using this botanical. However, efficacy for vasomotor symptoms has not been established.[2]

A 2007 Cochrane review examining studies of phytoestrogen supplementation (generally from soy or red clover) concluded that evidence has not yet established the efficacy of phytoestrogen supplements for the alleviation of menopausal symptoms.[6]

Black cohosh. Some studies have suggested that black cohosh improves vasomotor symptoms in women,[7] but a larger controlled clinical trial was unable to confirm any significant benefit.[8] Several cases of significant liver toxicity have been reported.[9-11]

Two other botanicals sometimes used for menopausal symptoms, **dong quai** (*Angelica sinensis*) and **chaste tree** (*Vitex agnus castus*), have not performed consistently well in controlled clinical trials.[12]

Low-fat diets. Some evidence suggests that a low-fat diet may be helpful. In an observational study, perimenopausal women following low-fat (~20%) diets scored significantly lower on the vasomotor symptoms subscale (including hot flashes and night sweats), compared with a control group following a diet containing ~30% fat.[13] These women also had reductions in serum cholesterol, estrogen levels, and mammographic densities. A beneficial effect of a low-fat diet on menopausal symptoms has not been established in controlled clinical trials.

Orders

See Basic Diet Orders chapter.

What to Tell the Family

It is useful for the patient and family to understand that menopause is a normal condition, not a disease or diagnosis. It can, however, be accompanied by symptoms and, in some cases, mood changes, all of which are temporary. Diet changes and exercise may reduce vasomotor symptoms, in addition to their other benefits.

References

1. Fugate SE, Church CO. Nonestrogen treatment modalities for vasomotor symptoms associated with menopause. *Ann Pharmacother.* 2004;38:1482-1499.

2. McKee J, Warber SL. Integrative therapies for menopause. *South Med J.* 2005;98:319-326.

3. Shanafelt TD, Barton DL, Adjei AA, Loprinzi CL. Pathophysiology and treatment of hot flashes. *Mayo Clin Proc.* 2002;77:1207-1218.

4. Huntley AL, Ernst E. Soy for the treatment of perimenopausal symptoms-a systematic review. *Maturitas.* 2004;47:1-9.

5. Viereck V, Emons G, Wuttke W. Black cohosh: just another phytoestrogen? *Trends Endocrinol Metab.* 2005;16:214-221.

6. Lethaby AE, Brown J, Marjoribanks J, Kronenberg F, Roberts H, Eden J. Phytoestrogens for vasomotor menopausal symptoms. *Cochrane Database Syst Rev.* 2007;(4):CD001395.

7. Frei-Kleiner S, Schaffner W, Rahlfs VW, Bodmer Ch, Birkhäuser M. Cimicifuga racemosa dried ethanolic extract in menopausal disorders: a double-blind placebo-controlled clinical trial. *Maturitas*. 2005;51:397-404.

8. Newton KM, Reed SD, LaCroix AZ, Grothaus LC, Ehrlich K, Guiltinan J. Treatment of vasomotor symptoms of menopause with black cohosh, multibotanicals, soy, hormone therapy, or placebo: a randomized trial. *Ann Intern Med*. 2006;145:869-789.

9. Nisbet BC, O'Connor RE. Black cohosh-induced hepatitis. *Del Med J*. 2007;79:441-444.

10. Cohen SM, O'Connor AM, Hart J, Merel NH, Te HS. Autoimmune hepatitis associated with the use of black cohosh: a case study. *Menopause*. 2004;11:575-577.

11. Lynch CR, Folkers ME, Hutson WR. Fulminant hepatic failure associated with the use of black cohosh: a case report. *Liver Transpl*. 2006;12:989-992.

12. Haimov-Kochman R, Hochner-Celnikier D. Hot flashes revisited: pharmacological and herbal options for hot flashes management. What does the evidence tell us? *Acta Obstet Gynecol Scand*. 2005;84:972-979.

13. Leyenaar J, Sutherland HJ, Lockwood GA, et al. Self-reported physical and emotional health of women in a low-fat, high-carbohydrate dietary trial (Canada). *Cancer Causes Control*. 1998;9:601-610.

SECTION XII: IMMUNOLOGY AND ALLERGY

67. Systemic Lupus Erythematosus

Systemic lupus erythematosus (SLE) is a chronic autoimmune disorder of uncertain etiology. Various immune changes occur, including B cell lymphocyte hyperreactivity, T cell lymphocyte defects, complement activation, and autoantibodies to nuclear and cellular antigens.

The clinical course is irregular, with periods of exacerbation and remission, and the severity of disease ranges from mild to life-threatening. Virtually any organ system of the body can be involved, notably the skin, joints, kidneys, lungs, nervous system, and serous membranes. Organ damage results from deposition of immune complexes within tissues and autoantibody-mediated destruction of host cells. The most common clinical presentations are skin changes, arthritis, and constitutional symptoms (eg, fever, fatigue, weight loss). But more serious manifestations are not uncommon, such as vasculitis (including of the central nervous system), nephritis, pleuritis, pericarditis, arterial and venous thromboses, anemia, leukopenia, and thrombocytopenia.

Risk Factors

The prevalence of SLE is 40 to 50 cases per 100,000 people. Incidence has tripled over the past half-century, but this is likely due to improved detection of mild cases.

Gender. Nearly 90% of cases occur in women, particularly during the childbearing years. The female-to-male ratio is 3:1 in children, approximately 15:1 in adults, and 8:1 in postmenopausal women.

Ethnicity. African Americans are most commonly affected and are 3 times more likely to have SLE than whites. Hispanic, Asian, and Native Americans also have an increased incidence compared with whites.

Geography. Prevalence varies significantly by geography. For example, SLE is rare in West Africa, increases in frequency in Central and Southern Africa, and has a high frequency in America and Europe. It is unclear whether this variation is related to environmental or genetic factors.

Age. Peak onset occurs between 20 and 50 years of age.

Genetics. There is an increased incidence in close relatives (SLE affects approximately 10% of relatives of index patients) and a strong correlation in monozygotic twins, but specific involved genes have yet to be determined.

Medications. Development of an SLE-like syndrome has been associated with use of hydralazine, isoniazid, methyldopa, and procainamide. However, clinical manifestations of drug-induced SLE tend to be less severe and often remit with removal of the offending agent.

Diagnosis

The American College of Rheumatology has established clinical and laboratory criteria to aid in diagnosis. At least 4 of the following 11 criteria should be present for diagnosis:

- Malar rash.
- Discoid rash.
- Photosensitivity.
- Oral or nasopharyngeal ulcers.
- Arthritis in more than 2 joints (in 90% of cases).
- Serositis (pleuritis or pleural effusion, pericarditis or pericardial effusion).
- Renal disorders (proteinuria).
- Neurologic disorders (seizure, psychosis).
- Hematologic disorders (anemia, leukopenia, thrombocytopenia).
- Immunologic disorders (anti-DNA antibodies, anti-Smith antibodies, antiphospholipid antibodies, false-positive syphilis serology).
- Antinuclear antibodies (ANA) (in 98% of cases).

Treatment

Dietary changes, physical activity, smoking cessation, and avoidance of sun exposure are proven nonmedical measures for managing SLE. Pregnancy should be avoided during active disease, due to a high risk of miscarriage and maternal complications.

Medical therapy is tailored to specific organ involvement:

Nonsteroidal antiinflammatory drugs (NSAIDs) are used in patients with arthritis, myalgias, fever, and mild serositis. However, sulfa-containing

NSAIDs (celecoxib) should be used with caution, as they may exacerbate the disease. The risk of adverse events associated with NSAIDs, especially COX-2 inhibitors, should be considered when prescribing these medications.

Steroids are frequently used during exacerbations and are particularly effective for pericarditis, nephritis, cerebritis, and arthritis. However, steroid-sparing therapy using disease-modifying antirheumatic drugs (see below) may be warranted to mitigate the long-term adverse effects of glucocorticoids. Because long-term steroid use can affect bone structure, dual energy x-ray absortiometry (DEXA) scanning may be helpful to monitor skeletal integrity.

Disease-modifying antirheumatic drugs (azathioprine, hydroxychloroquine, mycophenolate mofetil, cyclophosphamide) may be useful in cases refractory to NSAIDs and/or steroids. In particular, hydroxychloroquine is often beneficial for skin and musculoskeletal symptoms, and mycophenolate mofetil appears to have renal-protective effects. Cyclophosphamide is often used in situations of major organ involvement and life-threatening disease.

Experimental therapies under investigation include stem cell transplantation, anti-B-cell antibodies, other anticytokine antibodies, intravenous immune globulin, and thalidomide.

A number of drugs have reportedly exacerbated the disease or resulted in drug allergy. In particular, sulfonamides should be avoided, as they may exacerbate symptoms. There are also anecdotal reports of aseptic meningitis caused by ibuprofen.

Measures to protect against direct and indirect sunlight exposure should be emphasized, including using high-SPF sunscreen daily, wearing long-sleeved shirts and wide-brimmed hats, and avoiding midday sun.

Low-impact, weight-bearing exercise is important for maintaining cardiovascular and bone health.

Influenza vaccine is safe for SLE patients but less effective than for other individuals.

Nutritional Considerations

SLE is one of a number of autoimmune diseases that may be influenced by essential fatty acids, which are precursors of proinflammatory eicosanoids and cytokines. These hormone-like chemicals are a hallmark of disease activity in SLE, and some (thromboxane A2, tumor necrosis factor alpha [TNF α) increase the risk for other inflammatory conditions, including cardiovascular disease, in SLE patients. Although clinical trials have not established a role for diet therapy in preventing or treating SLE, some rationale exists for the use of a low-fat, low-cholesterol diet and a proportionately greater intake of omega-3 fatty acids. The primary nutritional issues are as follows:

Omega-3 fatty acids. Omega-3 fatty acids can reduce the production of the proinflammatory cytokines (TNF α, interleukin-1) that are implicated in SLE.[1,2] In patients with lupus nephritis, taking 30 to 45 grams per day of flax seed (a rich source of alpha-linoleic acid) reduced serum creatinine and proteinuria.[3,4] Similarly, supplementation with fish oils has been reported to improve disease activity[5] and to reduce triglycerides in pediatric SLE patients.[6] While these studies suggest that flax oil or other sources of omega-3 fatty acids may be helpful, they included a limited number of participants and require confirmation.

Antioxidants. Poorer antioxidant status is a risk factor for the development of SLE.[7] The oxidative stress that may accompany low antioxidant intake is a frequent finding in, as well as a possible contributor to, SLE and its complications.[8,9] Preliminary evidence suggests that antioxidant supplementation using proanthocyanidins may reduce disease activity[10] and, with vitamin C and vitamin E, decrease some measures of oxidative stress.[11] However, these findings require confirmation in larger controlled trials.

Low-saturated-fat, low-cholesterol diet. Patients with SLE frequently have dyslipidemia characterized by elevated triglyceride levels and low high-density lipoprotein (HDL)[12] and are at increased risk for cardiovascular events.[13] In recognition of these facts, an American Heart Association Expert Panel has provided recommendations for prevention and treatment of cardiovascular risk for pediatric patients with SLE, including evaluation and education by nutrition professionals.[14] Diet education for individuals with SLE and dyslipidemia should include meals low in saturated fat and cholesterol, and evidence indicates that such treatment produces significant reduction in LDL cholesterol in patients with SLE.[14,15] (See Dyslipidemias chapter.)

Two additional nutritional considerations merit discussion:

Patients with SLE are at risk for glucocorticoid-induced osteoporosis and fractures.[16] Glucocorticoids also increase the risk for diabetes,[17] thereby increasing cardiovascular risk for SLE patients. However, no evidence suggests that dietary treatment can prevent the development of insulin resistance in steroid-treated SLE patients.

Limited evidence shows that, at least in pediatric SLE patients, spinal bone density significantly improves with calcium and vitamin D supplementation.[18] Adult patients on chronic glucocorticoid therapy should supplement with calcium and vitamin D.

Some evidence suggests that patients benefit from dehydroepiandrosterone (DHEA). At doses of 200 mg/d, DHEA has been found to lower elevated levels of interleukin-6, improve assessments of disease activity, and reduce flares in lupus patients. Some studies have also found steroid-sparing effects and reductions in bone loss with only mild side effects (hirsutism, acne).[19,20] However, the potential adverse effects of DHEA on uterine health are not fully elucidated.

Orders

See Basic Diet Orders chapter.

Vitamin D and calcium supplementation, as appropriate.

What to Tell the Family

SLE is a serious autoimmune disorder that can be partly treated by lifestyle and nutritional changes. Smoking cessation, avoidance of sun exposure, and regular physical activity are important measures. Supplementation with omega-3 fatty acids may decrease the activity of the disease and, especially in conjunction with a low-fat, low-cholesterol diet, protect the heart. Patients using chronic steroid therapy are at risk for osteoporosis. These patients should have their bone density checked on a regular basis and should supplement their diets with calcium and vitamin D.

References

1. Aringer M, Smolen JS. Tumor necrosis factor and other pro-inflammatory cytokines in systemic lupus erythematosus: a rationale for therapeutic intervention. *Lupus.* 2004;13:344-347.

2. Kettler DB. Can manipulation of the ratios of essential fatty acids slow the rapid rate of postmenopausal bone loss? *Altern Med Rev.* 2001;6:61-77.

3. Clark WF, Kortas C, Heidenheim AP, Garland J, Spanner E, Parbtani A. Flaxseed in lupus nephritis: a two-year nonplacebo-controlled crossover study. *J Am Coll Nutr.* 2001;20:143-148.

4. Clark WF, Parbtani A, Huff MW, et al. Flaxseed: a potential treatment for lupus nephritis. *Kidney Int.* 1995;48:475-480.

5. Walton AJ, Snaith ML, Locniskar M, Cumberland AG, Morrow WJ, Isenberg DA. Dietary fish oil and the severity of symptoms in patients with systemic lupus erythematosus. *Ann Rheum Dis.* 1991;50:463-466.

6. Ilowite NT, Copperman N, Leicht T, Kwong T, Jacobson MS. Effects of dietary modification and fish oil supplementation on dyslipoproteinemia in pediatric systemic lupus erythematosus. *J Rheumatol.* 1995;22:1347-1351.

7. Comstock GW, Burke AE, Hoffman SC, et al. Serum concentrations of alpha tocopherol, beta-carotene, and retinol preceding the diagnosis of rheumatoid arthritis and systemic lupus erythematosus. *Ann Rheum Dis.* 1997;56:323-325.

8. Alves JD, Grima B. Oxidative stress in systemic lupus erythematosus and antiphospholipid syndrome: a gateway to atherosclerosis. *Curr Rheumatol Rep.* 2003;5:383-390.

9. Kovacic P, Jacintho JD. Systemic lupus erythematosus and other autoimmune diseases from endogenous and exogenous agents: unifying theme of oxidative stress. *Mini Rev Med Chem.* 2003;3:568-575.

10. Stefanescu M, Matache C, Onu A, et al. Pycnogenol efficacy in the treatment of systemic lupus erythematosus patients. *Phytother Res.* 2001;15:698-704.

11. Tam LS, Li EK, Leung VY, et al. Effects of vitamins C and E on oxidative stress markers and endothelial function in patients with systemic lupus erythematosus: a double-blind, placebo-controlled pilot study. *J Rheumatol.* 2005;32:275-282.

12. Svenungsson E, Gunnarsson I, Fei GZ, Lundberg IE, Klareskog L, Frostegard J. Elevated triglycerides and low levels of high-density lipoprotein as markers of disease activity in association with up-regulation of the tumor necrosis factor alpha/tumor necrosis factor receptor system in systemic lupus erythematosus. *Arthritis Rheum.* 2003;48:2533-2540.

13. Bessant R, Hingorani A, Patel L, MacGregor A, Isenberg DA, Rahman A. Risk of coronary heart disease and stroke in a large British cohort of patients with systemic lupus erythematosus. *Rheumatology* (Oxford). 2004;43:924-929.

14. Kavey RE, Allada V, Daniels SR, et al. Cardiovascular risk reduction in high-risk pediatric patients: a scientific statement from the American Heart Association Expert Panel on Population and Prevention Science; the Councils on Cardiovascular Disease in the Young, Epidemiology and Prevention, Nutrition, Physical Activity and Metabolism, High Blood Pressure Research, Cardiovascular Nursing, and the Kidney in Heart Disease; and the Interdisciplinary Working Group on Quality of Care and Outcomes Research: endorsed by the American Academy of Pediatrics. *Circulation.* 2006;114:2710-2738.

15. Shah M, Coyle Y, Kavanaugh A, Adams-Huet B, Lipsky PE. Development and initial evaluation of a culturally sensitive cholesterol-lowering diet program for Mexican and African American patients with systemic lupus erythematosus. *Arthritis Care Res.* 2000;13:205-212.

16. Di Munno O, Mazzantini M, Delle Sedie A, Mosca M, Bombardieri S. Risk factors for osteoporosis in female patients with systemic lupus erythematosus. *Lupus.* 2004;13:724-730.

17. Robinzon B, Cutolo M. Should dehydroepiandrosterone replacement therapy be provided with glucocorticoids? *Rheumatology* (Oxford). 1999;38:488-495.

18. Warady BD, Lindsley CB, Robinson FG, Lukert BP. Effects of nutritional supplementation on bone mineral status of children with rheumatic diseases receiving corticosteroid therapy. *J Rheumatol.* 1994;21:530-535.

19. Petri MA, Mease PJ, Merrill JT, et al. Effects of prasterone on disease activity and symptoms in women with active systemic lupus erythematosus. *Arthritis Rheum.* 2004;50:2858-2868.

20. Chang DM, Lan JL, Lin HY, Luo SF. Dehydroepiandrosterone treatment of women with mild-to-moderate systemic lupus erythematosus: a multicenter randomized, double-blind, placebo-controlled trial. *Arthritis Rheum.* 2002;46:2924-2927.

68. Anaphylaxis and Food Allergy

Anaphylaxis is a rapid, life-threatening, systemic reaction. In anaphylaxis, activation of mast cells and/or basophils initiates a cascade causing release of chemicals that lead to inflammation, vasodilation, bronchoconstriction or bronchospasm with airway edema, and mucus secretion involving the respiratory, cardiovascular, integumentary (skin), and gastrointestinal systems. Although anaphylaxis is usually due to an IgE-mediated (allergic antibody) immediate-type hypersensitivity reaction, similar symptoms can occur as a result of an antibody-independent or anaphylactoid-mediated activation. Common triggers in the hospital include drugs, blood products, and radiocontrast media. Outside the hospital, common triggers include venomous insect stings and certain foods, such as eggs, peanuts, dairy products, fish and shellfish, and tree nuts. Allergen-specific immunotherapy (allergy injections) also poses a risk of anaphylaxis.

Food proteins may initiate an immune response in sensitized individuals. The spectrum of symptoms due to allergy is broad, affecting the eyes, nose, throat, skin, and gastrointestinal tract. Respiratory symptoms are the most life-threatening and include swelling of the airway (angioedema), which can lead to asphyxiation and death.

Risk Factors

Atopy. Individuals with a history of allergic diseases are said to be atopic and may have greater risk of severe or fatal reactions to anaphylaxis triggers.

Age and gender. Allergy and anaphylaxis patterns vary by age and gender. For example, adults have more reactions to venomous insects, such as bees, because they are more likely to have been previously exposed, compared with children. Likewise, females are more likely to be sensitized to neuromuscular blockers through a similar chemical in cosmetics.

Exposure history. Intravenous exposure tends to cause more severe reactions, because it circumvents epithelial or endothelial exposure barriers. Severity also increases with intermittent dosing (as compared with continuous dosing) or with greater intensity of exposure, as in seasonal or frequent occupational exposures.

History of anaphylaxis. Previous (especially recent) anaphylaxis is a risk factor for recurrence.

Ulcer prophylaxis. Some evidence suggests that patients using H2-receptor blockers and proton pump inhibitors may have increased IgE reactivity to common dietary components, with increased risk of anaphylaxis. Further study is needed.[1]

Diagnosis

Anaphylaxis is a clinical diagnosis. Findings may include:

- Flushing.
- Urticaria.
- Angioedema.
- Wheezing/stridor.
- Pre-syncope/hypotension.
- Nausea/vomiting.
- Diaphoresis.
- Rhinitis.
- Change of mental status.
- Incontinence.
- Hypovolemic shock.

History of exposure to common triggers should be elicited. A serum antibody test, such as enzyme-linked immunosorbent assay (ELISA) or radioallergosorbent test (RAST), may be used to determine the IgE response to various allergens.

Skin testing and IgE levels may be used in diagnosis of food allergies. However, a double-blind, placebo-controlled food challenge may be needed to identify the inciting entity. When diagnosis of anaphylaxis is uncertain, testing for levels of plasma histamine, 24-hour urine N-methyl-histamine, and serum/urine tryptase may be helpful but will not indicate the etiology.

Treatment

Cardiopulmonary monitoring and assessment (with intubation, if required), oxygen, and 2 high-volume intravenous access sites are immediately needed. The inciting agent should be removed, if possible. A tourniquet above the site of a venom sting or site of an allergy shot injection may be helpful.

Epinephrine (1:1000) should be administered intramuscularly as soon as the diagnosis of anaphylaxis is suspected. It may be self-administered with an EpiPen or similar device and can be repeated at 15-minute intervals en route to an emergency department. Epinephrine (1:10000) is used intravenously or through an endotracheal tube for severe symptoms. Most fatalities occur when epinephrine administration is delayed. Glucagon is used intravenously in patients on beta-blockers who do not respond to epinephrine.[2]

Antihistaminic H1 and H2 blockers should also be used until anaphylaxis resolution. Diphenhydramine and cimetidine are given intravenously.

Oral agents should be considered when more intensive medical care is not immediately accessible.

Methylprednisolone may be administered intravenously.

Inhaled beta-agonists (eg, albuterol) may be used if bronchospasm is present.

If the patient is hypotensive, colloid or crystalloid intravenous fluid should be administered in large volumes. Pressors (dopamine, norepinephrine, phenylephrine, vasopressin) should be used for refractory hypotension.[3]

Patients with more than mild symptoms should be observed in the emergency department or admitted to the hospital for continued observation, due to risk of recrudescent symptoms after initial improvement.

Nutritional Considerations

Allergic Reactions to Foods

Approximately 5% to 10% of young children and 2% to 4% of adults are allergic to 1 or more foods.[4] The figure for adults is lower because most people outgrow childhood food allergies. Several studies suggest that the risk for developing sensitization to various foods may be reduced by late introduction of potentially allergenic foods and by avoidance of those foods by children whose parents have a known allergy to them.[5]

This remains controversial. Although allergic reactions can occur with almost any food, certain items, such as peanuts, tree nuts, and shellfish, are most often responsible for food-induced anaphylaxis. Unlike allergies to other foods, these are generally not outgrown.[4]

Common allergens include milk, egg, peanuts, tree nuts, seeds, wheat, soy, fish, and shellfish. Since these foods are responsible for the vast majority of allergic reactions,[6] avoidance or delayed introduction of them may be indicated to reduce risk of allergy, although the efficacy of this strategy has not been established. Allergic reactions to these foods have been implicated in food-induced asthma and eosinophilic esophagitis.[7,8] Cow's milk may also contribute to both otitis media and pulmonary hemosiderosis (Heiner syndrome) in young children.[9] Some patients react to the presence of the allergens in these foods in amounts as low as 1 mg.[10] Allergic reactions also appear to differentially affect people by age: Cow's milk, eggs, soybeans, and peanuts are frequent causes in children, whereas peanuts, tree nuts, fish, and shellfish are the most common ones in adults.

Fruits and vegetables may occasionally cause food allergy. Many healthful foods, vegetables among them, may cause food allergy. Celery and zucchini can produce allergic reactions even after thorough cooking.[11,12] As noted below, patients with pollen allergy often cross-react to many foods.

Sensitization may develop as a result of cross-reactivity to foods with similar antigens. Melon proteins may cross-react with pollen proteins[13] and are highly cross-reactive with proteins contained in peaches.[14] Adults with birch pollen allergy (manifesting as rhinitis or asthma) and eczema may exhibit late (>24 hours) reactions after ingestion of foods that cross-react with birch pollen; for example, apple, apricot, carrot, celery, cherry, hazelnut, and pear.[15]

Persons who are allergic to one fruit are often allergic to others in the same family. For instance, peach, melon, kiwi, apple, and banana frequently cross-react with avocado, apricot, and plum and may be diagnosed via skin prick testing,[16] although IgE testing may be negative. Patients allergic to latex are often allergic to tropical fruits, such as bananas, kiwi, and avocado. Allergy to citrus fruits, though less commonly reported, causes both oral allergy syndrome (a form of contact dermatitis of the lips, tongue, or other mouth tissues) and systemic allergic reaction.[17]

Interestingly, a lower frequency of allergic cross-reactivity occurs with the ingestion of plant foods than with the consumption of animal products. The frequency of cross-reactivity between peanuts and other legumes is <10%, and between wheat and other grains is <15%. By comparison, cross-reactivity between mammalian milks (ie, cow's milk vs goat's milk) occurs in approximately 90% of cases, and occurs between types of fish with a frequency of 50%.[18]

Omega-6 fatty acids (found in seed oils and animal products) may increase production of IgE, the main immunoglobulin involved in allergic reactions.[19,20] Omega-6 fatty acids may increase production of leukotrienes, which may facilitate the allergic response.[21,22] These findings suggest that there may be benefit in limiting intake of vegetable oils, margarines, and other sources of omega-6 fatty acids.

Dietary supplements may cause anaphylactic reactions. Royal jelly,[23] willow bark,[24] echinacea,[25] and fruit-containing herbal tea[26] have been known to cause anaphylactic reactions. Rarely, anaphylactic reactions to vitamin supplements have occurred, including reactions to synthetic folic acid,[27] synthetic vitamin B5 (dexpanthenol, the stable alcohol of pantothenic acid),[28] and synthetic forms of thiamine (vitamin B1) and riboflavin (vitamin B2).[29]

Reducing the Likelihood of Allergies

The following steps may help reduce the likelihood that children will develop allergies.

Breast-feeding. An American Academy of Pediatrics review concluded that breast-feeding for at least 4 months may prevent or delay the occurrence of atopic dermatitis, cow's milk allergy, and wheezing in early childhood, when compared with feeding formula made with intact cow milk protein.[30] If mothers cannot breast-feed, formula should be chosen carefully. Cow's milk allergy is common and may occur even with partially and extensively hydrolyzed whey formulas, which trigger IgE production. An amino acid–based formula, on the other hand, was found by one study to be less allergenic.[31]

Delayed introduction of potentially allergenic foods. Delaying the introduction of table foods until at least 4 to 6 months of age has been recommended by some authors.[5] However, the American Academy of Pediatrics has concluded that evidence is insufficient to document a protective effect of any dietary intervention beyond 4 to 6 months of age, and that the documented benefits of nutritional intervention are largely limited to infants at high risk of developing allergy.[30]

Caution regarding processed foods that may harbor many potential allergens. Patients may be allergic to several foods and food ingredients, and processed food products can be especially problematic. These foods often contain milk, egg, fish, beef, nuts, and seed proteins that are not listed on the product labels but can cause such reactions as oral allergy syndrome and anaphylaxis. Although processing of certain foods reduces their allergenicity (eg, cutting or heating fruit), most allergens remain stable after processing.[32] In some cases (eg, roasting peanuts), processing increases allergenicity.[4] Eating unprocessed, minimally processed, and homemade foods is likely to decrease this risk. In patients who suspect but cannot confirm food allergy, an elimination diet can be helpful (see below).

Elimination Diets

An antigen-avoidance diet for women who are breast-feeding may be used to reduce children's risk of developing atopic eczema in families with a significant family history.[33] In infants, older patients with elevated IgE levels, and persons diagnosed with food allergy who experienced atopic eczema/dermatitis, excluding certain foods (most often, cow's milk and eggs) has been shown to reduce symptoms of this skin condition.[34] Diet therapy has also frequently been effective (52% to 80% of patients) in severe or otherwise refractory cases of atopic eczema/dermatitis.[34] More than 50% of children experienced significant improvements in atopic dermatitis during dietary exclusion of cow's milk and eggs, and roughly one-third outgrow their allergies after 1 to 2 years of avoiding the offending foods, with the exception of nuts and shellfish, which typically continue to elicit reactions.[15] To identify foods that trigger atopic dermatitis, an elimination diet can be implemented on an outpatient basis. The procedure is described below.

Start with a baseline diet made up of only those foods not implicated in food allergy; that is, eliminate cow's milk, eggs, nuts, and wheat. Well-tolerated foods include:

Brown, white, and puffed rice.

Cooked and dried fruits: cherries, cranberries, pears, prunes, peaches, apricots, papaya, and plums, unless there is a documented allergy to these or to birch pollen.

Cooked green, yellow, and orange vegetables: artichokes, asparagus, broccoli, chard, collards, lettuce, spinach, squash, string beans, sweet potatoes, tapioca, and taro.

Plain and carbonated water.

Condiments: modest amounts of salt, maple syrup, or vanilla extract.

When the dermatitis has abated (usually within a week or so), the patient should keep a food diary and add in foods 1 group at a time in generous amounts every 3 to 5 days to observe which ones cause symptom recurrence. Foods listed above that are most commonly implicated in food allergy should be added last. If the food is associated with allergy symptoms, it should be removed from the diet for 1 to 2 weeks, and then reintroduced to see if the same reaction occurs. If no symptoms occur, that food can be kept in the diet. For individuals with a history of anaphylaxis, suspect foods should only be tried under the close supervision of a qualified physician.

Orders

See Basic Diet Orders chapter.

Nutrition consultation to instruct patient on avoiding triggers of food allergy and following an elimination diet, as well as to arrange follow-up.

What to Tell the Family

Food allergy, while common, can usually be diagnosed and treated through allergy testing and avoidance of the offending food(s). Anaphylaxis may occur with consumption of processed foods that contain hidden allergens, and persons who are predisposed to anaphylactic reactions should carry an injectable form of epinephrine, such as an EpiPen or EpiPen Jr. These medications must be stored properly, renewed annually, and kept available for emergencies. Patients and their families should be trained in their use. In families with a history of atopy, the risk for food allergy may be reduced by breast-feeding and late introduction of foods known to cause allergic reactions.

References

1. Untersmayr E, Bakos N, Scholl I, et al. Anti-ulcer drugs promote IgE formation toward dietary antigens in adult patients. *FASEB J.* 2005;19:656-658.

2. Zaloga GP, Delacey W, Holmboe E, Chernow B. Glucagon reversal of hypotension in a case of anaphylactoid shock. *Ann Intern Med.* 1986;105:65-66.

3. Kill C, Wranze E, Wulf H. Successful treatment of severe anaphylactic shock with vasopressin. Two case reports. *Int Arch Allergy Immunol.* 2004;134:260-261.

4. Nowak-Wegrzyn A, Sampson HA. Adverse reactions to foods. *Med Clin North Am.* 2006;90:97-127.

5. Arshad SH. Food allergen avoidance in primary prevention of food allergy. *Allergy.* 2001;56(suppl 67):113-116.

6. Beyer K, Teuber S. The mechanism of food allergy: what do we know today? *Curr Opin Allergy Clin Immunol.* 2004;4:197-199.

7. Heine RG. Pathophysiology, diagnosis and treatment of food protein-induced gastrointestinal diseases. *Curr Opin Allergy Clin Immunol.* 2004;4:221-229.

8. Spergel JM. Eosinophilic esophagitis in adults and children: evidence for a food allergy component in many patients. *Curr Opin Allergy Clin Immunol.* 2007;7:274-278.

9. James JM. Respiratory manifestations of food allergy. *Pediatrics.* 2003;111(pt 3):1625-1630.

10. Moneret-Vautrin DA, Kanny G. Update on threshold doses of food allergens: implications for patients and the food industry. *Curr Opin Allergy Clin Immunol.* 2004;4:215-219.

11. Ballmer-Weber BK, Hoffmann A, Wuthrich B, et al. Influence of food processing on the allergenicity of celery: DBPCFC with celery spice and cooked celery in patients with celery allergy. *Allergy.* 2002;57:228-235.

12. Reindl J, Anliker MD, Karamloo F, Vieths S, Wuthrich B. Allergy caused by ingestion of zucchini (Cucurbita pepo): characterization of allergens and cross-reactivity to pollen and other foods. *J Allergy Clin Immunol.* 2000;106:379-385.

13. Rodriguez J, Crespo JF, Burks W, et al. Randomized, double-blind, crossover challenge study in 53 subjects reporting adverse reactions to melon (Cucumis melo). *J Allergy Clin Immunol.* 2000;106:968-972.

14. Figueredo E, Cuesta-Herranz J, De-Miguel J, et al. Clinical characteristics of melon (Cucumis melo) allergy. *Ann Allergy Asthma Immunol.* 2003;91:303-308.

15. Werfel T, Breuer K. Role of food allergy in atopic dermatitis. *Curr Opin Allergy Clin Immunol.* 2004;4:379-385.

16. Crespo JF, Rodriguez J, James JM, Daroca P, Reano M, Vives R. Reactivity to potential cross-reactive foods in fruit-allergic patients: implications for prescribing food avoidance. *Allergy.* 2002;57:946-949.

17. Ibanez MD, Sastre J, San Ireneo MM, Laso MT, Barber D, Lombardero M. Different patterns of allergen recognition in children allergic to orange. *J Allergy Clin Immunol.* 2004;113:175-177.

18. James JM. Food allergy: opportunities and challenges in the clinical practice of allergy and immunology. *Clin Rev Allergy Immunol.* 2004;27:105-114.

19. Bolte G, Frye C, Hoelscher B, Meyer I, Wjst M, Heinrich J. Margarine consumption and allergy in children. *Am J Respir Crit Care Med.* 2001;163:277-279.

20. Kankaanpaa P, Sutas Y, Salminen S, Lichtenstein A, Isolauri E. Dietary fatty acids and allergy. *Ann Med.* 1999;31:282-287.

21. Di Lorenzo G, Pacor ML, Vignola AM, et al. Urinary metabolites of histamine and leukotrienes before and after placebo-controlled challenge with ASA and food additives in chronic urticaria patients. *Allergy.* 2002;57:1180-1186.

22. Worm M, Vieth W, Ehlers I, Sterry W, Zuberbier T. Increased leukotriene production by food additives in patients with atopic dermatitis and proven food intolerance. *Clin Exp Allergy.* 2001;31:265-273.

23. Takahama H, Shimazu T. Food-induced anaphylaxis caused by ingestion of royal jelly. *J Dermatol.* 2006;33:424-426.

24. Boullata JI, McDonnell PJ, Oliva CD. Anaphylactic reaction to a dietary supplement containing willow bark. *Ann Pharmacother.* 2003;37:832-835.

25. Mullins RJ. Echinacea-associated anaphylaxis. *Med J Aust.* 1998;168:170-171.

26. Lleonart R, Corominas M, Lombardero M. Tea infusion, another source of Rosaceae allergy. *Allergy.* 2007;62:89-90.

27. Smith J, Empson M, Wall C. Recurrent anaphylaxis to synthetic folic acid. *Lancet.* 2007;370:652.

28. Röckmann H, Goerdt S, Bayerl C. Anaphylaxis after dexpanthenol exposure by multi-vitamin tablets. *Clin Exp Dermatol.* 2005;30:714-716.

29. Ou LS, Kuo ML, Huang JL. Anaphylaxis to riboflavin (vitamin B2). *Ann Allergy Asthma Immunol.* 2001;87:430-433.

30. Greer FR, Sicherer SH, Burks AW; American Academy of Pediatrics Committee on Nutrition; American Academy of Pediatrics Section on Allergy and Immunology. Effects of early nutritional interventions on the development of atopic disease in infants and children: the role of maternal dietary restriction, breastfeeding, timing of introduction of complementary foods, and hydrolyzed formulas. *Pediatrics.* 2008;121:183-191.

31. Caffarelli C, Plebani A, Poiesi C, Petroccione T, Spattini A, Cavagni G. Determination of allergenicity to three cow's milk hydrolysates and an amino acid-derived formula in children with cow's milk allergy. *Clin Exp Allergy.* 2002;32:74-79.

32. Besler M, Steinhart H, Paschke A. Stability of food allergens and allergenicity of processed foods. *J Chromatogr B Biomed Sci Appl.* 2001;756:207-228.

33. Kramer MS, Kakuma R. Maternal dietary antigen avoidance during pregnancy and/or lactation for preventing or treating atopic disease in the child. *Cochrane Database Syst Rev.* 2003;(4):CD000133. Updated July 16, 2003.

34. Fiocchi A, Bouygue GR, Martelli A, Terracciano L, Sarratud T. Dietary treatment of childhood atopic eczema/dermatitis syndrome (AEDS). *Allergy.* 2004;59(suppl 78):78-85.

SECTION XIII: BONE, JOINT, CONNECTIVE TISSUE, AND RHEUMATIC DISEASES

69. Rheumatoid Arthritis

Rheumatoid arthritis (RA) is a chronic, systemic, autoimmune disease marked by inflammation of the joints, sometimes with prominent extra-articular manifestations. The disease is initially characterized by inflammation of the synovial membranes (synovitis) of peripheral joints. If RA is uncontrolled, many cases ultimately lead to destruction of the articular cartilage, bone erosions, and significant deformity, disability, and morbidity in 10 to 20 years from onset.

The etiology of rheumatoid arthritis is unknown, but likely involves interaction of genetic and environmental factors. The typical presentation consists of a gradual onset of polyarticular symmetric arthritis of small joints and is characterized by pain, morning stiffness, and joint swelling. Among the early articular sites of disease are the metacarpophalangeal and proximal interphalangeal joints of the fingers, the metacarpophalangeal and interphalangeal joints of the thumbs, the wrists, and the metatarsophalangeal joints of the toes. Extra-articular manifestations may include dry eye syndrome (which occurs with variable severity in up to 50% of patients), pericarditis, episcleritis, scleritis, subcutaneous nodules, vasculitis, splenomegaly, fatigue, and mild anemia.

Risk Factors

RA affects about 1% of the adult population in the United States. Prevalence varies widely among ethnic and regional groups. For example, far less than 1% of rural Africans are affected, compared with 5% of Pima Indians. Other risk factors include:

Age. The typical age of onset is 30 to 55 years, although the disease may occur at any age.

Gender. RA is 2 to 3 times more common in women than in men.

Genetics. The disease generally does not aggregate in families. Nonetheless, a multitude of genes may play a role in the development of RA. For example, the *HLA-DRB1* gene contains a short disease-conferring sequence.

Diagnosis

The diagnosis of rheumatoid arthritis is largely clinical; no single laboratory or imaging study is definitive. The American Rheumatism Association has established 7 clinical signs, 4 of which must be present for diagnosis:

- Morning stiffness in or around joints, lasting at least 1 hour before maximal improvement.

- Soft-tissue swelling and pain of 3 or more joint areas lasting at least 6 weeks.

- Swelling of the proximal interphalangeal, metacarpophalangeal, or wrist joints lasting at least 6 weeks.

- Symmetric swelling (arthritis) lasting at least 6 weeks.

- Rheumatoid nodules.

- Positive rheumatoid factor (found in about 85% of patients).

- Radiographic erosions and/or periarticular osteopenia in hand and/or wrist joints.

Anti-CCP antibodies. The pathological process of RA involves local production of antibodies to citrullinated proteins within the inflamed joint. These antibodies may be detected before clinical symptoms develop and are associated with more severe joint destruction and greater disease activity.[1]

Treatment

Treatment of rheumatoid arthritis generally includes physical therapy, dietary intervention (see Nutritional Considerations below), anti-inflammatory medication, and disease-modifying agents.

Extra-articular manifestations are treated according to the specific syndrome (eg, lubricating eyedrops for dry eye syndrome).

Weight loss should be encouraged for overweight patients to decrease stress on the weight-bearing joints. Adequate rest and smoking cessation are also beneficial. Surgery is reserved for severe, debilitating disease.

Physical Therapy

Regular low-impact exercise, including aerobic exercises, judicious strength training, and range-of-motion exercises, is important for preserving joint function and preventing contractures and muscle atrophy. Water-based exercise does not appear to increase the rate of large joint damage. A reasonable prescription for exercise in RA patients may emphasize low-intensity water-based (and sometimes land-based) exercises.[2] Heat and hydrotherapy, relaxation techniques, and passive and active joint exercises are also helpful.

Pharmacologic Therapy

Anti-inflammatory medications are first-line treatments. Steroids are more effective than NSAIDs for pain relief and suppression of inflammation. However, they should be used carefully, as patients are at significant risk for bone loss and other complications of prolonged steroid use. When steroids are used, dietary supplementation with adequate vitamin D and calcium should be instituted. Patients who require steroid therapy beyond 3 months may benefit from the addition of a bisphosphonate, such as alendronate.

Disease-modifying antirheumatic drugs (DMARDs) are a mainstay of rheumatoid arthritis therapy and may prevent joint damage, preserve joint integrity and function, improve quality of life, and reduce health care costs.[3] These drugs include hydroxychloroquine, sulfasalazine, methotrexate, leflunomide, gold salts, D-penicillamine, azathioprine, and cyclosporine. Many DMARDs have potentially serious side effects and require close monitoring.

Newer agents that have proven beneficial for rheumatoid arthritis include anti-tumor necrosis factor α (TNF-α) agents (etanercept, infliximab, adalimumab), selective costimulation modulators (abatacept), and interleukin-1 receptor antagonists (anakinra). Other biological agents targeting key cellular constituents of the immune system or cytokines are expected to be approved in the near future.

Nutritional Considerations

Rheumatoid arthritis may sometimes be ameliorated with proper diet. Studies have shown both symptomatic and laboratory evidence of improvement with vegetarian diets and various elimination diets. Omega-3 fatty acids may reduce pain and inflammation in RA. The key nutritional issues in RA are summarized below:

Vegetarian Diets

A body of evidence indicates that patients who follow vegan or vegetarian diets may experience significant improvement in rheumatoid arthritis symptoms. Improvement in laboratory values (rheumatoid factor, CRP) is a frequent finding on these diets and correlates with a reduction in antibodies to food antigens.[4,5] Conversely, higher intakes of meat[6,7] and elevated serum cholesterol concentrations[8] are associated with increased risk of developing this disease. Patients with RA are known to be at higher risk for cardiovascular disease and to have higher serum levels of oxidized low-density lipoprotein (LDL).[9]

Eliminating Diet Triggers

Clinical tests have shown that consumption of allergenic foods increases pro-inflammatory chemicals (cytokines) that are considered a hallmark of RA.[10] Studies have shown that eliminating certain foods brings symptomatic improvement.[11,12] To identify trigger foods, an elimination diet can easily be instituted on an outpatient basis. The procedure is as follows:

Start with a simple baseline diet, excluding foods that are more common triggers (dairy products, corn, meats, wheat, oats and rye, eggs, citrus fruits, potatoes, tomatoes, nuts, and coffee) and including only those foods not implicated in arthritis, listed below:

- Brown rice.

- Cooked or dried fruits (cherries, cranberries, pears, prunes).

- Cooked green, yellow, and orange vegetables (artichokes, asparagus, broccoli, chard, collards, lettuce, spinach, string beans, squash, sweet potatoes, tapioca, and taro).

- Plain or carbonated water.

- Condiments (modest amounts of salt, maple syrup, vanilla extract).

After approximately 4 weeks on this diet, if symptoms have improved or disappeared, patients may introduce previously eliminated foods one at a time, every 2 days. Patients should keep a food diary and add these foods in generous amounts to observe which ones cause arthritic symptoms. Foods listed above as common triggers should be added last. A newly added food associated with increased joint pain should be removed from the diet for 1 to 2 weeks, and then reintroduced to see if the same reaction occurs. If no symptoms are experienced, that food can be kept in the diet.

Antioxidants

Poor antioxidant status may be a risk factor for RA.[13] Studies have shown that a higher intake of certain carotenoids found in fruits and vegetables may protect against developing RA.[14,15] Foods containing beta-cryptoxanthin (eg, citrus fruits) and zeaxanthin (eg, green leafy vegetables) may be particularly helpful. The European Prospective Investigation of Cancer (EPIC)–Norfolk study of more than 25,000 individuals found that those consuming the highest amounts of these carotenoids had half the risk for developing inflammatory polyarthritis, compared with those consuming the least amount.[16] Lower serum levels of vitamin E and selenium were also found to predict the development of rheumatoid arthritis.[17]

Oil Intake

A diet low in arachidonic acid, an omega-6 fatty acid found in animal products, was found to ameliorate inflammation in patients with RA. This effect was strengthened by omega-3 fatty acid supplementation.[18] Studies have also found a lower incidence of arthritis in Mediterranean countries, which may be attributable to olive oil intake,[6,19] possibly because this fat negates the production of pro-inflammatory chemicals that affect RA patients. Supplementing with gamma-linolenic acid (GLA) was found to be an effective strategy for reducing the symptoms of RA,[20] and supplementation with a combination of GLA and omega-3 fatty acids was found to both reduce symptoms and decrease the need for NSAIDs in RA patients.[21,22] These fatty acids appear to work by blocking production of arachidonic acid-derived inflammatory mediators, an effect that is achievable with vegan diets as well (see above).

Folic Acid

Patients with RA are often treated with methotrexate, a folate antagonist that can increase plasma homocysteine concentrations.[23] Folate supplementation is recommended to prevent methotrexate-induced toxicity, folate deficiency, and hyperhomocysteinemia.[24]

Orders

Vegetarian diet, nondairy, to be tried on a prospective basis.

Nutrition consultation: to advise patient in the above diet, consider elimination diet to evaluate for occult food allergies, and arrange follow-up to assist patient in long-term dietary modifications.

Physical and occupational therapy consultations to recommend an individualized exercise program.

What to Tell the Family

Rheumatoid arthritis can be ameliorated through dietary measures and medication as needed to control symptoms. Due to the hereditary component of RA, family members may benefit from a similar diet. The patient should stay physically active through regular low-impact exercise, light strength training, and range-of-motion exercises. Exercises learned in physical therapy should be incorporated into the daily exercise routine.

References

1. Cantaert T, De Rycke L, Bongartz T, et al. Citrullinated proteins in rheumatoid arthritis. *Arthritis Rheum*. 2006;54:3381-3389.

2. De Jong, Vlieland. Safety of exercise in patients with rheumatoid arthritis. *Curr Opin Rheumatol*. 2005;17:177-182.

3. American College of Rheumatology Ad Hoc Committee on Clinical Guidelines. Guidelines for the management of rheumatoid arthritis: 2002 update. *Arthritis Rheum*. 2002;46:328.

4. McDougall J, Bruce B, Spiller G, Westerdahl J, McDougall M. Effects of a very low-fat, vegan diet in subjects with rheumatoid arthritis. *J Altern Complement Med*. 2002;8:71-75.

5. Hafstrom I, Ringertz B, Spangberg A, et al. A vegan diet free of gluten improves the signs and symptoms of rheumatoid arthritis: the effects on arthritis correlate with a reduction in antibodies to food antigens. *Rheumatology* (Oxford). 2001;40:1175-1179.

6. Pattison DJ, Symmons DP, Lunt M, et al. Dietary risk factors for the development of inflammatory polyarthritis: evidence for a role of high level of red meat consumption. *Arthritis Rheum*. 2004;50:3804-3812.

7. Grant WB. The role of meat in the expression of rheumatoid arthritis. *Br J Nutr*. 2000;84:589-595.

8. Heliovaara M, Aho K, Knekt P, Reunanen A, Aromaa A. Serum cholesterol and risk of rheumatoid arthritis in a cohort of 52,800 men and women. *Br J Rheumatol*. 1996;35:255-257.

9. Kim SH, Lee CK, Lee EY, et al. Serum oxidized low-density lipoproteins in rheumatoid arthritis. *Rheumatol Int*. 2004;24:230-233.

10. Karatay S, Erdem T, Yildirim K, et al. The effect of individualized diet challenges consisting of allergenic foods on TNF-alpha and IL-1beta levels in patients with rheumatoid arthritis. *Rheumatology* (Oxford). 2004;43:1429-1433.

11. van de Laar MA, Aalbers M, Bruins FG, van Dinther-Janssen AC, van der Korst JK, Meijer CJ. Food intolerance in rheumatoid arthritis. I. A double blind, controlled trial of the clinical effects of elimination of milk allergens and azo dyes. *Ann Rheum Dis*. 1992;51:298-302.

12. Kjeldsen-Kragh J, Haugen M, Borchgrevink CF, et al. Controlled trial of fasting and one-year vegetarian diet in rheumatoid arthritis. *Lancet*. 1991;338:899-902.

13. Heliovaara M, Knekt P, Aho K, Aaran RK, Alfthan G, Aromaa A. Serum antioxidants and risk of rheumatoid arthritis. *Ann Rheum Dis*. 1994;53:51-53.

14. Cerhan JR, Saag KG, Merlino LA, Mikuls TR, Criswell LA. Antioxidant micronutrients and risk of rheumatoid arthritis in a cohort of older women. *Am J Epidemiol*. 2003;157:345-354.

15. Comstock GW, Burke AE, Hoffman SC, et al. Serum concentrations of alpha tocopherol, beta carotene, and retinol preceding the diagnosis of rheumatoid arthritis and systemic lupus erythematosus. *Ann Rheum Dis*. 1997;56:323-325.

16. Pattison DJ, Symmons DP, Lunt M, et al. Dietary beta-cryptoxanthin and inflammatory polyarthritis: results from a population-based prospective study. *Am J Clin Nutr*. 2005;82:451-455.

17. Knekt P, Heliovaara M, Aho K, Alfthan G, Marniemi J, Aromaa A. Serum selenium, serum alpha-tocopherol, and the risk of rheumatoid arthritis. *Epidemiology*. 2000;11:402-405.

18. Adam O, Beringer C, Kless T, et al. Anti-inflammatory effects of a low arachidonic acid diet and fish oil in patients with rheumatoid arthritis. *Rheumatol Int*. 2003;3:27-36.

19. Linos A, Kaklamani VG, Kaklamani E, et al. Dietary factors in relation to rheumatoid arthritis: a role for olive oil and cooked vegetables? *Am J Clin Nutr*. 1999;70:1077-1082.

20. Little C, Parsons T. Herbal therapy for treating rheumatoid arthritis. *Cochrane Database Syst Rev*. 2001;(1):CD002948.

21. Lau CS, Morley KD, Belch JJ. Effects of fish oil supplementation on non-steroidal anti-inflammatory drug requirement in patients with mild rheumatoid arthritis--a double-blind placebo controlled study. *Br J Rheumatol*. 1993;32:982-989.

22. Belch JJ, Ansell D, Madhok R, O'Dowd A, Sturrock RD. Effects of altering dietary essential fatty acids on requirements for non-steroidal anti-inflammatory drugs in patients with rheumatoid arthritis: a double blind placebo controlled study. *Ann Rheum Dis*. 1988;47:96-104.

23. Whittle SL, Hughes RA. Folate supplementation and methotrexate treatment in rheumatoid arthritis: a review. *Rheumatology* (Oxford). 2004;43:267-271.

24. Morgan SL, Baggott JE, Lee JY, Alarcon GS. Folic acid supplementation prevents deficient blood folate levels and hyperhomocysteinemia during long-term, low-dose methotrexate therapy for rheumatoid arthritis: implications for cardiovascular disease prevention. *J Rheumatol*. 1998;25:441-446.

70. Osteoarthritis

Osteoarthritis (OA), also known as degenerative joint disease, is the most common joint disorder. It is characterized by hyaline cartilage degeneration and subchondral bone hypertrophy within a joint. Unlike rheumatoid arthritis, OA usually produces minimal inflammation. In severe cases, the articular joint surface may be destroyed, with resultant pain and disability.

OA may be idiopathic or secondary, and multiple factors generally influence its development. Idiopathic OA, although often considered a "wear and tear" disorder, is genetically driven. Secondary forms may occur due to endocrine abnormalities (eg, hypothyroidism, diabetes mellitus), other joint diseases (eg, rheumatoid arthritis, gout, infection), and bone pathology (eg, avascular necrosis, Paget disease).

OA begins with joint stiffness, typically lasting less than 15 minutes a day, and gradually progresses to pain with joint motion. The condition most commonly affects weight-bearing joints (knee, hip, or vertebra). When the hands are involved, the distal interphalangeal (DIP) and the first carpometacarpal (CMC) joints are most commonly affected.

OA rarely affects the elbow, wrist, ankle, and temporomandibular joints.

Risk Factors

Obesity. Knee and hip joints are particularly vulnerable in obese individuals.

Age. The condition is rare in young people, but common in middle-aged and older adults.[1] One-third of people older than 65 years have radiographic evidence of osteoarthritis in the knee.

Female gender. Females have nearly 3 times the risk of symptomatic disease, compared with men. The reason for this discrepancy is uncertain.[2]

Occupation. Certain occupations, such as construction work and carpentry, increase the risk for osteoarthritis of the hands, hips, and knees.

Genetics. An identical twin of an individual with hand or knee osteoarthritis has double the risk of having the same condition, compared with a fraternal twin.[3]

Trauma. Repetitive joint trauma presents a cumulative risk.

Preexisting or anatomical joint abnormality.

Knee laxity, poor proprioception, and significant quadriceps weakness increase the risk of osteoarthritis of the knee.

Diagnosis

The diagnosis of idiopathic OA is based on history, physical examination, laboratory studies, and imaging. An atypical presentation warrants inquiry into a secondary cause.

OA is usually asymmetrical, but it can be bilateral in small joints. The following findings may be present on physical exam:

- Tender joint.

- Crepitus during joint motion.

- Bony enlargements, especially of the distal interphalangeal joints (Heberden nodes) and proximal interphalangeal joints (Bouchard nodes).

- Flexion contracture or varus deformity of the knee.

Joint effusion, if present, is mild and is not typically associated with signs of inflammation. However, a variant of OA termed "inflammatory osteoarthritis" may present with joint effusion, redness, warmth, and morning stiffness.

No lab test is specific for osteoarthritis. The presence of an abnormal erythrocyte sedimentation rate, rheumatoid factor, or >2000 WBC/mm^3 in a joint aspirate suggests that an inflammatory arthritis, rather than OA, should be considered.

Radiographic imaging of affected joints may reveal joint space narrowing, osteophytes, or subchondral bone sclerosis.

Treatment

The choice of treatment depends partly on whether inflammation is present. Options include a supervised exercise/muscle-strengthening program, medication, and surgical intervention. Arthroscopy and joint replacement are usually reserved for patients with severe, functionally limiting disease.

Nonpharmacologic treatments, including low-impact exercise and physical therapy, may be sufficient for mild cases. Weight loss and shoe inserts, braces, or splints may be helpful for osteoarthritis of weight-bearing joints.

Capsaicin cream significantly reduces pain, possibly by depleting substance P.[4]

Glucosamine and chondroitin sulfate are popular but controversial oral supplements that may act as cartilage enhancers. They can be safely used with other treatments and may improve symptoms in some individuals. However, no convincing evidence has shown that the underlying disease process is ameliorated.

Nonsteroidal anti-inflammatory drugs (NSAIDs) and acetaminophen are the most commonly used treatments. Careful monitoring of blood pressure is necessary when using NSAIDs because of the potential for aggravating or causing hypertension, and a 2- to 4-week trial should be completed before increasing the dose. If analgesia is suboptimal after 2 to 4 weeks at the maximum dose, a different NSAID or a nonacetylated salicylate (eg, salsalate, nabumetone) may be tried. Chronic use may lead to gastrointestinal ulceration or kidney disease, especially if combined with aspirin.

COX-2 inhibitors are as effective as traditional NSAIDs but require further study to determine whether the benefits outweigh the potential cardiovascular risks.

Tramadol, another type of analgesic, may be combined with the above drugs.

Narcotics should be reserved for patients with short-term severe pain or those who are unresponsive to the above therapeutics.

Intra-articular steroid injections should be reserved for individuals who are unresponsive to NSAIDs or for whom NSAIDs are contraindicated. Adequate evidence for efficacy exists only for the knee joint, and injections should be limited to 3 or 4 times a year per joint. Infection should be ruled out prior to injection.

Injections of hyaluronic acid derivatives (Hyalgan or Synvisc) may be beneficial when noninvasive treatments achieve suboptimal results.

Surgical therapy may be indicated for severe cases. Joint replacement (arthroplasty) should be reserved for refractory cases in which activities of daily living are limited. Significant improvement in symptoms and function may occur after surgery. Arthroscopic debridement and synovectomy for OA have not been proven effective.

Nutritional Considerations

The role of nutrition in OA is mainly related to the effects of diet on body weight. Obesity increases the risk for osteoarthritis of the hip[5] and of the hand.[6] Conversely, weight loss was found to significantly improve functional mobility and knee pain.[7,8] Some evidence suggests that a reduction in body fat, independent of body weight, may help relieve OA symptoms.[9] To the extent that a low-fat, high-fiber diet in combination with exercise prevents weight gain, a nutrition-based approach is likely to be useful in preventing and treating OA.

Once the disease process is established, the combination of glucosamine sulfate (1500 mg/d) and chondroitin sulfate (1200 mg/d) has been suggested for knee osteoarthritis, based on favorable early studies.[10,11] Subsequent controlled trials, however, have yielded mixed results. A multicenter trial that concluded these compounds did not provide pain relief, with the possible exception of a subgroup of patients with moderate to severe knee pain.[12] However, these agents may slow disease progression, as indicated by radiographic changes in joint space narrowing.[13]

Elevated serum cholesterol was independently associated with generalized OA in one study[14] and with osteoarthritis of the knee in another study.[15]

Ginger may provide significant pain relief for osteoarthritis patients. Its effects appear to be attributable to inhibition of both cyclooxygenase and lipoxygenase and to subsequent reductions of inflammatory mediators, such as prostaglandin E2 (PGE2), nitric oxide,[16] and chemokines.[17] Effective doses range from 170 mg ginger extract 3 times per day to 250 mg 4 times per day.

Orders

See Basic Diet Orders chapter and Obesity chapter.

What to Tell the Family

Family members can help the patient with lifestyle changes that affect the joints. In some cases, OA may be preventable or treatable through maintenance of a healthy weight with diet changes and exercise. Muscle-strengthening and low-impact exercises are the best options to avoid exacerbating the disease.

References

1. Brandt, K. Osteoarthritis: Clinical patterns and pathology. In: Kelley WN, Harris ED Jr, Ruddy S, Sledge CE, eds. *Textbook of Rheumatology*. 5th ed. Philadelphia, Pa: WB Saunders; 1997:1383.

2. Davis MA, Ettinger WH, Neuhaus JM, Hauck WW. Sex differences in osteoarthritis of the knee: The role of obesity. *Am J Epidemiol*. 1988;127:1019-1030.

3. Spector TD, Cicuttini F, Baker J, Loughlin J, Hart D. Genetic influences on osteoarthritis in women: a twin study. *BMJ*. 1996;312:940-943.

4. Deal CL, Schnitzer TJ, Lipstein E, et al. Treatment of arthritis with topical capsaicin: a double-blind trial. *Clin Ther*. 1991;13:383-395.

5. Lievense AM, Bierma-Zeinstra SM, Verhagen AP, van Baar ME, Verhaar JA, Koes BW. Influence of obesity on the development of osteoarthritis of the hip: a systematic review. *Rheumatology* (Oxford). 2002;41:1155-1162.

6. Sayer AA, Poole J, Cox V, et al. Weight from birth to 53 years: a longitudinal study of the influence on clinical hand osteoarthritis. *Arthritis Rheum.* 2003;48:1030-1033.

7. Christensen R, Astrup A, Bliddal H. Weight loss: the treatment of choice for knee osteo-arthritis? A randomized trial. *Osteoarthritis Cartilage.* 2005;13:20-27.

8. Messier SP, Loeser RF, Miller GD, et al. Exercise and dietary weight loss in overweight and obese older adults with knee osteoarthritis: the Arthritis, Diet, and Activity Promotion Trial. *Arthritis Rheum.* 2004;50:1501-1510.

9. Toda Y, Toda T, Takemura S, Wada T, Morimoto T, Ogawa R. Change in body fat, but not body weight or metabolic correlates of obesity, is related to symptomatic relief of obese patients with knee osteoarthritis after a weight control program. *J Rheumatol.* 1998;25:2181-2186.

10. Bruyere O, Pavelka K, Rovati LC, et al. Glucosamine sulfate reduces osteoarthri-tis progression in postmenopausal women with knee osteoarthritis: evidence from two 3-year studies. *Menopause.* 2004;11:138-143.

11. Richy F, Bruyere O, Ethgen O, Cucherat M, Henrotin Y, Reginster JY. Structural and symptomatic efficacy of glucosamine and chondroitin in knee osteoarthritis: a compre-hensive meta-analysis. *Arch Intern Med.* 2003;163:1514-1522.

12. Clegg DO, Reda DJ, Harris CL, et al. Glucosamine, chondroitin sulfate, and the two in combination for painful knee osteoarthritis. *N Engl J Med.* 2006;354:795-808.

13. Bruyere O, Reginster JY. Glucosamine and chondroitin sulfate as therapeutic agents for knee and hip osteoarthritis. *Drugs Aging.* 2007;24:573-580.

14. Sturmer T, Sun Y, Sauerland S, et al. Serum cholesterol and osteoarthritis. The base-line examination of the Ulm Osteoarthritis Study. *J Rheumatol.* 1998;25:1827-1832.

15. Hart DJ, Doyle DV, Spector TD. Association between metabolic factors and knee osteoarthritis in women: the Chingford Study. *J Rheumatol.* 1995;22:1118-1123.

16. Shen CL, Hong KJ, Kim SW. Effects of ginger (Zingiber officinale Rosc.) on decreas-ing the production of inflammatory mediators in sow osteoarthrotic cartilage explants. *J Med Food.* 2003;6:323-328.

17. Phan PV, Sohrabi A, Polotsky A, Hungerford DS, Lindmark L, Frondoza CG. Ginger extract components suppress induction of chemokine expression in human synoviocytes. *J Altern Complement Med.* 2005;11:149-154.

71. Gout

Gout is a metabolic disease characterized by hyperuricemia and pre-cipitation and tissue deposition of urate crystals, resulting in inflamma-tion and tissue injury. Clinical manifestations include recurrent bouts of acute, often monoarticular arthritis, which most commonly affects the first metatarsophalangeal joint ("podagra"), knees, ankles, and wrists; nephrolithiasis; and palpable tophi.

Ninety percent of cases are due to decreased excretion of uric acid, usually secondary to chronic renal disease, low volume states, and diuretic use. The remaining 10% are due to excess uric acid production as may occur in the context of inherited enzyme abnormalities, psoriasis, hemoglobinopathies, and leukemias. Not all patients with hyperuricemia will develop gout. Indeed, about two-thirds of hyperuricemic patients will remain asymptomatic. Higher levels of serum uric acid and longer durations of exposure increase the risk of progression to clinical disease. However, some patients with clinical symptoms of gout have normal serum uric acid levels.

Risk Factors

Age. Incidence increases with age.

Gender. In younger populations, gout occurs more commonly in males, presumably because estrogen facilitates urinary excretion of urate in women. Gender does not affect risk in older patients.

Family history.

Dietary factors. See Nutritional Considerations below.

Obesity.

Medication. Diuretics, cyclosporine, low-dose aspirin, and niacin increase serum uric acid levels.

Stress, trauma, surgery. These factors may precipitate acute attacks.

Diagnosis

Signs and symptoms consistent with acute monoarticular arthritis suggest gout. However, definitive diagnosis requires demonstration of intracellular monosodium urate crystals in a synovial fluid or tophus aspirate.

Elevated serum uric acid level is present in most cases.

In gout, synovial fluid aspirate reveals negatively birefringent, needle-shaped crystals.

A 24-hour urine uric acid collection may help distinguish overproduction from underexcretion (>800 mg of uric acid/24 hours indicates overproduction).

Early in the disease, x-rays of the joints may appear normal. As the disease progresses, punched-out erosions with a rim of cortical bone may appear.

Treatment

Treatment of asymptomatic hyperuricemia, aside from the dietary adjustments noted below in Nutritional Considerations, is usually not indicated. Anti-inflammatory agents for acute attacks and prophylaxis for patients with high risk of recurrence are the cornerstones of therapy.

The treatment of choice for acute attacks in otherwise healthy adults is bed rest and nonsteroidal anti-inflammatory drugs (NSAIDs); indomethacin is often used.

Corticosteroids are reserved for severe disease or for patients who cannot take NSAIDs (eg, patients with renal failure). Monoarticular disease may be treated with intra-articular steroid administration. Polyarticular gout may be treated with oral or IV steroids.

Due to the high incidence of side effects, colchicine is now used less commonly.

Prophylactic medications to reduce the risk of further attacks include allopurinol, which inhibits xanthine oxidase to decrease uric acid production, and probenecid, which increases uric acid excretion. Caution must be exercised with the use of probenecid because it may increase the risk for nephrolithiasis. Rarely, allopurinol may cause Stevens-Johnson syndrome.

Febuxostat is a nonpurine inhibitor of xanthine oxidase that may be useful in patients with renal insufficiency because it is metabolized in the liver. Its use is associated with sustained lowering of serum uric acid, reduction of gout flares, and reduction of tophus area.[1]

Losartan lowers uric acid levels by virtue of direct inhibition of URAT1 (urate anion exchanger).[2]

Surgery is reserved for severe cases, including joint deformities, intractable pain, and nerve compression due to tophi.

Nutritional Considerations

Gout is significantly influenced by diet. A high intake of meat, for example, is a known risk factor for the elevated uric acid level that is associated with gout. Gout occurs more commonly in overweight persons, particularly those with the metabolic syndrome (see Obesity chapter).

The following factors are associated with decreased risk of gout:

Reducing or avoiding meat. Studies have found that, compared with persons eating the least red meat, poultry, or fish, those eating the highest amount have higher uric acid levels and a significantly greater risk for developing gout.[2,3]

In contrast, diets that provide protein from vegetable sources have resulted in significantly lower (~13%) uric acid levels, even when providing as much as 27% of calories from protein.[4]

Maintenance of healthy body weight. After adjustment for uric acid level, body mass index independently predicts gout risk.[5] Compared with men at or near their ideal weight, overweight men (BMI of 25 to 29.9) have almost double the risk for developing gout. Risk is nearly tripled for those with a BMI of 35 or greater.[6]

Avoidance of alcohol. Serum uric acid is associated with alcohol intake in men.[7] With the possible exception of moderate wine intake, the risk for gout appears to increase linearly with alcohol consumption.[8]

In addition, the following diet and lifestyle considerations should be noted:

Elevated lead levels. Elevated body lead burden increases serum uric acid and can compromise kidney function,[9] although evidence for a connection between lead exposure and the development of gout has not been established.[10] Lead exposure in adults can occur through many mechanisms, notably occupational exposures, storage of alcoholic beverages in lead crystal, and lead piping in older homes. For further details, see Foodborne Chemicals chapter. Chelation treatment to remove lead results in improved clearance of uric acid from the blood.[11]

Kidney stones. Gout appears to increase the risk for kidney stones,[12] and consuming 2 liters or more of water and water-based beverages per day may be helpful in reducing the risk of stone formation in gout patients.[13] (See also Nephrolithiasis chapter.)

Dairy intake. A study of nearly 15,000 individuals in the Third National Health and Nutrition Examination Survey found that individuals who consumed milk 1 or more times per day, or yogurt at least once every other day, had significantly lower serum uric acid concentrations than did those who did not drink milk.[2] In the Health Professionals Follow-up Study involving more than 47,000 men, the risk for gout was roughly 45% lower in men who consumed the most dairy products (2 or more glasses of skim milk per day), compared with those who consumed the least (less than 1 glass per month).[3] The effect appears to be caused by casein and lactalbumin, two milk proteins that have a uricosuric effect.[3] However, there are several caveats. First, the inverse association in the latter study was limited to the consumption of low-fat dairy products.[3] Second, the levels of dairy consumption associated with a reduced risk of gout are associated with significantly increased risk of other diseases (see Parkinson Disease and Prostate Cancer chapters). In addition, a protective effect of dairy products on the development of gout has not yet been found in women.

Orders

See Basic Diet Orders chapter.

Alcohol restriction.

Weight loss if indicated.

What to Tell the Family

Gout is a treatable disease that often responds well to a combination of diet therapy and medication. The family can help the patient in adhering to a healthful diet and can be most supportive by adopting the same dietary changes as the patient. Avoidance of alcohol and meat is important for lowering blood levels of uric acid and may also reduce the symptoms of the metabolic syndrome that often accompany elevated uric acid. Loss of excess weight may enhance treatment by improving the kidney's ability to clear uric acid from plasma.

References

1. Gelber AC. Febuxostat versus allopurinol for gout. *N Engl J Med*. 2006;354:1532-1533; author reply 1532-1533.

2. Choi HK, Liu S, Curhan G. Intake of purine-rich foods, protein, and dairy products and relationship to serum levels of uric acid: the Third National Health and Nutrition Examination Survey. *Arthritis Rheum*. 2005;52:283-289.

3. Choi HK, Atkinson K, Karlson EW, Willett W, Curhan G. Purine-rich foods, dairy and protein intake, and the risk of gout in men. *N Engl J Med*. 2004;350:1093-1103.

4. Jenkins DJ, Kendall CW, Vidgen E, et al. High-protein diets in hyperlipidemia: effect of wheat gluten on serum lipids, uric acid, and renal function. *Am J Clin Nutr*. 2001;74:57-63.

5. Lin KC, Lin HY, Chou P. Community-based epidemiological study on hyperuricemia and gout in Kin-Hu, Kinmen. *J Rheumatol*. 2000;27:1045-1050.

6. Choi HK, Atkinson K, Karlson EW, Curhan G. Obesity, weight change, hypertension, diuretic use, and risk of gout in men: the Health Professionals' Follow-Up Study. *Arch Intern Med*. 2005;165:742-748.

7. Loenen HM, Eshuis H, Lowik MR, et al. Serum uric acid correlates in elderly men and women with special reference to body composition and dietary intake (Dutch Nutrition Surveillance System). *J Clin Epidemiol.* 1990;43:1297-1303.

8. Choi HK, Atkinson K, Karlson EW, Willett W, Curhan G. Alcohol intake and risk of incident gout in men: a prospective study. *Lancet.* 2004;363:1277-1281.

9. Weaver VM, Jaar BG, Schwartz BS, et al. Associations among lead dose biomarkers, uric acid, and renal function in Korean lead workers. *Environ Health Perspect.* 2005;113:36-42.

10. Shadick NA, Kim R, Weiss S, Liang MH, Sparrow D, Hu H. Effect of low level lead exposure on hyperuricemia and gout among middle aged and elderly men: the normative aging study. *J Rheumatol.* 2000;27:1708-1712.

11. Lin JL, Yu CC, Lin-Tan DT, Ho HH. Lead chelation therapy and urate excretion in patients with chronic renal diseases and gout. *Kidney Int.* 2001;60:266-271.

12. Kramer HJ, Choi HK, Atkinson K, Stampfer M, Curhan GC. The association between gout and nephrolithiasis in men: The Health Professionals' Follow-Up Study. *Kidney Int.* 2003;64:1022-1026.

13. Asplin JR. Uric acid stones. *Semin Nephrol.* 1996;16:412-424.

72. Osteoporosis

Osteoporosis is a metabolic disease characterized by progressive thinning of the bone matrix and cortex. Fractures may result from decreased bone strength, and hip fractures are a significant cause of morbidity and mortality for aging adults. Primary osteoporosis reflects an imbalance in the coupling of osteoblasts and osteoclasts and commonly reflects natural hormonal and metabolic changes (eg, menopause). Secondary osteoporosis makes up 5% of cases and can be caused by hyperparathyroidism, hyperthyroidism, diabetes mellitus, chronic kidney disease, hepatic disease, malabsorption syndromes, pancreatic insufficiency, malignancy, and certain medications.

Risk Factors

In general, whites are at greater risk than persons of Latin American, Asian, or African heritage. Blacks have greater bone densities and a lower risk of fracture, compared with white Americans. African American women, however, have higher morbidity and mortality associated with fracture.[1]

Many risk factors are associated with osteoporosis. The following are among the most common:

Age. In postmenopausal women, fracture risk increases with age. Both men and women aged 70 and older have an increased risk of fracture.

Female gender. Primary osteoporosis is 6 times more common in women than in men. Also, osteoporosis begins earlier and tends to be more severe in women.

Body habitus. Persons with lower body mass have lower bone mineral density. Obesity reduces the risk of developing osteoporosis.

Sedentary lifestyle.

Genetic factors.

Previous fracture in the adult years.

Smoking.

Glucocorticoid, cyclosporine, and **methotrexate** treatment.

Medications. Vitamin A, heparin, aluminum-containing antacids, antidepressants, anticonvulsants, and **medroxyprogesterone** increase risk, whereas thiazide diuretics, estrogens, and androgens are protective.

High alcohol consumption. However, a moderate-to-low alcohol intake could be protective.[2]

Nulliparity.

Early onset of menopause.

Calcium or vitamin D deficiency.

Other dietary factors (see Nutritional Considerations below).

Diagnosis

Osteoporosis can lead to fragility fractures that most commonly occur in the vertebral body, wrist, and hip. Vertebral fracture is the most common clinical manifestation of osteoporosis or osteopenia (a diagnosis of less severe bone loss), typically presenting as an asymptomatic incidental finding on x-ray or at the time of a bone density measurement. Fracture of the vertebrae usually occurs in the lower thoracic or upper lumbar region and may occur after simple movements like bending over and lifting. Multiple fractures may result in pronounced thoracic kyphosis, sometimes called dowager's hump.[3] In the absence of fracture, pain is unlikely to be due to osteoporosis, but it could be due to osteomalacia or other bone disease.

In the absence of fragility fracture, radiological bone densitometry establishes the diagnosis of osteoporosis. Women 65 years or older and younger postmenopausal women with elevated risk should have a bone density scan. Bone biopsy, which can ensure histologic diagnosis, is rarely performed. A history of fracture is not necessary for diagnosis.

Laboratory tests, particularly thyroid-stimulating hormone, complete blood count (CBC), 25-hydroxy vitamin D, serum protein electrophoresis, urine calcium, and a comprehensive metabolic panel (including calcium and phosphate), can help determine if osteoporosis is primary or secondary. Because many disease processes can contribute to osteoporosis, disease-specific diagnostic evaluations are necessary, based on clinical presentation and screening tests.

Treatment

The clinical focus should be on prevention, symptomatic therapy, and inhibition of disease progression. Consuming adequate calcium and vitamin D and getting frequent weight-bearing exercise are most important (see Nutritional Considerations).

Regular weight-bearing and resistance exercise is helpful for increasing the bone mineral density (BMD) of the spine in postmenopausal women and for preventing and treating osteoporosis.[4,5]

Additional modifications include dietary changes (see Nutritional Considerations below), taking precautions to avoid falls, and smoking cessation. Smoking has an independent, dose-dependent effect on bone loss, which increases fracture risk in both sexes. Smoking increases the lifetime risk of developing a hip fracture by an estimated 31% in women and 40% in men and increases the lifetime risk for vertebral fracture by an estimated 13% in women and 32% in men. Risk declines among former smokers, but the benefit is not observed until 10 years after smoking cessation.[6,7]

Medications

In addition to ensuring adequate calcium intake and vitamin D status at every stage of life and getting regular weight-bearing exercise, the following medications may need to be used in specific situations:

Calcitonin decreases bone resorption, may reduce associated pain, and reduces future vertebral fractures. It is often used to treat osteopenia in order to prevent further progression of bone density loss.

Estrogen use, with or without progesterone, reduces bone resorption, slows progression of osteoporosis, and reduces the risk of fragility fractures. However, the benefits of estrogens must be weighed against the many possible adverse effects of estrogen therapy, particularly the increased risk of breast cancer and stroke.

Raloxifene, a selective estrogen receptor modulator (SERM), inhibits bone resorption, is useful for osteoporosis prevention, and reduces risk of vertebral fractures. Like tamoxifen, it reduces breast cancer risk, but, unlike tamoxifen, raloxifene does not increase the risk of endometrial cancer. Like calcitonin, it is used to treat osteopenia.

Testosterone may increase bone mass for men with osteoporosis (especially in males with low serum testosterone levels). If it is used, prostate-specific antigen (PSA) level should be monitored, due to the risk of progression of occult prostate cancer.

Thiazides decrease renal calcium loss and are associated with increased bone mass density, especially in those with hypercalciuria. However, they may increase the risk for electrolyte disturbances and postural hypotension.

Bisphosphonates (alendronate, pamidronate, risedronate, and ibandronate) decrease bone resorption and reduce risk of vertebral and hip fractures. When they are taken orally, esophagitis and gastrointestinal side effects may occur. Avascular necrosis of the jaw is a rare but serious side effect, most commonly seen in oncology patients treated with intravenous bisphosphonates.

Teriparatide, a recombinant human parathyroid hormone, primarily stimulates bone formation and is administered subcutaneously for a 2-year period.

Nutritional Considerations

Osteoporosis is more common where Western diets prevail.[8] The common belief that this complex disease is preventable or treatable by a high intake of calcium supplements or dairy products alone has not withstood scrutiny.[9] The Nurses' Health Study, following more than 72,000 women for 18 years, found no effect of either dairy products or a high-calcium diet on fracture risk.[10] Recent calcium-balance studies performed by U.S. Department of Agriculture scientists indicate that the mean daily calcium requirement is approximately 740 mg for both sexes, a figure that is considerably lower than previously proposed.[11]

Skeletal health involves dietary habits that support bone formation and retard bone resorption, in addition to regular exercise. The topic of daily calcium intake and its impact on bone metabolism remains highly controversial, as is the role of the quantity and quality of protein intake. In contrast, the role of other essential nutrients (eg, potassium and magnesium) in promoting bone health is becoming increasingly apparent.

The following factors are under investigation for their role in preventing or slowing osteoporosis:

Reduced animal protein intake. A relatively high protein intake is associated with increased bone mineral mass and reduced incidence of osteoporotic fracture.[12] However, the source of this protein is a matter of some controversy, and evidence indicates that the proportion of animal to plant protein has a considerable influence on bone health and fracture risk. Cross-cultural studies have found strong, positive relationships between animal protein intake and risk for hip fracture.[13] In one study, women with higher meat intake (≥5 servings per week) had a significantly increased risk for forearm fracture compared with women eating meat less than once per week.[14] In another, elderly women whose diets contained a high ratio of animal protein to vegetable protein had more rapid bone loss and greater risk for hip fracture than those with a low ratio.[15] Other studies found that bone mass was inversely associated with animal protein intake and positively related to intake of vegetable protein.[16]

Bone health appears to benefit from replacing animal protein with vegetable sources of protein, particularly soy. In clinical studies with postmenopausal women, soy products have been found to prevent bone loss.[17,18] The relatively high concentrations of isoflavones in plant-based proteins may be one of the many proposed reasons for their beneficial effect on bone metabolism.[19] Although isoflavones are commonly presumed to act in an estrogen-agonistic fashion, other mechanisms include inhibiting the formation of osteoclasts and suppressing the activity of existing osteoclasts.[20]

Increased fruit and vegetable intakes. Studies have shown that fruit and vegetable intakes are associated with bone mineral density in both women and men. These associations may be due to the buffering effect of potassium and magnesium in fruits and vegetables on the acid-base balance that partly determines bone resorption.[21,22] These foods also provide vitamin K, low intakes of which may contribute to osteoporosis and risk of hip fracture by causing undercarboxylation of osteocalcin.[23,24] In addition, fruits and vegetables are important sources of folic acid, a nutrient critical for normalizing blood levels of homocysteine that have been linked to osteoporotic fracture.[25] In the Hordaland Homocysteine Study involving over 3,000 women, elevated levels of homocysteine were inversely associated with bone density, and blood folate levels were significantly associated with bone density in the subgroup of elderly women.[26]

Reduced sodium intake. Some studies have found that habitually high sodium intake increases urinary calcium loss[27] and markers of bone resorption.[28] Although restricting dietary sodium reduces calcium loss and markers of bone resorption in postmenopausal (not premenopausal) women,[29] the effect of sodium restriction on long-term bone integrity and fracture risk remains unclear.

Low-fat diets. Studies have found that higher intake of fat is associated with a greater loss of bone[2] and greater fracture risk.[30] Possible mechanisms include the tendency of excess fat intake to reduce calcium absorption and to affect eicosanoid production. Specifically, the omega-6 polyunsaturated fatty acids linoleic acid and arachidonic acid act as precursors to prostaglandin E2 (PGE2), which favors osteoclast-induced bone resorption at the expense of osteoblast-induced bone formation.[31]

Moderation in caffeine use. Studies have found that women consuming the most caffeine have accelerated spinal bone loss.[32] The Nurses' Health Study found that those consuming more than 817 mg/d had nearly triple the risk for hip fracture, compared with those having the lowest intakes (0-192 mg/d).[33] In a study involving 489 elderly women given 3 different hormone replacement regimens, the risk for bone loss was greatest in women who consumed ≥18 ounces of coffee per day (or 300 mg caffeine from other sources) and was dependent on vitamin D receptor genotype.[32] It is possible, although not proven, that increased dietary calcium may offset the calciuretic effects of caffeine.[34]

Limiting alcohol intake. Alcohol decreases the endogenous production of calcitonin[35] and may displace important bone-forming nutrients. A study of nearly 16,000 women and men found that the risk for osteoporotic fracture in both sexes was approximately 40% higher among those having more than 1.5 drinks per day, compared with those having less than this amount.[35]

Limiting supplemental vitamin A. Studies have shown that the declines in bone density and risk for hip fracture are increased at as little as twice the recommended intake for retinol.[36] Risk for fracture also appears to be significantly higher in women consuming more food sources of retinol.[37] Vitamin A adequacy can instead be ensured with beta carotene from plant sources, particularly orange and yellow vegetables.

Combined supplemental vitamin D and calcium. Supplementing with calcium alone carries limited benefits for bone health and fracture risk. These include small positive effects on bone density, but only a trend toward reducing vertebral fractures, and no proof that it reduces nonvertebral fractures.[38] However, a meta-analysis of controlled trials of vitamin D supplementation (700 to 800 IU/d) found a reduced risk of hip and nonvertebral fractures of 26% and 23%, respectively, benefits that were not found at a dose of 400 IU per day.[39]

The benefit of a combination of calcium with vitamin D is more controversial. A Cochrane review concluded that the benefits of combined calcium and vitamin D supplementation on fracture prevention in women with involutional and postmenopausal osteoporosis were restricted mainly to those living in institutional care.[40] However, the best evidence of this combination may be the reduction of bone loss in patients with corticosteroid-induced osteoporosis.[41] Results of a calcium-vitamin D supplementation trial involving over 36,000 individuals in the Women's Health Initiative studies indicated small but significant improvement in hip bone density but no significant reduction in hip fracture.[42] Compliance with the treatment regimen appeared to be an issue for many women, possibly due to constipation caused by calcium supplementation.[43] In those women who took at least 80% of study medication, hip fracture risk was reduced by nearly 30%, and women over age 60 also experienced a significant risk reduction. However, those in the age group 50 to 59 had over twice the risk for hip fracture, and the risk for kidney stones increased by 17% in those taking calcium supplements.[42]

Vitamin K. There may also be a role for vitamin K supplementation. A systematic review and meta-analysis of vitamin K supplementation in Japanese adults indicated that optimizing intake of this vitamin might have a significant effect on bone integrity.[44] In women 40 to 78 years old, a series of studies revealed that 45 mg menadione (a vitamin K precursor) per day resulted in a 60%, 77%, and 81% lower risk for vertebral, hip, and nonvertebral fractures, respectively. Green leafy vegetables are rich in vitamin K.

Orders

See Basic Diet Orders chapter.

Low-sodium diet.

Restrict caffeine and alcohol consumption.

Female patients with osteoporosis should aim for a total calcium intake from diet and supplements of about 1500 mg/d in 3 or more divided doses, plus 800 IU/d of vitamin D. While supplemental calcium and vitamin D may benefit selected adult patients without osteoporosis, there is no theoretical basis for population-wide recommendations for high calcium intakes, particularly in males, due to associations between calcium or dairy intake and prostate cancer (see Prostate Cancer chapter).

Smoking cessation.

Exercise prescription with patient-appropriate weight-bearing exercises. Physical therapy or exercise physiology consultation as needed.

What to Tell the Family

Osteoporosis is a preventable and treatable disorder. Family members can help the patient maintain healthful dietary and exercise habits, and will be most supportive to the extent they follow these habits themselves.

References

1. Woodson GC. Risk factors for osteoporosis in postmenopausal African American women. *Current Medical Research & Opinion.* 2004;20:1681-1687.

2. Macdonald HM, New SA, Golden MH, Campbell MK, Reid DM. Nutritional associations with bone loss during the menopausal transition: evidence of a beneficial effect of calcium, alcohol, and fruit and vegetable nutrients and of a detrimental effect of fatty acids. *Am J Clin Nutr.* 2004;79:155-165.

3. Riggs BL, Melton LJ III. Involutional osteoporosis. *N Engl J Med.* 1986;314:1676-1686.

4. Bonaiuti D, Shea B, Iovine R, et al. Exercise for preventing and treating osteoporosis in postmenopausal women. *Cochrane Database Syst Rev.* 2002;(3):CD000333.

5. Prior JC, Barr SI, Chow R, Faulkner RA. Prevention and management of osteoporosis: consensus statements from the Scientific Advisory Board of the Osteoporosis Society of Canada. 5. Physical activity as therapy for osteoporosis. *CMAJ.* 1996;155:940-944.

6. Ward KD, Klesges RC. A meta-analysis of the effects of cigarette smoking on bone mineral density. *Calcif Tissue Int.* 2001;68:259-270.

7. Cornuz J, Feskanich D, Willett WC, Colditz GA. Smoking, smoking cessation, and risk of hip fracture in women. *Am J Med.* 1999;106:311-314.

8. Hegsted DM. Fractures, calcium, and the modern diet. *Am J Clin Nutr.* 2001;74:571-573.

9. Lanou AJ, Berkow SE, Barnard ND. Calcium, dairy products, and bone health in children and young adults: a reevaluation of the evidence. *Pediatrics.* 2005;115:736-743.

10. Feskanich D, Willett WC, Colditz GA. Calcium, vitamin D, milk consumption, and hip fractures: a prospective study among postmenopausal women. *Am J Clin Nutr.* 2003;77:504-511.

11. Hunt CD, Johnson LK. Calcium requirements: new estimations for men and women by cross-sectional statistical analyses of calcium balance data from metabolic studies. *Am J Clin Nutr.* 2007;86:1054-1063.

12. Bonjour JP. Dietary protein: an essential nutrient for bone health. *J Am Coll Nutr.* 2005;24(suppl 6):526S-536S.

13. Abelow BJ, Holford TR, Insogna KL. Cross-cultural association between dietary animal protein and hip fracture: a hypothesis. *Calcif Tissue Int.* 1992;50:14-18.

14. Feskanich D, Willett WC, Stampfer MJ, Colditz GA. Protein consumption and bone fractures in women. *Am J Epidemiol.* 1996;143:472-479.

15. Sellmeyer DE, Stone KL, Sebastian A, Cummings SR, for the Study of Osteoporotic Fractures Research Group. A high ratio of dietary animal to vegetable protein increases the rate of bone loss and the risk of fracture in postmenopausal women. *Am J Clin Nutr.* 2001;73:118-122.

16. Weikert C, Walter D, Hoffmann K, Kroke A, Bergmann MM, Boeing H. The relation between dietary protein, calcium and bone health in women: results from the EPIC-Potsdam cohort. *Ann Nutr Metab.* 2005;49:312-318.

17. Lydeking-Olsen E, Beck-Jensen JE, Setchell KD, Holm-Jensen T. Soymilk or progesterone for prevention of bone loss-a 2-year randomized, placebo-controlled trial. *Eur J Nutr.* 2004;43:246-257.

18. Ho SC, Woo J, Lam S, Chen Y, Sham A, Lau J. Soy protein consumption and bone mass in early postmenopausal Chinese women. *Osteoporos Int.* 2003;14:835-842.

19. Watkins BA, Reinwald S, Li Y, Seifert MF. Protective actions of soy isoflavones and n-3 PUFAs on bone mass in ovariectomized rats. J Nutr Biochem. 2005;16:478-488.

20. Valachovicova T, Slivova V, Sliva D. Cellular and physiological effects of soy flavonoids. *Mini Rev Med Chem.* 2004;4:881-887.

21. Tucker KL, Chen H, Hannan MT, et al. Bone mineral density and dietary patterns in older adults: the Framingham Osteoporosis Study. *Am J Clin Nutr.* 2002;76:245-252.

22. Tucker KL, Hannan MT, Chen H, Cupples LA, Wilson PW, Kiel DP. Potassium, magnesium, and fruit and vegetable intakes are associated with greater bone mineral density in elderly men and women. *Am J Clin Nutr.* 1999;69:727-736.

23. Ryan-Harshman M, Aldoori W. Bone health. New role for vitamin K? *Can Fam Physician.* 2004;50:993-997.

24. Feskanich D, Weber P, Willett WC, Rockett H, Booth SL, Colditz GA. Vitamin K intake and hip fractures in women: a prospective study. *Am J Clin Nutr.* 1999;69:74-79.

25. Cashman KD. Homocysteine and osteoporotic fracture risk: a potential role for B vitamins. *Nutr Rev.* 2005;63:29-36.

26. Gjesdal CG, Vollset SE, Ueland PM, et al. Plasma total homocysteine level and bone mineral density: the Hordaland Homocysteine Study. *Arch Intern Med.* 2006;166:88-94.

27. Ginty F, Flynn A, Cashman KD. The effect of dietary sodium intake on biochemical markers of bone metabolism in young women. *Br J Nutr.* 1998;79:343-350.

28. Itoh R, Suyama Y, Oguma Y, Yokota F. Dietary sodium, an independent determinant for urinary deoxypyridinoline in elderly women. A cross-sectional study on the effect of dietary factors on deoxypyridinoline excretion in 24-h urine specimens from 763 free-living healthy Japanese. *Eur J Clin Nutr.* 1999;53:886-890.

29. Nordin BE, Need AG, Morris HA, Horowitz M. The nature and significance of the relationship between urinary sodium and urinary calcium in women. *J Nutr.* 1993;123:1615-1622.

30. Kato I, Toniolo P, Zeleniuch-Jacquotte A, et al. Diet, smoking and anthropometric indices and postmenopausal bone fractures: a prospective study. *Int J Epidemiol.* 2000;29:85-92.

31. Requirand P, Gibert P, Tramini P, Cristol JP, Descomps B. Serum fatty acid imbalance in bone loss: example with periodontal disease. *Clin Nutr.* 2000;19:271-276.

32. Rapuri PB, Gallagher JC, Kinyamu HK, Ryschon KL. Caffeine intake increases the rate of bone loss in elderly women and interacts with vitamin D receptor genotypes. *Am J Clin Nutr.* 2001;74:694-700.

33. Hernandez-Avila M, Colditz GA, Stampfer MJ, Rosner B, Speizer FE, Willett WC. Caffeine, moderate alcohol intake, and risk of fractures of the hip and forearm in middle-aged women. *Am J Clin Nutr.* 1991;54:157-163.

34. Massey LK. Is caffeine a risk factor for bone loss in the elderly? *Am J Clin Nutr.* 2001;74:569-570.

35. Kanis JA, Johansson H, Johnell O, et al. Alcohol intake as a risk factor for fracture. *Osteoporos Int.* 2005;16:737-742.

36. Crandall C. Vitamin A intake and osteoporosis: a clinical review. *J Women's Health* (Larchmt). 2004;13:939-953.

37. Feskanich D, Singh V, Willett WC, Colditz GA. Vitamin A intake and hip fractures among postmenopausal women. *JAMA.* 2002;287:47-54.

38. Shea B, Wells G, Cranney A, et al. Calcium supplementation on bone loss in postmenopausal women. *Cochrane Database Syst Rev.* 2004;(1):CD004526.

39. Bischoff-Ferrari HA, Willett WC, Wong JB, Giovannucci E, Dietrich T, Dawson-Hughes B. Fracture prevention with vitamin D supplementation: a meta-analysis of randomized controlled trials. *JAMA.* 2005;293:2257-2264.

40. Avenell A, Gillespie WJ, Gillespie LD, O'Connell DL. Vitamin D and vitamin D analogues for preventing fractures associated with involutional and post-menopausal osteoporosis. *Cochrane Database Syst Rev.* 2005;(3):CD000227.

41. Homik J, Suarez-Almazor ME, Shea B, Cranney A, Wells G, Tugwell P. Calcium and vitamin D for corticosteroid-induced osteoporosis. *Cochrane Database Syst Rev.* 2000;(2):CD000952.

42. Jackson RD, LaCroix AZ, Gass M, et al. Calcium plus vitamin D supplementation and the risk of fractures. *N Engl J Med.* 2006;354:669-683.

43. Reid IR, Mason B, Horne A, et al. Randomized controlled trial of calcium in healthy older women. *Am J Med.* 2006;119:777-785.

44. Cockayne S, Adamson J, Lanham-New S, Shearer MJ, Gilbody S, Torgerson DJ. Vitamin K and the prevention of fractures: systematic review and meta-analysis of randomized controlled trials. *Arch Intern Med.* 2006;166:1256-1261.

73. Fibromyalgia

Fibromyalgia is a common but poorly understood pain syndrome that affects muscles, tendons, and ligaments. Some reports suggest the syndrome begins after trauma or illness.

Patients' histories and examinations present no explanation for the persistent pain. The condition may be related to an abnormality in pain perception. The most plausible hypothesis is that it occurs in genetically predisposed individuals who develop a heightened sense of pain and hypersensitivity to numerous stimuli.[1]

Nearly every fibromyalgia patient has fatigue, along with poor sleep quality that may include sleep apnea or other sleep abnormalities. One notable sleep abnormality has been determined to reflect alpha wave intrusions in delta sleep.[2] Other common concurrent illnesses include irritable bowel syndrome, depression or anxiety, and headache. Many other nonspecific symptoms may occur, including glossodynia (a burning or tingling sensation of the lips, tongue, or entire mouth), paresthesias without dermatomal distribution, environmental sensitivity (chemical and allergic), and difficulty concentrating.

Risk Factors

Gender. The condition is 10 times more common in women than in men.

Age. Incidence increases with age and peaks during middle age. The overall prevalence in the United States is approximately 2%, but many older adult populations have a prevalence approaching 10%.

Genetic factors. Specific genes relating to abnormal serotonin metabolism and transmission have been identified in fibromyalgia patients.

Diagnosis

Pain is generally diffuse and widespread. Screening for psychiatric conditions is appropriate, but a positive diagnosis does not exclude fibromyalgia as a separate diagnosis.

Physical examination reveals characteristic, symmetrical tender points. Palpation of these areas causes pain that is disproportionate to the intensity of palpation. Apart from muscle and tendon pain, the examination is otherwise normal except in individuals with coexisting conditions, such as rheumatoid arthritis, osteoarthritis, and lupus.

The diagnosis of fibromyalgia requires tenderness in 11 of 18 tender points.[3] Pressure should be applied gradually and with a dolorimeter (4kg/cm), or by using a finger to the point of blanching of the fingertip.[4] The following tender points should be palpated bilaterally:

- Superolateral quadrant of the gluteus maximus.
- Supraspinatus origin.
- Superior half of the trapezius.
- Suboccipital insertion.
- Sternocleidomastoid (posteroinferior).
- Second costochondral junction.
- Lateral epicondyle (approximately 2 cm distal).
- Greater trochanter.
- Medial knee (fat pad).

No abnormal laboratory or imaging findings are diagnostic of fibromyalgia, and inappropriate use of tests can lead to misdiagnosis. Initial laboratory tests that could help rule out other etiologies include erythrocyte sedimentation rate, complete blood count, thyroid function tests, Lyme disease titer, and creatine kinase. In appropriate at-risk individuals, vitamin D levels should be checked to rule out metabolic diseases, such as osteomalacia.[5]

Treatment

No single intervention is curative. However, multiple complementary modalities, along with consistent encouragement and reassurance by the physician can be very helpful. Commonly used treatments include both nonpharmacologic and drug therapies.

Nonpharmacologic Interventions[6]

Low-impact, incremental, cardiovascular exercise programs (3 times weekly).

Muscle strengthening and flexibility programs. Yoga often serves both purposes.

Hypnotherapy, cognitive behavioral therapy, electromyography (EMG) biofeedback, and meditation programs.

Acupuncture, TENS (transcutaneous electro-nerve stimulator) units, and trigger point needling (or injections with lidocaine) are under investigation.

Pharmacologic Interventions

Nonsteroidal anti-inflammatory drugs are no better than placebo when used as monotherapy. However, they may be effective in combination with centrally active medications.

Acetaminophen and/or tramadol in medication-naïve patients may be helpful, but efficacy in other clinical scenarios requires further study.

Cyclobenzaprine and tricyclic antidepressants, such as amitriptyline, may benefit a minority of patients. Efficacy may lessen over time. Small doses with gradual increase are advised, due to undesirable side effects (eg, dry mouth, urinary retention). Desipramine may have milder adverse side effects.

Selective serotonin reuptake inhibitors may be effective in treating pain and may act synergistically with tricyclics.[7]

Duloxetine and milnacipran, which inhibit catecholamine and serotonin reuptake, and muscle relaxants, such as carisoprodol (at bedtime), may be beneficial.

Emerging therapeutics, such as anticonvulsants and serotonin receptor blockers, may also be effective in treating pain and other symptoms. Pregabalin was recently approved for the treatment of fibromyalgia.[8]

Narcotics and benzodiazepines are usually contraindicated.

A multidisciplinary approach that includes physical therapy, good sleep hygiene, and mental health specialists may be indicated for optimal treatment because concomitant depressive symptoms and adjustment problems are often present. Patients also benefit from knowing that a hidden condition is not the cause of their symptoms.

Nutritional Considerations

Fibromyalgia is considered a rheumatic disease, one in which inflammatory cytokines (eg, interleukin-6) may be involved in triggering or increasing inflammation and its symptoms.[9] Markers of increased oxidative stress (malondialdehyde, advanced glycosylation end products)[10] and lower levels of the antioxidant enzyme superoxide dismutase have been found in patients with fibromyalgia.[11] Dietary manipulation can reduce oxidative stress and cytokine production (see Rheumatoid Arthritis chapter), but such treatments have yet to be tested in fibromyalgia patients. Limited evidence suggests that a vegan diet may improve subjective experience of joint pain and stiffness.[12,13] However, this impression requires confirmation in additional controlled clinical trials.

Fibromyalgia patients also have disturbed sleep and may have lower nocturnal melatonin production, which can increase daytime fatigue and pain perception.[14] Limited evidence indicates that supplemental melatonin (3 mg at bedtime) reduces tender points, pain severity, and sleep disturbances and results in improvement in both patient and physician assessment of global improvement.[15] Further studies are needed to assess the effects of diet changes and melatonin supplements on the condition.

Orders

See Basic Diet Orders.

Exercise prescription. Patient should be given an appropriate, sustainable, and enjoyable exercise routine.

What to Tell the Family

Fibromyalgia is a poorly understood condition that is treated symptomatically. General recommendations for a healthy exercise routine may be helpful to the patient and the entire family. Concomitant depression or other mental illness should be treated, but fibromyalgia is not an imaginary illness. Good sleep hygiene is also very important. Limited evidence suggests that some patients may respond well to a low-fat, vegan diet, and diet changes are easier to adopt when all family members make the change.

References

1. Banic B, Petersen-Felix S, Anderson OK, et al. Evidence for spinal cord hypersensitivity in chronic pain after whiplash injury and in fibromyalgia.

Pain. 2004;107:7-15.

2. Rothenberg R. Fibromyalgia. Documentation & Treatment. *Fibromyalgia Frontiers.* 2007;15:11-16.

3. Wolfe F, Smythe HA, Yunus MB, et al. The American College of Rheumatology 1990 criteria for the classification of fibromyalgia: report of the multicenter criteria committee. *Arthritis Rheum.* 1990;33:160-172.

4. Okifuji A, Turk DC, Sinclair JD, Starz TW, Marcus DA. A standardized manual tender point survey. I. Development and determination of a threshold point for the identification of positive tender points in fibromyalgia syndrome. *J Rheumatol.* 1997;24:377-383.

5. Shinchuk L, Holick MF. Vitamin d and rehabilitation: improving functional outcomes. *Nutr Clin Pract.* 2007;22:297-304.

6. Goldenberg DL, Burckhardt C, Crofford L. Management of fibromyalgia syndrome. *JAMA*. 2004;292:2388-2395.

7. Goldenberg DL, Mayskiy M, Mossey CJ, et al. A randomized, double-blind crossover trial of fluoxetine and amitriptyline in the treatment of fibromyalgia. *Arthritis Rheum*. 1996;39:1852.

8. Crofford LJ, Rowbotham MC, Mease PJ, et al. Pregabalin for the treatment of fibromyalgia syndrome: results of a randomized, double-blind, placebo-controlled trial. *Arthritis Rheum*. 2005;52:1264-1273.

9. Wallace DJ, Linker-Israeli M, Hallegua D, Silverman S, Silver D, Weisman MH. Cytokines play an aetiopathogenetic role in fibromyalgia: a hypothesis and pilot study. *Rheumatology* (Oxford). 2001;40:743-749.

10. Hein G, Franke S. Are advanced glycation end-product-modified proteins of pathogenetic importance in fibromyalgia? *Rheumatology* (Oxford). 2002;41:1163-1167.

11. Bagis S, Tamer L, Sahin G, et al. Free radicals and antioxidants in primary fibromyalgia: an oxidative stress disorder? *Rheumatol Int*. 2005;25:188-190.

12. Donaldson MS, Speight N, Loomis S. Fibromyalgia syndrome improved using a mostly raw vegetarian diet: an observational study. *BMC Complement Altern Med*. 2001;1:7.

13. Hanninen O, Kaartinen K, Rauma AL, et al. Antioxidants in vegan diet and rheumatic disorders. *Toxicology*. 2000;155:45-53.

14. Wikner J, Hirsch U, Wetterberg L, Rojdmark S. Fibromyalgia--a syndrome associated with decreased nocturnal melatonin secretion. *Clin Endocrinol* (Oxf). 1998;49:179-183.

15. Citera G, Arias MA, Maldonado-Cocco JA, et al. The effect of melatonin in patients with fibromyalgia: a pilot study. *Clin Rheumatol*. 2000;19:9-13.

SECTION XIV: ENDOCRINOLOGY AND METABOLISM

74. Diabetes Mellitus

Diabetes mellitus (DM) includes a group of metabolic diseases characterized by hyperglycemia, which is attributable to insulin deficiency and/or insulin resistance. It leads to a wide range of complications and, when poorly controlled, can contribute to significant morbidity and mortality (see Diabetes Complications chapter). Three main types of diabetes are recognized:

Type 1 diabetes, accounting for approximately 5% to 10% of total cases, occurs after destruction of the insulin-producing beta-islet cells of the pancreas (usually through an autoimmune process). Most cases present in childhood with polyuria and polydipsia, unexplained weight loss, fatigue, and blurred vision. The condition can also be diagnosed in adults. Type 1 diabetes requires insulin treatment.

Type 2 diabetes, which accounts for more than 80% of diabetes cases, usually presents in adults after a long, asymptomatic course. About 85% of patients are centrally obese, and insulin resistance is typically present. Diabetes manifests when insulin production fails to keep pace with the body's increased need. Prevalence in children is climbing rapidly due to increasing obesity. Type 2 diabetes is often accompanied by hypertension and lipid abnormalities and is part of the metabolic syndrome. Although symptoms upon initial presentation tend to be much milder in type 2 than in type 1 diabetes, complications are frequent and increase in prevalence over time if metabolic control is poor.

Gestational diabetes mellitus (GDM) accounts for about 2% of diabetes cases. As its name suggests, GDM first appears during pregnancy. Hormones secreted by the placenta—estrogen, progesterone, growth hormone, corticotrophin-releasing hormone, and prolactin—oppose insulin's function, and the pancreas struggles to produce enough insulin to compensate for the greater caloric intake during pregnancy. Treatment with dietary modification and/or drugs (usually insulin) is essential to prevent fetal complications. Although blood glucose levels usually normalize postpartum, many women with GDM eventually develop type 2 diabetes or have a delayed onset of type 1 diabetes.

Risk Factors

Risk factors for type 1 diabetes include:

- **Family history.** When a first-degree relative has diabetes, the risk of developing type 1 diabetes is about 10% to 15%. Many possible genes are under investigation.

- **Exposure to bovine milk proteins.** Consumption of cow's milk in early childhood has been under investigation as a contributing factor, although it has not yet been definitively established.

- **Fetal or childhood Coxsackie virus and enteroviral infections.**

- **Birth weight greater than 4,500 grams.**

- **Preeclampsia.**[1]

- **Maternal age greater than 25 years.**[1]

- **ABO incompatibility-induced jaundice.**[1]

Risk factors for type 2 diabetes include:

- **Family history of type 2 diabetes** in first- or second-degree relatives.

- **Older age.**[1]

- **Abdominal obesity.**[2]

- **History of gestational diabetes.**

- The presence of **hypertension** and **dyslipidemia.**

- **Ethnic background:** Blacks, Latinos, American Indian/Alaska Natives, and Asians and Pacific Islanders have a greater prevalence.

- **Previous impaired fasting glucose** or **impaired glucose tolerance.**

Risk factors for GDM are listed below. In addition, individuals of Asian, African, Native American, and Hispanic ancestry have greater prevalence of GDM than non-Hispanic whites.[3] The risk factors for GDM overlap with type 2 diabetes.

- **Family history of type 2 diabetes** in a first-degree relative.

- **A previous abnormal oral glucose tolerance test.**

- **Glucocorticoid use** during pregnancy.
- **Polycystic ovarian syndrome.**
- **Age greater than 25 years.**
- **A prepregnancy weight at least 10% above ideal body weight.**
- **Early postpubescent weight gain.**
- **Previous child with birth weight greater than 9 pounds.**
- **Previous idiopathic perinatal death** or **birth defect.**
- **Maternal birth weight greater than 9 pounds** or **less than 6 pounds.**[4]
- **Sedentary lifestyle.**

Other factors, such as chronic sleep loss, may worsen glycemic control among individuals with diabetes.[5]

Diagnosis

Endocrinopathies, such as Cushing disease, acromegaly, pheochromocytoma, and hyperthyroidism, may impair glucose tolerance and should be ruled out.

Type 1 and Type 2 Diabetes

Diabetes can be diagnosed by any of the following, assessed on 2 occasions:[6]

- A fasting plasma glucose concentration greater than 125 mg/dL.
- A 2-hour oral glucose tolerance test (GTT) result of 200 mg/dL or greater.
- A random plasma glucose of 200 mg/dL or greater when diabetes symptoms are present.

Normal fasting plasma glucose is less than 100 mg/dL, and the 2-hour GTT is less than 140 mg/dL. Intermediate results reflect impaired fasting glucose (impaired glucose tolerance in the case of GTT), which often precedes an eventual diabetes diagnosis ("pre-diabetes"). Hemoglobin A1c (A1c) is not currently accepted for diagnosis of diabetes because it is too insensitive, but it is crucial for clinical management.

Type 1 DM often presents with ketoacidosis, which is caused by partial or total insulin deficiency and normally requires hospital admission and intensive care. Type 1 DM can be confirmed by the identification of islet-cell antibodies or other autoantibodies (eg, antiglutamic acid de-hydrogenase [GAD] or anti-insulin antibodies). However, some patients have no identifiable cause of islet cell destruction.

Patients initially thought to have type 2 DM but with autoantibodies most likely have late-onset type 1 diabetes or late-onset autoimmune diabetes. They are unlikely to respond adequately to oral hypoglycemics and will likely require insulin.

Gestational Diabetes

Screening for GDM is a routine part of prenatal examinations. Several strategies may be used for diagnosis.

Screening typically occurs between 24 and 28 weeks of gestation and involves a 1-hour challenge with a 50-g carbohydrate load. A venous serum or plasma glucose greater than 129 or 139 (either threshold may be used),[7] with sensitivity of 90% and 80%, respectively, is abnormal and necessitates a 3-hour GTT (with 100-g carbohydrate load).

The Fourth International Workshop-Conference on Gestational Diabetes Mellitus established more stringent diagnostic criteria, which are based on the 3-hour GTT and require that 2 of the following 4 criteria be met:

- Fasting serum glucose concentration >95 mg/dL (5.3 mmol/L).

- One-hour serum glucose concentration >180 mg/dL (10 mmol/L).

- Two-hour serum glucose concentration >155 mg/dL (8.6 mmol/L).

- Three-hour serum glucose concentration >140 mg/dL (7.8 mmol/L).

In pregnancy, mildly abnormal glucose levels can lead to fetal complications, which is why fasting serum glucose greater than 95 mg/dL is considered abnormal and treatment is started very early. Treatment should be considered in women with fasting glucose greater than 90 mg/dL due to the increased risk of macrosomia, which can occur even with a normal GTT.[8]

Treatment

Dietary and lifestyle interventions are important for patients with all types of DM (see below). Education for diabetes self-management, which includes self-monitoring of blood glucose, is an important component of treatment.[9]

A1c Targets

For all types of diabetes, good blood-glucose control decreases the risk of complications. A1c testing should be used as an index of diabetes control. It provides a fairly accurate measurement of the average blood glucose during the previous 2 to 3 months. The A1c goal set by the American Diabetes Association is <7%.

However, this value is not a threshold; goals should be individualized. Some studies show that risk of complications appears to fall with lower A1c values. However, risk of hypoglycemia may be increased, depending on medications used. Moreover, the ACCORD (Action to Control Cardiovascular Risk in Diabetes) study including 10,251 participants, which compared intensive treatment (intended to reduce A1c to less than 6%) with less-intensive treatment, showed increased deaths in the intensively treated group, leading to an early termination of this part of the study in 2008.[10]

Type 1 Diabetes

Insulin is available in several forms that differ in duration of action.

- Long-acting insulins provide basal coverage. Glargine is usually administered daily; detemir may be given once or twice a day.

- NPH has an intermediate length of action and is often administered twice a day.

- Rapid-acting insulin analogs (or regular insulin) can be administered in boluses before meals to curb postprandial blood glucose elevations and to correct pre-meal elevations.

- Intermediate insulin is available premixed with short- or rapid-acting insulin when two insulin types are required.

- Premixed insulins are primarily used in patients with type 2 diabetes.

Amylin is a beta-cell hormone that is cosecreted with insulin. Pramlinitide, a synthetic amylin analog, is injected at mealtimes along with fast-acting insulin. It reduces postprandial rises in blood glucose concentrations and suppresses appetite, which may lead to weight loss.

Type 2 Diabetes

Oral Agents

Biguanides. Metformin is commonly used as a first-line agent, as it does not generally promote weight gain. It decreases hepatic gluconeogenesis and increases insulin sensitivity. It is contraindicated in heart failure, renal insufficiency, liver disease, excessive alcohol intake, serious infection and illness, and other disease processes. Gastrointestinal disturbances are common but usually abate over time.

Sulfonylureas. Glipizide, glyburide, and glimepride are the most commonly used oral antihyperglycemic medications. Glipizide is shorter-acting and may be preferable for geriatric patients or those with renal insufficiency. Sulfonylureas may cause hypoglycemia and weight gain, and they often cease to be effective within a few years.

Thiazolidinediones. Pioglitazone and rosiglitazone increase insulin sensitivity, decrease glucose production, and may also increase insulin secretion. They are contraindicated in heart failure. Weight gain and fluid retention are common side effects. Recent reports have raised concerns about possible cardiac risks of rosiglitazone. A 2007 meta-analysis showed a 43% increased risk of myocardial infarction, although contradictory studies have also been published.[11] Possible mechanisms include its tendency to boost low-density lipoprotein cholesterol (by an average of 19 percent in published studies), precipitate congestive heart failure, and reduce hemoglobin levels.[11] These concerns do not appear to apply to pioglitazone.

Meglitinides. Nateglinide and repaglinide stimulate insulin secretion but are shorter-acting than sulfonylureas and must be taken with meals.

Alpha-glucosidase inhibitors. Acarbose and miglitol inhibit the conversion of carbohydrates to monosaccharides and lower postprandial glucose values. Flatulence is a common side effect and may limit compliance, but it generally improves over time.

DPP-IV inhibitors (eg, sitagliptin) inhibit the enzyme that degrades endogenous incretin hormones. This results in increased glucose-dependent insulin secretion, decreased glucagon secretion, and delayed gastric emptying. Sitagliptin must be given at a lower dose for those with renal insufficiency.

Noninsulin Injectables

Incretin mimetic. Exenatide is an injectable synthetic used to increase mealtime insulin secretion in type 2 diabetes. It is less likely to cause hypoglycemia or weight gain, compared with insulin or insulin secretogogues, and may promote satiety, leading to decreased appetite and weight loss. Nausea is a common side effect.

Pramlintide (described above) may also be used in type 2 diabetes.

Insulin

The insulin formulations described above for type 1 diabetes are appropriate for use in type 2. The best regimen is the one that (1) results in good blood glucose control with a dosing schedule that is acceptable to the patient and (2) causes the fewest episodes of hypoglycemia. A new strategy uses insulin as first-line therapy at diagnosis. In some cases, it can later be withdrawn, with blood glucose levels maintained through lifestyle interventions alone.

A patient with presumed type 2 diabetes and autoantibodies is less likely to respond to the oral agents. Such patients may require insulin therapy (see type 1 diabetes) and are at increased risk of ketoacidosis.

Gestational Diabetes

Nutrition therapy is the first-line treatment for GDM. Adequate control is achieved if fasting plasma glucose is less than 90 mg/dL and 1-hour postprandial glucose is less than 120 mg/dL. When these goals are not met, insulin should be considered. Dietary interventions are discussed in detail under Nutritional Considerations below.

Insulin is the best-studied pharmaceutical agent for GDM, and it is the only recommended treatment in the United States. However, metformin is used by some obstetricians with some evidence of safety.

Role of Physical Activity

A sedentary lifestyle is associated with increased risk for impaired glucose tolerance and diabetes.[12] Exercise[13] and diet-exercise programs that produce weight loss significantly reduce the risk for type 2 diabetes.[14,15]

Exercise alone has little or no effect on body weight.[16] However, in persons with established diabetes, exercise reduces blood glucose and plasma lipid concentrations[17] and improves insulin sensitivity, independent of weight loss. Exercise also reduces cardiovascular complications of diabetes, including high blood pressure, left ventricular diastolic function, arterial stiffness, systemic inflammation, and left ventricular mass.[18]

Women who either have or are at risk for gestational diabetes can also benefit from exercise. Independent of body mass index, women who regularly engage in moderate exercise (eg, brisk walking) are at reduced risk of GDM.[19] In women with GDM, exercise has been found to be a useful strategy for helping to maintain blood glucose within the normal range and to control blood glucose without the use of insulin.[20] Note: Exercise must be stopped if contractions occur.

Medications, especially insulin acting during the time of the activity, may need to be adjusted or carbohydrate intake increased on days when exercise occurs.

Certain pharmaceuticals, such as beta-blockers, thiazides, oral contraceptives, niacin, and glucocorticoids, can impair glucose tolerance and raise A1c levels.

Nutritional Considerations

Prevention: Type 1 Diabetes

Dietary factors that may influence the risk of type 1 diabetes have been under investigation. The following considerations have emerged as potentially important candidates for preventive strategies, although none has been definitively established as such:

Breast-feeding. In some epidemiologic studies, breast-feeding is associated with reduced risk for developing insulin-dependent diabetes. Longer duration of breast-feeding may reduce risk for type 1 diabetes, presumably by increasing protection against infections, enhancing the infant's immune responses, increasing beta-cell proliferation, and delaying exposure to foreign food antigens.[21] An autoimmune mechanism may also be involved (see below). Although breast-feeding is the best choice for infant feeding, ethical and practical difficulties have prevented controlled trials of its effect on diabetes risk.

Avoidance of early introduction of cow's milk. Cow's milk has been temporally related to the diagnosis of diabetes,[22] and children with type 1 diabetes have higher levels of antibodies to cow's milk protein that represent independent risk markers for this condition.[23] Although it has not yet been proven conclusively that cow's milk is a trigger for type 1 diabetes, the American Academy of Pediatrics concluded that avoiding early exposure to cow's milk may reduce the risk.[24]

The question of whether the early ingestion of intact foreign proteins contained in cow's milk may increase type 1 diabetes risk may be answered in part by the Trial to Reduce Type 1 Diabetes in the Genetically at Risk (TRIGR) study. This international effort will test the hypothesis that weaning infants to an extensively hydrolyzed formula instead of cow's milk may delay or prevent the onset of type 1 diabetes in genetically susceptible children.[25] Although the results of this study are pending, TRIGR investigators have reported that the highest levels of insulin antibodies were found in infants fed exclusively cow's milk formula, compared with those who received both breast milk and cow's milk or breast milk alone.[26] A smaller study with a similar design found that this intervention resulted in a significant protection from positivity for islet cell antibodies.[27]

Avoiding early introduction of gluten-containing foods. In epidemiologic studies, supplementing infant diets with gluten-containing foods before 3 months of age is associated with increased risk for developing islet cell autoantibodies.[28] In some children, both early (before 3 months) and late (after 7 months) introduction of cereals was associated with increased risk of islet autoimmunity, suggesting that there may be a window of exposure to cereals, outside which initial exposure increases islet autoimmunity risk in genetically susceptible children.[29]

In first-degree relatives of patients with type 1 diabetes and evidence of autoimmunity-related type 1 diabetes, insulin response to intravenous glucose tolerance testing and insulin sensitivity improved on a gluten-free diet, despite the absence of changes in antibody titers.[30] A higher prevalence of celiac disease has been observed in children with type 1 diabetes compared with other children.[31]

Researchers are seeking ways to prevent autoimmune attacks of pancreatic beta-cells, with the goal of reducing the risk for developing insulin-dependent diabetes. So far, evidence suggests that the following dietary factors may influence the risk of type 1 diabetes: breast-feeding, vitamin D supplementation, and cod liver oil supplementation (a source of vitamin D) during both pregnancy and the infant's first year of life.[32] All of these actions are capable of modulating the production of proinflammatory cytokines that are known to be involved in the pathogenesis of type 1 diabetes.[33]

Prevention: Type 2 Diabetes

Although type 2 diabetes has a strong genetic component, diet and lifestyle significantly affect the likelihood that the disease will manifest and also influence its course after diagnosis. The risk for type 2 and gestational diabetes can be decreased by avoiding overweight and by following specific dietary and lifestyle practices. Notably, the Diabetes Prevention Program demonstrated that dietary changes designed to reduce body weight, combined with regular exercise, can significantly reduce the risk for type 2 diabetes. Risk reduction was 58% in the group that combined diet and exercise compared with placebo. Those on drug (metformin) treatment had a 31% reduction. In individuals age 60 and older, the risk reduction was 71% with diet and exercise.[14]

Individuals in Asia and Africa who follow traditional diets low in animal fat and high in complex carbohydrates and who remain physically active have a far lower incidence of diabetes than those who follow a Western diet and activity pattern.[34] Vegetarians also have a lower incidence of diabetes than their omnivorous counterparts.[35]

These results are probably due to several factors. Intake of saturated fat is associated with impaired glucose tolerance, insulin resistance, gestational diabetes, and type 2 diabetes.[36] In contrast, a higher intake of dietary fiber, particularly in the form of fruits and vegetables, results in lower postprandial glucose.[37-39] In addition, high-fiber diets often contain micronutrients important in glucose tolerance. Among these, magnesium may be especially important; a study of over 127,000 men and women found that consuming the highest amount of magnesium was associated with a roughly 35% lower risk for development of type 2 diabetes compared with consuming the least amount.[40]

High intake of heme iron (eg, in meat) is associated with a significantly increased risk of type 2 diabetes.[41]

Diets high in sugars and refined carbohydrates increase risk for GDM.[42]

Nutritional Management

Nutrition therapy may be beneficial in both type 1 and type 2 diabetes.

The goals of nutrition therapy in diabetes management include control of glucose to near-normal levels, normalization of serum lipids and blood pressure, and attainment of a healthy weight. Adherence to a healthful diet, regular exercise, and use of medications when necessary may achieve these goals and help minimize the risk of complications.

Current standards of care for nutrition therapy established by the American Diabetes Association recommend that individuals with diabetes receive individualized dietary counseling, monitor carbohydrate intake, limit saturated fat intake to <7% of total calories, minimize trans fat intake, lose weight if overweight and insulin-resistant, and limit alcohol to ≤1 drink/day for women and ≤2 drinks/day for men.[6]

Recent studies suggest that low-fat, plant-based diets may be more effective for both glycemic control and reduction of cardiovascular risk factors, particularly plasma cholesterol.[43,44] A randomized, controlled trial including 99 individuals with type 2 diabetes showed that among those whose diabetes medications remained stable throughout the 22-week trial, the drop in A1c was significantly greater with a low-fat, vegan diet, compared with a diet following American Diabetes Association guidelines (-1.2 vs 0.4 percentage points, P=0.01). The reductions in body weight, LDL cholesterol, and urinary albumin excretion were also greater on the vegan diet.[44] The diet used in the trial excluded all animal products, avoided added oils, and favored low–glycemic index foods.

A low-fat, plant-based diet influences nutrient intake and body composition in several ways that may, in turn, affect insulin sensitivity:

First, because such diets are low in fat and high in fiber, they typically cause covert reductions in energy density and energy intake, which are not fully compensated for by increased food intake.[45-47] The addition of 14 g of dietary fiber per day is associated with a 10% decrease in energy intake.[46] As a result, low-fat, vegan diets are associated with significant weight loss,[48] an important effect given that increased body fat, especially visceral fat, is associated with insulin resistance.[49]

Independent of their effect on body weight, reductions in total fat intake and in the proportion of dietary saturated fat to unsaturated fat increase insulin sensitivity.[50] Increased carbohydrate intake is associated with increased insulin sensitivity in healthy individuals and with improved glycemic control and reduced cardiovascular risk factors in individuals with type 2 diabetes.[43,51,52]

Carbohydrate type may influence glucose control. A review of 5 studies of individuals with type 1 or type 2 diabetes showed that diets with lower glycemic indices significantly reduced A1c concentrations.[53] Furthermore, diets richer in fiber tend to produce lower postprandial blood glucose concentrations compared with fiber-depleted diets, and high-fiber diets have been shown to improve glycemic control in individuals with type 2 diabetes.[54] Because vegan diets consist solely of plant-derived foods, they are typically high in fiber, compared with nonvegan diets,[55] provided the diet does not rely heavily on processed foods.

Finally, limited evidence suggests that elevated body iron stores are associated with insulin resistance, while reductions in iron stores by any means (eg, dietary alterations or phlebotomy) increase insulin sensitivity.[56] A vegan diet provides iron in its nonheme form, which is somewhat less absorbable than heme iron. A study comparing 30 ovolactovegetarians and 30 meat eaters, all of whom were healthy and had BMIs <23 kg/m^2, showed that the vegetarians had adequate, but lower, body iron stores compared with the meat eaters: serum ferritin concentration

35 μg/L (95% CI, 21-49) versus 72 μg/L (95% CI, 45-100). The vegetarians also demonstrated less insulin resistance than the meat eaters: steady-state plasma glucose concentration 4.1 mmol/L (95% CI, 3.5-5.0) versus 6.9 mmol/L (95% CI, 5.2-7.5).[56]

Similar dietary changes are helpful for patients with type 1 diabetes. A high-fiber diet results in lower insulin requirements and improved management of blood glucose and lipids.[57] The ability of plant-based diets to reduce cardiovascular risk factors is likely to be important in type 1 diabetes as well.

Further study is needed to establish optimal dietary interventions in gestational diabetes. Some evidence suggests that a diet limiting carbohydrates to 40% of calories, with fat providing 40% and protein providing the remaining 20%, improves glycemic control and reduces the need for exogenous insulin.[58] Calorie allowance, if used, should be based on prepregnancy percentage of ideal body weight. Breakfast should be small because of the normal hypercortisolemic morning state in pregnancy, which opposes insulin and raises blood glucose concentrations. Future studies are required to compare a carbohydrate-reduced diet with a low-fat, high-fiber diet, particularly a vegan diet.

Because lifestyle change must be permanent in diabetes, as in many other medical conditions, adherence is a clinical challenge. Researchers have long lamented the poor adherence achieved with typical diets for diabetes.[59] A potential weakness of such diets is that they require portion size limits for overweight persons, and limits on saturated fat intake are based on these limited energy intakes. As a result, individuals who exceed their prescribed energy intake limits with outsized portions can easily exceed recommended limits on saturated fat.

In this respect, vegan diets may present a clinical advantage. Because they include no animal fat, variations in food quantity are less likely to result in substantial increases in saturated fat intake. While vegetarian or vegan diets may sound restrictive, their acceptability in clinical studies is similar to that of seemingly more moderate therapeutic diets.[60-63] Because vegan diets are based on the elimination of certain foods, they require no specified limits on portions, calories, or carbohydrates and may be simpler to understand than regimens that limit quantities of certain foods without proscribing any. While individuals vary in their adherence to therapeutic diets, studies suggest that the more far-reaching the diet changes that are recommended by clinicians, the more changes patients actually make.[64]

Alcohol has mixed effects. Moderate alcohol intake (15 to 30 g of alcohol, equal to 1 to 2 drinks/day) improves insulin sensitivity and is associated with a lower risk for type 2 diabetes.[65,66] However, the association of alcohol intake with these purported benefits has not been proven in controlled clinical trials, and alcohol consumption is not without risks. Higher intakes (>30 g/day) are associated with significantly increased risk for diabetes.[66] For individuals treated with insulin or sulfonylureas, alcohol can increase the risk of hypoglycemia. In addition to potentially increasing breast cancer risk and potentially causing hazardous interactions with medications, alcoholic beverages consumed at mealtime can impair a patient's resolve to follow a healthful diet. Therefore, a physician should discuss alcohol consumption with individuals at risk for type 2 diabetes.

Dietary Supplements in Type 2 Diabetes

Several supplements have been investigated for their role in diabetes management, notably chromium and certain botanicals:

Chromium. The role of chromium as an insulin cofactor was discovered relatively recently.[67] In 1977, Canadian researchers described the case of a woman in her mid-30s who received nutrition parenterally as a result of prior intestinal surgery. Gradually worsening weight loss, hyperglycemia, and neuropathic symptoms led her doctors to institute treatment with increasing insulin doses. Eventually, the addition of chromium to her feeding regimen permitted discontinuance of insulin and marked symptomatic improvement.[68]

Until recently, the mechanism whereby chromium may improve indices of glucose metabolism was unknown. Current evidence indicates that this mineral works by increasing the presence of the main insulin-responsive glucose transporter (GLUT4) to the plasma membrane[69] and by enhancing tyrosine phosphorylation of the insulin receptor.[70]

Dietary Reference Intakes (DRI) for micronutrients do not take into account the increased need for certain nutrients caused by certain diseases, including diabetes. Plasma levels of chromium have been found to be 25% to 30% lower in diabetic persons with mild or severe hypoglycemia than in euglycemic individuals.[71]

Although correcting chromium deficiencies is essential for blood glucose control, it is not yet clear that additional chromium helps. Randomized trials in individuals with type 1, type 2, or gestational diabetes, including trials using daily doses as high as 1000 mcg, have yielded mixed results.[72-74] As a result, most diabetes authorities do not recommend chromium supplements.

According to the Food and Nutrition Board of the Institute of Medicine, the safe and adequate daily intakes of chromium for adults 19 to 50 years of age are 35 mcg for men and 25 mcg for women. For people over 50, the numbers are 30 mcg for men and 20 mcg for women. Most common multiple vitamins include chromium, usually in amounts ranging from 100 mcg to 200 mcg.

Magnesium. A meta-analysis of randomized controlled trials of supplemental magnesium found significant decreases in fasting glucose and improvements in HDL concentrations. The median dose was approximately 360 mg/day. Among treated groups, the mean fasting blood glucose concentration was approximately 10 mg/dL (0.56 mmol/L) lower, and HDL cholesterol was 3 mg/dL (0.08 mmol/L) higher, compared with untreated groups.[75] Apparently, magnesium increases insulin sensitivity and may also increase insulin secretion.

Increased magnesium intakes can be achieved through diet without the use of supplements. Foods rich in magnesium include whole grains (eg, brown rice, barley, and oats) and green vegetables, such as spinach and Swiss chard. Many bean varieties are also rich in magnesium. In the Harvard Nurses' Health Study, women who had more magnesium in their diets had a significantly lower likelihood of developing diabetes.[76] In the Harvard study, a "high" intake was about 400 milligrams per day.

Botanicals. The role of certain botanicals for patients with type 2 diabetes is also under investigation. Metformin, for example, was developed from *Galega officinalis* (French lilac).[77]

Cinnamon has been shown to cut fasting glucose levels by 10 percent to 29 percent.[78] Effects may be dose-dependent; researchers have observed no change in blood glucose at 1.8 g/d but a significant improvement in fasting glucose at 3g/d.[79] Some of cinnamon's helpful effects might be explained by polyphenol polymers, which have an insulin-like action.[80]

The production of nitric oxide (important in signaling glucose uptake in skeletal muscle) is increased by American ginseng,[81] which has been found in small studies to lower postprandial glucose in both diabetic and nondiabetic individuals.[82] Bitter melon (*Momordica charantia*), a botanical with insulin-mimetic and gluconeogenesis-inhibiting effects, has also demonstrated blood glucose-lowering effects in humans.[83]

In spite of these encouraging findings, problems remain with the use of botanicals in diabetes. Clinical trials of ginseng and bitter melon have included only small numbers of persons, and studies suffer from a lack of standardization of active ingredients.[84] Long-term safety and efficacy have not been established. Patients should be aware that, even in trials showing improvement in glycemic control, glucose levels typically do not return to normal, so medications will still be required.

Orders

A low-fat, nondairy vegetarian (vegan) diet may be preferable for patients with diabetes. An emphasis on low–glycemic index foods provides additional benefits. A diet following ADA guidelines may also be considered, particularly for those who have already had good success with this approach.

Pregnant patients should work closely with a dietitian to ensure adequate nutrient intake.

See also Basic Diet Orders chapter.

Nutrition consultation is essential for advising patient in above dietary recommendations and arranging follow-up.

Exercise prescription, individualized.

What to Tell the Family

The risk of developing type 2 and gestational diabetes can be reduced through healthful dietary habits and regular physical activity (see Basic Diet Orders chapter). These measures are important even in individuals who are not overweight. In established disease, the risk of complications is reduced through the healthful dietary habits, particularly a low-fat vegan diet emphasizing low–glycemic index foods. Exercise, self-monitoring of blood glucose, and use of appropriate oral medication and/or insulin are also key parts of diabetes management. Family members can help prevent and more effectively manage diabetes by following similar dietary recommendations.

References

1. Dahlquist GG, Patterson C, Soltesz G. Perinatal risk factors for childhood type 1 diabetes in Europe. The EURODIAB Substudy 2 Study Group. *Diabetes Care*. 1999;22:1698-1702.

2. Chan JM, Rimm EB, Colditz GA, et al. Obesity, fat distribution and weight gain as risk factors for clinical diabetes in men. *Diabetes Care*. 1994;17:961-969.

3. Centers for Disease Control. Prenatal care and pregnancies complicated by diabetes. US reporting areas, 1989. *MMWR CDC Surveill Summ.* 1993;42:119-122.

4. Innes KE, Byers TE, Marshall JA, et al. Association of a woman's own birth weight with subsequent risk for gestational diabetes. *JAMA.* 2002;287:2534-2541.

5. Knutson KL, Ryden AM, Mander BA, Van Cauter E. Role of sleep duration and quality in the risk and severity of type 2 diabetes mellitus. *Arch Intern Med.* 2006;166:1768-1774.

6. American Diabetes Association. Standards of Medical Care in Diabetes--2007. *Diabetes Care.* 2007;30:S4-S41.

7. American College of Obstetricians and Gynecologists. Gestational Diabetes. ACOG Practice Bulletin No. 30. Washington, DC: American College of Obstetricians and Gynecologists; 2001.

8. Schrader HM, Jovanovic-Peterson L, Bevier W, Peterson CM. Fasting plasma glucose and glycosylated protein at 24 to 28 weeks of gestation predict macrosomia in the general obstetric population. *Am J Perinatol.* 1995;12:247-251.

9. Strine TW, Okoro CA, Chapman DP, Beckles GL, Balluz L, Mokdad AH. The impact of formal diabetes education on the preventive health practices and behaviors of persons with type 2 diabetes. *Prev Med.* 2005;41:79-84.

10. National Heart, Lung, and Blood Institute changes intensive blood sugar treatment strategy in clinical trial of diabetes and cardiovascular diseases [press release]. National Institutes of Health website (NIH News). Available at: http://public.nhlbi.nih.gov/newsroom/home/GetPressRelease.aspx?id=2551. Accessed April 9, 2008.

11. Nissen SE, Wolski K. Effect of rosiglitazone on the risk of myocardial infarction and death from cardiovascular causes. *N Engl J Med.* 2007;356:2457-2471.

12. Dunstan DW, Salmon J, Owen N, et al. Physical activity and television viewing in relation to risk of undiagnosed abnormal glucose metabolism in adults. *Diabetes Care.* 2004;27:2603-2609.

13. Laaksonen DE, Lindstrom J, Lakka TA, et al. Physical activity in the prevention of type 2 diabetes: the Finnish diabetes prevention study. *Diabetes.* 2005;54:158-165.

14. Knowler WC, Barrett-Connor E, Fowler SE, et al. Reduction in the incidence of type 2 diabetes with lifestyle intervention or metformin. *N Engl J Med.* 2002;346:393-403.

15. Davey Smith G, Bracha Y, Svendsen KH, et al. Incidence of type 2 diabetes in the randomized multiple risk factor intervention trial. *Ann Intern Med.* 2005;142:313-322.

16. Boulé NG, Haddad E, Kenny GP, Wells GA, Sigal RJ. Effects of exercise on glycemic control and body mass in type 2 diabetes mellitus: a meta-analysis of controlled clinical trials. *JAMA.* 2001;286:1218-1227.

17. Santeusanio F, Di Loreto C, Lucidi P, et al. Diabetes and exercise. *J Endocrinol Invest.* 2003;26:937-940.

18. Stewart KJ. Role of exercise training on cardiovascular disease in persons who have type 2 diabetes and hypertension. *Cardiol Clin.* 2004;22:569-586.

19. Zhang C, Solomon CG, Manson JE, Hu FB. A prospective study of pregravid physical activity and sedentary behaviors in relation to the risk for gestational diabetes mellitus. *Arch Intern Med.* 2006;166:543-548.

20. Butte NF. Carbohydrate and lipid metabolism in pregnancy: normal compared with gestational diabetes mellitus. *Am J Clin Nutr.* 2000;71(suppl 5):1256S-1261S.

21. Virtanen SM, Knip M. Nutritional risk predictors of beta cell autoimmunity and type 1 diabetes at a young age. *Am J Clin Nutr.* 2003;78:1053-1067.

22. Akerblom HK, Vaarala O, Hyoty H, Ilonen J, Knip M. Environmental factors in the etiology of type 1 diabetes. *Am J Med Genet*. 2002;115:18-29.

23. Saukkonen T, Virtanen SM, Karppinen M, et al. Significance of cow's milk protein antibodies as risk factor for childhood IDDM: interactions with dietary cow's milk intake and HLA-DQB1 genotype. Childhood Diabetes in Finland Study Group. *Diabetologia*. 1998;41:72-78.

24. American Academy of Pediatrics. Infant feeding practices and their possible relationship to the etiology of diabetes mellitus. *Pediatrics*. 1994;94:752-754.

25. Rogers LM, Jovanovic L, Becker DJ. Should she or shouldn't she?: the relationship between infant feeding practices and type 1 diabetes in the genetically at risk. *Diabetes Care*. 2005;28:2809-2812.

26. Tiittanen M, Paronen J, Savilahti E, et al. Dietary insulin as an immunogen and tolerogen. *Pediatr Allergy Immunol*. 2006;17:538-543.

27. Akerblom HK, Virtanen SM, Ilonen J, et al. Dietary manipulation of beta cell autoimmunity in infants at increased risk of type 1 diabetes: a pilot study. *Diabetologia*. 2005;48:829-837.

28. Ziegler AG, Schmid S, Huber D, Hummel M, Bonifacio E. Early infant feeding and risk of developing type 1 diabetes-associated autoantibodies. *JAMA*. 2003;290:1721-1728.

29. Norris JM, Barriga K, Klingensmith G, et al. Timing of initial cereal exposure in infancy and risk of islet autoimmunity. *JAMA*. 2003;290:1713-1720.

30. Pastore MR, Bazzigaluppi E, Belloni C, Arcovio C, Bonifacio E, Bosi E. Six months of gluten-free diet do not influence autoantibody titers, but improve insulin secretion in subjects at high risk for type 1 diabetes. *J Clin Endocrinol Metab*. 2003;88:162-165.

31. Vitoria JC, Castano L, Rica I, Bilbao JR, Arrieta A, Garcia-Masdevall MD. Association of insulin-dependent diabetes mellitus and celiac disease: a study based on serologic markers. *J Pediatr Gastroenterol Nutr*. 1998;27:47-52.

32. Stene LC, Joner G, and the Norwegian Childhood Diabetes Study Group. Use of cod liver oil during the first year of life is associated with lower risk of childhood-onset type 1 diabetes: a large, population-based, case-control study. *Am J Clin Nutr*. 2003;78:1128-1134.

33. Rabinovitch A. An update on cytokines in the pathogenesis of insulin-dependent diabetes mellitus. *Diabetes Metab Rev*. 1998;14:129-151.

34. Fujimoto WY, Bergstrom RW, Boyko EJ, et al. Diabetes and diabetes risk factors in second- and third-generation Japanese Americans in Seattle, Washington. *Diabetes Res Clin Prac*. 1994;24(suppl):S43-S52.

35. Snowdon DA, Phillips RL. Does a vegetarian diet reduce the occurrence of diabetes? *Am J Public Health*. 1985;75:507-512.

36. Montonen J, Knekt P, Harkanen T, et al. Dietary patterns and the incidence of type 2 diabetes. *Am J Epidemiol*. 2005;161:219-227.

37. Liese AD, Schulz M, Moore CG, Mayer-Davis EJ. Dietary patterns, insulin sensitivity, and adiposity in the multi-ethnic Insulin Resistance Atherosclerosis Study population. *Br J Nutr*. 2004;92:973-984.

38. Ylonen K, Alfthan G, Groop L, Saloranta C, Aro A, Virtanen SM. Dietary intakes and plasma concentrations of carotenoids and tocopherols in relation to glucose metabolism in subjects at high risk of type 2 diabetes: the Botnia Dietary Study. *Am J Clin Nutr*. 2003;77:1434-1441.

39. Ford ES, Mokdad AH. Fruit and vegetable consumption and diabetes mellitus incidence among U.S. adults. *Prev Med.* 2001;32:33-39.

40. Lopez-Ridaura R, Willett WC, Rimm EB, et al. Magnesium intake and risk of type 2 diabetes in men and women. *Diabetes Care.* 2004;27:134-140.

41. Rajpathak S, Ma J, Manson J, Willett WC, Hu FB. Iron intake and the risk of type 2 diabetes in women: a prospective cohort study. *Diabetes Care.* 2006;29:1370-1376.

42. Zhang C, Schulze MB, Solomon CG, Hu FB. A prospective study of dietary patterns, meat intake and the risk of gestational diabetes mellitus. *Diabetologia.* 2006;49:2604-2613.

43. Barnard RJ, Jung T, Inkeles SB. Diet and exercise in the treatment of NIDDM: the need for early emphasis. *Diab Care.* 1994;17:1469-1472.

44. Barnard ND, Cohen J, Jenkins DJ, et al. A low-fat, vegan diet improves glycemic control and cardiovascular risk factors in a randomized clinical trial in individuals with type 2 diabetes. *Diab Care.* 2006;29:1777-1783.

45. Kendall A, Levitsky DA, Strupp BJ, Lissner L. Weight loss on a low-fat diet: consequence of the imprecision of the control of food intake in humans. *Am J Clin Nutr.* 1991;53:1124-1129.

46. Howarth NC, Saltzman E, Roberts SB. Dietary fiber and weight regulation. *Nutr Rev.* 2001;59:129-139.

47. Bell EA, Rolls BJ. Energy density of foods affects energy intake across multiple levels of fat content in lean and obese women. *Am J Clin Nutr.* 2001;73:1010-1018.

48. Barnard ND, Scialli AR, Turner-McGrievy G, Lanou AJ, Glass J. The effects of a low-fat, plant-based dietary intervention on body weight, metabolism, and insulin sensitivity. *Am J Med.* 2005;118:991-997.

49. Bonora E. Relationship between regional fat distribution and insulin resistance. *Int J Obes Relat Metab Disord.* 2000;24(suppl 2):S32-S35.

50. Lovejoy JC, Windhauser MM, Rood JC, de la Bretonne JA. Effect of a controlled high-fat versus low-fat diet on insulin sensitivity and leptin levels in African-American and Caucasian women. *Metab.* 1998;47:1520-1524.

51. Brunzell JD, Lerner RL, Hazzard WR, Porte D, Bierman EL. Improved glucose tolerance with high carbohydrate feeding in mild diabetes. *N Eng J Med.* 1971;284:521-524.

52. Fukagawa NK, Anderson JW, Hageman G, Young VR, Minaker KL. High-carbohydrate, high-fiber diets increase peripheral insulin sensitivity in healthy young and old adults. *Am J Clin Nutr.* 1990;52:524-528.

53. Brand Miller JC. Importance of glycemic index in diabetes. *Am J Clin Nutr.* 1994;59(suppl):747S-752S.

54. Chandalia M, Garg A, Lutjohann D, von Bergmann K, Grundy SM, Brinkley LJ. Beneficial effects of high dietary fiber intake in patients with type 2 diabetes mellitus. *N Engl J Med.* 2000;342:1392-1398.

55. Turner-McGrievy GM, Barnard ND, Scialli AR, Lanou AJ. Effects of a low-fat, vegan diet and a Step II diet on macro- and micronutrient intakes in overweight, postmenopausal women. *Nutrition.* 2004;20:738-746.

56. Hua NW, Stoohs RA, Facchini FS. Low iron status and enhanced insulin sensitivity in lacto-ovo-vegetarians. *Br J Nutr.* 2001;86:515-519.

57. Anderson JW, Randles KM, Kendall CWC, Jenkins DJA. Carbohydrate and fiber recommendations for individuals with diabetes: a quantitative assessment and meta-analysis of the evidence. *J Am Coll Nutr.* 2004;23:5-17.

58. Major CA, Henry MJ, De Veciana M, Morgan MA. The effects of carbohydrate restriction in patients with diet-controlled gestational diabetes. *Obstet Gynecol.* 1998;91:600-604.

59. Laitinen JH, Ahola IE, Sarkkinen ES, Winberg RL, Harmaakorpi-Iivonen PA, Uusitupa MI. Impact of intensified dietary therapy on energy and nutrient intakes and fatty acid composition of serum lipids in patients with recently diagnosed non-insulin-dependent diabetes mellitus. *J Am Diet Assoc.* 1993;93:276-283.

60. Franklin TL, Kolasa KM, Griffin K, Mayo C, Badenhop DT. Adherence to very-low-fat diet by a group of cardiac rehabilitation patients in the rural southeastern United States. *Arch Fam Med.* 1995;4:551-554.

61. Toobert DJ, Glasgow RE, Radcliffe JL. Physiologic and related behavioral outcomes from the Women's Lifestyle Heart Trial. *Ann Behav Med.* 2000;22:1-9.

62. Ornish DM, Lee KL, Fair WR, Pettengill EB, Carroll PR. Dietary trial in prostate cancer: Early experience and implications for clinical trial design. *Urology.* 2001;57(suppl 1):200-201.

63. Barnard ND, Scialli AR, Turner-McGrievy GM, Lanou AJ. Acceptability of a very-low-fat, vegan diet compares favorably to a more moderate low-fat diet in a randomized, controlled trial. *J Cardiopulm Rehab.* 2004;24:229-235.

64. Barnard ND, Akhtar A, Nicholson A. Factors that facilitate compliance to lower fat intake. *Arch Fam Med.* 1995;4:153-158.

65. Beulens JW, Stolk RP, van der Schouw YT, Grobbee DE, Hendriks HF, Bots ML. Alcohol consumption and risk of type 2 diabetes among older women. *Diabetes Care.* 2005;28:2933-2938.

66. van de Wiel A. Diabetes mellitus and alcohol. *Diabetes Metab Res Rev.* 2004;20:263-267.

67. Mertz W. Chromium occurrence and function in biological systems. *Physiol Rev.* 1969;49:163-239.

68. Jeejeebhoy KN, Chu RC, Marliss EB, Greenberg GR, Bruce-Robertson A. Chromium deficiency, glucose intolerance, and neuropathy reversed by chromium supplementation, in a patient receiving long-term total parenteral nutrition. *Am J Clin Nutr.* 1977;30:531-538.

69. Chen G, Liu P, Pattar GR, et al. Chromium activates GLUT4 trafficking and enhances insulin-stimulated glucose transport in 3T3-L1 adipocytes via a cholesterol-dependent mechanism. *Mol Endocrinol.* 2005;20:857- 870.

70. Wang H, Kruszewski A, Brautigan DL. Cellular chromium enhances activation of insulin receptor kinase. *Biochemistry.* 2005;44:8167-8175.

71. Cheng HH, Lai MH, Hou WC, Huang CL. Antioxidant effects of chromium supplementation with type 2 diabetes mellitus and euglycemic subjects. *J Agric Food Chem.* 2004;52:1385-1389.

72. Ryan GJ, Wanko NS, Redman AR, Cook CB. Chromium as adjunctive treatment for type 2 diabetes. *Ann Pharmacother.* 2003;37:876-885.

73. Cefalu WT, Hu FB. Role of chromium in human health and in diabetes. *Diabetes Care.* 2004;27:2741-2751.

74. Kleefstra N, Houweling ST, Jansman FG, et al. Chromium treatment has no effect in patients with poorly controlled, insulin-treated type 2 diabetes in an obese Western population: a randomized, double-blind, placebo-controlled trial. *Diabetes Care.* 2006;29:521-525.

75. Song Y, He K, Levitan EB, Manson JE, Liu S. Effects of oral magnesium supplementation on glycaemic control in Type 2 diabetes: a meta-analysis of randomized double-blind controlled trials. *Diabet Med.* 2006;23:1050-1056.

76. Song Y, Manson JE, Buring JE, Liu S. Dietary magnesium intake in relation to plasma insulin levels and risk of type 2 diabetes in women. *Diab Care.* 2004;27:59-65.

77. Vuksan V, Sievenpiper JL. Herbal remedies in the management of diabetes: lessons learned from the study of ginseng. *Nutr Metab Cardiovasc Dis.* 2005;15:149-160.

78. Khan A, Safdar M, Khan MMA, Khattak KN, Anderson RA. Cinnamon improves glucose and lipids of people with type 2 diabetes. *Diabetes Care.* 2003;26:3215-3218.

79. Altschuler JA, Casella SJ, MacKenzie TA, Curtis KM. The effect of cinnamon on A1C among adolescents with type 1 diabetes. *Diabetes Care.* 2007;30:813-816.

80. Anderson RA, Broadhurst CL, Polansky MM, et al. Isolation and characterization of polyphenol type-A polymers from cinnamon with insulin-like biological activity. *J Agric Food Chem.* 2004;52:65-70.

81. Han K, Shin IC, Choi KJ, Yun YP, Hong JT, Oh KW. Korea red ginseng water extract increases nitric oxide concentrations in exhaled breath. *Nitric Oxide.* 2005;12:159-162.

82. Yeh GY, Eisenberg DM, Kaptchuk TJ, Phillips RS. Systematic review of herbs and dietary supplements for glycemic control in diabetes. *Diabetes Care.* 2003;26:1277-1294.

83. Dey L, Attele AS, Yuan CS. Alternative therapies for type 2 diabetes. *Altern Med Rev.* 2002;7:45-58.

84. Sievenpiper JL, Arnason JT, Vidgen E, Leiter LA, Vuksan V. A systematic quantitative analysis of the literature of the high variability in ginseng (Panax spp.): Should ginseng be trusted in diabetes? *Diabetes Care.* 2004;27:839-840.

75. Complications of Diabetes Mellitus

Diabetes mellitus (DM), both type 1 and type 2, affects many organ systems, particularly the heart, eyes, kidneys, and the peripheral and autonomic nervous systems. Also, macrosomia and birth complications occur more often in infants born to women with inadequately controlled diabetes mellitus.

Prevention of macrovascular complications depends on control of the major risk factors for cardiac disease, such as smoking, blood pressure, and blood lipid concentrations; blood glucose control has been less effective in controlled trials. For prevention of microvascular damage, glycemic control is essential. Control of blood pressure and other vascular parameters is also important.

1. Cardiac Complications[1]

Cardiovascular disease (CVD) is the leading cause of mortality in individuals with diabetes. Morbidity due to CVD is also common.

Control of cardiac risk factors is therefore critical, particularly smoking, hypertension, and dyslipidemias (see CHD, Hypertension, and Dyslipidemias chapters).

Risk Factors

Smoking.

Hypertension.

Dyslipidemia.

Obesity.

Microalbuminuria.

Hyperglycemia.

Gender. Women with diabetes have greater risk of cardiac complications.

Diagnosis

Patients with diabetes may have atypical presentations for CVD. Screening with electrocardiogram or cardiac stress tests may be appropriate in some patients.

Hypertension

Blood pressure control is particularly important for individuals with diabetes. The goal blood pressure should be less than 130/80 mm Hg, and further lowering may be beneficial (see Hypertension chapter).

Hyperlipidemia

The goals for blood lipid concentrations are also somewhat different for patients with diabetes. LDL should be less than 100 mg/dL, and in certain patients (especially those with known CVD), the goal may be less than 70 mg/dL. In known cases of CVD, triglycerides should be less than 150 and HDL greater than 40 mg/dL. HDL greater than 50 mg/dL may be an appropriate goal for women (see Dyslipidemias chapter).

Treatment

Dietary and behavioral modifications, including smoking cessation, regular exercise, and loss of excess weight, are critical for the prevention and management of cardiac complications in diabetes patients.

When further therapy is needed, specific medicines are usually helpful.

Aspirin therapy (75–325 mg/d) is recommended for most persons older than 30 years, particularly in the presence of additional cardiovascular risk factors or documented cardiovascular disease. Potential side effects, including bleeding, must be considered. Because of the risk of Reye syndrome, aspirin therapy should not be instituted in patients under 21 years.

Hypertension

Hypertension in diabetes should be treated with an angiotensin-converting enzyme (ACE) inhibitor or angiotensin receptor blocker (ARB). Further drugs to lower blood pressure may be required. These include diuretics, beta-blockers, and calcium channel blockers (see Hypertension chapter).

Hyperlipidemia

Statins and fibrates are likely to be effective in reducing cardiovascular events, and other lipid-lowering therapies may also be tried in combination (see Dyslipidemias chapter).

Nutritional Considerations

To reduce the risk of cardiac complications, the appropriate dietary changes are those that improve plasma lipid concentrations, reduce blood pressure, and control glycemia. These steps are discussed in detail in the chapters on coronary heart disease, hyperlipidemia, hypertension, and diabetes.

A substantial body of evidence suggests that a combination of a vegetarian diet, regular exercise, smoking cessation, and stress management yields greater improvements in indices of cardiovascular disease, compared with other regimens.[2,3] The Multicenter Lifestyle Demonstration Project, which included 440 patients with coronary artery disease, of whom 91 also had diabetes, showed that such a regimen is effective in individuals with diabetes, just as it is for those without diabetes.[4] In a randomized, controlled trial of individuals with type 2 diabetes, a low-fat, vegan diet reduced LDL cholesterol concentrations by 21% and reduced triglycerides by 16% among participants whose lipid-lowering medications were held constant.[5] The type of carbohydrate that predominates in the therapeutic diet may be clinically important. Diets high in refined carbohydrate may increase triglyceride concentrations for some individuals, but high-carbohydrate diets that are drawn from high-fiber and low—glycemic index foods appear to have the opposite result.[6]

A randomized controlled clinical trial of alpha-lipoic acid, administered at 800 mg/d for 4 months, showed improvements in symptoms of cardiac autonomic neuropathy.[7] Further study with a larger number of individuals is required before this treatment can be recommended.

2. Ophthalmic Complications

Glaucoma and Cataracts

Glaucoma and cataracts may develop earlier in diabetes patients, compared with those without diabetes (see Glaucoma and Cataract chapters).

Retinopathy

In diabetes, pathologic changes in the retinal vasculature pose a major long-term threat to vision. In nonproliferative diabetic retinopathy, microaneurysms, small "dot and blot" hemorrhages, hard exudates (lipid material that can be toxic to the retina), and retinal infarcts known as "cotton wool spots" appear. These changes tend to concentrate in the macula, where they can blur and distort central vision.

In proliferative retinopathy (neovascularization), fragile, abnormal vessels grow into the vitreous, presumably in response to ischemia. Vitreous hemorrhage causes symptoms ranging from "floaters" to complete visual obscuration. Ultimately, tractional retinal detachment can result. Retinopathy is not painful, so the condition can progress undetected by the patient.

Good blood glucose control, as indicated by a low hemoglobin A1c, can reduce the risk of ophthalmic involvement and slow its progression.[8-12] Similarly, blood pressure control is important, as poorly controlled hypertension increases the severity of retinopathy.[13-15]

Risk Factors

Poor blood glucose control.

Hypertension.

Duration of diabetes.

Smoking.

Diagnosis

Retinopathy can be diagnosed by ophthalmoscopy with dilated pupils.

Use of a fundus lens at the slit lamp allows a stereoscopic view and facilitates diagnosis of macular edema.

In fluorescein angiography, an intravenous injection of fluorescein followed by serial photography of the fundus reveals leakage from microaneurysms, nonperfusion, and other useful information to guide therapy.

Treatment

For proliferative retinopathy where vitreous hemorrhage appears likely, panretinal laser photocoagulation often stabilizes neovascularization or even causes it to regress.

When diabetic retinopathy causes clinically significant macular edema (defined by severity of leakage and proximity to the central macula), photocoagulation can slow progression.[16] Individual microaneurysms can be obliterated, or a broader grid photocoagulated, if the leakage pattern is diffuse. Intravitreal steroids and vascular endothelial growth factor inhibitors may also play a role in treatment.

Nutritional Considerations

Nutritional interventions that improve control of blood glucose, blood pressure, and lipid concentrations may help prevent or slow ophthalmic complications.

Glaucoma

Most individuals with diabetes are known to be insulin resistant, and evidence indicates that 85% of persons with type 2 diabetes also have the metabolic syndrome.[17] Both of these conditions are associated with elevated intraocular pressure, a well-known risk factor for glaucoma.[18] Control of high blood pressure (a component of the metabolic syndrome) is also important in the care of glaucoma (see Glaucoma chapter). Dietary treatments that address these underlying conditions have not yet been found to prevent or treat glaucoma.

Cataract

Individuals with diabetes are at increased risk for cataract. However, no controlled clinical trials using nutrition therapies indicate that diet changes reduce this risk among individuals with diabetes. In the general population, a number of dietary factors are associated with lower cataract risk, including maintenance of ideal weight and normal lipid levels, high intake of antioxidant-containing foods, avoidance of alcohol, and avoidance of sources of galactose (ie, dairy products) (see Cataract chapter).

Retinopathy

Evidence indicates that control of blood glucose,[11,12] blood pressure,[19] and blood cholesterol[20] reduces the onset and progression of diabetic retinopathy.[21,22] A specific diet therapy suitable for prevention of retinopathy has not yet been established. However, evidence from the Diabetes Complications and Control Trial (DCCT) associated diets high in fat and low in fiber with progression of retinopathy,[23] suggesting that low-fat, high-fiber diets diet may have promise for reducing retinopathy risk.

3. Nephropathy

Diabetic nephropathy involves pathologic changes to the kidney vasculature. If uncontrolled, the disease progresses from microalbuminuria to macroalbuminuria and an elevated plasma creatinine concentration, and eventually to end-stage disease requiring dialysis or transplant. Pathogenesis involves hypertension, ischemia, hyperglycemia, and advanced glycosylation end products. Persistently elevated blood glucose, blood pressure, and cholesterol and triglyceride concentrations are associated with microalbuminuria.[24]

Risk Factors

All individuals with diabetes are at risk for nephropathy. Pima Indians with type 2 diabetes have a particularly high susceptibility to nephropathy, with incidence of up to 50% after 20 years. However, Pimas living in the United States are at much higher risk compared with Pimas in Mexico, suggesting that the risk among Pimas may be partly mediated by diet and lifestyle rather than genetic factors. African Americans with type 2 DM appear to have more than 4 times the risk of end-stage renal disease compared with Caucasians.[25] This may also be true for Native Americans and Mexican Americans.[26]

Risk factors include:

Family history of diabetes nephropathy.

Poor blood glucose control.

Concomitant hypertension.

Elevated glomerular filtration rate.

Dietary factors (see Nutritional Considerations below).

Other possible risk factors include obesity, increasing age, duration of DM, and smoking.

Diagnosis

Microalbuminuria, defined as a persistent loss of albumin in the urine of 30 to 299 mg/d, is the first indication of nephropathy. Macroalbuminuria is diagnosed when urinary albumin losses are ≥300 mg/d.

A random urine specimen with an albumin concentration of greater than 30 mg/L suggests microalbuminuria. False-negative or false-positive results may occur due to urine volume at time of collection.

A urine albumin-creatinine ratio with a value of 30 μg/mg or greater also suggests microalbuminuria.

Transient microalbuminuria may occur with hyperglycemia, exercise, heart failure, and febrile illness.

When screening suggests microalbuminuria, a repeat specimen (albumin-creatinine ratio) should be obtained after waiting at least 1 to 2 weeks. A standard urine test strip can usually detect macroalbuminuria (1+ or greater). Albumin-specific test strips can detect microalbuminuria. However, false-negatives and false-positives are possible when using test strips. Twenty-four-hour urine samples are not required to make these diagnoses.

Treatment

Treatment recommendations for nephropathy are similar in type 1 and type 2 diabetes.

Glycemic control is essential for preventing further kidney damage.

Treatment with angiotensin-converting enzyme (ACE) inhibitors and/or angiotensin receptor blockers (ARBs) helps prevent the progression of microalbuminuria to more severe renal disease. This approach is especially important if hypertension is present, and target blood pressure to reduce vascular complications is less than 130/80 mm Hg. Diltiazem, verapamil, and low-dose diuretics (because hypertension in diabetes is often volume dependent) may also be indicated.

Control of plasma cholesterol and triglyceride concentrations is important (see Dyslipidemias chapter for details on optimizing LDL, HDL, and triglycerides).

Weight loss is helpful, perhaps because of its beneficial effects on glucose, blood pressure, and lipid control.[27]

Nutritional Considerations

Reducing saturated fat, cholesterol, and animal protein intake may reduce the risk for or progression of nephropathy. Elevated cholesterol is a risk factor for nephropathy[28] and end-stage renal disease.[29] Cholesterol-lowering treatment was found to retard the progression of diabetic nephropathy.[30]

Restriction of animal protein reduces the progression of diabetic nephropathy.[31] Excessive intake of total protein and animal protein has been shown to increase urinary albumin excretion.[32] In short-term studies, proteinuria has been reduced through the use of vegetarian diets[33] and diets deriving protein primarily from soy and other plant sources.[34] These diets also facilitate blood pressure control,[3] which further helps reduce diabetic nephropathy progression.[35]

Dietary sodium restriction is indicated for a number of reasons, including prevention or treatment of microalbuminuria. It is also important because sodium excess may offset both the antihypertensive and antiproteinuric effects of renin-angiotensin system-blocking drugs.[36]

4. Neuropathy

Neuropathy is a particularly common diabetes complication, affecting approximately half of all diabetes patients. Distal symmetric polyneuropathy is the most common presentation; however, neuropathy can also involve the autonomic nervous system and individual nerves.

The disease may present with sensory loss but also with paresthesia and dysesthesia in the affected areas. Pathogenesis may occur due to ischemia and metabolic factors, including advanced glycosylation end products. Progression is likely. If severe, neuropathy may lead to joint deformities and infections that ultimately require amputation.

Risk Factors

Poor blood glucose control. Good glycemic control helps prevent neuropathy, and improvement of previously poor glycemic control can improve neuropathic symptoms.[10]

Duration of diabetes.

Smoking, dyslipidemia, hypertension, and obesity may also contribute to risk.

Diagnosis

The presence of distal symmetric polyneuropathy can be assessed with simple clinical tests. Altered sensation, whether vibration (128 Hz tuning fork), pain (pin-prick), temperature, or pressure (10-g monofilament at dorsal aspect of great toe), or absence of ankle reflexes suggests neuropathy. The use of more than one test increases diagnostic accuracy.[1] Electrophysiologic studies, such as nerve conduction tests, can confirm the diagnosis.

The presence of autonomic neuropathy can often be assessed by history and physical examination. Constipation, incontinence, erectile dysfunction, tachycardia, pupillary dysfunction, and orthostatic hypotension, among other abnormalities, suggest autonomic neuropathy.

Treatment

Diabetes neuropathy is best addressed through primary prevention, which requires tight glycemic control. In cases of pre-existing neuropathy, symptoms may improve with diet and lifestyle changes, as noted below.

In addition to optimized glycemic control, foot care is essential. Properly fitted shoes, foot hygiene, daily foot inspection (special mirrors can help patients who have mobility problems), regular nail care (without cutting nails too short), and immediate consultation with a health care provider whenever an abnormality occurs are all important.

Medications also may help alleviate pain symptoms of diabetes neuropathy. Examples include:

Tricyclic antidepressants.

Duloxetine, a dual serotonin and norepinephrine reuptake inhibitor.

Topical lidocaine and **capsaicin cream.**

Anticonvulsants such as gabapentin, carbamazepine, and lamotrigine. Pregabalin is structurally similar to gabapentin but has a different mechanism of action and may be more effective.

Mexiletine may be tried in consultation with a cardiologist, if pain persists.

Long-acting narcotics and **tramadol** may be used in patients for whom addiction is not a concern.

Medications may treat autonomic symptoms, such as erectile dysfunction, gastric abnormalities, and incontinence. These treatments usually improve quality of life but do not alter the disease course.

Nutritional Considerations

A combination of a vegetarian diet and exercise may have particular value in treating neuropathy. In a study of 21 individuals with painful neuropathy, symptoms completely disappeared in 17 and improved in the remainder using a vegan diet along with regular walking.[37] Evidence suggests that in addition to the effect of vegetarian diets on glycemic control, their effect on body weight, blood pressure, lipids, and blood rheology may be relevant to neuropathy.[38,39] Future clinical trials are needed to determine the value of dietary modifications for this condition.

In addition to the benefits of a diet and exercise regimen, some nutritional supplements have shown potential benefit. Alpha-lipoic acid, in both intravenous and oral forms ($\geq$600 mg/d), appears to be safe and effective for improving symptoms of diabetic neuropathy in clinical trials.[40,41] In a multicenter controlled trial that included 181 patients, a combined symptom score (including stabbing pain, burning pain, paresthesia, and numbness) was significantly reduced by oral lipoic acid dosed at 600 mg/d.[42] Long-term safety and efficacy have yet to be established. Although an antioxidant action is presumed, alpha-lipoic acid also improves microcirculation.[43]

Oral supplementation of the acetyl form of the amino compound L-carnitine (acetyl-L-carnitine, ALC) has also been found helpful for peripheral neuropathy in diabetes. An analysis of two double-blind, placebo-controlled, randomized multi-center trials in which roughly 1,300 patients were given 500 mg or 1,000 mg ALC 3 times daily for 1 year found significant improvements in pain, sural nerve fiber numbers, and nerve fiber regeneration. Some improvement in vibration perception was also noted, although nerve conduction velocities and amplitudes did not improve.[44] Another double-blind, placebo-controlled, randomized multi-center trial of 333 patients given 2,000 mg of ALC per day found that, compared with placebo, ALC provided a statistically significant improvement in nerve conduction velocity and amplitude and significantly improved pain scores.[45]

Other supplements under investigation for neuropathy treatment include gammalinolenic acid [46,47] and magnesium.[48]

5. Complications for the Newborn

Women with diabetes should plan their pregnancies so blood glucose can be well controlled prior to conception. Good glucose control during pregnancy decreases the risk of complications, such as congenital anomalies, miscarriage, macrosomia, and birth trauma, and reduces the need for cesarean section.

Because of the insulin antagonist effect of pregnancy, some women develop DM only during pregnancy (gestational diabetes). Although gestational diabetes is not associated with an increase in congenital anomalies or miscarriage, it can cause the other difficulties noted above. Complications of delivery, including shoulder dystocia, increase with newborns that are more than 4,000 grams (macrosomic). Control of blood sugar (eg, with insulin) reduces this risk.[49,50]

See the Diabetes Mellitus chapter for more treatment information.

Nutritional Considerations

Guidelines set forth by the American Diabetes Association (ADA) suggest that all women with gestational diabetes receive nutritional counseling by a registered dietitian that is individualized to meet maternal weight, height, and pregnancy needs, consistent with the maternal blood glucose goals that have been established. ADA guidelines further recommend that obese (BMI >30 kg/m^2) women with gestational diabetes restrict calories by 33% (to ~25 kcal/kg actual weight per day). Restriction of carbohydrates to 35% to 40% of calories is also recommended, owing to evidence that doing so decreases maternal glucose levels and improves maternal and fetal outcomes.[51]

Some evidence suggests that a high-fiber diet may be useful for preventing gestational diabetes and its complications. A study of over 13,000 women found that higher fiber intakes are associated with lower risk for gestational diabetes, while low-fiber diets increase risk.[52] Thus, the *type* of carbohydrate (rather than the *amount*) may require consideration for its effect on maternal blood glucose control. No randomized controlled study has yet compared low carbohydrate, low-fiber diets with diets higher in carbohydrates and fiber.

Orders

See Diabetes Mellitus chapter.

What to Tell the Family

The best way to prevent diabetes complications is through aggressive control of blood glucose and cardiovascular risk factors. Diet plays an important role, along with exercise and appropriate medications. Encouraging the entire family to adopt a healthy diet is important, not only to support dietary adherence by the patient, but also to reduce the family's risk of disease.

All diabetes patients should be screened yearly for retinopathy by an ophthalmologist and have lab work done to monitor for nephropathy. Neuropathy is most likely to be discovered by the patient, but the family can help monitor for blisters or calluses. Special shoes may be needed to prevent infections.

It is important for the family and patient to understand that because diabetes complications can greatly reduce quality of life, aggressive prevention and/or treatment is imperative.

References

1. American Diabetes Association. Standards of medical care in diabetes—2006. *Diabetes Care*. 2006;29:S4-S42.

2. Ornish D, Scherwitz LW, Billings JH, et al. Intensive lifestyle changes for reversal of coronary heart disease. *JAMA*. 1998;280:2001-2007.

3. Berkow SE, Barnard ND. Blood pressure regulation and vegetarian diets. *Nutr Rev*. 2005;63:1-8.

4. Pischke CR, Weidner G, Elliott-Eller M, et al. Comparison of coronary risk factors and quality of life in coronary artery disease patients with versus without diabetes mellitus. *Am J Cardiol*. 2006;97:1267-1273

5. Barnard ND, Cohen J, Jenkins DJ, et al. A low-fat, vegan diet improves glycemic control and cardiovascular risk factors in a randomized clinical trial in individuals with type 2 diabetes. *Diabetes Care*. 2006;29:1777-1783.

6. Jenkins DJ, Wolever TM, Kalmusky J, et al. Low-glycemic index diet in hyperlipidemia: use of traditional starchy foods. *Am J Clin Nutr*. 1987;46:66-71.

7. Ziegler D, Gries FA. Alpha-lipoic acid in the treatment of diabetic peripheral and cardiac autonomic neuropathy. *Diabetes*. 1997;46(suppl 2):S62-S66.

8. Klein R, Klein BEK, Moss SE, Davis MD, DeMets DL. Glycosylated hemoglobin predicts the incidence and progression of diabetic retinopathy. *JAMA*. 1988;260:2864-2871.

9. Reichard P, Nilsson B-Y, Rosenqvist U. The effect of long-term intensified insulin treatment on the development of microvascular complications of diabetes mellitus. *N Engl J Med*. 1993;329:304-309.

10. Diabetes Control and Complications Trial Research Group. The effect of intensive treatment of diabetes on the development and progression of long-term complications in insulin-dependent diabetes mellitus. *N Engl J Med*. 1993;329:977-986.

11. UK Prospective Diabetes Study (UKPDS) Group. Effect of intensive blood-glucose control with metformin on complications in overweight patients with type 2 diabetes (UKPDS 34). *Lancet.* 1998;352:854-865.

12. UK Prospective Diabetes Study (UKPDS) Group. Intensive blood-glucose control with sulphonylureas or insulin compared with conventional treatment and risk of complications in patients with type 2 diabetes (UKPDS 33). *Lancet.* 1998;352:837-853.

13. Knowler WC, Bennett PH, Ballintine EJ. Increased incidence of retinopathy in diabetics with elevated blood pressure. *N Engl J Med.* 1980;302:645-650.

14. Klein R, Klein BE, Moss SE, Davis MD, DeMets DL. Wisconsin Epidemiologic Study of Diabetic Retinopathy: III. Prevalence and risk of diabetic retinopathy when age at diagnosis is 30 or more years. *Arch Ophthalmol.* 1984;102:527-532.

15. Kohner EM, Aldington SJ, Stratton IM, et al. United Kingdom Prospective Diabetes Study, 30: Diabetic retinopathy at diagnosis of non-insulin-dependent diabetes mellitus and associated risk factors. *Arch Ophthalmol.* 1998;116:297-303.

16. Early Treatment Diabetic Retinopathy Study Research Group. Photocoagulation for diabetic macular edema. *Arch Ophthalmol.* 1985;103:1796-1806.

17. Alexander CM, Landsman PB, Teutsch SM, Haffner SM. 2003 NCEP-defined metabolic syndrome, diabetes, and prevalence of coronary heart disease among NHANES III participants age 50 years and older. *Diabetes.* 2003;52:1210–1214.

18. Oh SW, Lee S, Park C, Kim DJ. Elevated intraocular pressure is associated with insulin resistance and metabolic syndrome. *Diabetes Metab Res Rev.* 2005;21:434-440.

19. Mathews JP, Mathews D, Lavin MJ. The management of diabetic retinopathy. *Practitioner.* 2004;248:34,38-40,42.

20. Chew EY, Klein ML, Ferris FL III, et al. Association of elevated serum lipid levels with retinal hard exudate in diabetic retinopathy. Early Treatment Diabetic Retinopathy Study (ETDRS) Report 22. *Arch Ophthalmol.* 1996;114:1079-1084.

21. Ohkubo Y, Kishikawa H, Araki E, et al. Intensive insulin therapy prevents the progression of diabetic microvascular complications in Japanese patients with non-insulin-dependent diabetes mellitus: a randomized prospective 6-year study. *Diabetes Res Clin Pract.* 1995;28:103-117.

22. Rowe S, MacLean CH, Shekelle PG. Preventing visual loss from chronic eye disease in primary care: scientific review. *JAMA.* 2004;291:1487-1495.

23. Cundiff DK, Nigg CR. Diet and diabetic retinopathy: insights from the Diabetes Control and Complications Trial (DCCT). *MedGenMed.* 2005;7:3.

24. Perkins BA, Ficociello LH, Silva KH, Finkelstein DM. Regression of microalbuminuria in type 1 diabetes. *N Engl J Med.* 2003;348:2285-2293.

25. Brancati FL, Whittle JC, Whelton PK, et al. The excess incidence of diabetic end-stage renal disease among blacks. A population-based study of potential explanatory factors. *JAMA.* 1992;268:3079-3084.

26. Smith SR, Svetkey LP, Dennis VW. Racial differences in the incidence and progression of renal diseases. *Kidney Int.* 1991;40:815-822.

27. Morales E, Valero MA, Leon M, Hernandez E, Praga M. Beneficial effects of weight loss in overweight patients with chronic proteinuric nephropathies. *Am J Kidney Dis.* 2003;41:319-327.

28. Gall MA, Hougaard P, Borch-Johnsen K, Parving HH. Risk factors for development of incipient and overt diabetic nephropathy in patients with non-insulin dependent diabetes mellitus: prospective, observational study. *BMJ*. 1997;314:783-788.

29. Appel GB, Radhakrishnan J, Avram MM, et al. Analysis of metabolic parameters as predictors of risk in the RENAAL study. *Diabetes Care*. 2003;26:1402-1407.

30. Lam KS, Cheng IK, Janus ED, Pang RW. Cholesterol-lowering therapy may retard the progression of diabetic nephropathy. *Diabetologia*. 1995;38:604-609.

31. Pedrini MT, Levey AS, Lau J, Chalmers TC, Wang PH. The effects of dietary protein restriction on the progression of diabetic and non-diabetic renal disease: a meta-analysis. *Ann Intern Med*. 1996;124:627-632.

32. Toeller M, Buyken A, Heitkamp G, et al. Protein intake and urinary albumin excretion rates in the EURODIAB IDDM Complications Study. *Diabetologia*. 1997;40:1219-1226.

33. Jibani MM, Bloodworth LL, Foden E, Griffiths KD, Galpin OP. Predominantly vegetarian diet in patients with incipient and early clinical diabetic nephropathy: effects on albumin excretion rate and nutritional status. *Diabet Med*. 1991;8:949-953.

34. Azadbakht L, Shakerhosseini R, Atabak S, Jamshidian M, Mehrabi Y, Esmaill-Zadeh A. Beneficiary effect of dietary soy protein on lowering plasma levels of lipid and improving kidney function in type II diabetes with nephropathy. *Eur J Clin Nutr*. 2003;57:1292-1294.

35. Parving HH, Hovind P. Microalbuminuria in type 1 and type 2 diabetes mellitus: evidence with angiotensin converting enzyme inhibitors and angiotensin II receptor blockers for treating early and preventing clinical nephropathy. *Curr Hypertens Rep*. 2002;4:387-393.

36. Weir MR. Dietary salt, blood pressure, and microalbuminuria. *J Clin Hypertens* (Greenwich). 2004;6(suppl 3):23-26.

37. Crane MG, Sample C. Regression of diabetic neuropathy with total vegetarian (vegan) diet. *J Nutr Med*. 1994;4:431-439.

38. McCarty MF. Favorable impact of a vegan diet with exercise on hemorheology: implications for control of diabetic neuropathy. *Med Hypotheses*. 2002;58:476-486.

39. Bansal V, Kalita J, Misra UK. Diabetic neuropathy. *Postgrad Med J*. 2006;82:95-100.

40. Ziegler D, Reljanovic M, Mehnert H, Gries FA. Normal ranges and reproducibility of statistical, geometric, frequency domain, and non-linear measures of 24-hour heart rate variability. *Horm Metab Res*. 1999;31:672-679.

41. Reljanovic M, Reichel G, Rett K, et al. Treatment of diabetic polyneuropathy with the antioxidant thioctic acid (alpha-lipoic acid): a two year multicenter randomized double-blind placebo-controlled trial (ALADIN II). Alpha Lipoic Acid in Diabetic Neuropathy. *Free Radic Res*. 1999;31:171-179.

42. Ziegler D, Ametov A, Barinov A, et al. Oral Treatment with α-Lipoic Acid Improves Symptomatic Diabetic Polyneuropathy: The SYDNEY 2 trial. *Diabetes Care*. 2006;29:2365-2370.

43. Haak E, Usadel KH, Kusterer K, et al. Effects of alpha-lipoic acid on microcirculation in patients with peripheral diabetic neuropathy. *Exp Clin Endocrinol Diabetes*. 2000;108:168-174.

44. Sima AA, Calvani M, Mehra M, Amato A, and the Acetyl-L-Carnitine Study Group. Acetyl-L-carnitine improves pain, nerve regeneration, and vibratory perception in patients with chronic diabetic neuropathy: an analysis of two randomized placebo-controlled trials. *Diabetes Care*. 2005;28:89-94.

45. De Grandis D, Minardi C. Acetyl-L-carnitine (levacecarnine) in the treatment of diabetic neuropathy. A long-term, randomised, double-blind, placebo-controlled study. *Drugs R D.* 2002;3:223-231.

46. Keen H, Payan J, Allawi J, et al. Treatment of diabetic neuropathy with gamma-linolenic acid. The gamma-Linolenic Acid Multicenter Trial Group. *Diabetes Care.* 1993;16:8-15.

47. Horrobin DF. Essential fatty acids in the management of impaired nerve function in diabetes. *Diabetes.* 1997;46(suppl 2):S90-S93.

48. De Leeuw I, Engelen W, De Block C, Van Gaal L. Long term magnesium supplementation influences favourably the natural evolution of neuropathy in Mg-depleted type 1 diabetic patients (T1dm). *Magnes Res.* 2004;17:109-114.

49. Di Cianni G, Miccoli R, Volpe L, et al. Maternal triglyceride levels and newborn weight in pregnant women with normal glucose tolerance. *Diabet Med.* 2005;22:21-25.

50. Kitajima M, Oka S, Yasuhi I, Fukuda M, Rii Y, Ishimaru T. Maternal serum triglyceride at 24-32 weeks' gestation and newborn weight in nondiabetic women with positive diabetic screens. *Obstet Gynecol.* 2001;97:776-780.

51. American Diabetes Association. Gestational diabetes. *Diabetes Care.* 2004;27:S88-S90.

52. Zhang C, Liu S, Solomon CG, Hu FB. Dietary fiber intake, dietary glycemic load, and the risk for gestational diabetes mellitus. *Diabetes Care.* 2006;29:2223-2230.

76. Hypothyroidism

Hypothyroidism is a condition in which the thyroid gland fails to secrete sufficient thyroxine (T_4) and triiodothyronine (T_3). The disease may reflect intrinsic thyroid dysfunction (primary hypothyroidism), or it may result from insufficient stimulation of the thyroid gland by thyroid-stimulating hormone (TSH) due to a malfunction in the pituitary (secondary hypothyroidism) or hypothalamus (tertiary hypothyroidism).

Clinical manifestations may be subtle and nonspecific, including weakness, fatigue, and weight gain. However, chronic or severe disease can manifest with goiter, dull facial expression, drooping eyelids, hoarse speech, thinning or dry, brittle hair, dry skin, myxedema (swelling of the skin and soft tissues), menstrual disorders, bradycardia, pericardial effusion, constipation, depression, paresthesias, ataxia, and anemia.

Hypothyroidism affects about 5 million Americans. The most common cause worldwide is iodine deficiency. However, in the United States, where iodized salt is commonly used, most cases are due to autoimmune thyroiditis (Hashimoto's disease), in which CD8+ lymphocytes and antithyroid antibodies impair the normal functioning of the thyroid gland. Other causes include drugs (lithium, amiodarone), genetic mutations of thyroglobulin and thyroid peroxidase molecules, congenital hypothyroidism, neck surgery, and radiothyroid ablation therapy. Hypothyroidism may also rarely result from hypothalamic or pituitary disorders, such as pituitary tumors, postpartum pituitary necrosis, and head trauma, in which the production or release of TSH is impaired.

Some, but not all, patients with hypothyroidism develop a goiter. The clinical presentation of goiter depends on its size and location. Most patients with a goiter have no related symptoms. However, some may experience cough, dyspnea, and wheezing due to tracheal compression; dysphagia due to esophageal compression; hoarseness resulting from laryngeal nerve compression; and Horner syndrome if the cervical sympathetic chain is involved.

Myxedema coma is a rare, life-threatening complication of severe hypothyroidism manifested by mental status changes, often accompanied by hypotension, hypothermia, hypoventilation, and, though rarely, coma. (Its name is actually a misnomer, because patients typically exhibit neither the nonpitting swelling of the skin referred to as myxedema, nor coma.) Precipitants of myxedema coma include infection, myocardial infarction, stroke, trauma (including surgery and burns), hypoglycemia, hyponatremia, hemorrhage, noncompliance with thyroid medications, and various drugs (eg, beta-blockers, sedatives, narcotics, and phenothiazines).

Risk Factors

Gender. The majority of cases occur in women.

Age. Risk of hypothyroidism and myxedema coma increases with age.

Genetics. Hypothyroidism is associated with several polymorphisms in the genes for human leukocyte antigen (HLA), T-cell antigen receptors, and other immunomodulatory molecules.

Diagnosis

Because clinical presentation is highly variable, diagnosis relies on laboratory testing. Several factors may lead to altered thyroid test results in the absence of thyroid disease. These include malnutrition, chronic illness, severe acute illness, drugs, and pregnancy.

Initial laboratory testing includes serum TSH plus an estimate of free T_4 levels.

- Serum TSH is increased in primary hypothyroidism. This is the most sensitive test for primary hypothyroidism, but it is not useful for secondary hypothyroidism, in which TSH is usually decreased, but may also be normal or elevated.

- Serum free T_4 or T_4 index is decreased. A normal value, in the context of elevated TSH, represents subclinical hypothyroidism.

- Further laboratory testing may be useful in selected cases.

- Thyroid autoantibodies are present in Hashimoto's thyroiditis.

- Radioactive iodine uptake may be low in cases of hypothyroidism. However, this study is more useful for evaluating cases of hyperthyroidism.

- Elevated cholesterol, triglycerides, and creatine phosphokinase may occur, but are nonspecific markers of hypothyroidism.

Radioimaging can evaluate the size, shape, and iodine distribution of the thyroid gland and evaluate for compression of vital structures.

Treatment

In most cases, hypothyroidism requires lifelong thyroid hormone replacement (L-thyroxine). The usual regimen begins at 50μg/day (12.5-25μg/day in elderly patients) and increases by 25 to 50μg/day every 4 to 8 weeks until a maintenance dose is reached. The dose is adjusted until a normal TSH level is attained.

Treatment of subclinical hypothyroidism is not always necessary and should be considered on a case-by-case basis.

Iodine deficiency is treated with potassium iodide.

Myxedema coma is treated initially with intravenous L-thyroxine, L-triiodothyronine, and corticosteroids, followed by maintenance doses of oral thyroid hormones.

Nutritional Considerations

Genetic factors apparently account for approximately 80% of the risk for developing autoimmune thyroid disease. Environmental factors also play a role in many cases. Individuals and populations ingesting inadequate amounts of iodine appear to be particularly at risk, as are patients with autoimmune diseases.

The use of iodized salt is a well-accepted public health strategy for decreasing the incidence of iodine deficiency disorders.[1] Although mild iodine deficiency results in enlarged thyroid glands, evidence of clinical hypothyroidism does not necessarily follow.[2] Conversely, even mildly to moderately excessive iodine intake (≥220 μg/day) through foods, dietary supplements, topical medications, and/or iodinated contrast media[3] can increase risk for hypothyroidism.[4] Iodine excess causes a hypothyroid state partly because of a decrease in the sodium/iodide symporter[5] that is responsible for transport of iodide into thyrocytes (Wolff-Chaikoff Effect), a fundamental step in thyroid hormone biosynthesis.[6]

Hypothyroidism is not uncommonly found in patients with celiac disease (CD);[7] for example, 8% of patients with CD were found to be hypothyroid in one study.[8] The prevalence of autoantibodies to the thyroid is significantly higher in patients with undiagnosed celiac disease than in celiac patients on a gluten-free diet.[9,10] These autoantibodies appear to be gluten-dependent, disappearing after adoption of a gluten-free diet.[9] Although evidence is limited, clinical trials found that most patients who strictly followed a gluten-free diet for one year experienced a normalization of subclinical hypothyroidism[11] and reduced need for thyroxine.[12]

Iron deficiency may also contribute to thyroid disease risk. Although Western, meat-eating populations have greater iron stores than non-Western populations, some individuals may experience poor iron status. Plasma thyroxine and triiodothyronine concentrations were significantly lower in women with iron-deficiency anemia, compared with controls.[13] Iron-deficiency anemia blunts the effect of iodine supplementation on thyroid function, and iron supplementation improves it.[14] However, iron supplements should be taken apart from levothyroxine (see below).

Selenium is a micronutrient with important roles in thyroid functioning. Selenoproteins include the iodothyronine selenodeiodinases, D1 and D2, which are responsible for the production of biologically active T3. Low selenium blood levels are associated with lymphocyte infiltration of the thyroid,[15] suggesting a link between this mineral and autoimmune thyroid disease. Selenium supplementation appears to be of some benefit in patients with autoimmune thyroiditis (AIT) on L-thyroxine. Controlled clinical trials, using 200 μg/day for several weeks showed 25%-55% reductions in thyroid peroxidase (an enzyme that catalyzes iodination of T_4 and T_3) antibody concentrations.[16,17] However, none have demonstrated a thyroid hormone-sparing effect thus far.

Organochlorine pollutants (eg, dioxins, PCBs) are ubiquitous toxins often found in fish, meat, eggs, and dairy products.[18] Evidence suggests that PCBs have several antithyroid effects.[19] Thus far, most of these effects have been demonstrated only in humans exposed to these pollutants by accident or through occupational exposure. However, a weight loss study in humans found significant correlations between an increase in plasma organochlorine concentrations and decreases in triiodothyronine concentration and resting metabolic rate, even after statistical adjustment for the known effect of weight loss on T_3 levels.[20] Additional study is required to determine to what degree these pollutants might affect hypothyroidism.

When thyroid medication is used, it should be taken on an empty stomach. Meals can delay gut absorption of levothyroxine, with a particularly noticeable effect from high-fiber meals.[21,22] Both calcium carbonate and iron supplements can significantly reduce absorption of levothyroxine and reduce its effectiveness.[23,24] This may have particular relevance for older women, who are more likely to need thyroid hormone replacement and to take calcium supplements.

Orders

See Basic Diet Orders chapter.

Dietitian should instruct patient on ways to avoid diet-medication interactions that may influence TSH and T_3.

What to Tell the Family

Hypothyroidism is common and treatable, in most cases with excellent outcome. Prevention of hypothyroidism requires adequate dietary intake of iodine at recommended levels. Patients who live in countries where iodine is scarce may need supplements of these minerals. In patients with established hypothyroidism, hormone replacement is needed to normalize T_3 and TSH levels.

References

1. Delange F, Burgi H, Chen ZP, Dunn JT. World status of monitoring iodine deficiency disorders control programs. *Thyroid.* 2002;12:915-924.

2. Thomson CD. Selenium and iodine intakes and status in New Zealand and Australia. *Br J Nutr.* 2004;91:661-672.

3. Pennington JA. A review of iodine toxicity reports. *J Am Diet Assoc.* 1990;90:1571-1581.

4. Laurberg P, Bulow Pedersen I, Knudsen N, Ovesen L, Andersen S. Environmental iodine intake affects the type of nonmalignant thyroid disease. *Thyroid.* 2001;11:457-469.

5. Wolff J. Physiology and pharmacology of iodized oil in goiter prophylaxis. *Medicine* (Baltimore). 2001;80:20-36.

6. Ferreira AC, Lima LP, Araujo RL, et al. Rapid regulation of thyroid sodium-iodide symporter activity by thyrotrophin and iodine. *J Endocrinol.* 2005;184:69-76.

7. Cardenas A, Kelly CP. Celiac sprue. *Semin Gastrointest Dis.* 2002;13:232-244.

8. Ansaldi N, Palmas T, Corrias A, et al. Autoimmune thyroid disease and celiac disease in children. *J Pediatr Gastroenterol Nutr.* 2003;37:63-66.

9. Ventura A, Neri E, Ughi C, Leopaldi A, Citta A, Not T. Gluten-dependent diabetes-related and thyroid-related autoantibodies in patients with celiac disease. *J Pediatr.* 2000;137:263-265.

10. Bonamico M, Anastasi E, Calvani L, et al. Endocrine autoimmunity and functionin adolescent celiac patients: importance of the diet. *J Pediatr Gastroenterol Nutr.* 1997;24:463.

11. Sategna-Guidetti C, Volta U, Ciacci C, et al. Prevalence of thyroid disorders in untreated adult celiac disease patients and effect of gluten withdrawal: an Italian multicenter study. *Am J Gastroenterol.* 2001;96:751-757.

12. Valentino R, Savastano S, Tommaselli AP, et al. Prevalence of coeliac disease in patients with thyroid autoimmunity. *Horm Res.* 1999;51:124-127.

13. Beard JL, Borel MJ, Derr J. Impaired thermoregulation and thyroid function in iron-deficiency anemia. *Am J Clin Nutr.* 1990;52:813-819.

14. Zimmermann MB, Kohrle J. The impact of iron and selenium deficiencies on iodine and thyroid metabolism: biochemistry and relevance to public health. *Thyroid.* 2002;12:867-878.

15. Prummel MF, Strieder T, Wiersinga WM. The environment and autoimmune thyroid diseases. *Eur J Endocrinol.* 2004;150:605-618.

16. Turker O, Kumanlioglu K, Karapolat I, Dogan I. Selenium treatment in autoimmune thyroiditis: 9-month follow-up with variable doses. *J Endocrinol.* 2006;190:151-156.

17. Duntas LH, Mantzou E, Koutras DA. Effects of a six month treatment with selenomethionine in patients with autoimmune thyroiditis. *Eur J Endocrinol.* 2003;148:389-393.

18. Schell LM, Gallo MV, Denham M, Ravenscroft J. Effects of pollution on human growth and development: an introduction. *J Physiol Anthropol.* 2006;25:103-112.

19. Langer P. Review: persistent organochlorinated pollutants (POPs) and human thyroid—2005. *Endocr Regul.* 2005;39:53-68.

20. Pelletier C, Doucet E, Imbeault P, Tremblay A. Associations between weight loss-induced changes in plasma organochlorine concentrations, serum T(3) concentration, and resting metabolic rate. *Toxicol Sci.* 2002;67:46-51.

21. Liel Y, Harman-Boehm I, Shany S. Evidence for a clinically important adverse effect of fiber-enriched diet on the bioavailability of levothyroxine in adult hypothyroid patients. *J Clin Endocrinol Metab.* 1996;81:857-859.

22. Benvenga S, Bartolone L, Squadrito S, et al. Delayed intestinal absorption of levothyroxine. *Thyroid.* 1995;5:249-253.

23. Singh N, Singh PN, Hershman JM. Effect of calcium carbonate on the absorption of levothyroxine. *JAMA.* 2000;283:2822-2825.

24. Campbell NR, Hasinoff BB, Stalts H, Rao B, Wong NC. Ferrous sulfate reduces thyroxine efficacy in patients with hypothyroidism. *Ann Intern Med.* 1992;117:1010-1013.

77. Hyperthyroidism

Hyperthyroidism is a condition of excess thyroid hormone. It may be caused by intrinsic thyroid dysfunction or, rarely, by excessive stimulation of the thyroid gland by an autonomous source of thyroid-stimulating hormone (TSH). Approximately 85% of hyperthyroidism cases result from Graves disease, in which autoantibodies to the TSH receptor continually stimulate the thyroid gland to overproduce thyroid hormone. Other common causes include toxic multinodular thyroid, toxic adenoma, and thyroiditis. Hyperthyroidism may also be caused by excessive ingestion of exogenous thyroid hormone or iodine. Rarely, hyperthyroidism may be caused by a TSH-secreting anterior pituitary adenoma or struma ovarii.

Graves hyperthyroidism may be associated with other autoimmune diseases, including Addison disease and type 1 diabetes mellitus. Hyperthyroid symptoms may also result when physiologically high doses of levothyroxine are used during treatment for thyroid malignancy in order to suppress TSH.

Clinical manifestations of hyperthyroidism vary significantly from patient to patient, with symptom severity often correlating with circulating thyroid hormone concentrations. The most common signs and symptoms include tachycardia, palpitations, heat intolerance, weight loss, and menstrual irregularities. Less common are nausea, vomiting, restlessness, anxiety, tremor, and atrial fibrillation. Further signs and symptoms depend on the etiology and severity of hyperthyroidism. In Graves disease, for example, typical symptoms are a diffuse, symmetric goiter; ophthalmopathy (including lid lag and irreversible exophthalmos); and dermopathy (including pretibial myxedema, a thickening and redness of the pretibial skin).

The most severe form of hyperthyroidism is thyroid storm, which can be precipitated by thyroidectomy, acute stress (eg, infection, trauma, nonthyroid surgery), or an acute iodine load. Presentation may include extreme fever (up to 40°C to 41°C/104°F to 106°F), severe nausea, vomiting, jaundice, rigidity, agitation, or delirium. These symptoms may progress to seizures and coma, tachycardia, congestive heart failure, and frank shock.

Risk Factors

Gender. Hyperthyroidism is more common in females.

Genetics. Certain *HLA-D* subtypes increase risk for Graves disease.

Iodine. Excess dietary iodine intake and iodine-rich medication (amiodarone) use may cause hyperthyroidism. Amiodarone may also cause thyroiditis.

Diagnosis

TSH is the most cost-effective assay for hyperthyroidism and should be the initial screening test. TSH is decreased in all types of hyperthyroidism, except when pituitary tumors produce TSH or the thyroid hormone feedback loop malfunctions.

Free T_4 concentration is increased; the magnitude of T_4 elevation is correlated with the degree of biochemical disease. A total T_3:T_4 ratio greater than 20 is common in Graves disease.

Once hyperthyroidism has been diagnosed, further testing can determine the underlying etiology. Thyroid stimulating immunoglobulins, antithyroglobin, and antithyroid peroxidase levels are often elevated in Graves disease—high titers can help establish the etiology of hyperthyroidism. A 24-hour radioactive iodine uptake scan is often necessary for diagnosis of Graves disease and exclusion of other disorders. Uptake is increased in Graves disease, toxic adenoma, and multinodular goiter and is decreased in thyroiditis, excessive iodine consumption, and overmedication with thyroid hormone supplementation.

Radioimaging can define the shape and size of the thyroid and determine where "hot" nodules are distributed (iodine will concentrate in "hot" nodules). Functional nodules may represent toxic adenoma or multinodular goiter. Diffuse uptake is seen in Graves disease. Absence of uptake strongly suggests thyroiditis, exogenous thyroid hormone ingestion, or, rarely, struma ovarii.

Treatment

Initial therapy often uses a beta-blocker to oppose the adrenergic effects of thyroid hormone.

Antithyroid drugs (eg, propylthiouracil, methimazole) interfere with thyroid hormone production. Although antithyroid drugs must generally be continued for at least 1 to 2 years, they may be a useful temporizing measure in anticipation of spontaneous remission of hyperthyroidism, which occurs in <50% of patients with Graves disease over 1 to 2 years.

Radioactive iodine (I131) to ablate thyroid tissue is a definitive treatment with excellent success rates; it is the most commonly used treatment. It cannot, however, be used in pregnancy, and breast-feeding mothers must pump and dispose of their milk for about 5 days after treatment. Complete destruction of the thyroid gland then requires thyroid hormone replacement to reestablish a euthyroid state.

Surgical removal of the thyroid (thyroidectomy) is also an effective treatment. It is often indicated in hyperthyroid patients who have an obstructive goiter.

Lifelong thyroid hormone supplementation will be necessary after ablation or thyroidectomy due to resultant hypothyroidism.

Thyroid storm treatment is generally similar to that for hyperthyroidism but with closer monitoring and higher medication doses. Treatment with glucocorticoids or potassium iodine may be indicated (excess iodine reduces release of stored thyroid hormone into the circulation). Intensive care unit observation is essential.

Nutritional Considerations

Iodine-induced hyperthyroidism has been reported in patients after treatment for previous thyroid diseases. Specifically, patients treated with antithyroid drugs for Graves disease are prone to develop iodine-induced hyperthyroidism.[1-3] Excess iodine exposure may occur through drugs, antiseptics, food preservatives, and contrast media.[1] Cow's milk is a primary source of dietary iodine in the United States.[4] Certain breads and milk contained up to 587 µg and 110 µg iodine per serving, respectively,[4] which would provide a large excess when compared with the Recommended Dietary Allowance for adults of 150 µg.

Patients with celiac disease have an increased prevalence of autoimmune disease, including Graves disease.[5,6] It is unclear whether the association is due to a common genetic basis for the two conditions[7] or to an as-yet unidentified cause-and-effect relationship. Limited evidence indicates that antithyroid antibody production abates in celiac patients after 3 to 6 months on a gluten-free diet.[8]

Orders

See Basic Diet Orders chapter.

Nutrition consultation to assist patient in planning appropriate iodine intake.

What to Tell the Family

Hyperthyroidism is common and generally responds well to medical therapy. In some cases, the disease spontaneously remits. In others, radioactive iodine therapy, antithyroid drugs, or surgery are indicated to remove or destroy overactive thyroid cells, which may necessitate lifelong thyroid hormone replacement to maintain a normal hormone level. Patients with mild to moderate disease could attempt a trial period of avoiding foods that contain high concentrations of iodine (including dairy products, bread made with iodate dough conditioners, iodized salt, sea salt, fish and shellfish, and eggs) and foods that contain iodides, iodate, algin, alginates, carrageen, agar, and red dye number 3.

References

1. Roti E, Uberti ED. Iodine excess and hyperthyroidism. *Thyroid*. 2001;11:493-500.

2. Garcia-Mayor RV, Paramo C, Luna Cano R, Perez Mendez LF, Galofre JC, Andrade A. Antithyroid drug and Graves' hyperthyroidism. Significance of treatment duration and TRAb determination on lasting remission. *J Endocrinol Invest*. 1992;15:815-820.

3. Solomon BL, Evaul JE, Burman KD, Wartofsky L. Remission rates with antithyroid drug therapy: continuing influence of iodine intake? *Ann Intern Med*. 1987;107:510-512.

4. Pearce EN, Pino S, He X, Bazrafshan HR, Lee SL, Braverman LE. Sources of dietary iodine: bread, cows' milk, and infant formula in the Boston area. *J Clin Endocrinol Metab*. 2004;89:3421-3424.

5. King AL, Moodie SJ, Fraser JS, et al. Coeliac disease: investigation of proposed causal variants in the CTLA4 gene region. *Eur J Immunogenet*. 2003;30:427-432.

6. Daly P. Thyroid Disease: Why Do Celiacs Have It? Celiac Sprue Association, 2004. Available at: http://www.csaceliacs.org/library/whythyroid.php. Accessed May 6, 2006.

7. Ch'ng CL, Biswas M, Benton A, Jones MK, Kingham JG. Prospective screening for coeliac disease in patients with Graves' hyperthyroidism using anti-gliadin and tissue transglutaminase antibodies. *Clin Endocrinol* (Oxf). 2005;62:303-306.

8. Berti I, Trevisiol C, Tommasini A, et al. Usefulness of screening program for celiac disease in autoimmune thyroiditis. *Dig Dis Sci*. 2000;45:403-406.

SECTION XV: NEUROLOGICAL DISORDERS

78. Migraine

Migraine is a recurrent condition marked by moderate to severe episodic headaches, other neurologic manifestations, or both. Migraine may be caused by dysfunction of the trigeminovascular system and is attended by a wave of hyperpolarization of cells and hypoperfusion across the cerebral cortex. These events can cause the patient to experience an "aura," a state characterized by unusual visual or other sensory phenomena. The headache is believed to result from multiple factors, including sensitization of trigeminal sensory neurons and activation of the trigeminovascular system, altered serotonin metabolism, and the release of vasoactive polypeptides such as substance P, causing inflammation of the meninges and cranial vessels.[1-3]

In approximately 60% of cases, the headache is unilateral, but it can occur globally and bifrontally, as well as (rarely) in other patterns. Pain escalation is usually gradual, progressing from dull to severe and throbbing in most cases, and can be exacerbated by light, sound, and activity. Nausea is common, and vomiting may result. Explosive onsets of headaches should be investigated for alternative causes, although this pattern, too, may represent migraine.

Migraines typically begin in the teenage years or early adulthood; they rarely commence after age 40. There are uncommon variants of migraine including retinal, ophthalmoplegic, and familial hemiplegic. Migraine without aura ("common" migraine) makes up about 80% of all cases. Migraine with aura ("classic" migraine) is the second most common type.

Aura is caused by neuronal dysfunction. The most common manifestations are visual phenomena (flashing lights, jagged lines, and scotomata, usually still visible with the eyes closed) with other sensory symptoms (eg, tingling or numbness in the hand and mouth, altered taste or smell, or dizziness). Migraines with motor symptoms are classified as familial or sporadic hemiplegic migraine. Auras typically last no more than an hour, except in cases of motor dysfunction. In complicated migraines, neurologic symptoms may last weeks or may be permanent (usually with evidence of a stroke). Aura without headache (acephalgic migraine or "atypical" migraine) may also occur.

Symptoms that suggest a headache may be migraine include:

- Multiple headaches of moderate-to-severe intensity, lasting from hours to days.

- Unilateral, throbbing quality.

- Photophobia, phonophobia.

- Nausea/vomiting.

- Aggravation of headache by activity.

- Autonomic features such as rhinorrhea or congestion, tearing, changes in pupil size, and others (these occur occasionally, not routinely).[4]

- Pain sensation with normal stimuli (cutaneous allodynia).

Triggers may include menses, fasting, bright lights, overexertion, sleep deprivation, head trauma, changes in weather, changes in eating or sleeping schedules, stress, and substances in food or beverages, such as nitrites, glutamate, aspartate, and tyramine. Other identified triggers are excessive vitamin A intake, histamine, corticosteroid withdrawal, caffeine or analgesic withdrawal, and strong odors.[5] Triggers may act as vasodilators[2,6] or through allergic reactions.[7,8]

Risk Factors

Up to 60% of migraine cases are familial, with specific gene abnormalities in some cases. Women are affected about 3 times more often than men.[9] Persons with right-to-left cardiac shunts (usually due to patent foramen ovale) have increased migraine prevalence,[10-12] for unknown reasons.

Some studies have linked obesity to the frequency and severity of migraine attacks,[13] although not all studies are in agreement. A study of over 30,000 individuals found no association with obesity.[14] The odds of developing chronic daily headache were found to be more than 5 times greater in obese compared with normal-weight individuals.[13]

Estrogen withdrawal may precipitate migraine. This may occur with normal menstrual cycles, with menopause, or with variation in oral exogenous doses (eg, missed pills or drug interactions that affect estrogen concentrations).[15]

Diagnosis

Migraine is a clinical diagnosis. Neuroimaging is only necessary if another etiology is suspected due to the presence of neurologic abnormalities, an atypical pattern of headache, or progression of symptoms despite appropriate treatment. Providers may consider a CT scan and lumbar puncture for patients with rapid or explosive onset of severe headache (to rule out subarachnoid hemorrhage). MRI scanning is more effective in patients with focal neurologic signs, gait instability, or other findings inconsistent with migraine.

Migraine without Aura[16]

A clinical diagnosis of migraine is indicated for patients who experience 5 or more episodes fulfilling the following criteria:

- Duration of 4 to 72 hours.

- Two or more of the following: unilateral location, pulsating quality, moderate or severe pain intensity, aggravation by routine physical activity.

- At least 1 of the following:

  1. nausea and/or vomiting

  2. photophobia and phonophobia.

- Headache not attributed to another disorder.

Migraine with Aura[16]

The following criteria, occurring on 2 or more occasions, establish the clinical diagnosis of migraine with aura:

- Aura consisting of 1 or more of the following and without motor weakness: fully reversible visual symptoms, fully reversible sensory symptoms, or fully reversible speech disturbance.

- Two or more of the following: homonymous (same field defect in both eyes) visual symptoms or unilateral sensory symptoms, at least 1 aura developing gradually over 5 or more minutes or different auras developing in succession over at least 5 minutes, or each aura lasting between 5 and 60 minutes.

- Headache fulfilling the criteria for "migraine without aura" begins during or within 1 hour of the aura(s).

- Headache not attributed to any other disorder.

Probable Migraine[16]

Headaches that have many of the features of migraine but lack one of the criteria described above are termed "probable migraine." They typically respond to treatments that are effective for migraine.

Treatment

Prevention is the mainstay of migraine therapy. The patient may benefit from avoiding situations that trigger or exacerbate migraines; for example, by maintaining appropriate sleep patterns, avoiding fasting and trigger foods, and participating in stress management.

The absorption of oral medicines may be decreased due to migraine-induced gastric stasis.

Abortive Therapy

Abortive therapies are more effective when given early and in larger appropriate doses, although frequent use (more than 10 times per month) can lead to medication-overuse headaches. All short-acting analgesic medications can result in these headaches (also called analgesic rebound headaches or transformed migraine). Non-oral (suppository, intranasal, intramuscular, or intravenous) drugs may work better for patients who suffer from nausea and vomiting during episodes. The following agents are commonly used:

Analgesics. Aspirin, other NSAIDs including indomethacin, and acetaminophen. Chronic use can lead to overuse headaches. NSAIDs may be combined with acetaminophen. A combined naproxen-sumatriptan formulation is available.

Triptans (sumatriptan, rizatriptan, almotriptan, zolmitriptan). These serotonin receptor agonists are for moderate-to-severe migraine when vascular disease and uncontrolled hypertension are absent. Triptans inhibit vasoactive peptide release, cause vasoconstriction, and block pain pathways in the brainstem.[17] Sensitization may decrease effect. They should be avoided in pregnancy and in hemiplegic or basilar migraine. Serotonin syndrome is possible, especially when used with selective serotonin reuptake inhibitors.

Dihydroergotamine (intranasal or injectable) is effective for moderate-to-severe attacks when vascular disease and hypertension are absent. Administration may require antiemetic premedication. It should not be used during pregnancy or within 24 hours of triptans due to risk of myocardial infarction.

Aspirin and/or acetaminophen with caffeine. Note: Caffeine withdrawal is a very common migraine trigger.

Isometheptene (a vasoconstrictor) and **dichloralphenazone** (a mild sedative). Both are components of the drug Midrin.

Intranasal **lidocaine** solution (4%).

Antiemetics, prochlorperazine and metoclopramide. These can be administered intravenously, as monotherapy, or as an adjunct to above therapies.

Benzodiazepines, narcotics, and barbiturates should be used sparingly, due to their habit-forming qualities and the high potential for analgesic-overuse (analgesic-rebound) headache.[18,19] This can result from the frequent use of any short-acting analgesic but is more common and severe with narcotics, barbiturates, and benzodiazepines.

Prophylactic Therapy

Daily prophylaxis is indicated if headaches occur twice per week or more frequently, or when they are particularly prolonged or have associated severe disability or complications. It may be several weeks before benefits are evident. Many prophylactic agents are pharmaceuticals, although there is also good evidence for effectiveness of some botanicals, vitamins, and minerals.[20] The following agents are commonly used:

Beta-adrenergic blockers, such as propranolol or timolol. Propranolol increases rizatriptan levels, so doses of rizatriptan being used to abort migraine should be halved.

Anticonvulsants, such as topiramate, gabapentin, levetiracetam, or valproic acid.

Calcium channel blockers, such as verapamil.

Nonsteroidal antiinflammatory drugs (NSAIDs), such as naproxen.[21] These agents are most useful when there is a short period of migraine susceptibility each month.

Antidepressants. Tricyclic antidepressants, such as amitriptyline or nortriptyline, and serotonin antagonists are effective. Selective serotonin reuptake inhibitors (SSRI) need further study, but they are often helpful when there is comorbid depression.

Angiotensin-converting enzyme (ACE) inhibitors or **angiotensin receptor blockers (ARBs).**

Riboflavin (see Nutritional Considerations below).

Cognitive and **behavioral therapy.**

Two medicinal botanicals, **petasites**[22] and **feverfew,**[23] are under study for their efficacy in migraine treatment.

Butterbur *(Petasites hybridus* root). In double-blind, randomized clinical trials, butterbur reduced migraine frequency by roughly half compared with placebo. Although this effect was achieved with 25 mg BID in one study,[24] a second trial with a larger number of patients found that only a higher dose (75 mg BID) resulted in a statistically significant reduction in migraine frequency (~50% fewer attacks over a 4-month period) when compared with 50 mg BID.[22] Similar results were obtained in a multicenter prospective open-label study with children and adolescents.[25]

The mechanisms by which this botanical may reduce migraine attacks have not been established but may include spasmolytic and anti-leukotriene effects and an effect on calcium channels.[24] So far, *Petasites* has a good safety record; belching is its most common side effect.[26] However, the long-term safety of this agent has not been established. Efficacy comparisons with commonly prescribed medications for migraine have yet to be performed.

Feverfew is an herb with antiinflammatory properties. Research studies have yielded mixed verdicts as to its efficacy for migraines. Some clinical trials have suggested efficacy of the native herb or its extracts in preventing or aborting migraines, while others have yielded inconclusive results, perhaps due to variations in preparations tested.[27] However, a recent randomized, double-blind, multicenter, parallel-group study found that a feverfew extract (6.25 mg TID) decreased migraine attacks by 40%, compared with a 27% reduction for placebo (P=.05).[28]

Nutritional Considerations

Nutritional approaches to migraine are often effective and are appealing to patients. They can be particularly attractive when treating pregnant women, for whom pharmacologic interventions are generally contraindicated.

Foods containing tyramine and other biogenic amines have long been suspected of triggering migraine. Although a review of randomized, double-blind, placebo-controlled studies failed to establish these as a cause of either headache or migraine,[29] other studies (see below) indicate that dietary treatment may still be helpful for preventing migraine in certain individuals. Additional controlled clinical trials are required to firmly establish the role for diet in the causation or prevention of migraine. Nevertheless, dietary treatment may be considered first as a low-cost, low-risk treatment before medication is used or in patients who either do not respond to or tolerate medication well.

Elimination diets. Avoidance of foods found to trigger migraine can reduce or eliminate headache in approximately 20% to 50% of patients.[30,31] Foods commonly identified as migraine triggers include (in order of importance): dairy products (eg, cheese), chocolate, eggs, citrus fruits, meat, wheat, nuts and peanuts, tomatoes, onions, corn, apples, and bananas.[32] Tyramine- and phenylalanine-containing foods, such as aged cheese, beer, and red wine, have also been implicated in migraine.[31,32] Although evidence is limited, dietary treatment of pediatric migraine with an allergen-free diet was effective in over 90% of subjects.[33] Elimination of certain food additives, including MSG, aspartame, and sodium nitrate, may also be helpful.[34,35]

To identify trigger foods, an elimination diet may be conducted on an outpatient basis if the patient can control his or her diet for several weeks.

The procedure is as follows: Start with a baseline diet including only those foods not implicated in migraine:

- Brown rice.

- Cooked or dried fruits, such as cherries, cranberries, pears, or prunes (avoid citrus fruits).

- Cooked green, yellow, and orange vegetables (artichokes, asparagus, broccoli, chard, collards, lettuce, spinach, string beans, squash, sweet potatoes, tapioca, and taro).

- Plain or carbonated water.

- Condiments (modest amounts of salt, maple syrup, and vanilla extract).

Wean from caffeine-containing beverages gradually, or avoid caffeine if not habitually consumed.

When migraines have stopped or diminished (usually within a week or so), the patient should keep a food diary and add in foods one at a time in generous amounts every other day to observe which cause migraine recurrence.

Foods listed above that are the most common triggers of migraine attacks should be added last. If the food is associated with a migraine attack, it should be removed from the diet for 1 to 2 weeks and then reintroduced to see if the same reaction occurs. If no symptoms are experienced, that food can remain in the diet.

Some evidence suggests that reducing total and omega-6 fat in the diet may reduce migraine occurrence in some patients. In an open trial including 54 migraine patients, reducing total fat intake from 66 grams to 28 grams per day resulted in a significant decrease in headache frequency, intensity, duration, and medication intake.[36] It is not clear if the effect was due to reduced fat intake or to the exclusion of specific high-fat foods.

One suggested mechanism relates to arachidonic acid. This omega-6 fatty acid, found in animal products and derived to a lesser degree from the intake of the polyunsaturated fat linoleic acid, is a precursor for both prostaglandin E2 (PGE2) and leukotriene B4 (LTB4), levels of which are elevated during migraine attacks.[37,38] Although inhibition of the production of these eicosanoids by NSAIDs (see above Treatment section) and by antileukotriene drugs[39] has been found effective for migraine prevention, changes in diet that limit the intake of omega-6 fats may have a similar biological action.

Caffeine. Some patients report anecdotally that 1 to 2 cups of strong black coffee may stop an evolving migraine. Caffeine withdrawal appears to trigger headache[40] that is abated by coffee drinking.[41] However, daily use may contribute to development of frequent and resistant headaches.[42]

Heart health-promoting diets. Individuals with frequent migraines appear to be at higher risk for coronary heart disease compared with people without migraines. In the Women's Health Study, which included nearly 28,000 individuals, those with a history of migraine had more than twice the risk for myocardial infarction compared with women who had no migraine history.[43] Similarly, the Physicians Health Study of over 20,000 individuals found that those with a history of migraine had a more than 40% greater risk for MI compared with other people.[44] (See also Coronary Heart Disease chapter.)

Supplements. Several supplements have shown promise for migraine prevention or treatment, although some have been investigated with greater rigor than others. A particular complication of migraine research is the strong placebo effect, which requires sound experimental design.

Vitamin B₂. Studies have found significant reductions in headache frequency and headache days with daily pharmacologic doses (400 mg) of riboflavin.[45,46]

Magnesium. Magnesium deficiency is a common finding in patients with menstrual migraine.[47] Migraine patients retain more magnesium after an oral load, compared with control patients, also suggesting systemic magnesium deficiency.[48] Magnesium therapy has been found to improve migraine symptoms when given intravenously[49] and to reduce the number of headache days in children given oral magnesium.[50] Magnesium has also been used intravenously to abort severe migraine attacks in the emergency room. Whether this is by a different mechanism than its prophylactic effect is not known.

Supplemental fatty acids. The rationale for use of essential fatty acids originated in their purported antiinflammatory and platelet-stabilizing effects. However, promising early reports[51,52] were followed by a negative report,[53] suggesting that a strong placebo effect may influence research findings.

Orders

Nutrition consultation to help identify food triggers, prescribe elimination diet as described above, formulate meal plans, and for help with attaining a healthy body weight. (See also Coronary Heart Disease chapter.)

Consider allergist referral on an outpatient basis.

What to Tell the Family

The patient's family should be taught about the possible role of dietary and environmental triggers and how family members can assist the patient in avoiding them. Among individuals with identified triggers, even minor exposures can cause migraines. The family can assist and encourage the patient to keep a headache and diet diary to better identify headache-provoking foods and substances. The whole family can use the elimination diet short-term. This will help the patient comply with the diet. Riboflavin and magnesium supplements may also be considered.

References

1. Welch KM, Cutrer FM, Goadsby PJ. Migraine pathogenesis: Neural and vascular mechanisms. *Neurology.* 2003;60:9-14.

2. Martin VT, Behbehani MM. Headache: Towards a rational understanding of migraine trigger factors. *Medical Clinics of North America.* 2001;85:911-941.

3. Bolay H, Reuter U, Dunn AK, et al. Intrinsic brain activity triggers trigeminal meningeal afferents in a migraine model. *Nat Med.* 2002;8:136-142.

4. Nappi G, Micielli G, Tassorelli C, et al. Effectiveness of piroxicam fast dissolving formulation sublingually administered in the symptomatic treatment of migraine without aura. *Headache.* 1993;33:296-300.

5. Chabriat H, Joire JE, Danchot J, et al. Combined oral lysine acetylsalicylate and metochopranide in the acute treatment of migraine: A multicenter double-blind placebo-controlled study. *Cephalalgia.* 1994;14:297-300.

6. Diamond S, Prager J, Freitag FG. Diet and headache: Is there a link? *Postgraduate Medicine.* 1986;79:279-286.

7. Egger J, Carter CM, Soothill JF, Wilson J. Oligoantigenic diet treatment of children with epilepsy and migraine. *J Pediatr.* 1989;114:51-58.

8. Monro J, Carini C, Brostoff J, Zilkha K. Food allergy in migraine. Study of dietary exclusion and RAST. *Lancet.* 1980;2:1-4.

9. Rasmussen BK. Epidemiology of headache. *Cephalalgia.* 2001;21:774-777.

10. Lamy C, Giannesini C, Zuber M, et al. Clinical and imaging findings in cryptogenic stroke patients with and without patent foramen ovale: the PFO-ASA Study. Atrial Septal Aneurysm. *Stroke.* 2002;33:706-711.

11. Anzola GP, Magoni M, Guindani M, et al. Potential source of cerebral embolism in migraine with aura: a transcranial Doppler study. *Neurology.* 1999;52:1622-1625.

12. Del Sette M, Angeli S, Leandri M, et al. Migraine with aura and right-to-left shunt on transcranial Doppler: a case-control study. *Cerebrovasc Dis.* 1998;8:327-330.

13. Bigal ME, Liberman JN, Lipton RB. Obesity and migraine: a population study. *Neurology.* 2006;66:545-550.

14. Scher AI, Stewart WF, Ricci JA, Lipton RB. Factors associated with the onset and remission of chronic daily headache in a population-based study. *Pain.* 2003;106;81- 89.

15. Ashkenazi A, Silberstein S. Menstrual migraine: a review of hormonal causes, prophylaxis and treatment. *Expert Opinion on Pharmacotherapy.* 2007;8:1605-1613.

16. International Headache Society. IHS Classification ICHD-II. Migraine without aura, and typical aura with migraine headache. Available at: http://ihs-classification.org/en/02_klassifikation/02_teil1/01.02.00_migraine.html. Accessed August 8, 2007.

17. Tfelt-Hansen P, De Vries P, Saxena PR. Triptans in migraine: a comparative review of pharmacology, pharmacokinetics and efficacy. *Drugs.* 2000;60:1259-1287.

18. Couch JR. Rebound-withdrawal headache (medication overuse headache). *Current Treatment Options in Neurology.* 2006;8:11-19.

19. Zidverc-Trajkovic J, Pekmezovic T, Jovanovic Z, et al. Medication overuse headache: clinical features predicting treatment outcome at 1-year follow-up. *Cephalalgia.* 2007;27:1219-1225.

20. Evans RW, Taylor FR. "Natural" or alternative medications for migraine prevention. *Headache.* 2006;46:1012-1018.

21. Welch KM, Ellis DJ, Keenan PA. Successful migraine prophylaxis with naproxen sodium. *Neurology.* 1985;35:1304-1310.

22. Lipton RB, Gobel H, Einhaupl KM, Wilks K, Mauskop A. Petasites hybridus root (butterbur) is an effective preventive treatment for migraine. *Neurology.* 2004;63:2240-2244.

23. Vogler BK, Pittler MH, Ernst E. Feverfew as a preventive treatment for migraine: a systematic review. *Cephalalgia*. 1998;18:704-708.

24. Diener HC, Rahlfs VW, Danesch U. The first placebo-controlled trial of a special butterbur root extract for the prevention of migraine: reanalysis of efficacy criteria. *Eur Neurol*. 2004;51:89-97.

25. Pothmann R, Danesch U. Migraine prevention in children and adolescents: results of an open study with a special butterbur root extract. *Headache*. 2005;45:196-203.

26. Danesch U, Rittinghausen R. Safety of a patented special butterbur root extract for migraine prevention. *Headache*. 2003;43:76-78.

27. Pittler MH, Ernst E. Feverfew for preventing migraine. *Cochrane Database Syst Rev*. 2004;(1):CD002286.

28. Diener HC, Pfaffenrath V, Schnitker J, Friede M, Henneicke-von Zepelin HH. Efficacy and safety of 6.25 mg t.i.d. feverfew CO2-extract (MIG-99) in migraine prevention-a randomized, double-blind, multicentre, placebo-controlled study. *Cephalalgia*. 2005;25:1031-1041.

29. Jansen SC, van Dusseldorp M, Bottema KC, Dubois AE. Intolerance to dietary biogenic amines: a review. *Ann Allergy Asthma Immunol*. 2003;91:233-240.

30. Vaughan TR. The role of food in the pathogenesis of migraine headache. *Clin Rev Allergy*. 1994;12:167-180.

31. Mansfield LE, Vaughan TR, Waller SF, Haverly RW, Ting S. Food allergy and adult migraine: double-blind and mediator confirmation of an allergic etiology. *Ann Allergy*. 1985;55:126-129.

32. Barnard N. *Foods That Fight Pain*. New York: Harmony Books; 1998.

33. Egger J, Carter CM, Wilson J, Turner MW, Soothill JF. Is migraine food allergy? A double-blind controlled trial of oligoantigenic diet treatment. *Lancet*. 1983;2:865-869.

34. Millichap JG, Yee MM. The diet factor in pediatric and adolescent migraine. *Pediatr Neurol*. 2003;28:9-15.

35. Sinclair S. Migraine headaches: nutritional, botanical and other alternative approaches. *Altern Med Rev*. 1999;4:86-95.

36. Bic Z, Blix GG, Hopp HP, Leslie FM, Schell MJ. The influence of a low-fat diet on incidence and severity of migraine headaches. *J Women's Health Gend Based Med*. 1999;8:623-630.

37. Davis RJ, Murdoch CE, Ali M, et al. EP4 prostanoid receptor-mediated vasodilatation of human middle cerebral arteries. *Br J Pharmacol*. 2004;141:580-585.

38. LaMancusa R, Pulcinelli FM, Ferroni P, et al. Blood leukotrienes in headache: correlation with platelet activity. *Headache*. 1991;31:409-414.

39. Riccioni G, Di Ilio C, Conti P, Theoharides TC, D'Orazio N. Advances in therapy with antileukotriene drugs. *Ann Clin Lab Sci*. 2004;34:379-387.

40. Awada A, al Jumah M. The first-of-Ramadan headache. *Headache*. 1999;39:490-493.

41. Sjaastad O, Bakketeig LS. Caffeine-withdrawal headache. The Vaga study of headache epidemiology. *Cephalalgia*. 2004;24:241-249.

42. Hering-Hanit R, Gadoth N. Caffeine-induced headache in children and adolescents. *Cephalalgia*. 2003;23:332-335.

43. Kurth T, Gaziano JM, Cook NR, Logroscino G, Diener HC, Buring JE. Migraine and risk of cardiovascular disease in women. *JAMA*. 2006;296:283-291.

44. Kurth T, Gaziano JM, Cook NR, et al. Migraine and risk of cardiovascular disease in men. *Arch Intern Med.* 2007;167:795-801.

45. Boehnke C, Reuter U, Flach U, Schuh-Hofer S, Einhaupl KM, Arnold G. High-dose riboflavin treatment is efficacious in migraine prophylaxis: an open study in a tertiary care centre. *Eur J Neurol.* 2004;11:475-477.

46. Schoenen J, Jacquy J, Lenaerts M. Effectiveness of high-dose riboflavin in migraine prophylaxis. *Neurology.* 1998;50:466-470.

47. Mauskop A, Altura BT, Altura BM. Serum ionized magnesium levels and serum ionized calcium/ionized magnesium ratios in women with menstrual migraine. *Headache.* 2002;42:242-248.

48. Trauninger A, Pfund Z, Koszegi T, Czopf J. Oral magnesium load test in patients with migraine. *Headache.* 2002;42:114-119.

49. Bigal ME, Bordini CA, Tepper SJ, Speciali JG. Intravenous magnesium sulphate in the acute treatment of migraine without aura and migraine with aura. A randomized, double-blind, placebo-controlled study. *Cephalalgia.* 2002;22:345-353.

50. Wang F, Van Den Eeden SK, Ackerson LM, Salk SE, Reince RH, Elin RJ. Oral magnesium oxide prophylaxis of frequent migrainous headache in children: a randomized, double-blind, placebo-controlled trial. *Headache.* 2003;43:601-610.

51. Black KL, Culp B, Madison D, et al. The protective effects of dietary fish oil on focal cerebral infarction. *Prostaglandin Med.* 1979;5:247-252.

52. McCarren T, Hitzemann R, Smith R, et al. Amelioration of severe migraine by fish oil (omega-3) fatty acids. *Am J Clin Nutr* 1985;41:874.

53. Pradalier A, Bakouche P, Baudesson G, et al. Failure of omega-3 polyunsaturated fatty acids in prevention of migraine: a double-blind study versus placebo. *Cephalalgia.* 2001;21:818-822.

79. Multiple Sclerosis

Multiple sclerosis (MS) is an autoimmune disease of the central nervous system (CNS). The pathological process involves white-matter inflammation in many scattered areas of the CNS, along with demyelination, oligodendrocyte loss, glial scarring, and eventual axonal destruction. MS may shorten life span by 10 or more years, compared with national averages. The disease may present in several ways. The most common form is relapsing-remitting, often with incomplete remission and some accumulating disability. It may be progressive from the outset (primary progressive) or may later become progressive after a period of relapses and remissions (secondary progressive). In a rarer form of the disease, the progressive relapsing form, progressive disability is apparent from the outset of the condition, although clear exacerbations also occur and are usually followed by partial remission. In a minority of patients, the disease is relatively benign with no or little evidence of accumulating disability between exacerbations.

It remains to be determined whether primary progressive MS has the same pathophysiology as the more common types.

The age of MS onset is typically the mid-to-late 20s for the relapsing-remitting type and mid-to-late 30s for the primary-progressive type (although the age range is large). Persons with relapsing-remitting MS can convert to progressive MS, typically in their early 40s. The age of peak onset is 5 years earlier for women than for men, and women with MS typically outnumber men by 2 to 3 times.[1,2]

Symptoms and signs of the disease depend upon the part of the central nervous system affected. MRI studies show that most lesions are asymptomatic, although the effect of lesions may be cumulative, and the condition of some patients rapidly deteriorates.

Presenting symptoms in approximate descending order of frequency are:

- Sensory change in extremities.
- Optic neuritis.
- Motor symptoms including weakness, spasm, and paraplegia.
- Diplopia or internuclear ophthalmoplegia.
- Gait difficulties.
- Bladder/bowel dysfunction, vertigo, or pain.

Other vague symptoms, such as fatigue or cognitive difficulty, may become prominent with time and may correlate with the pathologic progression.

Risk Factors

No exact list of risk factors has been identified for MS. However, the following demographic and other factors are relevant:

Race and ethnicity. Risk varies dramatically among racial and ethnic groups. Among affected individuals, whites outnumber blacks by a 9:1 ratio. The condition is particularly common among Palestinians, Parsis, and Sardinians, and rare among Chinese and Japanese individuals, African blacks, and certain other ethnic groups.[3]

Geography. Risk depends on place of residence during the prepubertal years, increasing with distance from the equator. However, this finding may represent genetic susceptibility or vitamin D activity.

Low vitamin D intake. Supplementation of vitamin D is associated with reduced risk.[4,5]

Smoking. Smoking increases risk.[6]

Heredity. Monozygotic twins have a 20% to 39% risk when one twin has MS, as compared with non-twin siblings or dizygotic twins, who have a 3% to 5% risk.[7] Maternal origin of a hereditary factor is suggested.[8]

Stress. Stressful life events are associated with MS exacerbations.[9,10]

There have been some epidemiologic associations between MS and certain infectious agents, including Epstein-Barr virus[11,12] and *Chlamydia pneumoniae*.[13,14] However, no definitive causal links have been established,[15] and treatment trials directed at infection have not so far been successful.

Despite recent questions regarding potential links between MS and the hepatitis B vaccine, the evidence for any such causal link is weak.[16,17] For persons who have MS, vaccines are believed to be safe.[18,19]

Diagnosis

Two or more clinically distinct episodes of dysfunction of white matter pathways (ie, separated in space and time) as described above, in a person of the appropriate age, strongly suggest MS. These tracts include the optic nerves, sensory and motor tracts of the spinal cord and brain stem, and those of the cerebellum. Subcortical and periventricular white matter is most commonly involved, although lesions are often silent in these areas.

Presenting symptoms were listed previously. Some additional symptoms include:

- Fatigue.

- Heat intolerance. Elevated body temperatures exacerbate symptoms (Uhthoff syndrome).

- Radiating "electric shock" with movement of the neck (Lhermitte sign).

- Depression and/or cognitive dysfunction.

- Dysarthria, dysphagia, and/or nystagmus.

- Sexual dysfunction.

Diagnostic tests can also help confirm a clinical diagnosis:

Brain MRI is the test of choice and may show multiple white-matter lesions. A lesion's potential to represent an MS plaque corresponds directly to its size and proximity or relationship to the cerebral ventricles. Enhancement of a lesion indicates that it has been active within the past 3 months. Other disease processes such as ischemia and lupus can also cause white-matter lesions. Established MRI criteria are quite accurate in determining patients who are likely to have MS.[20,21]

Spinal MRI may aid diagnosis.[22] Fewer abnormalities are apparent on spinal cord imaging than on imaging of the brain in MS patients. However, this test may help satisfy the criterion of dissemination in space when few or no abnormalities are seen above the foramen magnum.[23]

Lumbar puncture may show oligoclonal bands, myelin basic protein, or IgG abnormalities in 80% to 85% of patients with active MS.

Abnormal **visual-evoked, somatosensory-evoked, or auditory-evoked potentials** may be identified; visual and somatosensory findings are most helpful for diagnostic purposes.

In a patient with a first episode of optic neuritis (clinically isolated syndrome), an MRI showing one or more white-matter lesions larger than 3 mm is associated with a greater than 50% chance of developing MS within 10 years (compared with a 22% chance for those without such lesions).[24] Overall, 39% of optic neuritis patients have been shown to develop MS within 10 years, and 60% have developed it within 40 years.[25] The presence of oligoclonal bands in the cerebrospinal fluid at the time of initial presentation with optic neuritis also increases the likelihood that patients will develop MS.

Treatment

No pharmacologic therapy has been proven to affect the course of primary progressive disease, although clinical trials continue to assess immune-suppressant medications.

Although there is no known cure for MS, the following treatments are used, with some efficacy:[26-28]

Corticosteroids may be used to treat acute attacks. They appear to shorten an attack but do not seem to affect its ultimate outcome. Typical regimens include intravenous methylprednisolone for 3 to 5 days, followed by an optional short course of prednisone taper. Oral steroid therapy may be efficacious; however, a study of patients with optic neuritis suggested that oral treatment may be detrimental.[29,30]

A relapsing-remitting diagnosis warrants the use of **interferon, glatiramer acetate,** or **natalizumab.** [26-28] Interferon is available as beta 1a and beta 1b. The drug choice depends on an individualized risk-benefit assessment for each patient. Interferon use is limited by its potential to create neutralizing antibodies, which are thought to decrease efficacy. Natalizumab use may raise the risk of progressive multifocal leukoencephalopathy and requires patient counseling and extensive monitoring.

Plasma exchange and **human immune globulin infusion**[31,32] are being investigated in rapidly worsening relapsing-remitting MS and as part of other immune treatment regimens.

Monoclonal antibodies targeting various presumptive aspects of MS pathophysiology are in development. In addition to Natalizumab, **Daclizumab** appears to be effective for relapsing-remitting MS and may hold some promise for secondary progressive MS.

Treatment options for progressive disease are severely limited.[26-28] **Immunosuppressive therapies,** such as steroids, methotrexate, cyclophosphamide, cladribine, interferon, total lymphoid irradiation, mitoxantrone, and human immune globulin infusion, are possible options. Long-term use is limited by risk of infection and malignancy.

Mitoxantrone[33,34] is effective for relapsing-remitting MS and probably also delays progression in progressive forms, but it is usually reserved for severe or rapidly deteriorating disease due to its potential for cardiac toxicity.

In addition to the disease-modifying treatments noted above, treatments may also be directed at specific symptoms.[35,36] Paroxysmal symptoms, such as spasms, sensory deficits, dysarthria/ataxia, and pain disorders, have shown some response to **anticonvulsants** such as valproic acid, carbamazepine, and gabapentin. Seizures, while not a common symptom of MS, are more common than in the general population.

Several medications, including **benzodiazepines, baclofen,** and **tizanidine**, may reduce muscle spasticity and, especially, painful spasms.

Modafinil or **amantadine** may help symptoms of fatigue.

Bladder spasticity may be treated with **anticholinergic** or other bladder **antispasmodic** medications. In cases of bladder dyssynergia, these medications can cause urinary retention.

Physiotherapy may improve movement, but benefits are usually short-lived.

Interferon beta 1a has shown some benefit with regard to preserving cognitive function in patients with relapsing-remitting MS.[37]

Cannabis and similar pharmaceutical agents have shown inconsistent results.

Statins, normally used to lower cholesterol, and some other emerging treatments may have benefit, but they require further study.

Nutritional Considerations

Several dietary factors have emerged in studies on the risk of developing MS or on its progression after diagnosis.

Supplemental Vitamin D

Limited evidence suggests that vitamin D may play a preventive role.[38] In the Nurses' Health Study I and II, regular use of a vitamin D supplement, typically within a multiple vitamin, resulted in a 40% reduction in MS risk.[5] The effect of vitamin D may be related to an increase in the antiinflammatory cytokine TGF-β and a reduction in Th1 cells that are known to be involved in the progression of autoimmune diseases, including MS.[39] Despite theoretical concerns about the possibility of toxic effects of excessive vitamin D, there were no reported instances of hypercalcemia or hypercalcuria in a 28-week trial of gradually escalating doses (28,000-280,000 IU/wk) of vitamin D_3 in 12 MS patients.[40]

Low-Saturated-Fat Diet

Several investigations testing the impact of diet in MS etiology have noted a higher prevalence of MS in correlation with greater intakes of energy, fat, and protein.[41] Specifically, higher intake of saturated fat found in foods of animal (not plant) origin, including meat, milk, butter, and eggs, was associated with the prevalence of MS.[41] The incidence of MS is low in Japan and in various African countries, where saturated fat intake is typically very low.[42-44]

Diets high in saturated fat might be involved in MS in various ways. One explanation suggests that meals high in saturated fat reduce oxygen availability to the CNS, resulting in activation of lysing enzymes in cells that may increase the permeability of the blood-brain barrier to potential toxins.[45] The tendency of saturated fats to elevate blood cholesterol concentrations may also play a role, as suggested by a reduction in MS lesions in patients treated with certain cholesterol-lowering drugs.[46] Saturated fats interfere with the conversion of essential fatty acids to their long-chain derivatives (eg, arachidonic acid [AA], eicosapentanoic acid [EPA], docosahexanoic acid [DHA]).[42] These derivatives reduce the production of proinflammatory cytokines[47] that play key roles in MS.[42]

Additionally, evidence indicates that during relapse, both low density lipoprotein (LDL) oxidizability and autoantibodies to oxidized LDL are increased.[48] The known proinflammatory effects of oxidized LDL[49] might explain the relationship between saturated fat-induced increases in LDL and MS. The reduced amount of LDL that would be expected in the blood of patients on diets very low in saturated fat might explain the benefit of such a diet in MS.

In 1948, neurologist Roy Swank, of the Montreal Neurological Institute, hypothesized that a low-saturated-fat diet would retard the progression of MS and tested this diet in 264 people.[45] His experimental diet restricted total and saturated fat intake, the latter to no more than 15 grams per day. It excluded dairy products that were more than 1% fat and fattier cuts of meat. The diet also included 15 grams of vegetable oils and 5 grams of cod liver oil daily, and patients could use an additional 5 grams of vegetable oils, as long as fat intake did not exceed 40 grams per day (not counting the small amounts of fat naturally present in cereal grains, fruits, and vegetables). Swank noted in a longitudinal study over 50 years that patients following this regimen strictly (ie, those who consumed no more than 30 grams of fat per day) experienced substantial decreases in MS exacerbation, lower mortality rates, and better functional capacity, compared with individuals whose fat intakes were higher.[50] Although this study has been criticized for selection bias and a lack of controls, masking, and randomization, the reported results are impressive. Diets that are low in total and saturated fat have additional benefits, including their potential to control obesity (which is a frequent finding in individuals with MS) and to reduce cardiovascular mortality.[41]

Dairy Avoidance

Epidemiologic studies have repeatedly associated milk and dairy product intake with MS prevalence. Two theories have emerged to explain this association. First, some evidence suggests that an immunologic phenomenon may be involved. MS patients are known to have an enhanced antibody response to myelin oligodendrocyte glycoprotein (MOG).[51] These antibodies have been found to cross-react with the bovine milk protein butyrophilin, a process that would not normally occur due to the development of oral tolerance to this protein early in life. Some have suggested that, when gastrointestinal infections or other factors prevent the development of tolerance *to this protein,* exposure to butyrophilin early in life may lead to susceptibility to MS. A second theory suggests that dairy calcium may suppress the production of $1,25(OH)_2D_3$,[52] the active hormone form of vitamin D that may be protective against MS, as noted above.

Lipid-Supplemented Diets

Several studies have revealed lower levels of essential fatty acids (eg, linoleic acid, an omega-6 fatty acid) or long-chain omega-3 fatty acids (eg, EPA) in red blood cells, adipose tissue, plasma lipids, and CSF of patients with MS.[41] Theoretically, supplementation with linoleic acid might be of benefit not only by preventing deficiency, but also by suppressing the type I immune response[53] that partly characterizes the immune response in MS.[54]

However, clinical trials of omega-6 fatty acid treatment for MS have not yielded convincing results. These studies provided patients with 17 to 20 grams of sunflower oil per day in capsule form for 24 to 30 months.

Numerous trials have been conducted in which omega-3 fatty acid supplements (eg, fish oils, EPA and DHA acid, 6 to 10 grams per day for 1 to 2 years) were given to patients with MS, and symptoms were rated on the Disability Status Score (DSS). Both the quality of evidence and the outcome of these studies have been reviewed by the Agency for Healthcare Research and Quality (AHRQ).[55] AHRQ concluded that, although some trials with weaker study designs found a reduction in MS incidence or progression, aggregate data are insufficient to draw conclusions about the effects of omega-3 fats on MS incidence, and evidence regarding the progression of MS is inconsistent and inconclusive.[55] A recent Cochrane Collaboration review concluded that there does not appear to be any short-term benefit of polyunsaturated fatty acids, although the data are insufficient to conclude that supplements are ineffective.[56]

Orders

See Basic Diet Orders chapter.

A low saturated fat (<10 g/d), low cholesterol diet may be tried prospectively. This is most effectively accomplished with a low-fat, vegan diet.

Nutrition consultation will be helpful in implementing this diet and arranging outpatient follow-up.

Smoking cessation.

Stress reduction exercises, such as yoga and meditation, may be useful.

What to Tell the Family

Although there is no known cure for MS, some clinical studies show that disease progression may be slowed if the saturated fat intake is less than 10 grams daily. Family members can assist the patient in reducing saturated fat and may improve their own health by following a similar diet. Limiting or avoiding animal products (red meat, chicken, fish, eggs, and dairy products) and tropical oils (palm, palm kernel, and coconut) is usually necessary to reach this goal, and a nutritionist can aid in following this diet regimen.

References

1. Irizarry MC. Multiple Sclerosis. In: Cudkowicz ME, Irizarry MC, eds. *Neurologic Disorders in Women*. Boston, Ma: Butterworth-Heinemann; 1997:85.

2. Wallin MT, Page WF, Kurtzke JF. Multiple sclerosis in US veterans of the Vietnam era and later military service: race, sex, and geography. *Ann Neurol*. 2004;55:65-71.

3. Rosati G. The prevalence of multiple sclerosis in the world: an update. *Neurological Sciences*. 2001;22:117-139.

4. Van der Mei IA, Ponsonby AL, Dwyer T, et al. Past exposure to sun, skin phenotype, and risk of multiple sclerosis: case-control study. *BMJ*. 2003;327:316.

5. Munger KL, Zhang SM, O'Reilly E, et al. Vitamin D intake and incidence of multiple sclerosis. *Neurology*. 2004;62:60-65.

6. Franklin GM, Nelson L. Environmental risk factors in multiple sclerosis: causes, triggers, and patient autonomy. *Neurology*. 2003;61:1032-1034.

7. Sadovnick AD, Armstrong H, Rice GP, et al. A population-based study of multiple sclerosis in twins: update. *Ann Neurol*. 1993;33:281-285.

8. Ebers GC, Sadovnick AD, Dyment DA, et al. Parent-of-origin effect in multiple sclerosis: observations in half-siblings. *Lancet*. 2004;363:1773-1774.

9. Mohr DC, Hart SL, Julian L, Cox D, Pelletier D. Association between stressful life events and exacerbation in multiple sclerosis: a meta-analysis. *BMJ*. 2004;328:731.

10. Ackerman KD, Stover A, Heyman R, et al. 2002 Robert Ader New Investigator award. Relationship of cardiovascular reactivity, stressful life events, and multiple sclerosis disease activity. *Brain Behav Immun*. 2003;17:141-151.

11. Thacker EL, Mirzaei F, Ascherio A. Infectious mononucleosis and risk for multiple sclerosis: a meta-analysis. *Ann Neurol*. 2006;59:499-503.

12. Lunemann JD, Munz C. Epstein-Barr virus and multiple sclerosis. *Current Neurology & Neuroscience Reports.* 2007;7:253-258.

13. Bagos PG, Nikolopoulos G, Ioannidis A. Chlamydia pneumoniae infection and the risk of multiple sclerosis: a meta-analysis. *Multiple Sclerosis.* 2006;12:397-411.

14. Munger KL, Peeling RW, Hernan MA, et al. Infection with Chlamydia pneumoniae and risk of multiple sclerosis. *Epidemiology.* 2003;14:141-147.

15. Hernan MA, Zhang SM, Lipworth L, et al. Multiple sclerosis and age at infection with common viruses. *Epidemiology.* 2001;12:301-306.

16. Schattner A. Consequence or coincidence? The occurrence, pathogenesis and significance of autoimmune manifestations after viral vaccines. *Vaccine.* 2005;23:3876-3886.

17. Hocine MN, Farrington CP, Touze E, et al. Hepatitis B vaccination and first central nervous system demyelinating events: reanalysis of a case-control study using the self-controlled case series method. *Vaccine.* 2007;25:5938-5943.

18. Rutschmann OT, McCrory DC, Matchar DB. Immunization and MS: a summary of published evidence and recommendations. *Neurology.* 2002;59:1837-1843.

19. DeStefano F, Verstraeten T, Jackson LA, et al. Vaccinations and risk of central nervous system demyelinating diseases in adults. *Arch Neurol.* 2003;60:504-509.

20. Swanton JK, Rovira A, Tintore M, et al. MRI criteria for multiple sclerosis in patients presenting with clinically isolated syndromes: a multicentre retrospective study. *Lancet Neurology.* 2007;6:677-686.

21. Filippi M, Rocca MA. Conventional MRI in multiple sclerosis. *J Neuroimaging.* 2007;17(suppl 1):3S-9S.

22. Kidd D, Thorpe JW, Thompson AJ, et al. Spinal cord MRI using multi-array coils and fast spin echo. II. Findings in multiple sclerosis. *Neurology.* 1993;43:2632.

23. Bot JC, Barkhof F, Polman CH, et al. Spinal cord abnormalities in recently diagnosed MS patients: added value of spinal MRI examination. *Neurology.* 2004;62:226-233.

24. Beck RW, Trobe JD, Moke PS, et al. High- and low-risk profiles for the development of multiple sclerosis within 10 years after optic neuritis: experience of the Optic Neuritis Treatment Trial. *Arch Ophthalmol.* 2003;121:944-949.

25. Rodriguez M, Siva A, Cross SA, et al. Optic neuritis: a population-based study in Olmsted County, Minnesota. *Neurology.* 1995;45:244-250.

26. Kieseier BC, Wiendl H, Hemmer B, Hartung HP. Treatment and treatment trials in multiple sclerosis. *Current Opinion in Neurology.* 2007;20:286-293.

27. Korniychuk E, Dempster JM, O'Connor E, et al. Evolving therapies for multiple sclerosis. *Int Rev Neurobiol.* 2007;79:571-588.

28. Freedman MS. Disease-modifying drugs for multiple sclerosis: current and future aspects. *Expert Opinion on Pharmacotherapy.* 2006;7(suppl 1):S1-S9.

29. Beck RW, Cleary PA, Anderson MM Jr, et al. A randomized, controlled trial of corticosteroids in the treatment of acute optic neuritis. The Optic Neuritis Study Group. *N Engl J Med.* 1992;326:581-588.

30. Beck RW, Cleary PA. Optic neuritis treatment trial. One-year follow-up results. *Arch Ophthalmol.* 1993;111:773-775.

31. Soelberg-Sorensen P. Intravenous polyclonal human immunoglobulins in multiple sclerosis. *Neurodegenerative Dis.* 2008;5:8-15.

32. Fazekas F, Strasser-Fuchs S, Hommes OR. Intravenous immunoglobulin in MS: promise or failure? *J Neurol Sci.* 2007;259:61-66.

33. Perini P, Calabrese M, Tiberio M, et al. Mitoxantrone versus cyclophosphamide in secondary-progressive multiple sclerosis: a comparative study. *J Neurol.* 2006;253:1034-1040.

34. Fox EJ. Management of worsening multiple sclerosis with mitoxantrone: a review. *Clin Ther.* 2006;28:461-474.

35. Boissy AR, Cohen JA. Multiple sclerosis symptom management. *Expert Rev Neurother.* 2007;7:1213-1222.

36. Henze T. What is new in symptom management? *Int MS J.* 2007;14:22-27.

37. Fischer JS, Priore RL, Jacobs LD, et al. Neuropsychological effects of interferon beta-1a in relapsing multiple sclerosis. Multiple Sclerosis Collaborative Research Group. *Ann Neurol.* 2000;48:885-892.

38. Brown SJ. The role of vitamin D in multiple sclerosis. *Ann Pharmacother.* 2007;40:1158-1161.

39. Cantorna MT, Mahon BD. Mounting evidence for vitamin D as an environmental factor affecting autoimmune disease prevalence. *Exp Biol Med* (Maywood). 2004;229:1136-1142.

40. Kimball SM, Ursell MR, O'Connor P, Vieth R. Safety of vitamin D_3 in adults with multiple sclerosis. *Am J Clin Nutr.* 2007;86:645-651.

41. Schwarz S, Leweling H. Multiple sclerosis and nutrition. *Mult Scler.* 2005;11:24-32.

42. Das UN. Is there a role for saturated and long-chain fatty acids in multiple sclerosis? *Nutrition.* 2003;19:163-168.

43. Malosse D, Perron H, Sasco A, Seigneurin JM. Correlation between milk and dairy product consumption and multiple sclerosis prevalence: a worldwide study. *Neuroepidemiology.* 1992;11:304-312.

44. Ghadirian P, Jain M, Ducic S, Shatenstein B, Morisset R. Nutritional factors in the aetiology of multiple sclerosis: a case-control study in Montreal, Canada. *Int J Epidemiol.* 1998;27:845-852.

45. Swank RL, Grimsgaard A. Multiple sclerosis: the lipid relationship. *Am J Clin Nutr.* 1988;48:1387-1393.

46. Vollmer T, Key L, Durkalski V, et al. Oral simvastatin treatment in relapsing-remitting multiple sclerosis. *Lancet.* 2004;363:1607-1608.

47. Calder PC. n-3 polyunsaturated fatty acids, inflammation, and inflammatory diseases. *Am J Clin Nutr.* 2006;83(suppl):1505S-1519S.

48. Besler HT, Comoglu S. Lipoprotein oxidation, plasma total antioxidant capacity and homocysteine level in patients with multiple sclerosis. *Nutr Neurosci.* 2003;6:189-196.

49. Paoletti R, Gotto AM Jr, Hajjar DP. Inflammation in atherosclerosis and implications for therapy. *Circulation.* 2004;109:III20-III26.

50. Swank RL, Goodwin J. Review of MS patient survival on a Swank low saturated fat diet. *Nutrition.* 2003;19:161-162.

51. Guggenmos J, Schubart AS, Ogg S, et al. Antibody cross-reactivity between myelin oligodendrocyte glycoprotein and the milk protein butyrophilin in multiple sclerosis. *J Immunol.* 2004;172:661-668.

52. Chan JM, Stampfer MJ, Ma J, Gann PH, Gaziano JM, Giovannucci EL. Dairy products, calcium, and prostate cancer risk in the Physicians' Health Study. *Am J Clin Nutr.* 2001;74:549-554.

53. Namazi MR. The beneficial and detrimental effects of linoleic acid on autoimmune disorders. *Autoimmunity*. 2004;37:73-75.

54. Knutson KL, Disis ML. Tumor antigen-specific T helper cells in cancer immunity and immunotherapy. *Cancer Immunol Immunother*. 2005;54:721-728.

55. MacLean CH, Issa AM, Newberry SJ, et al. Effects of Omega-3 fatty acids on cognitive function with aging, dementia, and neurological diseases. Rockville, MD: Agency for Healthcare Research and Quality, US Dept of Health and Human Services; 2005. AHRQ publication 05-E011-2.

56. Farinotti M, Simi S, DiPietrantonj C, et al. Dietary interventions for multiple sclerosis. *Cochrane Database Syst Rev*. 2007;(1):CD004192.

80. Parkinson Disease

Parkinson disease (idiopathic paralysis agitans) is a progressive, degenerative disorder of the brain that is associated with a loss of dopaminergic neurons in the substantia nigra; neurodegeneration in other areas of the central nervous system (CNS), such as the locus ceruleus and the cerebral cortex; and the presence of Lewy bodies. Loss of dopamine stimulation causes an imbalance between excitation and inhibition pathways of the basal ganglia (that coordinate motor activity), resulting in impairment in the voluntary control of movement.

Hallmarks of the disease include muscular ("cogwheel") rigidity, slowed initiation of movement (bradykinesia), and an unstable, flexed posture. Despite instability, the gait is narrow-based. A resting tremor that decreases with movement appears in about two-thirds of patients and most often manifests in a classic "pill-rolling" tremor of the thumb and forefinger. This tremor disappears with the initiation of movement, only to return with sustained postures or rest. Patients exhibit a shuffling gait and slowed movements and usually show progressive difficulties with activities of daily living (eg, eating, dressing, writing). Depression is common, and hallucinations may appear with more advanced disease, sometimes as an adverse side effect of medications used to treat the condition. Dementia occurs in about one-third of cases and often appears as Alzheimer disease. However, prominent hallucinations may indicate diffuse Lewy body disease. Autonomic dysfunction, including postural hypotension, is common late in the course of disease.

Most cases are idiopathic. However, there are many conditions that present as parkinsonism, most of which do not include tremor. Some of these are degenerations of the basal ganglia systems but without dominant degeneration of substantia nigra seen in idiopathic Parkinson. Parkinsonism may also result from exposure to toxins (MPTP, a contaminant of poorly synthesized opioid narcotics; pesticides; manganese toxicity), head trauma, CNS infection, and postsynaptic dopamine-receptor blockers, such as antiemetics, antipsychotics, and reserpine.

Risk Factors

Age. About 1% of Americans over age 50 are affected, and prevalence increases with age. Typical age of onset is the late 50s, although 10% of cases present before age 40.

Although genetics has been postulated to play a role (and, in rare families, a specific genetic defect can be identified), familial disease is uncommon.

Environmental factors, such as pesticides and heavy metals, are being studied for possible roles in Parkinson disease, especially because specific toxins are known to target the substantia nigra.

Diagnosis

Diagnosis of Parkinson disease is generally made by the characteristic clinical presentation, including history, physical examination, and neurologic examination. Presentation is often unilateral or asymmetrical, especially at disease onset.

Although there are no commonly available laboratory tests or imaging modalities, clinical response to a dopamine agonist is strong supportive evidence for the diagnosis.

A CT scan, MRI, and/or laboratory testing may be indicated in equivocal cases to rule out other diagnoses (Wilson disease, Huntington disease, cerebrovascular disease, normal pressure hydrocephalus, mass lesions). However, imaging is generally indicated only if the presentation is atypical or if focal symptoms are present.

Treatment

Parkinson disease follows a progressive course. The disease advances in all cases, but the rate of progression varies, with younger patients often progressing more rapidly. While there is no definitive cure, medical treatment can alleviate many of the symptoms. Medications should be used at their lowest effective dose.

Adjuvant Therapies

Physical, occupational, and speech therapies are often beneficial, and social work consultation can help make daily living at home easier for the patient and prevent further disability. Exercise has been shown to be beneficial at all stages of the condition and can help mood as much as mobility. Exercises should focus on conditioning, strengthening, and stretching (20 minutes at least three times weekly is a reasonable target). As balance worsens, appropriate precautions must be taken.

Medications

Medications that might cause parkinsonian symptoms should be discontinued and alternative drugs used if necessary. Treatment is primarily aimed at increasing the availability of dopamine to the CNS and reducing symptoms. To date, there are no proven methods to slow disease progression.

Levodopa (a dopamine metabolic precursor) plus **carbidoba** (which antagonizes the dopa decarboxylase enzyme that would otherwise convert levodopa to dopamine prior to reaching the brain) have proven to be the most effective therapy to improve symptoms. Concern about potentially speeding Parkinson deterioration by early use of levodopa is probably unfounded. Extended use of levodopa is correlated with development of symptoms of dopamine excess, such as dyskinesias.

Dopamine agonists (bromocriptine, pramipexole, ropinerole, apomorphine) improve symptoms and can delay levodopa therapy. Apomorhine, an injectable, can rescue patients from sudden akinesia.

Monoamine oxidase inhibitors (type B) (Selegiline and Rasagiline) impede the breakdown of dopamine and may also prolong the action of levodopa.

Catecholamine-O-methyl-transferase (COMT) inhibitors (entacapone, tolcapone) may slow the breakdown of dopamine, which is often helpful if the effect of levodopa therapy is too short. However, tolcapone is associated with liver toxicity that can be fatal.

Amantidine may be useful not only for its mild anti-Parkinson effects, but also as a mild psychostimulant and a treatment for severe dyskinesias.

Some evidence suggests that **low-dose estrogen** may reduce motor symptoms in postmenopausal women. Further study is warranted.

Hallucinations may be treated with clozapine or quetiapine, tremor with benztropine or trihexyphenidyl, and depression with amitriptyline.

Surgery

Surgical approaches (deep brain stimulation, or on rare occasion, thalamotomy or pallidotomy) may have a role in advanced disease, especially in patients with severe intractable dyskinesia, tremor, or rigidity.

Nutritional Considerations

Nutritional links to Parkinson disease have been identified, although the mechanisms explaining these associations are not entirely clear.

Nutritional Factors in Prevention

In epidemiologic studies, the following factors have been associated with reduced risk of developing Parkinson disease:

Low-fat diets. The prevalence of Parkinson disease correlates with intake of animal fat,[1,2] and with total and saturated fat.[3]

Minimizing dairy products. The Health Professionals Follow-Up Study found a higher risk for Parkinson disease in men with high intakes of dairy products (roughly 3 servings per day).[4] Positive associations with Parkinson disease risk were found for dairy protein, dairy calcium, dairy vitamin D, and lactose, and not for other sources of these nutrients. Similarly, the Honolulu-Asia Aging Study, which included approximately 7,500 men, also found a risk from dairy intake; those consuming >16 oz/day of milk had more than twice the risk for Parkinson disease, compared with those who drank no milk.[5] The largest study relating dairy products to Parkinson disease (more than 130,000 men and women were involved in the American Cancer Society's Cancer Prevention Study II Nutrition Cohort) found that individuals who consumed between 134 g and 502 g of milk per day (roughly 4-16 oz/day) had a 40% greater risk, compared with those who consumed less. In those persons whose intake exceeded 16 oz/day, the risk was 60% greater.[6]

Caffeinated beverages. Observational studies have found protective effects of frequent consumption of coffee or tea,[7-9] although some evidence suggests that benefits are limited to men, and to women who do not use postmenopausal hormone-replacement therapy.

Nutritional Factors in Treatment

The most immediate nutritional concerns in Parkinson disease treatment include changes in the absorption rate, blood levels, and CNS uptake of L-dopa. The protein content of meals, and particularly the distribution of protein intake throughout the day, has emerged as an important consideration in the effectiveness of L-dopa for many patients.[10-13]

Patients with PD have a 4-fold increase in risk for weight loss of 10 lbs or more compared with age-matched controls for a variety of reasons, including dysphagia, dyskinesias, depression, and cognitive impairment. Conversely, excess weight gain may occur due to an increase in sedentary behavior.[14] Individuals with chewing or swallowing difficulties should be referred to a speech therapist for appropriate changes in diet texture. A registered dietitian can help families plan meals that are also adequate in fluid and fiber (particularly insoluble fiber), an important concern to prevent constipation.[14]

Timing of Protein Intake

Most patients do not note a major effect of food on their response to medication. Those who do appreciate an effect of food can usually avoid problems by taking levodopa a half an hour before, or more than an hour after, meals. However, some patients with Parkinson disease note a major interaction in which high-protein meals blunt the response to medication, particularly L-dopa, reflecting competition for neutral amino acid carriers across the blood-brain barrier. The beneficial effects of a protein-reduced diet, or the redistribution of almost all protein to evening meals on L-dopa availability (and subsequent control of dyskinesias), have been subsequently documented in patients who experience erratic responses to levodopa therapy.[10-13] In these studies, reducing protein intake to amounts as low as 10 g/d (or 0.5g/kg body weight) resulted in an improved therapeutic response in many (though not all) individuals. Low-protein diets resulted in improvements in neurologic scoring.[12]

Similarly, redistributing all but 7 grams of protein intake to the evening meal resulted in improvement in the Northwest Disability and AIMS Dyskinesia Scale.[11] Both low-protein diets and diets reserving protein for evening meals were associated with significant reductions in the need for L-dopa.[11,12] A more recent study that both decreased protein intake to the Recommended Daily Allowance (ie, 0.8 g/kg body weight) and distributed almost all protein to the evening meal (through the use of special low-protein starches) demonstrated a similar benefit. Specifically, postprandial and total "off" phases (consisting of dyskinesias and complaints of pain, paresthesias, sweating, constipation or shortness of breath) were reduced from a mean of 79 to 49 minutes, while total 'off' time was decreased from a mean of 271 to 164 minutes by the protein redistribution diet, reductions of 38% and 39% in "off" time, respectively.[10] In addition, the midday dosage of L-dopa was reduced in one-third of patients by an average of 9%. Caution may be required because the results of protein redistribution can be so effective that an excess of L-dopa may enter the brain and trigger dyskinesia.[15]

A protein restriction-induced decrease in requirement for L-dopa may offer more than symptomatic benefit. It is well known that oxidative stress is central to the pathology of PD, and autoxidation of L-dopa increases oxidative stress in the substantia nigra.[16] In addition, higher cumulative levodopa doses have been associated with the earlier occurrence of motor complications.[17] Therefore, measures that reduce L-dopa dosages may prolong the period during which patients benefit from drug therapy. In addition, high-protein meals raise blood levels of homocysteine,[18] a possible risk factor for vascular disease known to be elevated in PD patients as a side-effect of L-dopa.[19]

Due to the risk of nutrient insufficiencies on protein-restricted diets,[20] multiple-vitamin-mineral supplementation has been suggested.[14] Physicians interested in referring patients for a protein redistribution diet that meets both energy and micronutrient needs should contact a registered dietitian, who can help patients and families plan appropriate meals.

Botanicals

The seed powder of the plant *Mucuna pruriens* contains significant amounts of L-dopa, and has long been used in Ayurvedic (East Indian) medicine for the treatment of movement disorders.[21] Although several open trials and one double-blind, placebo-controlled trial demonstrated effectiveness, a report by the American Academy of Neurology concluded that there is currently insufficient evidence to support or refute the use of *Mucuna pruriens*.[22] However, considering the commercial availability of *Mucuna pruriens*, in addition to the growing number of East Indian immigrants to the United States,[23] physicians may well encounter patients who are using this product.

Oxidative Stress and Parkinson Disease

Several factors have led to the theory that oxidative stress contributes to the risk for development of Parkinson disease,[24] possibly by causing mitochondrial damage.[25] This has resulted in trials of both medications that inhibit oxidation and supplements that scavenge free radicals.

Vitamin E. Some evidence suggests that dietary vitamin E intake is inversely correlated with risk of developing Parkinson disease, and lower levels of vitamin E have been found in the cerebrospinal fluid of patients with the condition, when compared with patients who have other neurologic diseases.[26] However, vitamin E supplements have not been shown to be effective, either in preventing or slowing the progression of the condition.[27]

Coenzyme Q10. The neuroprotective effects of coenzyme Q10 (300, 600, or 1200 mg/day) are under investigation for a potential role in Parkinson disease treatment, but significant benefits have not yet been demonstrated.[22]

Orders

See Basic Diet Orders chapter.

A nutrition consultation would be appropriate to assist the patient in restricting protein prior to the evening hours.

What to Tell the Family

To minimize deconditioning, patients should maintain an active lifestyle to the extent possible. Also, patients should be aware that Parkinson disease often causes weight loss. Family members can help reduce severe weight loss risk by providing breakfast, lunch, and between-meal snacks that are high in calories from whole grains (100% whole oats, oat bran, bulgur, barley, brown rice), fruits, 100% fruit juices, and vegetables. The family should ensure proper nutrient intake and be advised that protein deficiency is unlikely if adequate calories are consumed. Family members can improve the effectiveness of L-dopa therapy by reserving high-protein foods for evening meals. A qualified nutrition professional (eg, registered dietitian) may be helpful in accomplishing these aims.

References

1. Anderson C, Checkoway H, Franklin GM, Beresford S, Smith-Weller T, Swanson PD. Dietary factors in Parkinson's disease: the role of food groups and specific foods. *Movement Disorder.* 1999;14:21-27.

2. Logroscino G, Marder K, Cote L, Tang M-X, Shea S, Mayeux R. Dietary lipids and antioxidants in Parkinson's disease: a population-based, case-control study. *Ann Neurol.* 1996;39:89-94.

3. Johnson CC, Gorell JM, Rybicki BA, Sanders K, Peterson EL. Adult nutrient intake as a risk factor for Parkinson's disease. *Int J Epidemiol.* 1999;28:1102-1109.

4. Chen H, Zhang SM, Hernan MA, Willett WC, Ascherio A. Diet and Parkinson's disease: a potential role of dairy products in men. *Ann Neurol.* 2002;52:793-801.

5. Park M, Ross GW, Petrovitch H, et al. Consumption of milk and calcium in midlife and the future risk of Parkinson disease. *Neurology*. 2005;64:1047-1051.

6. Chen H, O'Reilly E, McCullough ML, et al. Consumption of dairy products and risk of Parkinson's disease. *Am J Epidemiol*. 2007;165:998-1006.

7. Ascherio A, Weisskopf MG, O'Reilly EJ, et al. Coffee consumption, gender, and Parkinson's disease mortality in the cancer prevention study II cohort: the modifying effects of estrogen. *Am J Epidemiol*. 2004;160:977-984.

8. Ascherio A, Chen H, Schwarzschild MA, Zhang SM, Colditz GA, Speizer FE. Caffeine, postmenopausal estrogen, and risk of Parkinson's disease. *Neurology*. 2003;60:790-795.

9. Tan EK, Tan C, Fook-Chong SM, et al. Dose-dependent protective effect of coffee, tea, and smoking in Parkinson's disease: a study in ethnic Chinese. *J Neurol Sci*. 2003;216:163-167.

10. Barichella M, Marczewska A, De Notaris R, et al. Special low-protein foods ameliorate postprandial off in patients with advanced Parkinson's disease. *Mov Disord*. 2006;21:1682-1687.

11. Pincus JH, Barry K. Protein redistribution diet restores motor function in patients with dopa-resistant "off" periods. *Neurology*. 1988;38:481-483.

12. Mena I, Cotzias GC. Protein intake and treatment of Parkinson's disease with levodopa. *N Engl J Med*. 1975;292:181-184.

13. Gillespie NG, Mena L, Cotzias GC, Bell MA. Diets affecting treatment of parkinsonism with levodopa. *J Am Diet Assoc*. 1973;62:525-528.

14. Olanow CW, Watts RL, Koller WC. An algorithm (decision tree) for the management of Parkinson's disease (2001): treatment guidelines. *Neurology*. 2001;56:S1-S88.

15. Berry EM, Growdon JH, Wurtman JJ, Caballero B, Wurtman RJ. A balanced carbohydrate: protein diet in the management of Parkinson's disease. *Neurology*. 1991;41:1295-1297.

16. Di Stefano A, Sozio P, Cocco A, et al. L-dopa- and dopamine-(R)-alpha-lipoic acid conjugates as multifunctional codrugs with antioxidant properties. *J Med Chem*. 2006;49:1486-1493.

17. Hauser RA, McDermott MP, Messing S. Factors associated with the development of motor fluctuations and dyskinesias in Parkinson disease. *Arch Neurol*. 2006;63:1756-1760.

18 [was 15]. Verhoef P, de Groot LC. Dietary determinants of plasma homocysteine concentrations. *Semin Vasc Med*. 2005;5:110-123.

19. Lamberti P, Zoccolello S, Armanese E, et al. Hyperhomocysteinemia in L-dopa treated Parkinson's disease patients: effect of cobalamin and folate administration. *Eur J Neurol*. 2005;12:365-368.

20. Kempster PA, Wahlqvist ML. Dietary factors in the management of Parkinson's disease. *Nutr Rev*. 1994;52(pt 1):51-58.

21. Katzenschlager R, Evans A, Manson A. Mucuna pruriens in Parkinson's disease: a double blind clinical and pharmacological study. *J Neurol Neurosurg Psychiatry*. 2004;75:1672-1677.

22. Sucherowsky O, Gronseth G, Perlmutter J, et al. Practice parameter: neuroprotective strategies and alternative therapies for Parkinson disease (an evidence-based review): report of the Quality Standards Subcommittee of the American Academy of Neurology. *Neurology*. 2006;66:976-982.

23. Camarota SA, McArdle N. Where immigrants live: an examination of state residency of the foreign born by country of origin in 1990 and 2000. Center for Immigration Studies Web site. http://www.cis.org/articles/2003/back1203.html#table1. Published 2003. Accessed July 1, 2006.

24. Hald A, Lotharius J. Oxidative stress and inflammation in Parkinson's disease: is there a causal link? *Exp Neurol.* 2005;193:279-290.

25. Liu J, Ames BN. Reducing mitochondrial decay with mitochondrial nutrients to delay and treat cognitive dysfunction, Alzheimer's disease, and Parkinson's disease. *Nutr Neurosci.* 2005;8:67-89.

26. Buhmann C, Arlt S, Kontush A, et al. Plasma and CSF markers of oxidative stress are increased in Parkinson's disease and influenced by antiparkinsonian medication. *Neurobiol Dis.* 2004;15:160-170.

27. Pham DQ, Plakogiannis R. Vitamin E supplementation in Alzheimer's disease, Parkinson's disease, tardive dyskinesia, and cataract: part 2. *Ann Pharmacother.* 2005;39:2065-2072.

81. Alzheimer Disease

Alzheimer disease is a slowly progressive dementia characterized by cognitive decline and behavioral changes. Pathological changes in the brain include atrophy of the cerebral cortex (particularly in the temporal and parietal lobes), the presence of neurofibrillary tangles and senile (amyloid) plaques, a loss of cholinergic neurons in the brain, and reduced activity of choline acetyltransferase (the enzyme responsible for acetylcholine production) in the cerebral cortex and hippocampus. Pathogenesis is not well understood but involves neurotoxicity, inflammation and, likely, apoptosis.

The disease typically progresses from mild memory impairment to severe cognitive loss with personality/behavioral changes, sometimes including irritability, delusions, and hallucinations. The patient often experiences language problems (particularly with generation of nouns [dysnomia]), and spatial disorientation is common. Alzheimer disease reduces life expectancy by as much as 50% following initial diagnosis.[1]

Risk Factors

Alzheimer disease disproportionately affects women and African Americans. Evidence suggests that Alzheimer disease is associated with the following:

Older age. Results of a US community study (n=3,623) estimated prevalence at 3% for ages 65 to 74, 18.7% for ages 75 to 84, and 47.2%

for those over 85.[2] In 2000, 4.5 million people in the United States had Alzheimer disease, and that number is expected to triple by 2050.[3]

Family history. Risk is inversely proportional to the age of onset in a first-degree relative.

Genetics. Certain genetic abnormalities (particularly with the presenilin and amyloid precursor protein genes) place individuals at high risk of early onset Alzheimer disease. However, these represent only a small fraction of cases. More commonly, late onset Alzheimer disease is associated with certain subtypes of apo E4, among other genes. Trisomy 21 is also associated with increased risk.[4]

Hypercholesterolemia.[4] Of the 1,037 postmenopausal women enrolled in the Heart and Estrogen/Progestin Replacement Study, those with LDL cholesterol levels in the top 25% had 76% greater odds of developing cognitive impairment, compared with women who had lower LDL levels.[5]

Overweight. Women over the age of 70 had a 36% increased risk for Alzheimer disease for every one point increase in body mass index.[6] This finding has not been replicated in men.

Hypertension,[4] **declining blood pressure over time, cerebrovascular and cardiovascular disease, diabetes, smoking, and persistently elevated alcohol use.** All these factors are associated with cerebral atrophy. Excess body weight may exacerbate these factors or lead to cerebral atrophy directly.[7]

Elevated homocysteine[8,9] **and the metabolic syndrome** may also increase risk.

Diagnosis

Pathologic findings cannot be demonstrated except by autopsy (or, rarely, by brain biopsy); therefore, definitive diagnosis of Alzheimer disease is not possible in normal clinical practice. Current evaluation of the patient with suspected Alzheimer disease focuses on identifying potentially reversible disorders that can produce cognitive deficits.

Routine neuroimaging, particularly magnetic resonance imaging, can help rule out certain causes of dementia, such as vascular dementia, hydrocephaly, chronic subdural hematoma, and brain tumors. Occasionally, such conditions are identified even in the absence of other clinical indicators. Therefore, neuroimaging should be considered in all cases of progressive cognitive deterioration. Tests of potential metabolic abnormalities (eg, hypothyroidism, vitamin B_{12} deficiency, electrolyte abnormalities) should be included in the workup. Occasionally, lumbar puncture may be needed, particularly in atypical cases (such as those associated with somnolence or confusion at the outset) or those with rapid progression. Electroencephalography, which is usually normal early in Alzheimer disease, may provide useful clues to alternative diagnosis in unusual cases.

Severe sleep disorders, disorders of liver and renal function, and side effects of various medications can produce cognitive dysfunction, as can depression (pseudodementia). Neuropsychiatric testing may be useful to aid in the diagnosis of Alzheimer disease or to evaluate its progression. Such testing may be particularly helpful if the presentation is atypical.

Overlap with other causes of dementia does occur (eg, Lewy body dementia and Pick disease). However, because treatment is generally based on symptoms, biopsy is not commonly performed.

Treatment

People who **exercise, participate in intellectually stimulating activities, and remain active in social networks** appear to be at lower risk for Alzheimer disease,[10] and those affected may slow its progression through these activities.

Drugs may have a modest effect.

Memantine, an N-methyl-D-aspartate receptor antagonist along with **galantamine**, may slow the loss of mental and physical function. Memantine has modest effects in patients with moderate-to-advanced disease.

Some evidence suggests that **nonsteroidal anti-inflammatory drugs (NSAIDs)** may help prevent Alzheimer disease.[11] This finding requires further study.

The benefits of **acetylcholinesterase inhibitors**, such as **donepezil**, are modest, especially in advanced cases.[12]

Ginkgo biloba may provide a modest benefit. A ginkgo biloba extract known as EGb761 appears to act by a mechanism similar to that of cholinesterase inhibitors for mild-to-moderate Alzheimer disease,[13,14] and it showed a small benefit over a placebo in clinical trials.[15-17]

HMG-CoA reductase inhibitors (statins) are under investigation for a possible role in prevention of Alzheimer disease. In addition, huperzine

A, an anticholinergic herb used in traditional Chinese medicine,[18] and other herbs[19] are under study for possible use in Alzheimer disease prevention and treatment.

Nutritional Considerations

Several epidemiological studies have examined associations between diet and the risk of Alzheimer disease and cognitive decline.[20-22] The following factors are under study for a possible role in reducing risk:

Low Plasma Cholesterol

Elevated cholesterol levels are associated with increased risk for Alzheimer disease, even after controlling for the presence of the apo E4 allele.[23] Use of lipid-lowering agents has been found in several epidemiological studies to be associated with a lower risk of dementia,[24,25] although clinical trials have not yet supported this conclusion or established a mechanism by which such an improvement would occur.

Reduced Saturated and Trans Fatty Acids

High intake of saturated fats and trans fats is associated with risk of Alzheimer disease.[26-28] In contrast, limited evidence suggests that diets high in omega-3 fatty acids may reduce Alzheimer disease risk.[29]

Adherence to a Mediterranean diet is associated with reduced Alzheimer risk.[30]

Some have suggested that the regular consumption of fatty fish (ie, more than twice per week) may be associated with lower risk for AD in individuals without the ε4 allele.[31] However, a systematic review by the Agency for Healthcare Research and Quality (AHRQ) concluded that data are inadequate to justify conclusions.[32]

Maintaining Healthy Weight

Avoidance of overeating and maintenance of ideal weight may lower risk for Alzheimer disease. Reduced energy intake may reduce the risk for Alzheimer disease, especially in people carrying the apo E4 allele.[33] An 18-year follow-up study found that women diagnosed with dementia had higher average body mass index than that of women not diagnosed with dementia.[6]

Antioxidants

Evidence is mixed regarding the role of antioxidants in reducing risk of Alzheimer disease. Two prospective studies found that greater intakes of antioxidant-rich foods may lower the risk for Alzheimer disease.[34,35] One was a four-year study of 815 community-dwelling residents. Among those who were negative for apo E4, the highest dietary vitamin E intake was associated with a 70% lower risk for Alzheimer disease.[34] The Rotterdam Study of more than 5,000 individuals found that a high intake of dietary vitamins C and E was associated with a roughly 20% lower risk for this disease.[35]

With respect to antioxidant supplements, some evidence indicates that a combination of vitamins C and E (as alpha-tocopherol) is associated with an 80% lower risk for Alzheimer disease.[36] Other evidence suggests that the effect of pharmacologic dosages of vitamin E may be similar to that of selegine in treating Alzheimer disease.[37] However, a review of clinical trials concluded that evidence for the use of supplementary alpha-tocopherol in Alzheimer disease is as yet insufficient.[38] Additional evidence that supplementation with alpha-tocopherol alone is unlikely to be beneficial comes from studies of patients with mild cognitive impairment (a risk factor for Alzheimer disease), in which vitamin E supplementation did not affect the rate of progression to clinical Alzheimer disease.[39]

Good sources of vitamin C include citrus fruits, kiwi, melons, and many vegetables. Good sources of vitamin E include wheat germ, peanuts, and sunflower seeds.

B Vitamins

An adequate intake of folate, B_6, and B_{12} may reduce risk of Alzheimer disease. Inadequate intakes of these B vitamins can cause a rise in plasma homocysteine, which in turn is a strong and independent risk factor for the development of Alzheimer disease.[8,40] Findings suggest that low folate or B_{12} status may precede the onset of Alzheimer disease.[20,41] In one large prospective study, older individuals with the highest intake of folate had significantly lower risk of developing Alzheimer disease during the study period.[42]

Avoiding Aluminum

Some evidence suggests that avoiding dietary or environmental exposure to aluminum may reduce the risk for Alzheimer disease. Although aluminum is not yet established as a direct cause of Alzheimer disease in humans,[43,44] epidemiological studies have found statistically significant relationships between aluminum in drinking water and Alzheimer disease.[45] Also, some evidence exists that patients with Alzheimer disease have increased absorption of aluminum even when they are on normal diets.[46] Aluminum has caused neurotoxic effects in individuals who have been exposed to the metal occupationally, by dialysis, or through the use of aluminum-containing medications, although the pathologic changes in these cases is not identical to those of Alzheimer disease.[43,47]

Nevertheless, this remains a topic of significant controversy and ongoing research.[48]

Avoiding Excess Iron

Excess iron intake may contribute to Alzheimer risk. Iron accumulates in the brain with aging, and evidence suggests that iron contributes to the beta-amyloid deposition, amyloid precursor protein, free radicals, and neurofibrillary tangles that characterize this disease. In addition, the brains of Alzheimer patients appear to exhibit numerous defects in iron storage, binding, and mobilization not seen in the brains of healthy control participants.[49] Evidence of the role of iron and aluminum in Alzheimer disease is partly confirmed by previous studies[50,51] and more recent investigations[52] that revealed improvement in Alzheimer patients treated with chelating agents that remove excess aluminum, iron, and copper.

Moderate Alcohol Consumption

Although alcohol intake as low as 20 grams per day (1.25 servings) is a known risk factor for certain cancers, hypertension, and several other diseases,[53] recent studies show that people who consume 1 to 3 drinks per day have a lower risk for Alzheimer disease, compared with teetotalers.[54] In most of these studies, risk reduction was associated with wine and not alcohol per se,[20] and a cause-and-effect relationship has not been established.

Benefits of moderate alcohol consumption, if any, are thought to derive from alterations in blood lipids and platelet aggregation (which result from consumption of alcohol in any form), as well as from antioxidant flavonoids present in red wine. Heavy alcohol use is associated with cognitive decline. It is not clear whether alcohol accelerates the progression of Alzheimer disease or causes cognitive impairment by a separate mechanism.[55]

Orders

See Basic Diet Orders chapter.

Physical and occupational therapy consultation for home safety evaluation and needs assessment.

What to Tell the Family

Although no cure for Alzheimer disease is known, drug treatment may slow progression. Additionally, behavioral changes that include mental and physical exercise may help slow the disease process. A diet low in saturated fat, cholesterol, and trans fatty acids will help prevent other age-related debilitating diseases in the patient. This diet is also ideal for the general health of the whole family, and some evidence suggests that it may help prevent the occurrence of Alzheimer disease in family members.

Safety precautions for Alzheimer patients are important at all times. Connection with social services or a support group may also help ease the burden of care for a person with Alzheimer disease. Although routine genetic testing is not typically recommended, family members may want to be tested for the presence of the apo E4 allele. At minimum, they should be encouraged to mitigate their future risk of Alzheimer disease by noting the above recommendations.

References

1. Larson EB, Shadlen MF, Wang L, et al. Survival after initial diagnosis of Alzheimer's disease. *Ann Intern Med.* 2004;140:501-509.

2. Evans DA, Funkenstein HH, Albert MS, et al. Prevalence of Alzheimer's disease in a community population of older persons: higher than previously reported. *JAMA.* 1989;262:2551-2556.

3. Hebert LE, Scherr PA, Bienias JL, Bennett DA, Evans DA. Alzheimer's disease in the US population: prevalence estimates using the 2000 census. *Arch Neurol.* 2003;60:1119-1122.

4. Kivipelto M, Helkala EL, Laakso MP, et al. Apolipoprotein E epsilon4 allele, elevated midlife total cholesterol level, and high midlife systolic blood pressure are independent risk factors for late-life Alzheimer's disease. *Ann Intern Med.* 2002;137:149-155.

5. Yaffe K, Barrett-Connor E, Lin F, Grady D. Serum lipoprotein levels, statin use, and cognitive function in older women. *Arch Neurol.* 2002;59:378-384.

6. Gustafson D. An 18-year follow-up of overweight and risk of Alzheimer's disease. *Arch Intern Med.* 2003;163:1524-1528.

7. Gustafson D, Lissner L, Bengtsson C, Björkelund C, Skoog I. A 24-year follow-up of body mass index and cerebral atrophy. *Neurology.* 2004;63:1876-1881.

8. den Heijer T, Vermeer SE, Clarke R, et al. Homocysteine and brain atrophy on MRI of nondemented elderly. *Brain.* 2003;126(pt 1):170-175.

9. Seshadri S, Beiser A, Selhub J, et al. Plasma homocysteine as a risk factor for dementia and Alzheimer's disease. *N Engl J Med.* 2002;346:476-483.

10. Fratiglioni L, Paillard-Borg S, Winblad B. An active and socially integrated lifestyle in late life might protect against dementia. *Lancet Neurol.* 2004;3:343-353.

11. in't Veld BA, Ruitenberg A, Hofman A, et al. Nonsteroidal anti-inflammatory drugs and the risk of Alzheimer's disease. *N Engl J Med.* 2001;345:1515-1521.

12. Courtney C, Farrell D, Gray R, et al. Long-term donepezil treatment in 565 patients with Alzheimer's disease (AD2000): randomised double-blind trial. *Lancet.* 2004;363:2105-2115.

13. Wettstein A. Cholinesterase inhibitors and Gingko extracts—are they comparable in the treatment of dementia? Comparison of published placebo-controlled efficacy studies of at least six months' duration. *Phytomedicine.* 2000;6:393-401.

14. Mazza M, Capuano A, Bria P, Mazza S. Ginkgo biloba and donepezil: a comparison in the treatment of Alzheimer's dementia in a randomized placebo-controlled double-blind study. *Eur J Neurol.* 2006;13:981-985.

15. Le Bars PL, Kieser M, Itil KZ. A 26-week analysis of a double-blind, placebo-controlled trial of the ginkgo biloba extract EGb 761 in dementia. *Dement Geriatr Cogn Disord.* 2000;11:230-237.

16. Kanowski S, Hoerr R. Ginkgo biloba extract EGb 761 in dementia: intent-to-treat analyses of a 24-week, multicenter, double-blind, placebo-controlled, randomized trial. *Pharmacopsychiatry.* 2003;36:297-303.

17. Birks J, Grimley EV, Van Dongen M. Ginkgo biloba for cognitive impairment and dementia. *Cochrane Database Syst Rev.* 2002;(4):CD003120.

18. Zhang HY, Tang XC. Neuroprotective effects of huperzine A: new therapeutic targets for neurodegenerative disease. *Trends Pharmacol Sci.* 2006;27:619-625.

19. Kim DSHL, Kim J-Y, Han YS. Alzheimer's disease drug discovery from herbs: neuroprotectivity from -amyloid (1-42) insult. *J Alternative Complementary Med.* 2007;13:333-340.

20. Luchsinger JA, Mayeux R. Dietary factors and Alzheimer's disease. *Lancet Neurol.* 2004;3:579-587.

21. Gillette-Guyonnet S, Abellan Van Kan G, Andrieu S, et al. IANA task force on nutrition and cognitive decline with aging. *J Nutr Health Aging.* 2007;11:132-152.

22. Donini LM, De Felice MR, Cannella C. Nutritional status determinants and cognition in the elderly. *Arch Gerontol Geriatr.* 2007;44(suppl 1):143-153.

23. Notkola IL, Sulkava R, Pekkanen J, et al. Serum total cholesterol, apolipoprotein E 4 allele, and Alzheimer's disease. *Neuroepidemiology.* 1998;17:14-20.

24. Rockwood K, Kirkland S, Hogan DB, et al. Use of lipid-lowering agents, indication bias, and the risk of dementia in community-dwelling elderly people. *Arch Neurol.* 2002;59:223-227.

25. Simons M, Keller P, Dichgans J, Schulz JB. Cholesterol and Alzheimer's disease. *Neurology.* 2001;57:1089-1093.

26. Morris MC, Evans DA, Bienias JL, et al. Dietary fats and the risk of incident Alzheimer's disease. *Arch Neurol.* 2003;60:194-200.

27. Kalmijn S, Launer LJ, Ott A, Witteman JC, Hofman A, Breteler MM. Dietary fat intake and the risk of incident dementia in the Rotterdam Study. *Ann Neurol.* 1997;42:776-782.

28. Giem P, Beeson WL, Fraser GE. The incidence of dementia and intake of animal products: preliminary findings from the Adventist Health Study. *Neuroepidemiology.* 1993;12:28-36.

29. Morris MC, Evans DA, Bienias JL, et al. Consumption of fish and n-3 fatty acids and risk of incident Alzheimer's disease. *Arch Neurol.* 2003;60:940-946.

30. Scarmeas N, Stern Y, Tang MX, Mayeux R, Luchsinger JA. Mediterranean diet and risk for Alzheimer's disease. *Ann Neurol.* 2006;59:912-921.

31. Huang TL, Zandi PP, Tucker KL, et al. Benefits of fatty fish on dementia risk are stronger for those without APOE epsilon4. *Neurology.* 2005;65:1409-1414.

32. MacLean CH, Issa AM, Newberry SJ, et al. Effects of omega-3 fatty acids on cognitive function with aging, dementia, and neurological diseases. Rockville, MD: Agency for Healthcare Research and Quality, US Dept of Health and Human Services; 2005. AHRQ publication 05-E011-2.

33. Luchsinger JA, Tang M-X, Shea S, Mayeux R. Caloric intake and the risk of Alzheimer's disease. *Arch Neurol.* 2002;59:1258-1263.

34. Morris MC, Evans DA, Bienias JL, et al. Dietary intake of antioxidant nutrients and the risk of incident Alzheimer's disease in a biracial community study. *JAMA.* 2002;287:3230-3237.

35. Engelhart MJ, Geerlings MI, Ruitenberg A, et al. Dietary intake of antioxidants and risk of Alzheimer's disease. *JAMA.* 2002;287:3223-3229.

36. Zandi PP, Anthony JC, Khachaturian AS, et al. Reduced risk of Alzheimer disease in users of antioxidant vitamin supplements: the Cache County Study. *Arch Neurol.* 2004;61:82-88.

37. Sano M, Ernesto C, Thomas RG. A controlled trial of selegiline, alpha-tocopherol, or both as treatment for Alzheimer's disease. *N Engl J Med.* 1997;336:1216-1222.

38. Tabet N, Birks J, Grimley Evans J. Vitamin E for Alzheimer's disease. *Cochrane Database Syst Rev.* 2000;(4):CD002854.

39. Petersen R, Thomas RG, Grundman M, et al. Vitamin E and donepezil for the treatment of mild cognitive impairment. *New Engl J Med.* 2005;352:2379-2388.

40. Mattson MP. Will caloric restriction and folate protect against AD and PD? *Neurology.* 2003;60:690-695.

41. Quadri P, Fragiacomo C, Pezzati R, et al. Homocysteine, folate, and vitamin B-12 in mild cognitive impairment, Alzheimer's disease, and vascular dementia. *Am J Clin Nutr.* 2004;80:114-122.

42. Luchsinger JA, Tang MX, Miller J, et al. Relation of higher folate intake to lower risk of Alzheimer disease in the elderly. *Arch Neurol.* 2007;64:86-92.

43. Campbell A. The potential role of aluminum in Alzheimer's disease. *Nephrol Dial Transplant.* 2002;17(suppl 2):17-20.

44. Yokel RA. The toxicology of aluminum in the brain: a review. *Neurotoxicology.* 2000;21:813-828.

45. Flaten TP. Aluminum as a risk factor in Alzheimer's disease, with emphasis on drinking water. *Brain Res Bull.* 2001;55:187-196.

46. Solfrizzi V, Panza F, Capurso A. The role of diet in cognitive decline. *J Neural Transm.* 2003;110:95-110.

47. Soni MG, White SM, Flamm WG, Burdock GA. Safety evaluation of dietary aluminum. *Regul Toxicol Pharmacol.* 2001;33:66-79.

48. Shcherbatykh I, Carpenter DO. The role of metals in the etiology of Alzheimer's disease. *J Alzheimer Dis.* 2007;11:191-205.

49. Thompson KJ, Shoham S, Connor JR. Iron and neurodegenerative disorders. *Brain Res Bull.* 2001;55:155-164.

50. McLachlan DR, Smith WL, Kruck TP. Desferrioxamine and Alzheimer's disease: video home behavior assessment of clinical course and measures of brain aluminum. *Ther Drug Monit.* 1993;15:602-607.

51. Crapper-McLachlan DR, Dalton AJ, Kruck TP, et al. Intramuscular desferrioxamine in patients with Alzheimer's disease. *Lancet.* 1991;337:1304-1308.

52. Ritchie CW, Bush AI, Mackinnon A, et al. Metal-protein attenuation with iodochlorhydroxyquin (clioquinol) targeting Abeta amyloid deposition and toxicity in Alzheimer disease: a pilot phase 2 clinical trial. *Arch Neurol.* 2003;60:1685-1691.

53. Rehm J, Gmel G, Sempos CT, Trevisan M. Alcohol-related morbidity and mortality. *Alcohol Res Health.* 2003;27:39-51.

54. Letenneur L, Larrieu S, Barberger-Gateau P. Alcohol and tobacco consumption as risk factors of dementia: a review of epidemiological studies. *Biomed Pharmacother.* 2004;58:95-99.

55. Tyas SL. Alcohol use and the risk of developing Alzheimer's disease. National Institute on Alcohol Abuse & Alcoholism. *Alcohol Res Health.* 2001;25:299-306.

82. Stroke

Stroke, an infarct in the brain, is the third-leading cause of death in the United States. About 80% of strokes are ischemic in origin and generally result from occlusion of a major cerebral artery by an embolus or thrombus. Global ischemia can occur after respiratory arrest or after cardiac events such as asystole or ventricular fibrillation. Hemorrhagic strokes occur when blood from a ruptured vessel (eg, an aneurysm) compresses and damages brain tissue. Venous strokes, due to thrombosis of the venous dural sinuses, are less common but may be associated with hypercoagulability, dehydration, and the use of estrogen.

A transient ischemic attack (TIA) produces similar signs and symptoms but is transitory. It often resolves completely within 30 to 60 minutes, although symptoms may last several hours. Occurrence of a TIA indicates a need for thorough neurologic and cardiovascular evaluation of stroke risk.

Warning signs of stroke include the following sudden changes:

- Numbness (paresthesia) or weakness (paresis) of the face, arm, or leg, usually on one side of the body.

- Confusion, difficulty speaking (dysarthria or aphasia) or understanding.

- Visual disturbances, which may include partial or complete vision loss.

- Dizziness and/or ataxia.

- Severe headache with no known cause—particularly with hemorrhagic strokes.

Risk Factors

Compared with whites, blacks and Native Americans have higher a prevalence of stroke, and blacks, Asians, Native Americans, and Latinos have higher stroke mortality.[1] It is unclear whether these differences are due to environmental (eg, differential access to medical care) or genetic causes. Other risk factors include:

Age. The risk of stroke doubles every 10 years beyond age 55.[2,3]

Gender. Women have a slightly higher incidence of stroke, compared with men, and case-fatality rates due to stroke are also higher in women.[4]

Hypertension. As the most important modifiable risk factor, especially for hemorrhagic stroke, both systolic hypertension and diastolic hypertension are associated with an increased risk. (For more information, see Hypertension chapter.)

Smoking. Cigarette smoking increases risk for ischemic stroke, intracerebral hemorrhage, and subarachnoid hemorrhage. The risk is reduced to that of a nonsmoker within 2 to 5 years of smoking cessation.

Overweight. Excess body weight is associated with increased ischemic stroke risk.

Diabetes.

Dyslipidemia.

Sedentary lifestyle. Higher levels of occupational or leisure-time physical activity protect against stroke.[5] A study of women undergoing coronary angiography found that those with higher activity levels were at significantly lower risk for cardiovascular events, including stroke.[6]

Poor nutrition. High-fat, high-sodium diets and a lack of key nutrients such as folic acid have been associated with increased risk for stroke (see Nutritional Considerations below).

Carotid stenosis. Both symptomatic and asymptomatic stenoses of the internal carotid arteries are associated with increased risk for ischemic stroke.[7]

Atrial fibrillation. In the Framingham Study, patients with atrial fibrillation had 5-fold greater risk of stroke than did their healthy counterparts.[8] Further, the attributable risk of stroke due to atrial fibrillation increased with age from 1.5% for persons aged 50 to 59 years, to 23.5% for those aged 80 to 89 years.[8]

Sickle cell disease.

Migraine. Studies have found that migraines with aura were strongly associated with risk of stroke and TIA.[9] Hemiplegic and basilar migraines are also risk factors.

Alcohol abuse.

Drug abuse. Use of cocaine and amphetamines may result in hemorrhage.

Hormone replacement therapy. Combined and unopposed estrogen therapies raise stroke risk, although low-dose contraceptives do not appear to carry this risk.

Heart disease, vasculitis, elevated homocysteine levels, anticoagulant use, and **bleeding disorders** also raise the risk of stroke. Stroke risk is elevated during pregnancy and the postpartum period.

Diagnosis

Evaluation should include a detailed history of symptom onset, a thorough physical (including neurologic) examination, and imaging tests to determine whether the stroke is hemorrhagic or ischemic. Evaluation of the cardiac rhythm is also essential. Paroxysmal atrial fibrillation may easily be missed if the patient is not closely monitored.

Laboratory tests normally include a complete blood count (CBC), blood glucose, erythrocyte sedimentation rate (elevated in temporal arteritis or other vasculitides), lipoprotein and triglyceride levels, and coagulation tests. Young patients and those without cardiovascular risk factors may have abnormal antiphospholipid antibodies (specifically, lupus anticoagulant). Lumbar puncture may help diagnose small subarachnoid hemorrhages, if computed tomography (CT) scan or magnetic resonance imaging (MRI) is negative.

A noncontrast CT scan of the brain helps determine whether a stroke is hemorrhagic or ischemic and is the initial study of choice. However, areas of infarct due to ischemia are often not acutely visible. CT is necessary before considering thrombolysis, which must be performed within

3 hours of the earliest symptom onset. Newer intravascular techniques may extend this window, but currently they are available only in tertiary care settings.

Subarachnoid hemorrhage on CT scan strongly suggests an aneurysm, although an arteriovenous malformation is also a possibility. Aneurysms and other vascular malformations can often be identified by CT scan or by MRI, but cerebral angiogram (conventional or CT angiogram) is the preferred method, particularly for identification of aneurysms. MRI (diffusion- and perfusion-weighted images) is best for detecting ischemic strokes and can show damaged areas that are at risk even at the earliest stages of stroke.

Carotid duplex ultrasonagraphy, arteriography, or magnetic resonance angiography (MRA) of the carotid system may determine if stroke has occurred as a result of carotid occlusion. MRA is generally more accurate than carotid duplex studies.

Treatment

Daily aspirin prophylaxis is generally recommended in patients at risk for stroke, assuming that they are not at high risk for side effects (eg, gastrointestinal bleeding).

Basic supportive treatment is important in suspected stroke. Fever should be treated, blood pressure and hyperglycemia should be regulated so as to be neither high nor low, and intubation is sometimes necessary.

A stroke-outcomes assessment should be performed daily to monitor the level of impairment.[10]

Because the intensity of stroke rehabilitation efforts is associated with the degree of recovery, many hospitals have specialized stroke-recovery units.[11] Speech therapy, physical therapy, and occupational therapy are important treatments during rehabilitation.

Transient Ischemic Attack

Because the risk of recurrent strokes is high in patients who have suffered a transient ischemic attack (TIA) or stroke, it is essential to identify the cause and implement therapy to reduce risk.

- Antiplatelet therapy with aspirin or its alternatives (eg, clopidogrel, ticlopidine, or aspirin plus dipyridamole) can reduce stroke risk.
- Warfarin should be considered if cardiac thrombi or atrial fibrillation is involved. Investigation for cardiac abnormalities (including

right to left shunts) should be considered, particularly in young patients with stroke or TIA, or if there is a high index of suspicion for embolus.

- Patients at high risk for stroke may require carotid endarterectomy within 2 weeks of the TIA if stenosis is >70% (and sometimes >50%) on the symptomatic side. Treatment of stenosis in asymptomatic patients remains controversial; very high-grade stenoses may warrant intervention if surgical risks are low. Intravascular procedures, such as stenting, have not proven superior to endarterectomy, but they may be an option in high-risk surgical patients.

- If hypercoagulability is suspected (particularly in young individuals with few stroke risk factors), screening for hypercoagulability is appropriate.

Ischemic Stroke

Ischemic stroke may lead to rapid (2 to 5 days) neurologic deterioration resulting from cerebral edema or hemorrhagic conversion of infarct, and patients may be at risk for brain herniation. Close monitoring should occur in the intensive care unit using the Glasgow coma scale, regular CT imaging, and possibly intracranial pressure monitoring.

Thrombolytic agents (alteplase) dissolve artery-blocking clots in the brain during the critical early stages of stroke. They are of proven benefit only when administered within 3 hours of stroke onset and when patients meet restrictive criteria. After this time, the risk of intracerebral hemorrhage outweighs benefit. Some intravascular procedures may extend this window, although they should be administered only in a stroke center.

Antiplatelet agents (eg, aspirin, aspirin-dipyridamole, clopidogrel, ticlopidine) should be given within 48 hours of stroke if there is no contraindication. Of these, only aspirin has been well-studied.

Treatment with low-molecular-weight heparin and/or warfarin is generally reserved for strokes with ongoing thromboembolism. In addition, their use requires initial evaluation to exclude intracranial hemorrhage and baseline evaluation of the international normalized ratio (INR), partial thromboplastin time, platelet count, and other tests to assess coagulation status, if indicated.

Some studies have also found emergency carotid endarterectomy to be effective in rare circumstances.

There is growing recognition of the value of aggressive lipid lowering for stroke prevention in at-risk patients and for the management of acute ischemic strokes.[12] In most circumstances, patients should be considered for interventions immediately after recognition of their high-risk status. Beginning treatment very early after a cerebrovascular event leads to better outcomes.

Neuroprotective agents have failed to show benefits, thus far, in clinical trials.

Hemorrhagic Stroke

Treatment of intracerebral hemorrhage depends on the extent of the hemorrhage, as well as its cause and location. Medical or surgical decompression may be indicated.

Subarachnoid hemorrhage due to an aneurysm or arteriovenous malformation requires urgent evaluation and may warrant surgery, depending on the patient's age, clinical status, and risk of rebleeding.

Nutritional Considerations

The role of dietary factors in stroke is apparent from the disorder's pathophysiology. Because ischemic strokes are caused by atherosclerosis, they are more common in the presence of high blood cholesterol concentrations, which, in turn, are strongly linked to dietary saturated fat and cholesterol and a low fiber intake, among other contributors to cardiovascular risk. Similarly, hypertension contributes to both ischemic and hemorrhagic stroke, so diets that are high in saturated fat or sodium or low in potassium would tend to increase risk. A diet high in potassium, low in sodium, and rich in vegetables, fruits, cereal fiber, and whole grains may be ideal for reducing stroke risk.[13]

In epidemiologic studies, the following factors are associated with reduced stroke risk:

Reduced dietary fat and cholesterol. Individuals with higher blood cholesterol concentrations tend to have higher stroke risk.[14,15] In women with diabetes sampled from the Nurses' Health Study, higher intakes of saturated fat and cholesterol—which raise blood cholesterol concentrations—were related to an increased risk for cardiovascular disease (CVD), including stroke.[16]

Diets rich in fruits, vegetables, and whole grains. Higher intakes of fruits and vegetables not only reduce fat and cholesterol intake, but also are associated with reduced risk for stroke.[17] These foods provide carotenoids, vitamin C, vitamin E, and folate, all of which have been associated with reduced stroke risk in epidemiologic studies.[18-23] A meta-analysis of cohort studies of fruit and vegetable intake that included 257,551 individuals concluded that, compared with individuals eating less than 3 servings per day, the risk for stroke was roughly 10% less for persons eating 3 to 5 servings per day and 25% less for those having more than 5 servings per day.[24] High intake of cereal fiber was associated with lower risk for both total and hemorrhagic stroke in some studies,[25,26] and with a lower risk for ischemic stroke in others.[27]

Consuming less sodium and more potassium. In addition to decreasing the risk for hypertension, lower sodium intake has been found to decrease stroke incidence and mortality.[28,29] When compared with persons consuming the lowest amounts of potassium, those eating the highest amounts had the lowest stroke mortality.[30,31]

Maintenance of healthy body weight. The risk for stroke increases with the degree of overweight,[32,33] although evidence to date is stronger for men than for women.[34,35] The same dietary changes that reduce cholesterol and blood pressure also tend to reduce body weight (see Dyslipidemias and Hypertension chapters). Clinical trials have not yet tested the extent to which weight reduction may reduce stroke risk.[36]

Limiting alcohol consumption. High alcohol intake (30 to 60 grams, or 3 to 6 drinks, per day) is associated with a greater risk of stroke.[37,38] Consuming moderate amounts of alcohol (1 to 2 drinks per day) appears to reduce stroke risk,[37,39] but may aggravate risk for other conditions, such as breast cancer.

After stroke occurs, adequate nutrition is an essential part of clinical care. In the FOOD Trial Collaboration, poor nutritional status was associated with worse outcomes at 6 months post-stroke.[40] Two additional issues are being addressed in research studies:

Folate supplementation. Elevated homocysteine levels are associated with heightened stroke risk. Because dietary supplementation with folic acid, pyridoxine, and vitamin B_{12} reduces homocysteine levels, 2 large supplementation trials were carried out with these vitamins. Despite the strong theoretical basis, there was no observable decrease in stroke risk.[41,42]

However, a meta-analysis of controlled trials examining the role of folate supplementation in primary prevention of stroke found a significant 18% lower stroke risk in individuals given folate in amounts ranging from 0.5 mg/d to 15 mg/d. Persons most likely to benefit were those taking folic acid for >36 months, those who experienced a decrease in homocysteine concentration of more than 20%, individuals whose habitual diets omitted folate-fortified grain products, and those without a history of previous stroke.[43] Folate supplementation has not been shown to be effective for stroke prevention in patients with preexisting vascular diseases.[44]

Antioxidants. Antioxidant concentrations are often low in patients with ischemic stroke, and low intake of foods rich in antioxidants is associated with elevated stroke risk. However, despite the fact that antioxidant-rich diets appear to have some preventive effects, supplementation with specific antioxidants has not been shown to significantly reduce risk.

Patients who have had a stroke should have an assessment of their swallowing ability before resuming eating or drinking. If they cannot take food and fluids orally, they should receive enteral feedings using a nasogastric, nasoduodenal, or PEG tube to maintain hydration and nutrition while undergoing efforts to restore swallowing.[45] Typically, adequate swallowing mechanics return within the first 2 weeks post-stroke. Nutritional supplements do not appear to be necessary or beneficial in these patients, unless required for an indication other than stroke.

Orders

See Basic Diet Orders chapter.

Sodium intake less than 2 grams daily.

Physical/occupational therapy consultation for home safety evaluation.

Stroke rehabilitation, speech and swallowing therapy, as appropriate.

What to Tell the Family

Stroke occurs more frequently among those of advanced age and those who have blood vessel disease, family or previous history of stroke, and poor blood pressure control. However, persons who eat diets rich in fruits, vegetables, and fiber and low in saturated fat, cholesterol, and sodium decrease their risk for stroke, as do those who quit smoking, drink alcohol minimally, and engage in regular physical activity. It is important for the patient and family to follow a similar, healthful diet in order to decrease the risk of future stroke. In addition, family members should be aware of the warning signs of stroke and immediately call 911 if these signs occur. Timing of care is critical to treatment success.

References

1. Centers for Disease Control and Prevention (CDC). Prevalence of Stroke—United States, 2005. *MMWR Morb Mortal Wkly Rep.* 2007;56:469-474.

2. Brown RD, Whisnant JP, Sicks JD, et al. Stroke incidence, prevalence, and survival: secular trends in Rochester, Minnesota, through 1989. *Stroke.* 1996;27:373-380.

3. Whisnant JP. Modeling of risk factors for ischemic stroke. The Willis Lecture. *Stroke.* 1997;28:1840-1844.

4. American Heart Association. Women, Heart disease and Stroke. Available at: http://www.americanheart.org/presenter.jhtml?identifier=4786. Accessed June 28, 2007.

5. Wendel-Vos GC, Schuit AJ, Feskens EJ, et al. Physical activity and stroke. A meta-analysis of observational data. *Int J Epidemiol.* 2004;33:787-798.

6. Wessel TR, Arant CB, Olson MB, et al. Relationship of physical fitness vs. body mass index with coronary artery disease and cardiovascular events in women. *JAMA.* 2004;292:1179-1187.

7. Barnett HJ, Gunton RW, Eliasziw M, et al. Causes and severity of ischemic stroke in patients with internal carotid artery stenosis. *JAMA.* 2000;283:1429-1436.

8. Wolf PA, Abbott RD, Kannel WB. Atrial fibrillation as an independent risk factor for stroke: the Framingham Study. *Stroke.* 1991;22:983-988.

9. Stang PE, Carson AP, Rose KM, et al. Headache, cerebrovascular symptoms, and stroke: the Atherosclerosis Risk in Communities Study. *Neurology.* 2005;64:1573-1577.

10. American Heart Association. Stroke outcome classification. Available at: http://www.americanheart.org/presenter.jhtml?identifier=1859. Accessed May 30, 2005.

11. Kwakkel G, Wagenaar RC, Koelman TW, et al. Effects of intensity of rehabilitation after stroke: a research synthesis. *Stroke.* 1997;28:1550-1556.

12. Paciaroni M, Hennerici M, Agnelli G, Bogousslavsky J. Statins and stroke prevention. *Cerebrovascular Diseases.* 2007;24:170-182.

13. Ding EL, Mozaffarian D. Optimal dietary habits for the prevention of stroke. *Semin Neurol.* 2006;26:11-23.

14. Koren-Morag N, Tanne D, Graff E, Goldbourt U. Low- and high-density lipoprotein cholesterol and ischemic cerebrovascular disease: the bezafibrate infarction prevention registry. *Arch Intern Med.* 2002;162:993-999.

15. Leppala JM, Virtamo J, Fogelholm R, Albanes D, Heinonen OP. Different risk factors for different stroke subtypes: association of blood pressure, cholesterol, and antioxidants. *Stroke.* 1999;30:2535-2540.

16. Tanasescu M, Cho E, Manson JE, Hu FB. Dietary fat and cholesterol and the risk of cardiovascular disease among women with type 2 diabetes. *Am J Clin Nutr.* 2004;79:999-1005.

17. Gillman MW, Cupples LA, Gagnon D, et al. Protective effect of fruits and vegetables on development of stroke in men. *JAMA.* 1995;273:1113-1117.

18. Hak AE, Ma J, Powell CB, et al. Prospective study of plasma carotenoids and tocopherols in relation to risk of ischemic stroke. *Stroke.* 2004;35:1584-1588.

19. Hirvonen T, Virtamo J, Korhonen P, Albanes D, Pietinen P. Intake of flavonoids, carotenoids, vitamins C and E, and risk of stroke in male smokers. *Stroke.* 2000;31:2301-2306.

20. Voko Z, Hollander M, Hofman A, Koudstaal PJ, Breteler MM. Dietary antioxidants and the risk of ischemic stroke: the Rotterdam Study. *Neurology.* 2003;61:1273-1275.

21. Yochum LA, Folsom AR, Kushi LH. Intake of antioxidant vitamins and risk of death from stroke in postmenopausal women. *Am J Clin Nutr.* 2000;72:476-483.

22. He K, Merchant A, Rimm EB, et al. Folate, vitamin B_6, and B_{12} intakes in relation to risk of stroke among men. *Stroke.* 2004;35:169-174.

23. Bazzano LA, He J, Ogden LG, et al. Dietary intake of folate and risk of stroke in US men and women: NHANES Epidemiologic Follow-up Study. National Health and Nutrition Examination Survey. *Stroke.* 2002;33:1183-1188.

24. He FJ, Nowson CA, MacGregor GA. Fruit and vegetable consumption and stroke: meta-analysis of cohort studies. *Lancet.* 2006;367:320-326.

25. Oh K, Hu FB, Cho E, et al. Carbohydrate intake, glycemic index, glycemic load, and dietary fiber in relation to risk of stroke in women. *Am J Epidemiol.* 2005;161:161-169.

26. Ascherio A, Rimm EB, Hernan MA, et al. Intake of potassium, magnesium, calcium, and fiber and risk of stroke among U.S. men. *Circulation.* 1998;98:1198-1204.

27. Liu S, Manson JE, Stampfer MJ, et al. Whole grain consumption and risk of ischemic stroke in women: A prospective study. *JAMA.* 2000;284:1534-1540.

28. Nagata C, Takatsuka N, Shimizu N, Shimizu H. Sodium intake and risk of death from stroke in Japanese men and women. *Stroke.* 2004;35:1543-1547.

29. He J, Ogden LG, Vupputuri S, Bazzano LA, Loria C, Whelton PK. Dietary sodium intake and subsequent risk of cardiovascular disease in overweight adults. *JAMA.* 1999;282:2027-2034.

30. Fang J, Madhavan S, Alderman MH. Dietary potassium intake and stroke mortality. *Stroke.* 2000;31:1532-1537.

31. Khaw KT, Barrett-Connor E. Dietary potassium and stroke-associated mortality. A 12-year prospective population study. *N Engl J Med.* 1987;316:235-240.

32. Suk SH, Sacco RL, Boden-Albala B, et al. Abdominal obesity and risk of ischemic stroke: the Northern Manhattan Stroke Study. *Stroke.* 2003;34:1586-1592.

33. Zhou BF. Effect of body mass index on all-cause mortality and incidence of cardiovascular diseases-report for meta-analysis of prospective studies open optimal cut-off points of body mass index in Chinese adults. *Biomed Environ Sci.* 2002;15:245-252.

34. Rosengren A, Wilhelmsen L, Lappas G, Johansson S. Body mass index, coronary heart disease and stroke in Swedish women. A prospective 19-year follow-up in the BEDA study. *Eur J Cardiovasc Prev Rehabil.* 2003;10:443-450.

35. Field AE, Coakley EH, Must A, et al. Impact of overweight on the risk of developing common chronic diseases during a 10-year period. *Arch Intern Med.* 2001;161:1581-1586.

36. Curioni C, André C, Veras R. Weight reduction for primary prevention of stroke in adults with overweight or obesity. *Cochrane Database Syst Rev.* 2006;(4):CD006062.

37. Mukamal KJ, Ascherio A, Mittleman MA, et al. Alcohol and risk for ischemic stroke in men: the role of drinking patterns and usual beverage. *Ann Intern Med.* 2005;142:11-19.

38. Reynolds K, Lewis B, Nolen JD, Kinney GL, Sathya B, He J. Alcohol consumption and risk of stroke: a meta-analysis. *JAMA.* 2003;289:579-588.

39. Klatsky AL, Armstrong MA, Friedman GD, Sidney S. Alcohol drinking and risk of hospitalization for ischemic stroke. *Am J Cardiol.* 2001;88:703-706.

40. FOOD Trial Collaboration. Poor nutritional status on admission predicts poor outcomes after stroke: observational data from the FOOD trial. *Stroke.* 2003;34:1450-1456.

41. Toole JF, Malinow MR, Chambless LE, et al. Lowering homocysteine in patients with ischemic stroke to prevent recurrent stroke, myocardial infarction, and death: the Vitamin Intervention for Stroke Prevention (VISP) randomized controlled trial. *JAMA.* 2004;291:565-575.

42. Lonn E, Yusuf S, Arnold MJ, et al. Homocysteine lowering with folic acid and B vitamins in vascular disease. *N Engl J Med.* 2006;354:1567-1577.

43. Wang X, Qin X, Demirtas H, et al. Efficacy of folic acid supplementation in stroke prevention: a meta-analysis. *Lancet.* 2007;369:1876-1882.

44. Bazzano LA, Reynolds K, Holder KN, He J. Effect of folic acid supplementation on risk of cardiovascular diseases: a meta-analysis of randomized controlled trials. *JAMA.* 2006;296:2720-2726.

45. Adams HP Jr, del Zoppo G, Alberts MJ, et al. Guidelines for the early management of adults with ischemic stroke: a guideline from the American Heart Association/American Stroke Association Stroke Council, Clinical Cardiology Council, Cardiovascular Radiology and Intervention Council, and the Atherosclerotic Peripheral Vascular Disease and Quality of Care Outcomes in Research Interdisciplinary Working Groups: the American Academy of Neurology affirms the value of this guideline as an educational tool for neurologists. *Stroke.* 2007;38:1655-1711.

SECTION XVI: INTEGUMENTARY CONDITIONS

83. Acne Vulgaris

Acne is the most common skin disorder in the United States, affecting more than 17 million Americans. Most adolescents in Western countries experience some degree of acne, which generally resolves as androgen levels decline. Some cases, however, persist into adulthood or have their onset in adulthood.

Common acne, as it appears in adolescents, is associated with many factors, including genetic predisposition, hormonal abnormalities, and clogged pilosebaceous follicles. Plugs found in follicles of patients with acne are composed of a mixture of lipids secreted by sebaceous glands and keratin that accumulates from surrounding keratinocytes.

Acne may appear as closed comedones ("whiteheads") or, when excessive distention forces open the follicular orifice, open comedones ("blackheads"). Oxidation of the lipid and melanin cause the darkened appearance of open comedones. Increased production of androgens during puberty leads to sebaceous gland growth and increased sebum production, providing an anaerobic lipid-rich medium that is optimal for bacterial growth. *Propionibacterium acnes* (an anaerobic diptheroid) proliferates and can incite an inflammatory reaction that results in the characteristic acne lesions.

Acne most commonly affects areas of the body with the greatest number of sebaceous glands. These include the face, upper back, neck, chest, and upper arms. Mild acne is not inflammatory and involves only a small number of open or closed comedones. Moderate-to-severe acne involves inflammation of the dermis surrounding the pilosebaceous unit. This inflammation is due to follicular rupture, spilling of free fatty acids (resulting from the hydrolysis of triglycerides by *P acnes*), and the release of lysosomal enzymes from neutrophils attracted by chemotactic factors released by *P acnes*. This process results in the formation of pustules, papules, or nodules that cover a large area of skin. Scarring and hyperpigmentation can also occur, usually in patients with darker complexions.

Risk Factors

Cosmetics. Skin and hair products that contain oils or dyes can exacerbate acne lesions. Water-based cosmetics are less comedogenic.

Repetitive skin trauma. Rubbing (even with cleansing agents), scrubbing, or occlusive clothing (eg, bra straps, helmets, turtlenecks) can promote inflammatory reactions in the lesions.

Environmental exposures. Humidity and sweating can exacerbate acne. Exposure to certain chemicals (eg, dioxin and other halogenated hydrocarbons) that are found in herbicides and other industrial products can cause severe inflammatory acne and scarring.

Drugs. Certain drugs are likely to cause acne, including corticosteroids, phenytoin, isoniazid, disulfiram, lithium, and B vitamins.

Diet. Milk intake, in particular, has been linked to acne (see Nutritional Considerations below).

Genetics. Genetics likely plays a role in the manifestation of acne, especially in persistent and late-onset cases.[1]

Stress. Stress is believed to be associated with acne exacerbations, but further study is required to establish this connection.

Hormones. Endocrine disorders marked by excess androgens, such as congenital adrenal hyperplasia and polycystic ovarian syndrome, may trigger the development of acne vulgaris.

Diagnosis

Acne vulgaris is a clinical diagnosis. History and dermatologic examination are necessary to characterize the distribution and types of acne lesions and to evaluate underlying medical disorders.

Fever and arthralgia in a patient with severe inflammatory acne suggest acne fulminans, a serious disease that requires immediate treatment with systemic corticosteroids and isotretinoin (see below).

Women with oligomenorrhea, hirsutism, male- or female-pattern alopecia, infertility, acanthosis nigricans, and truncal obesity should be evaluated for hyperandrogenism, which may occur due to polycystic ovarian syndrome or an androgen-secreting tumor.

Treatment

Treatment should address both the physical and psychological effects of acne and should be guided by the severity and type of lesions. Light and laser therapies may be used to treat acne in the future.

Noninflammatory Acne

A number of topical therapies are used to treat noninflammatory acne.

Retinoids (eg, tretinoin, adapalene, tazarotene) decrease follicle hyperkeratinization. Treatment for 8 weeks is required before assessing efficacy, and acne may initially worsen. Retinoids are available in various preparations, including creams, gels and microgels (which are less irritating), solutions, and pads. Skin irritation and photosensitivity may occur. Tazarotene is contraindicated during pregnancy.

Acid preparations (eg, salicylic acid, azelaic acid, glycolic acid) also decrease follicle hyperkeratinization. Salicylic acid is the most commonly used acid and is available over-the-counter. Azelaic acid may be effective for acne-induced hyperpigmentation.

Benzoyl peroxide is an effective topical treatment that has antibacterial and comedolytic properties. In patients with inflammatory lesions, it may be used in combination with a topical antibiotic, such as erythromycin, or a topical retinoid.

Extraction of comedones may also be performed by a trained clinician.

Inflammatory Acne

Inflammatory acne is often treated with multiple topical therapies, which are more effective than either agent alone.[2] Benzoyl peroxide, topical antibiotics (eg, erythromycin, tetracycline, azealic acid, clindamycin), retinoids, and acids are commonly used.

Antibiotics attack the proprionibacterium in the hair follicles. Bacterial resistance may occur but is reduced by combination therapy with benzoyl peroxide.[2-4]

Severe Acne

Severe acne can be treated with intensive topical treatment, but it may require oral therapy.

Oral antibiotics are usually prescribed for 3 to 6 months. Resistance may occur with prolonged therapy.

Isotretinoin is usually reserved for the most severe cases of nodulocystic acne, or acne that is refractory to combination treatment. It is extremely effective, but is expensive and has many potential adverse effects, including teratogenicity. Close follow-up is necessary for laboratory work, including pregnancy tests, liver function tests, lipid panels, and complete blood counts. Treatment usually lasts 6 months and may result in permanent remission.

Systemic corticosteroids should be added if the acne worsens with initiation of isotretinoin.

Nutritional Considerations

Several studies suggest that acne occurs more commonly in countries following Westernized diets.[5-7] However, the role of specific nutritional factors remains unclear. For years, dermatologists advised patients to avoid chocolate, fried foods, and fatty foods, although proof of their pathogenic role was lacking. Acne may not be worse in individuals with a higher intake of table sugar or chocolate,[6] although recent evidence suggests that diet may indeed contribute to hormone-related acne.

Western Diets and Acne

Indigenous populations that eat plant-based diets composed mainly of unprocessed or minimally processed foods high in carbohydrate and fiber, and emphasizing unsaturated, rather than saturated, fats, are largely free of acne. Such foods include tubers, fruit, vegetables, peanuts, corn, and rice. In contrast, the vast majority of teenagers and 40% to 54% of the adult (>25 years) population in Western societies have some degree of facial acne.[5] Evidence also suggests that as immigrants become acculturated to a typical Western diet, their previously low incidence of acne rises to the levels found in Western societies.[6] The following dietary aspects have been under investigation:

Excess fat and calories. Dietary fat contributes to sebum production, and excesses of both fat and carbohydrate contribute to increased lipid secretion in human skin. In contrast, restricting calories can reduce sebum production by as much as 40%.[6]

Diets high in saturated fat,[8] meat,[9] and milk[7] increase blood concentrations of insulin-like growth factor I (IGF-I), which, in turn, stimulates the production of androgens known to increase sebum production.[5,6] Plant-based diets, low-fat diets, high-fiber diets, and vegetarian diets lower IGF-I and increase IGF-binding proteins.[5,9,10]

High-glycemic index foods. A clinical trial of 43 Australian male acne sufferers showed that a diet moderately low in carbohydrate and glycemic index for 12 weeks reduced acne lesions by 24%.[11] The dietary intervention also reduced blood concentrations of free androgens and increased IGF-binding proteins.[12]

Dairy products. In the Nurses Health Study II, more than 47,000 women completed questionnaires in 1998 that were based on recalling their diet during high school, and associations were estimated between various food groups and diagnosis of teenage acne. Women who consumed more than 2 glasses of skim milk per day during their teen years (ie, ages 13 to 18) had a 40% greater prevalence of teenage acne, compared with those drinking less than 1 glass per week.[7,13] A similar finding emerged from the Growing Up Today Study involving 9,039 girls and 7,843 boys aged 9 to 15 years. Those consuming 2 or more milk servings per day had a 20% higher risk for acne, compared with those consuming <1 serving per week.[14]

Controlled trials testing this relationship are in progress. While mechanisms that might explain the association have not been established, several possibilities have been suggested. Milk contains both hormones and hormone-like chemicals (eg, IGF-I) that may survive processing and affect the pilosebaceous glands. Apart from the hormones found in milk, hormones or growth factors may be produced in the human body in response to milk ingestion. For instance, regular milk ingestion by adults is associated with an elevation of blood concentrations of IGF-I,[15] which stimulates proliferation of basal keratinocytes.[14]

Orders

See Basic Diet Orders chapter.

Low-fat, high-fiber, nondairy diet may be tried on a prospective basis.

What to Tell the Family

Acne is a distressing condition. Some evidence suggests that it may be in some measure preventable by dietary changes. In particular, dairy intake has been associated with the development and worsening of acne in women and could also play a role in men. Likewise, a high-fat diet may be implicated in acne formation. In addition, the use of oil-based cosmetics, excessive scrubbing or rubbing, and occlusive clothing (tight bras, turtlenecks) may worsen the acne lesions. Family members can assist patients with acne by helping them stay on a healthful diet. Moreover, following such a diet themselves may reduce family members' own risk for diet-related conditions.

References

1. Goulden V, Clark SM, Cunliffe WJ. Post-adolescent acne: a review of clinical features. *Br J Dermatol.* 1997;136:66-70.

2. Strauss JS, Krowchuk DP, Leyden JJ, et al. Guidelines of care for acne vulgaris management. *J Am Acad Dermatol.* 2007;56:651-663.

3. Eady EA, Bojar RA, Jones CE, Cove JH, Holland KT, Cunliffe WJ. The effects of acne treatment with a combination of benzoyl peroxide and erythromycin on skin carriage of erythromycin-resistant propionibacteria. *Br J Dermatol.* 1996;134:107-113.

4. Purdy S. Acne. *BMJ.* 2006;333:949.

5. Cordain L, Lindeberg S, Hurtado M, Hill K, Eaton SB, Brand-Miller J. Acne vulgaris: a disease of Western civilization. *Arch Dermatol.* 2002;138:1584-1590.

6. Wolf R, Matz H, Orion E. Acne and diet. *Clin Dermatol.* 2004;22:387-393.

7. Adebamowo CA, Spiegelman D, Danby FW, Frazier AL, Willett WC, Holmes MD. High school dietary dairy intake and teenage acne. *J Am Acad Dermatol.* 2005;52:207-214.

8. Heald AH, Cade JE, Cruickshank JK, Anderson S, White A, Gibson JM. The influence of dietary intake on the insulin-like growth factor (IGF) system across three ethnic groups: a population-based study. *Public Health Nutr.* 2003;6:175-180.

9. Allen NE, Appleby PN, Davey GK, Kaaks R, Rinaldi S, Key TJ. The associations of diet with serum insulin-like growth factor I and its main binding proteins in 292 women meat-eaters, vegetarians, and vegans. *Cancer Epidemiol Biomarkers Prev.* 2002;11:1441-1448.

10. Kaaks R, Bellati C, Venturelli E, et al. Effects of dietary intervention on IGF-I and IGF-binding proteins, and related alterations in sex steroid metabolism: the Diet and Androgens (DIANA) Randomised Trial. *Eur J Clin Nutr.* 2003;5:1079-1088.

11. Smith RN, Mann NJ, Braue A, Makelainen H, Varigos GA. A low-glycemic-load diet improves symptoms in acne vulgaris patients: a randomized controlled trial. *Am J Clin Nutr.* 2007;86:107-115.

12. Smith RN, Mann NJ, Braue A, Mäkeläinen H, Varigos GA. The effect of a high-protein, low glycemic-load diet versus a conventional, high glycemic-load diet on biochemical parameters associated with acne vulgaris: A randomized, investigator-masked, controlled trial. *J Am Acad Dermatol.* 2007;57:247-256.

13. Danby FW. Acne and milk, the diet myth, and beyond. *J Am Acad Dermatol.* 2005; 52:360-362.

14. Adebamowo CA, Spiegelman D, Berkey CS, et al. Milk consumption and acne in adolescent girls. *Dermatol Online J.* 2006;12:1.

15. Heaney RP, McCarron DA, Dawson-Hughes B, et al. Dietary changes favorably affect bone remodeling in older adults. *J Am Dietetic Assoc.* 1999;99:1228-1233.

---

84. Psoriasis

Psoriasis, a chronic disorder involving inflammation and hyperproliferation of the epidermis, affects more than 5 million Americans and up to 200 million people worldwide. Normally, epidermal cells are sloughed and replaced within 27 days. In psoriatic skin, the life cycle lasts only

4 days. The etiology is multifactorial, involving genetic predispositions and associated T-cell dysfunction, pro-inflammatory cytokines, activated growth factors, and neutrophil recruitment. Psoriasis has autoimmune features, but the antigen trigger is not known (however, see Nutrition Considerations below).

Plaque psoriasis (also known as psoriasis vulgaris) is the most common form, accounting for 80% of cases. The remaining cases are guttate, pustular, and inverse (flexural). Plaque psoriasis is marked by symmetrically distributed, thick, erythematous skin plaques and silvery scales that occur primarily on extensor surfaces, including the elbows and knees as well as the scalp, lower back, and intertriginous areas. Nail changes are present in 50% to 80% of cases, and they are rarely the only sign of disease. The changes manifest as pitting, deformations, thickening, onycholysis, or unusual nail coloration.

Most cases follow a relapsing-remitting course, which may be influenced by certain medications, trauma, stress, alcohol, and tobacco use. The lesions can be painful and disfiguring. In severe cases, lesions cover more than 10% of the body and can have a significant effect on self-esteem and quality of life, contributing to depression and suicidal ideation. More severe symptoms, including psoriatic arthritis, occur in 10% to 25% of patients, sometimes resulting in permanent joint deformity if left untreated.

Risk Factors

Psoriasis can occur at any age, although most cases present between 20 and 40 years. All races are affected, but the disorder is less common in African Americans and rare in indigenous populations of North America and South America. Other factors associated with risk follow:

Genetics. There is a clear, although complex, genetic predisposition. Nearly half of psoriasis patients have an affected first-degree relative. The most consistent association is with *HLA-Cw6*, which can increase the risk of disease 10-fold.

Medication use. Medications known to exacerbate symptoms include lithium, beta-blockers, angiotensin-converting enzyme (ACE) inhibitors, terbinafine, and nonsteroidal anti-inflammatory drugs (NSAIDs).

Steroid therapy withdrawal. Abrupt cessation of steroid therapy can result in the sudden worsening of psoriasis; therefore, steroids are usually contraindicated.

Infection. Patients with human immunodeficiency virus (HIV) and children with recurring infections, particularly streptococcal pharyngitis, are at increased risk.

Stress. Emotional and physiologic stress (trauma) has been linked to exacerbations, which may occur up to a month after the stressful event.

Obesity. See Nutritional Considerations below.

Climate. Moderate amounts of sunlight can improve psoriasis. However, excessive sun exposure can trigger or exacerbate the disease.

Alcohol intake (see below) and **tobacco** use are also important risk factors.

Additional factors are under investigation. For example, rubella vaccination was positively associated with psoriatic arthritis in a case-control study in the United Kingdom.[1]

Diagnosis

Psoriasis is usually diagnosed by the classic appearance and location of plaques. Laboratory tests are not available to confirm or exclude the diagnosis. In equivocal cases, skin biopsy may aid diagnosis.

Psoriatic arthritis—also known as distal arthritis, which primarily affects the distal interphalangeal joints—is diagnosed by history, physical examination, and exclusion of other arthritic disorders such as rheumatoid arthritis, gout, and ankylosing spondylitis. It is a seronegative arthritic disorder and may affect joints symmetrically or asymmetrically.

Treatment

Despite a wide range of therapeutic options, psoriasis can be a challenge to treat. Treatments are based on the type of psoriasis, severity, and areas of skin affected.

Topical Therapies

Topical moisturizing creams and ointments are the initial therapy for mild to moderate disease and may reduce itching and scaling; however, lotions have the opposite effect. **Medicated shampoos, foams, or solutions** are used for scalp lesions.

Topical corticosteroids are especially useful for local and widespread plaques and lesions that are resistant to other therapies. Low-potency steroids may be used on the face and intertriginous areas, whereas more potent steroids are reserved for the scalp and thick plaques on extensor surfaces. However, resistance to steroid creams can develop quickly, and withdrawal may cause exacerbation of disease. Long-term or excessive use can lead to thinning of skin, easy bruising, and systemic side effects.

Vitamin D analogues (eg, calcipotriene) slow keratinocyte growth, flatten lesions, and remove scale; these may be used in combination with topical steroids.

Anthralin has been used effectively for more than a century. It slows proliferation of skin cells through inhibition of DNA synthesis.

Tazarotene, a retinoid, slows proliferation of skin cells but may cause skin irritation and is contraindicated in women who are pregnant or who may become pregnant. Short contact therapy (20 minutes) followed by washing has been shown to be better tolerated than and as effective as traditional tazarotene therapy.[2]

Coal tar is probably the oldest known treatment and is generally used to reduce inflammation, itching, and scaling. It can be compounded with steroid creams or ointments and is available as a shampoo. Some preparations may also be as effective as vitamin D analogues.[3]

Topical calcineurin inhibitors are second-line agents that may be most useful for facial and intertriginous areas.[4,5] There may be an increased risk of cancer with their use (see Atopic Dermatitis chapter).

Phototherapy is known to be beneficial and is used especially for generalized disease. More common options include natural sunlight (lesions usually improve during the summer), ultraviolet B radiation, and psoralen plus ultraviolet A radiation (PUVA). High-energy excimer laser treatment has been shown to be effective and safe for targeting localized psoriasis while requiring fewer office visits and sparing uninvolved skin.[6] Phototherapy may be combined with other treatments to increase efficacy. An increased risk of skin cancer may occur with phototherapy.

Systemic therapy may be required for severe or treatment-resistant psoriasis or patients with psoriatic arthritis. Options include oral retinoids (acitretin), methotrexate with folic acid, azathioprine, cyclosporine, sulfasalazine, and hydroxyurea. These can have significant side effects and are contraindicated in pregnant women. Immune-modulating drugs (eg, alefacept, efalizumab, etanercept) are now being used for psoriatic arthritis and severe and refractory cases.

Psychological approaches may be valuable in individuals with psoriasis. Stress plays an important role in the onset, exacerbation, and prolongation of psoriasis[7] and appears to impair the clearance of lesions in phototherapy-treated patients.[8] Some evidence indicates that hypnosis[7] and cognitive-behavioral stress management programs[9] reduce symptom severity.

Psoriatic arthritis is usually treated with nonsteroidal anti-inflammatory drugs, which do not appear to exacerbate skin lesions. When NSAIDs are insufficient, disease-modifying anti-rheumatic drugs are necessary. Options include the systemic therapies listed above, as well as antimalarial drugs, gold compounds, and leflunomide.

Nutritional Considerations

Dietary strategies are aimed at eliminating inciting factors, reducing inflammation, and limiting calories.

Fasting, low-calorie diets, and vegetarian diets have all demonstrated effectiveness in reducing psoriasis symptoms.[10] Part of the effectiveness is likely explained by weight loss. Obesity is significantly more common in patients with psoriasis than in control subjects.[11] Recent evidence indicates that the odds ratio for developing psoriasis is 1.6 in those who are overweight (body mass index [BMI] of 26-29) and 1.9 in persons with a BMI greater than 29,[12] compared with normal-weight individuals.

These dietary adjustments may have other consequences of benefit in psoriasis, including lower production of proinflammatory leukotrienes (eg, LTB4) as a result of decreased arachidonic acid intake, declines in inflammation,[13] and reduced levels of insulin-like growth factor I (IGF-1).[14] A vegetarian regimen may help to counteract the hyperlipidemia that is frequently associated with retinoid treatment.[10]

Anti-gliadin antibodies are a frequent finding in patients with psoriasis,[15] and the psoriasis area and severity index (PASI) improves significantly in these patients on gluten-free diets.[16] Patients with palmar plantar pustulosis may benefit from elimination of gluten in their diets.[17] Similarly, in patients with celiac disease, a gluten-free diet may offer relief of psoriatic symptoms.[10]

Essential fatty acids. Patients with psoriasis may demonstrate linoleic acid deficiency and elevated skin levels of pro-inflammatory arachidonic acid,[10] an omega-6 fatty acid found in meat, eggs, and milk.

Higher intakes of linoleic acid (an omega-6 fatty acid) are important for production of prostaglandin E2, an eicosanoid important for inhibition of the type 1 helper T cells (Th1) involved in psoriasis.[18] Intake of omega-3 fatty acids may also provide similar benefits with regard to these pro-inflammatory metabolites. Although smaller clinical trials of a combination of omega-6 and omega-3 fatty acids found no significant improvement in the severity of psoriasis,[19] others have found that omega-3 fatty acids improve the effectiveness of standard treatments, reduce the hyperlipidemia caused by etretinate (an oral retinoid), prolong the beneficial effects of phototherapy, and reduce the nephrotoxicity of cyclosporin.[20] Additional clinical trials are required before either omega-6 or omega-3 fatty acid supplements are recommended for the treatment of psoriasis, and moderation is advised regarding a substantial increase in either supplement, due to the risk for weight gain and the potential for polyunsaturated fats to increase oxidative stress.[21]

Alcohol avoidance. Excess alcohol intake is an important risk factor for psoriasis,[22] possibly because alcohol can increase histamine production in psoriatic lesions[10] and enhance proliferation of epidermal cells. In alcohol abusers, the disease often remits with abstinence and recurs upon resumed alcohol use.[23] Even in light to moderate alcohol users, alcohol consumption is correlated with disease severity.[24]

Orders

See Basic Diet Orders chapter.

Gluten-free diet in patients with anti-gliadin antibodies.

Smoking cessation.

Alcohol restriction, as appropriate.

Consider dermatologist referral.

What to Tell the Family

The family can play an important role in improving psoriasis symptoms. Family members can encourage the patient to use medications as directed. When a therapeutic diet is prescribed, family members can help by adopting a similar diet. Doing so facilitates adherence and may also reduce the family's health risks.

References

1. Pattison EJ, Harrison BJ, Griffiths CE, Silman AJ, Bruce IN. Environmental risk factors for the development of psoriatic arthritis: results from a case control study. *Ann Rheum Dis.* 2007 Sep 6; [Epub ahead of print].

2. Veraldi S, Caputo R, Pacifico A, Peris K, Soda R, Chimenti S. Short contact therapy with tazarotene in psoriasis vulgaris. *Dermatology*. 2006;212:235-237.

3. Tzaneva S, Honigsmann H, Tanew A. Observer-blind, randomized, intrapatient comparison of a novel 1% coal tar preparation (Exorex) and calcipotriol cream in the treatment of plaque type psoriasis. *Br J Dermatol*. 2003;149:350-353.

4. Lebwohl M, Freeman AK, Chapman MS, Feldman SR, Hartle JE, Henning A. Tacrolimus ointment is effective for facial and intertriginous psoriasis. *J Am Acad Dermatol*. 2004;51:723-730.

5. Gribetz C, Ling M, Lebwohl M, et al. Pimecrolimus cream 1% in the treatment of intertriginous psoriasis: a double-blind, randomized study. *J Am Acad Dermatol*. 2004;51:731-738.

6. Feldman SR, Mellen BG, Housman TS, et al. Efficacy of the 308-nm excimer laser for treatment of psoriasis: results of a multicenter study. *J Am Acad Dermatol*. 2002;46:900-906.

7. Shenefelt PD. Hypnosis in dermatology. *Arch Dermatol*. 2000;136:393-399.

8. Fortune DG, Richards HL, Kirby B, et al. Psychological distress impairs clearance of psoriasis in patients treated with photochemotherapy. *Arch Dermatol*. 2003;139:752-756.

9. Fortune DG, Richards HL, Kirby B, Bowcock S, Main CJ, Griffiths CE. A cognitive-behavioural symptom management programme as an adjunct in psoriasis therapy. *Br J Dermatol*. 2002;146:458-465.

10. Wolters M. Diet and psoriasis: experimental data and clinical evidence. *Br J Dermatol*. 2005;153:706-714.

11. Henseler T, Christophers E. Disease concomitance in psoriasis. *J Am Acad Dermatol*. 1995;32:982-986.

12. Naldi L, Chatenoud L, Linder D, et al. Cigarette smoking, body mass index, and stressful life events as risk factors for psoriasis: results from an Italian case-control study. *J Invest Dermatol*. 2005;125:61-67.

13. Fuchs J, Zollner TM, Kaufmann R, Podda M. Redox-modulated pathways in inflammatory skin diseases. *Free Radic Biol Med*. 2001;30:337-353.

14. Krane JF, Gottlieb AB, Carter DM, Krueger JG. The insulin-like growth factor I receptor is overexpressed in psoriatic epidermis, but is differentially regulated from the epidermal growth factor receptor. *J Exp Med*. 1992;175:1081-1090.

15. Woo WK, McMillan SA, Watson RG, McCluggage WG, Sloan JM, McMillan JC. Coeliac disease-associated antibodies correlate with psoriasis activity. *Br J Dermatol*. 2004;151:891-894.

16. Michaelsson G, Gerden B, Hagforsen E, et al. Psoriasis patients with antibodies to gliadin can be improved by a gluten-free diet. *Br J Dermatol*. 2000;142:44-51.

17. Michaëlsson, G. Palmoplantar pustulosis and gluten sensitivity: a study of serum antibodies against gliadin and tissue transglutaminase, the duodenal mucosa and effects of gluten-free diet. *Br J Dermatol*. 2007;156:659.

18. Namazi MR. The beneficial and detrimental effects of linoleic acid on autoimmune disorders. *Autoimmunity*. 2004;37:73-75.

19. Oliwiecki S, Burton JL. Evening primrose oil and marine oil in the treatment of psoriasis. *Clin Exp Dermatol*. 1994;19:127-129.

20. Simopoulos AP. Omega-3 fatty acids in inflammation and autoimmune diseases. *J Am Coll Nutr*. 2002;21:495-505.

21. Jenkinson A, Franklin MF, Wahle K, Duthie GG. Dietary intakes of polyunsaturated fatty acids and indices of oxidative stress in human volunteers. *Eur J Clin Nutr.* 1999;53:523-528.

22. Zheng GY, Wei SC, Shi TL, Li YX. Association between alcohol, smoking and HLA-DQA1*0201 genotype in psoriasis. *Acta Biochim Biophys Sin* (Shanghai). 2004;36:597-602.

23. Smith KE, Fenske NA. Cutaneous manifestations of alcohol abuse. *J Am Acad Dermatol.* 2000;43(pt 1):1-16.

24. Wolf R, Wolf D, Ruocco V. Alcohol intake and psoriasis. *Clin Dermatol.* 1999;17:423-430.

85. Atopic Dermatitis

Atopic dermatitis, frequently described as eczema, is a common chronic skin disease that affects about 20% of people worldwide. It is associated with other markers of atopy, such as asthma, allergic rhinitis, and food allergy. Pathogenesis is not well understood. Signs of disease (inflammation) usually occur early in life and resolve by 6 years of age. However, a significant population has atopic dermatitis that may persist indefinitely.

Presentation varies, depending on patient age and disease severity. In general, children have itching and subsequent erythematous plaques or patches with scaling and papular features on the upper body. Adults tend to have thickened skin with lichenification and excoriated and fibrotic papules, reflecting the chronicity of the disease. Severe cases may present in any distribution. Patients with atopic dermatitis are at increased risk for skin infections.

Risk Factors

Family or personal history of atopy. Maternal disease seems to be a stronger risk factor than paternal disease.[1] About half of those with atopic dermatitis have a relative with allergic asthma. A history of food allergy, allergic rhinitis, or asthma is associated with atopic dermatitis.

Antigens. Variations in antigen exposure may affect risk of disease. Developed countries appear to have higher rates of disease.[2]

Some evidence suggests that exclusive breast-feeding for at least the first 3 months of life may be associated with reduced risk among infants with a family history of atopy.[3]

Diagnosis

Major diagnostic criteria for atopic dermatitis include pruritus, relapsing disease, age-appropriate distribution of lesions (face and extensor surfaces in children and flexor surfaces in adults), and a family history of atopy. Nonspecific minor criteria that may aid diagnosis include periorbital darkening, dry skin, and keratosis pilaris on the skin over the triceps region.[4] Other diseases, such as hyperimmunoglobulin E syndrome and scabies, can resemble atopic dermatitis in appearance. In atopic dermatitis, intertriginous regions are not usually affected (unlike psoriasis, in which these areas may be involved.)

No laboratory tests definitively diagnose atopic dermatitis. However, up to 80% of patients will have an elevated serum immunoglobulin E (IgE) and positive skin tests for immediate hypersensitivity reactions to common allergens.[5] These tests are not required for diagnosis.

Recurrent skin infections may occur in atopic dermatitis-damaged skin, and they may also exacerbate disease. Skin infections occur much more commonly in atopic dermatitis patients than in psoriasis patients,[6] suggesting that factors aside from skin breakdown are involved in predisposition to skin infection.

Treatment

Initial treatment of atopic dermatitis should seek to eliminate exacerbating agents, such as soaps and detergents, food allergens, and cosmetics. Excessive bathing or use of lotions should be discouraged, as evaporation of water from the skin exacerbates atopic dermatitis. Some patients may be surprised to learn that water-based lotions actually increase evaporation of water from the skin. Humidifiers may be tried in dry climates.

Emollient creams or ointments should be applied liberally, especially after bathing to lock in moisture. Occlusive bandages, gloves, or socks can be worn nightly to aid skin hydration.

Psychological approaches to mitigate stress may help avoid exacerbations.[7]

Antihistamines may relieve itching symptoms.

Antibiotics may be effective when patients develop a bacterial infection in the affected area or have pustular disease.

Topical corticosteroids should be used in the lowest possible therapeutic strength to treat active atopic dermatitis. Occasional use of topical steroids between episodes reduces the likelihood of recurrence.

Systemic corticosteroids, such as prednisone, may be used for a short duration when exacerbations occur.

Topical tacrolimus and other topical calcineurin inhibitors are second-line agents. They are used less commonly because of concerns about their carcinogenic potential. They may be used in children 2 years old and older who have not responded to other agents. Unlike corticosteroids, topical calcineurin inhibitors do not cause skin atrophy, so they can be used on sensitive areas, such as the face, eyelids, and underarms. Patients treated with tacrolimus ointment should be aware that a facial flush reaction can occur within 5 to 15 minutes of alcohol ingestion.[8]

Topical cromolyn (cromoglycate) sodium has fewer potential side effects.

Severe Disease

Oral tacrolimus and cyclosporine may be used for severe cases, with close monitoring for systemic side effects. It should be noted, however, that a possible risk of skin and lymph cancers is associated with calcineurin inhibitors.

Methotrexate, azathioprine, and mycophenolate mofetil are other immunosuppressants that may be occasionally prescribed by a dermatologist for severe cases. These therapies should be generally avoided in children.

Monoclonal antibodies (omalizumab) may help in refractory cases.

Phototherapy using ultraviolet light (UVA, UVB, and narrow-band UVB) is usually successful but may raise the risk of melanoma and other skin cancer.

Desensitization through immunotherapy is not a successful treatment option.

Herbal preparations, including *Flos lonicerae, Herba menthae, Cortex moutan, Rhizoma atractylodis,* and *Cortex phellodendri*, are under study as possible treatment options.[9]

Nutritional Considerations

Nutritional modifications that may improve atopic dermatitis have been under study for many years. The following factors are under investigation:

Avoiding alcohol during pregnancy. In cases in which both parents had allergic diseases, maternal alcohol intake equivalent to 4 or more drinks per week increased the risk for atopic dermatitis 4-fold.[10] Alcohol use during pregnancy carries other major risks and should be avoided completely.

Breast-feeding. Breast-feeding allows infants to avoid exposure to cow's milk proteins, except insofar as they may be transmitted from the maternal diet through breast milk, as has been demonstrated in studies of colicky infants (see Colic chapter).

Avoidance of allergenic foods (eg, eggs, cow's milk, soy, and wheat) by a breast-feeding mother may further reduce risk of atopy in the infant. Some have suggested that breast milk supplies specific protective factors as well, notably transforming growth factor 2, a cytokine that provides anti-allergenic immunoprotection. Diminished production of this cytokine has been reported in persons with atopic eczema and in the breast milk from mothers with atopy.[11] Exclusive breast-feeding for the first 6 months, with introduction of solid foods thereafter, has been recommended by some investigators.[12] In contrast, exclusive breast-feeding for periods longer than 9 months were associated with increased risk of atopy.[12]

Extensively hydrolyzed whey protein formulas. Hydrolyzed formulas have been used in children who are not breast-fed to reduce the incidence of atopic dermatitis, and they are tolerated by at least 90% of infants with documented allergy to cow's milk protein.[13] However, these formulas retain some allergenicity, and only amino acid–based formulas can be considered completely nonallergenic.[14]

Delayed introduction of solid foods. Avoiding the introduction of solid foods until infants have reached 4 to 6 months of age appears to reduce the risk of atopy. A combination of breast-feeding (or hypoallergenic formula) and delayed introduction of solid food appears to be the most effective regimen for atopy prevention in infants.[15] This approach may be augmented by environmental controls, such as polyvinyl mattress covers and anti–dust mite sprays. In a clinical trial, these combined steps were associated with a 67% reduction in dermatitis incidence, compared with a control population.[16,17]

Eliminating allergy-causing foods. Only a small fraction of patients with atopic dermatitis have documented food allergy. Of the food allergies identified in children with atopic dermatitis, roughly 90% are due to eggs, cow's milk, soy, and wheat.[18] More than 50% of children with diet-related atopic dermatitis experience both a significant improvement during periods of dietary exclusion and an exacerbation of their condition when challenged with allergen-containing foods.[18]

Adults with eczema are more likely than children with the condition to experience exacerbations when exposed to foods containing birch pollen, such as apple, carrots, celery, and hazelnuts.[18] (See Rheumatoid Arthritis and Anaphylaxis and Food Allergy chapters for instructions on elimination diets.)

Double-blind, placebo-controlled food challenges have found that a small fraction of children and adults experience skin reactions when given various additives. These include nitrite, benzoate, and tartrazine, balsam of Peru, and both natural and artificial vanilla.[19,20] More than 50% of patients have been reported to improve on diets low in allergens.[19]

Vegetarian diets. Preliminary evidence indicates that a vegetarian diet results in significant improvement in symptoms of atopic eczema, as judged by SCORAD (SCORing Atopic Dermatitis), a clinical tool for objectively assessing the severity of atopic dermatitis. This improvement appears to be related to reductions in circulating blood levels of eosinophils and neutrophils and decreased monocyte production of PGE2, an inducer of IgE and T helper 2 (Th2) cell production.[21] A low-energy diet (55% of estimated energy needs) conferred similar benefit to individuals with atopic dermatitis,[22] although the practicality of energy-restricted regimens for long-term use is not established.

Probiotic therapy. Probiotics (mainly *Lactobacillus rhamnosus*) are orally administered microorganisms that have been used for atopic diseases because they may have anti-inflammatory and antiallergic properties by stimulating Th1 cytokines[23] and by down-regulating CD34+ cells involved in the symptoms of dermatitis, while increasing those with anti-inflammatory effects (eg, interferon-γ).[24] In earlier studies, prenatal treatment with *Lactobacillus* in mothers with a family history of atopic disease, combined with postnatal probiotic treatment of their infants, reduced the incidence of infant atopic dermatitis by 50%.[24] Probiotic therapy also significantly reduced symptoms, as indicated by a change in SCORAD, in infants[23] and in children.[25] More recent data continue to support the possible usefulness of probiotics in prevention of infant atopic dermatitis,[26] but more recent data have not been as consistent for treating established atopic dermatitis.[27,28]

Avoidance of stevia extract. Stevia (*Stevia rebaundiana Bertoni*) is a natural noncaloric sweetener frequently used by individuals who want to avoid synthetic sugar substitutes such as aspartame. Although healthy infants have not been found to react negatively to stevia, 64% of a group of 50 infants displayed allergy to stevia upon skin prick test, and one experienced an anaphylactic reaction.[29]

Orders

See Basic Diet Orders chapter.

Elimination diet if specific triggers for dermatitis have not been found.

What to Tell the Family

Atopic dermatitis is a persistent ailment with a significant hereditary component. Some evidence indicates that the risk for developing this disease can be moderated through breast-feeding and allergen avoidance. In persons with established disease, effective management of symptoms is possible through combinations of topical ointments, diet modification, dietary supplements, and, if necessary, systemic anti-inflammatory (corticosteroid) treatment.

References

1. Ruiz RG, Kemeny DM, Price JF. Higher risk of infantile atopic dermatitis from maternal atopy than from paternal atopy. *Clin Exp Allergy.* 1992;22:762-766.

2. Trepka MJ, Heinrich J, Wichmann HE. The epidemiology of atopic diseases in Germany: an east-west comparison. *Rev Environ Health.* 1996;11:119-131.

3. Gdalevich M, Mimouni D, David M, Mimouni M. Breast-feeding and the onset of atopic dermatitis in childhood: A systematic review and meta-analysis of prospective studies. *J Am Acad Dermatol.* 2001;45:520-527.

4. Hanifin JM, Rajka G. Diagnostic features of atopic dermatitis. *Acta Dermatol Venereol.* 1980;92:44-47.

5. Jones SM, Sampson HA. The role of allergens in atopic dermatitis. *Clin Rev Allergy.* 1993;11:471-490.

6. Christophers E, Henseler T. Contrasting disease patterns in psoriasis and atopic dermatitis. *Arch Dermatol Res.* 1987;279:S48-S51.

7. Pallanti S, Lotti T, Urpe M. Psychoneuroimmunodermatology of atopic dermatitis: from empiric data to the evolutionary hypothesis. *Dermatol Clin.* 2005;23:695-701.

8. Milingou M, Antille C, Sorg O, Saurat JH, Lubbe J. Alcohol intolerance and facial flushing in patients treated with topical tacrolimus. *Arch Dermatol.* 2004;140:1542-1544.

9. Hon KL, Lee VW, Leung TF, et al. Corticosteroids are not present in a traditional Chinese medicine formulation for atopic dermatitis in children. *Ann Acad Med Singapore.* 2006;35:759-763.

10. Linneberg A, Petersen J, Gronbaek M, Benn CS. Alcohol during pregnancy and atopic dermatitis in the offspring. *Clin Exp Allergy.* 2004;34:1678-1683.

11. Rautava S, Isolauri E. Cow's milk allergy in infants with atopic eczema is associated with aberrant production of interleukin-4 during oral cow's milk challenge. *J Pediatr Gastroenterol Nutr.* 2004;39:529-535.

12. Pesonen M, Kallio MJ, Ranki A, Siimes MA. Prolonged exclusive breastfeeding is associated with increased atopic dermatitis: a prospective follow-up study of unselected healthy newborns from birth to age 20 years. *Clin. Exp Allergy.* 2006;36:1011-1018.

13. Host A, Halken S. Hypoallergenic formulas-when, to whom and how long: after more than 15 years we know the right indication! *Allergy.* 2004;59(suppl 78):45-52.

14. Caffarelli C, Plebani A, Poiesi C, Petroccione T, Spattini A, Cavagni G. Determination of allergenicity to three cow's milk hydrolysates and an amino acid-derived formula in children with cow's milk allergy. *Clin Exp Allergy.* 2002;32:74-79.

15. Muraro A, Dreborg S, Halken S, et al. Dietary prevention of allergic diseases in infants and small children. Part III: Critical review of published peer-reviewed observational and interventional studies and final recommendations. *Pediatr Allergy Immunol.* 2004;15:291-307.

16. Arshad SH. Primary prevention of asthma and allergy. *J Allergy Clin Immunol.* 2005;116:3-14.

17. Arshad SH, Bateman B, Sadeghnejad A, Gant C, Matthews SM. Prevention of allergic disease during childhood by allergen avoidance: the Isle of Wight prevention study. *J Allergy Clin Immunol.* 2007;119:307-313.

18. Werfel T, Breuer K. Role of food allergy in atopic dermatitis. *Curr Opin Allergy Clin Immunol.* 2004;4:379-385.

19. Worm M, Vieth W, Ehlers I, Sterry W, Zuberbier T. Increased leukotriene production by food additives in patients with atopic dermatitis and proven food intolerance. *Clin Exp Allergy.* 2001;31:265-273.

20. Kanny G, Hatahet R, Moneret-Vautrin DA, Kohler C, Bellut A. Allergy and intolerance to flavouring agents in atopic dermatitis in young children. *Allerg Immunol* (Paris). 1994;26:204-206, 209-210.

21. Tanaka T, Kouda K, Kotani M, et al. Vegetarian diet ameliorates symptoms of atopic dermatitis through reduction of the number of peripheral eosinophils and of PGE2 synthesis by monocytes. *J Physiol Anthropol Appl Human Sci.* 2001;20:353-361.

22. Kouda K, Tanaka T, Kouda M, et al. Low-energy diet in atopic dermatitis patients: clinical findings and DNA damage. *J Physiol Anthropol Appl Human Sci.* 2000;19:225-228.

23. Viljanen M, Savilahti E, Haahtela T, et al. Probiotic effects on fecal inflammatory markers and on fecal IgA in food allergic atopic eczema/dermatitis syndrome infants. *Pediatr Allergy Immunol.* 2005;16:65-71.

24. Ogden NS, Bielory L. Probiotics: a complementary approach in the treatment and prevention of pediatric atopic disease. *Curr Opin Allergy Clin Immunol.* 2005;5:179-184.

25. Weston S, Halbert A, Richmond P, Prescott SL. Effects of probiotics on atopic dermatitis: a randomised controlled trial. *Arch Dis Child.* 2005;90:892-897.

26. Kukkonen K, Savilahti E, Haahtela T, et al. Probiotics and prebiotic galacto-oligosaccharides in the prevention of allergic diseases: a randomized, double-blind, placebo-controlled trial. *J Allergy Clin Immunol.* 2007;119:192-198.

27. Brouwer ML, Wolt-Plompen SA, Dubois AE, et al. No effects of probiotics on atopic dermatitis in infancy: a randomized placebo-controlled trial. *Clin Exp Allergy.* 2006;36:899-906.

28. Viljanen M, Savilahti E, Haahtela T, et al. Probiotics in the treatment of atopic eczema/dermatitis syndrome in infants: a double-blind placebo-controlled trial. *Allergy.* 2005;60:494-500.

29. Kimata H. Anaphylaxis by stevioside in infants with atopic eczema. *Allergy.* 2007;62:565-566.

86. Burns

Burn injuries are among the leading causes of accidental death. Every year, an estimated 500,000 people in the United States suffer burn injuries requiring medical attention, and up to 50,000 require hospitalization.[1] Hospital stays may be lengthy and may involve multiple surgical procedures.

Burns can result from thermal, chemical, and electrical injuries. Each type is treated differently, as described below.

Serious burns are complex injuries affecting skin, muscles, tendons, bones, nerves, and blood vessels. Skin damage impairs the body's normal fluid and electrolyte balance, thermal regulation, and ability to fight infection. Long-term effects include diminished muscle and joint function and impaired manual dexterity. Involvement of the respiratory system can lead to airway obstruction and respiratory failure and arrest. Burns can also cause permanent disfigurement with concomitant sexual and psychological concerns regarding intimacy and self-esteem.

Risk Factors

Certain populations in the United States are at higher risk of becoming injured by a burn. In a recent study, for example, African American children in Ohio had nearly 8 times the burn risk, compared with white children.[2]

Additional risk factors include:

Use of wood stoves.

Exposed heating sources or **electrical cords.**

Unsafe storage of flammable or caustic materials.

Careless smoking. Cigarettes are the leading cause of house fires.

Water heaters set above 120°F.

Microwave-heated foods and containers.

Age. Children under 4, especially those who are poorly supervised, are at particular risk.

Gender. Males are more than twice as likely to suffer burn injuries.

Substandard or **older housing.**

Substance abuse. Use of alcohol and illegal drugs increases risk.

Absent or **nonfunctioning smoke detectors.** The presence of a functioning detector decreases risk of death by fire by 60%.

Diagnosis

A detailed history will assess the mechanism, duration, and timing of the burn. Physical examination will ascertain burn location and severity and check for dehydration, disfigurement, and infection. Biopsy is rarely needed to verify infection. Even minor burns can exacerbate diabetes, hypertension, and cardiac disease; patients with these conditions should usually be referred to a burn center. Fires in enclosed spaces should raise the suspicion for smoke-inhalation injury. Clinicians should also be attentive to injuries that suggest physical abuse.

Burns are classified based on the mechanism and depth. The depth is classified as superficial, superficial partial-thickness, deep partial-thickness, or full thickness.

Superficial Burns

Burns that affect only the epidermis are superficial and are characterized by erythema or discoloration, mild swelling, and pain. These burns do not cause blisters. Sun overexposure is a common cause. Injuries heal in 3 to 6 days.

Superficial Partial-Thickness Burns

These burns affect the epidermis and superficial layers of the dermis, causing a red color and blistering. Fluid is lost through damaged skin, and the burns are painful and tender since nerve endings are still intact. These burns will blanch with pressure. Injuries heal in 1 to 3 weeks. Scarring is uncommon, but skin color changes can persist for several months after the burn is healed.

Deep Partial-Thickness Burns

Burns affecting the deep layers of dermis are termed deep partial-thickness burns. Blisters are present, but the skin usually has a mottled appearance. It will still blanch with pressure and is both painful and tender.

Sometimes a deep partial-thickness burn is hard to distinguish from a full-thickness burn. Healing takes >3 weeks, and scarring is common.

Full-Thickness Burns

Burns that penetrate beyond the dermis are classified as full-thickness burns. Fat, muscle, tendon, and bone may be affected. Injuries may have a charred appearance and/or contain white or gray patches. Occasionally, they appear red but will not blanch with pressure. Burns are often not tender, as cutaneous nerve endings have been destroyed. However, partial-thickness burns often coexist with full-thickness burns and can be extremely painful. Healing occurs only at the wound edges, and by secondary intention. Scarring is significant, unless skin grafting is performed.

Treatment

Burn patients require specialized care and support. The American Burn Association (ABA) estimates the level of care required for burns according to the location, depth, and percentage of total body surface area (TBSA) affected.

The types of burn cases that should be referred to a burn unit include:[3]

- Partial-thickness burns covering more than 10% TBSA.

- Burns involving the face, hands, feet, genitalia, perineum, or major joints.

- Full-thickness burns.

- Electrical burns.

- Chemical burns.

- Inhalation injuries.

- Patients with preexisting medical disorders that could complicate management or recovery.

- Patients with concomitant trauma (such as fractures) in which the burn injury poses the greatest risk of morbidity or mortality.

- Patients who will require special social, emotional, or long-term rehabilitative intervention.

Immediate care can be lifesaving. Before burns are treated, the burning agent must be prevented from inflicting further damage. Materials such as melted synthetic shirts, hot tar, or chemicals should be immediately removed, or, in special cases (eg, hydrofluoric acid), chemically inactivated.

Burns should be thoroughly cleaned (under local anesthesia if necessary) with mild soap and water. Sterile dressings may be applied, although minor burns may need only topical treatment (see below). Tetanus vaccination and analgesics may be administered as needed. Burns that do not heal as predicted or that match the ABA referral criteria above require a specialist consultation or referral.

Superficial Burns

Superficial burns should be immersed immediately in cool water if possible, or a cool moist cloth can be applied until pain subsides. Very cold water and ice should not be used, as these will damage skin. Once a minor burn is completely cooled, a fragrance-free lotion or moisturizer can be applied to prevent drying. Additional topical treatments may also be helpful. Aloe vera gel may help achieve more rapid healing, compared with petroleum jelly.[4] However, many aloe vera gels dry the skin.

Partial-Thickness Burns (Superficial and Deep)

Blisters should be left intact only if they are smaller than 2 cm. Inflammatory cytokines delay healing in larger blisters. Dead skin, broken blisters, and blisters larger than 2 cm should be debrided and cleaned regularly to prevent infection and to speed healing.

Partial-thickness burns are the hardest to evaluate. Depending on the depth, these burns can be treated with collagenase ointment, silvadene cream, artificial membranes, or surgery. For superficial partial-thickness burns, in general, the best cosmesis will result from conservative care. Deeper partial-thickness burns may require surgery for good cosmesis and function. Consultation with a burn center may determine the best mode of therapy.

Elevation of the burned area above heart level aids healing and decreases painful throbbing and swelling. Physical and occupational therapy may be needed to prevent joint immobility caused by scarring, even from moderate burns.

Full-Thickness Burns

Surgery is usually required for full-thickness burns, since they have no viable skin structures remaining that can help heal the wound.

During the first hours after a major burn, massive capillary leakage may result in profound shock if not treated. Most burn surgeons begin fluid resuscitation using the Parkland Formula. Burns can be better assessed if they are not covered with cream. Therefore, major burns are best dressed with dry gauze only, before transferring the patient to a burn unit.

Large doses of narcotics and anxiolytics may be required to keep the patient comfortable. Often, promotility agents, stool softeners, or cathartics are needed to maintain bowel function. An insulin drip may be necessary to prevent hyperglycemia.

Also, beta-blockade with propanolol and anabolic steroid support with oxandrolone can decrease muscle wasting and weight loss due to hypermetabolism.[5]

In addition, an escharotomy (which involves cutting through burned tissue until healthy tissue is reached) may be needed to allow chest expansion or to prevent compartment syndromes in the extremities.

Inhalation Injuries

Inhalation burns are often identified by the following triad:

- The patient was in an enclosed space with smoke.

- Carbonaceous sputum and singed oropharynx are present.

- Elevated carboxyhemoglobin is detected by arterial blood gas analysis.

Inhalation injuries are frequently accompanied by carbon monoxide poisoning and require hospitalization. Other substances in smoke that can cause toxicity include benzenes, aldehydes, ammonia, acrolein, nitrogen oxide, and hydrogen cyanide produced by burning wool, nylon, plastics, and even cotton. Antidotes to suspected cyanide poisoning are available and should be administered immediately.

Superheated steam or gas causes airway edema or bronchospasm resembling an asthmatic attack. Intubation is often necessary. Necrotic tissue in the lungs also predisposes to pneumonia, or acute respiratory distress syndrome, and requires intensive monitoring and treatment.

Chemical Burns

With chemical burns, it is imperative to identify the source, ascertain whether the agent has been ingested through inhalation or swallowing, and determine the duration of contact. Health care workers must observe universal precautions to avoid exposure.

Any chemical burn requires a call to a burn center. Most chemical burns can be treated with copious water irrigation. However, many chemicals complicate care through metabolic derangement and respiratory failure. Do not induce emesis, as it can further injure the esophagus and lungs.

A burn center or poison control center can provide useful information on treatment of chemical burns, including neutralization methods, if indicated, and warn of expected systemic effects of the burn.

Electrical Burns

Any electrical injury requires a call to a burn center. Electrical injuries damage multiple organs, including the cardiovascular, gastrointestinal, renal, visual, and musculoskeletal systems. Special attention must be paid to fluid status. Two types of electrical injuries are caused by direct and alternating current.

The most common direct-current electrical injury is lightning, which is fatal in approximately one-third of cases. When the patient survives, trauma injuries (from muscle contractures or the patient's being thrown) are common. Urinalysis or serum creatine phosphokinase (CPK) levels are mandatory to rule out myoglobinuria or rhabdomyolysis. Other direct-current injuries come from batteries, especially car batteries.

Injuries from alternating current arise from domestic or industrial wiring and can be classified as low or high voltage (>1,000 volts). Because the current is alternating and an electrical surge moves into and out of the entire body with each cycle of current, the whole body is subjected to its effects. There are no entrance and exit points, only contact points.

Any electrical skin burns should be regarded solely as contact points. Contact points are often full-thickness burns that need referral to a burn center. Most of the damage is underneath the skin, as the current courses through muscles, nerves, blood vessels, and the periostium. For example, patients may lose most of their forearm musculature, despite an initial clinical exam showing only a small palmar contact point. Compartment syndromes are common and must be treated aggressively. Urinalysis or serum CPK measurement should be performed.

Nutritional Considerations

Nutritional support is a key component of burn care. Elevations in metabolic rate ranging between 118% and 210% of that predicted by the Harris-Benedict equation occur in adults with a burn covering 25% of total body surface area (TBSA). Resting metabolic rate (RMR) is approximately 180% of basal rate during acute admission in these patients, and their calorie needs may exceed 5,000 kcal/day.[6] Patients with a surface burn of 40% can lose 25% of preadmission weight in 3 weeks without nutrition support;[6] losses exceeding 10% are associated with significantly poorer outcome, including impaired immunity and delayed healing.[7]

Energy and Macronutrient Support

Significant weight loss is preventable with nutritional support. Recommended daily energy intake is as follows: for adults, 25 kcal/kg plus 40 kcal per each percent of burn area; for children, 1,800 kcal plus 2,200 calories per m^2 of burn area.[6] Individualized nutrition assessment is recommended for patients with burns on >20% of TBSA.[8]

Enteral nutrition support with a high-protein, high-carbohydrate diet is recommended, and timing may be critical. Feedings started within ~4 to 36 hours following injury appear to have advantages over delayed (>48 hours) feedings. If patients are hemodynamically stable (a prerequisite for prevention of bowel ischemia), these benefits include reductions in sepsis associated with gut permeability and clinical infection, as well as significantly shortened hospital stays.[9] Enteral support can reduce the burn-related increase in secretion of catabolic hormones and help maintain gut mucosal integrity. The duodenal route is better tolerated than gastric feeding, due to an 18% failure rate in the latter from regurgitation.[7] Total parenteral nutrition (TPN) is not recommended, due to its ineffectiveness in preventing the catabolic response to burns.[7] TPN also impairs immunity and liver function and increases mortality, when compared with enteral nutrition.[6]

High-carbohydrate, low-fat diets for burn patients result in less proteolysis and more improvement in lean body mass and may reduce infectious morbidity and shorten hospitalization time when compared with a high-fat regimen.[6,8] However, the benefit of a high-carbohydrate formula must be balanced against the risk for hyperglycemia, which can negatively influence the outcome of critically ill patients.[7] Nearly all burn patients experience insulin resistance as part of their hypermetabolic response and will need to be placed on an insulin drip to maintain tight control of blood glucose.

Protein and fluid needs must also be considered carefully. Protein oxidation rates are 50% higher in burn patients, and protein needs are ~1.5 to 2.0 grams/kg.[6]

Water loss can be as much as 4 liters/m^2/day[6] and a range of 30 to 50 ml/hour is given depending on the size of the burn, degree of hypernatremia, and urine output.[10]

Micronutrient Support

Additional vitamin-mineral supplements may be indicated. Levels of the fat-soluble vitamins A and E and carotenoids fall below normal in burn injury patients.[11] In one study, vitamin E treatment reduced elevation in lipid peroxide levels in burn patients, although improved outcome was not noted as a result.[12] Vitamin D synthesis is impaired in the skin of burn patients, both acutely and long-term. Blood levels appear to continue to fall, are below the normal range several years after recovery, and may negatively affect lumbar spine bone mineral density. Consequently, supplementation with the recommended dietary allowance of 400 IU of vitamin D per day has been suggested for patients with significant burns.[13]

Patients with major burns also suffer acute trace-element deficiencies, at least partly because of large exudative losses through the burned areas.[14] A lack of certain trace elements (eg, selenium and zinc) can exacerbate poor immunity, and burns are the second-leading cause of immunodeficiency (after HIV infection).[6] Although a role for free radicals and lipid peroxides in burn trauma has been established,[15] little research has been done on the effects of antioxidant supplements in human burn injury. However, the addition of selenium, zinc, and copper to a standard trace element formula and enteral nutrition was associated with a significant decrease in the number of bronchopneumonia infections and with a shorter hospital stay.[14]

Evaluating Nutritional Response to Feeding

The response of burn patients to their nutritional intake should be evaluated weekly or biweekly. Nitrogen balance studies are not useful, as a large amount of protein is extruded from the wound beds daily. In addition, standard measures of nutritional repletion, such as visceral proteins (eg, albumin and ferritin), are influenced not only by nutritional status, but also by inflammatory processes. When low concentrations are observed, the simultaneous concentrations of acute phase reactants, such as C-reactive protein, must be compared with their own reference standard to separate nutritional effects from inflammatory effects. Nevertheless, weekly or biweekly pre-albumin levels can guide nutritional status.[16]

Orders

Low-fat, high-protein, high-carbohydrate, enteral tube feedings with appropriate caloric content. Weekly or biweekly assessments of nutritional status.

Nutrition consultation.

Physical therapy, occupational therapy, and mental health consultations, as appropriate.

What to Tell the Family

Burn injuries are very traumatic. It is important for the family to know that the patient will need a great deal of support. This is especially true for deep partial-thickness (2nd degree) and full-thickness (3rd or 4th degree) burns. In general, a burn patient will be in the hospital 1 to 2 days for each percent of TBSA burned. Therefore, a person with a 50% TBSA burn may be hospitalized for two months and may undergo 10 to 20 surgeries. In severe burns, the patient will be physically incapacitated and emotionally traumatized. The family will play an essential role supporting the patient.

References

1. American Burn Association. Burn Incidence and Treatment in the US: 2007 Fact Sheet. Available at: http://www.ameriburn.org/resources_factsheet.php. Accessed May 2, 2007.

2. Hayes JR, Groner JI. Minority status and the risk of serious childhood injury and death. *J Natl Med Assoc*. 2005;97:362-369.

3. American College of Surgeons. Resources for optimal care of the injured patient. In: *Guidelines for the Operation of Burn Units*. Chicago, Ill: Committee on Trauma, American College of Surgeons; 1999:55-62.

4. Visuthikosol V, Sukwanarat Y, Chowchuen B, Sriurairatana S, Boonpucknavig V. Effect of aloe vera gel to healing of burn wound: a clinical and histologic study. *J Med Assoc Thai*. 1995;78:403-409.

5. Pereira CT, Herndon DN. The pharmacologic modulation of the hypermetabolic response to burns. *Adv Surg*. 2005;39:245-261.

6. Herndon DN, Tompkins RG. Support of the metabolic response to burn injury. *Lancet*. 2004;363:1895-1902.

7. Andel H, Kamolz LP, Horauf K, Zimpfer M. Nutrition and anabolic agents in burned patients. *Burns*. 2003;29:592-595.

8. De-Souza DA, Greene LJ. Pharmacological nutrition after burn injury. *J Nutr*. 1998;128:797-803.

9. McClave SA, Marsano LS, Lukan JK. Enteral access for nutritional support: rationale for utilization. *J Clin Gastroenterol*. 2002;35:209-213.

10. Cancio LC, Chavez S, Alvarado-Ortega M, et al. Predicting increased fluid requirements during the resuscitation of thermally injured patients. *J Trauma*. 2004;56:404-413.

11. Pintaudi AM, Tesoriere L, D'Arpa N, et al. Oxidative stress after moderate to extensive burning in humans. *Free Radic Res*. 2000;33:139-146.

12. Latha B, Babu M. The involvement of free radicals in burn injury: a review. *Burns*. 2001;27:309-317.

13. Klein GL, Chen TC, Holick MF, et al. Synthesis of vitamin D in skin after burns. *Lancet.* 2004;363:291-292.

14. Berger MM, Spertini F, Shenkin A, et al. Trace element supplementation modulates pulmonary infection rates after major burns: a double-blind, placebo-controlled trial. Am *J Clin Nutr.* 1998;68:365-371.

15. Horton JW. Free radicals and lipid peroxidation mediated injury in burn trauma: the role of antioxidant therapy. *Toxicology.* 2003;189:75-88.

16. Manelli JC, Badetti C, Botti G, Golstein MM, Bernini V, Bernard D. A reference standard for plasma proteins is required for nutritional assessment of adult burn patients. *Burns.* 1998;24:337-345.

SECTION XVII: ENVIRONMENTAL ILLNESSES

87. Foodborne and Waterborne Illness

Foodborne and waterborne illnesses are common but often unrecognized. They cause an estimated 76 million illnesses, 300,000 hospitalizations, and 5,000 deaths yearly in the United States.[1,2] The most prominent symptom is acute diarrhea, but the associated dehydration may lead to electrolyte irregularities, acute renal failure, and encephalopathy. Rarely, food or waterborne illness may be associated with prolonged or more severe complications, such as anemia, shock, hemolytic-uremic syndrome, spontaneous abortion, seizures, and liver, heart, or lung disease. Many illnesses carried by food or water are particularly common in the developing world, due to poor sanitation, polluted water, and lack of refrigeration. However, developed countries are by no means exempt. About 20% of all US diarrheal episodes are believed to be caused by foodborne or waterborne illness.[3]

This chapter focuses mainly on acute diarrheal illnesses but also includes information on prions and other rare diseases that are part of the full scope of foodborne and waterborne illness.

Risk Factors

Risk factors for specific pathogens are presented below.

Age. Young children are the most likely to have acute diarrhea. Institutionalized elderly persons are also at higher risk.

Medications. Antibiotic use alters the normal gut flora, and H2-receptor blockers or other medications may increase gastric pH. Both of these factors increase susceptibility to foodborne illness.

Undercooked meat. Intentionally undercooked or raw meats and fish (eg, steak tartare, sushi, and oysters) increase the risk of foodborne illness. This is of particular concern in patients with advanced liver disease (who may develop *Vibrio vulnificus* sepsis after ingestion of raw oysters) and immunocompromised individuals, such as transplant recipients or persons with HIV infection.

Hygiene. Spread of disease is facilitated by environments where raw sewage, from either humans or animals, contaminates water used for drinking or irrigation. Infected food handlers may contaminate food during preparation after inadequate hand washing. Child daycare facilities are common sources of infection, as hand washing may not be sufficiently thorough.

Diagnosis

A detailed history to assess changes in the patient's bowel pattern and temporal relationships with exposures to food, antibiotics, sick persons, or travel (including hiking and camping) is important. The history may help determine whether the condition is likely to be self-limited or requires treatment. In addition, the history points toward likely causative organisms that may be candidates for testing. For example, a history of blood or mucus in the diarrhea warrants stool examination and direct visualization of the colon. Laboratory evaluation usually includes culture, leukocyte count, fecal occult blood testing, and possibly screening for ova and parasites. In patients who have recently used antibiotics, stool evaluation for *Clostridium difficile* toxin is indicated.

Acute diarrhea diagnosis in the clinical setting is based on an increased frequency and looser consistency of stools. Diarrhea is defined as 6 or more soft or waterlike daily stools, although episodes vary considerably. Severe bacterial cases may cause diarrhea every 30 minutes. Viruses, especially noroviruses, cause the majority of gastroenteritis cases. The major clinical decision for severe or persistent diarrhea is whether supportive therapy (ie, oral or intravenous rehydration therapy for volume depletion) is sufficient, or whether pathogen-focused antibiotics are required. In most cases, antibiotics are not indicated, and they may cause antibiotic-associated diarrhea or *Clostridium difficile* colitis. In cases of salmonellosis, antibiotics may result in a chronic carrier state in the gallbladder.

Irritable bowel syndrome, inflammatory bowel disease, malabsorption syndromes (eg, celiac sprue, gluten, and other food intolerances), and hyperthyroidism should be considered in the differential if the diarrhea does not resolve within 1 to 2 weeks.

Diarrheal Illness

Viral gastroenteritis. Norovirus is the most common viral cause of gastroenteritis and may cause vomiting and explosive diarrhea. It occurs in families and among persons living in other close quarters, such as cruise ships and daycare settings. Viruses can be transmitted through the air and via the fecal-oral route. Rotavirus, adenovirus, and astrovirus are other common viral causes of intestinal illness.

Salmonella. This widespread foodborne illness occurs in 2 main types: typhoid fever and nontyphoidal infection. Typhoid fever classically presents systemically with fever, hepatomegaly, and splenomegaly, and a tender abdomen, but it may also include rash (ie, a classic "rose spot" skin lesion) and diarrhea or constipation. Nontyphoidal salmonella infection typically presents with nausea, vomiting, diarrhea, and fever and is the most common cause of foodborne gastroenteritis in the United States. Illness usually occurs due to undercooked poultry, cross-contamination of other foods or cooking surfaces, and raw or undercooked eggs (including egg-containing products, such as mayonnaise and custards, left at room temperature).

Milk, meat, and fecally contaminated fresh produce, such as alfalfa sprouts, may also transmit disease, as can pet reptiles such as turtles. Disease occurs more commonly in the summer and fall. Particularly susceptible are individuals with inflammatory bowel disease, lymphomas, and altered bowel flora (eg, due to antibiotics). Bloody diarrhea may occur.

Carriers of *Salmonella typhi* (eg, the infamous cook "Typhoid Mary" in early 20th century New York) occasionally cause typhoid fever epidemics.

Campylobacter. The second most common cause of foodborne illness in the United States is *Campylobacter jejuni*. Undercooked poultry and cross-contamination of other foods are the most likely sources. On average, 60% of retail poultry products throughout the world[4] and up to 88% in the United States[5] are contaminated with campylobacter. Bloody diarrhea may also occur with campylobacter infection.

Shigella. The third most common cause of foodborne illness in the United States, *Shigella flexneri*, is a highly infectious (an inoculum of just 10 organisms can cause infection) and pathogenic bacterium that spreads through food, water, or person-to-person contact. It is common in nursing homes and daycare settings. It often causes bloody diarrhea. Other complications include hemolytic uremic syndrome and thrombotic thrombocytopenic purpura. *Shigella dysenteriae* is found in underdeveloped countries and may result in bloody diarrhea and shock.

Cryptosporidium parvum. This parasite is transmitted through ingestion of *C parvum* eggs in contaminated or inadequately filtered water, or exposure to cows and their manure. In addition to being a common water contaminant, it can contaminate produce and unpasteurized milk. Cryptosporidium is a common infectious agent in pools and spas and can also spread from person to person.[6] Self-limited diarrhea is common in immunocompetent individuals. In persons with HIV, diarrhea can be chronic and debilitating.

Escherichia coli. The *E coli* O157:H7 strain is spread most often through undercooked hamburger. Unpasteurized juice and raw produce contaminated by cattle manure may also be sources. It may cause bloody diarrhea and can lead to the hemolytic uremic syndrome and thrombotic thrombocytopenic purpura. Like salmonella, it usually occurs in the summer and fall. Other more common *E coli* strains may also cause diarrheal illness.

Yersinia enterocolitica. This bacterium may produce pharyngitis and diarrhea, and typically comes from undercooked pork, unpasteurized milk, or contaminated water.

Vibrio cholerae. This often severe bacterial infection results in a secretory diarrhea. It occasionally occurs along the Gulf Coast from contaminated water. *Vibrio parahaemolyticus* and *vulnificus* infection is due to ingestion of contaminated shellfish, and may cause sepsis and shock in patients with advanced liver disease.

Cyclospora cayetanensis. This parasitic infection is acquired from produce exposed to contaminated water and person-to-person contact. It may cause prolonged diarrhea, upper gastrointestinal symptoms, and systemic symptoms, such as fatigue.

Bacillus cereus. This bacterium can multiply in underheated foods, such as rice, vanilla sauce, gravies, or foods left under heating lamps at suboptimal temperatures. *B cereus* produces toxins that typically cause rapid-onset, self-limited vomiting and may also cause diarrhea.

Staphylococcus aureus. Ingestion of toxins produced by *S aureus* may cause symptoms similar to those caused by *B cereus* within 6 to 10 hours. Common sources include contaminated salads, eggs, meat, and dairy products that have been prepared and left at room temperature.

Clostridium perfringens. Found in contaminated meat and poultry, it produces toxins after ingestion.

Giardia lamblia. This very common intestinal parasite is often found in mountain streams due to fecal contamination by beavers and bears. It is also spread through food and person-to-person (fecal-oral) contact, and causes upper gastrointestinal symptoms, along with diarrhea and foul-smelling flatulence.

Entamoeba histolytica. An infection occurring worldwide, it is prevalent in tropical regions. In addition to causing painful profuse diarrhea with blood and mucus, amoebic infection may also cause ulcers on the anus, and liver, lung, heart and brain abscesses with systemic symptoms. It can be transmitted sexually, as well as by consumption of contaminated water.

Nondiarrheal Illness

Hepatitis A. This virus can be contracted through water, contaminated produce (eg, strawberries and cantaloupe), milk, and raw shellfish. Spread usually occurs through cross-contamination by an infected food handler, particularly one who does not practice good hand washing, at any point from the farm to the plate. Fecal-oral transmission may also occur through sexual contact.

Listeria monocytogenes causes listeriosis and is fatal in nearly 20% of cases. The most common manifestations include bacteremia and meningitis, particularly in infants and the elderly. This organism is the basis for the warning to pregnant women not to consume unpasteurized soft cheeses, particularly from Latin America. Raw hot dogs, cole slaw, and deli meats are also high-risk foods. Less commonly, one may develop gastroenteritis related to listeriosis. Immunocompromised patients, particularly renal transplant recipients, are at increased risk for listeriosis.

Clostridium botulinum causes a life-threatening paralysis and may result from home canning, fish fermentation, and extended use of food warmers. Infants less than 12 months of age may develop life-threatening botulism from ingestion of spores present in honey or corn syrup. These products should not be used in this age group.

Toxoplasma gondii infection may occur through ingestion of raw beef or lamb or through cross-contamination from cat feces (eg, in infrequently cleaned litter boxes and gardens). Infection is generally self-limited and asymptomatic, except in immunocompromised patients. However, primary infection with toxoplasmosis during pregnancy is dangerous to the fetus. Immunocompetent individuals may develop a mononucleosis-like syndrome. In individuals with T-cell immunodeficiencies, such as HIV patients or heart transplant recipients, the organism often causes brain, retinal, lung, and muscle lesions (commonly due to reactivation of previous infection, rather than new infections).

Trichinosis. This disease is caused by ingestion of encysted larvae in undercooked pork and wild carnivorous game, such as bear. Cattle and horse meat can be cross-contaminated. Trichinosis rarely causes diarrhea but may cause ocular, cardiac, neurologic, and muscular symptoms such as muscle swelling and pain after larval migration. It is now rare in the United States due to regulatory controls on the feeding of pigs, but is seen more commonly in developing countries.

Echinococcus. This parasite may be ingested in water contaminated by wild and domestic canines (eg, foxes and wolves), particularly in the Middle East, Greece, Africa, and Asia. Cysts may infect the liver and lungs and may cause symptoms decades after the initial infection.

Brucellosis. Brucellosis, particularly *B abortus, B melitensis*, and *B suis*, is found in contaminated dairy and meat products, commonly from Latin America. Brucellosis may result in high fevers, septicemia, septic arthritis, meningitis, endocarditis, osteomyelitis, and rashes.

Tapeworms can be found in raw fish, beef, and pork. *Taenia solium* may be acquired through ingestion of infected raw pork or soil, resulting in cysticercosis or neurocysticercosis. With neurocysticercosis, patients will commonly present with new-onset seizures, even after death of the parasite. Migration to the skin and liver may also occur. In rare instances, fish tapeworms may cause pernicious anemia due to vitamin B_{12} malabsorption. Beef tapeworms are asymptomatic.

Fish toxins cause several kinds of illness. Ciguatera poisoning occurs after ingesting fish that have eaten toxic microalgae. It is associated with neurologic and cardiovascular complications, including circumoral paresthesias and paralysis. Scombroid, or histamine poisoning, results from the bacterial decomposition of muscle proteins of certain finfish (eg, tuna and mackerel). Tetrodotoxin in puffer fish is often fatal due to multiorgan system collapse.

Prions are abnormal proteins that cause slowly progressive spongiform encephalopathies, including Creutzfeldt-Jakob disease and bovine spongiform encephalopathy (BSE, or "mad cow disease"). The latter disease emerged in the mid-1990s in Great Britain, presumably due to the practice of feeding cattle the remains of other ruminants, particularly sheep (sheep are susceptible to a similar spongiform encephalopathy called scrapie). Evidence suggests that human cases of variant Creutzfeldt-Jakob disease have been due to prion transmission through consumption of infected cattle.[7] The risk to humans has been reduced by regulations for livestock feeding and processing that help prevent ingestion of concentrated neural material (ie, brain and spinal cord). Similar diseases occur in other animals, such as chronic wasting disease in deer and elk.

Prevention and Treatment

Prevention is the most effective way to limit the morbidity and mortality associated with food and waterborne illness. Essential to prevention efforts are clean drinking water, restaurant and meat inspection, temperature monitoring, appropriate sewage processing, monitoring of public waterways for contamination, and public education on proper hygiene. The public should be cautioned about foods presenting particular risk and given instruction in proper food handling and preparation.

Vaccines are available for hepatitis A and typhoid fever.

All patients with suspected foodborne illness should be instructed in proper hand-washing techniques to protect others with whom they are in contact. Diagnosis of foodborne illness generally requires notification of the public health department.

Most acute diarrheal episodes are self-limited. Oral (or intravenous) rehydration therapy (ORT) may be needed. Patients treating their conditions at home can prepare ORT using 1 teaspoon of salt, 1 teaspoon of baking soda, and 8 tablespoons of sugar mixed in 2 liters of clean water. Some outcomes may be improved or the disease course shortened through antibiotic treatment, but only when a specific diagnosis is suspected. Antimotility drugs (eg, loperamide) may be useful in viral diarrhea, or when easy access to a restroom is limited, but are otherwise not generally recommended.

Note: Travelers may use ciprofloxacin (500mg twice daily) or azithromycin (1 gram) in case of severe diarrhea. Therapy may be needed for 3 days if not resolved in 24 hours.[8] Bismuth subsalicylate may also be used (using an equivalent of ~1 gram [liquid or tablets] every 30 minutes for up to 8 doses). Toxicity is possible, especially in aspirin users, and manifests as tinnitus, vertigo, vomiting, and diarrhea, which can potentially confuse the clinical picture.

Salmonella (nontyphoidal) is usually self-limited, although antibiotic treatment should be used in very sick individuals, such as those with concurrent immunocompromised states or vascular disease or at the extremes of age.

Typhoid fever may be multidrug resistant. Fluoroquinolones or third-generation cephalosporins are generally effective, although resistance to many antibiotics has emerged and varies according to the country of exposure.

Campylobacter may be treated with antibiotics, which may shorten the duration of illness, but are not usually required. Typically, fluoroquinolones, erythromycin, and tetracycline are effective. However, many studies have verified growing resistance to fluoroquinolones.[9]

Shigella, like salmonella and campylobacter, is treated with antibiotics when patients are very sick, immunocompromised, or a risk to public health (ie, food handlers, daycare attendees, hospital workers). Antibiotic choice depends on the age of the patient and resistance patterns. Typical antibiotics are fluoroquinolones, trimethoprim-sulfamethoxazole (if sensitive), and azithromycin. Ceftriaxone is used in children.

Cryptosporidiosis treatment is rarely necessary in immunocompetent persons. In immunocompromised patients, such as those infected with HIV, paromomycin with azithromycin and nitazoxanide has been used with varying success.

E coli (O157:H7) should generally not be treated with antibiotics, as their lack of efficacy is well-documented and treatment has been linked with a higher incidence of hemolytic uremic syndrome. Other *E coli* infections may require supportive therapy. Traveler's diarrhea is often caused by *E coli* (see above).

Yersinia requires antibiotics in complicated illness only.

For **Vibrio** infections, oral rehydration therapy is essential due to the risk of severe diarrhea resulting in volume loss and shock. Antibiotics may shorten the course of diarrhea and Vibrio excretion, and may be used as a therapy adjunct. Doxycycline, tetracycline, and fluoroquinolones are possible choices. Macrolides are commonly used for children. Mortality can exceed 50% when Vibrio infections are untreated.

Listeria should be treated promptly with intravenous antibiotics, such as penicillin G or trimethoprim-sulfamethoxazole. A 2-week treatment is generally prescribed, except in immunocompromised patients, for whom longer courses are required. Gentamicin can be added for severe infections once its potential toxicity is considered.

Botulism usually requires treatment with an antitoxin. Enemas and laxatives are helpful, and antibiotics may be used, although they have uncertain efficacy. Intense monitoring in a hospital is required.

Toxoplasma gondii infection should be treated in pregnant and immunocompromised patients or in the presence of severe or prolonged symptoms. Pyrimethamine and sulfadiazine (folic acid antagonists) are the drugs of choice, along with folinic acid to prevent sulfadiazine-associated bone marrow suppression.

Cyclospora can be treated with trimethoprim and sulfamethoxazole.

Tapeworms can be prevented by cooking or freezing meat prior to ingestion and by avoiding cross-contamination. Albendazole or praziquantel may be used for active disease, but risks may outweigh benefits. Anticonvulsants are required in the presence of seizure activity. Surgery is rarely required.

Amoeba and **giardiasis** may be treated with metronidazole.

Echinococcus calls for cyst injection with hypertonic saline or ethanol prior to excision (marsupialization), and/or oral albendazole treatment. Spillage of cyst contents into the peritoneal cavity may result in anaphylaxis; therefore, expertise with this procedure is required.

Trichinosis can usually be prevented by freezing meat. For individuals who consume pork or other at-risk meats, thorough cooking also kills these pathogens. Treatment is not usually necessary, but mebendazole and albendazole are generally effective. Symptomatic treatment of pain and fever and systemic steroids are often helpful.

Brucellosis is related to unpasteurized dairy products and contact with animals on farms or in slaughterhouses. Infections are commonly treated with a regimen of doxycycline plus rifampin, gentamicin, or streptomycin.

Nutritional Considerations

Foods of animal origin, particularly meat and eggs, are most often implicated in cases of foodborne illness.[10] Scientists at the CDC's Foodborne and Diarrheal Diseases Branch have observed that foodborne illness starts near the bottom of the food chain in the form of contamination of animal feed with *Salmonella enterica*.[11] Other investigators working with the Food and Drug Administration's (FDA) Division of Animal and Food Microbiology Office have documented that resistant strains of salmonella are common in retail ground meats, including ground chicken, beef, turkey, and pork.[12]

Consumers may believe that choosing white meat in place of red meat will reduce their risk for foodborne infection. However, a multistate investigation linked an outbreak of listeria to processed turkey meat, resulting in a recall of 16 million pounds of the product.[13] Eating chicken in restaurants has been noted as the most common cause of infection with campylobacter, a bacterium that is a common cause of gastroenteritis in the United States.[14]

Raw oysters and other shellfish eaten by approximately 10% of adults each year may be a source of Vibrio gastroenteritis if harvested from contaminated waters, particularly the Gulf of Mexico.[15] The US Department of Agriculture's (USDA) Food Safety and Inspection Service listed eggborne infection with *Salmonella enteritidis* as an important public health problem in the United States in 2000.[16] However, the problem appears to be ongoing, partly as a result of food-handling practices and specifically due to ingestion of products containing undercooked eggs, such as mayonnaise, ice cream, and custards. In addition, better food handling will not prevent infections passed in intact eggs.[17]

The USDA's Animal Disease Research Unit has found that dairy farms are a potential source of *Listeria monocytogenes*, a zoonotic foodborne pathogen that is responsible for 28% of U.S. food-related deaths every year.[18] Other studies have found that dairy farms using antibiotics are also a reservoir for multidrug-resistant *Salmonella typhimurium*,[19] *E coli* (O157:H7),[20] and *Yersinia enterocolitica*,[21] as well as other pathogenic organisms.[22]

Produce may become contaminated with fecal pathogens during planting, irrigating, harvesting, processing, and shipping, or through contaminated water.[23]

Food-service establishments can be a frequent source of foodborne infection, although the risk is also present in homes and any other setting that allows for poor temperature control in preparing, cooking, and storing food.[10] A 2005 survey of food-service personnel found that more than 50% did not always wear gloves while touching ready-to-eat foods; almost 25% did not follow appropriate hand-washing guidelines; more than 33% did not always change gloves between handling raw meat and ready-to-eat foods; and more than 50% did not use a thermometer to check food temperatures.[24] All these precautions should be used in any setting where food is prepared.

The CDC, FDA, and USDA have established the Foodborne Diseases Active Surveillance Network (FoodNet) as a component of the CDC's Emerging Infections Program (EIP). FoodNet's purpose is to monitor trends in foodborne diseases, determine the societal burden caused by these diseases, and assess which diseases are attributable to specific foods and settings in the United States. Data listed on FoodNet's Web site clearly indicate that the routine practice of using antibiotics in animal feed selects for the development of antimicrobial resistance.[25] The site lists US farms and dairies in violation of guidelines to avoid antibiotic use. Tracing the origin of contaminated meat by FoodNet is complicated by the fact that a single hamburger might contain meat from many cows and the fact that the beef is handled at multiple facilities.[1] These factors make it extremely difficult to identify the origin of contamination. Extensive research into flash gamma irradiation has shown effective eradication of bacterial contamination. However, low public acceptance has resulted in slow implementation of this process.[26]

Orders

See Basic Diet Orders chapter.

What to Tell the Family

Complete avoidance of foodborne illness may not be possible. However, risk can be minimized through proper cooking and handling to avoid cross-contamination. Risk is further reduced by avoiding foods of animal origin. However, certain plant foods may also be contaminated during production, processing, or handling.

In the case of immunocompromised patients, ingestion of raw fish and raw meat is associated with a higher risk of foodborne illnesses. Patients with chronic liver disease should be strongly encouraged to avoid raw shellfish, including oysters, clams, and shrimp.

References

1. Kuehn BM. Surveillance and coordination key to reducing foodborne illness. *JAMA*. 2005;294:2683-2684.

2. Centers for Disease Control and Prevention. Diagnosis and Management of Foodborne Illness. A Primer for Physicians and Other Health Care Professionals. *MMWR*. 2004;53(RR-4):1-33.

3. Imhoff B, Morse D, Shiferaw B, et al. Burden of self-reported acute diarrheal illness in FoodNet surveillance areas, 1998-1999. *Clin Infect Dis*. 2004;38(suppl 3):S219-S226.

4. Cui S, Ge B, Zheng J, Meng J. Prevalence and antimicrobial resistance of Campylobacter spp. and Salmonella serovars in organic chickens from Maryland retail stores. *Appl Environ Microbiol*. 2005;71:4108-4111.

5. Smith KE, Besser JM, Hedberg CW, et al. Quinolone-resistant *Campylobacter jejuni* infections in Minnesota, 1992-1998. *N Engl J Med*. 1999;340:1525-1532.

6. Centers for Disease Control and Prevention. Surveillance for waterborne-disease outbreaks associated with recreational water in the United States, 2001-2002. *MMWR.* 2004;53(SS-8):1-22.

7. Collinge J. Variant Creutzfeldt-Jakob disease. *Lancet.* 1999;354:317-323.

8. Hill DR, Ericsson CD, Pearson RD, et al. The practice of travel medicine: guidelines by the Infectious Diseases Society of America. *Clin Infect Dis.* 2006;43:1499-1539.

9. Gupta A, Nelson JM, Barrett TJ, et al. Antimicrobial resistance among Campylobacter strains, United States, 1997-2001. *Emerg Infect Dis.* 2004;10:1102-1109.

10. Todd EC. Epidemiology of foodborne diseases: a worldwide review. *World Health Stat Q.* 1997;50:30-50.

11. Crump JA, Griffin PM, Angulo FJ. Bacterial contamination of animal feed and its relationship to human foodborne illness. *Clin Infect Dis.* 2002;35:859-865.

12. White DG, Zhao S, Sudler R, et al. The isolation of antibiotic-resistant salmonella from retail ground meats. *N Engl J Med.* 2001;345:1147-1154.

13. Olsen SJ, Patrick M, Hunter SB, et al. Multistate outbreak of Listeria monocytogenes infection linked to delicatessen turkey meat. *Clin Infect Dis.* 2005;40:962-967.

14. Friedman CR, Hoekstra RM, Samuel M, et al. Risk factors for sporadic Campylobacter infection in the United States: A case-control study in FoodNet sites. *Clin Infect Dis.* 2004;38(suppl 3):S285-S296.

15. Altekruse SF, Bishop RD, Baldy LM, et al. Vibrio gastroenteritis in the US Gulf of Mexico region: the role of raw oysters. *Epidemiol Infect.* 2000;124:489-495.

16. Schroeder CM, Naugle AL, Schlosser WD, et al. Estimate of illnesses from Salmonella enteritidis in eggs, United States, 2000. *Emerg Infect Dis.* 2005;11:113-115.

17. Lee R, Beatty ME, Bogard AK, et al. Prevalence of high-risk egg-preparation practices in restaurants that prepare breakfast egg entrees: an EHS-Net study. *J Food Prot.* 2004;67:1444-1450.

18. Borucki MK, Reynolds J, Gay CC, et al. Dairy farm reservoir of Listeria monocytogenes sporadic and epidemic strains. *J Food Prot.* 2004;67:2496-2499.

19. Villar RG, Macek MD, Simons S, et al. Investigation of multidrug-resistant Salmonella serotype typhimurium DT104 infections linked to raw-milk cheese in Washington State. *JAMA.* 1999;281:1811-1816.

20. Murinda SE, Nguyen LT, Ivey SJ, et al. Prevalence and molecular characterization of Escherichia coli O157:H7 in bulk tank milk and fecal samples from cull cows: a 12-month survey of dairy farms in east Tennessee. *J. Food Prot.* 2002;65:752-759.

21. Ackers ML, Schoenfeld S, Markman J, et al. An outbreak of Yersinia enterocolitica O:8 infections associated with pasteurized milk. *J Infect Dis.* 2000;181:1834-1837.

22. Altekruse SF, Timbo BB, Mowbray JC, Bean NH, Potter ME. Cheese-associated outbreaks of human illness in the United States, 1973 to 1992: sanitary manufacturing practices protect consumers. *J Food Prot.* 1998;61:1405-1407.

23. Dentinger CM, Bower WA, Nainan OV, et al. An outbreak of hepatitis A associated with green onions. *J Infect Dis.* 2001;183:1273-1276.

24. Green L, Selman C, Banerjee A, et al. Food service workers' self-reported food preparation practices: an EHS-Net study. *Int J Hyg Environ Health.* 2005;208:27-35.

25. Centers for Disease Control and Prevention. FoodNet-Foodborne Diseases Active Surveillance Network. Available at: http://www.cdc.gov/foodnet/. Accessed December 26, 2005.

26. Oldfield EC III. Emerging foodborne pathogens: keeping your patients and your families safe. *Rev Gastroenterol Disord.* 2001;1:177-186.

88. Foodborne Chemicals

Chemicals and chemical reactions are an integral part of everyday life. Photosynthesis occurs in plants, acids aid digestion, buffers balance the pH of blood, and, of course, industry uses many chemical reactions to produce modern products. However, more and more potentially toxic chemicals are becoming concentrated in our environment due to the continued and rapid industrialization of the world.

Products of industry, whether byproducts of manufacturing, such as heavy metals and polychlorinated biphenyls (PCBs), or finished products, such as antibiotics, pesticides, herbicides, batteries, fuels, and electronic equipment, are all potential toxins. Ground and surface waters used for drinking and fishing, soil used for agriculture purposes, and farmed animals raised with growth/production stimulators are all potential reservoirs of chemicals that can harm human health.

Heavy Metals

Public health agencies and clinicians should educate the public regarding ways to minimize heavy metal exposures. Known exposures should be discussed immediately with a local poison control authority.

Elemental mercury is a well-known toxin. It is used in medical instruments, although less commonly today than in the past, and in dental amalgam fillings. Family physicians may encounter patients who have inhaled elemental mercury resulting from spills at home or in schools, although these exposures may not lead to toxicity. Mercury also forms several compounds and is a common environmental pollutant as a result of industrial processes.

Aside from occupational exposures, the main exposure route is through ingestion of fish, especially those high on the food chain, such as shark, tuna, and swordfish, and certain fish taken from some freshwaters. Dental fillings are not believed to present a public health hazard, although alternatives to amalgam fillings are available. Some vaccines may contain thimerosal (DTaP, Hib, Hep B), a compound that includes mercury. However, the amount of mercury in vaccines is not considered unsafe. Thimerosal-free vaccines are available.

Mercury poisoning may cause digestive, respiratory, renal, and neurologic disorders and can be lethal. (The phrase "mad as a hatter" refers to neurologic sequelae of mercury exposures in the felt hat industry of the 19th century.) Some evidence links mercury to cardiovascular disease. Mercury easily crosses the placenta in pregnant women and may cause birth defects, even in the absence of maternal symptoms.

Mercury toxicity is usually diagnosed by a blood test. Chelation is available for acute mercury toxicity.

Cadmium, a heavy metal common in the environment, can cause kidney, bone, and lung disease and is considered a probable carcinogen by the federal Environmental Protection Agency (EPA). Cigarettes are a common source of cadmium exposure. Incineration of household waste, particularly batteries, may release cadmium into the atmosphere, and industrial processes such as mining and land applications of sewage sludge can pollute water and air. Phosphate fertilizers commonly contain cadmium, and grain and vegetable crops easily absorb the metal through polluted irrigation waters.

Fish concentrate cadmium in their livers and kidneys, leading to toxicity in populations that commonly consume whole fish, especially fish taken from urban waters. Shellfish also concentrate cadmium.

Cadmium toxicity can be diagnosed through urine and blood tests, although blood generally shows evidence of acute exposures only. For this reason, prevention of excess exposure is of paramount importance. No well-studied and accepted chelating agent is available for cadmium in humans.

Lead is very common in landfills harboring old electronic devices (solder) and cathode ray tubes, in mine runoff areas, and in manufacturing facilities where lead is used in batteries, radiators, lead glazes, and other products. Groundwater and waterways may become contaminated from these sources, and many old houses still use lead pipes to connect to city water mains. In addition, older houses often have lead-based paint, which may flake and be consumed by small children.

Lead may also be present in toy jewelry, radiographs (if stored in lead-lined boxes), household crystal and glazed pottery used for serving foods and beverages, imported Mexican candy, and traditional medicines. For example, some Ayurvedic and Chinese medicines may contain lead, mercury, and arsenic.[1,2] Air emissions, especially in areas where leaded gasoline is still available, may cause surface contamination of crops.

Lead poisoning can lead to nervous system and kidney damage and can cause several nonspecific symptoms. It may also adversely affect fetal and childhood development and fertility in men. During pregnancy and lactation, women can mobilize lead stored in bone from past exposures.

Lead poisoning is diagnosed through blood lead concentrations, among other laboratory findings, and chelation agents are available for treatment of patients with high levels or acute symptoms.

High-calcium diets may protect against lead accumulation by reducing gastrointestinal absorption of this mineral.[3] High blood levels of vitamin C are also independently associated with lower prevalence of elevated blood lead concentrations.[4] However, neither calcium nor vitamin C has yet been found to reduce body lead burden in randomized controlled clinical trials.

Arsenic is present in some pesticides, treated wood, and mining runoff. Exposures may also come from the smelting process. Arsenic is also a component of chicken feed supplements used to treat parasites[5] and often reaches drinking water, especially untreated well water. Exposure through water is of particular concern, because the arsenic compounds formed are readily bioavailable. Exposure may also result from occupational inhalation.

Long-term exposure is related to hyperkeratosis,[6] neurologic and cardiovascular problems, as well as increased risk of skin, lung, and other cancers. Arsenic poisoning is commonly diagnosed through urine tests, although hair and nail samples can also reveal exposure. Chelation therapy is available.

Polychlorinated Biphenyls and Dioxins[7,8]

PCBs are synthetic organic chemicals that were used in many products before 1977, when domestic PCB production was banned in the United States. Over 1.5 billion pounds were produced in the United States. PCBs now represent an environmental contaminant concentrated in fatty fish and other animal products (dairy products, eggs, and meats) and are also detectable in human tissues.

Evidence strongly suggests that PCBs are human carcinogens and adversely affect the immune, reproductive, nervous, and endocrine systems of animals and humans. PCBs can cross the placenta and may contribute to cognitive problems in children.[9] PCBs also enter breast milk, although the contribution of this route of exposure to health effects in infants is not well established, and breast-feeding is still encouraged.[10]

Dioxins are usually byproducts of industrial processes, including incineration, although they also result from volcanic eruptions. Like PCBs, they are found mostly in animal products near the top of the food chain and ultimately can affect animal and human immune, reproductive, nervous, and endocrine systems. Although less than 10% of dioxins are considered significantly toxic, their long half-life—about 7 years in the human body—makes them an important public health concern. Destroying dioxins requires incineration at temperatures above 850° to 1000° centigrade.[11]

Pesticides[12]

Pesticides (including herbicides) are agents that can both beneficially and adversely affect public health. They are beneficial in that they can restrict the spread of disease. On the other hand, over 4 billion pounds of pesticides are applied annually in the United States, so the prevention of unnecessary and accidental exposure through direct contact, or through water and food sources, is essential.

Several common classes of pesticides have the potential for adverse effects on the central nervous system: carbamates (carbaryl), organochlorines (lindane, DDT), organophosphates (malathion), and pyrethroids (permethrin). DEET is also commonly used to prevent mosquito and tick bites and can be toxic if not used as directed or if ingested; hand-washing after application is essential.

Lindane and permethrin are available by prescription for the treatment of scabies. Permethrin is safer for infants, children, and during pregnancy and is also available as an antilice shampoo.

It is estimated that 50% of lifetime pesticide exposure occurs in the first 5 years of life.[13] Developing fetuses and children are at high risk of pesticide toxicity due to their rapid growth and developmental vulnerability. Some pesticides have the potential to disrupt endocrine pathways involving estrogen, androgen, and thyroid receptors. In addition, young children are particularly vulnerable, because they spend more time outdoors, often put their hands in their mouths, and ingest a much greater amount of food per unit body weight. For some pesticide residues, breast milk may contain several times the concentrations found in maternal blood samples.[14]

Acute pesticide ingestion can be treated with gastric lavage, charcoal, pralidoxime (for organophosphates), and atropine. Diazepam may also help prevent seizures.

Antibiotics

Untreated pharmaceuticals, such as the antihelminthic morantel, which is used widely in animal agriculture, may pass easily into soil and water supplies once released into the environment.[15] Public health authorities are concerned that antibiotic use on farms may spawn antibiotic resistance. In Oklahoma, turkey, cattle, and chicken farms and retail meats showed multi-antibiotic-resistant *Klebsiella pneumonia* bacteria, which could transfer the gene for resistance to *E coli*.[16]

In developed countries, studies have suggested an association between antimicrobial use in farmed animals and the development of antibiotic resistance in humans.[17] Some experts believe antibiotic resistance is more commonly due to antibiotic use in human patients or to contact with hospital environments.[18] Others have suggested that the development of resistance in humans may be due, in some cases, to antibiotic-resistant microflora of farm animals contaminating products entering the human food supply and passing resistance genes on to human microflora.[19] Antimicrobial use to increase yields for plants, such as lettuce[20] and aquaculture,[21] spreads similar risk of antimicrobial resistance in humans.

Heterocyclic Amines[22,23]

Heterocyclic amines (HCAs) are carcinogenic compounds that form during cooking of all meats, including fish. HCAs are capable of inducing genetic damage after ingestion. In general, grilling causes the greatest amount of HCA formation, followed by pan-frying. Chicken products contribute the greatest quantity of HCAs in North American diets, compared with other meats, in part due to the quantity of chicken products consumed. Several cancers are associated with HCAs, including those arising in the colon and rectum, stomach, breast, lung, and prostate. Modification of cooking methods (such as microwaving) and reducing meat consumption are effective preventive steps.

The intake of cruciferous vegetables, such as broccoli and Brussels sprouts, has been found to increase HCA metabolism in humans by induction of hepatic detoxification enzymes.[24-26]

Nitrates

Nitrates and nitrites are used as preservatives in hot dogs, pickled meats and vegetables, some cheeses, and other foods. They are metabolized in the body to form *N*-nitroso compounds, which are associated with gastric and esophageal cancer. New evidence also links nitrate ingestion to a raised COPD risk. *N*-nitroso compounds also form during smoking of foods, such as fish. Nitrates are also a natural component of many vegetables, and produce commonly contains nitrate residues from fertilizers. However, despite the presence of nitrates in and on many fruits and vegetables, protection from gastric cancer is afforded by the consumption of these foods, presumably because of the inhibitory effect of vitamin C on the formation of *N*-nitroso compounds.

Other foods and nutrients also inhibit *N*-nitroso compound formation. These include polyphenolic compounds in fruits and vegetables;[27] garlic and other *allium* species;[28] and vitamin E and selenium.[29]

Orders

See Basic Diet Orders chapter.

What to Tell the Family

Many toxic chemicals are concentrated in fatty animal tissues (including fish liver and kidneys) or produced during cooking. To reduce exposure to these toxic chemicals, it is best to reduce consumption (and trim visible fat) as described in the basic diet orders.

Certain fish species are common sources of toxic exposures. While some evidence shows fish to be more healthful than other meats for various health outcomes (such as cardiovascular events), the toxic load of some fish species raises important concerns. This is of particular relevance for women prior to and during their childbearing years and for pregnant and lactating women. Despite the presence of some toxic chemicals in breast milk, the benefits of breast-feeding outweigh the presumed risks to the baby.

Organic produce is increasingly available. Nonorganically produced fruits and vegetables can be washed thoroughly with warm water and a soft brush to reduce pesticide residues. Certain fruits and vegetables, such as apples, berries, tomatoes, and grapes, tend to carry larger pesticide residues.

Household pesticides, if used at all, should be carefully stored. When they are used, family members and domestic animals should be protected from exposure for the period of time specified in the product instructions.

References

1. Saper RB, Kales SN, Paquin J, et al. Heavy metal content of ayurvedic herbal medicine products. *JAMA*. 2004;292:2868-2873.

2. US Department of Human Services, Centers for Disease Control and Prevention, National Center for Environmental Health, frequently asked questions. Lead in folk medicine: questions and answers. Available at: http://www.cdc.gov/nceh/lead/faq/folk%20 meds.htm. Accessed April 9, 2007.

3. Chuang HY, Tsai SY, Chao KY, et al. The influence of milk intake on the lead toxicity to the sensory nervous system in lead workers. *Neurotoxicology*. 2004;25:941-949.

4. Simon JA, Hudes ES. Relationship of ascorbic acid to blood lead levels. *JAMA*. 1999;281:2289-2293.

5. Lasky T, Sun W, Kadry A, Hoffman MK. Mean total arsenic concentrations in chicken 1989-2000 and estimated exposures for consumers of chicken. *Environ Health Perspect*. 2004;112:18-21.

6. US Department of Health and Human Services, Centers for Disease Control and Prevention, Agency for Toxic Substances and Disease Registry. ToxFAQs for arsenic. Available at: http://www.atsdr.cdc.gov/tfacts2.html. Accessed April 9, 2007.

7. US Environmental Protection Agency. Polychlorinated biphenyls (PCBs). Available at: http://www.epa.gov/opptintr/pcb/pubs/effects.html. Accessed April 9, 2007.

8. World Health Organization. Dioxins and their effects on human health (fact sheet No. 225, June 1999). Available at: http://www.who.int/mediacentre/factsheets/fs225/en/ index.html.

9. Jacobson JL, Jacobson SW. Intellectual impairment in children exposed to polychlorinated biphenyls in utero. *N Engl J Med*. 1996;335:783-789.

10. US Department of Health and Human Services, Centers for Disease Control and Prevention, Agency for Toxic Substances and Disease Registry. Toxicological profile for polychlorinated biphenyls (PCBs). Available at: http://www.atsdr.cdc.gov/toxprofiles/tp17. html. Accessed April 9, 2007.

11. US Department of Health and Human Services, Centers for Disease Control and Prevention, Agency for Toxic Substances and Disease Registry. Toxicological profile for chlorinated dibenzo-p-dioxins (CDDs). Available at: http://www.atsdr.cdc.gov/toxprofiles/ tp104.html. Accessed April 9, 2007.

12. Weiss B, Amler S, Amler RW. Pesticides. *Pediatrics*. 2004;113:1030-1036.

13. Landrigan PJ, Mattison DR, Babich HJ, et al, for the Committee on Pesticides in the Diets of Infants and Children. Report on pesticides in the diets of infants and children. National Research Council. Washington, DC: National Academy Press; 1993.

14. Wolff M. Occupationally derived chemicals in breast milk. *Am J Ind Med*. 1983;4:259-281.

15. Konek CT, Illg KD, Al-Abadleh HA, et al. Nonlinear optical studies of the agricultural antibiotic morantel interacting with silica/water interfaces. *J Am Chem Soc.* 2005;127:15771-15777.

16. Kim SH, Wei CI, Tzou YM, An H. Multidrug-resistant Klebsiella pneumoniae isolated from farm environments and retail products in Oklahoma. *J Food Prot.* 2005;68:2022-2029.

17. Padungton P, Kaneene JB. Campylobacter spp in humans, chickens, pigs and their antimicrobial resistance. *J Vet Med Sci.* 2003;65:161-170.

18. Berends BR, van den Bogaard AE, Van Knapen F, Snijders JM. Human health hazards associated with the administration of antimicrobials to slaughter animals. Part II. An assessment of the risks of resistant bacteria in pigs and pork. *Vet Q.* 2001;23:10-21.

19. Teuber M. Spread of antibiotic resistance with food-borne pathogens. *Cell Mol Life Sci.* 1999;56:755-763.

20. Rodriguez C, Lang L, Wang A, Altendorf K, Garcia F, Lipski A. Lettuce for human consumption collected in Coosta Rica contains complex communities of culturable oxytetracycline- and gentamicin-resistant bacteria. *Appl Environ Microbiol.* 2006;72:5870-5876.

21. Cabello FC. Heavy use of prophylactic antibiotics in aquaculture: a growing problem for human and animal health and for the environment. *Environ Microbiol.* 2006;8:1137-1144.

22. Keating GA, Bogen KT. Estimates of heterocyclic amine intake in the US population. *Journal of Chromatography B.* 2004;802:127-133.

23. Sugimura T, Wakabayashi K, Nakagama H, Nagao M. Heterocyclic amines: Mutagens/carcinogens produced during cooking of meat and fish. *Cancer Sci.* 2004;95:290-299.

24. Knize MG, Kulp KS, Salmon CP, Keating GA, Felton JS. Factors affecting human heterocyclic amine intake and the metabolism of PhIP. *Mutat Res.* 2002;506-507:153-162.

25. Walters DG, Young PJ, Agus C, et al. Cruciferous vegetable consumption alters the metabolism of the dietary carcinogen 2-amino-1-methyl-6-phenylimidazo[4,5-b]pyridine (PhIP) in humans. *Carcinogenesis.* 2004;25:1659-1669.

26. Murray S, Lake BG, Gray S, et al. Effect of cruciferous vegetable consumption on heterocyclic aromatic amine metabolism in man. *Carcinogenesis.* 2001;22:1413-1420.

27. Potter JD, Steinmetz K. Vegetables, fruit and phytoestrogens as preventive agents. *IARC Sci Publ.* 1996;139:61-90.

28. Milner JA. A historical perspective on garlic and cancer. *J Nutr.* 2001;131(suppl 3):1027S-1031S.

29. Chow CK, Hong CB. Dietary vitamin E and selenium and toxicity of nitrite and nitrate. *Toxicology.* 2002;180:195-207.

SECTION XVIII: PSYCHIATRIC CONDITIONS

89. Attention Deficit Hyperactivity Disorder

Attention deficit hyperactivity disorder (ADHD) is characterized by inattentiveness, hyperactivity, and poor impulse control. It is estimated to affect 5% to 10% of children, and up to 70% of cases persist into adolescence and adulthood. It can affect cognitive, academic, behavioral, emotional, and social functioning and may be associated with comorbid psychiatric conditions, such as oppositional-defiant and conduct disorders, learning disabilities, anxiety, depression, and, later in life, substance-use disorders.

This neurobehavioral disorder is probably of multifactorial origin; that is, it may be caused by a combination of genetic and environmental factors. Neurotransmitter abnormalities have been postulated, focusing on catecholamine metabolism in the cerebral cortex and basal ganglia. An imbalance between norepinephrine and dopamine in the prefrontal cortex is suspected. Methylphenidate, a stimulant that is effective in treating ADHD symptoms, is known to increase synaptic dopamine concentrations.

Inattention may present as disorganization, forgetfulness, frequent misplacing of things, inability to follow instructions, academic underachievement, distractibility, inability to finish tasks, poor concentration, careless mistakes, or poor attention to detail. Hyperactivity is identified by fidgeting, restlessness, difficulty remaining seated, and talking excessively or inability to remain quiet when appropriate.

Impulsivity is noted by difficulty waiting turns, disruptive classroom behavior, interrupting others, peer rejection, and attempting risky activities without considering consequences. Affected adults may show inattention and impulsivity, rather than hyperactivity, and may have difficulty keeping a schedule, managing money, staying with a job, or maintaining a relationship.

Risk Factors

Male gender. ADHD is identified 2 to 3 times more frequently in boys than in girls.

Age. About half of cases present earlier than age 4. Although some will remit by adolescence, others persist into adulthood. At present, no "adult-onset" variety is recognized; symptoms must have been present before 7 years old to meet diagnostic criteria.

Genetics. Some studies indicate that as much as 75% to 80% of risk may be genetic. Studies of twins reveal a 90% concordance in monozygotic twins. Several genes have been identified as possible candidates, notably dopamine receptor and transporter genes.

Environmental factors. Early lead exposure or head injury may increase risk.

Diagnosis

For a diagnosis of ADHD, the American Psychiatric Association requires at least 6 symptoms of inattention or at least 6 symptoms of hyperactivity and impulsivity, which are listed below.[1] Symptoms must have lasted for at least 6 months, must have begun prior to age 7, and must be present in at least 2 settings (eg, school and home). Also, there must be clear evidence of clinically significant impairment in social, academic, or occupational functioning.

Symptoms of Inattention

- Often fails to give close attention to details or makes careless mistakes in schoolwork, work, or other activities.
- Often has difficulty sustaining attention in tasks or at play.
- Often does not seem to listen when spoken to directly.
- Often does not follow through on instructions and fails to finish schoolwork, chores, or duties in the workplace.
- Often has difficulty organizing tasks and activities.
- Often avoids, dislikes, or is reluctant to engage in tasks that require sustained mental effort.
- Often loses things necessary for tasks or activities.
- Is often easily distracted by extraneous stimuli.
- Is often forgetful in daily activities.

Symptoms of Hyperactivity and Impulsivity

- Often fidgets with hands or feet or squirms in seat.

- Often leaves seat in classroom or in other situations in which remaining seated is expected.

- Often runs about or climbs excessively in situations in which these behaviors are inappropriate (in adolescents, or adults, may be limited to subjective feelings of restlessness).

- Often has difficulty playing or engaging in leisure activities quietly.

- Is often "on the go" or acts as if "driven by a motor."

- Often talks excessively.

- Often blurts out answers before questions have been completed.

- Often has difficulty awaiting turn.

- Often interrupts or intrudes on others (eg, butts into conversations or games).

A medical, neurologic, psychological, and cognitive evaluation should be performed to rule out underlying medical contributors, cognitive deficiencies, and mimicking disorders. Diagnosis of adult ADHD is similar to that in children but may be complicated by a more subtle presentation, usually lacking the hyperactivity component.

Treatment

A cardiac assessment is recommended prior to initiation of stimulants.

Pharmacologic Treatments[2]

Stimulants. Methylphenidate and **dextroamphetamine** are effective in 60%-70% of children with ADHD. They increase catecholamine release from presynaptic neurons. Sustained-release preparations and longer-acting medications, such as dexmethylphenidate, minimize rebound symptoms and irritability, as well as minimize disruptions in the school day caused by twice-daily or three-times-daily dosing schedules. Side effects may include decreased appetite, insomnia, anxiety, irritability, or headache. Moreover, sympathomimetic agents raise blood pressure and heart rate, potentially contributing to risk of sudden cardiac death.[3]

Lisdexamfetamine is a new stimulant, activated in the gut, that may prevent potential abuse (snorting, injection).

Modafinil is not yet approved for treatment of ADHD, due to several case reports of an association with Stevens-Johnson syndrome (a potentially fatal rash) in children.

Nonstimulants. Several classes of nonstimulant medications may be effective, although controlled studies are limited. Nonstimulants are generally used in patients who do not respond to or cannot tolerate stimulants.

Atomoxetine is a selective norepinephrine reuptake inhibitor and is the only FDA-approved nonstimulant for ADHD. The FDA has warned that this medication may cause hepatotoxicity, suicidal thinking, and serotonin syndrome (when used along with fluoxetine). It should be discontinued in patients who develop jaundice or laboratory evidence of hepatotoxicity.

Among **antidepressant** medications, tricyclic antidepressants (eg, imipramine, nortriptyline) and dopamine reuptake inhibitors (eg, bupropion) have both been used with some anecdotal success but are not approved for use in children because of concerns about sudden cardiac death. Bupropion is used frequently in adults as a first-line treatment because it is not a stimulant per se. Moreover, many adult patients have comorbid depression. Bupropion is not habit forming and is less likely to be abused than stimulants. Selective serotonin reuptake inhibitors do not appear to have as much effect as other antidepressants.

Clonidine is an alpha-2 adrenergic agonist that may be useful in easily frustrated, highly aroused, and aggressive patients, as well as in children and adolescents with tic disorders. Side effects may include dizziness, syncope, palpitations, diaphoresis, pedal edema, or urinary changes. In addition, several drugs may interact with clonidine, including alcohol, barbiturates, beta-blockers, digoxin, and cold medicines. Combined use with methylphenidate requires monitoring of blood pressure and pulse.

Gaunfacine is an alpha-2 adrenergic agonist with fewer side effects than clonidine. Its use remains investigational.

Anticholinesterase inhibitors, such as tacrine and donepezil, and nicotinic analogues are currently being investigated.

Nonpharmacologic Treatments

Behavioral interventions are useful for many patients, particularly children. These might include seating near the teacher, daily report card with home reinforcement, and extended time to complete tasks.

Replacing television viewing with exercise may be a promising preventive approach. A growing body of evidence indicates that small children who watch relatively little television have a significantly lower risk for developing ADHD compared with other children.[4] In contrast to watching TV and other sedentary activities, physical activity in children plays a critical role in their growth and development.[5] A meta-analytic review of studies found significant reductions in disruptive behavior in children who exercised regularly, particularly those with ADHD.[6] The improvements may be partially explained by findings of a dopamine-agonistic effect of exercise.[7] Also, sports and other social activities help children learn appropriate social skills.

Biofeedback. Electroencephalographic (EEG) biofeedback training may be a promising investigational treatment. Research studies have demonstrated that some individuals who have ADHD have excess slow-wave activity and reduced fast-wave activity compared with matched peers. Using video and auditory feedback, individuals can learn to reduce their slow-wave activity and/or increase their fast-wave activity.[8] Case series report that approximately 75% of patients have a positive clinical response.[9]

Nutritional Considerations

The role of diet in ADHD has been controversial ever since it was first proposed in the book *Why Your Child Is Hyperactive* by pediatrician Ben Feingold, MD.[10] Dr. Feingold demonstrated that the removal of synthetic colorings, flavorings, and preservatives from the diet led to a marked improvement in many children. (Feingold suspected a much wider array of dietary sensitivities, but those 3 were the easiest to study.) Later researchers failed to replicate these effects.

However, subsequent studies have reasserted the role of diet, suggesting that the list of offending agents may go beyond the food dyes, flavorings, and preservatives that were originally studied. Children with ADHD often have an allergic or other hypersensitive response to artificial colors, flavors, or preservatives,[11] and recent studies suggest that a histamine response may underlie ADHD symptoms in some children (see below). In addition, some studies have suggested a contributory role of nutrient-poor meals and snacks.[11] Such diets may contribute to the deficiency of nutrients (eg, iron and zinc) that has been documented in children with ADHD.[12] These nutrients are known to be required for neurotransmitter production.

The following nutritional factors are under study for their effect on ADHD:

Diets free of artificial flavorings, colors, and common allergens. At least 8 controlled studies have demonstrated either significant behavioral improvement on oligoantigenic diets compared with regular diets or behavioral deterioration on a placebo-controlled challenge with foods suspected of aggravating symptoms. In one of these studies, parental reports indicated that more than half the subjects exhibited a reliable improvement in behavior on an oliogoantigenic diet.[13] Typical oligoantigenic diets used previously included only lamb, chicken, potatoes, rice, banana, apple, cabbage, cauliflower, Brussels sprouts, broccoli, cucumber, celery, carrots, parsnip, salt, pepper, calcium, and vitamins.[14] The therapeutic basis for such a regimen may lie in an allergic response (ie, histamine production) to artificial colors, flavors, and dyes. Histamine is a neurotransmitter; antagonism of its actions improves cognitive performance. Notably, the antihistamine diphenhydramine (Benadryl) was once a treatment for ADHD, although it was not as effective as stimulants. Other histamine receptor antagonists are currently being evaluated for potential application in ADHD.[15]

A meta-analysis of double-blind, placebo-controlled trials concluded that artificial food colors contribute one-third to one-half of the behavioral deterioration that would be observable when hyperactive children are taken off psychostimulants.[16]

Omega-3 fatty acids. Both omega-3 and omega-6 fatty acids have been reported to be lower in children with ADHD compared with other children, and limited data suggest that certain fatty acids (eg, eicosapentaenoic acid [EPA] and docosahexanoic acid [DHA]) can affect behavior. However, clinical trials of polyunsaturated essential fatty acids in children with ADHD have produced inconsistent results.[14] Of 6 published placebo-controlled trials of polyunsaturated essential fatty acids, 2 with gamma-linolenic acid were equivocal; 1 with DHA was negative; and 3 with a combination of GLA, EPA, and DHA were positive on some measures.[14]

Zinc. As a cofactor for neurotransmitters, zinc influences regulation of γ-aminobutyric acid (GABA), serotonin, and dopamine, all of which may play roles in ADHD.[17] Poor zinc status is common and can delay cognitive development; it has been found with greater frequency in hyperactive children compared with controls.[17] Zinc status has been reported in a small sample to correlate with response to amphetamine treatment,[17] and controlled clinical trials in the Middle East, an area of zinc deficiency, support the possibility that supplemental zinc (55-150 mg ZnSO4/day) may improve response to methylphenidate[18] or improve symptoms of hyperactivity and impulsiveness when used as monotherapy.[19] However, these reports leave questions about sample retention and data analysis, and further controlled clinical trials are required.

Aspartame or sucrose restriction and mineral supplements. Controlled trials of sugar-restricted diets found no effect on behavioral symptoms in ADHD, even in children thought to be sugar-sensitive.[14,20] Deficiency of several minerals (iron, copper, zinc, calcium) may influence neurotransmission in the central nervous system, and several studies have demonstrated mineral deficiencies in children with ADHD. However, controlled studies have not established a clear benefit of supplementation in individuals with ADHD.[12] Similarly, studies have not supported a causal role for aspartame in ADHD.[21]

Orders

See Basic Diet Orders chapter and Nutritional Requirements Throughout the Life Cycle chapter.

What to Tell the Family

ADHD can impair learning, work performance, and social relationships. However, several effective treatments are available. Although many parents have understandable concerns about drug therapy, medications are highly effective and generally provide rapid and dramatic relief. Other options—behavioral treatment, special educational programming, and, for a subset, oligoantigenic diet—may be tried separately or in combination with medication.

References

1. American Psychiatric Association. *Diagnostic and Statistical Manual of Mental Disorders.* 4th ed. Arlington, Va: American Psychiatric Association; 1994:78-85.

2. Pliszka S; AACAP Work Group on Quality Issues. Practice parameter for the assessment and treatment of children and adolescents with attention-deficit/hyperactivity disorder. *J Am Acad Child Adolesc Psychiatry.* 2007;46:894-921.

3. Nissen SE. ADHD drugs and cardiovascular risk. *N Eng J Med.* 2006;354:1445-1448.

4. Christakis DA, Zimmerman FJ, DiGiuseppe DL, McCarty CA. Early television exposure and subsequent attentional problems in children. *Pediatrics.* 2004;113:708-713.

5. Cooper DM, Nemet D, Galassetti P. Exercise, stress, and inflammation in the growing child: from the bench to the playground. *Curr Opin Pediatr.* 2004;16:286-292.

6. Barkley RA. Adolescents with attention-deficit/hyperactivity disorder: an overview of empirically based treatments. *J Psychiatr Pract.* 2004;10:39-56.

7. Tantillo M, Kesick CM, Hynd GW, Dishman RK. The effects of exercise on children with attention-deficit hyperactivity disorder. *Med Sci Sports Exerc.* 2002;34:203-212.

8. Butnik SM. Neurofeedback in adolescents and adults with attention deficit hyperactivity disorder. *J Clin Psychol.* 2005;61:621-625.

9. Monastra VJ. Electroencephalographic biofeedback (neurotherapy) as a treatment for attention deficit hyperactivity disorder: rationale and empirical foundation. *Child Adolesc Psychiatr Clin N Am.* 2005;14:55-82.

10. Feingold B. *Why Your Child Is Hyperactive.* New York: Random House; 1974.

11. Boris M, Mandel FS. Foods and additives are common causes of the attention deficit hyperactive disorder in children. *Ann Allergy.* 1994;72:462-468.

12. Daley KC. Update on attention-deficit/hyperactivity disorder. *Curr Opin Pediatr.* 2004;16:217-226.

13. Kaplan BJ, McNicol J, Conte RA, Moghadam HK. Overall nutrient intake of preschool hyperactive and normal boys. *J Abnorm Child Psychol.* 1989;17:127-132.

14. Arnold LE. Alternative treatments for adults with attention-deficit hyperactivity disorder (ADHD). *Ann NY Acad Sci.* 2001;931:310-341.

15. Leurs R, Bakker RA, Timmerman H, de Esch IJ. The histamine H3 receptor: from gene cloning to H3 receptor drugs. *Nat Rev Drug Discov.* 2005;4:107-120.

16. Schab DW, Trinh NH. Do artificial food colors promote hyperactivity in children with hyperactive syndromes? A meta-analysis of double-blind placebo-controlled trials. *J Dev Behav Pediatr.* 2004;25:423-434.

17. Arnold LE, DiSilvestro RA. Zinc in attention-deficit/hyperactivity disorder. *J Child Adolesc Psychopharmacol.* 2005;15:619-627.

18. Akhondzadeh S, Mohammadi MR, Khademi M. Zinc sulfate as an adjunct to methylphenidate for the treatment of attention deficit hyperactivity disorder in children: a double blind and randomized trial. *BMC Psychiatry.* 2004;4:9.

19. Bilici M, Yildirim F, Kandil S, et al. Double-blind, placebo-controlled study of zinc sulfate in the treatment of attention deficit hyperactivity disorder. *Prog Neuropsychopharmacol Biol Psychiatry.* 2004;28:181-190.

20. Wolraich ML, Lindgren SD, Stumbo PJ, Stegink LD, Appelbaum MI, Kiritsy MC. Effects of diets high in sucrose or aspartame on the behavior and cognitive performance of children. *N Engl J Med.* 1994;330:301-307.

21. American Dietetic Association. Position of the American Dietetic Association: use of nutritive and nonnutritive sweeteners. *J Am Diet Assoc.* 2004;104:255-275.

90. Schizophrenia

Schizophrenia is characterized by the presence of delusions and/or hallucinations, as well as disorganized speech and behavior. It is also marked by the loss of normal functions, particularly emotional expression, productivity of thought and speech, and goal-directed behavior. Although it is discussed here as a single entity, schizophrenia is likely composed of a group of disorders that are heterogenous in origin despite similar symptomatology. An excess of brain dopamine activity is presumed to underlie these symptoms, but its etiology is likely multifactorial and remains an area of ongoing research.

The disorder affects about 1% of people worldwide. Schizophrenia occurs across all socioeconomic groups and cultures, although patients are often socially and economically marginalized as a result of the disease and its accompanying stigma, resulting in lowered socioeconomic status. Additionally, schizophrenia appears to have a better prognosis in developing countries, where patients are more fully integrated into their communities and family units.

Risk Factors

Age. The onset of schizophrenia is typically before age 25, and the illness persists throughout life. Although the lifetime risk for men and women is similar, onset is often later in women than in men, with a second peak onset around menopause, suggesting a protective role for estrogen. Peak onset for men is age 10 to 25, and for women it is age 25 to 35. Less than 10% of women present after age 40.

Genetic factors. Approximately half of monozygotic twins are affected when the other twin has schizophrenia. Monozygotic twins reared by adoptive parents have similar rates of schizophrenia as their twin siblings raised by their biological parents, suggesting the primary importance of genetic factors. First-degree relatives of affected individuals have a ten-fold increased risk for developing schizophrenia. However, no specific gene has been isolated, and several genes may play a role.

Early developmental influences. Analgesic use during the second trimester[1] or hypertension and diuretic use during the third trimester of pregnancy may be associated with increased risk of schizophrenia for the newborn.[2] Fetal malnutrition, paternal age over 50 years,[3] and winter and spring births (presumably related to viral infections) are also associated with increased risk. Persons who were not breast-fed for at least 2 weeks have been shown to have increased prevalence of schizophrenia,[4] and a child with a genetic predisposition to schizophrenia may have a further increased risk if a childhood head injury occurs.

Toxoplasma gondii. This organism may infect the central nervous system and may be associated with schizophrenia.

Diagnosis

The history will clarify acute symptoms, and physical examination may help rule out other causes of psychosis. The diagnostic criteria of the American Psychiatric Association call for 2 or more of the following, each present for a significant portion of time during a 1-month period:

- Delusions.

- Hallucinations.

- Disorganized speech.

- Grossly disorganized or catatonic behavior.

- Negative symptoms: affective flattening, reduced productivity of thought or speech, or reduced goal-directed behavior.

To establish the diagnosis, the patient must also demonstrate marked social or occupational dysfunction, signs of illness must be present for at least 6 months, and the condition cannot be attributable to substance abuse, a medical condition, or other mental health problems, such as depression and bipolar disorder.

Schizophrenia cannot be diagnosed through laboratory tests or imaging. However, some brain-imaging studies reveal increased ventricular and decreased frontal lobe volume.

Treatment

Treatment for schizophrenia is lifelong and multidisciplinary, aiming to reduce symptoms, maximize functioning, and prevent relapse. This is often challenging because affected individuals may not recognize their illness or seek treatment and may stop treatment because of undesirable side effects, limited financial resources, or lack of access to mental health services.

Ideally, a person can maintain a fairly normal lifestyle once properly treated. Emotional and physical support is an important component of treatment, and patients often have superior outcomes when direct family or community support is part of their overall treatment plan.

Pharmacologic Therapy

Medications are the most effective treatment. Antipsychotics act as dopamine receptor antagonists. Discontinuation of antipsychotics typically results in symptom recurrence. However, relapse is common even with continuous treatment. The disease is characterized by a waxing and waning of symptoms, necessitating close follow-up and continued support.

Typical antipsychotics (or neuroleptics), such as haloperidol or chlorpromazine, can be very effective, but they carry greater risk of tardive dyskinesia and other serious adverse effects, compared with newer drugs.

Second-generation (atypical) antipsychotics, such as olanzapine, risperidone, ziprasidone, aripiprazole, and quetiapine, generally carry less risk of tardive dyskinesia and neuroleptic malignant syndrome. Olanzapine, although generally well tolerated, often results in significant weight gain (approximately 20 to 30 pounds), as well as the development of the metabolic syndrome and its accompanying health consequences. Aripiprazole and ziprasidone are the least likely to cause weight gain and sedation, but they are more likely to be associated with akathesia and agitation. Risperidone now carries a black box warning for increased risk of cerebrovascular events. Sedation is often a side effect of risperidone, quetiapine, and olanzapine, although it subsides with continued use. Hyperlipidemia and weight gain can also be significant with both seroquel and risperdal, although less so than with olanzapine. Atypical antipsychotics are associated with increased risk of all-cause mortality in older patients.

Clozapine may be used for refractory cases. It also helps treat suicidal ideation, an important consideration given that as many as 40% of persons with schizophrenia will attempt suicide. Physicians need special authorization to use clozapine. Clozapine has several serious potential adverse effects, including life-threatening agranulocytosis, making weekly blood draws mandatory. Additional adverse effects include weight gain, anticholinergic effects, and increased risk of seizures.

Nonpharmacologic Therapy

Cognitive-behavioral therapy and family therapy are intended to help the patient and family identify warning signs of relapse and its consequences and improve treatment adherence. Family therapy has been shown to reduce relapse and rehospitalization.[5]

Group therapy, job training, and social skills training may improve quality of life and social functioning.[6,7]

Nutritional Considerations

Among the sequelae of schizophrenia is an increased risk of cardiovascular disease. The greater risk results from several factors. Patients' diets are often poor, smoking and physical inactivity are common, and antipsychotic medications may contribute to weight gain, hyperglycemia, and hypertriglyceridemia.[8-11] As a result, patients benefit from heart-healthy diets. Evidence indicates that behavioral interventions can improve weight control in persons with schizophrenia.[9,12]

Aside from cardiovascular risk, there may be other reasons for patients with schizophrenia to avoid typical Western (ie, high-fat, high-sugar) diets. These diets reduce hippocampal expression of brain-derived neurotrophic factor (BDNF), an important growth and maintenance factor for dendrites, which is reduced in the prefrontal cortex of patients with schizophrenia. Low concentrations of BDNF have also been implicated in both coronary atherosclerosis and insulin-resistance syndrome.[13] The latter is twice as common in schizophrenia patients as it is in the general U.S. adult population and helps explain the greater incidence of coronary heart disease in these patients.[14] Clarification of these issues awaits further research.

Regarding the causation of schizophrenia, epidemiologic studies have adduced interesting but inconclusive links between schizophrenia and environmental factors, including diet. Some evidence indicates that maternal exposure to *Toxoplasma gondii* is a risk factor for schizophrenia in offspring.[15,16] Humans can become infected with *T gondii* in a variety of ways, including ingestion of animal tissues. *T gondii* can also be spread when cat litter is not promptly cleaned.

Researchers have speculated that Westernized diets may play a role, citing a lower prevalence of schizophrenia in unindustrialized cultures and Asian populations. During the Industrial Revolution, intakes of saturated fat, meat, dairy products, and refined sugars paralleled an increase in schizophrenia.[8] However, these geographic differences may have been influenced by underreporting. Moreover, significant social changes have occurred simultaneously with nutritional changes; the role of nutrition, therefore, remains speculative.

Several studies have suggested that individuals with schizophrenia have lower levels of certain polyunsaturated fats in the central nervous system, compared with other people, and that eicosapentanoic acid supplements may reduce symptoms of schizophrenia, as measured by the Positive and Negative Symptoms Scale (PANSS).[17] However, these studies were generally small and should be repeated in larger populations.

One group of investigators has found a reduction in tardive dyskinesia symptoms with the use of branched-chain amino acid formulas.[18-20] Tardive dyskinesia is associated with deficient clearance of phenylalanine, an excess of which may increase production of catecholamines and indolamines, which may drive the hyperkinetic movements of tardive dyskinesia.[18] Branched-chain amino acids compete with phenylalanine at the blood-brain barrier, reduce the entry of phenylalanine into the

CNS, and subsequently reduce production of catecholamines and indolamines.

Vitamins E[21] and B6[22] are under investigation for possible effects on the progression of tardive dyskinesia.

Orders

See Basic Diet Orders chapter.

What to Tell the Family

Schizophrenia is a lifelong illness that requires medication and support from both mental health professionals and family members. Persons with schizophrenia are at greater than average risk for cardiovascular disease from a combination of medication, sedentary lifestyle, poor diet, and smoking. Family members can support the affected person by providing a healthful diet and a smoke-free environment, and by encouraging participation in regular physical activity. The potential benefit of additional nutritional interventions is a matter of ongoing research.

References

1. Sørensen HJ, Mortensen EL, Reinisch JM, Mednick SA. Association between prenatal exposure to analgesics and risk of schizophrenia. *Br J Psychiatry.* 2004;185:366-371.

2. Sørensen HJ, Mortensen EL, Reinisch JM, Mednick SA. Do hypertension and diuretic treatment in pregnancy increase the risk of schizophrenia in offspring? *American Journal of Psychiatry.* 2003;160:464-468.

3. Byrne M, Agerbo E, Ewald H, Eaton WW, Mortensen PB. Parental age and risk of schizophrenia. *Archives of General Psychiatry.* 2003;60:673-678.

4. Sørensen HJ, Mortensen EL, Reinisch JM, Mednick SA. Breastfeeding and risk of schizophrenia in the Copenhagen Perinatal Cohort. *Acta Psychiatr Scand.* 2005;112:26-29.

5. Bustillo J, Lauriello J, Horan W, Keith S. The psychosocial treatment of schizophrenia: an update. *Am J Psychiatry.* 2001;158:163-175.

6. Eckman TA, Wirshing WC, Marder SR, et al. Technique for training schizophrenic patients in illness self-management: a controlled trial. *Am J Psychiatry.* 1992;149:1549-1555.

7. Marder SR, Wirshing WC, Mintz J, et al. Two-year outcome of social skills training and group psychotherapy for outpatients with schizophrenia. *Am J Psychiatry.* 1996;153:1585-1592.

8. Peet M. Diet, diabetes and schizophrenia: review and hypothesis. *Br J Psychiatry.* 2004;184(suppl 47):S102-S105.

9. Faulkner G, Soundy AA, Lloyd K. Schizophrenia and weight management: a systematic review of interventions to control weight. *Acta Psychiatr Scand.* 2003;108:324-332.

10. Mahadik SP, Evans D, Lal H. Oxidative stress and role of antioxidant and omega-3 essential fatty acid supplementation in schizophrenia. *Prog Neuropsychopharmacol Biol Psychiatry.* 2001;25:463-493.

11. Haupt DW, Newcomer JW. Hyperglycemia and antipsychotic medications. *J Clin Psychiatry.* 2001;62(suppl 27):15-26, discussion 40-41.

12. O'Keefe CD, Noordsy DL, Liss TB, Weiss H. Reversal of antipsychotic-associated weight gain. *J Clin Psychiatry.* 2003;64:907-912.

13. Chaldakov GN, Fiore M, Stankulov IS, et al. NGF, BDNF, leptin, and mast cells in human coronary atherosclerosis and metabolic syndrome. *Arch Physiol Biochem.* 2001;109:357-360.

14. Cohn T, Prud'homme D, Streiner D, Kameh H, Remington G. Characterizing coronary heart disease risk in chronic schizophrenia: high prevalence of the metabolic syndrome. *Can J Psychiatry.* 2004;49:753-760.

15. Brown AS, Schaefer CA, Quesenberry CP Jr, Liu L, Babulas VP, Susser ES. Maternal exposure to toxoplasmosis and risk of schizophrenia in adult offspring. *Am J Psychiatry.* 2005;162:767-773.

16. Torrey EF, Yolken RH. Toxoplasma gondii and Schizophrenia. *Emerg Infect Dis.* 2003;9:1375-1380.

17. Peet M. Nutrition and schizophrenia: beyond omega-3 fatty acids. *Prostaglandins Leukot Essent Fatty Acids.* 2004;70:417-422.

18. Richardson MA, Bevans ML, Read LL, et al. Efficacy of the branched-chain amino acids in the treatment of tardive dyskinesia in men. *Am J Psychiatry.* 2003;160:1117-1124.

19. Richardson MA, Small AM, Read LL, Chao HM, Clelland JD. Branched chain amino acid treatment of tardive dyskinesia in children and adolescents. *J Clin Psychiatry.* 2004;65:92-96.

20. Richardson MA, Bevans ML, Weber JB, et al. Branched chain amino acids decrease tardive dyskinesia symptoms. *Psychopharmacology* (Berl). 1999;143:358-364.

21. Pham DQ, Plakogiannis R. Vitamin E supplementation in Alzheimer's disease, Parkinson's disease, tardive dyskinesia, and cataract: Part 2. *Ann Pharmacother.* 2005;39:2065-2072.

22. Lerner V, Miodownik C, Kaptsan A, et al. Vitamin B(6) in the treatment of tardive dyskinesia: a double-blind, placebo-controlled, crossover study. *Am J Psychiatry.* 2001;158:1511-1514.

91. Mood Disorders

Mood and anxiety symptoms occur normally in the course of any eventful life and likely have important evolutionary functions. However, they become pathologic when they interfere with daily functioning, maintenance of relationships, work or school performance, and other important activities of daily living.

Mood and anxiety disorders are distinct conditions, but their biological underpinnings and clinical presentations frequently overlap. Because the nutritional considerations related to these disorders are similar, the conditions are described in a single chapter.

Depression is a common disorder marked by sadness and loss of interest or pleasure. Associated symptoms may include poor concentration, excessive feelings of guilt, sleep disturbance, fatigue or loss of energy, appetite disturbance, sexual dysfunction, delusions, psychomotor changes (eg, slowed thoughts and movements, slumped posture), and/or recurrent thoughts of death. The pathophysiology of depression is believed to involve a combination of abnormal neurotransmitter (eg, serotonin, norepinephrine, and dopamine) activity, hormonal (eg, cortisol, thyroid) abnormalities, genetic traits, and environmental and psychological factors.

Bipolar disorders include 1 or more manic episodes (when the mood is abnormally elevated, expansive, or irritable) or mixed episodes (in which the criteria are met for both a manic episode and a depressive episode nearly every day). Associated symptoms may include grandiosity, decreased need for sleep, pressured speech, racing thoughts, distractibility, and risky behavior such as excessive spending and sexual indiscretions.[1]

Anxiety is marked by physiological arousal (motor tension, autonomic hyperactivity) and psychological arousal (excessive worry, increased vigilance). Norepinephrine, serotonin, and gamma-aminobutyric acid (GABA) may be involved in its pathophysiology, and both genetic predispositions and environmental factors are believed to play a role.

Risk Factors

Significant mood symptoms are present in up to 40% of primary care patients in the United States. Major depression occurs in about 15% of people (lifetime risk), and medical inpatients have increased prevalence.

The following factors are associated with increased risk:

Gender. There is approximately a two-fold greater incidence of depression in women than in men, independent of country or culture. Lifetime prevalence of major depressive disorder is 10% to 25% for women and 5% to 12% for men.[1] In contrast, Bipolar I Disorder has an equal prevalence in men and women, and manic episodes are more common in men. Women also have a higher incidence of the rapid cycling subtype (>4 episodes/year) of bipolar disorder than men.

Family history. It is important to consider both diagnosed and undiagnosed indicators of mood disorder, especially in first-degree relatives.

Inadequate social supports. Examples include living alone or having few friends.

Stressful life events. These include life transitions such as retirement and events of painful loss, such as the death of a spouse.

Coexisting medical illness. Some studies show that up to 30% of patients who present to physicians with a physical symptom had either a depressive or anxiety disorder.[2] Common coexisting illnesses associated with depression include coronary disease, cancer, neurologic disease, and endocrine disease (eg, hypothyroidism). Common coexisting illnesses associated with anxiety include angina, myocardial infarction, arrhythmias, congestive heart failure, mitral valve prolapse, asthma, chronic obstructive pulmonary disease (COPD), hyperthyroidism, hypoglycemia, Cushing syndrome, Parkinson disease, and cancer. Depression and anxiety often occur concurrently.

Medications. Drugs associated with exacerbation of anxiety include bronchodilators and theophylline, antidepressants (anxiety symptoms associated with starting an antidepressant usually abate after several weeks of use), various antihypertensive medications (although beta-blockers are sometimes used to decrease the physical symptoms of anxiety), steroids, psychostimulants (eg, methylphenidate), over-the-counter medications that contain caffeine, and pseudoephedrine.

Drug intoxication or withdrawal. Drugs that may contribute to symptoms of anxiety include caffeine, alcohol, cannabis, cocaine, methamphetamine, and nicotine. Some medications that are used to treat anxiety, notably benzodiazepines, can cause rebound anxiety, in which individuals feel more anxious after the medication wears off than they did before taking it. This often leads to a cycle of escalating use.

Suicide attempts are common in individuals with depression or bipolar disorders, as well as in those with other psychiatric illnesses. One-quarter to one-half of bipolar patients attempt suicide, and approximately 15% will die as a result.[3] Additional risk factors for suicide include the following:

- A history of suicide attempts.
- Suicidal ideation.
- Family history of suicide or attempts.
- Access to weapons.
- Substance abuse.

- Underlying medical illness.
- Male gender.
- Increasing age.
- Presence of panic attacks.

Diagnosis

A detailed history, including psychiatric history, medication use, substance abuse, and social history, should be taken for all patients. Physical examination should include a thorough neurologic examination and should rule out disorders that are associated with depression or anxiety, especially cardiac and endocrine disease.

Particular attention should be paid to medication history as many medications may contribute to mood and anxiety disorders. Isotretinoin, for example, is under investigation for its contribution to depression and suicidal ideation, and some older antihypertensive medications cause depression that is indistinguishable from primary depression.

All patients should be asked about suicidal ideation. In patients deemed at risk, immediate psychiatric attention (which may include hospitalization) is necessary.

Physiologic or laboratory testing is generally not necessary except to evaluate for medical disorders (eg, electrocardiogram, thyroid function tests, complete blood count, blood chemistries). A urine toxicology screen may be appropriate in some patients to evaluate for drug use.

Diagnosis of Major Depressive Disorder

Major Depressive Disorder is characterized by 1 or more major depressive episodes. According to the *Diagnostic and Statistical Manual of Mental Disorders*, 4th edition, diagnosis of a major depressive episode includes at least 5 of the following symptoms occurring on most days within the same 2-week period, and representing a change from previous functioning, causing significant distress or impairment, and not accounted for by effects of a medication, substance abuse, or bereavement:[1]

- Depressed mood most of the day, nearly every day.
- Markedly diminished interest in or pleasure from most activities.
- Significant weight loss or gain or change in appetite.
- Altered sleep patterns (insomnia or hypersomnia).

- Psychomotor agitation or retardation observable to others.

- Fatigue or loss of energy.

- Feelings of worthlessness or excessive guilt.

- Diminished ability to think or concentrate; indecisiveness.

- Recurrent thoughts of death or suicidal ideation, plan, or attempt.

Diagnosis of Bipolar Disorder (DSM IV)

The essential feature for the diagnosis of bipolar disorder is 1 or more manic or mixed (meeting criteria for both manic and depressive episodes) episodes. The criteria for a manic episode are summarized here:

- A distinct period of abnormally and persistently elevated, expansive, or irritable mood, lasting at least 1 week (or any duration if hospitalization is necessary).

- During the period of mood disturbance, 3 (or more) of the following symptoms are present to a significant degree (4 are required when the mood is only irritable):

    - Inflated self-esteem or grandiosity.

    * Decreased need for sleep.

    - More talkative than usual or pressured speech.

    - Flight of ideas or racing thoughts.

    - Distractibility.

    - Increase in goal-directed activity or psychomotor agitation.

    - Excessive involvement in pleasurable activities that have a high. potential for painful consequences, such as buying sprees or sexual indiscretions.

- The mood disturbance is severe enough to cause marked impairment in social or occupational functioning or to necessitate hospitalization, or there are psychotic features.

- The symptoms are not directly due to substance use or a general medical illness.

Bipolar II Disorder is characterized by a clinical course that includes 1 or more major depressive episodes and 1 or more hypomanic episodes. Hypomanic episodes are similar to manic episodes but are not severe enough to cause marked impairment in social or occupational functioning or to necessitate hospitalization. There are no psychotic features.

Diagnosis of Generalized Anxiety Disorder

Generalized Anxiety Disorder is characterized by excessive anxiety and worry occurring more days than not for at least 6 months. The patient finds it difficult to control the worry and has at least 3 of the following symptoms:

- Restlessness.

- Fatigue.

- Difficulty concentrating or mind going blank.

- Irritability.

- Muscle tension.

- Sleep disturbance.

The anxiety or physical symptoms cause clinically significant distress or impairment in social, occupational, or other areas of function, and the disturbance is not due to a medical condition or substance abuse.[1]

Treatment

Treatment usually includes pharmacologic and nonpharmacologic therapies, along with treatment of any coexisting medical and psychiatric conditions.

For **depressive disorders**, selective serotonin reuptake inhibitors, serotonin-norepinephrine reuptake inhibitors, bupropion, and tricyclic antidepressants are most commonly used. Up to 6 to 8 weeks of treatment are usually necessary before the full benefit of medications is apparent. Successful relief of symptoms occurs in about half of patients.

For **anxiety disorders**, antidepressants, benzodiazepines, and buspirone are commonly used.

For **bipolar disorders,** valproate, lithium, and carbamazepine are used as preventives, and antipsychotics may be used during exacerbations with psychotic features. Monitoring of drug levels and of other common blood tests is required.

In some cases of mood or anxiety disorders, psychotherapy may be effective, used alone or in combination with medications, and it improves the outcome of medication treatments. Interpersonal psychotherapy and cognitive-behavioral therapy can be as effective as medications in the acute treatment of depressed outpatients, and the latter has an enduring effect that reduces the risk for relapse. Treatment with a combination of medication and psychotherapy may enhance the probability of response over either treatment alone, especially in persons with chronic depression.[4] Cognitive-behavioral therapy is also a well-established effective treatment for generalized anxiety disorder.[5]

Studies suggest that exercise may be as efficacious as medications for the treatment of depression over both the short term and the long term. The apparent antidepressant effect of exercise has been attributed to the correction of dysregulation of the central monoamines, reduction of stress-induced hypothalamic-pituitary axis hyperactivity, distraction from negative emotions, and improvement in self-esteem and self-efficacy.[6]

Avoidance of caffeine, alcohol, and recreational drugs can help prevent exacerbations of mood disorders and anxiety. In addition, self-hypnosis, meditation, exercise, and relaxation techniques are helpful in treating anxiety disorders.[7]

Due to the evidence that major depression and anxiety disorders are associated with nicotine dependence,[8] referral to a smoking cessation program may be indicated. Treatment with certain antidepressants (eg, bupropion) may facilitate smoking cessation.[9]

Nutritional Considerations

Diet may influence mood in several ways. Caffeine and alcohol have pronounced nervous system effects. Weight loss in obese persons is associated with improvement in mood.[10] In addition, certain amino acids and other nutrients act as cofactors in the production of neurotransmitters. Dietary carbohydrate and protein influence the rate at which neurotransmitter precursors enter the central nervous system from the blood. Specifically, carbohydrate-containing meals that raise blood glucose and insulin secretion result in a drop in plasma amino acids. In turn, this means that fewer amino acids compete with tryptophan for transport through the blood-brain barrier. Tryptophan is a serotonin precursor.[11]

Diabetes is associated with depression. Presumably, this is primarily because diabetes and its complications are likely contributors to depressive symptoms. However, poor metabolic control may exacerbate depression and diminish the response to antidepressants, and clinical studies have shown that, as metabolic control improves, so does depression.[12] In addition, persons who are depressed are at increased risk for diabetes. A 2006 meta-analysis of 9 longitudinal studies found that individuals with major depressive disorder have a 37% increased risk of developing diabetes, compared with other persons.[13]

The following nutrients are under investigation for their role in mood disorders:

Folate and Other B Vitamins

Low blood concentrations of folate and vitamin B_{12} correlate with depression in the general population.[14] The association between folate and depression may be mediated in part by elevated homocysteine levels, which are frequently found in depressed persons.[14,15] High plasma homocysteine has been associated with reduced levels of cerebrospinal fluid amine metabolites 5-hydroxyindole acetic acid (5-HIAA), homovanillic acid (HVA), and 3-methyl, 4-hydroxy phenylglycol.[16]

A common variant of the enzyme 5, 10-methylenetetrahydrofolate reductase (MTHFR) is significantly more common in individuals with elevated homocysteine or depression.[17]

Folic acid is important in the production of tetrahydrobiopterin (BH4), a cofactor in the conversion of phenylalanine to tyrosine and in the hydroxylation of tyrosine and tryptophan, rate-limiting steps in the synthesis of dopamine, norepinephrine, and serotonin. BH4 is also involved in regulating the presynaptic release of neurotransmitters from nerve terminals.[16] Low blood-folate concentrations are associated with significantly greater risk for relapse in persons on antidepressant therapy,[18] and folate status predicts response to antidepressant treatment in the elderly.[19] Two clinical trials adding methyltetrahydrofolate (one at 500 μg/d, the other at 15 mg/d) to an antidepressant regimen further reduced depressive symptoms, as indicated by the Hamilton Depression Rating Scale.[20]

Observations that depression is associated with low levels of both vitamin B_{12}[21] and pyridoxal phosphate[22] indicate that increasing dietary (and perhaps supplemental) intakes of these vitamins may be important in preventing or treating depression. Limited evidence suggests that geriatric patients with depression and cognitive dysfunction respond better to antidepressant medication when given supplemental vitamins B_1, B_2, and B_6, compared with antidepressant treatment alone.[23]

These observations may help explain why consuming a traditional Chinese diet, which is high in folate, is associated with lower rates of major depression.[14]

Omega-3 Fatty Acids

Depression is associated with lower levels of long-chain omega-3 fatty acids (ie, eicosapentanoic and docosahexanoic acids) in red blood cell membranes.[24] Some, but not all, studies have found that in countries where intake of these fatty acids is higher, depression is less prevalent.[25] Among individuals in the Arctic, the abandonment of traditional diets high in omega-3 fatty acids has been associated with increasing rates of depression and anxiety,[26] although other biological and social factors may confound this interpretation.

Blood levels of polyunsaturated fatty acids have predicted cerebrospinal fluid levels of both 5-HIAA and HVA.[27] Limited trials have indicated improvements in depression rating scales when fish oils were administered with standard antidepressants.[25,28,29] This result has not been confirmed in large trials, and it is not known whether botanical sources of omega-3s, such as flax oil, might have the same effect.

Botanical Treatments

St. John's Wort is effective in 50% to 70% of outpatients with mild depression.[30] For major depression, results have been mixed, with some reviews indicating minimal benefits;[31] more recent studies suggest an efficacy similar to that of antidepressant medications.[32,33]

Passion flower (*Passiflora incarnata*), chamomile (*Matricaria recutita*), and lemon balm *(Melissa officinalis)* contain flavonoids that bind to benzodiazepine receptors, but evidence of their anxiolytic effects is modest.[7,30]

Kava is an herbal treatment with an apparent anxiolytic effect. Some kava users have developed liver toxicity, which may have been attributable to excessive doses or to contamination. However, the safety of the compound is not yet established.[34]

It is important to ask patients if they are using any herb treatment. St. John's Wort, for example, taken at high doses in addition to an SSRI may cause serotonin syndrome, which is potentially fatal.[35]

The following treatments may be helpful but require more study:

S-adenosylmethionine (SAMe)

Elevated concentrations of homocysteine often found in depressed persons (see above) may increase central nervous system (CNS) levels of S-adenosylhomocysteine, which has been shown to inhibit monoamine neurotransmitter metabolism. As the sole methyl donor in the

CNS, SAMe is involved in the creation of monoamine neurotransmitters, membrane phospholipids, and proteins and nucleoproteins. In 19 controlled trials, SAMe has shown effects similar to those of medication in treating depression.[36] SAMe may have the advantages of a faster onset of action and fewer side effects, compared with selective serotonin reuptake inhibitors.[37]

Inositol

Inositol, a substance found in many foods (eg, whole-grain cereals and legumes) is a key intermediate of the phosphatidyl-inositol (PI) cycle, a second-messenger system used by several noradrenergic, serotonergic, and cholinergic receptors. Limited studies have suggested that at doses of 12 to 18 grams per day, inositol reduces anxiety symptoms as effectively as selective serotonin reuptake inhibitors, with a low incidence of side effects.[38,39]

Orders

See Basic Diet Orders chapter.

What to Tell the Family

It is important for the family to understand that mood disorder symptoms are not simply volitional or temporary states of mind that can be easily changed. Depression in particular may arise from other diseases, and the presence of both disorders may indicate a need for more aggressive monitoring. Although they are medical disorders, depression, anxiety and bipolar illnesses respond well in many cases to both medication and psychotherapy, which will often include a role for the family. Combining pharmacologic and psychotherapeutic treatments may be particularly effective. Family members can also assist the patient in informing the physician about the use of any supplements, such as St. John's Wort, because of the risk of serotonin syndrome when some are used in combination with common medications.

References

1. American Psychiatric Association. *Diagnostic and Statistical Manual of Mental Disorders*. 4th ed. Arlington, Va: American Psychiatric Association; 1994.

2. Kroenke K, Jackson JL, Chamberlin J. Depressive and anxiety disorders in patients presenting with physical complaints: clinical predictors and outcome. *Am J Med.* 1997;103:339-347.

3. Jamison KR. Suicide and bipolar disorder. *J Clin Psychiatry.* 2000;61(suppl 9):47-51.

4. Hollon SD, Jarrett RB, Nierenberg AA, Thase ME, Trivedi M, Rush AJ. Psychotherapy and medication in the treatment of adult and geriatric depression: which monotherapy or combined treatment? *J Clin Psychiatry.* 2005;66:455-468.

5. Butler AC, Chapman JE, Forman EM, Beck AT. The empirical status of cognitive-behavioral therapy: A review of meta-analyses. *Clin Psychol Rev.* 2006;26:17-31.

6. Barbour KA, Blumenthal JA. Exercise training and depression in older adults. *Neurobiol Aging.* 2005;26(suppl 1):119-123.

7. Jorm AF, Christensen H, Griffiths KM, Parslow RA, Rodgers B, Blewitt KA. Effectiveness of complementary and self-help treatments for anxiety disorders. *Med J Aust.* 2004;181(suppl 7):S29-S46.

8. Bergen AW, Caporaso N. Cigarette smoking. *J Natl Cancer Inst.* 1999;91:1365-1375.

9. Tonstad S, Johnston JA. Does bupropion have advantages over other medical therapies in the cessation of smoking? *Expert Opin Pharmacother.* 2004;5:727-734.

10. Evans DL, Charney DS, Lewis L, et al. Mood disorders in the medically ill: scientific review and recommendations. *Biol Psychiatry.* 2005;58:175-189.

11. Huffman DM, Altena TS, Mawhinney TP, Thomas TR. Effect of n-3 fatty acids on free tryptophan and exercise fatigue. *Eur J Appl Physiol.* 2004;92:584-591.

12. Lustman PJ, Clouse RE. Depression in diabetic patients: the relationship between mood and glycemic control. *J Diabetes Complications.* 2005;19:113-122.

13. Knol MJ, Twisk JWR, Beekman ATF, Heine RJ, Snoek FJ, Pouwer F. Depression as a risk factor for the onset of type 2 diabetes mellitus. A meta-analysis. *Diabetologia.* 2006;49:837-845.

14. Coppen A, Bolander-Gouaille C. Treatment of depression: time to consider folic acid and vitamin B_{12}. *J Psychopharmacol.* 2005;19:59-65.

15. Bjelland I, Tell GS, Vollset SE, Refsum H, Ueland PM. Folate, vitamin B_{12}, homocysteine, and the MTHFR 677C->T polymorphism in anxiety and depression: the Hordaland Homocysteine Study. *Arch Gen Psychiatry.* 2003;60:618-626.

16. Paul RT, McDonnell AP, Kelly CB. Folic acid: neurochemistry, metabolism and relationship to depression. *Hum Psychopharmacol.* 2004;19:477-488.

17. Kelly CB, McDonnell AP, Johnston TG, et al. The MTHFR C677T polymorphism is associated with depressive episodes in patients from Northern Ireland. *J Psychopharmacol.* 2004;18:567-571.

18. Papakostas GI, Petersen T, Mischoulon D, et al. Serum folate, vitamin B_{12}, and homocysteine in major depressive disorder, Part 2: predictors of relapse during the continuation phase of pharmacotherapy. *J Clin Psychiatry.* 2004;65:1096-1098.

19. D'Anci KE, Rosenberg IH. Folate and brain function in the elderly. *Curr Opin Clin Nutr Metab Care.* 2004;7:659-664.

20. Taylor MJ, Carney S, Geddes J, Goodwin G. Folate for depressive disorders. *Cochrane Database Syst Rev.* 2003;(2):CD003390.

21. Wolters M, Strohle A, Hahn A. Cobalamin: a critical vitamin in the elderly. *Prev Med.* 2004;39:1256-1266.

22. Hvas AM, Juul S, Lauritzen L, Nexo E, Ellegaard J. Vitamin B_6 level is associated with symptoms of depression. *Psychother Psychosom.* 2004;73:340-343.

23. Bell IR, Edman JS, Morrow FD, et al. Brief communication. Vitamin B_1, B_2, and B_6 augmentation of tricyclic antidepressant treatment in geriatric depression with cognitive dysfunction. *J Am Coll Nutr.* 1992;11:159-163.

24. Maes M, Christophe A, Delanghe J, Altamura C, Neels H, Meltzer HY. Lowered omega3 polyunsaturated fatty acids in serum phospholipids and cholesteryl esters of depressed patients. *Psychiatry Res*. 1999;85:275-291.

25. Nemets B, Stahl Z, Belmaker RH. Addition of omega-3 fatty acid to maintenance medication treatment for recurrent unipolar depressive disorder. *Am J Psychiatry*. 2002;159:477-479.

26. McGrath-Hanna NK, Greene DM, Tavernier RJ, Bult-Ito A. Diet and mental health in the Arctic: is diet an important risk factor for mental health in circumpolar peoples?— a review. *Int J Circumpolar Health*. 2003;62:228-241.

27. Hibbeln JR, Linnoila M, Umhau JC, Rawlings R, George DT, Salem N Jr. Essential fatty acids predict metabolites of serotonin and dopamine in cerebrospinal fluid among healthy control subjects, and early- and late-onset alcoholics. *Biol Psychiatry*. 1998;44:235-242.

28. Su KP, Huang SY, Chiu CC, Shen WW. Omega-3 fatty acids in major depressive disorder. A preliminary double-blind, placebo-controlled trial. *Eur Neuropsychopharmacol*. 2003;13:267-271.

29. Peet M, Horrobin DF. Dose-ranging study of the effects of ethyl-eicosapentaenoate in patients with ongoing depression despite apparently adequate treatment with standard drugs. *Arch Gen Psychiatry*. 2002;59:913-919.

30. Brown RP, Gerbarg PL. Herbs and nutrients in the treatment of depression, anxiety, insomnia, migraine, and obesity. *J Psychiatr Pract*. 2001;7:75-91.

31. Linde K, Mulrow CD, Berner M, Egger M. St John's wort for depression. *Cochrane Database Syst Rev*. 2005;(2):CD000448.

32. Kasper S, Anghelescu IG, Szegedi A, Dienel A, Kieser M. Superior efficacy of St John's wort extract WS 5570 compared to placebo in patients with major depression: a randomized, double-blind, placebo-controlled, multi-center trial [ISRCTN77277298]. *BMC Med*. 2006;4:14.

33. Anghelescu IG, Kohnen R, Szegedi A, Klement S, Kieser M. Comparison of Hypericum extract WS 5570 and paroxetine in ongoing treatment after recovery from an episode of moderate to severe depression: results from a randomized multicenter study. *Pharmacopsychiatry*. 2006;39:213-219.

34. Brown AC, Onopa J, Holck P, et al. Traditional kava beverage consumption and liver function tests in a predominantly Tongan population in Hawaii. *Clin Toxicol* (Phila). 2007;45:549-556.

35. Zhou S, Chan E, Pan SQ, Huang M, Lee EJ. Pharmacokinetic interactions of drugs with St John's wort. *J Psychopharmacol*. 2004;18:262-276.

36. Fetrow CW, Avila JR. Efficacy of the dietary supplement S-adenosyl-L-methionine. *Ann Pharmacother*. 2001;35:1414-1425.

37. Shippy RA, Mendez D, Jones K, Cergnul I, Karpiak SE. S-adenosylmethionine (SAM-e) for the treatment of depression in people living with HIV/AIDS. *BMC Psychiatry*. 2004;4:38.

38. Palatnik A, Frolov K, Fux M, Benjamin J. Double-blind, controlled, crossover trial of inositol versus fluvoxamine for the treatment of panic disorder. *J Clin Psychopharmacol*. 2001;21:335-339.

39. Benjamin J, Levine J, Fux M, Aviv A, Levy D, Belmaker RH. Double-blind, placebo-controlled, crossover trial of inositol treatment for panic disorder. *Am J Psychiatry*. 1995;152:1084-1086.

92. Eating Disorders

Up to 3% of American women meet diagnostic criteria for an eating disorder, and up to 20% of college-aged women engage in some form of binging and purging behavior.[1] Anorexia nervosa and bulimia nervosa are the most well known eating disorders.

Anorexia nervosa is characterized by a refusal to maintain normal body weight. Patients have a distorted body image, a body weight less than 15% below the expected value, amenorrhea, and abnormal eating behaviors that may include binge eating, purging, and restricted food intake. About half of patients develop concurrent bulimic symptoms.

Bulimia nervosa is characterized by recurrent episodes of binge eating and inappropriate compensatory behaviors intended to prevent weight gain or cause weight loss, such as self-induced vomiting and laxative abuse.

The etiology of eating disorders is likely multifactorial, with genetic, psychological, environmental, and social factors implicated. Some clinicians have speculated that a cultural preoccupation with thinness and dieting in the United States and other Western countries has set the stage for eating disorders. Equally plausible is the possibility that the increasing prevalence of overweight and obesity in the United States and other countries has triggered an unhealthy response to weight problems. Up to 40% of adolescent girls in the United States believe they are overweight, and approximately 60% are attempting to lose weight. A substantial number of these girls have reported that they tried vomiting or laxatives to control their weight.[2]

Significant morbidity and mortality are associated with severe or long-standing eating disorders, including osteoporosis, decreased gray matter, electrolyte and metabolic abnormalities, heart disorders, gastrointestinal dysfunction, dental erosion, and infertility. Osteoporosis, decreased gray matter, and dental erosion are often not reversible, even with appropriate treatment and weight recovery. Comorbid psychiatric disorders, including depression, anxiety, and obsessive-compulsive disorder, are present in more than half of patients.

Risk Factors

About 90% of cases of eating disorders occur in women, with onset typically occurring in late adolescence and early adulthood. Additional risk factors include:

History of obesity and/or dieting. A history of obesity is linked to increased risk for eating disorders. Adolescents who reported dieting during mid-adolescence were significantly more likely to develop eating disorders.[3]

Participation in activities that emphasize leanness. Examples include ballet, gymnastics, running, and wrestling.

Family history. Women who have a first-degree relative with an eating disorder are up to 10 times more likely to develop an eating disorder themselves.[4] Eating disorders are also associated with a family history of depression.

Psychiatric history. Histories that include depression, substance abuse, sexual abuse, weight dissatisfaction, and low self-esteem are linked to higher risk for eating disorders.

Early puberty. Early sexual development may lead to increased self-consciousness regarding body image and is associated with subsequent dieting behaviors.

Diagnosis

The American Psychiatric Association's diagnostic criteria for anorexia nervosa are summarized as follows:[1]

- Refusal to maintain body weight at or above a minimally normal weight for age and height (eg, weight loss leading to maintenance of body weight less than 85% of that expected; or failure to make expected weight gain during period of growth, leading to body weight less than 85% of expected).

- Intense fear of gaining weight or becoming fat, despite being significantly underweight.

- Disturbance in the way in which one's body weight or shape is experienced, undue influence of body weight or shape on self-evaluation, or denial of the seriousness of the current low body weight.

- In postmenarcheal females, amenorrhea; ie, the absence of at least 3 consecutive menstrual cycles.

- The condition is subclassified as either the *restricting type* or the *binge-eating/purging type*, depending on whether the individual regularly engages in binge-eating or purging behavior (eg, self-induced vomiting or the misuse of laxatives, diuretics, or enemas).

The diagnostic criteria for bulimia nervosa are summarized below:

- Recurrent episodes of binge eating during discrete periods of time (eg, within any 2-hour period), characterized by eating an amount of food that is definitely larger than most people would eat during a similar period of time, and a sense of lack of control over eating during the episode.

- Recurrent inappropriate compensatory behavior to prevent weight gain, such as self-induced vomiting; misuse of laxatives, diuretics, enemas, or other medications; fasting; or excessive exercise.

- Episodes of binge eating and inappropriate compensatory behaviors occurring, on average, at least twice a week for 3 months.

- Self-evaluation is unduly influenced by body shape and weight.

- The disturbance does not occur exclusively during episodes of anorexia nervosa.

The disorder is subclassified by type. The *purging type* is characterized by self-induced vomiting or misuse of laxatives, diuretics, or enemas. The *nonpurging type* is characterized by other compensatory mechanisms, such as fasting or excessive exercise.

Several screening questionnaires are available for primary care clinicians. For example, in the questionnaire below, developed at St. George's Hospital Medical School in London in 1999, positive responses to 2 or more questions indicated a diagnosis of anorexia or bulimia nervosa, with a sensitivity and specificity of 100% and 87.5%, respectively.[5]

1. Do you make yourself sick because you feel uncomfortably full?

2. Do you worry you have lost control over how much you eat?

3. Have you recently lost more than 14 pounds in a 3-month period?

4. Do you believe yourself to be fat when others say you are too thin?

5. Would you say that food dominates your life?

Initial laboratory studies should include a complete blood count, electrolytes, calcium, magnesium, phosphorous, blood urea nitrogen, creatinine, urinalysis, and thyroid function tests. A baseline electrocardiogram and pregnancy testing are indicated in all females with amenorrhea. Bone-density testing and MRI of the brain may be indicated if osteoporosis or impaired cognition is suspected.

Treatment

Medical comorbidities, including electrolyte disturbances and dehydration, should be treated and, when possible, prevented.

Hospitalization is indicated for severe malnutrition (body weight less than 75% of ideal), suicidal ideation, electrolyte disturbances, dehydration, abnormal vital signs (eg, bradycardia, hypothermia), cardiac arrhythmias, and failure of outpatient treatment.

Vitamin and mineral supplementation may be necessary. An inpatient or outpatient structured eating program may help restore healthy eating habits.

Psychotherapy is a mainstay of treatment for certain eating disorders. Because drug therapy is, for the most part, ineffective for anorexia nervosa,[6] psychotherapy is often the treatment of choice. However, not all forms of therapy have undergone rigorous testing. Family-based therapy appears to be more effective in anorexic adolescents (but not adults) than other therapeutic modalities. In adults, psychotherapy has been found to reduce anorexic behaviors in up to 60% of patients. However, more stringent assessment of the effects of cognitive-behavioral therapy indicated that only 17% of patients treated with this modality could be considered fully recovered.[7]

In persons with binge-eating disorder, a disorder characterized by excessive bingeing without compensatory behavior, cognitive-behavioral therapy and interpersonal therapy reduced binge eating by 48% to 98%[8] and produced abstinence rates of about 60%.[6] Medications such as antidepressants and anticonvulsants may also play a role.

Most studies show cognitive-behavioral therapy to be more effective than drug therapy for persons with bulimia nervosa.[9] Fluoxetine was approved for treatment of bulimia by the FDA and is significantly efficacious in about 60% of cases. Combining medication with psychotherapy improves the effectiveness of both treatments.[6] Also, self-help manuals appear to be as effective as psychotherapy in reducing binge episodes for some patients.[10]

Group support in a structured setting is a useful intervention. Groups based on principles of cognitive-behavioral or dialectic behavioral therapy have been shown to be effective. Twelve-step programs such as Overeaters Anonymous are often effective as well.

Nutritional Considerations

Nutrition therapy is indicated for patients with eating disorders, including anorexia nervosa, bulimia nervosa, and binge-eating disorder.[11] The degree to which nutrition professionals should be involved depends on the seriousness of the disorder. For instance, individuals who meet some but not all diagnostic criteria for anorexia or bulimia[12] may not face the same mortality risk as an individual with a more clearly defined and serious eating disorder. Similarly, individuals with the "restricting" subtype of anorexia who are significantly below ideal body weight and have disordered electrolyte concentrations are at greater risk of life-threatening arrhythmias[13] compared with anorexic individuals who present with the bingeing/purging subtype.

Refeeding

Particularly in persons who are significantly underweight, electrolytes should be carefully monitored and refeeding introduced gradually and progressively. Hypokalemia has been reported in 14% of patients with bulimia nervosa, and hyponatremia may be brought on by the use of diuretics, vomiting, and/or excessive water intake. Patients often ingest excessive water to curb hunger or provide the false impression of weight stability during weight checks at medical appointments. If patients are aggressively fed and rehydrated, hypophosphatemia-induced refeeding syndrome may occur, potentially involving dysrhythmias, respiratory failure, rhabdomyolysis, seizures, coma, heart failure, weakness, hemolysis, hypotension, ileus, metabolic acidosis, and sudden death.[14] High sodium intake increases the risk of fluid overexpansion.[15] Limiting sodium intake to required amounts (500 mg/d) is recommended.

To further assist in preventing refeeding syndrome, supplemental phosphorus should be started early and serum levels maintained above 3.0 mg/dL.[16] Hypomagnesemia occurs in approximately 1 in 6 patients with anorexia nervosa and may persist for weeks after refeeding.[17] Although weight gain is an eventual goal for anorexic patients, calories should be secondary to protein during initial refeeding. Suggested guidelines include providing 1.2 grams of protein per kilogram of ideal body weight/day for the first week and no more than 20 kcal/kilogram/day during the first week to avoid refeeding syndrome.[15] A reasonable weight regain goal is 0.5 to 1.0 pound per week.[13]

In addition to the need for a hypercaloric diet during weight restoration, evidence suggests that individuals with anorexia nervosa require

200 to 400 calories per day more than matched controls in order to maintain weight.[13]

It is essential to avoid power struggles with patients over diet choices or weight gain. Aggregate results of surveys of eating-disordered patients found that they rated support, understanding, and empathic relationships as critically important. Psychological approaches were viewed as the most helpful, while medical interventions focused exclusively on weight were viewed as not helpful.[13]

Patients who follow vegetarian diets should not be pushed to alter that preference. In addition, pressuring patients to make commitments to improve (eg, to enroll in treatment or gain weight) has not been demonstrated as effective and may be counterproductive.

Instruments used to assess patients' readiness to stop restricting foods, purging, or bingeing have been found to be good predictors of clinical outcome in patients with anorexia nervosa.[13]

Weight-Loss Treatments

Weight-loss treatments are effective for patients with binge-eating disorder. Studies of the effects of both dietary and behavioral approaches to weight loss show that weight-loss treatments reduce binge-eating frequency.[10] Although it was once suspected that attempts at weight loss preceded binge episodes, the structured meal plans provided for weight loss may give binge eaters a feeling of greater control over food intake. Spontaneous remission of binge eating has also been reported.[8]

Vitamin/Mineral Deficiency

Vitamin/mineral deficiency is a frequent finding for patients with eating disorders, requiring diagnosis and treatment. More than half of patients with anorexia nervosa failed to meet the recommended dietary allowance (RDA) for vitamin D, calcium, folate, vitamin B_{12}, zinc, magnesium, and copper when assessed by diet history.[18] Deficiencies are also commonly found for several vitamins, including thiamine, B_2, niacin, B_6, folate, C, E, and K.[19-21] There have been case reports of patients with anorexia nervosa who were diagnosed with pellagra due to niacin deficiency[22] and scurvy due to vitamin C deficiency.[23] There are also case studies of patients with bulimia nervosa presenting with folate deficiency[24] and coagulation abnormalities due to vitamin K deficiency.[25]

Replacement of these and other nutrients is an important part of nutrition therapy. Zinc in particular has been found to enhance the rate of recovery in anorexics by increasing weight gain and improving anxiety and depression.[26] Weight gain itself reduces bone turnover in patients with anorexia nervosa.[27] In one study, treating bone disease in anorexic patients with calcium and vitamin D supplements was as effective as etidronate for reversing osteoporosis.[28]

Orders

Nutritional consultation and supplementation as indicated.

Psychiatric consultation for evaluation and to arrange appropriate follow-up.

What to Tell the Family

Eating disorders are typically precipitated and perpetuated by a combination of genetic, developmental, and psychological factors, requiring a multidisciplinary team approach (physician, psychiatrist, psychologist, dietitian) to treatment. Anorexia nervosa is particularly difficult to treat, often necessitating repeated episodes of hospitalization to prevent extreme weight loss. Bulimia nervosa is usually not life threatening and may respond well to cognitive-behavioral therapy, medication, or a combination of the two. Binge-eating disorder often responds well to behavior modification weight-loss strategies alone. Family members can render assistance by providing regular, well-balanced meals and emotional support.

References

1. American Psychiatric Association. Eating disorders. In: *Diagnostic and Statistical Manual of Mental Disorders*. 4th ed. Arlington, Va: American Psychiatric Association; 1994: 539-550.

2. Grunbaum JA, Kann L, Kinchen S, et al. Youth risk behavior surveillance--United States, 2003. *MMWR Surveill Summ*. 2004;53:1-96.

3. Patton GC, Selzer R, Coffey C, Carlin JB, Wolfe R. Onset of adolescent eating disorders: population based cohort study over 3 years. *BMJ*. 1999;318:765-768.

4. Woodside DB. A review of anorexia nervosa and bulimia nervosa. *Curr Probl Pediatr*. 1995;25:67-89.

5. Morgan JF, Reid F, Lacey JH. The SCOFF questionnaire: assessment of a new screening tool for eating disorders. *BMJ*. 1999;319:1467-1468.

6. Williamson DA, Martin CK, Stewart T. Psychological aspects of eating disorders. *Best Pract Res Clin Gastroenterol*. 2004;18:1073-1088.

7. Le Grange D, Lock J. The dearth of psychological treatment studies for anorexia nervosa. *Int J Eat Disord*. 2005;37:79-91.

8. Stunkard AJ, Allison KC. Two forms of disordered eating in obesity: binge eating and night eating. *Int J Obes Relat Metab Disord*. 2003;27:1-12.

9. Ricca V, Mannucci E, Zucchi T, Rotella CM, Faravelli C. Cognitive-behavioural therapy for bulimia nervosa and binge eating disorder. A review. *Psychother Psychosom*. 2000;69:287-295.

10. Carter JC, Olmsted MP, Kaplan AS, McCabe RE, Mills JS, Aime A. Self-help for bulimia nervosa: a randomized controlled trial. *Am J Psychiatry*. 2003;160:973-978.

11. Keel PK, Haedt A, Edler C. Purging disorder: an ominous variant of bulimia nervosa? *Int J Eat Disord*. 2005;38:191-199.

12. Chamay-Weber C, Narring F, Michaud PA. Partial eating disorders among adolescents: A review. *J Adolescent Health*. 2005;37:417-427.

13. Yager J, Devlin KJ, Halmi KA, et al. *Practice Guidelines for the Treatment of Patients with Eating Disorders*. 3rd ed. [American Psychiatric Association online publication] 2006. Available at: http://www.psych.org/psych_pract/treatg/pg/EatingDisorders3ePG_04-28-06.pdf. Accessed July 20, 2006.

14. Judge BS, Eisenga BH. Disorders of fuel metabolism: medical complications associated with starvation, eating disorders, dietary fads, and supplements. *Emerg Med Clin North Am*. 2005;23:789-813.

15. Melchior JC. From malnutrition to refeeding during anorexia nervosa. *Curr Opin Clin Nutr Metab Care*. 1998;1:481-485.

16. Kohn MR, Golden NH, Shenker IR. Cardiac arrest and delirium: presentations of the refeeding syndrome in severely malnourished adolescents with anorexia nervosa. *J Adolesc Health*. 1998;22:239-243.

17. Birmingham CL, Puddicombe D, Hlynsky J. Hypomagnesemia during refeeding in anorexia nervosa. *Eat Weight Disord*. 2004;9:236-237.

18. Hadigan CM, Anderson EJ, Miller KK, et al. Assessment of macronutrient and micronutrient intake in women with anorexia nervosa. *Int J Eat Disord*. 2000;28:284-292.

19. Winston AP, Jamieson CP, Madira W, Gatward NM, Palmer RL. Prevalence of thiamin deficiency in anorexia nervosa. *Int J Eat Disord*. 2000;28:451-454.

20. Moyano D, Sierra C, Brandi N, et al. Antioxidant status in anorexia nervosa. *Int J Eat Disord*. 1999;25:99-103.

21. Rock CL, Vasantharajan S. Vitamin status of eating disorder patients: relationship to clinical indices and effect of treatment. *Int J Eat Disord*. 1995;18:257-262.

22. Prousky JE. Pellagra may be a rare secondary complication of anorexia nervosa: a systematic review of the literature. *Altern Med Rev*. 2003;8:180-185.

23. Christopher K, Tammaro D, Wing EJ. Early scurvy complicating anorexia nervosa. *South Med J*. 2002;95:1065-1066.

24. Eedy DJ, Curran JG, Andrews WJ. A patient with bulimia nervosa and profound folate deficiency. *Postgrad Med J*. 1986;62:853-854.

25. Niiya K, Kitagawa T, Fujishita M, et al. Bulimia nervosa complicated by deficiency of vitamin K-dependent coagulation factors. *JAMA*. 1983;250:792-793.

26. Su JC, Birmingham CL. Zinc supplementation in the treatment of anorexia nervosa. *Eat Weight Disord*. 2002;7:20-22.

27. Heer M, Mika C, Grzella I, Drummer C, Herpetz-Dahlmann B. Changes in bone turnover in patients with anorexia nervosa during eleven weeks of inpatient dietary treatment. *Clinical Chemistry*. 2002;48:754-760.

28. Nakahara T, Nagai N, Tanaka M, et al. The effects of bone therapy on tibial bone loss in young women with anorexia nervosa. *Int J Eat Disord.* 2006;39:20-26.

93. Insomnia

Insomnia is characterized by difficulties in initiating sleep, maintaining sleep, or feeling restored after sleep. It is the most common sleep disorder in the United States, affecting about one-third of adults at some point in their lives. Approximately 10% of those with symptoms experience persistent insomnia.

Patients often report impairments in daytime function in addition to the nocturnal symptoms. They may experience daytime fatigue, inability to concentrate, irritability, anxiety, depression, and forgetfulness, and may have an increased risk of automobile accidents.[1] Further, these patients often have associated psychosomatic symptoms, such as nonspecific aches and pains.

Insomnia has been described as transient (less than 1 week of symptoms), short-term (1-3 weeks), and chronic (longer than 3 weeks).[2] Dozens of possible etiologies may explain each type. Sleep impairment lasting only a few days to a few weeks may be the result of poor or altered sleep environments, such as excessive noise or light and disagreeable room temperature. It may result from lifestyle changes, such as jet lag, change in work shift, acute illness, and stressful life events. Also, taking medications with stimulant properties and withdrawal from drugs or alcohol may contribute to impaired sleep. Insomnia lasting more than a few weeks may be associated with chronic drug or alcohol abuse, medical disorders, or psychiatric disorders, or it may result from primary sleep disorders, such as restless legs syndrome and sleep apnea.

Risk Factors

Insomnia occurs disproportionately in women and in people who are divorced, widowed, or separated. Additional risk factors include:

Age. Prevalence increases with age. Age is the most important risk factor for developing insomnia.

Psychiatric comorbidities. Sleep disturbances are more common in patients with mood disorders, such as major depression, dysthymia, and bipolar affective disorder, as well as in those with anxiety disorders, schizophrenia, and acute stress.

Drugs and alcohol. Abuse may be associated with impaired sleep.

Stimulants. Use of medications and other substances with stimulant properties is a common cause of insomnia. These include caffeine, theophylline, thyroxine, corticosteroids, bronchodilators, antidepressants, and methylphenidate.

Nicotine withdrawal is associated with sleep fragmentation. Insomnia is also a frequent side effect of nicotine patches[3] and of bupropion, an antidepressant often used for smoking cessation.[4]

Diagnosis

History and physical examination, including a sleep history and psychiatric history, should include evaluation of sleep habits, sleep environment, drug and alcohol use, medical and medication history, and family medical history. It is often helpful to interview the patient's bed partner and to ask the patient to keep a sleep log.

Laboratory testing may identify medical disorders (such as endocrinopathies) that can contribute to sleep difficulties.

Sleep testing is used in some patients. Polysomnography can identify sleep-related breathing disorders. Multiple sleep latency testing evaluates for inappropriate daytime sleepiness. Actigraphy measures motion during sleep.

Treatment

Underlying medical, surgical, or psychiatric disorders should be treated as appropriate.

It is helpful to ask the patient to maintain good sleep hygiene, the essentials of which are to exercise regularly but not before bedtime, avoid caffeine, and limit alcohol, particularly near bedtime.[3] Exercise has been shown to improve total sleep duration, sleep onset latency, and global sleep quality.[5] However, timing is important. Physical activity early in the day is generally not associated with improved sleep, and exercise taken shortly before bedtime can delay sleep onset.[3]

Other beneficial practices include sleeping only as much as necessary to feel rested, keeping a regular sleep schedule, avoiding smoking, and adjusting the bedroom environment as needed. Many individuals with insomnia report poorer sleep hygiene practices, including increased use of alcohol, smoking near bedtime, and taking frequent daytime naps.[6] Proper sleep hygiene is an often overlooked high-yield, low-risk means of helping patients with insomnia.

Nonpharmacologic Therapy

Maladaptive behaviors or thought patterns can sustain insomnia symptoms, independent of the initial underlying cause. Cognitive-behavioral sleep therapy addresses these problems and has proven more effective over the long term than pharmacologic therapy.[7] Although additional evidence from controlled trials is needed, cognitive-behavior therapy was also found effective for insomnia related to a spectrum of medical and psychiatric conditions (eg, cancer, chronic pain, human immunodeficiency virus [HIV], depression, posttraumatic stress disorder, alcoholism, bipolar disorder, eating disorders, generalized anxiety, and obsessive compulsive disorder).[8]

Disruptions of circadian rhythm can be treated with phototherapy (bright lights used at bedtime or on awakening) or chronotherapy (a stepwise advance of the bedtime and waking time later and later).

Warm-bath immersion to the mid-thorax, with water temperature at 40° to 41° C, for 30 minutes in the evening was shown to increase slow-wave sleep (deep sleep) in healthy elderly women with insomnia.[9]

Pharmacologic Therapy

Zolpidem, zaleplon, and eszopiclone are often the first drugs prescribed for sleep. Other frequently prescribed drugs are benzodiazepines (eg, temazepam, lorazepam, flurazepam), antihistamines (eg, diphenhydramine), and antidepressants (eg, amitriptyline, trazodone). In most cases, however, these drugs do not improve the quality of sleep.

Benzodiazepines are contraindicated in women who are pregnant and in patients with renal, hepatic, or pulmonary disease. They should be used with caution in patients who consume alcohol.

Ramelteon, a melatonin-receptor agonist, has been approved by the Federal Drug Administration (FDA) for insomnia treatment, but evidence of efficacy is weak. Supplemental use of melatonin and valerian may also be effective for sleep disorders (see Nutritional Considerations below).

Nutritional Considerations

Healthy natural sleep should follow as a consequence of the normal physical and mental fatigue people typically experience during an active life. However, sleep deprivation is increasingly common, and it may be attributed to poor lifestyle choices. Chief among these are excesses of caffeine and alcohol and inadequate physical activity. Steps to be considered are discussed below.

Avoiding alcohol. Small amounts of alcohol (eg, 1 standard drink per evening) may not have negative effects on sleep for most people. However, people soon develop tolerance to its sedative effects, thus making it less useful for inducing sleep.[10] Alcohol may increase the risk of insomnia by several mechanisms. Excess or chronic alcohol intake (ie, alcohol abuse or dependence) can decrease REM phase sleep in a dose-dependent manner.[11] Alcohol consumption in the amount of 0.5 or 1.0 g/kg (3-6 standard drinks) also causes disruption of normal circadian rhythms,[12] probably through inhibiting melatonin secretion by more than 40%.[13] Alcohol may cause rebound excitation through an increase in the number or sensitivity of receptors for glutamate, an excitatory neurotransmitter.[12] As alcohol is metabolized, it produces aldehydes, which can have stimulating effects.[14] Alcohol hangover, an excitatory state despite its reputation as one involving malaise, may be related to acetaldehyde.[12] Alcohol may also increase the level of histamine, a known excitatory neurotransmitter, in the central nervous system (CNS).[15]

Limiting caffeine. Caffeine produces varying effects in individuals. In middle-aged persons drinking up to 7 cups of coffee per day (600 mg) and in subjects to whom caffeine was acutely administered, few or no effects on sleep were noted.[3,16] However, some persons are more sensitive to the effects of caffeine, particularly elderly persons, who often unknowingly consume caffeine in over-the-counter medications.[17] Slower blood clearance and higher blood concentrations of caffeine at midnight have been found in individuals with caffeine-related insomnia than in those not adversely affected by caffeine, indicating that differences in caffeine metabolism may be a cause of sleep disturbance.[18] In persons with suspected or documented caffeine-sensitive sleep insomnia, discontinuing coffee alone may not be effective. This strategy may underestimate total caffeine intake from all sources, which include cola beverages, tea, chocolate, and medications.[19]

Avoiding milk if intolerant. Infants with cow's milk allergy have been found to have frequent arousals during sleep, shorter sleep cycles, and larger amounts of non-rapid eye movement (NREM) sleep with easy awakening. After elimination of cow's milk for several weeks, a significant decrease in the number of arousals occurred, while total sleep time and time spent in NREM2 and NREM3 sleep all increased significantly.[20] Further study by the same researchers using double-blind, crossover methodology also found normalization of sleep in a group of children <5 years of age.[21] Although confirmation from other investigators is indicated before cow's milk elimination can be deemed proven for children with sleep disorders, it is a low-cost, no-risk strategy that can be tried before more invasive evaluation methods.

Carbohydrates. Tryptophan and 5-hydroxytryptophan are precursors of melatonin through the serotonin pathway and have some efficacy in the treatment of insomnia. However, neither can be recommended, due to previous findings of contamination with a compound that has caused eosinophilia-myalgia syndrome (EMS).[22] The passage of tryptophan across the blood-brain barrier depends on the extent to which it must compete with other amino acids. In this context, carbohydrate-rich foods may prove helpful. Over the short run, they stimulate the release of insulin, which reduces blood concentrations of competing amino acids, fostering tryptophan's passage across the blood-brain barrier.[23]

Avoiding over-the-counter weight-loss products. Products that contain ephedra alkaloids (eg, ma huang) in combination with caffeine have been increasingly used for weight loss, but they have been found to cause insomnia when compared with a placebo.[24]

Rectifying poor iron status. Insomnia is a frequent problem in patients with restless legs syndrome. Iron deficiency, even at levels insufficient to cause anemia, has been associated with this syndrome, and iron deficiency anemia is also associated with insomnia in pregnancy.[25] Although more research is needed, available evidence implicates low brain iron concentration caused by the inadequate transportation of iron from the blood to the central nervous system as a cause of dopaminergic dysfunction in these patients.[26] Iron supplementation was found effective for improving insomnia in teens with low iron stores.[27]

The following 2 supplements are under investigation for their roles in treating insomnia:

Melatonin. Disturbances in circadian rhythm and melatonin production are more common among both the elderly and shift workers, and evidence suggests that this can be partly ameliorated by supplemental melatonin. Although studies suggest that melatonin is safe and effective for treating delayed sleep phase syndrome, most evidence does not support its effectiveness for the majority of primary and secondary sleep disorders.[28] However, melatonin appears to help patients, particularly the elderly, discontinue their reliance on benzodiazepines. This was found to be an effective strategy in 78% of patients using melatonin, compared with 25% using a placebo.[29]

Valerian. Valerian's sedative and hypnotic effects probably result from increases in the secretion of the neurotransmitter γ-aminobutyric acid (GABA) and inhibition of its uptake. Valerian binds to the same receptors as benzodiazepines but with less efficiency and milder effects; this difference may account for the lack of residual morning sedation that is a common side effect of hypnotics.[30] Doses of 400 to 500 mg/day have been found to significantly decrease sleep latency and improve subjective sleep quality. However, not all studies have found valerian to be effective. In addition, caution is warranted to avoid side effects, which may include headache, hangover, paradoxical stimulation, restlessness, and cardiac disturbances, as well as potentially dangerous interactions with barbiturates, benzodiazepines, opiates, and alcohol.[30]

Orders

See Basic Diet Orders chapter.

What to Tell the Family

Insomnia can be caused by several factors, the most common involving caffeine and alcohol intake, lack of exercise, and poor sleep hygiene. Family members can often help the patient alter habits relating to these contributors. When chronic, insomnia can adversely affect quality of life and should be discussed with a physician to rule out underlying medical or psychiatric etiologies.

References

1. National Sleep Foundation. 2005 Sleep in America Poll. National Sleep Foundation Web site. Available at: http://www.sleepfoundation.org/atf/cf/%7BF6BF2668-A1B4-4FE8-8D1A-A5D39340D9CB%7D/Sleep_Segments.pdf. Accessed December 2, 2005.

2. National Institutes of Health. Manifestations and Management of Chronic Insomnia in Adults. State-of-the-Science Conference, Final Statement: August 18, 2005. Available at: http://consensus.nih.gov/2005/2005InsomniaSOS026PDF.pdf.Accessed April 10, 2006.

3. Stepanski EJ, Wyatt JK. Use of sleep hygiene in the treatment of insomnia. *Sleep Med Rev.* 2003;7:215-225.

4. Fava M, Rush AJ, Thase ME, et al. 15 years of clinical experience with bupropion HCl: from bupropion to bupropion SR to bupropion XL. *Prim Care Companion J Clin Psychiatry.* 2005;7:106-113.

5. Montgomery P, Dennis J. Physical exercise for sleep problems in adults aged 60+. *Cochrane Database Syst Rev.* 2002;(4):CD003404.

6. Jefferson CD, Drake CL, Scofield HM, et al. Sleep hygiene practices in a population-based sample of insomniacs. *Sleep.* 2005;28:611-615.

7. Morin CM, Colecchi C, Stone J, Sood R, Brink D. Behavioral and pharmacological therapies for late-life insomnia: a randomized controlled trial. *JAMA.* 1999;281:991-999.

8. Smith MT, Huang MI, Manber R. Cognitive behavior therapy for chronic insomnia occurring within the context of medical and psychiatric disorders. *Clin Psychol Rev.* 2005;25:559-592.

9. Liao WC. Effects of passive body heating on body temperature and sleep regulation in the elderly: a systematic review. *Int J Nurs Stud.* 2002;39:803-810.

10. Roehrs T, Roth T. Sleep, sleepiness, and alcohol use. *Alcohol Res Health.* 2001;25:101-109.

11. Brower KJ. Insomnia, alcoholism and relapse. *Sleep Med Rev.* 2003;7:523-539.

12. Swift R, Davidson D. Alcohol hangover: mechanisms and mediators. *Alcohol Health Res World.* 1998;22:54-60.

13. Ekman AC, Leppaluoto J, Huttunen P, et al. Ethanol inhibits melatonin secretion in healthy volunteers in a dose-dependent randomized double blind cross-over study. *J Clin Endocrinol Metab.* 1993;77:780-783.

14. von Wartburg JP, Buhler R. Biology of disease. Alcoholism and aldehydism: new biomedical concepts. *Lab Invest.* 1984;50:5-15.

15. Zimatkin SM, Anichtchik OV. Alcohol-histamine interactions. *Alcohol.* 1999;34:141-147.

16. Sanchez-Ortuno M, Moore N, Taillard J, et al. Sleep duration and caffeine consumption in a French middle-aged working population. *Sleep Med.* 2005;6:247-251.

17. Brown SL, Salive ME, Pahor M, et al. Occult caffeine as a source of sleep problems in an older population. *J Am Geriatr Soc.* 1995;43:860-864.

18. Levy M, Zylber-Katz E. Caffeine metabolism and coffee-attributed sleep disturbances. *Clin Pharmacol Ther.* 1983;33:770-775.

19. Brown J, Kreiger N, Darlington GA, Sloan M. Misclassification of exposure: coffee as a surrogate for caffeine intake. *Am J Epidemiol.* 2001;153:815-820.

20. Kahn A, Francois G, Sottiaux M, et al. Sleep characteristics in milk-intolerant infants. *Sleep.* 1988;11:291-297.

21. Kahn A, Mozin MJ, Rebuffat E, Sottiaux M, Muller MF. Milk intolerance in children with persistent sleeplessness: a prospective double-blind crossover evaluation. *Pediatrics.* 1989;84:595-603.

22. Birdsall TC. 5-Hydroxytryptophan: a clinically-effective serotonin precursor. *Altern Med Rev.* 1998;3:271-280.

23. Hudson C, Hudson SP, Hecht T, MacKenzie J. Protein source tryptophan versus pharmaceutical grade tryptophan as an efficacious treatment for chronic insomnia. *Nutr Neurosci.* 2005;8:121-127.

24. Boozer CN, Daly PA, Homel P, et al. Herbal ephedra/caffeine for weight loss: a 6-month randomized safety and efficacy trial. *Int J Obes Relat Metab Disord.* 2002;26:593-604.

25. Sifakis S, Angelakis E, Papadopoulou E, Stratoudakis G, Fragouli Y, Koumantakis E. The efficacy and tolerability of iron protein succinylate in the treatment of iron-deficiency anemia in pregnancy. *Clin Exp Obstet Gynecol.* 2005;32:117-122.

26. Mizuno S, Mihara T, Miyaoka T, Inagaki T, Horiguchi J. CSF iron, ferritin and transferrin levels in restless legs syndrome. *J Sleep Res.* 2005;14:43-47.

27. Kotagal S, Silber MH. Childhood-onset restless legs syndrome. *Ann Neurol.* 2004;56:803-807.

28. Buscemi N, Vandermeer B, Pandya R, et al. Melatonin for treatment of sleep disorders. *Evid Rep Technol Assess* (Summ). 2004;108:1-7.

29. Garfinkel D, Zisapel N, Wainstein J, Laudon M. Facilitation of benzodiazepine discontinuation by melatonin: a new clinical approach. *Arch Intern Med.* 1999;159:2456-2460.

30. Tesch BJ. Herbs commonly used by women: an evidence-based review. *Am J Obstet Gynecol.* 2003;188(suppl 5):S44-S55.

Index